REAL COUNTRY VOLUME II
NORTHEAST AND EAST CENTRAL SCOTT COUNTY

Ann Bolton Bevins

Parson's Porch Books

www.parsonsporchbooks.com

Real Country Volume II: Northeast and East Central Scott County

ISBN: Hard Cover 978-1-951472-65-8

Copyright © 2021 by Ann Bolton Bevins

All rights reserved. No part of this book may be reproduced or transmitted in any form or by any means, electronic or mechanical, including photocopying, recording, or by any information storage and retrieval system, without permission in writing from the publisher.

Books in This Series

Real Country I Rural Northwest and West Central Scott County, Kentucky

Real Country II Rural Northeast and East Central Scott County, Kentucky

Real Country III Scott County South Triangle, West

Real Country IV Scott County South Triangle, Central and East

Ann Bolton Bevins is author of a *History of Scott County as Told by Selected Buildings* (1981); *The First Christian-Disciples Church: First Christian Church of Georgetown, Kentucky* (1981). *One Hundred Years at First National and Four Component Banks* (1983). She is co-author at *That Troublesome Parish: St. Francis/St. Pius Church Of White Sulphur* (1985); *Scott County, Kentucky* (1993); and *Images Of America: Georgetown And Scott County* (1998).

Edited by Robert L. Bevins.

Library of Congress cataloging-in-publication (cip) data

Bevins, Ann Bolton

Real Country I, II, III, IV

Includes annotations, bibliography, glossary, and index.

ISBN:

1. Architectural history – rural domestic, agricultural, industrial, educational complexes

2. General history (Kentucky and local)

3. Biography

REAL COUNTRY VOLUME II
NORTHEAST AND EAST CENTRAL SCOTT COUNTY

To
William Bevins, Sr. (1919-2014)
William Bevins, Jr., M.D. (1957-2016)
And my friend, Nancy B. Brown
and
All who persisted in their determination that I complete this work

A special acknowledgment in behalf of all those persons to whom I have promised this book
through the years and who have since passed away, many during the present year.
For them I pursued this work with dedication, save for competing efforts needing immediate attention.

Ann Bolton Bevins

2021

Epigraph

" . . . God keep me from ever completing anything. This whole book is but a draught* – nay, but the draught of a draught. Oh, Time, Strength, Cash, and Patience! "

Herman Melville, *Moby-Dick*

*draught is archaism for draft

Real Country II
Northeast and East Central Scott County

Acknowledgments and Introduction

Dear Reader: A special request from the author: this volume, Real Country II, and the three additional volumes, have been "under construction" for about ten years. Several times the information has been brought up to date with extended title searches and new discoveries. This is a process that could be extended interminably. Therefore, I ask for you to consider that this work was complete at the end of 2015. Your additional investigation takes off from this point. abb

Scott County, first settled by Europeans and Africans in 1775 and 1783, had its formal beginning on June 22, 1792 when Woodford County, established by the newly created Commonwealth of Kentucky from Fayette in 1789, was divided longitudinally. At the time of their creation, Scott and Woodford counties extended to the Ohio River. That extreme size did not last long. As population grew and demanded access to county seats, Scott yielded territory to the formation of all of present Boone, Kenton, and Grant counties and portions of Gallatin, Owen, Pendleton, and Harrison. Scott was not to achieve its present size until 1819 with the creation of Owen County. Today's Scott County encompasses 284 square miles.[1]

This volume relates to the northeast quadrant of Scott County. This territory includes parts of two of Scott County's three geophysical sections – the Lowell-Nicholson soils of the middle segment (the waistband) of Scott County, and the Eden Shale northern sector. The region is rich in history from the settlement period (c. 1785-1825) and the antebellum period (c. 1825 to 1865) into the late nineteenth and early twentieth centuries, the ultimate focus of this work. Founding families who claimed large grants of land or who bought them once they got here are treated at length in these pages. A major challenge has been indexing names of the individuals comprising these families, and their descendants, so that you, the reader, will be able to locate them and their activities as the decades moved forward.

Names that come to mind among the original European-derived settlers of the Northeast Scott County region include: John Pack, Richard F. Pack, Joseph and Sarah Smith Burgess, Edward "Ned" Burgess, T.J. Burgess, William and Lavinia Pack Penn, Joseph Fields, Zephaniah Fields, William Emison, Thomas Emison, William "Billy" Hinton, Henry Antle, James Reed, Jacob Mulberry, George Vallandingham, Jesse Hall, , J.R. Stowers, Richard Robinson, W.F. Eads, John Kitchen, J.T. Stone, Richard D. Faulconer, George M. Swinford, Clinton Barnhill, Bradford Munson, Shelby Munson, Thomas Price, William Price, John Hall, John Osborne, S.T. Giles, John Reed, and William Vance, among others. These families gave and in many cases continue to give the northeast county region its character.

Sadieville became the leading community of northeast Scott County. The more prominent villages included Holdings Mill/Mount Gilead Church, Turkeyfoot, Rogers Gap, Straight Fork/Davis, Alberta/Boyers Chapel, Muddy Ford, Delapain, and Hinton.

---

[1] See Lindsey Apple, Rick Johnston, and Ann Bevins, *Scott County, Kentucky: A History* (Georgetown: Scott County Historical Society, 1993), 45.

The author by herself could not have researched and written this four volume "tome," much less this second volume of the four. Writing local history with its mix of architecture, politics, struggles and the people who struggled, wartime and peace, farming, mechanization and its results, and industrialization, and commerce, is many faceted. Support and encouragement of friends and family over many years are paramount. "How is your book coming?" husband Bill queried year after year as I would get involved in scores of other causes. Our wish that we did not achieve was that I would finish it while Bill was alive to enjoy it. That opportunity passed us by, though Bill is always present in my realm of thought. Researchers such as I would be helpless without the professionals in the various libraries and archives, and in Property Valuation Administrator Tim Jenkins's and County Clerk Rebecca Johnson's offices, to provide guidance and encouragement..

Over many years traveling companions joined me and kept me from running off the road. Among them in ages past were Betty Hollingsworth, Edith Clifton, Judy McDowell, and Emma Jean Adams. Emma Jean, who was from Magoffin County, called our Eden Shale hills "mountains." Individuals with whom I worked on a professional level were Helen Powell, landscape architect and architectural historian, and Joy Barlow, social studies teacher.

Nancy Brown is the faithful and tolerant friend who kept me focused on the fact that if I were actually going to publish, I must not be allowed to "run off the road." Therefore Nancy drove many miles to photograph the properties herein depicted, wary that if I were to do the driving that we might roll down one or more of Scott County's roadside hills or into one or more of our county's many creeks and branches. Scott County's countryside is inhabited by fascinating people; we met many of them. Others questioned our relative safety; our defense was "Who's going to bother a couple of old ladies taking pictures of old houses?" But we continued, "onward and upward," as Nancy likes to say.

Dr. Ellen Emerick, professor of history at Georgetown College, is an incredibly wonderful addition to those individuals who have made this work more meaningful. Her knowledge and appreciation relate to my role as a returning student to Georgetown College with this work's inclusion as independent study. I am grateful for her knowledgeable contribution to interpreting this work about rural architecture and life, and for acceptance of my work by my faculty advisor/academic dean/provost/president pro tem Dr. Rosemary Allen.

Thank you, Scott County property owners, for allowing me to wander about your yards and farms to photograph your wonderful landmarks. It has been one of my life's greatest adventures getting to know you and the historic resources held in your trust. Previous owners and users are also among those whom I have known, if only in the realm of spirit and the recorded word.

A related concern was finding people with minds and hearts to read the text written over these many years. The most committed of the crew of proofreaders who gathered around my dining room table were Ellie Caroland, Mary Ann Hollingsworth, and of course Nancy Brown. Ellie evidenced similar heart during the many years that she worked with local folk and tourists alike using her hundreds of research assists in Scott County Public Library's Kentucky Room. Ellie has written a major volume related to her family's story and shares in the Lexington Carnegie Center's summer writing workshops. Joining our crew was Amanda Graham Kincaid, a many talented archaeologist anthropologist preservation administrator as well as mom. Winnie Bratcher made a significant contribution to proofreading.

And do keep in mind that these words have been written over time. There may be present tense references to buildings, places, and owners that are no more. There may be totally different owners of a particular building or site. In these cases, please forgive me for my oversight.

Thank you, dear friends. Your contributions will journey on with this work!

Ann Bolton Bevins
2021

Real Country II
Locations by Chapters

1. Agricultural Buildings

2. African American Communities
   Black, Boydtown, Cranetown, Sadieville Main Street, Roberts Lane in Sadieville

3. Northeast Scott County
   Roads: Boyers Chapel, Sadieville-Davis, Davis-Turkeyfoot, Burgess Smith, Elk Lick Church, Old Kentucky 32, Double Culvert, Sadieville-Hinton, Luke, Stone Lane, South Rays Fork, Kentucky 922/Muddy Ford, Mt. Gilead, Rogers Gap, Barkley Road, Barkley Lane, Hinton Cemetery, Finnell, Bailey, Gunnell, Morris, Dividing Ridge

4. North East Central Scott County
   Roads: Oxford-Muddy Ford, Old Turkeyfoot, Delaplain, Anderson, Barkley Lane

5. Northeast and East Central Crossroads Communities
   Hinton, Straight Fork/Davis, Alberta/Boyers Chapel, Muddy Ford, Turkeyfoot, Rogers Gap, Delaplain, Holdings Mill/Mount Gilead Church

6. Oxford

7. Sadieville

Foreword

Real Country is an amazing gift to all Scott Countians from Ann Bolton Bevins, widely accepted as the area's foremost authority on local history and architecture, as well as the genealogy of those who built, occupied, and authored the history which she chronicles.

It is a monumental four volume work based on extensive research and accompanied by her photography, which greatly enhances her work.

For the reader unfamiliar with Mrs. Bevins's work, some background might be helpful. For many years Scott County lacked a comprehensive and truly authoritative history. Through inclusion in statewide encyclopedic or textbook-style volumes, one could piece together basic information, and with some effort and a visit to the courthouse or public library, one could flesh out an "armchair" or casual historian's understanding. But for the most part, all the elements that bring history to life were lacking or were so piece meal as to be a daunting undertaking. In 1981 with the publication of *A History of Scott County As Told By Selected Buildings*, Ann began to fill that void and turn things around, making history exciting, personal, and interesting to both the casual and accomplished historian.

Based on her beliefs that old houses as well as religious, industrial, and commercial buildings have a way of communicating with us, and coupled with intensive research, utilizing all types of public records such as deeds and wills, as well as private sources such as letters, diaries, and interviews with family members and other historians, combined with a deep appreciation and understanding of human nature, Mrs. Bevins compiled the most comprehensive record to date of the life and times of Georgetown and Scott County throughout its history. Now, almost twenty-five years later, she has surpassed her earlier success to include all of rural Scott County – a work so massive as to require a multi-volume presentation with each volume dedicated to the unique features of the roughly four quadrants of the area.

Volume I covers the northwest and north central areas of Scott County, with special attention to agricultural influences, African American communities, crossroads communities, and the City of Stamping Ground, encompassing a huge and extremely varied area.

Volume II covers the northeast and east central areas with special attention to the community of Oxford and the City of Sadieville. It also addresses the crossroads communities of Hinton, Davis, Boyers Chapel/Alberta, Muddy Ford, Turkeyfoot, Rogers Gap, Delaplain, Holdings Mill/Mount Gilead Church, and the African American communities of Black, Boydtown, Cranetown, and areas of Sadieville.

Volume III is devoted to Scott County's "South Triangle's West," beginning with a requiem for all of the losses that have taken place in the contemporary era due to rapid growth and development. Like volumes one and two, it explores agricultural areas and the crossroads communities of White Sulphur and Payne's Depot. African American communities including Zion Hill, Trottertown, Payne's Depot, Lloyd Pike, McIntyre Settlement, and Hummonstown are detailed with photographs and narratives. The volume also covers Great Crossings and its people in depth.

Volume IV is devoted to Scott County's Southern Triangle's Central and Eastern Sectors and like *Volume III* begins with a Requiem for recent losses. Included are the African American communities of New Zion, Pleasant Point/Clabber Bottom, and Cartertown, as well as the crossroads communities of Lemon's Mill and Newtown.

In each volume the author covers all accessible public roads and explores as many of the architectural treasures as possible. Special attention is also paid to the influences that determined early and later development and to the churches and gathering places where the exchange of ideas and commerce define the areas' unique features. In her analysis of each of the selected properties, Mrs. Bevins incorporates criteria established by the National Register of Historic Places, which includes elements such as location, topography/setting, design, materials, workmanship, and overall effect.

Because Scott County is the fastest growing county in the state and because new influences and trends are appearing in the tide of history, it is essential for Scott County to evaluate its commitment to preservation whenever possible. In the years since 1981, many buildings both sound and diminished have become endangered or have disappeared entirely, and the rural landscape has changed dramatically. *Real Country* is a clarion call for commitment to preserving Scott County's heritage at least as it currently exists. More than anything, however, it is a gift of love and appreciation for the area and for its people, past, present, and future.

Nancy B. Brown

Robert Bevins has been a real force in the development of Real Country I, II, III, and IV, using his talent in design and the technical processes of organizing tables of content, turning alt text notes into figure citations for the early volumes, and indexing. Robert holds a Ph.D. with honors in toxicology from the University of Kentucky. He has always maintained a perceptive study of history and all things literary. His dissertation was entitled *Potentiation of camptothecin cytotoxicity by the sequential addition of histone deacetylase inhibitors.* (Published 2005, UK, Graduate Center for Toxicology).

Robert Bevins

Appreciation

Real Country I, II, III, and IV had their beginning perhaps as many as twenty years ago. Work on it moved with numerous interruptions over the decades. Nancy Brown (see previous pages) provided amazing and energetic support during the final phase, as did son Dr. Robert Bevins. When author Ann Bevins decided two years ago that her life would not be complete should she not finish her college degree that began in 1954, Dr. Rosemary Allen, Georgetown College provost and academic dean, not only welcomed Ann as a returning student but took on the responsibility of being her faculty advisor and included Real Country as independent study. History professor Dr. Ellen Emerick agreed to supervise this independent study. Without the support and input of these two scholars, this work would not have arrived at this point that gives it to you the readers.

Ann Bolton Bevins

Dr. Rosemary Allen

Ann Bolton Bevins has spent a lifetime collecting the stories that define Scott County, and the stories in Real Country bring that history to life. The photographs provide invaluable context, but my favorite part of her work is always the stories that go with the pictures. The details of everyday life and human experience provide a way for the imagination to supplement these still pictures with dimensions and movement that evoke days gone by. I loved, for instance, envisioning Mrs. Askew's teahouse, and above all I loved the story of Henry Viley Johnson. The collection of all of these pieces of gold makes Real Country a treasure for all of those who love history.

The practice of history has changed significantly over the last century. The life stories of powerful men, the unfolding of military battles, or the conditions of treaties that ended significant wars has broadened considerably to include everyday people's lives and concerns. Our problem, of course, is that for so long no one was actively preserving the "stuff" of everyday life, making it difficult to recapture the realities of that life. Kentucky is blessed to have, in these four volumes, an extraordinary history of its architectural development, spanning its history across both time and space. Preserved here for present and future generations are the settings that Kentuckians of all classes saw as "home". The breadth of this work cannot be overstated. Decades of searching out details that would be lost to us, indeed continue to be lost yearly, have produced both word paintings and photographic images of the domestic settings so integral to the lives of the people who built and occupied them.

Dr. Ellen Emerick

List of Illustrations

Figure 1. Buford Hall dry stone battered water tower that provided water for the entire farm. 40
Figure 2. Agricultural storage buildings formerly located near front of Buford Hall farm. 41
Figure 3. Picturesque line of cribs formerly located near front of Buford Hall farm near highway. 41
Figure 4. Two large battened cribs located near the front of Buford Hall agricultural complex. 41
Figure 5. Historic log house with centered chimney on Buford Hall Farm. 42
Figure 6. Typical later Buford Hall tenant house. 42
Figure 7. Racing barn central to Burgess Smith Farm on Burgess-Smith Road. 43
Figure 8. Burgess Smith hog barn has elegant pegged joinery. 43
Figure 9. Burgess Smith side-entered tobacco barn has similar pegged joinery. 43
Figure 10. Detail of historic Kitchen farm's small log crib barn. 44
Figure 11. John and Richard Pack double log crib barn. 44
Figure 12. Edward Burgess barn with octagonal cupola. Other photos reveal detail including (a) tower from inside log crib; (b) log crib exterior detail; (c) hog trough attached to outside of log crib. 45
Figure 13. View of main façade of first Elk Lick Particular Baptist Church now protected inside of extended log barn. Below - Exterior photo of expanded former Elk Lick Particular Baptist Church with log corn crib at right. 46
Figure 14. Barn of later Joseph Burgess near Davis. 46
Figure 15. Joseph Burgess barn near Cincinnati Road. 47
Figure 16. Foundation detail of Cincinnati Road Joseph Burgess barn. 47
Figure 17. Older barn on the Hugh Wilhoite farm. 47
Figure 18. A second, much altered, barn on Hugh Wilhoite farm. 47
Figure 19. W.V. "Bunk" Mulberry, Davis Road barn with continuous raised ridgeline. 48
Figure 20. William McIntyre surveys historic relics left in last house of Black neighborhood. 51
Figure 21. William Black, Opera Happy house facing Cynthiana Road. 52
Figure 22. Stephen Jones bungalow, a feature of the Boydtown community. 53
Figure 23. John Nichols house in Boydtown community. 54
Figure 24. Former Boydtown United Methodist Church, and at right, Boydtown schoolhouse. 55
Figure 25. Boydtown's Rosenwald School is a residence today. 55
Figure 26. Sallie Mason surveys her former neighborhood of Cranetown. 56
Figure 27. View of main street of Cranetown. 57
Figure 28. House on Cranetown Lane. 57
Figure 29. View of larger house in Cranetown. 57
Figure 30. Historic Mount Olive Baptist Church enhanced with brick facing and expanded brick addition. Nicodemus, Kansas 58
Figure 31. Nicodemus, Kansas, in its heyday. 59
Figure 32. (a) Surviving example of dugout house in Nicodemus vicinity. (b) Angela Bates; park ranger Michelle Huff; and historian Ann Bevins at Nicodemus National Park Service Visitors Center. (c) Verle Switzer, Nicodemus farmer and the first African American to crash the professional football color barrier as a Green Bay Packer. 60
Figure 33. (a) Home near Nicodemus of former slave of Richard M. Johnson.and (b) Original Nicodemus schoolhouse will be restored. 60
Figure 34. Historic photo of Sadieville's Rosenwald schoolhouse. 62
Figure 35. Levi Craig house with interesting walkway constructed with stone slabs. 62
Figure 36. Childhood home of Bess Dallas and Cora Frye. 63
Figure 37. Later home of Bess Dallas. 63

Figure 38. Henry and May Scott house has porch supported by tapered posts. 64
Figure 39. Cindy Foster, former Sadieville clerk who put together the city's Rosenwald School history...............64
Figure 40. (a) Alicestyne Adams as Rosenwald teacher. (b) Angela Bates discusses Sadieville's relationship to Nicodemus, Kansas. 64
Figure 41. Roberts-Williams house and its modern extension. 65
Figure 42. Roy and Adeline Brooks house; the Brookses were parents of Robert Brooks of World War II renown. 65
Figure 43. Lane leading past Brooks farm buildings..65
Figure 44. Circa 1938 Craftsman style house relates to Hurley and Henry families. 66
Figure 45. Ben Offutt house on Roberts Lane has recessed entryway. 66
Figure 46. Harold and Nannie Roberts house has wraparound porch. 66
Figure 47. Railroad underpasses built by masons E.C. Muddiman and E.E. Muddman. (a) The Double Culvert Road underpass. (b) Luke Road underpass. (c) Shawnee Run underpass located on present farm of Ron Vance. ..67
Figure 48. Mark Elliott makes notes about Reed-Munson graveyard on his farm south of Alberta. 70
Figure 49. (a) John Pack log house east of Sadieville; (b) close-up view of John Pack house; (c) Early Kentucky style mantel in John Pack house. 71
Figure 50. (a) Rear elevation of Richard and Sadie Pack house; (b) outbuilding, possible servants' quarters, or schoolhouse, of Pack property; (c) Pack smokehouse. 72
Figure 51. Richard and Sarah Emison Pack's Charity Hill. 72
Figure 52. Detail of Richard-Sadie Pack house...72
Figure 53. Intricately detailed rock wall along Sadieville-Davis turnpike, boundary of Pack farm, ascribed to Herbert W. "Hub" Antle and/or Frank Gillispie...73
Figure 54. William Penn house was one of the best built and most stylish houses in northern Scott County. 73
Figure 55. Stairwell of William Penn house had Early Kentucky and Greek Revival era refinements. 74
Figure 56. John W. Penn house on Sadieville-Davis Road has Princess Anne roof profile......................................74
Figure 57. Least altered of the Penn family houses has Princess Anne roof pattern...75
Figure 58. Former Penn house on Sadieville-Davis Road is brick veneered and has Craftsman style porch. 75
Figure 59. Nannie L. Penn gained title to a farm near Davis with Gothic Revival styling. The house has battened vertical siding. 76
Figure 60. Edward Caesar Burgess's log house served by shouldered chimney burned several decades ago. The late Burgess Swope, a granddaughter, recalled the smaller building as the plantation schoolhouse. 77
Figure 61. Small log buildings along the road leading toward Turkeyfoot were important to travelers, as was the small iron bridge..77
Figure 62. Burgess Smith's residential tract once included an elaborate house. Only the tenant house remains, along with a multipurpose barn and cattle handling pens..78
Figure 63. Two small houses are joined and are identified on the 1879 Beers & Lanagan map as the property of "J. Fields."..78
Figure 64. Small closeted stairway of the Edward Burgess property is an outstanding example. 78
Figure 65. The exterior of the small Burgess house has small shouldered chimney...78
Figure 66. Rodney Courtney house, Penn farm...79
Figure 67. Elk Lick Church site, home of Robert and Christina Gillispie. 80
Figure 68. Former property of Lancaster and Bryant..80
Figure 69. Façade of first Elk Lick Particular Baptist Church. 80
Figure 71. Addison Thomson bungalow. 81
Figure 71. Smokehouse near Addison Thomson Grayland house..81
Figure 72. William Thomson house. 81
Figure 73. Bungalow of T.J. Burgess, III, and his wife, Louise..82

Figure 74. Davis-Crenshaw/Mrs. Gordon Fightmaster house. 83
Figure 75. Emison Mill site and Charles Fields house. 83
Figure 76. (a) Dorothy Core, dog, and Robert Bevins at Emison mill site. (b) Emison miller's house. 84
Figure 77. Emison-Barkley mill owners' house. 85
Figure 78. Emison-Barkley mill. 85
Figure 79. A.B. Barkley family picnic at old home site. 86
Figure 80. Giles family trust house. 87
Figure 81. Azalia B. Giles house. 87
Figure 82. The Hinton-Tucker house was acquired by Nannie E. Tucker from two groups of William Hinton heirs. 88
Figure 83. Asher Hinton house. 89
Figure 84. Cam Skinner house. 89
Figure 85. Asher Hinton graveyard is next to his house. 90
Figure 86. Laura Hinton Wells house. 90
Figure 87. Hinton-Doris Reed house. 90
Figure 88. Hinton-Doris Reed house. 90
Figure 89. Antle-Driskell house. 91
Figure 90. Diana Reed and W.E. Bates house. 91
Figure 91. Gillispie and African American cemetery. 91
Figure 92. W.E. Bates barn and dry stone foundation. 92
Figure 93. James and Diana Reed and J.E. and Martha Vallandingham house. 92
Figure 94. Barn on Reed-Vallandingham farm. 93
Figure 95. Hinton Road School Site. schoolhouse. 93
Figure 96. Reed-Vallandingham smokehouse. 93
Figure 97. Jacob Mulberry house. 94
Figure 98. Mulberry-Grigg house. 94
Figure 99. Mulberry-Swinford house. 95
Figure 100. Walter V. "Bunk" Mulberry house. 95
Figure 101. Walter V. "Bunk" Mulberry cellar/workshop. 95
Figure 102. Leonard Mulberry house. 96
Figure 103. R.T. and Laura Etta V. Nelson log house. 96
Figure 104. McGuirk/Fightmaster house. 97
Figure 105. W.F. Eads house. 97
Figure 106. W.F. Eads landscape features. 98
Figure 107. John Kitchen house, smokehouse. 98
Figure 108. Thomas Kitchen house. 99
Figure 109. Faulconer-Dunaway Farm. 99
Figure 110. Mollie and J.E. Faulconer and Lancaster farm. 100
Figure 111. Richard D. Faulconer house. 101
Figure 112. John and Pauline Henry bungalow. 101
Figure 113. Christine Wilderson and Dorothy Green in the log Stowers house. 102
Figure 114. Christine Wilderson and Dorothy Green and the stone chimney. 102
Figure 115. Stowers farmland. 102
Figure 116. Stower-Lowery house. 103
Figure 117. Photo of Green-Wilderson house. 103
Figure 118a. Later barns on Robinson-Lowery farm. 103
Figure 119. Tim and Kris Lowery log house. 104

Figure 120. Sadieville's Ben Offutt, Spanish American War veteran. 104
Figure 121. Benjamin and Edna Offutt house. 104
Figure 122. F.W. and Lucinda Davis house. 105
Figure 123. Polcer Hiles-J.W. Davis house. 106
Figure 124. Giles-Reffitt house. 106
Figure 125. Below-grade house near Sadieville. 106
Figure 126. Shepherd's Crossing, Muddy Ford Road: Clinton Barnhill house. 108
Figure 127. Barnhill-Dawson house. 108
Figure 128. Clinton Barnhill house. 109
Figure 129. Barnhill-Lacy house 110
Figure 130. Corda Johnson Reed house. 110
Figure 131. Martha J. Burgess house. 111
Figure 132. Darius Foxworthy house. 111
Figure 133. Martha J. Burgess/John, Sally, and Joe Henderson house. 112
Figure 134. Ray and Cephas Tucker house. 113
Figure 135. Margaret Munson and Rollie Hinton house. 114
Figure 136. Carl and Thelma Vance house. 114
Figure 137. Pierce Munson log house: Shawnee Run Farm. 115
Figure 138. Historic photo of Pierce Munson log house. 116
Figure 139. Commercial features of Shawnee Run Farm. 116
Figure 140. Bridge over Shawnee Run at historic Munson farm. 116
Figure 141. Room of Munson house with logs exposed. 117
Figure 142. Shelby Munson house, near Turkeyfoot. 117
Figure 143. House, third on historic Price-Hiles site, was built with sensitivity to history by David and Linda Harris. 118
Figure 144. Historic smokehouse or storage building on present site of David and Linda Harris house. 118
Figure 145. Carl and Thelma Vance's setting of T.C. White historic Turkeyfoot property. 119
Figure 146. Ron Vance, historian, built a contemporary style home on the site of the first Vance house, home of his ancestors, in Turkeyfoot. 120
Figure 147. Thomas B. and Nannie Mallory Hiles were individual owners of the Craftsman style house and "wishing well" in the yard. 120
Figure 148. Walker and Sally Fields owned the Craftsman era house in Rogers Gap. 121
Figure 149. Buford Hall, II, extended and improved his historic family property and built the two story classical revival style house at Rogers Gap. 121
Figure 150. Barkley Road bungalow is historically associated with the Henry Clay and Nannie Morris Fields family. 123
Figure 151. Williamson family members owned the sturdily built nineteenth century frame house well into the twentieth century. 124
Figure 152. Jamie and Janene Hoffman built picturesque house on Barkley Road, using fabric salvaged from demolition of house on Georgetown's North Hamilton and East Washington streets. 125
Figure 153. Historic Lynn West property on North Hamilton and Washington streets survives in the Barkley Road home of Jamie and Janene Hoffman. 125
Figure 154. View of gable end of Hoffman house looking down Barkley Road to surviving agricultural features from earlier Williamson farm. 126
Figure 155. Barkley-Grizzle house, older bungalow with full basement and wraparound balcony. 126
Figure 156. The part log Dudley Williamson house, thought to date from 1855. 127

Figure 157. Three friendly dogs greeted passers-by at the Jesse Duncan house, purchased by Stephen E. and Jennifer Gariepy. 127
Figure 158. Earlier owned by J.B. Wells, Ellen Gregg Scobey owned the above property at her death in 2017. ..128
Figure 159. Ellen Gregg Scobey built the family's picnic shelter as a tribute to the Gregg family. 128
Figure 160. Samuel T. Giles house owners included present owners Circuit Judge Paul Isaacs and his wife Anna, also an attorney but at heart a practicing farmer. 129
Figure 161. Basement entrance to the older log house of the historic Giles family. 130
Figure 162. The log house occupies a corner of the historic spread. 130
Figure 163. View of the Samuel T. Giles spread from Giles Hill on Barkley Road. 131
Figure 164. Historic R.P. and Anna Giles house located at the entrance of North Mount Gilead Road. 131
Figure 165. (a) Willie A. Reed House, a Giles family property owned by Rich A. and Victoria Aurelius. (b) View of the Willie A. Red outbuildings as seen from the house. 133
Figure 166. Historic photo of Giles-Humphrey Farm, courtesy L. Denver Humphrey, author of contributed poem. Photo of Giles-Humphrey Farm courtesy L. Denver Humphrey. 134
Figure 167. Sarah J. Sharp house on Barkley Road. 134
Figure 168. Coppage-Giles house continues as part of the Giles family landscape. 135
Figure 169. Marie Minus Hamon of the James Amos Hamon family passed the property on to Mattie H. Ewing. 135
Figure 170. John Reed acquired county line property from Isaac Shuff in 1869. A barn and lake were included in the Shuff to Reed deed. 136
Figure 171. William Wells, Sr. and Willie Wells were owners of the Princess Anne style frame house. 136
Figure 172. O.R. and Gertrude Wells house was left by Nancy Anderson to S.L. Warth in 1901. 137
Figure 173. W.C. and Noah Hanna, father and son, owned the L-shaped house from 1911 to 1955. 137
Figure 174. Frank and Kay Wiseman house on Finnell Pike has full dovetail notches, the craftsmanship of Dr. Wiseman. 139
Figure 175. Sign designating the Wiseman Kentucky spread "Shenandoah" after Wiseman's former home; 138
Figure 176. Smokehouse/storage with high stone foundation. 138
Figure 177. Shenandoah's rear wing. 139
Figure 179. Gregory and Elizabeth Trotter house, a present-era Victorian style house with towers and handmade stained-glass windows. Gregory Trotter built the weathervane 140
Figure 181. View of stained glass window crafted by Gregory Trotter. 140
Figure 182. Letha and John J. Holland's circa 1930 house. 141
Figure 183. Gregg-Bailey house with combined log and timber frame sections. 142
Figure 184. Joseph Bailey log smokehouse propped up for the immediate future. 142
Figure 185. Joseph Bailey house on its "last leg." 143
Figure 186. Joseph and Noah Bailey house on Mount Gilead Road. 143
Figure 187. Willis W. Gunnell house was renovated by Ray and Lorrene Alexander. 144
Figure 188. Gunnell-Alexander house Craftsman mantel with over-mirror and historic tile. 145
Figure 189. Stairwell of Gunnell-Alexander house recalls the Craftsman building era. 145
Figure 191. Pastoral view of Gunnell Pike setting of the Gunnell-Alexander farm. 146
Figure 190. Perhaps the original Gunnell log house under camouflaged covering on Gunnell Road. 146
Figure 192. B.F. Sharon house on Gunnell Road. 147
Figure 193. Dutch Colonial Revival house attributed to W.T. Juett. 148
Figure 194. Square-plan dwelling with hip roof with Griggs-Gregg relationship. 148
Figure 195. Moody-Morris house has log component. 149
Figure 196. Dorothy Stuard and the Griggs house and its outbuilding were the perfect match. 149
Figure 197. Decorated stairwell of the Moody-Morris house. 151

Figure 198. Mantelpiece in older section of Moody-Morris house. 151
Figure 199. Elversia Fields and Fannie Houston house. 152
Figure 200. Cemetery across road from Fields-Houston house. 152
Figure 201. Historic Hinton Cemetery on Hinton Road. 152
Figure 202. Older house on Double Culvert Road may relate to William Griffith. 153
Figure 203. J.L. Luke house ruin provides shelter for modern Charolais herd. 154
Figure 204. Alice Baird and her husband Dr. J.W. Baird were owners of the Luke Pike property. 154
Figure 205. Pack-Luke house on Luke Pike. 155
Figure 206. Older house on Luke-Swinford farm. 156
Figure 207. Larger house on Luke-Swinford farm. 156
Figure 208. House deeded by Thomas and Nancy Griffith to H. Bascom Griffith in 1873. 156
Figure 209. Historic log house owned in earlier years by John Kitchen. 157
Figure 210. Edna Juett Sherritt bungalow on Muddy Ford Road. 158
Figure 211. Effie Juett Hall's house is one of the older dwellings of the Juett spread. 159
Figure 212. The red oak tree on the lawn of the Effie Juett Hall house is said to be two centuries old. 159
Figure 213. The stylish W.T. Juett log house became the home of the Elroy Mallard family in 1966. 160
Figure 214. Ward E. Juett house is a Masonite-sided bungalow on a stone foundation. 161
Figure 215. Sanborn map of Indian Oil Refinery recalls one of Georgetown's most exciting eras. 162
Figure 216. The Indian Oil Refinery office was redone for the home of James R. and Lily May Lewis. 163
Figure 217. Rear elevation of Indian Oil Refinery office and an outbuilding. 164
Figure 218. Tower that survived the refinery's demolition. 165
Figure 219. Two older postcards' views of DeGaris Mill and the mill dam. 167
Figure 220. Norman Hambrick bungalow. 167
Figure 221. Scott County's last county infirmary has become a comfortable family dwelling. 168
Figure 222. Historic barn associated with county infirmary operation. 168
Figure 223. County infirmary's smokehouse was another attractive feature of the operation. 168
Figure 224. R.C. Muntz house on Delaplain Road. 170
Figure 225. R.H. and Crawford Moore house on Delaplain Road. 170
Figure 226. Annie T. Glenn, C.F. and Martha Glenn, and Remus Mason house. 171
Figure 227. Drawing of Valentine Rogers house on Sims Road by Edith Linn Clifton. 171
Figure 228. R.C. Muntz house on Delaplain Road. 172
Figure 229. Kent Walters house on historic Crawford Moore land. 173
Figure 230. Detail of Valentine Rogers house. 174
Figure 231. Rita Jones house on Anderson Road. 174
Figure 232. Stairwell of Rita Jones house on Anderson Road. 174
Figure 233. Margaret and Evermont Hambrick, Les and Lee Gilkey, and Marcie Beatty house of several eras. 175
Figure 234. Craftsman period garage of Muntz family on Anderson Road. 175
Figure 235. Later house on Sarah Risk Farm. 176
Figure 236. Cincinnati Southern Railroad overpass near Hinton. 177
Figure 237. McLoney house, no longer standing, near Hinton. 177
Figure 238. Three Hinton houses photographed circa 1980. 178
Figure 239. Four Hinton houses dating from circa 1980. 178
Figure 240. L-shaped decorated cottage resides on picturesque hilltop. 178
Figure 241. Much remodeled Hinton Methodist Church. 179
Figure 242. Hinton house with large windows and picket fence. 179
Figure 243. Historical photograph of Davis village showing schoolhouse, church, cemetery, and store. ...180
Figure 244. House on Davis property purchased by Dr. M.D. Sanford in 1895. 181

Figure 245. Davis Store was purchased by Laura Conner to save the property. 181
Figure 246. Historic Beard Church at Davis, is said to have been one of the prettiest of such churches 182
Figure 247. Exterior detail of Beard Church. 183
Figure 248. Beautiful interior of church. 183
Figure 249. Wooden pews. 183
Figure 250. Pulpit area of Beard Church. 183
Figure 251. Photograph of Davis School during its last years. 184
Figure 252. Joshua and John May house and store in Davis. 184
Figure 253. W.T. Smith family house on Davis's Harrison County side. 184
Figure 254. Winding lane leading into village of Alberta on the Scott and Harrison county line. 185
Figure 255. Albert and Harriet Stevens's multi-gabled house in Alberta. 185
Figure 256. Alberta's Batey-Swinford Store. 186
Figure 257. Boyers Chapel Methodist Church with later portico. 187
Figure 258. Elizabeth Maddox-Joe Sutton house on edge of Muddy Ford. 187
Figure 259. Eli Muddiman house in Muddy Ford. 188
Figure 260. Muddy Ford Robertson Store as rebuilt following devastating fire. 188
Figure 261. Fannee Fields Hilander posing on the old rock fence by the white house on the hill. 189
Figure 262. Muddy Ford School with its large student body. 190
Figure 263. Muddy Ford's Bethesda Presbyterian Church. 191
Figure 264. Early Turkeyfoot house, possibly the home of Henry Hinton. 192
Figure 265. Turkeyfoot Christian Church. 193
Figure 266. Turkeyfoot School was a decorative version of a traditional school design. 194
Figure 267. Iconic photo of Turkeyfoot church. 194
Figure 268. Photo of second Turkeyfoot school with students grouped in front. 194
Figure 269. Historic photo of Shelby Munson house. From left Shelby's daughter Almira (Allie) who married Joseph Franklin Barkley, Ron Vance's great grandfather, grandson of Oxford's Robert Barkley. Shelby's house burned circa 1945-1946. 195
Figure 270. Rogers Gap village site. 195
Figure 271. T.R. Clark bungalow at Rogers Gap may date from as late as 1955 196
Figure 272. Walter and Sallie Fields house at Rogers Gap. 196
Figure 273. Third building of Dry Run Baptist Church was built in 1958. 197
Figure 274. Dry Run School on Cincinnati Road. 198
Figure 275. E.E. Muddiman store at Delaplain had a distinguishing design. 198
Figure 276. Hiram Wood house at Delaplain. 199
Figure 277. Mount Gilead Methodist Church served the community known sequentially as Holdings Mill, Finnell, Star, and Mount Gilead. 200
Figure 278. Rhoda Gregg Roehrig, since deceased, and Judy McLoney McDowell check out the tombstone of their ancestor Lutitia Holding Hamon in the Mount Gilead cemetery. 201
Figure 279. Two-story house of Amanda M. Penn or her husband has been owned by the family since construction. 202
Figure 280. Fannee Fields Hilander and Shirley Houston check out a log house that they visited frequently in childhood. 203
Figure 281. Early house n Holdings Mill community possibly originally owned by Penn or Holding family and discussed in Fannee Hilander's Hold Back the Spring. 203
Figure 282. The John F. Giles complex later owned by the Cummins and Roehrig families. 205
Figure 283. Gothic Revival house in Finnell relates to businessman/farmer James Amos Hamon. 206
Figure 284. James Amos Hamon barn in Finnell/Star had showy horizontal siding. 206

Figure 285. Robert and Mildred Gregory's front-gabled house. The Gregorys were farmers and leaders in the Mount Gilead and Scott County community. 206
Figure 286. James Amos Hamon's "Cheap Store" was preserved overtime by Robert Gregory. 206
Figure 287. Hilltop barn of James Amos Hamon in Mount Gilead community. 207
Figure 288. Oxford sidewalks are believed to have been the work of E.C. and E.E. Muddiman. 208
Figure 289. Rains home in Oxford was a former home of W.C. Owens, winner of the 1894 Congressional election. 210
Figure 290. Former Oxford School. 210
Figure 291. Shoemaker Isaiah Bailey's house was bought by Jacob Price and later was Presbyterian manse. 211
Figure 292. Cast iron steps of Presbyterian Church were inherited from Cynthiana Christian Church. 211
Figure 293. Oxford Presbyterian Church was an outstanding design of E.C. Muddiman. 212
Figure 294. Oxford's Masonic Lodge was the work of Hartwell E. Boswell. 214
Figure 295. Reuben Anderson house and tavern with entrances from Muddy Ford Road (house) and Cynthiana Road (tavern). 215
Figure 296. Removal of the Anderson building provided a lot for the relocation of a log house from the barn of Hiram Wood. 215
Figure 297. James and Sarah Risk's Italianate style house and interior chimneys and brackets in the soffit. 216
Figure 298. Greek Revival period house of William Gray dates from 1840. 216
Figure 299. Oxford Christian Church is another masterpiece of E.C. Muddiman. 217
Figure 300. Thomas C. Peacher passed on his home to daughter Lottie Barkley. The Barkleys deeded the property her sister Fannie Cannon. 218
Figure 301. By 1908 J.W. Hiten owned the L-shaped frame house and lot in central Oxford. 218
Figure 302. Jim and Wilma Ewbank owned the brick Italianate style house possibly built by E.C. Muddiman...219
Figure 303. E.C. Muddiman probably built the stylish country store that Wilma and Jim Ewbank christened "The Wee Shop of Oxford." 219
Figure 304. In the 1980s and 1990s Oxford hosted annual festivals in the fall. (The building at left was a Jacob Price outbuilding.) 220
Figure 305. Jane Frankie Risk and her husband Dr. W.T. Hendricks had the Victorian Italianate building as their home. Outbuildings at the right relate to the farm and Dr. Hendricks's medical practice. 221
Figure 306. Aaron Gaylor owned the house at the left and the store later owned by W.E. Davis. 221
Figure 307. The partial house was known as the Bradford Holland garage. 222
Figure 308. W.S. Dickerson constructed the Cape Cod style house on 195 acres that he purchased in 1944. Billy and Carrie Hall Green were recent owners. 222
Figure 309. James G. Davis owned the house of John and Lena True for three decades. 223
Figure 310. Lula Ethel Juett and her son Hugh Frank Juett willed their home to farm manager James W. Cannon. 223
Figure 311. The two houses on Newtown Road were sold by A. Dudley Hamon to Douglas P. and Mary F. Moore. 224
Figure 312. E.C. Muddiman may have built the brick house owned in recent years by Doctors James R. and Audrey Rooney. 224
Figure 313. Dr. F.M. Cannon house has Carpenter Gothic styling and a later addition. 225
Figure 314. Dr. C.T. Hendricks may have been the original owner of the Carpenter Gothic style house facing Muddy Ford Road. 226
Figure 315. Oxford Methodist Church was a 1905 masterwork of E.C. Muddiman. 227
Figure 316. Mattie A. and Charlie Smith house has two front gables with soffit trim at the gables' apex. 228
Figure 317. Oxford's vocational agriculture chapter house was built by students of E.W. Walton using bricks from former Great Crossings schoolhouse. 228

Figure 318. Oxford's Craftsman Style school building began with four rooms constructed in 1928. 229
Figure 319. Helen F. Juett's house is richly embellished with Victorian trim. The picture window is an addition. 231
Figure 320. Light recreation can be enjoyed at Warring Pavilion..232
Figure 321. Early Sadieville buildings lining Pike Street are across the road from the modern city park............232
Figure 322. Sadieville's relocated depot is now City Hall. 232
Figure 323. Sadieville's leading resource may be the railroad underpass with a view of the mill. Photo by Sandra Whelan, former city clerk..233
Figure 324. Cincinnati Southern Railroad became Cincinnati New Orleans and Texas Pacific and is now known as Norfolk Southern. It is a very busy railroad. 234
Figure 325. The current Sadieville Milling Company succeeded the original mill on nearby Eagle Creek. 235
Figure 326. Plat of Sadieville as filed in Scott County Will Book S...236
Figure 327. The former Pike Street building known as the "Corner House" no longer stands...............................236
Figure 328. Warring Picnic Pavilion is a gathering place for Sadieville events. 237
Figure 329. Arthur Lancaster's drug store during earlier years had a railed balcony. 237
Figure 330. Leonard Mulberry owned the large store that became Sadieville Baptist Church. 237
Figure 331. Harriet Kaley Hotel in earlier years attracted railroad travelers. 238
Figure 332. Sadieville Deposit Bank was designed and built by African American builder James Bailey. 239
Figure 333. Leander Risk's popular hotel dated from 1885. The photo depicts a 1970s festival..........................241
Figure 334. George B. Johnson house was built following an historic Sunday morning fire. 242
Figure 335. John M. Theobald house dates from 1888. 242
Figure 336. F.T. Mansfield, business leader, lived here until 1937. W.T. and Frances Warring became owners in 1956...244
Figure 337. R.E. Lee bought the lot for this house in 1898. Joseph and Nell Burgess bought it in 1936. 244
Figure 338. Rodham and Fannie Fields were the original owners of the house at 223 Main Street. 245
Figure 339. Vera Hinton later Van Cleve stands in foreground of the earlier W.A. Hinton home. 246
Figure 340. W.T. Mefford built the two-story house in 1886. 246
Figure 341. Founded and constructed in 1893, Sadieville Christian Church has long been served by outstanding ministers. 247
Figure 342. Judith A. Stone's one-story house dates from 1897..247
Figure 343. Earlier view of Sadieville City Hall and Cornish Hall next door..248
Figure 344. Historic photo of Main Street and Sadieville's early commercial life. 248
Figure 345. Charales W. Cornish provided funds in his will for a joint hall for Sadieville's two lodges. The building dates from 1895..248
Figure 346. Jimmie Jones's house was perhaps Sadieville's first store. 249
Figure 347. Older view of Jimmie Jones's house..249
Figure 348. The former depot was relocated by Joseph Burgess and turned into City Hall. 250
Figure 349. Site of the 1901 foot bridge...250
Figure 350. The well organized Kaley Hotel advertised on the 1879 Beers & Lanagan map. 250
Figure 351. Jimmie Jones's dwelling house on Pike Street...250
Figure 352. Jasper Rose bought the former brick hotel at auction in 1906. It was one of the city's most popular destinations...251
Figure 353. John Cottingam's house before recent renovation. 252
Figure 354. Former S.T. and Lucy Connellee dwelling and store house. 252
Figure 355. House sold in 1910 by Lucille and B.B. Barnett to Emma Nelson..253
Figure 356. The Nathaniel McLoney-W.W. Hutchcraft house. 253
Figure 357. John Crosthwait bought this house in 1900. 253

Figure 358. Building with shop relates to 1915 sale by R.H. McCabe to E.S. Baldwin. 254
Figure 359. Front-gabled ell style house was sold in 1931 by G.N. Robertson. 254
Figure 360. Manlius Price bought the small outlying farm from R. and Fannie Fields. 254
Figure 361. The tall unembellished house occupies a lot owned by Mary K. Gillispie in 1936. 255
Figure 362. The C.L. Neale house on the site of the home of Zephaniah and Gabriella Fields. 255
Figure 363. C. L. Neale house. 255
Figure 364 Early Home of Granville Kelly 255
Figure 365. The Marshall family house's early deeds called for "room to turn a team." 256
Figure 366. Polk Fields house was long considered Sadieville's first house. 256
Figure 367. The former home of Scott County Sheriff R.H. McCabe is one of Sadieville's best designs. 257
Figure 368. J.W. Hamilton house is pictured in B.O. Gaines's History of Scott County. 257
Figure 369. House on lot sold by Polk Fields to C.S. Davis in 1905. 257
Figure 370. Polk Fields sold the lot for 145 Vine Street to Leonard Mulberry. 258
Figure 371. Early house of James F. Rose 258
Figure 372. Early McCabe house became the home of Elizabeth Craig. 258
Figure 373. The Marshall family were longtime owners of the L-shaped house on Vine Street. ..259
Figure 374. John A. and Frances McCabe bought the lot for this house in 1898. 259
Figure 375. The McCabes' cellar with a storage building above occupied the back of their Vine Street lot. 260
Figure 376. The McCabes' barn served farmland adjacent to their Sadieville lot. 260
Figure 377. Lavina McCabe was the original owner of the houses at 229 Vine. 260
Figure 378. Hotel owner J.O. Rose and his family owned the property from 1925 to 1935. 261
Figure 379. The Robert Carlisle family owned the property on the north side of Vine. 261
Figure 380. C.W. Cornish bought the lot for this house in 1899 from S.B. Jones. 262
Figure 381. Hamilton and Sheehan sold this house in 1924 to J.T. Cunningham. 262
Figure 382. This was the home of historian and mail carrier W.A. "Bill" Mashall. 263
Figure 383. Silas B. Jones sold this house to blacksmith and handyman W.A. Maines and William McCoy 263
Figure 384. . J.C. and Lottie Lancaster sold this house in 1930 to Roy Fightmaster. 264
Figure 385. Granville and Fannie Kelly were longtime owners of the house at Vine and Bridge. ..264
Figure 386. J.M. Henry sold the T-shaped house to Dixie Zeysing, mother of Richard W. Zeysing. 265
Figure 387. The Methodist Episcopal Church was Sadieville's first church. 265
Figure 388. Lucy Thompson's house has a high dry stone foundation. 265
Figure 389. Sadieville Baptist Church was a large building with a balcony and a large bell tower. 265
Figure 390. The west wing of the house at 216 Church Street briefly served as a schoolhouse. ..266
Figure 391. The Church Street house during its later years. 266
Figure 392. R.W. Chowning built the Pamelia Parker house in 1906 from her heirs. 266
Figure 393. The Methodist Church parsonage was jointly owned by the trustees of the Salem, Sadieville, and Hinton congregations..266
Figure 394. Dr. J.W. Baird's house shares features of the Craftsman and Princess Anne styles. ..267
Figure 395. Mose Burgess's large barn served as warehouse for items to be shipped on the railroad. 267
Figure 396. In Sadievlle's early years, this building housed city hall upstairs and the jail downstairs.................268
Figure 397. George and Letha Marshall were among the Sadieville young people who became lifelong sweethearts after high school..269
Figure 398. This historic photo of College Street shows Sadieville School at the apex and to the east the J.W. Burgess barn that was a landmark in deeds to neighborhood properties............................269
Figure 399. Sadieville's 1904 school building during its later years. 270
Figure 400. Sadieville School's vaulted-roofed gymnasium was built in 1957. 271
Figure 401. A.H. Creighton house on College Street has a Craftsman style porch....................272

Figure 402. Stafford and Nancy Hughes's house on College Street. 272
Figure 403. J.H. Truitt house on College Street. 272
Figure 404. One of Sadieville's stellar dwellings is the Craftsman style brick house of T.F. and Carrie Sherritt on College Street. 273
Figure 405. Stylish A.L. McCabe house was the family's home from 1905 to 1962. 274
Figure 406. Lucy Lancaster family home from 1899 to 1984. 274
Figure 407. Sallie Sherritt's American Foursquare style house. 275
Figure 408. W.H. and Sadie Truitt house, circa 1894. 275
Figure 409. Pike Street commercial building of W.H. and Sadie Truitt. 275
Figure 410. Sadieville's unique lodge building and movie theater. 276
Figure 411. . J.C. and Lettie Swinford's Dutch Colonial Revival style house, circa 1914. 277
Figure 412. Llewellyn Price house dates from early twentieth century. 277
Figure 413. R.E. Chowning house, circa 1919. 277
Figure 414. W.C. and Nettie Faulconer house on Cunningham Avenue. 278
Figure 415. Lorena Hamilton house, circa 1914, is one of Sadieville's most attractive dwellings. 279
Figure 416. Lorena Hamilton sold this house to Mary E. Mulberry, mother of Carrie Sherritt and Gertrude Davis. 279
Figure 417. Charles and Mamie May's house has a unique high roof. 279
Figure 418. Masons and builders Herbert and George Antle, Charley May, and John Neal are shown building the foundation of a house for Tom Hamilton's mother, Lorena Hamilton. Photo courtesy Ron Vance. 280
Figure 419. C.T. Covington house on Railroad Lane. 280
Figure 420. Clarence and Gertrude Davis house was constructed of Tyrone limestone in a Dutch Colonial Revival style. 281
Figure 421. Sadieville water tower, dismantled in 2016. 282
Figure 422. Gauging station on Eagle Creek related to Sadieville's earlier water works. 282
Figure 423. Entrance to Sadieville Knights of Pythias Cemetery. 282
Figure 424. Early view of Cincinnati Southern railroad station and Main Street. 283

Contents

Foreword 13

Appreciation 15

Chapter 1 40

Agricultural Buildings and Complexes of Northeast and East Central Scott County 40

    Complexes 40

        Buford Hall, I, and Buford Hall, II, Agricultural Complex. 40

        Burgess Smith Barns. 43

        Burgess Smith "Racing Barn." 43

        Burgess Smith Hog Barn. 44

        Burgess Smith Side-Entered Tobacco Barn. 44

    Log Crib Barns 44

        Kitchen Log Crib Barn. 44

        John and Richard Pack Log Crib Barn. 45

        Edward Burgess Log Crib Barn, Davis-Turkeyfoot Road. 46

        Joseph Burgess Barn, Sadieville-Davis Road. 47

        Hugh Willhoite Barns. 48

        W.V. "Bunk" Mulberry Barn. 48

        J. Fields Barn. 48

        Kitchen Family "Mad Fence." 48

Chapter 2 African American Communities of Northeast and North Central Scott County 50

    Oxford Area African American Communities 50

    William Innis Farm and the Mary and Thomas Black Settlement 50

        William Black/ William and Opera Happy House, 3332 Cynthiana Road. 52

    Boydtown, Muddy Ford Road 52

        Boydtown, Wesley Boyd Tracts. 52

        Stephen Jones Tracts -- 4690 Muddy Ford Road. 53

        John Nichols House, 4720 Muddy Ford Road. 54

        Hurley House, 4738 Muddy Ford Road. 54

        Boydtown United Methodist Church. 54

        Boydtown [Rosenwald] School, 4770 Muddy Ford Road. 55

    Cranetown 56

    Cartertown 58

    Mount Olive Church and Scott County's Kansas Suburb, Nicodemus 58

REAL COUNTRY II. NORTHEAST AND EAST CENTRAL SCOTT COUNTY

Mount Olive Baptist Church/Dry Run Missionary Baptist Church, and Nicodemus, our "Kansas Suburb." ...58

Sadieville's African American Community ...60

    Cora Frye House, 824 Pike Street. ...63

    Bess Dallas House, 832 Pike Street. ...64

    Levi Craig House, 836 Pike Street. ...64

    York Smith House, Pike Street. ...64

    Harry and May Scott House, 852 Pike Street. ...64

    Roy Brooks' House, Farm buildings, 858 Pike Street. ...65

    Hurley-Henry House, 684 Pike Street. ...65

Roberts Lane ...65

    Roberts-Williams House, 111 Roberts Lane. ...65

    Ben Offutt House, 117 Roberts Lane. ...66

    Harold and Nannie Roberts House, 125 Roberts Lane. ...66

Chapter 3 Rural Northeast Scott County Late Nineteenth and Early Twentieth Century Survivors ...67

    Dividing Ridge Road, North and South. ...67

    Double Culvert, and Luke Roads, and Shawnee Run Cincinnati Southern Tunnels. ...67

    Fields Road, Harrison County's Unity Precinct, and Connersville. ...68

    South Ray's Fork (Hinton-Stonewall) Road. ...69

    Hinton and Northeast County Line Roads. ...69

    Collard School Site. ...69

    Elk Lick Church Road. ...69

    Burgess Smith Road. ...69

    Davis-Turkeyfoot and Boyers Chapel Roads. ...69

Boyers Chapel Road Properties ...70

Pack and Penn Family Properties ...71

    Richard F. and Sarah Martha "Sadie" Emison Pack House Site and Farm, Davis Road. ...71

    T.J. Burgess Stone Walls by Herbert Antle and/or Frank Gillispie, Sadieville-Davis Road. ...73

    William Penn House Site, Sadieville-Davis Road. ...74

    John W. Penn House, Sadieville-Davis Road. ...75

    Penn Houses, 2060, 2100 Davis Road. ...75

    Joe and Addie Penn House, 2200 Davis Road. ...76

Burgess Properties ...77

    Early Burgess houses. ...78

    655 and 867 Burgess Smith Road -- Burgess Smith Home Site. ...79

    Penn-Courtney Tract and Side-Entered Tobacco Barn, 800 Burgess Smith Road. ...79

- Elk Lick Particular Baptist Church Site, Davis-Turkeyfoot Road...80
- Elk Lick Church on Sadieville-Connersville Road. 80
- Elk Lick Church Site, 841 Elk Lick Church Road: Robert and Christina Gillispie House. 80
- Lancaster-Bryant House, 1411 Elk Lick Church Road. 81
- Joe S. and Richard L. Burgess House, Old Kentucky 32. 81
- Grayland Farm/K.C., Ella B., G.D., Addison Thomson House, 1101 Davis-Turkeyfoot Road..............81
- T.J., III, and Louise Burgess, House, 224 Sadieville Road/Old Kentucky 32.................................82

Emison and Emison Mills Properties 82
- Charles P. Fields House, 285 Elk Lick Church Road..82
- Davis/Crenshaw House, 589 Elk Lick Church Road. 83
- Emison Mill Site, Eagle Creek and Elk Lick Church Road. 83
- A.B. Barkley Mill Operation. 84

Hinton Family Properties 85
- William "Billy" Hinton. 85
- Ralph C. Giles Farm, Double Culvert Road. 87
- Farm, 1220 Double Culvert Road..87
- Hinton-Tucker House, 1310 Double Culvert Road. 88
- Asher Hinton Residential and Agricultural Complex, 375 Burgess Smith Road. 89
- Hinton- Reed House, Davis-turkeyfoot Road..90
- Laura Hinton Wells House, 495 Davis-Turkeyfoot Road. 90
- Doane Antle/James Willis Hinton House, 1030 Burgess Smith Road. 91
- William E. and Ann E. Reed Bates House, Farm, 763 Sadieville-Hinton Road. 91
- Reed/Vallandingham House, 548 Elk Lick Church Road. 92
- Hinton Road School Site. 93

Mulberry Properties..94
- W. V. "Bunk" Mulberry House, Davis Road. 95
- Leonard Mulberry House, Farm, 1751 Davis Road. 96
- Vallandingham-Nelson House, 280 Double Culvert Road..96
- McGuirk-Swinford House, 644 Hinton-Sadieville Road. 97
- W.F. Eads/A.J. and Juanita Lancaster House, 1236 Elk Lick Church Road. 97

Kitchen Properties 98
- John Kitchen House, Davis Road. 98
- Thomas Kitchen House, 2376 Davis Road..98
- Stone Family Farm, 555 Stone Lane. 99
- Faulconer-Dunaway House, 680 Stone Lane. 100

Real Country II. Northeast and East Central Scott County

- Lancaster Properties 101
  - Lancaster House, 984 Stone Lane. 101
  - John and Pauline J. Henry House, 120 South Rays Fork Road. 101
- Stowers and Robinson Farms, 155 and 227 South Rays Fork Road 102
  - Stowers-Wilderson House, 155 South Rays Fork Road. 102
  - The Robinson-Lowry Farm, South Rays Fork Road. 103
  - F.W. and Lucinda Davis House, 285 South Rays Fork Road 104
  - Benjamin and Edna Offutt House and Farm, 615 Hinton-Sadieville Road. 104
  - Brise Hiten House, Sadieville-Davis Road. 105
- Hiles, Giles, and Davis Houses 105
  - Hiles-Davis House, Sadieville-Davis Road. 105
  - 2111 Davis Road. 106
- Kentucky 922/Muddy Ford Road 106
  - Lee Gilkey Farm, Muddy Ford Road. 107
- Barnhill and Sharon Properties 107
  - Shepherd's Crossing/Clinton Barnhill House, 5000 Muddy Ford Road. 108
  - Barnhill-Dawson House, 5032 Muddy Ford Road. 109
  - Barnhill-Lacy House, 437 Rogers Gap Road. 109
  - Barnhill-Morris House, 781 Gunnell Pike. 110
- Burgess Properties 110
  - Martha Burgess House, 5219 Muddy Ford Road. 110
  - Corda Johnson Reed House, 5343 Muddy Ford Road. 110
  - Burgess/Henderson, 5253 Muddy Ford Road. 112
  - 6787 Muddy Ford Road. 113
- Munson Properties 113
  - Margaret Munson and Rollie Hinton House, 1366 Rogers Gap Road. 113
  - Munson-Hinton-Vance House, 1312 Rogers Gap Road. 114
  - Shelby Munson Farm, 7103 Muddy Ford Road. 117
- Price-Hiles Properties, Rogers Gap/Turkeyfoot Road 118
  - Ron Vance House, 1450 Rogers Gap Road. 119
  - Thomas B. and Nannie Mallory Hiles House, 1050 Rogers Gap Road. 120
- Buford Hall Family Properties 121
  - Buford Hall, II, House, 383 Rogers Gap Road. 121
  - The Hall Family 122
  - Henry Clay Fields Farm, 123 Barkley Road. 123

R.H. Williamson Farm, 493 Barkley Road.	124
Barkley/Grizzle House, 1155 Barkley Road.	126
Williamson-Duncan House, 576 Hinton Cemetery Road.	127
Wells-Duncan Houses, 571-577-583 Finnell Road.	127
Jesse Duncan House, 388 Hinton Cemetery Road.	128
Samuel T. Giles House II, 1588 Barkley Road.	129
Samuel T. Giles House I, 1468 Barkley Pike.	130
Samuel W. Giles House, 1495 Barkley Road.	131
Giles-Humphrey House, 131 North Mount Gilead Church Road.	132
Willie A. Reed House, 767 Mount Gilead Church Road.	133
Coppage-Giles House, 787 Hinton Cemetery Road.	134
Sarah J. Sharp House, 1889 Barkley Road.	134
John Reed-Humphrey House, 2024 Barkley Road.	135
Finnell Road	136
Hamon Properties	136
W.T. and Sue Hamon House, Finnell Road.	136
Mattie H., James K. Ewing House, 850 Finnell Road.	136
Warth-Conner House, 525 Finnell Road.	137
Hannah/Hanna	138
W.C., Noah Hanna House, 423 Finnell Road.	138
W.C. and Noah Hanna House, 333-339 Finnell Road. On the former	138
Shenandoah: Frank and Kay Wiseman Log House and Related Buildings, Finnell Road	138
L.S. Milner House, 239 South Mount Gilead Church Road.	139
Gregory W. and Elizabeth Trotter, 425 South Mount Gilead Road.	140
Stonewall J. Holland House, 805 North Mount Gilead Road.	141
Bailey Properties	141
Noah and Joseph Bailey House, 450 Mount Gilead Church Road.	143
Gunnell-Alexander House, 425 Gunnell Road.	144
Richard, William Gunnell House, 925 Gunnell Road.	146
W.T. Juett House, 426 Gunnell Road.	147
Griggs/Gregg Properties	148
Griggs House, Root Cellar, 1153-1155 Gunnell Road.	149
Moody-Morris House, 933 Morris Road.	149
Hinton Properties, Hinton Cemetery Road	152
Houston House, 539 Hinton Cemetery Road.	152

- Double Culvert and Luke Roads 153
  - 338 Double Culvert Road. 153
  - Dr. J.W. and Alice Baird House, 1050 Luke Pike. 153
  - Sowers-Giles House, 1075 Double Culvert Road. 154
- Luke Family Properties 154
  - Pack-Luke House, 576 Luke Pike. 155
  - Luke-Swinford Historic House Ruin and House, 711 Luke Pike. 156
  - Griffith House, 213 Luke Pike. 156
- Dividing Ridge Road, North. 157
  - John Kitchen House, 159 North Dividing Ridge Road. 157

Chapter 4 East Central Scott County 158
- Oxford-Muddy Ford Road. 158
  - The Nichols-Juett Properties. 158
  - Sherritt House, 4511 Muddy Ford Road. 158
  - William T. Juett House, 4671 and 4673 Muddy Ford Road. 159
- Old Turkeyfoot Road. 161
  - Indian Oil Refinery Site, North Hamilton Street/Old Turkeyfoot Road. 161
  - Prewitt-DeGaris Mill, DeGaris Mill Road. 167
- Delaplain Road 167
  - N.W. Hambrick Bungalow, 656 Delaplain Road. 167
  - Scott County Infirmary/ "Poor House," 714 Delaplain Road. 168
- Sims Road. 172
  - Valentine Rogers House, 664 Sims Road. 172
- Anderson Road 173
  - Crawford Moore Family Property, 235 Anderson Road. 173
  - Muntz House, 328 Anderson Road. 175
  - Barkley House, 526 Barkley Lane. 176

Chapter 5 Northeast and East Central Scott Crossroads and Railroad Villages 177
- Hinton 177
  - 120 Hinton Road, Gillispie House. 178
  - Lutes-Whitson House, 561 Hinton Road. 179
  - Rawlins-Whitson House, 581 Hinton Road. 179
  - Hinton Church Sites. 180
  - 4681 Hinton Road. 180
  - Dr. M.D. Sanford House, 2494 Davis Road. 180

- Laura Conner-William T. Smith Store, 2512 Davis Road..................181
- Beard Church and Cemetery..................181
  - Beard Presbyterian Church and Cemetery..................181
  - Joshua and John May House, Store, 2704 Davis Road..................184
  - Smith Bungalow, Davis Road..................184
- Alberta/Boyers Chapel..................185
  - Batey-Swinford Store, Shop, House, 1227 Boyers Chapel Pike..................186
  - Boyers Chapel Methodist Church..................187
- Muddy Ford..................187
  - Elizabeth Vance- Joe Sutton Property, 5411 Muddy Ford Road..................187
  - Eli Muddiman House Site, Muddy Ford..................188
  - Muddy Ford/ Robertson Store Site, 689 Barkley Road..................188
  - Muddy Ford Store Fire..................189
  - Muddy Ford School..................190
  - Bethesda Presbyterian Church, Muddy Ford Road..................190
- Turkeyfoot Village..................191
  - Turkeyfoot Christian Church..................192
- Rogers Gap..................195
  - Fields House, 1031 Rogers Gap Road..................196
- Dry Run/Delaplain..................196
  - Dry Run Baptist Church, 2109 Cincinnati Road..................197
  - Dry Run School, Cincinnati Road..................198
  - E.E. Muddiman Store Site, Delaplain, near former Cincinnati Rail Depot..................198
  - Hiram Wood House Site, Delaplain Road..................199
  - Mount Gilead Cemetery..................200
  - The Holdings..................201
  - Grangers Hall Site..................202
  - Warth Farm Log House Site..................203
  - John F. Giles Farm/ Cummins/Roehrig House, 1353 Finnell Road..................205

Chapter 6 Oxford Village..................208
- Oxford Village Lane, North Side..................210
  - Owens-Fleming-Rains house Site, 2780 Oxford Village Lane..................210
  - 212
- Former Providence Presbyterian Church/Jarvis Antiques, Oxford Village Lane..................212
  - Masonic Lodge, Tavern, Store, Post Office, Church Education Building, Oxford Village Lane..................214

Reuben Anderson House/Tavern Site, 2740 Oxford Village Lane. ...215
James Risk House, 2720 Oxford Village Lane. ...216
Thomas C. Peacher House, 2733 Oxford Village Lane. ...218
Lottie Barkley House, 2731 Oxford Village Lane. ...218
Muddiman/Hamon/Ewbank House, 2727 Oxford Village Lane. ...219
Jane Frankie Risk and Dr. W.T. Hendricks House, 2721 Oxford Village Lane. ...221
Blacksmith Shop/Grocery, House Site, 2693 Oxford Village Lane. ...222
Juett-Cannon House, 2489 Oxford Village Lane. ...223
Oxford-Newtown Road ...224
    G.B. and Belle Cannon House, 4313 Newtown Road. ...224
    Moore-Hamon Houses, 4347 Newtown Road. ...224
    F.M. Cannon House, 4330 Newtown Road. ...225
Muddy Ford Road ...227
    Hendricks-Barkley-Holland House, 4381 Muddy Ford Road. ...227
Delaplain Road ...228
    Vocational Agriculture/FFA Building, 1442 Delaplain Road. ...228
    Oxford High School, Graves Lumber Yard, 1446 Delaplain Road. ...229
    Helen F. Juett House, Delaplain Road. ...231
    Oxford Historic District. ...231

Chapter 7 Sadieville ...232
    Sadieville Railroad Underpass. ...234
    Sadieville Milling Company/New Era Milling Company, 350 Pike Street. ...235
Main Street – "Downtown" ...236
    Site, Former "Corner House" – Marshall-McCabe Furniture Store. ...236
    Warring Pavilion, City Park, Bandstand Site, Firehouse Site. ...237
    123 Main Street – Leonard Mulberry Store/Sadieville Baptist Church. ...238
    125 Main Street – Arthur Lancaster Drug Store. ...238
    127 Main Street – Harriet Kaley Hotel. ...239
    133 Main Street – Deposit Bank. ...239
    137 Main Street – Leander Risk Hotel. ...241
Main Street Residential Block ...242
    207 Main Street – George B. Johnson House. ...242
    211 Main Street – John M. Theobald House. ...243
    215 Main Street – F.T. Mansfield/W.T. and Frances P. Warring House. ...244
    219 Main Street – R.E. Lee/J.S. and Nell Burgess House. ...244

223 Main Street/Rodham and Fannie Fields House. 245

231 Main Street – Mefford/Daugherty/Hinton House. 246

Sadieville Christian Church – 241 Main Street, and Christian Church Parsonage, 245 Main Street. 246

311 Main Street—Judith A. Stone House. 248

Pike Street - south side 248

   Cornish Hall, 205 Pike Street. 248

   Queen City Railroad Depot/Sadieville City Hall. 249

   Jimmie Jones Dwelling and Storehouse, 615 Pike Street. 250

   Pike Street 1901 Footbridge Abutment Site. 250

   John Kaley Hotel, 625 Pike Street. 251

   John Cottingham Building, 631 Pike Street. 251

   Barnes-Rose Hotel (and Saloon), 639 Pike Street. 252

   643 Pike Street – Connellee-Crosthwait Dwelling and Store. 252

   667 Pike Street – Mabel Gann House Site. 253

   683 Pike Street – Nathaniel McLoney House. 253

   685 Pike Street – Barnett-Nelson House. 253

   695 Pike Street – Commercial Building. 254

   723 Pike Street – Bailey-Robertson House. 254

Pike Street - north Side 254

   662 Pike Street – Crosthwait-Risk House. 254

   668 Pike Street – Price-Parker House. 254

   730 Pike Street – Faulconer-Roberts House. 255

Vine Street – South Side 255

   117 Vine Street -- Neale-Willhoite House. 255

   J. Polk Fields House, 151 Vine Street. 256

   C.S. Davis House, 141 Vine Street. 256

   R.H. McCabe/Bob Davis House, 219 Vine Street. 258

   John A. and Frances McCabe House, 225 Vine Street. 260

   Lavina McCabe House, 239 Vine Street. 260

   Jacob Mulberry House, 247 Vine Street. 261

Vine Street – North Side 261

   Robert M. and Ella Nora Carlisle House, 152 Vine Street. 261

   C.W. Cornish House, 210 Vine Street. 262

   Hamilton and Sheehan House, 214 Vine Street. 263

   W.A. "Bill" Marshall House, 220 Vine Street. 263

J.O. and Laura Rose House, 222 Vine Street.	264
McCabe-Swinford House, 228 Vine Street.	264

Church Street/Gano Avenue ... 265

Sadieville Methodist Church Site.	265
Former Methodist Church Parsonage, 109 Gano Avenue.	265
117 Gano Avenue – Dr. Baird house.	266
Sadieville District 13 School, 216 Church Street.	267
Jail -- "Temple of Justice," Corner of Church (Mulberry) and Johnson Alley.	268

College Street ... 268

Sadieville Schools.	268
Sadieville City School.	270
A.H. Creighton House, 224 College Street.	272
Stafford and Nancy Hughes House, 228 College Street.	272
J.W. Truitt House, 236 College Street.	273
T.F. Sherritt - Brooker House, 302 College Street.	273
A.L. McCabe House, 306 College Street.	274
Lucy Lancaster House, 308 College Street.	275
Sallie Sherritt House, 312 College Street.	275
316 College Street.	275
William H. and Sadie Truitt Commercial Building, 326 College Street.	276
Lodge Building, Theater, 213 Cunningham Avenue.	276
Truitt-Warring House, 203 Cunningham Avenue.	277
J.C. and Lettie A. Swinford House, 219 Cunningham Avenue.	277
Faulconer House, 204 Cunningham Avenue.	278
Mary E. Mulberry House, 208 Cunningham Avenue.	279
Lorena Hamilton House, 214 Cunningham Avenue.	279
220 Cunningham Avenue.	280

Railroad Lane ... 280

Former Section House.	281

Eagle Bend Road --The Sadie Burgess Whitney Estate ... 281

Clarence S. and Gertrude Davis House, 105 Eagle Bend Drive.	281
Sadieville Water Works.	282

Conclusion ... 283

Photograph of G.H. Nunnelley Hardware lot south of Cincinnati Southern Railroad depicting assembled materials for building lodge and store at Biddle. Photo courtesy of Ann Glass.

CHAPTER 1

AGRICULTURAL BUILDINGS AND COMPLEXES OF NORTHEAST AND EAST CENTRAL SCOTT COUNTY

The age of great barns in Scott County and Central Kentucky peaked during the late nineteenth and early twentieth centuries. The earlier years also brought forth a series of folk barns. World War II's era of international industry and the growth that accompanied it resulted indirectly in a huge decline in the number of great and folk barns. Some historic barns fell into decay as many owners, in good faith, could not find funds to save them. Others became victims of the development mania, of individuals and companies bent on removing them in the face of construction of properties that could never equal in quality and attractiveness those that they replaced.

Discernable differences exist between the built agricultural resources of southern Scott County from those in the northern portion of the county. On southern Scott County's Maury-McAfee soils, most of the tobacco barns until approximately 1920 were constructed of heavy milled timbers with time honored mortise and tenon joints secured with large wooden pegs. A few mortised grain barns and corn cribs remain. Most surviving examples of these agricultural resource types in northern Scott County, with notable exceptions, have basic notched and nailed joints, sturdy and strong, more utilitarian than beautiful.

COMPLEXES

BUFORD HALL, I, AND BUFORD HALL, II, AGRICULTURAL COMPLEX. One of Scott County's most extensive agricultural complexes of the late nineteenth and early twentieth centuries was the farm developed by Buford Hall, I (1827-1896), and Buford Hall, II (1879-1946), on a vast acreage of soils transitional between Lowell-Nicholson (a small amount) to Eden Shale (a large sector). These soils supported the Halls' extensive sheep operation and the younger Hall's cattle establishment, supplemented on the not so hilly sections by tobacco farming and the growing of corn and grains.

In 1987 as part of a general study of

Figure 1. Buford Hall dry stone battered water tower that provided water for the entire farm.

properties along U.S. 25 in Scott County, the author with architectural historian and landscape architect Helen Powell, working under a grant provided to the Georgetown-Scott County Planning Commission by the Kentucky Heritage Council, spent an afternoon guided by Jeff Brashear, who with other members of his family were operating the farm for the corporation that had bought it from Marion Hall. We visited and photographed each of the thirty-six built properties on this vast farm. The PVA 1980 inventory listed 3,126.87 acres. Buildings

Figure 2. Agricultural storage buildings formerly located near front of Buford Hall farm.

Figure 3. Picturesque line of cribs formerly located near front of Buford Hall farm near highway.

Figure 4. Two large battened cribs located near the front of Buford Hall agricultural complex.

maintained in mint condition during the years of Hall family ownership began to deteriorate after the sale, underscoring the importance of periodic maintenance, repair, and upkeep. It was during this period that Marion Hall explained to us his grandfather's and father's roles in the farm's development.

The agricultural operation ambitiously undertaken by Buford Hall between 1827 and 1896 continued with the expansion from 2,170 acres in 1879 to 4,180 acres during the era of his son Buford Hall, Jr., and his grandson Marion Hall. The vast spread extended north and south of Rogers Gap Road, east and west of Cincinnati Road, and south of Double Culvert Road. The southern portion of the farm, including one hundred acres south of Rogers Gap village, contains a pattern of Lowell-Nicholson soils as the geographical transition is made from the Inner Bluegrass to the Eden Hills's Eden Shale soils. The low-lying lands of the eastern part of the farm are watered by Eagle Creek's Shawnee Branch and Rogers Gap Creek. The easternmost acreage, more amenable to cultivation, was the location of much of the Halls' tobacco, corn, grains, and hay cultivation. Sheep and cattle grazing the higher elevations received water from large low tanks spaced across the spread and filled from a picturesque water tower (previous page) on a high point. By the time of his death the elder Hall was grazing 1,200 to 1,500 sheep a year, mostly of the Cotswold breed. His sheep were sold in the Eastern United States. The George Vanderbilt farm near Baltimore was stocked with Hall sheep. [2]

After the death of Buford Hall, Sr., Buford Hall, Jr., took advantage of the burgeoning burley tobacco economy and built four state of the art tobacco barns and acquired another. Hall's barns were constructed, in the spirit of regional estate farms, with heavy milled timbers secured with pegged mortise and tenon joints. Unlike many barns of this type, however, Hall's barns rested on continuous poured concrete footings and poured piers. After the early years, mixed sheep breeds became more common on the Hall land as Western ewes were bred with Suffolk and Hampshire sires. After his father's death, Marion Hall managed the farm until its conclusion in 1985. He was grazing about 400 sheep and a large herd of cattle at the time of the sale to Beluga, a corporation operated by Pavia & Harcourt of New York City. [3]

---

[2] Bevins and Powell, "Buford Hall Farm," SC472 and SC472A-M, November 20 - December 4, 1987; Information from Marion Hall; B.O. Gaines, *The B.O. Gaines History of Scott County* 1 (Georgetown, 1904), reprinted by Frye Printing Company, 1981, 61, 81; M.R. Burgess, *The House of the Burgesses* (San Bernardino, California, 1983), 54.

[3] Information from Marion Hall; tour of Hall farm by Helen Powell and the author with farm employee Jeff Brashear.

The stunning introduction to the Hall farm for many travelers was the collection of agricultural buildings and lined-up corn cribs (pictured on the previous page) in view of Interstate Highway 75. Various other components of the agricultural complex stood at strategic points across the Hall land. Sheep barns, except for the example with a foundation of molded concrete blocks located near the farm shops, have poured foundations. The four sheep barns located near grazing areas have nearby low watering troughs with water pumped from deep wells. Eleven tenant houses remained on the farm during the 1987 study. All but two dated from the late nineteenth and early twentieth centuries. The scales house stood near the southwest corner of the farm. A farm shop and blacksmith shop, built on high dry stone foundations, served the operation for many years. Near them were a sheep barn, a large drive-in crib, a large granary, a wagon house with a trussed roof, and a hayshed.

Figure 5. Historic log house with centered chimney on Buford Hall Farm.

There were at least two small log houses on the farm. The log house pictured at the right was last owned by M.B. Carr. It has an address of 150 Rogers Gap Road. During its early years it belonged to Margaret Vance, who married Joseph Carr. She was a grandmother of historian Ronald T. Vance. The next log house upstream belonged to Martin Sellers, who married Catherine Vance, a sister of Margaret Vance Carr.[4]

The stellar quality of the closely managed Hall agricultural complex and the neatness and thoroughness with which the Halls maintained the barns, cribs, and tenant houses, declined after the purchase of the farm by Beluga, Inc. Beluga acquired the estate as an investment, however, and continued to look for a successor owner or owners and a future use or multiple uses, while operating the farm with the assistance of tenants and leasing it for hunting. Their search concluded when RLF Lexington Properties, co-owned by Stanford banker Jesse Correll, a major political contributor, bought the 3,127 acres in 2007 for $7.5 million or $2,398 an acre. The Commonwealth of Kentucky purchased 2,497 acres of this land on December 7, 2012 for $2,500 an acre with a plan for a conservation management area of Kentucky Fish and Wildlife. Fish and Wildlife, which considered buying the farm in 2002 or 2003, owns land across Kentucky for the stated purpose of protecting rural land from development and providing outdoor recreation for Kentuckians. The property's location between Lexington and Cincinnati was a factor in the commission's interest in acquiring the farm.[5]

Figure 6. Typical later Buford Hall tenant house.

RLF sold about 500 acres of the farm to a private landfill company and retained one hundred acres. Fish and Wildlife paid for the land with funds from the Wetland and Stream Mitigation Fund that included $3.25 million and federal grants, committing at the same time to restore nineteen miles of streams and headwaters on the property. The fund is managed by the U.S. Army Corps of Engineers, U.S. Fish and Wildlife Service, U.S. Environmental Protection Agency, and the

---

[4] Information from Ronald T. Vance.
[5] John Cheves, "Land sale sweet for political donor," *Lexington Herald Leader*, December 19, 2011, A1 and A2.

Kentucky Division of Water. The office of Governor Steve Beshear stressed that no state tax revenues were used. In the meantime, veterans' organizations got involved to help develop the conservation effort in honor of the nation's veterans and the liberty that Americans enjoy due to their efforts and sacrifices. The area was christened Veterans Memorial Wildlife Management Area in a special dedication ceremony in July 2012, with Kentucky Lieutenant Governor Jerry Abramson, Kentucky Fish and Wildlife Commissioner Jonathan Gassett, State Senator Damon Thayer, Congressman Ben Chandler, and State Representative Ryan Quarles sharing in the ceremony.[6]

Figure 7. Racing barn central to Burgess Smith Farm on Burgess-Smith Road.

The recreational area is seventy-four percent forested and has five designated parking areas. The governor's office press release stipulated that it "has a variety of important habitat types for game species and declining [species and numbers of] migratory birds, reptiles, and amphibians, [and] a variety of hardwood forests, shrub lands, and grasslands." One of the first groups to sponsor events in the recreation area was the Double Eagle Chapter of the National Wild Turkey Federation with an event entitled "Juniors Acquiring Knowledge, Ethics, and Sportsmanship." Among the activities were conservation exhibitions, archery, air rifle and air pistol, fishing, skeet, fly tying, and turkey calling."[7]

BURGESS SMITH BARNS, BURGESS SMITH ROAD

BURGESS SMITH BARNS. Three of northeast Scott County's stellar barns were originally owned by Burgess Smith, grandson of Joseph Burgess (1809-1892) and son of Evaline Burgess (1840-1931) and Sterling Paul Smith. They include a racing barn, a hog barn, and a side-entered tobacco barn.[8]

Figure 8. Burgess Smith hog barn has elegant pegged joinery.

BURGESS SMITH "RACING BARN." The cruciform "racing barn" on the Burgess Smith spread on Eagle Creek was central to a racetrack encircling a flat forty acres with a mound at the center traditionally referred to as an Indian mound. The agricultural region for this unique resource is the characteristically hilly Eden Shale section of Scott County. The barn measures forty by eighty-four feet. Each joint of the ten-inch-square posts, cut with a circular saw, is secured by four pegs of uniform size. Tier rails are uniformly pegged four by six-inch timbers. Decoratively shaped boards in the front gable end and five round metal ventilators along the ridgeline complete the design. The barn is pictured at the upper right.[9]

Burgess Smith lived in a large frame house on the road that bears his name. Reported to have had considerable gingerbread trim,

Figure 9. Burgess Smith side-entered tobacco barn has similar pegged joinery.

---

[6] John Cheves, Nancy Royden, *Georgetown News-Graphic*, July 17, 2012.
[7] John Cheves.
[8] M.R. Burgess, *House of the Burgesses* (San Bernadino, California: Borgo Press (1983), 54.
[9] Ann Bolton Bevins, *A History of Scott County As Told By Selected Buildings* (Georgetown: Kreative Grafiks, Ink., 1981), 304-305; Ann Bolton Bevins, "Historical Development of Agricultural Buildings With Specific Focus on Agricultural Resources of Scott County, Kentucky," report prepared for Kentucky Heritage Council (1985), 130-131.

the house burned several decades ago, though some of its material was conserved for reuse.

BURGESS SMITH HOG BARN. Burgess Smith's pegged hog barn, center photo, constructed with heavy timbers with tenoned mortise joints, remains Scott County's best hog barn example. Previous owner, the late Edgar Penn, described it as being of "rack and pole" construction. It has four open driveways and with large doors, raised ridgeline ventilators, and stall windows (now boxed in), and was well ventilated.[10]

BURGESS SMITH SIDE-ENTERED TOBACCO BARN. A surviving model rack tobacco barn is the Burgess Smith barn on Burgess-Smith Pike. The barn has three driveways entered through doors on the long sides. Its major joints are mortised and secured with wooden pegs. Its support by two large open heavy timber pens, positioned between the driveways, suggests that the early rack barn may have been a design descendant of the double log crib barn. It is the third of the barns pictured on the previous page.[11]

LOG CRIB BARNS

Log crib barns, perhaps once common to the farmscape, are most assuredly becoming rare. These wonderful nostalgia-inducing structures probably evolved much as the interior corn and grain cribs did, from need. Innately versatile, the sheltered crib could serve as a livestock shelter or could be adapted to store hay and other farm products. With rails, the log crib could be used for air curing tobacco. As the old log crib barns fell into disuse and were replaced by more efficient barn types, some owners found a new mythology to describe them. This writer has heard some of them called "hemp barns" by individuals drawing from both tradition and supposition.[12]

Figure 10. Detail of historic Kitchen farm's small log crib barn.

We are grateful to the farmers who refused to demolish these vestiges of their pasts, allowing today's architectural historians and other admirers to have a chance to appreciate them.

KITCHEN LOG CRIB BARN. The smallest such barn observed by the survey team was standing on the Kitchen farm on the Sadieville-Davis farm in 1987 when the writer was engaged in the study project about agricultural buildings. Emory Kitchen, father of Judy Smith, who worked with the study, drove us in a four-wheel drive truck to the old barn, in a state of

Figure 11. John and Richard Pack double log crib barn.

---

[10] *Selected Buildings*, 131.

[11] *Selected Buildings*.

[12] The barn on the Davis-Turkeyfoot Road with an octagonal cupola was called a prizing barn by one farmer and may have served as such. Prizing barns were centrally located warehouses to which growers brought produce or tobacco for "pricing" incidental to sales, marketing, and shipping.

ruin but with sufficient fabric for interpretation. The crib measured approximately eight by twelve feet. Some of the siding had rotted away, especially on the north side. The comparatively small crib had a wooden floor. There had been an earlier home site on this farm, with the present house that stands near the Sadieville-Davis Road dating from 1865.[13]

JOHN AND RICHARD PACK LOG CRIB BARN. East of Sadieville on the historic John and Lucinda Mulberry Pack and Richard F. and Sarah "Sadie" Emison Pack farm stood a model two crib barn. The cribs were aligned vertically; driveways extended along both sides of the superstructure. The larger crib measured twenty by twenty-eight feet. The smaller crib had a chute. A log wall connects the upper portions of the cribs that are separated by a drive-through space. The larger crib has a high hand-through slit in the logs and an attached pegged trough. Near this barn is a drive-through crib/granary put together with square headed nails. The nearby house was a very early

Figure 12. Edward Burgess barn with octagonal cupola. Other photos reveal detail including (a) tower from inside log crib; (b) log crib exterior detail; (c) hog trough attached to outside of log crib.

log example. The Packs' daughter Josephine married T.J. Burgess, one of the largest farm operators in northern Scott County and a founder of the City of Sadieville. Their daughter Laura Stevenson, who married her cousin N. Moses Burgess, next inherited the historic property. T.J. Burgess, their son, passed it on to the previous owners, Mrs. T.J. Burgess, and her son Tom Burgess.[14]

---

[13] Bevins, "Agricultural Buildings," 124.
[14] *Agricultural Buildings*, 122, 123, 128.

EDWARD BURGESS LOG CRIB BARN, DAVIS-TURKEYFOOT ROAD. By far the most elaborate log crib barn is the one that Edward Burgess (1816-1898) built on Eagle Creek across the Davis-Turkeyfoot Road from his log house. This is a section of northern Scott County once known as Sulphur Well. Atop the square superstructure is an elegant octagonal spire mounted on the upper logs of the crib. The crib, measuring roughly twenty-four feet square, is a marvel itself. The logs have adze and ax marks and have weathered to silver tones. Pegged to the interior wall is a hewn trough. The crib has a loft sheathed with closely butted boards, enabling the storage of small grains. Some of the whittled manger poles remain intact, and there is also a manger attached to one of the crib's outside walls. Burgess was a son of Edward C. "Ned" Burgess and a brother of Joseph Fields Burgess, owner of the large farm with the high style Greek Revival mansion at Stonewall.[15] It is an overwhelming experience to stand in the crib and look overhead at the complex support structure. This Burgess log crib barn has long been the jewel of regional barns, making the statement that the Burgesses did things in no small way.

Figure 13. View of main façade of first Elk Lick Particular Baptist Church now protected inside of extended log barn. Below - Exterior photo of expanded former Elk Lick Particular Baptist Church with log corn crib at right.

The nearby former church and its barn extension and the diminutive log corn crib stand nearby. The farm's small log houses added immeasurably to the character of this little road. This northerly section of this road to Turkeyfoot will live on in the memories of those of us who have received the gift of traveling along it.

ELK LICK PARTICULAR BAPTIST CHURCH /BARN. Beside the small Elk Lick Branch that flows into Eagle Creek near the Davis-Turkeyfoot Road is a tobacco barn that incorporates Scott County's oldest surviving church building, the Elk Lick Particular Baptist Church. Organizers of the church in 1799 were Jacob and John Mulberry, James Riley, Taylor Noel, and Edward C. Burgess. Other early members, according to late historian of the Eagle Hills William A. Marshall, were Dudley and John Davis and Richard Pendleton. By 1801, the congregation had grown to forty members, and by 1818, to fifty-nine members. The church affiliated with the Licking Association, an organization of Baptist churches called "particular" or "primitive" and holding specific Biblical tenets regarding the doctrines of election and conversion. In 1801 the congregation bought four acres from John Hawkins in the names

Figure 14. Barn of later Joseph Burgess near Davis.

---

[15] *House of the Burgesses*, 51-61; Bevins, "Agricultural Buildings," 122-123.

of Jacob Mulberry, trustee, and John Mulberry. Boundaries were given as lands of John Bows "on two sides" and Abram Fields and Charles Malery [sic] "on the other two sides."[16]

Figure 15. Joseph Burgess barn near Cincinnati Road.

The congregation relocated in 1849 to a Davis Road site described by William Marshall as across the road from the W.V. "Bunk" Mulberry house and barn. The new site led the congregation to change its name to "Flat Rock." After selling the property in 1848 to Joseph Burgess for ninety-eight dollars, the church moved to a site on a road that then assumed the name "Elk Lick Church Road."

Figure 16. Foundation detail of Cincinnati Road Joseph Burgess barn.

The original log church survives with additions on its south and east sides. The church entrance appears to have been on the west side. A break in the stone foundation on the protected south end suggests the changing of plans for stairs or a chimney at this point. The barn is used for housing tobacco and storing livestock feed. A delightful log corn crib, still in use, stands off to the side.[17]

Figure 17. Older barn on the Hugh Wilhoite farm.

JOSEPH BURGESS BARN, SADIEVILLE-DAVIS ROAD. On the east side of the intersection of the Davis and Burgess Smith roads is a circa 1920 barn six bents long and six tier rails high. Its banked driveway parallels the road. The roof is of the half-monitor type. It is a barn type found on other Burgess farms.[18]

Figure 18. A second, much altered, barn on Hugh Wilhoite farm.

---

[16] William A. Marshall, "Elk Lick Particular Baptist Church," *Scott County Church Histories: A Collection* (Georgetown: Scott County Bicentennial Commission, 1979), 16-18.
[17] Bevins, *Agricultural Buildings*, 125.
[18] Bevins, *Agricultural Buildings*, 129.

JOSEPH BURGESS/EVALINE SMITH/S.F. GANO BARNS. Joseph Burgess's estate on the Cincinnati Road at Stonewall grew from his purchase of land from several owners who included the Lemon and Ireland families. The Irelands owned a tavern in the area that may have been the predecessor to the Greek Revival style Joseph Burgess house with the stone kitchen likely remaining from the Ireland years.

Figure 19. W.V. "Bunk" Mulberry, Davis Road barn with continuous raised ridgeline.

Though not as dramatic as the barns of her brother Burgess Smith, Sarah Smith Gano's farm contains several barns joined with pegged mortised joints. The farm is owned today by the Sally Gano Hays family.[19]

HUGH WILLHOITE BARNS. This is the farm where late farmer and community leader Bob Davis once hunted along apparently abandoned roads, leading him to recall, "One of my happiest memories as a boy was hunting along that road with the view from the ridge and seeing that beautiful house and those big barns." The farm offers vistas of the Cincinnati Southern Railroad and the forests to the north.

The historic Hugh Willhoite farm's resources include the foundation of a burned log house, a tall tobacco barn, and a large stock barn with ten stalls on each side of the driveway. Sides of the tobacco barn rise fourteen feet; the large doors hang on decorative rollers. A raised ventilator runs the length of the ridgeline. There are vestiges of battening on the former stock barn.[20]

W.V. "BUNK" MULBERRY BARN. On the Eads farm, earlier owned by W.V. "Bunk" Mulberry, listed on the 1879 map as having included a blacksmith shop, is a curious barn with a roof with a raised ventilator. The barn is supported by some posts with ax marks. A nearby smokehouse is mounted on stacked stone piers. The property also includes drylaid stone fences, a story and half dwelling with a foundation of straight squared stones, a stone-walled spring that reportedly seldom if ever went dry, and a dry cellar with a workshop mounted on the cellar foundation.[21]

J. FIELDS BARN. Formerly owned by R.W. Mahan, a farmstead labeled "J. Fields" on the 1879 map contains a barn with a banked drive reinforced by a dry stone retaining wall. Tier rails are positioned across the drive while the rails above the other two driveways are parallel to the ridgeline. Near a probably early through road is a spring with a curved drylaid stone wall. This resource stands west of the northern section of the Davis-Turkeyfoot Road and includes a one-story house with a log ell. In the yard is a dry cellar with stone shelves built into the walls.[22]

KITCHEN FAMILY "MAD FENCE." The family of John Kitchen was located in the area of East Eagle Creek prior to 1819. The ruins of an older house occupy a high point in the interior of the now rugged farm, looking down on the log crib barn discussed earlier in this chapter. Among the stone fences on the farm is the "mad fence," two parallel diagonally laid rock walls erected by two reportedly angry brothers. The main barn is a mortised side-entry structure with an interior crib, large log sills, and tier "racks." The present house, located near Davis, dates from 1865; it has decorative millwork and shaped shingles. At one time the Kitchens operated the store, post office, and toll house for the village known first as Straight Fork.[23]

---

[19] Bevins, *Agricultural Buildings*, 123-124.
[20] Bevins, *Agricultural Buildings*, 129-130.
[21] Bevins, *Agricultural Buildings*, 129.
[22] Bevins, *Agricultural Buildings*, 131.
[23] Bevins, *Agricultural Buildings*, 124, 129.

CHAPTER 2
AFRICAN AMERICAN COMMUNITIES
OF NORTHEAST AND NORTH CENTRAL SCOTT COUNTY

Communities of free African Americans blossomed during the years following the Civil War and adoption of amendments to the United States Constitution enforcing voting and economic rights to the formerly enslaved. Churches and lodges were formative in the development of these neighborhoods. Schools were important to African American families from the beginning of their new lives as freedpersons. Leading the way to understanding and making use of this liberty were individuals who had become free during the settlement and antebellum periods. We will look at the neighborhoods that excelled and survived into the current era in the northeast and east central portions of Scott County.

OXFORD AREA AFRICAN AMERICAN COMMUNITIES

A fascinating pair of African American neighborhoods grew up on both sides of the Cynthiana Road on the former farm of William Innis, a descendant of some of Scott County's earliest families. Innes willed his farm to two of his slaves, Mary Black, who gave her surname to the neighborhood known as Black, and Richard Innis. Other African American neighborhoods that emerged in the vicinity of Oxford in eastern Scott County were Boydtown, north of Oxford on the Muddy Ford section of Turkeyfoot Road, and Cranetown off Delaplain Road west of Oxford.

WILLIAM INNIS FARM AND THE MARY AND THOMAS BLACK SETTLEMENT

Near the Scott- Harrison county line on both sides of Cynthiana Road are the two sections of the former William Innis farm, including his family home, devised by William Innis to former slaves Dick Innes/Innis and Mary Black. William Innis died in 1850.[24]

In addition to providing for his slaves, Innis asked that his books be sent to his cousins named Innis in Rush County, Indiana. Nieces Laurinda Cheek and Elizabeth McHatton were to receive $500 and $300. The bulk of Innis's will, however, related to his former and current slaves. "Dick Innis, "formerly my slave," was to receive sixty acres of his farm along with his house, outbuildings, horses, and the cows, calves, sheep, and hogs on the place. . . "Also my wagon and four pair of wagon gear; also a harrow, log chain, wheat fan, hand saw, drawing knife, steelyards, two plows, all the growing corn on hand at my death, and all the pork, bacon, groceries on hand at that time." Thomas Wesley was to live with and serve Dick and at the age of twenty-one "be emancipated and set free," when he should also have one hundred dollars placed in trust for him. Thomas was also to receive "the Highlander filly and a cow and calf." Milly was to be set free, receiving a cow about three years old, a quilt, and twenty dollars. Innis named John Ireland executor. Richard "Dick" Innis died in 1887, his will providing that his real estate except that of his wife be rented for two years, the proceeds to pay his debts. Land was then to be divided into three parts among Anika, his wife; his daughter Mariah Smith, and daughter Pattie Ann Allen, the latter with remainder to her children.[25]

William Innis's estate sale took place in June 1850. Richard Innis bought three bags and a half bushel of corn for $1.87. Thomas Black bought a wheel and kettle. Henry Edmundson, a minister and landowner known

---

[24] Will Book L-221.
[25] Will Book S-248.

through the years as a friend to African Americans, was present and made several purchases, as did former slave Milly. The sale netted $123.86. Thomas Black and Richard Innis were recorded as having paid $800 for land.[26]

In 1853, Jesse Hall, commissioner and guardian of the children of Tom and Mary Black, free persons of color, and a next friend of Mary Black, sold thirty-one acres on Cherry Run bounded by J.J.R. Flournoy, Richard Innis, P. Shropshire, and John Hall, for $1,755.34.[27]

Hall was involved in the various transactions related to the Blacks for about three decades following William Innis's death. In 1866 Hall acquired for $3552 the 113 acres on the south side of Cynthiana Road that he sold to Mary Black in 1877 for $3,500, having bought it from William A. Thompson. J.J. Ireland, Innis's executor, had sold the land in 1856 to Thompson. One wonders if perhaps Thompson and Hall held the property awaiting Mrs. Black's ability to pay for it.[28]

During the next several years, Mary Black and her family formed a community called "Black" along Black's Lane. The neighborhood had its own social and economic structure including a school and a restaurant. Mrs. Black died in 1894, having written her will seven months earlier, declaring herself to have been "of sound mind and memory. . . bless the Almighty God for the same." She left her son Thomas Black "what is known to the family as the big field." Jacob Black was to receive land along the lane "to the end of my picket fence." Dividing the remainder of her farm were Sarah, Jackson, and William Black. William Black purchased a number of parcels on both sides of the Cynthiana Road during the next several years. In 1939 he sold 19.5 acres to Opera and Willliam Happy for $12,000; over time the lane came to be called Happy Lane. Mrs. Black had stipulated that the road leading from the turnpike to her dwelling "forever remain a passway." She also left twelve acres and a house on the road leading to Hammond's store [the present Finnell Road] to Mrs. Will Mitchell, asking that Gusty Black have a lifetime interest in the house "at or on the property."[29]

Figure 20. William McIntyre surveys historic relics left in last house of Black neighborhood.

Though the community of Black was a viable one in its day, one by one its dwellings were torn down and replaced with modern examples. The writer had the privilege of visiting the community's next to last vestige

---

[26] Will Book L-349, 350; M-90.
[27] Deed Book 1-672
[28] Deed Book 1-672, 3-57.
[29] Will Book S-434; Deed Book 64-164. In most African American communities, a church was established early. Some churches had antecedents organized during the slavery era.

Figure 21. William Black, Opera Happy house facing Cynthiana Road.

(pictured on the previous page) when several items were sold, including a sign to the restaurant. A ring and items relating to the Spanish American War career of Ben Savage, also a prominent landowner in Georgetown's Boston, were discovered in the last house to survive in the main neighborhood.

WILLIAM BLACK/ WILLIAM AND OPERA HAPPY HOUSE, 3332 CYNTHIANA ROAD. The William Black/William and Opera Happy house, considered part of the community of Black though a feature of Cynthiana Road, crowns a crest near the Scott-Harrison county line. In 1939 William Black sold Opera and William Happy 19.5 acres located on the portion of the farm on the north side of the highway for $12,000. The three bays wide Black/Happy house has an enclosed front porch. There are other additions to the back of the house. William Happy deeded the house and thirty-five acres to Naomi Smith in 2004. [30]

BOYDTOWN, MUDDY FORD ROAD

BOYDTOWN, WESLEY BOYD TRACTS. Only remnants survive of the once thriving village initially called Boydsville and subsequently Boydtown in honor of founder Wesley Boyd. Boydtown is located a short distance east of Cranetown, its sister community on the Oxford-Muddy Ford Road (KY 922). Both neighborhoods were served by the Boydtown Methodist Chapel as early as 1869. The community evolved following the 1875 purchase by African American John Wesley Boyd of seventeen acres two rods from estate farmer William N. Atkins for $806.25 and two acres from C.J. Ward. During the next two decades the community popularly known as Boydsville spawned homes, small farms, a Methodist Church, and a school. In 1921 a new school financed by the Rosenwald Fund replaced the original school building. Boydtown's church, pictured on the next page, was dismantled in August 2015. The Rosenwald school, converted into a residence, survives, along with three other historic era dwellings.[31]

---

[30] Deed Book 285-326.
[31] Apple, Johnston, and Bevins, *Scott County, Kentucky,* 220, 245, 370; Deed Books 14-377, 14-6, 18-351, 34-540.

Among the lots that J. Wesley Boyd sold were: 1887, to Mary Frances Bowman, one and one-half acres twelve poles, ninety dollars; 1887, to Martin Graves, "sixty poles in the town of Boydsville," thirty dollars; 1893, to Urias Hurley, two acres, lot adjacent to church lot; 1893; Elizabeth Scott, sixty dollars, 1901, Boyd's widow to Trustees of the Colored School District at or near Oxford, one-fourth acre, twenty dollars.

STEPHEN JONES TRACTS -- 4690 MUDDY FORD ROAD. In 1877 another area farmer, John H. Barkley, sold Stephen Jones, an African American, twenty acres. Like most African Americans in the post-Emancipation era, Stephen Jones subdivided the twenty acres two rods ten poles that he bought in 1877 from the Barkley family for sixty-five dollars an acre. In 1905 Rilda Banks and Frankie Jones, heirs of Stephen Jones, deeded lot number three to Cora Graves, wife of Martin Graves. The house on this lot is a nicely designed bungalow on a dry stone foundation. Its extended dormer has two double windows. The house has a side porch and patio connected to the shed-roofed front porch, which is currently supported by tapered square posts. This property along with several other neighboring lots was sold in 1965 by Howard M. Graves and Friday Brown, heirs of Cora and Martin Graves, to Alva C. and Virginia Elizabeth True for $1,000. In 1980 the Trues sold the bungalow to Richard C. and Linda H. Haggin, who sold it in 1987 to Paul and Tammy Parker. Charles J. Reeder bought the house and 2.61 acres in 1991 for $56,100. It is currently owned by Charles J. and Wendy Reeder.[32]

Figure 22. Stephen Jones bungalow, a feature of the Boydtown community.

---

[32] Deed Books 37-86, 18-351, 98-458, 94-548, 125-535, 146-717, 172-676, 206-283, 191-052.

JOHN NICHOLS HOUSE, 4720 MUDDY FORD ROAD. John Nichols owned a generous share of Boydtown properties, including a one story four bay house with a stone foundation, located well off the Muddy Ford Road. In 1974 his estate representatives sold to V. Emma Nichols and Vivian Wilson a small farm of seven acres one rod. Granting the title were Opera Nichols and William Happy, Cora Nichols, Russell and Norma Nichols, V. Emma Nichols Wilson, Emma Elizabeth and Raymond Ellison, and Russell Clay Givens. A house was standing when Elisha Alexander sold Nichols property in two tracts, including a house and lot in Boydsville along with seven acres. Alexander acquired the house from Amanda Thomas in 1898 and a lot from J.A. Shropshire. [33]

Figure 23. John Nichols house in Boydtown community.

HURLEY HOUSE, 4738 MUDDY FORD ROAD. Urias Hurley, administrator, with family members Robert, Charles, and Reuben Hurley, Virgie Allen, Julia Hurley, Daisie Hurley, and Alexander Hurley, sold two tracts in Boydtown in 1905 to Gabe Hurley. In 1962 Norma U. and Russell Nichols and others sold five lots in Boydtown including the Hurley lot to James K. and Corinne Fisher. James Fisher died in 1989, asking that the property be sold with proceeds divided among his three children – James K. Fisher, Norma U. Nichols, and Zelma Bishop. In 1989 James K. Fisher and Henrietta E. Fender sold the accumulated 8.5 acres in Boydtown to James E. and Henrietta Fender for $40,000. The house on this lot was an impressive example of a substantial African American village dwelling. It was built on a stone foundation, was one and one-half stories tall, and had a centered chimney and a porch supported by turned posts.[34]

BOYDTOWN UNITED METHODIST CHURCH. Boydtown United Methodist Church's story was lovingly told in the 1979 *Scott County Church Histories: A Collection* by Opera Happy.

Mrs. Happy wrote, "The First Methodist Church of Boydtown was organized in the year 1869 in a log school house on the farm of Mrs. Mary Black on the Cynthiana Road. The church was spiritually organized in the hearts and minds of the folks in the little village of Boydtown." Mrs. Happy explained that when the matter of securing ground for the church was taken up, "Mr. Wesley Boyd permitted the residents of the village to choose any site . . . for the church and burying ground and granted them the deed." The church and community grew

---

[33] Deed Books 125-535, 47-373, 63-195, 32-346, 31-178.
[34] Deed Books 37-69, 92-27, 182-013; Will Book X-635, 5-711.

Figure 24. Former Boydtown United Methodist Church, and at right, Boydtown schoolhouse.

together. "We glorify God today in memory of those who sacrificed and struggled here in the beginning." The church was rebuilt following destruction of the first meetinghouse by fire.

Charter members of the Boydtown ongregation were Steve Jones, Pleas Smith, Ike Chinn, Alex Hurley, Mary Chinn, Mary Jan Conner, Wesley Boyd, and Martha Gilkey. In 1875 the title was extended when W.N. Atkins for one hundred dollars deeded to Isaac Chinn, Wesley Boyd, Alex Hurley, Curtis Allen, and Stephen Jones, trustees of the Methodist Church, two acres on the Muddy Ford Road. Other members "who worshiped and served this church and community until God called them to rest" included Henry Carter, George Deshay, the Reverend William Nutter, Jane Nutter, Virgie Allen, Narcissa Desha, Gabe Henderson, Louisa Hurley, Charles Hurley, Barney Henderson, Stella Fisher, James Fisher, Dave Fox, and Howard Graves. Among the early ministers were the Reverends Felix Ross, Clarence Coleman, and Baldwin David. Officers and trustees in 1979 were William Happy, John K. Nichols, Cora Nichols, James Happy, Emma Wilson, Jeremiah Wilson, Opera Happy, Vivian Wilson, and Naomi Smith. Pastors included the Reverends Jessie Scott, Taylor Seals, and R.M. Palmer.[35] The historic church was demolished in August 2015.

Figure 25. Boydtown's Rosenwald School is a residence today.

BOYDTOWN [ROSENWALD] SCHOOL, 4770 MUDDY FORD ROAD. In 1917 Julius Rosenwald, born in 1862 in Springfield, Illinois, son of German Jewish immigrants and president of Sears, Roebuck and Company since 1908, established the Julius Rosenwald Fund as a non-profit organization to promote "the wellbeing of mankind." In 1920 he reorganized the southern school building initiative inspired by his friend and education associate Booker T. Washington (1856-1915) and his wife, Margaret Murray Washington of Tuskegee, locating the headquarters at Peabody College in Memphis in 1920. From that time until

---

[35] Opera Happy, "Boydtown Methodist Church," *Scott County Church Histories*, (1979), 112; Deed Book 14-377.

1937, the fund provided grants to local districts for building and expanding qualified school buildings for African American students. The initiative yielded $28,408,520 toward construction of 5,357 African American public schools, shops, and teachers' homes in 883 southern counties in fifteen southern states. In Kentucky, there were 184 school building projects.[36]

Almost immediately after the establishment of the Rosenwald Fund, the Scott County Board of Education began applying Rosenwald standards to its buildings and seeking funding for schools for African American students. The records of the Rosenwald Fund were studied by Georgetown College's Alicestyne Adams to determine specifics about funding for Kentucky African American school building projects. Her research revealed construction projects at Sadieville, 1917-1920, $2,500; Boydtown, 1920-1921, $1,500; Great Crossing, 1920-1921, $2,700; Watkinsville, 1921-1922, $2,000; New Zion, 1927-1928, $1,800; and Zion Hill, 1929-1930, $3,200. According to the chart of Kentucky schools benefitting from the fund, Boydtown had a portrait of Rosenwald on display, and Zion Hill carried $2,000 insurance, the latter a requirement for schools for potential damage by fire. A 1929 effort to qualify the Boston school in Georgetown did not succeed.[37]

On June 4, 1921, J.M. Risk received the contract to build a school for $558 on the Boydtown site. In September, the board merged the Dry Run and Boydtown districts with the understanding that materials from the Dry Run site would be used in construction of the Boydtown School. In January 1922 the board took action to change the windows at Watkinsville to meet requirements for the Rosenwald Fund for Colored Schools and in March the superintendent was authorized to secure an estimate for the Perry School. In May the board voted to use the Rosenwald plan for one room schools at Perry and Stamping Ground – "boxed, weatherboarded, ceiled, concrete foundation." Windows at Watkinsville were changed to meet Rosenwald Fund requirements. In June the Brockman Brothers received the contract to build Perry School for $1,240, using first class material and workmanship.[38]

In 1901 Wesley Boyd deeded a village lot to the board of education for the community school. The 1904 B.O. Gaines *History of Scott County* list of county schools does not include a school for Boydtown; area students would have attended African American schools at Oxford, Dry Run, or at Black on the Cynthiana Road. In 1955 the county board of education sold the building to George May, who in 1971 sold it to C.T. and Norma Egbert. In 1984 John L. Barnes sold it to John L. and Diedre A. Smith Barnes, who sold it in 1988 to Christopher S. and Diane Higgins. The historic schoolhouse now serves as a lovely rural home for the Higgins family.[39]

Cranetown

Cranetown, a once thriving African American community, became for a time a most intriguing ghost town nestled well off the Delaplain-Oxford Road. Some of the earliest African American Cranetown property owners were Al Crane, who bought four acres in 1881 from Willis and Martha A. Gunnell; John and Edmund Henderson, two and one-half acres from Fannie Atkins in 1883; William Gilkey, one acre in 1885 from John

Figure 26. Sallie Mason surveys her former neighborhood of Cranetown.

---

[36] Alicestyne Adams, Director Underground Railroad Research Institute, *Rosenwald Schools in Kentucky* (Georgetown: African American Forum, Inc., Georgetown College, and Underground Railroad Research Institute, 2007), 6-10.
[37] Alicestyne Adams, 25.
[38] Bevins, notes from minutes of Scott County Board of Education, Office of the Superintendent, Scott County Schools.
[39] Gaines History 1:83; Deed Books 34-540, 82-142, 115-694, 140-283, 158-290, 176-727.

Henderson; John Gilkey, five acres from W.N. Atkins in 1891; and Joe Mason, 1750 square yards in 1900 and 1.5 acres in 1902 from John and Georgia Gilkey.[40]

Figure 27. View of main street of Cranetown.

Figure 28. House on Cranetown Lane.

Figure 29. View of larger house in Cranetown.

About twenty years ago the writer visited Cranetown with Sallie Mason, other members of her family, and Wilma Ewbank. We wistfully traveled the narrow lane leading to the once thriving little community and walked through the abandoned dwellings as Mrs. Mason told us about the people who lived there. You sensed Cranetown's presence in a day gone by when most inhabitants worked nearby. Since that day many families have moved away, many to northern cities and some into Georgetown. Those who choose to give attention to their former dwellings do so "for old time's sake."

Mrs. Mason told us that in 1925 the house where she and her husband Joe lived was moved from the spring near the bottom to the hill and that "we stayed here till 1974."

"Mattie Shaw also left around 1974," she added. The Masons added two rooms to the house. She pointed to a grey house with two-over-two-pane sash, once the home of Will and Sally White. Mrs. Mason also pointed out the house of George and Narcissus Deshay, who "were here in 1925." She led us past four more houses and two more on the main road. People associated with them included "Aunt Frank (Caroline) Chinn." Albert Crane had a prominent residence, while over the hill was the home of Ed Henderson. Alex Kirtley was on the back lane, as was Dean, a daughter of Mr. Deshay. The burial ground was "up the road."

Residents of nearby Boydtown whom Mrs. Mason recalled included Charlie Conner, Willie D. Allen, Jimmy Fisher, V. Emma Wilson, and Amos Pugh. She also discussed a short man who drove a two-wheel sulkey. When the Boydtown school closed, children from Cranetown attended the two-room school at New Zion. Nearby churches were Mount Olive on Cincinnati Road and the Boydtown church.

---

[40] Deed Books 20-39; 22-77, 78; 26-308; 33-605.

The earliest Cranetown deed discovered in this research process was the 1881 sale from the Gunnell family to Albert Crane, John Henderson, and Ed Henderson. Crane and his wife Kitty sold a house and lot in 1908 to Will White, a major neighborhood property owner. White bought other nearby parcels from James Shropshire, Will Deshay, the Preston Cole estate, John White heirs, and Evaline Fox. In 1980 Katie S. Edwards sold some of this property to Ed Lewis and Edna M. Thompson. Joseph Mason made several purchases from the Gilkeys: one acre in 1899, 1,750 square yards in 1900, and 1.5 acres in 1902.[41]

At the time of our visit, Ed Louis Thompson owned twenty-seven acres in Cranetown, and the Masons, eight acres. Cranetown contains building lots for today's population.

CARTERTOWN

Discussed by Mrs. Sallie Mason during the visit to Cranetown was the nearby settlement of Gladys and John C. Fisher called Cartertown. It had three houses, of which one remains. Names connected with the settlement were Aaron Wilson, a Mr. Tibbs, and Arthur Lee Taylor who married a Wilson.

MOUNT OLIVE CHURCH AND SCOTT COUNTY'S KANSAS SUBURB, NICODEMUS

Figure 30. Historic Mount Olive Baptist Church enhanced with brick facing and expanded brick addition.

MOUNT OLIVE BAPTIST CHURCH/DRY RUN MISSIONARY BAPTIST CHURCH, AND NICODEMUS, OUR "KANSAS SUBURB." Buford Hall employed a large number of African Americans on his extensive agricultural spread on the Rogers Gap-Turkeyfoot and Cincinnati roads and encouraged them to organize their Baptist Church. In July 1870 a group of farmers gathered under a sycamore tree on the lawn of Jeret Smith, who lived on the Hall farm. Under the leadership of the Reverend Morris Bell and a Reverend Charles, they organized the Mount Olive Baptist Church and chose C.C. Coleman, Jerry Scruggs, Ras Kirtley, Thornton Williams, Merit Hix, Abe Timberlake, and William King as deacons. The first trustees were Minor Lewis, Ed Smith, and Wyatt Griffin. Early members also included Mary Jan Hawkins, Mary Sims, Leathy Penny, Emily Moore, Phyllis Allen, Marie Spencer, Harriet Timberlake, Cynthia Fox, Lewis Smith, Mitchell Smith, Sam Penny, the Reverend Don Hickman, Jack Riley, Will Gilkey, Albert Crane, Easter Alexandra, John Robinson, and Joseph Lewis.[42]

Shortly after organizing, the congregation built a meetinghouse on the Hall farm. A second building, the present structure, rose on the site of the first, which burned. Mrs. Gossey reported that at the time that she wrote

---

[41] Deed Books 20-39, 33-205, 35-139, 39-260, 87-518.
[42] Ethel M. Gossey, "Mount Olive Baptist Church, Dry Run" in Bevins and Snyder (eds.), *Scott County Church Histories,* 34.

Figure 31. Nicodemus, Kansas, in its heyday.

the historical account, the congregation had forty-nine members and two deacons. "For our church we are grateful and thankful," she wrote. "Lord, we thank Thee for our church, tho it's small and members are few, but we know someone worked hard and long to give us a place to worship You."[43]

The circa 1900 Scott County Mount Olive meetinghouse, a small weatherboarded chapel, is preserved within the present brick faced complex. It had three windows along the long sides and a small square vestibule.[44]

In 1978 some of the members of the Mount Olive congregation found a new church home in Georgetown, buying a grocery building on Chambers Avenue and Bourbon Street. Trustees receiving title to the $20,000 property were Jesse Mason, Willie Gossey, and Willie Gossey, Jr. Members remaining at the older location adopted the name Dry Run Missionary Baptist Church.[45]

Scott County's Mount Olive Church was a center for the mid-1870s movement among Central Kentucky African Americans, catalyzed by circulars promoting a proposed community to be called Nicodemus on the high plains of northwest Kansas. The Mount Olive congregation promoted the migration of large numbers of freedpersons to Kansas. A main leader was Daniel Hickman, one of ten siblings who also included Benjamin Hickman, one of Georgetown's first black physicians. Daniel Hickman made his profession of faith in 1862 and became a minister in 1866, serving the Owens Baptist Church on Big Eagle and Mount Olive on Dry Run in Scott County.

A former carriage driver and chore employee, Hickman learned to read by saving scraps of paper with print, discarded by others. Twenty-four years old at the close of the Civil War, he rented land from a man who helped him develop his reading skills. Hickman read the newspapers to his fellow workers. Narratives about African American settlers in Nicodemus and their earlier lives in Kentucky are included in the Lula Craig Papers, a collection of interviews by the former teacher, archived by the University of Kansas. Craig was an ancestor of Angela Bates, leader of the successful movement to preserve Nicodemus as the oldest surviving black community in the American West as a National Park Site.

In 1865 Hickman married Willina Lewis, who converted to Christianity in 1867 at the Baptist Church at Dry Run. Willina and Daniel Hickman, Pastor Bell, and about 150 other people from Scott County equipped themselves with tools that they could carry with them and headed for the Promised Land in 1878. They traveled by train to Hays, Kansas, and then set out on foot to the site of Nicodemus. Willina's words on arriving at Nicodemus have become immortal and have been published far and wide in brochures and in books.

Willina learned millinery, dressmaking, and tailoring, and in Nicodemus she pioneered construction of hats from blue-stem grass, using four types of braids. Years later she told the following story to historian Lula Craig: "When we got in sight of Nicodemus the men shouted, 'There is Nicodemus!' Being very sick, I hailed

---

[43] Gossey, 35.
[44] Bevins and Powell, "Mount Olive/Dry Run Missionary Baptist Church," Kentucky Inventory Form SC474, December 4, 1987.
[45] Gossey, 35.

Figure 32. (a) Surviving example of dugout house in Nicodemus vicinity. (b) Angela Bates; park ranger Michelle Huff; and historian Ann Bevins at Nicodemus National Park Service Visitors Center. (c) Verle Switzer, Nicodemus farmer and the first African American to crash the professional football color barrier as a Green Bay Packer.

this news with gladness. I looked with all the eyes I had. I said, 'Where is Nicodemus? I don't see it.' My husband pointed out various smokes coming out of the ground and he said, 'That is Nicodemus.' The families lived in dugouts... The scenery was not at all inviting, and I began to cry."

Dugouts, similar to the example pictured at the left, were homes carved into the ground with shovels in the spirit of the Hobbits later made legendary by J.R.R. Tolkien. The 300 people living in dugouts crafted after their fall 1877 arrival in Kansas used borrowed tools for their sod, stone, and wooden houses. The 1878 Scott County immigrants carried tools with them.

Daniel Hickman and Morris Bell established Mount Olive Baptist Church, Nicodemus's first church. On returning to Kentucky, Bell left Hickman in charge of the congregation. Hickman distributed Sunday school and church literature for the American Baptist Publications Society of Philadelphia and preached the first sermon at nearby Hill City. He also organized neighboring Hill City's First and Second Baptist churches. The latter had a largely white congregation. North of nearby Bogue he founded the Mount Olivet Church, its name with a spelling variation honoring his old church in Kentucky. In all, Daniel Hickman spent fifty-one years in ministry. He was involved in local politics, was chair of the county commission, and was Graham County's first coroner. In 1903, Hickman moved to Topeka where he was custodian for the state capitol. He then accepted a call to a church in Junction City. He died in 1917 and was buried in the Mount Olivet cemetery.

Figure 33. (a) Home near Nicodemus of former slave of Richard M. Johnson. and (b) Original Nicodemus schoolhouse will be restored.

SADIEVILLE'S AFRICAN AMERICAN COMMUNITY

Mount Pleasant Baptist Church and the Sadieville Rosenwald School, standing side-by-side in the east Pike Street neighborhood, are among Sadieville's crowning features. Token dwellings of Sadieville's once dense black community also survive east of Vine Street along Roberts Lane. All give depth to the stories that grew up in the church and school.

Figure 34. Sadieville Mount Pleasant Baptist Church with congregation.

Figure 35. Interior of Sadieville's Mount Pleasant Baptist Church.

Figure 36. Sadieville Mount Pleasant Baptist Church, and behind it, the Rosenwald schoolhouse.

Two decades ago Nancy Brooks, Sadieville columnist for the *Georgetown News-Times*, Bess Dallas, and Bess's sister Cora Frye, and the author met on the lawn of Mount Pleasant Baptist Church to discuss Mrs. Dallas's and Mrs. Frye's experiences during their many years as residents of Sadieville. Bess and Cora at the time were among the few members of the dwindling Mount Pleasant congregation. At the time, Nancy was contributing a popular series of columns, among them notable classics, of daily life in and around Sadieville. In the back of our minds was trying to come up with ideas of how to save the church and schoolhouse.

Though Nancy and I learned a great deal that morning about Sadieville's African American community, none of us sharing in this wonderful discussion, was aware that the schoolhouse turned fellowship hall had been built with funding in part provided by the Julius Rosenwald Fund. However, we valued it as the school where Sadieville's black children received their education. We considered its preservation paramount.[46]

That crucial piece of information relating the school to the Rosenwald movement would await the research of Dr. Alicestyne Turley Adams, director of Georgetown College's Underground Railroad Research Institute. Dr. Adams's resulting exhibit and book about Kentucky's Rosenwald schools were completed in 2007. Former Sadieville city clerk Cindy Foster was a major force in bringing the school and church restoration project to reality. During this period Angela Bates, director of the Nicodemus, Kansas National Park Site project, journeyed to Sadieville for a presentation about Sadieville African Americans' role in settling and developing Nicodemus.[47]

An early community of African Americans who found employment in the Sadieville area developed on the Hinton Road

---

[46] Nancy Brooks, *Georgetown News & Times*, September 28, 1988.
[47] Alicestyne Adams, *Rosenwald Schools in Kentucky*.

during the post-Emancipation years. A black cemetery survives on the east side of the road a short distance from Sadieville. Another neighborhood was on the east end of Sadieville's Pike Street, which took its name from the turnpike of which it was part. The triangular piece of land formed by the junction of Angle Street with Pike Street once included a dense African American neighborhood essentially eliminated by Urban Renewal.

Figure 34. Historic photo of Sadieville's Rosenwald schoolhouse.

Cora, Bess, and Emma Frances were daughters of Elizabeth Nutter, affectionately called "Mammy Liz," and sisters of builder/stonemason Bill Spears. "He couldn't read, but he could thoroughly understand blueprints," elaborated Bess. Their mother had been a slave of Lafe and T.J. Burgess. Spears built Cora's house as well as the fences that line some of Sadieville lots and Burgess farms.

One of the first things you notice about Sadieville is the necessary existence of retaining walls, all beautifully engineered. Several rock walls also exist along the boundaries of some of the building lots. Many of them were the work of Ben Offutt and his son Harry. Benjamin and Edna Offutt were the original owners of the bungalow at 615 Hinton-Sadieville Road. The house is distinguished by classical Arts and Crafts style tapered posts set atop brick piers. Ben Offutt was both mason and carpenter; he brought up his son Harry in those trades. He died in 1951, leaving Edna, sons Graham and Harry C., and daughter, Mae Etta O. Holmes.

Organized in 1872, Mount Pleasant Baptist Church was until its recent closing Sadieville's oldest congregation, still enjoying the city's oldest meetinghouse. In 1884 T.J. and Josie Burgess sold the congregation trustees John Harrison, George Washington, and William Hurley the one hundred by 150-foot lot "for the purpose of erecting a house of worship."[48] Cora explained that the church's very fine foundation was the work of Harry Offutt, who died in 1982, and Chris Offutt. The pair also constructed the stone retaining wall along the front of the church lot.

Built between 1917 and 1920, Sadieville School was constructed by the Scott County Board of Education with a $2,500 grant from the Julius Rosenwald Fund, the organization responsible for funding schools for African American children throughout the South. The Sadieville

Figure 35. Levi Craig house with interesting walkway constructed with stone slabs.

school was one of six Scott County schools that achieved the elite status of qualifying for Rosenwald funding. Criteria for funding included the size of the school, availability of separate restroom or outhouse facilities for boys and girls, construction requirements, adequate lighting, and playground space.[49]

---

[48] Deed Book 24-37; "Mount Pleasant Baptist Church," *Scott County Church Histories,* 38.
[49] Adams, "Rosenwald Schools in Kentucky," 25.

Figure 36. Childhood home of Bess Dallas and Cora Frye.

In Sadieville, according to the 1904 B.O. Gaines history, there were sixty-eight black students. Celia O. Gaskins was the teacher, and York Smith, John Harrison, and Stafford Howard were trustees. [50]

In June 2008, the City of Sadieville purchased the church and school for $15,000. Mayor Rob Wagoner advised the commission that the transfer of ownership was necessary to qualify the property for a grant for preserving Rosenwald Schools through the National Trust for Historic Preservation and the Kentucky Heritage Council. The Reverend Anthony Roberts and his mother Nanni Roberts, eighty-seven, the last known trustees of the church, signed the purchase agreement. Mrs. Roberts explained that she had been a member of the church since she was thirteen years old. Her husband was a nephew of stonemason Bill Spears.[51]

CORA FRYE HOUSE, 824 PIKE STREET. Next door to the church is the childhood home of Bess Dallas and Cora Frye. Two catalpa trees in the yard, since removed, recalled an Arbor Day distribution to school children. Cora later moved further down Pike Street. Bess explained that Roy Vance, white, and Henry Harrison, African American, built the rock wall that lines the sidewalk in front of her house, as well as the dwelling's foundation. Some neighborhood houses are mounted on either wooden or stacked stone piers. Cora's husband, John, purchased their second house and lot

Figure 37. Later home of Bess Dallas.

in 1925 from Abe and Susie Williams. Earlier owners included Hollie and Hannah Johnson, E.B. Fightmaster, and Elizabeth F. Craig.[52] Cora died January 14, 1992, leaving her property to Charlesetta Miller. George E. Parker, who bought it in 2005, sold it in 2008 to Ronald and Christine Wright.[53]

---

[50] Gaines History 1: 83.
[51] Gayle Deaton, "Sadieville buys historic church," *Georgetown News-Graphic*, August 11, 2008; additional information from Frances (Mrs. W.T.) Warring.
[52] Deed Books 43-276, 43-275, 50-248, 52-133, 145-678, 146-205, 282-312.
[53] Deed Book 282-312, 321-783.

Figure 39. Cindy Foster, former Sadieville clerk who put together the city's Rosenwald School history.

Figure 38. Henry and Mary Scott house has porch supported by tapered posts.

BESS DALLAS HOUSE, 832 PIKE STREET. Bess Dallas's house next door to that of her sister, Cora Frye, stands on property sold to her by William Scott in 1958. The chain of title is fascinating. In 1899 S.T. and Lucy A. Connellee, co-founders of Sadieville, sold the lot for sixty dollars to John N. and Rebecca S. A. Henry. In 1901 John Newt Henry sold it to Pat Corrigan for $150. In 1904 Pat and Susie Corrigan sold it to William Scott, who sold it to Bess Dallas. Bess, like her sister, willed her house to Charlesetta Miller.[54] Mrs. Dallas's house has a stone foundation and a stone retaining wall behind the house. The rock wall that lined the sidewalk in front of the sisters' houses had diagonally laid coping. The fence begins at the steps leading into Bess's yard. Eight steps lead to her porch. The three-bay hall-parlor plan dwelling had a central chimney.

LEVI CRAIG HOUSE, 836 PIKE STREET. The three-bay house retains a portion of its streetside rock wall minus the coping, and the stone steps and walkway leading to the porch. It traces to the 1900 sale by Levi Craig to Richard and Sally Ignight. Craig published the newspaper known as *The Sadieville Sunshine.* The Ignites sold the property in 1923 to J.C.B. Fightmaster. In 1986 Agnes L. Parrish sold it to Sadieville Urban Renewal, which in 1990 sold it to John L. Greatbatch. Paul Wallace, a recent owner, sold it to Gilbert Hernandez.[55]

YORK SMITH HOUSE, PIKE STREET. The next house east on the Davis Road occupied a lot that the Connellees sold to Elizabeth Hurley, daughter of Charity Henderson, in 1902. Her heirs sold it to N. Mose Burgess, who in 1919 sold it to York Smith. Smith sold to Marvin Moore in 1935, and in 1961 the Moores sold to George and Odella McGee. Later owners included R.H. King, Bonnie Jean King, David Abrams, Charles Carpenter, Leonardo Sanchez, and Gilbert Hernandez in 1999.[56]

HARRY AND MARY SCOTT HOUSE, 852 PIKE STREET. A three-bay house with a porch supported by tall tapered posts relates to a 1905 sale by the Connellees to Harry Scott and Mary Scott, his daughter. In 1911 Ben Offutt acquired the property and in 1917 sold it for $1,100 to Mary Jones. Jones willed it to Susie Williams, who in 1952 sold it to Harold and Nannie C. Roberts. Urban Renewal acquired it in 1983 for $3,250 and sold it in 1983 to Joe B. Carr. Gilbert and Kathy Hernandez purchased it in 2005.[57]

Figure 40. (a) Alicestyne Adams as Rosenwald teacher. (b) Angela Bates discusses Sadieville's relationship to Nicodemus, Kansas.

---

[54] Deed Books 33-164, 34-255, 62-28, 272-307; Will Book 13-92.
[55] Deed Books 33-242, 34-530, 65-592, 165-710, 187-462, 204-541, 212-757, PVA files.
[56] Deed Books 35-197, 43-585, 50-624, 62-404, 91-332, 116-121, 163-539, 188-672, 244-406, 245-31, 253-662, 245-036.
[57] Deed Books 37-557, 69-318, 58-108, 79-17, 83-563, 90-221, 93-491, 95-234, 100-147, 154-218, 155-680, 293-20.

ROY BROOKS' HOUSE, FARM BUILDINGS, 858 PIKE STREET. Roy and Adeline Brooks were parents of Robert Brooks, the first member of the Fort Knox Armored Division to die in action in the Pacific Theater of World War II. In 1944 the Brookses bought the house at 858 Pike Street from Ben Offutt, trustee for the heirs of York Smith. Smith acquired the property in 1896 from S.T. Connellee. Annie Roberts and Jessie Banks quitclaimed their interest to Offutt, who sold the property to Mr. and Mrs. Brooks. In 1970 Roy Brooks, Jr. and his wife Valerie, and other heirs sold it to Earl K. and Lee L. Vance. Later owners include Charles D. and Betty Jean Ison, Lawrence McConnell, Edith C. Jones, Earl Gene Jones, and Glenda Sue Jones, who acquired the 1.79-acre tract in 1998. East of the house are agricultural buildings. This is the most easterly property on the north side of Pike Street.[58]

Figure 41. Roberts-Williams house and its modern extension.

HURLEY-HENRY HOUSE, 684 PIKE STREET. The Arts and Crafts style house occupying the lot owned in the early years of the twentieth century by T.J. and Josie Burgess and Leonard and Estella Mulberry has had better days and years. At the same time that the Burgesses sold the Pike Street lot to Mulberry, they also sold him a lot near the railroad in south Sadieville. In 1906 the Mulberrys sold the property to W.T. and Alma Brashears, who sold it two years later to Lewis and Ann Hurley and others. It remained the Hurley house until 1937 when heirs sold it to Henry W. and Nannie J. Henry. The Henrys sold it to Samuel Kelly and Lou Ella Gann in 1972, the year that Samuel Gann sold it to Lou Etta Wigglesworth.[59]

ROBERTS LANE

Begun as an extension of Vine Street, Roberts Lane contains several older houses identified with the community's African Americans. It takes its name from the Roberts family, one of whom, James Roberts, purchased a house and lot in 1901 described as being on the south side of Vine Street.

ROBERTS-WILLIAMS HOUSE, 111 ROBERTS LANE. In 1907 James and Alice Roberts sold Lue Dundery the house and lot that Roberts purchased in 1901 from Jasper and Laura Rose. In 1945 Susie Williams and others sold it to Richard Bowman. The property combined two tracts, a house bought in 1918 from Harrison and Mollie Keene, and the other, in 1925 from German Gillispie. In 1929 R.H. McCabe, Mary E. McCabe, and Ernest and Edith Davis sold the property to Abe and Susie Williams for $350. This property incorporates a four-bay vinyl sided remodeled house on a block foundation.[60]

Figure 42. Roy and Adeline Brooks house; the Brookses were parents of Robert Brooks of World War II renown.

Figure 43. Lane leading past Brooks farm buildings.

---

[58] Deed Books 69-300, 69-327, 112-274, 121-491, 128-189, 130-702, 238-692, 236-558.
[59] Deed Books 36-101, 38-317, 42-243, 90-94, 56-607, 119-4, 119-83.
[60] Deed Books 70-494, 50-373, 38-280, 36-18, 57-573, 50-373, 38-80.

BEN OFFUTT HOUSE, 117 ROBERTS LANE. In 1911 Wade and Stella H. Davis sold William Smith an L-shaped house then regarded as located on Vine Street. In 1928 Oscar and Ruth Smith and William Frank and Hazel C. Smith sold the property to stone mason and carpenter Ben Offutt. Offutt owned the house, which has a recessed entryway and porch approached by four steps, until his death in 1951, leaving it to his sons Graham Offutt and Harry Offutt. Graham died in 1958 and left the property to his widow Edna and his daughter Mae Etta Holmes. Harry Offutt and Mae Etta and her husband George Holmes conveyed their interest to Edna Offutt in 1983.[61] After Edna Offutt's death, in 1995, Mrs. Holmes as executor sold the house and lot to William H. and Valeria Miller. Subsequently it was sold to the United States Housing and Urban Development (HUD) agency, which in 2005 sold it to Barbara and Galen R. Rowe of Madisonville.[62]

Figure 44. Circa 1938 Craftsman style house relates to Hurley and Henry families.

HAROLD AND NANNIE ROBERTS HOUSE, 125 ROBERTS LANE. Harold and Nannie Roberts are the owners of the three-bay house (pictured below) that has a picture window and an extended wraparound porch. Floyd C. and Shirley B. McQueen sold it in 1971 to Karl M. and Bertha L. Forrest Baker. Cook purchased it in 1970 from Valerie McCabe and S.D. Guy, Mary McCabe having purchased it in 1941 from James H. Covington. The five-acre lot was sold in 1884 by T.J. Burgess to C.T. Covington for $360.[63]

Figure 45. Ben Offutt house on Roberts Lane has recessed entryway.

Figure 46. Harold and Nannie Roberts house has wraparound porch.

---

[61] Deed Books 42-155, 154-394, 213-256.
[62] Deed Books 214-195, 287-490, 290-776; Will Book 8-385.
[63] Deed Books 317-438, 119-95, 126-682, 114-309, 113-382, 66-284, and 22-25.

CHAPTER 3
RURAL NORTHEAST SCOTT COUNTY
LATE NINETEENTH AND EARLY TWENTIETH CENTURY SURVIVORS

Partiality to one's home county is a decided demographic reality. In many ways, we take special pride in and participate in the lives of our specific towns and line-defined counties. This relationship also exists within sections of counties that border other counties' lines. Most Kentucky counties, as they were chiseled into their present shapes, were drawn with interestingly irregular lines, making possible their quick recognition on maps of the Commonwealth or sections thereof. In its earliest years, the once huge county of Scott extended from Woodford, and before Woodford, Fayette, north to the Ohio River. Scott County's present eastern and western boundaries now come to an interesting northern terminus– not quite a point -- on the southern edge of our northern neighbor, Grant County, in the community bearing the name Corinth. We infrequently remember that a very small group of Corinth properties are in Scott County, creating a challenge for persons having to choose political and sports loyalty to one county or another.

From Corinth and Grant County eastward, the Scott boundary line follows an irregular southeast course that in the 1870s was taken up by the Cincinnati Southern Railroad toward the once very lively village of Hinton. At that point the ridge follows a southeast course along the road successively known as Fields Road, Hinton Road South, Northeast County Line Road, Dryden Road, and Dividing Ridge Road.

DIVIDING RIDGE ROAD, NORTH AND SOUTH. Dividing Ridge Road North and Dividing Ridge Road South, before terminating into Dividing Ridge Road per se, is bordered by Scott County on the ridge's east side and by Harrison on the west. At Highway U.S. 62, the Georgetown- Cynthiana Road, the Bourbon County line takes up where the Harrison County line leaves off. The western side of the northern point of Scott follows a relatively straight line southwest, making only a few slight changes of direction. The tri-county intersection of Grant, Owen, and Scott happens a short distance west of Ray's Fork, Scott County's neighbor to the west being Owen County. Scott, Owen, and Franklin counties' junction at the western bend of Minors Branch Road places Franklin as our western neighbor, a relationship that concludes with the merger of Elko-Bell Lane with North Elkhorn Creek just south of US460 (Georgetown-Frankfort Road) where the Scott, Franklin, and Woodford lines join at an obtuse angle.

DOUBLE CULVERT, AND LUKE ROADS, AND SHAWNEE RUN CINCINNATI SOUTHERN TUNNELS. E.C. and E.E. Muddiman, father and son, were expert masons and builders responsible for constructing many buildings, including the three brick churches and several houses of Oxford, the Oxford stone sidewalks, several buildings in downtown Georgetown, and a decorative brick store (no longer standing) in Delaplain. They were also among the most enterprising businessmen in the county. E.C. Muddiman established a store and attractive home at Muddy

Figure 47. Railroad underpasses built by masons E.C. Muddiman and E.E. Muddman. (a) The Double Culvert Road underpass. (b) Luke Road underpass. (c) Shawnee Run underpass located on present farm of Ron Vance.

Ford at the crossroads of Georgetown-Turkeyfoot Road, the Anderson Road, and the road then known as Turkeyfoot and now as Barkley. The Muddimans were the craftsmen who built the trio of picturesque stone railroad underpasses, pictured on the previous page, on the connected Double Culvert and Luke roads, and a third tunnel on Shawnee Run on a no-longer-existing road near the village of Turkeyfoot. The second of the two tunnels has a construction date of between 1874 and 1877. The third is an anomaly, being situated on the farm presently owned by Ronald T. Vance near Shawnee Run. That tunnel may have enjoyed a limited amount of traffic during its early years after which it was discontinued.[64]

Now almost legendary is the cost of building Cincinnati Southern Railroad through the Eagle Hills. The price tag was approximately $70,000 a mile (in uninflated postbellum dollars) while the cost of constructing the railroad between Lexington and Rogers Gap averaged about $17,000 a mile. The road was called "the heaviest mile between Cincinnati and Lexington," requiring bridges across Eagle Creek and its branches, and in many places on weakly underpinned clay soil that perennially challenges the best of engineers. One of the few places in the area where solid building stone could be found was two miles south of the Eagle Creek crossing. Stone quarried there was hauled to select sites where masons would joyfully receive it to construct culverts for the rugged Eden Shale vicinity.[65]

FIELDS ROAD, HARRISON COUNTY'S UNITY PRECINCT, AND CONNERSVILLE. Fields Road, a section of the earlier "Old Mulberry Dirt Road," jousts with Cincinnati Southern Railroad as it cuts its way south with properties on the east side in Harrison County and those on the west in Scott. Harrison County lands bordering northern Scott are part of that county's Unity Precinct. The first settlers in that area included Buck Cason and Charles Courtney of Virginia and Adam Renaker from Maryland. Among the early clergy were Benjamin Conrad and John Conner of the Old School Baptists. Most of the residents of the precinct were farmers; a few had small distilleries, and Benjamin Conrad established a mill near Connersville. One of the first magistrates was George Lemon.[66]

Harrison County's Connersville, discussed by Perrin as the most important village in the precinct, is positioned near the line in the extreme southern part of the county, about seven miles southeast of Cynthiana. Its first store was operated by John H. Conner, whose name became attached to the community circa 1830. Lewis Conner operated a tavern, and E.M. Bailey was the first postmaster. About 125 people lived in Connersville in 1880, providing a customer base for three general stores, one physician, one shoemaker, two hotels, two blacksmith shops, and one cooper shop. Boyers and Pemberton operated a mill and distillery. Unity, another nearby community, also seven miles from Cynthiana, was called "Trickum," possibly due to its role of being the setting for elections.[67] The several churches in the precinct in 1882 included Twin Creek Particular Baptist Church, Salem Chapel Methodist Church, and Mount Zion Chapel Methodist. Salem Church may have been the precinct's first. Standing three miles northeast of Connersville, its pastor in 1882 was the Reverend J.R. Lancaster. William Conrad, John Conner, and J.J. Gilbert were among Twin Creek's leading ministers. Mount Zion Church had as its first pastor the Reverend Josiah Whittaker. One of the early teachers was Christopher Whitson, who taught in the Cason neighborhood around 1820. All the congregations had participants from Scott County across the road and across the line.[68]

---

[64] Mary Celestine "Tine" Burgess, a daughter of Edward Burgess, married Edmond Caesar Muddiman in 1876 and died in 1886. M.R. Burgess, *House of the Burgesses* (San Bernardino, California: The Borgo Press, 1988, 59). Other information from Ronald T. Vance, historian and resident of Turkeyfoot. Photograph courtesy Ronald T. Vance.

[65] Apple, Johnston, and Bevins, eds., *Scott County, Kentucky: A History*, 233.

[66] Perrin, ed., *History of Bourbon, Scott, Harrison, and Nicholas Counties;* Gayle Deaton, "Sadieville buys historic church," *Georgetown News-Graphic*, August 11, 2008; additional information from Frances (Mrs. W.T.) Warring.

[67] Perrin, ed., *Bourbon, Scott, Harrison, and Nicholas Counties*, 322.

[68] Perrin, 322.

SOUTH RAY'S FORK (HINTON-STONEWALL) ROAD. Rays Fork of Eagle Creek is a dominant watershed in very northern Scott County on both sides of the Cincinnati Road. It was and is a valuable setting where some notable landowners plied the trades of farming and milling. (North Rays Fork Road's properties are discussed in Volume 1, which relates to northwest Scott County.) Stonewall is the main surviving community south of Corinth and was a significant commercial hub until replaced as a shipping center by Hinton on the Cincinnati Southern Railroad. This road connects the Stonewall and Hinton communities. Around 1928 Tom and Hallie Fisher purchased several large farms in the Rays Fork neighborhood and established Fisher's Camp, a major tourist attraction between that date and the opening of Interstate Highway 75. The camp had a large restaurant and thirty-one cabins by the time of World War II. Fisher's Camp with its lake, gasoline station, and service facilities became a popular setting for honeymoons, vacations, or simply dining out. It is further discussed in volume one in the section relating to Cincinnati Road properties.

HINTON AND NORTHEAST COUNTY LINE ROADS. Hinton Road leads from the junction of South Ray's Fork Road with Fields Road and extends through the village of Hinton at the junction of Stone Lane and the Harrison County line, where the road bends from southeast to south and leads to Sadieville. The road following the county line at this point is called the Northeast County Line Road. Several significant farms and houses are found on this road as it bends toward Sadieville.

COLLARD SCHOOL SITE. In 1917 John K. Butler deeded Desmon and James Dungan a one-fourth acre lot just south of the first overhead bridge north of Hinton and extending south 300 yards to the railroad and an adjacent tract described as the Collard School lot. Dungan sold the property in 1920 to Alonzo Fightmaster.[69]

ELK LICK CHURCH ROAD. The northern portion of Elk Lick Church Road is comparatively new, postdating 1879 and the publication that year of the Beers & Lanagan map. Several factors contributed to its development as a through road: discontinuation of the road between the Sadieville-Connersville Turnpike to Emison's Mill, intersecting with a then secondary road following the present route of the road to the county line road and the Sadieville-Connersville Road; newly developed farms on the northern portion of the present Elk Lick Church Road; and construction of Cincinnati Southern Railroad and its major station at Sadieville and secondary station at Hinton. The road's name relates to it as the third location of Elk Lick Primitive Baptist Church on the southern part of the road just north and west of the intersection with the Sadieville-Connersville turnpike. In more recent times the road is simply called "Elk Lick Road," though we must keep in mind that Elk Lick is actually a branch of Eagle Creek near the Davis-Turkeyfoot Road.

BURGESS SMITH ROAD. Extending along Eagle Creek as it flows northward to embrace Sadieville before crossing Cincinnati Pike on the way to Owen County is a road with picturesque contours that connects and serves Burgess and Smith family landmarks including those of Burgess Smith, grandson of Joseph Burgess and son of Eva B. and Sterling Price Smith. Burgess Smith developed his home place on a 534 acre farm that his grandfather purchased in 1838 from Richard W. and Polly Pack; it had earlier been part of 1000 acres patented to Robert Todd. It earlier belonged to the Packs' daughter Josephine and her husband T.J. Burgess, a son of Joseph Burgess of Stonewall. T.J. Burgess was Burgess Smith's uncle.

DAVIS-TURKEYFOOT AND BOYERS CHAPEL ROADS. The narrow road leading from the mere shadow of the former bustling village of Davis, formerly known as Straight Fork in honor of the branch of Eagle Creek that passes through it, leads to the mere shadow of the once busy village of Turkeyfoot. It is a fascinating thoroughfare, though its landmarks are successively slipping away. Boyers Chapel Road extends northeast from the Sadieville-Davis Road, leading to Boyers Methodist chapel in Harrison County, and the community of Alberta, probably named in honor of Albert Stevens. The county line village is discussed in this volume in the chapter on crossroads villages.

---

[69] Deed Books 47-369, 59-57.

Boyers Chapel Road Properties

Reed-Garton Homesite and Cemetery, 876 Boyers Chapel Road.
"The properties we own in many ways determine who we are," Mark Elliott muses regarding the developing countryside where he built a grand house in 2007 on 10.85554 acres on Boyers Chapel Road near Alberta. A brief distance uphill from Elliott's home is a graveyard that provides major hints about the site's history. Pursuing clues offered by the few legible writings on the stones, Elliott explored the internet, beginning with a search related to a Union soldier from Missouri who settled, married, and was buried there.

Figure 48. Mark Elliott makes notes about Reed-Munson graveyard on his farm south of Alberta. Sadieville-Davis Road

The gravestone of Hiram Garton in the small square tree shaded graveyard, shown in the photograph at the left with Elliott, is the only one of the several stones in the former enclosure that can be read. Another retains scored decoration at the top of the stone. Still another fragment has lettering stylistically like the lined etchings and reads: "of . . . ian," suggesting that it must represent a portion of the name of "Louisiana" (Louisa) Munson. Known generally as Louisa, she was a daughter of Cornelius Butler and Sally Fisher. Widow of Sanford Munson, she married Ebenezer Reed after the death of Reed's first wife, Harriet Weakley, daughter of Jeremiah Weakley. After Reed's death, Louisiana married Hiram Garton. Reed, who acquired the land from his father, is believed to have died while fighting for the Confederacy. Eben and Louisiana's children included a son Andrew and a daughter who became Mrs. John Romans, as reported in Louisiana's obituary in the Cynthiana *Democrat* on March 16, 1911.

In 1907 Andrew and his wife signed over the family property to their son Andrew with the stipulation that Louisiana could live on and control the property until her death. Later the elder Reed and his son were living, according to a later census, in Turkeyfoot, with Tom and Mary Hedger and a woman whose surname was Hork. Eben (variously spelled Eben and Ebon) Reed's father, is cited as one of the first settlers of Turkey Foot Precinct in William Henry Perrin's *History of Scott, Bourbon, Harrison, and Nicholas Counties*. The narrative states that Reed settled near the Turkey Foot post office circa 1790. In 1880 Thomas Reed and Ann E. Reed sold James N. Reed of Owen County for $1,500 "our half of the tract where Ebon Reed has resided . . . near Turkeyfoot."

Ebenezer is listed in the "Reed/Bailey" entry in the family history section of *Families & History, Scott County, Kentucky* as a son of Samuel Reed, a British seaman born in 1761, who settled in Lincoln, Virginia on a land grant. He and his wife Jane reared nine children: Ebenezer, James, Isaac, Jefferson, Sarah, Jane, Nancy, Samuel, and Mary. Ebenezer was born in 1804 and his first wife Harriet Weakley, married in 1830, had nine children: Catherine, Adeline, K. Jane, Martha, James N., Thomas, Harriet, Sarah Dianna, and Amanda. Eben spent a major portion of his life in the Turkeyfoot area. In April 1847 he sold land on Dividing Ridge for a school. He gave each of his children one hundred acres, all in Owen and Scott Counties. Following the death of his first wife in 1858, he married Louisiana (Louisa) Munson in 1859. When the Civil War broke out, Reed is said to have buried all his money on what was known as Reed Hill in Turkeyfoot. "Although many have tried, no one has located this money," recalls the family history account. Ebenezer Reed is pictured in the publication in a frock cost and ruffled shirt.[70]

William D. and Chasity Farrar acquired the farm in 2004 from Darrel G. and Lois J. Schell and Donald T. and Linda Johnson sold it in 1985 and 1987 to Elliott.

ALBERTA AND DAVIS -- COUNTY LINE VILLAGES. *Refer to the chapter on Crossroads Villages and Country Stores and Churches for a discussion of the Scott and Harrison county line communities of Straight Fork/Davis and Alberta.*

PACK AND PENN FAMILY PROPERTIES

Figure 49. (a) John Pack log house east of Sadieville; (b) close-up view of John Pack house; (c) Early Kentucky style mantel in John Pack house.

RICHARD F. AND SARAH MARTHA "SADIE" EMISON PACK HOUSE SITE AND FARM, DAVIS ROAD.

Northern Scott County's grand houses included two outstanding estate houses on the Sadieville-Davis Road, both removed in recent years. As this is written, the Joseph Burgess house at Stonewall on the Cincinnati Road is north Scott's lone great house survivor.

John Pack, one of the region's earliest settlers, lived in a superbly built early Kentucky log house on the farm where his son, Richard F. Pack, in the 1870s, was to establish his own estate farm that he and his wife Sadie named "Charity Hill." Serving both establishments was a double crib log barn and a crib/granary joined with square headed nails. John Pack's children, Lavinia and her husband William Penn, and Richard F. and his wife Sarah Martha "Sadie" Emison, divided Pack's estate in 1849, Richard receiving 1,057 acres valued at $12.88 an acre, and the Penns, 930 acres appraised at eight dollars an acre. The Penns also inherited the balance of the Witherspoon tract surveyed in 1831, also located on Straight Fork of Eagle Creek. Both couples and their families established homes on this land, their homes defining grand levels of accomplishment and culture.[71]

---

[70] "Reed/Bailey" and "Reed/Lusby," by Kathy Reed in *Families & History: Scott County, Kentucky* (Paducah: Turner Publishing Company for Scott County Genealogical Society, 1996), 231.
[71] Deed Book V-439.

Richard F. Pack, reported the *Georgetown Weekly Times* in the fall of 1873, "is building a fine residence." The Packs engaged Wood Brothers of Lexington to construct their Italianate style dwelling, pictured at the left and lower right, with a view to the south of Big Eagle Creek's confluence with Straight Fork. The dwelling's imposing main façade's crowning features included an octagonal roofed two story bay window in the front gable ell. First story windows had segmental arches, while those on the second story were round arched. Railed porches spanned both stories of the recessed block, the upper level porch having turned balusters, and the lower story, detail consisting of lozenges centered with crosspieces. A set of wide steps led to the porch with milled detail. Windows extended across the main block of the house as well as across the upper level of the front ell. Paired brackets were placed along the second story soffit. Completing the picture were elegantly tooled chimneys; a porch with milled posts, cornices and railing; and a second story balcony on the front with milled balusters. Siding was attached with square headed nails.[72]

Figure 52. Detail of Richard-Sadie Pack house.

Figure 51. Richard and Sarah Emison Pack's Charity Hill.

Figure 50. (a) Rear elevation of Richard and Sadie Pack house; (b) outbuilding, possible servants' quarters, or schoolhouse, of Pack property; (c) Pack smokehouse.

---

[72] *Georgetown Weekly Times*, September 10, October 22, 1873.

Behind the house was a small two story weatherboarded building that may have been servants' quarters or a school, with dwelling space on the second level. A small corner porch contained a stairway to the second level. Doors on the first level led to a room in the back and to the room on the right. Walls and ceiling were plastered and attached to sawn lath. The building was served by a saddlebag chimney with shelving on either side of the fireplace. Wainscoting applied around the room to a height of four feet created a schoolroom feeling. In the back yard stood a smokehouse on a raised stone foundation, its eaves having semi-circular milled trim. Weatherboarding was attached with square headed nails. Rope for hanging hams remained in place during the field survey of the property. Here too square headed nails were used.[73]

An abundance of stone walls lines the road in front of the estate, mostly horizontally coursed with diagonally laid coping. In several cases such fences meet the more regionally typical Hills of the Bluegrass slab stones laid vertically at a slant.

Figure 53. Intricately detailed rock wall along Sadieville-Davis turnpike, boundary of Pack farm, ascribed to Herbert W. "Hub" Antle and/or Frank Gillispie.

In 1893 the Richard F. Pack devisees – Sarah M. Pack, John E. Pack, L.D. and Sallie Burgess, and Josie Burgess -- called for a partition of the family's real estate. Josie, wife of T.J. Burgess, received 372 acres on the Dividing Ridge Road and 112 acres on the North Fork Pike and the Big Eagle-Connersville Pike (the Sadieville-Davis Road). Her lands were bordered by those of Jacob and Elizabeth Perkins, McKenney, Mrs. Rodgers, and William Harrison. Sallie Burgess's share extended along the Big Eagle-Connersville Pike and had as boundaries Big Eagle Creek and the land of J.S. Stone, William Parker, W.G. Haydon, the Offutt heirs, William Nelson, S.B. Jones, and T.J. Burgess. Excluded from her title was the old Elk Lick Baptist Church lot. She also received seventy-five acres on Eagle bounded by the Jacob Mulberry County Road, Jones and Smith, and the Pack dower. The Packs' son, John E. Pack, who practiced medicine in Georgetown, received 146 acres with boundaries including lands of Buford Hall, Cincinnati Southern Railroad, S.T. Connellee, and Mrs. Lancaster, and fifty-one acres bounded by Luke and J.V. Mulberry.[74]

T.J. BURGESS STONE WALLS BY HERBERT ANTLE AND/OR FRANK GILLISPIE, SADIEVILLE-DAVIS ROAD. Francis "Frank" Gillispie, according to some sources, or Herbert W. Antle (1878 – 1944), an important area stonemason, also known as Hub, constructed the finely coursed stone fences along Davis Road in front of the Burgess property. Gillispie's family has a tradition that Frank Gillispie was engaged by T.J. Burgess to build a stone fence along the front of his farm. Gillispie is recalled as having pursued this work with excellence at a cost of forty cents a rod (16 1/2/ feet)

Figure 54. William Penn house was one of the best built and most stylish houses in northern Scott County.

---

[73] Joy Barlow, field notes for 1985 agricultural buildings study.
[74] Deed Books 28-259, 261, 263.

between 1905 and 1915. He was a farmer and also served as custodian of Sadieville School.[75] It is possible that both men worked on different sections of the stone walls.

WILLIAM PENN HOUSE SITE, SADIEVILLE-DAVIS ROAD. Majestically positioned near the top of a hill with a south face toward Straight Fork was the William Penn house with a wealth of style dating from the early Kentucky and Greek Revival eras to the Italianate. The entry porch had a decided Eastlake flair. The side veranda was classic, as was the house interior with Greek Revival detail on the main staircase, pictured at right. Hugh Wallace Mason, transferred by his company to Utica, Indiana, made renovations on weekends and during vacation time and encouraged neighbors to look after the property. Aging of the latter, precluding their ability to take care of the property, resulted in weather damage as well as vandals invading this great house and taking a cruel toll.

Figure 55. Stairwell of William Penn house had Early Kentucky and Greek Revival era refinements.

The Penns' 930 acres of the John Pack estate included the balance of the Witherspoon tract on the north side of Straight Fork surveyed in 1831 and bounded by the land of John Gibson. Both families developed beautiful homes on their portions of the land and in 1888 at William Penn's death, his wife inherited "the homestead whereon we reside" with remainder to Millard F. Penn. Other heirs were Samuel Penn, Susan Mary Boswell, John W. Penn, Richard F. Penn, Joel M. Penn, Henry C. Penn, and LuCinda Hall (a granddaughter). In 1896 M.F. and Mary E. Penn sold the 200 acre family tract to Robert E. Lee for $5,000. The Lee family, including Mary G. Lee and Edward Gano Lee, Owen S. Lee, Rebecca Smith Lee, and the Owen S. Lee estate, owned the farm until 1966 when Rebecca Smith Lee, author and biographer of Mary Austin Holley, wife of Transylvania's Horace Holley, sold it to Elkhorn Farms, Inc. That organization sold it to Austin Harp Masonry and Land Company in 1969.[76]

Figure 56. John W. Penn house on Sadieville-Davis Road has Princess Anne roof profile.

---

[75] Information from Jeffrey Gillispie, grandson of Frank Gillispie.
[76] Deed Books V-439, 31-108, 71-302, 100-538, 110-54; Will Book S-275; Rebecca Smith Lee, *Mary Austin Holley, a Biography* (Austin: University of Texas Press, 1962).

JOHN W. PENN HOUSE, SADIEVILLE-DAVIS ROAD. An older house owned by the Giles family at this writing traces to an 1890 sale by John W. and Jennie K. Penn to James H. and Catharine Tucker. John W. Penn was one of the eight children of William Penn listed in Penn's will, written in 1883 and probated in 1888. In 1918 the Tuckers sold it to Alice and Sadocia A. Wells. The house was part of the Straight Fork tract on the bridge at the Big Eagle and Harrison County Turnpike (another name for this road.) In 1942 M.D. Sandford purchased the property at a master commissioner's sale resulting from the action of Lula Miley vs. Scott Burgess. Sandford left it to Eugenia S. Smith, his daughter, and to her children, with the stipulation that no mobile homes be allowed on the property for ninety-nine years. In 2005 Linda Smith, Todd Goepper, and others sold the 29.4-acre tract with the house to David A. and Patricia Giles and Lloyd D. and Annabel Giles.[77]

PENN HOUSES, 2060, 2100 DAVIS ROAD. In earlier years, as the writer was studying Scott County properties for the Kentucky Heritage Council survey, she enjoyed a history and geography lesson from Stanley Giles about the community extending along Straight Fork Branch of Eagle Creek between Sadieville and Davis. Mr. Giles explained that hilltop locations were preferred in the region because the relatively small Straight Fork Branch was capable of rapidly flooding the valley and the road. Thus, he said, the two very similar Princess Anne style houses justly thrived on their hilltops.

Figure 58. Former Penn house on Sadieville-Davis Road is brick veneered and has Craftsman style porch.

Figure 57. Least altered of the Penn family houses has Princess Anne roof pattern.

---

[77] Deed Books 25-463, 52-368, 99-104, 297-609; 297-609; Will Books S-275, X-104, 14-546.

Today the houses bear some but not total resemblance to their former selves, having been altered, in one case with later exterior materials; and in the other case, renovated with interesting respect to the Princess Anne style form with modern stylistic detailing. The house at 2060 Davis Road was owned by David and Patricia Giles and Lloyd D. Giles and is currently owned by Karen and Stuart Winburn. Identified with the Giles family from 1952, it retains the attractive foundation with peck hammered stone blocks with raised rounded mortar joints. Princess Anne styling includes the Queen Anne era's pyramidal roof form with extended gabled ells, popular though into the 1920s in the understated Princess Anne style. Charles and Lillian Giles and Stanley and Mildred Giles purchased the one hundred-acre spread containing the house at 2100 Davis Road from William A. Hinton, executor of the estate of Laura A. Conner. Mrs. Conner bought the property in 1944 from the estate of William Clark Courtney, who acquired it in 1928 from George W., Sr., and Belle Antle, whose title emanated from George M. Antle, Sr., purchaser in 1912 from Nannie L. and George M. Penn. The Penns were among the children of Annie M. and J.M. Penn, who in 1908 traded inherited parcels. Heirs also included Jodie S. and Addie Penn, Charley and Belle Penn, and Robert and Iva Penn. This house was sold by Daniel W. and Julie Siegel to Matthew and Emily Onorato in 2016. The formerly mirrored likeness is now clad in brick and has a variety of embellishments of modern vintage.[78]

Figure 59. Nannie L. Penn gained title to a farm near Davis with Gothic Revival styling. The house has battened vertical siding.

JOE AND ADDIE PENN HOUSE, 2200 DAVIS ROAD. As part of the Penn family division, Nannie L. Penn gained title to a farm near Davis containing an imposing house set on a level lawn on the north or Penn side of the road earlier called the Sadieville-Connersville Road. Its siding has been altered with board and batten in recent years. The two-story house is one room deep and has a central gable containing shaped shingles. Sash is two over two panes. Window surrounds are pedimented. The house has a stone foundation.

---

[78] Deed Books 39-267, 40-750, 42-304, 44-437, 56-372, 69-296, 78-598, 129-160, 144-724, 181-207, 184-525, 194-483, 225-85, 265-787, 274-728, 359-504, 382-85.

In 1908 the various Penn heirs made their several property divisions that are recorded in Deed Book 39 beginning with page 264. The 136-acre farm followed a line of initial transfer to Nannie Penn. In 1919 Nannie L. and G.M. Penn sold 124 acres to Joe S. and Addie Penn, the purchase price payable to Buford H. and Bennie Penn. Joe and Addie Penn sold the property in 1932 to Herbert Tomlinson who in 1934 sold it to J.M. and Anna B. Bronston, who owned it until 1943. Later owners have included: Sherman and Josie Parker, 1943; O.R. and Cordia V. Kelly, 1943; Laura Conner, 1945; William Hoskins, 1952; George Hoskins, 1953; Forrest and Edna Cox, 1958; and Ed Mosley, Jr., 1989.[79]

Figure 60. Edward Caesar Burgess's log house served by shouldered chimney burned several decades ago. The late Burgess Swope, a granddaughter, recalled the smaller building as the plantation schoolhouse.

BURGESS PROPERTIES

EDWARD "NED" BURGESS HOMESTEAD SITE AND BARN, DAVIS-TURKEYFOOT ROAD.

Edward "Ned" Burgess, patriarch of the Scott County Burgess families, lived in a log house across Eagle Creek and the Davis-Turkeyfoot Road from his unique log crib barn with an octagonal cupola, discussed in the first chapter of this volume. His youngest son, Edward Burgess, Jr., succeeded him as owner of the homestead. The main house burned in 1960. The ruins are pictured above, along with the picturesque log eighteen by twenty-foot Ned Burgess schoolhouse. To its west was an elaborate twelve by sixteen-foot root cellar faced with large squared stone blocks. A contemporary brick house has been built next to it in recent years.

Figure 61. Small log buildings along the road leading toward Turkeyfoot were important to travelers, as was the small iron bridge.

Above the house and schoolhouse on the hilltop was an older barn resting on large mud posts and joists that retained bark on their uncut undersides. Squared posts rose to the rafters. Near this barn was a corn crib mounted on stone pillars and having a two-foot overhang over the door. Along the road were two small log buildings, one pictured at lower left. Neither no longer stands. One can only hope that the one of a kind log crib barn capped with an octagonal cupola across the creek will survive for many more ages, and that the barn in the field several hundred yards to the northeast that accommodates the building first occupied by the Elk Lick Primitive Baptist Church will have similar immortality. This underscores awareness that surviving

---

[79] Deed Books 39-264, 42-566, 49-77, 59-419, 60-395, 65-239, 67-631, 67-633, 70-52, 79-86, 80-310, 86-608, 179-004.

Figure 62. Burgess Smith's residential tract once included an elaborate house. Only the tenant house remains, along with a multipurpose barn and cattle handling pens.

buildings, even ruins, inspire the retelling of history's stories, and that when the buildings or ruins are gone, the stories will diminish and ultimately cease to be told or recalled. These structures are discussed in this volume's chapter on agricultural buildings.[80]

Edward "Ned" Burgess was born in 1777 in Stafford County, Virginia and traveled to Kentucky around 1786 with his stepfather, Ralph Hughes, who settled in Bourbon County near Paris. Burgess married Sarah Fields in 1800 in Bourbon County. Sarah, a daughter of Revolutionary War veteran Joseph Fields and Nancy Noland, and her brother, Greenberry Fields (their parents died before 1784), were brought to Kentucky by their uncle, Abraham Fields. Ned Burgess appears on the Scott County tax lists of 1799-1800; he added his various parcels of land piece by piece. Sarah died in 1839 and Ned in 1858. Their children were Nancy, born in 1801, who married Cyrus Jaco in 1821; William Calvin, known as Calvin, born in 1802, who settled near Turkeyfoot, dying in 1859; Bathsheba, born in 1804, wife of Henry Bruce Drake; Mariah, born in 1804, who married George William Bates in 1827 and died in 1868; Joseph Fields, born in 1809, who married Elizabeth Sharp in 1831 (she died six weeks later), and Miranda Penn in 1839;[81] Margaret Ann, born in 1811, who married Jesse Dungan about 1850; James Henry born 1814 and died 1826; and Edward Caesar, born in 1816, who married Mary Ann Adams in 1836 (she died in 1858), and married second Sarah Elizabeth Davis, who died in 1898.[82]

Figure 63. Two small houses are joined and are identified on the 1879 Beers & Lanagan map as the property of "J. Fields."

Figure 64. Small closeted stairway of the Edward Burgess property is an outstanding example.

J. FIELDS HOUSE. On the back of the Mahan farm stands an ancient log and timber frame house, small in scale, on a stone foundation. The house was visited by the author and survey associate Joy Barlow in 1985 with farm owner James Ritchie. The front room was finished inside with vertical boards. The former kitchen, constructed of logs, had been heated by a large stone chimney. Two frame rooms were appended to it. An outhouse and a battened shed with a gable roof stood behind the dwelling. The 1879 map identifies the site as "J. Fields."

Figure 65. The exterior of the small Burgess house has small shouldered chimney.

EARLY BURGESS HOUSES. A small log house with a perfectly crafted early Kentucky interior stands in a field on the Addison Thomson farm. The photographs provide an interesting depiction of the settlement era dwelling. Edward Burgess, Jr., wrote his will in 1889 and

---

[80] Burgess (Mrs. Felix) Swope, a descendant of Edward Burgess, conveyed to the writer many years ago her recollection of the little building on the hill as the family schoolhouse.
[81] Refer to discussion of Joseph Burgess in the chapter entitled "Along the Northern Dry Ridge."
[82] M.R. Burgess, *House of the Burgesses* (San Bernardino: Borgo Press, 1983), 51-55. This work was expanded several years later.

codicils in 1889 and 1897, and died in 1898. He left to his sons by his first wife Mary Ann Adams the tract on "the east or south side" of the farm, "provided that they pay $500 each to the children of James G. Burgess, deceased." They were listed as John C. Burgess; Mary T., wife of W.V. Mulberry; and the children of Sallie Powers and Mary E. Duncan. He left his wife Sarah E. Burgess one-third of the remainder of land around the homestead, the balance to be divided among their children.[83]

In 1997 Carey O. and Lisa W. Shirey purchased the 433.16-acre Edward Burgess farm from Robert William Mahan, Jr., anticipating using the barn with the octagonal cupola as a centerpiece for their proposed winery. Thus the Shireys came to own two of the stellar Burgess Smith barns, along with the Edward Burgess barn. Mahan acquired the farm as a gift from his parents in 1973; they purchased it between 1966 and 1968 from Fred Bach of Columbus, Indiana, who bought the farm in three parcels from Alpheus McKenney, George North, and George Hoskins. The latter tract, consisting of 361.23 acres, came by way of Hoskins's partnership with Laura Hinton Conner as owners of this farm and of the 687-acre farm inherited by Penelope "Neppie" Musselman and her husband James F. Musselman, daughter and son-in-law of Joseph Burgess.[84]

655 AND 867 BURGESS SMITH ROAD -- BURGESS SMITH HOME SITE. Although Burgess Smith's home burned many years ago, the family corporation of John Buford Penn, John Blackford Penn, and Edgar Duke Penn persisted in preserving the barns and other buildings of the historic farm. Smith's three stellar barns are among Scott County's best agricultural building examples and are discussed in this volume's Chapter 1. All three barns and the home site are located on the Burgess Smith Road.

The writer's late friend Marjorie Penn, Edgar's wife, enthusiastically recalled the elegant Victorian beauty of Smith's home. It would be a wonderful experience to have a likeness of it. Some of its components are incorporated in the renovated and expanded Christopher Lee house in southern Scott County. These barns and the Edward Burgess log crib barn are supported by heavy timbers secured with wooden pegged mortised joints.

In 1942 Smith conveyed to Hugh R. Taylor, who agreed to carry two mortgages as part of the sale price, the 648.157 acres he inherited from his mother Eva B. Smith, and the tract purchased from G.M. Antle. Three months later Taylor and his wife Julia sold the farm to William F. Marshall, whose conveyance to Penn Farms took place in 1947. Joining the January 12, 1993 sale of the farm's 494.75 acres to the Shireys were Frank and Virginia Penn, William M. and Anne M. Arvin, Catherine "Katie" Penn and William D. Turner, and Anison Penn and Jeffrey Davis. The widespread operation's historic boundaries included Mrs. Holland, R.W. Hinton, Giles, Mrs. Antle, Joe Clark, a bridge, and Addison Thomson. A dwelling located on this property is a one story three bay house with turned posts carrying the porch's roof. Barns included in the Shirey purchase were the high style hog barn and the barn on the edge of the race track.[85]

Figure 66. Rodney Courtney house, Penn farm.

PENN-COURTNEY TRACT AND SIDE-ENTERED TOBACCO BARN, 800 BURGESS SMITH ROAD. Louella Penn, sister of Edgar and John, and her husband, J.T. Bowling, sold the remaining portion of the Penn Farms' Burgess Smith farm to Rodney D. and Pam Faye Courtney in 1993. Courtney served for many years as manager of the farm for the Penns and lived in the house on the 151.18-acre portion of the farm that he purchased from

---

[83] Will Book T-157.
[84] Deed Books 229-727, 123-467, 121-142, 90-41, 109-126, 101-393, 79-29, 51-201, 55-204, 59-577.
[85] Deed Books 198-371, 198-251, 72-418, 67-154, 66-607, and Will Book W-560.

Mrs. Bowling. The sources of this farm's purchase by John B. Penn, Sr. in 1948 were J.B. Wright and Earl Wright, who bought it from William F. Marshall the prior year. Marshall received title in 1942 from Hugh R. Taylor. The side entered tobacco barn is pictured in the chapter on agricultural buildings in this volume.[86]

ELK LICK PARTICULAR BAPTIST CHURCH SITE, DAVIS-TURKEYFOOT ROAD. Elk Lick Particular Baptist Church, which organized in 1799 on Elk Lick Branch of Eagle Creek in an area known as Sulphur Spring, was on the Edward Burgess settlement. Laura Hinton Conner, who purchased several properties related to the William Hinton family, willed the circa 3.5 acres to the William Hinton descendants, hoping that they would use it for reunions and other celebrations. The church and its attendant log and frame barn are discussed in Chapter 1 of this volume.[87]

ELK LICK CHURCH ON SADIEVILLE-CONNERSVILLE ROAD. The congregation relocated in 1848 to the Sadieville-Connersville Road, one and three-fourths miles east of Sadieville, on the fabled "flat rock" on the farm of John Pack and across the road from the land of Jacob Mulberry and W.V. "Bunk" Mulberry. The congregation moved again in 1874 to a site deeded by John Pack and the William and Nancy Emison estate to trustees Joseph Burgess, William Mulberry, Jacob Mulberry, and Jacob B. Neale. The third church, a two-door meetinghouse with Italianate brackets under the eaves and bracketed hoodmolds over the doors and windows, was dedicated March 12, 1875. The original church building is further discussed in this volume's Chapter 1 relating to agricultural complexes and buildings.

Figure 67. Elk Lick Church site, home of Robert and Christina Gillispie.

Elk Lick Church concluded its existence at the Elk Lick Road Church site in July 1937 when Billy Mulberry, W.S. Mulberry, and W.V. Mulberry, trustees, sold the building and its two acre and two poles lot to N.M. "Mose" Burgess for $500. Burgess sold that property to Henry Wilder for a Seventh Day Adventist Church. In October 1937 the trustees of the church bought a lot on College Street in Sadieville and in 1946 sold that property to the Scott County Board of Education. "Thus ended the Particular Baptist Church of Elk Lick, Flat Rock, and again Elk Lick, which lived from 1799 to 1946, a reign of 147 years," wrote historian William A. Marshall. "The sands of time," Marshall concluded, "ran out for a great society for the promoting of the interest of a place of divine worship. . ."[88]

ELK LICK CHURCH SITE, 841 ELK LICK CHURCH ROAD: ROBERT AND CHRISTINA GILLISPIE HOUSE. In 1958 Henry Wilder sold the old church site to Robert and Christine Gillispie. There the Gillispies constructed a ranch style house clad in Bedford stone, using lumber from the church building for the framework. The stone faced one story ranch style Gillispie house has a gable roofed porch with square posts mounted on stone piers on the entry end. The house has a large picture window left of the side entrance and four bays to the right of the doorway.

Figure 68. Former property of Lancaster and Bryant.

Figure 69. Façade of first Elk Lick Particular Baptist Church.

---

[86] Deed Books 199-443, 74-101, 72-502, 67-154; Will Book Y-93.
[87] Information from Ronald T. Vance, historian.
[88] William A. "Bill" Marshall, "Elk Lick Particular Baptist Church," *Scott County Church Histories: A Collection* (1981), 16-18.

LANCASTER-BRYANT HOUSE, 1411 ELK LICK CHURCH ROAD. An interesting L-shaped house on Elk Lick Church Road has two ell-end gables with fish scale shingles and a porch sheltering the door and windows. A.J. Lancaster sold the house and 12.4 acres in 1987 to Thomas and Ruth Bryant. Though the PVA description gives the construction date as 1996, the house appears older.[89]

JOE S. AND RICHARD L. BURGESS HOUSE, OLD KENTUCKY 32. A decorated cottage (not pictured) faced, from a distance, the old Sadieville Road cut off from the previous road along Elk Lick Church Road and Big Eagle Creek by construction of the present road leading into Sadieville from U.S. 25. Richard and Joe Burgess acquired the property in 1943 from Helena Burgess, who with Jessie Shirley and Mary Alma Paxton Thomas, inherited it from Richard L. and Vivian Burgess. In 1960 Joe S. and Nell Burgess deeded their interest in the entire 601 acres to Richard's widow and daughters. In 1983 Helena Burgess, Jessie Burgess Shirley, and Mary Alma Paxton Thomas sold 375 acres of that land to Douglas L. Ragland.[90]

WILLIAM THOMSON HOUSE, 917 DAVIS-TURKEYFOOT ROAD. A one- story L-shaped house, complete with shaped shingles in the front gable ell, likely dates from the late 1890s. PVA records list William Thomson as owner. Bill Brumley, whose wife decorated the house and yard with multiple lawn adornments, welcomed the writer and her associate, Emma Jean Adams, to the site during a photographic survey of the countryside.

Figure 71. Addison Thomson bungalow.

Figure 71a. Smokehouse near Addison Thomson Grayland house.

GRAYLAND FARM/K.C., ELLA B., G.D., ADDISON THOMSON HOUSE, 1101 DAVIS-TURKEYFOOT ROAD. Two houses remain on the portion of the Edward Burgess farm inherited by Ella Burgess and other children of Edward Burgess, Jr.'s marriage to his second wife, Sarah Edward Burgess. The main dwelling is an Arts and Crafts era house three bays wide with deep roof overhangs. A large extended dormer with a band of four windows provides lighting and head room for the loft. Edward Burgess's sixteenth child and progenitor of the present owner of the farm was Helena Ellen "Ella," born in 1873; she married Keller Current Thomson, Sr. in 1903 and died in Harrison County in 1962, the last of her large family to pass away. She wrote a short history of her family based on memories of her father and his siblings. The farm was next owned by her son G.D. Thomson and then by their son, Addison Thomson, who married Margaret Gray. Mrs. Thomson inherited the farm and accumulated family papers. The farm carries the name Grayland.[91]

Figure 72. William Thomson house.

---

[89] Deed Book 170-358.
[90] Deed Books 68-96, 89-452, 153-762; Will Book X-531.
[91] Burgess, (1983), 61; Deed Book 96-237; Will Book T-157.

T.J., III, AND LOUISE BURGESS, HOUSE, 224 SADIEVILLE ROAD/OLD KENTUCKY 32.

Occupying a distinguished vantage point that offers a spectacular view of the surrounding countryside, much Burgess owned, is the early twentieth century bungalow of T.J. "Jed" Burgess, III. Burgess and his family trace to Joseph Burgess, whose estate house and farm remain prominent landmarks on the Cincinnati Road. Joseph Burgess's son Thomas Jefferson Burgess I, and his daughters Evaline "Eva" [Sterling Paul] Smith, Nancy "Nannie" [Buford] Hall, Penelope "Neppie" [James F.] Musselman, became prominent landowners in the region in the spirit established earlier by their parents.[92]

Figure 73. Bungalow of T.J. Burgess, III, and his wife, Louise.

The succession of T.J. Burgesses began with T.J. Burgess, I, who was born in 1849 and died in 1923. He married Josephine "Josie" C. Pack, daughter of Dr. Richard F. and Sarah Martha "Sadie" Emison Pack, who inherited her father's estate farm "Charity Hill," where the couple lived. Their daughter Laura Stevenson (1882-1936) married her first cousin once removed, Noble Moses "Mose" Burgess (1880-1953). Mose Burgess was a farmer, businessman, and prominent Sadieville property owner. Mose and Laura were parents of T.J. "Jed" Burgess, II (1936-1972), who like his predecessors bearing his name was one of Scott County's leading landowners and farmers. He married first Pauline Giles (1904-1939), and second, Louise Mulberry Osborne. His son T.J. III "Tom," born in 1942, next managed the family lands of circa 3,000 acres. Mrs. Burgess (Louise) continues to own the family farm and the attractive and stylish bungalow with its splendid view of the road leading into Sadieville.[93]

The Burgess bungalow is built of dark red wire scored bricks. It has deep eaves decorated with singularly spaced brackets. The front porch, sheltered by a continuation of the house's gabled roof, is supported by square brick piers and has a classical style railing intermediate to the posts. On each side of the centered door flanked by sidelights is a triple window. A stylish Palladian window is centered in the extended gabled dormer with a keystone above the arch.

EMISON AND EMISON MILLS PROPERTIES

CHARLES P. FIELDS HOUSE, 285 ELK LICK CHURCH ROAD.

An imposing American Foursquare style house, three bays wide and two stories tall, presides over the historic farm of William Emison and James E. Emison, whose families lived in a large log house and operated the nearby mill, both on the nearby banks of Eagle Creek. Emison's Mill gave the section of the road closest to Sadieville its earlier name and was the commercial precursor to the City of Sadieville. The present Arts and Crafts style house was originally owned by Charles P. Fields, Sadieville banker, who built it circa 1929 following purchase of the farm from Voris Vallandingham. John Core and his wife, Dorothy "Dot" bought the seventy-two acres in 1965 from Charles P. and Morah W. Fields. Mrs. Core, an artist in the medium of pastels, sold the property to Darrell W. and Laura L. Roberts. John Core died in 1973. Several of Dorothy Core's works hang in Sadieville City Hall.

---

[92] Burgess, 54-59.
[93] Burgess, 61.

DAVIS/CRENSHAW HOUSE, 589 ELK LICK CHURCH ROAD. An attractive yellow vinyl clad bungalow in a pastoral tree shaded setting occupies another portion of the 476.97-acre tract inherited by Sadie Burgess Whitney from the Richard F. Pack estate. In 1925 Mrs. Whitney deeded the entire parcel on the Davis and Elk Lick Church roads and Big Eagle Creek to Clarence S. Davis for $17,512. Davis and his wife Gertrude sold eighty-five acres of that land to Roy D. Mulberry and his wife, who in 1937 sold it as part of 109 acres to J. Nelson and Ruby Crenshaw. The Davises or the Crenshaws were the apparent builders of the bungalow. The Crenshaws sold the same acreage in 1939 to Lucille Kroness, who sold it in 1943 to the Fightmasters. In 1962 the Nunnelley-Berman heirs deeded it to Mrs. Gordon Fightmaster.[94]

Figure 74. Davis-Crenshaw/Mrs. Gordon Fightmaster house.

Figure 75. Emison Mill site and Charles Fields house.

EMISON MILL SITE, EAGLE CREEK AND ELK LICK CHURCH ROAD. Between 1807 and 1815 Ash Emison, one of the first settlers on lower Dry Run of North Elkhorn Creek, built a mill on Big Eagle Creek about a mile northwest of present Sadieville. The road leading to the mill was called Emison's Mill Road. Emison earlier built a milling complex for grinding grains and sawing lumber on Dry Run on the land grant where he settled; its site is owned today by Betty Lou Lowery Graves. In 1805 Thomas Emison, son of Ash's brother Hugh, acquired a right to build a grist mill on Poplar Fork of Eagle Creek. The mill north of Sadieville remained an important landmark in that area well into the late nineteenth century. The likenesses of the mill and the Emison dwelling pictured on page 85 are taken from the J.R. Herring Collection, now owned by the Georgetown and Scott County Museum. The photos of the miller's house and artist Dorothy Core, her dog, and Robert Bevins at the mill site, then owned by Mrs. Core, were taken by the author circa 1980.[95]

---

[94] Deed Books 53-636, 55-83, 58-228, 63-159, 65-65, 67-546, 129-40.
[95] James Wade Emison, Jr., *Supplement to The Emison Families Revised (1954)* (Vincennes, Indiana, 1962), 24.

Figure 76. (a) Dorothy Core, dog, and Robert Bevins at Emison mill site. (b) Emison miller's house.

William Emison took over operation of the mill from his father. Emison's will, probated in 1878, left a life estate to his wife Nancy with remainder to the couple's three daughters, Mary Mallory, Sarah Pack, and Margaret Harwood, or their descendants. Emison explained in his will that his son James Edward had already received his "proper share." James E. Emison's will was also probated in 1878; he left funds for support of his parents if necessary and after their deaths to his sisters Mary Mallory and Sallie Pack or their children (his sister Margaret died a few days after the death of her brother James Edward). Ash's son, William Emison, operated the mill until his death in 1875, at which time his son-in-law Greenberry F. Mallory, husband of Mary Elizabeth Emison, became owner and operator.[96]

The city of Sadieville was named in honor of William Emison's daughter Sarah Martha "Sadie" Emison, who married Richard F. Pack, in 1848. Sadieville was developed and incorporated in the 1870s as a major shipping center on the new Cincinnati Southern Railroad. Charity Hill, the Pack home, was a gathering center for railroad executives and engineers as the rail line was under construction.[97] James Edward Emison was popularly known as "Mayor Jim Bob." He was Scott County sheriff and was recalled by his friends as a splendid fox hunter. He never married after his romance with a daughter of Bishop W.H. Forsythe was "blighted, due to the Civil War."[98]

A.B. BARKLEY MILL OPERATION. Mary Barkley Herring wrote that her father during the pre-Civil War era built a mill on the old Cincinnati Road in the northern part of Scott County and moved his growing family to the site. The question remains as to whether he rebuilt or leased and improved the mill of Ash Emison and his son William. After their father's death in 1863, the Barkley children were taken in by other family members. Later in

---

[96] Emison, 24. Photos from the J.R. Herring Collection, Georgetown and Scott County Museum earlier provided to author by historian Ron Vance.

[97] Emison, *Supplement*, 24, 322.

[98] Emison, *Emison Families Revised*, 126.

the century they gathered at the mill and home site and preserved the event with photographs located in the H.G. Herring Collection at the Georgetown and Scott County Museum.[99]

Figure 77. Emison-Barkley mill owners' house.   Figure 78. Emison-Barkley mill.

A.B. Barkley was shot "point blank" on January 1, 1863 by James F. Robinson, Jr., son of Kentucky Governor James F. Robinson, in Cal Barlow's jewelry store in Georgetown. The death was later declared an act of war. Barkley's estate was appraised in October of that year and recorded November 10. The appraisement listed "one steam grist mill and distillery, $1,000." Also cited were notes payable to Barkley and Bell, J.W. Fryman, John E. Sherritt, W.C. White, E.F. Osborne, Zachariah Thomson, and J.L. West. Listed as payable to Barkley and Lemon were notes from E.M. Hambrick, R.S. Hopkins, E.F. Cantrill, W.L. Richardson, Ruben Powell, and William W. Abbott. There was also a group of open accounts. Five slaves had a value of $2,375. Georgetown houses and a lot in Georgetown received a valuation of $800.[100]

Barkley's estate sale on January 29, 1864 yielded only $1,081.80. The mill and distillery were not among the items sold. Among the articles that were sold were: a log chain bought for $3.25 by Dr. Jo Emison; one "big plow" bought by E. Reed for $1.75; a sofa and chair, by T.B. Hiles, $5.00; one press, $1.75; a table for $6 and a bed and bedstead for $4.40 by J. Sherritt; a stove for $6.25 by James Reed; a sideboard for $3.00 and a bed and bedstead for $10.00 by J. Zeising; and beds and bedsteads by T.J. Marshall and J. Lancaster for $13.25 and $16.25. Neighbors buying livestock included T.J. Marshall and Henry Green, a yoke of red oxen, forty-one dollars; T.J. Marshall, a yoke of oxen, seventy dollars; and John R. Ewing, an ox wagon, twenty-five dollars.[101]

The Barkley children were placed in several homes and essentially separated after their father's death. In later years the family got together for a reunion at the old home place at Emison Mill. A photograph of the dress-up picnic, reproduced here, is from the J.G. Herring Collection, Georgetown and Scott County Museum.

Hinton Family Properties

William "Billy" Hinton.
William Hinton, progenitor of a large and illustrious clan, died in 1891, leaving "all of which I die possessed" to his wife Sarah. After her death it was to be divided, taking advancements into consideration, among their children -- Benjamin F. Hinton, Thomas Hinton, James Willis Hinton, George W. Hinton, John Asher Hinton, Mandeville Hinton, Henry Mitchell Hinton, Richard M. Hinton, Ferdinand Hinton, Nannie Tucker, Martha Noel, Aletha Jane Holland, and Laura Hinton. In his will William Hinton requested that his widow involve their sons Ferdinand and Henry Mitchell Hinton in management, under her direction, of the

---

[99] A copy of the Mary Barkley Herring letter was presented to the Sisters of the Visitation at Cardome by Evelyn Herring Harman of the Cardome Academy Class of 1942 and provided to the writer by Mother Jane Frances Blakely of the Visitation.
[100] Will Book O-227.
[101] Will Book O-227, 230.

estate "herein devised to her, in cultivation of the land, and with the buying, selling and trading necessary for her singular benefit." The portion of the estate designated for Aletha Jane was to be established "separate from the control of her husband."[102]

Figure 79. A.B. Barkley family picnic at old home site.

Division of a greater part of William Hinton's lands took place during the March 1892 term of court. A large portion of this land lay along the road that we now know as Double Culvert. The large dower tract was north of the road. Sons and daughters receiving land at that time were James W. Hinton, 110 acres bounded by the road, James Smith, L. Luke, and Richard Pack; Nannie Tucker, 110 acres bounded by the road, railroad, and Richard Pack; John Asher Hinton, 135 acres bounded by Daniel Gano; Laura Conner, one hundred acres bounded by the dower and Eagle Creek; Jane Holland, 115 acres bounded by Conner and James Smith; Martha Noel, ninety acres bounded by the road; and George Hinton; Ferdinand F. Hinton, sixty-seven acres "known as the Cox land" and bounded by C. Barnhill and Risk; Henry M. Hinton, one hundred acres, bounded by Eagle Creek, and also a three acre lot in Turkeyfoot; and George W. Hinton, 115 acres, bounded by Williamson.[103]

A biographical sketch of businesswoman and farmer Laura Conner, located via internet surfing by David Hawkins who lives amidst Hinton tradition on Burgess Smith Road, recalls the extent of Hinton family influence in the hills of Eagle Creek. William Hinton, Mrs. Conner's father, the account reads, was born, grew to manhood and married on his father Asher Hinton's farm. After declining his father's tradition bound offer of twenty acres of land or its equivalent in money, he moved "up the run a short way," purchasing a small tract that ultimately grew into a large farm. There he and his wife Sarah Sinclair, daughter of Benjamin and Priscilla Griffith Sinclair, reared a family of sixteen children. One of several traditions relating to Billy Hinton is that at the birth of each child, he set a commemorative cedar tree behind his home, which no longer stands, and that "there were no cedar trees in Turkeyfoot until he introduced them," a perhaps apocryphal assertion. As his children grew up and left home, he gave each a farm. All remained in Scott County, embracing the Hinton family lands and heritage.[104]

Billy Hinton, continued Hawkins's research, "prospered exceedingly, becoming an extensive stock owner, raising short horn cattle and fine horses." He was "very approachable and popular in the county and was known as Uncle Billy." He died with a reputation of having never taken a drink of liquor, sworn an oath, nor fired a gun. He was a member of Mt. Gilead Methodist Episcopal church from the age of nineteen "and lived up to its doctrines."

Over time the Hinton family amassed some 4,000 acres of land. The small railroad community of Hinton was named in honor of Asher Hinton's son, George W. Hinton. It is more than likely that both houses on this tract related to the Kenneth Hinton and D.T. and Lula Hinton era and that the two ancient houses in advanced stages of deterioration in this neck of the woods relate to other heirs of William Hinton and his children as well as of the heirs of his father Asher Hinton. In 1892 in a petition in Scott Circuit Court styled L.B. Hinton versus H.M. Hinton and others, the lands of William Hinton were formally divided. John A. Hinton received 135 acres in the division, a part of which Bernard Hinton inherited and passed on to his heirs.[105]

---

[102] Will Book S-345, 387; other information provided by Ronald T. Vance.
[103] Will Book S-387.
[104] Quoted from an email message entitled "Asher Hinton" from "Diamond Dave" to Jim Bevins, August 31, 2009. The statement about Asher Hinton contains at least two apocryphal allusions.
[105] Deed Book 27-404.

William Hinton stayed busy from the mid-nineteenth century until his later years acquiring land. Properties related to these acquisitions are discussed on the following pages.

Figure 81. Azalia B. Giles house.   Figure 80. Giles family trust house.

RALPH C. GILES FARM, DOUBLE CULVERT ROAD. An L-shaped one and one-half story house and a story and half bungalow were part of the farm owned by the Ralph C. Giles Trust, for which David Martin and Constance Sowers are trustees. The trust includes some of the extensive and far ranging lands of Asher and William Hinton and their large families. The house pictured at left is owned by Larry Riddle.[106]

In 2001 Bonnie Jane Lugar, Charlene Cheatham, and Carlene and Danny Perkins, heirs of Bonnie, Fred, and Constance Giles Sowers, sold to the Ralph C. Giles Trust their inherited 126 acres on Turkeyfoot Pike and Southern Railroad. Kenneth A. and Dorothy K. Hinton sold the first parcel of 111 acres minus five acres in 1945 to the Sowerses, who in 1950 purchased the smaller property from Nannie J. and W.W. McCabe, representing their interest in the William Hinton estate. Bernard Hinton and other heirs deeded land deriving from that branch of the Hinton family in 1921 to the McCabes. Part of their interest in the property came by way of adverse possession by Henry Sherman Sowers. In 2003 the Sowers heirs sold James and Rhonda Cross 51.495 acres that Fred and Constance Sowers bought in 1945 from Leonard Barnhill, Orris and Geneva Barnhill, and Margaret and Zelma Fightmaster. Carrie H. Barnhill acquired the tracts from the B.T. Hinton heirs and Laura Conner, both having inherited them it from William Hinton.

FARM, 1220 DOUBLE CULVERT ROAD. An L-shaped one and one-half story house and a story and half bungalow were part of the farm owned by the Ralph C. Giles Trust, of which David Martin and Ralph C. Giles, Jr., were trustees. A portion of the properties were jointly part of the former farm of Fred and Constance Sowers and included some of the extensive and far ranging lands of Asher and William Hinton and their large families. The house pictured here is owned by Larry Riddle.[107]

In 2001 Bonnie Jane Lugar, Charlene Cheatham, and Carlene and Danny Perkins, heirs of Bonnie, Fred, and Constance Giles Sowers, sold to the Ralph C. Giles Trust their inherited 126 acres on Turkeyfoot Pike and Southern Railroad. Kenneth A. and Dorothy K. Hinton sold the first parcel of 111 acres minus five acres in 1945 to the Sowerses, who in 1950 purchased the smaller property from Nannie J. and W.W. McCabe, representing their interest in the William Hinton estate. Bernard Hinton and other heirs deeded land deriving from that branch

---

[106] Deed Books 260-652, 282-542, 270-466, 69-450; 258-832, 70-431.
[107] Deed Books 260-652, 282-542, 270-466, 69-450; 258-832, 70-431.

of the Hinton family in 1921 to the McCabes. Part of their interest in the property came by way of adverse possession by Henry Sherman Sowers.[108]

In 2003 the Sowers heirs sold James and Rhonda Cross 51.495 acres that Fred and Constance Sowers bought in 1945 from Leonard Barnhill, Orris and Geneva Barnhill, and Margaret and Zelma Fightmaster. Carrie H. Barnhill acquired the tracts from the B.T. Hinton heirs and Laura Conner, both having inherited them from William Hinton.[109]

HINTON-TUCKER HOUSE, 1310 DOUBLE CULVERT ROAD. Nannie E. Tucker's lands are paramount in the story of a very nice two-story L-shaped house on a stone foundation. The background of ownership of this country estate is told in the 1892 and 1909 actions of the various William Hinton heirs regarding division of the lands of their ancestor. The grantors in the 1892 conveyance of 102 acres to Mrs. Tucker were J.W. Hinton, John A. Hinton, Aletha and John Hall, Laura and John L. Conner, Mandeville Hinton, B.F. Hinton, and Richard Hinton. Nannie was described in the deed as the "wife of Henry Tucker." Grantors of the 1909 action -- Henry Mitchell Hinton; John Asher Hinton; James W. Hinton; Lela, Noble, Noda, and John C. Noel; Aletha Jane Holland and her children; George W. Hinton; Ferdinand Hinton, B.T. Hinton, Laura Conner, and Mandeville Hinton -- deeded thirty-two acres to Nannie Tucker.[110]

Figure 82. The Hinton-Tucker house was acquired by Nannie E. Tucker from two groups of William Hinton heirs.

In 1925 Mrs. Tucker's heirs petitioned for her land to be divided. Enumerated in the document were E.D. and Willie Tucker, Willie and Scott Burgess, Azalia and George Giles, George W. and Sallie B. Tucker, Martha and Noda Noel, and A.F. and S.M. Powers. In 1978 Martha Noel Rutledge transferred to Taylor Rutledge the 17.5 and forty-acre tracts thus conveyed. Deward L. Noel and Laura F. Noel became the next owners, and in 2005 Deward Noel and others deeded the 57.5 acres with the two-story dwelling to Patricia Ann Noel. In 2012 Gary and Dawn Oaks purchased the property.[111]

---

[108] Deed Books 69-450, 76-161, 51-199, 51-268.
[109] Deed Books 270-466; 258-832; 70-431; 54-200, 203, 199.
[110] Deed Books 39-501, 54-524, 28-65.
[111] Deed Books 55-252, 253; 193-859; 141-288; 140-395; 296-727, 345-648.

ASHER HINTON RESIDENTIAL AND AGRICULTURAL COMPLEX, 375 BURGESS SMITH ROAD. Joe and Doris Clark, longtime owners of the home and agricultural buildings attributed to Asher Hinton, parted with their beloved rural property in 1993, selling it to David L. and Karen D. Hawkins, whose affection for the property rivals that of its previous owners.[112] Prior to the 1976 purchase by the Clarks, the farm on Eagle Creek with a rich pastoral view from the road known earlier as the Sadieville-Hinton Pike had been owned by Scott County's first Asher Hinton (1782-1856) and his heirs. His wife was Nancy Mitchell; she, like her husband, was of Virginian ancestry. They are buried in the side yard of the house now occupied by the Hawkinses. The elder Hintons lived in a log house not far from the present house established by Richard "Dick" Hinton, using the flooring from the log house in an upstairs room.[113]

Figure 83. Dick Hinton house near site of Asher Hinton house.

Asher Hinton was a son of James Hinton, who settled with his wife Catharine in the Turkeyfoot neighborhood circa 1792. After living several years in Scott County, James Hinton moved to Harrison County, dying there in August 1828 and leaving his property to his wife Rebecca. Sons named in James Hinton's will were Solomon, Jeremiah, James, Asher, and William; daughters were Rebecca, Deborah, Polly, Eleanor, and Caty. Hinton and other family members are buried in the small cemetery next to his house.[114]

Figure 84. Cam Skinner house.

---

[112] Deed Books 202-549, 132-131.
[113] Doris Reed for Rollie Hinton, *Families & History*, 193.
[114] *Hinton*.

Partition of Asher Hinton's estate took place in 1909. Among the heirs were John Asher Hinton, James W. Hinton, Lela Noel, John C. Noel, Aletha Jane Holland, George W. Hinton, Ferdinand Hinton, B.T. Hinton, Nannie Tucker, Laura Conner, Mandeville Hinton, and Richard "Dick" Hinton, children of his son William. Dick Hinton inherited the 121.5 acres on which he and his wife the former Luizah "Lulu" Vance, built their home, the two-story frame house now enhancing the ancestral home site. His heirs sold the home place in 1976 to the Clarks. Transferring the property were Dick Hinton's heirs Lottie and Buford Munson, Hallie and Richard Fightmaster, Tommie McKinney, Frank and Marian Hinton, Rollie and Jean Hinton, and Ellen and James Moreland.[115]

Figure 85. Asher Hinton graveyard is next to his house.

HINTON/CAM SKINNER PLACE, 318 DAVIS-TURKEYFOOT ROAD. Set well back from the road nearly opposite 917 Davis-Turkeyfoot Road is a very interesting older house with a huge stone chimney rising above the rear roofline at the second bay. The front bay of the formerly transverse porch is enclosed and has a small window. The fenestration of the part of the main façade that is not enclosed has two doors separated from a window, the door to the left having been enclosed. The remaining door is painted red and offers an intended welcoming effect. Cam Skinner was born in Missouri in 1870, son of Salathiel Parker Skinner and Nancy E. Fields. His grandfather, John R. Skinner, was a brother of Hezekiah Skinner, who owned considerable property on the northern portion of Cincinnati Road.

Figure 87. Hinton-Doris Reed house.

Figure 86. Laura Hinton Wells house.

HINTON-REED HOUSE, DAVIS-TURKEYFOOT ROAD. Unoccupied for several years is the ruin of a flood prone three bay story and half house covered with sheet roofing. Door and window spaces occupy the center and right bays and a small window lights the left bay. The once upon a time substantial house is owned by Hinton descendant Doris Reed.[116]

LAURA HINTON WELLS HOUSE, 495 DAVIS-TURKEYFOOT ROAD. An aluminum sided L-shaped house described by PVA files as having been built in 1930 is owned by Laura H. Wells. Her title came from Laura Conner, a daughter of William Hinton, and an important property owner in northern Scott County. An Antle house, which is part of the Sulphur Well property on Elk Lick Branch, is pictured at the left. The primary

Figure 88. Historic Antle family house.

---

[115] Deed Books 49-487, 202-549, 132-131.
[116] Information from Ronald T. Vance.

property on this site is the original Elk Lick Church building, partially enclosed within a barn.[117]

DOANE ANTLE/JAMES WILLIS HINTON HOUSE, 1030 BURGESS SMITH ROAD. The historic three bay dwelling known historically as the Doane Antle House and also as the James Willis Hinton Place is distinguished with nicely tooled chimneys on the gable ends and the end of the ell. An ancient photograph in the Antle collection now owned by Ron Vance (upper photo) pictures the house at its remote location described as "not far from Sadieville and before you get to Davis, up a hollow on right going to Davis." Clayton Smith purchased it in 2010.

Figure 89. Antle-Driskell house.

Next door stood the earlier home of Macedonia Antle, last of the homes of the historic Antle family. The farm's title traces to sale in 1938 by James Antle to Lizziebeth Fight/Fightmaster, who deeded the farm to Beal Fightmaster. The house burned while Fighmaster owned it.

Figure 90. Diana Reed and W.E. Bates house.

In 1988 Langley DeRossitt sold the farm to Geneva Driskell and Sheri Duncan, the description noting its location as adjacent to the land of Richard Antle and north of James Hinton's. It source was given as the property deeded to Macedonia Antle from J.V. Antle, with Henry Antle also as an earlier source.[118] Twenty-four graves are in the Antle Cemetery, also on Burgess Smith Road, including that of J.V. Antle (1826-1910). The earliest stone listed in the cemetery record is of an infant, born and died on October 26, 1859. In 1860 two-year-old Rufus K. Antle died. In 1871 thirty-three year- old Sara Jane Antle, wife of Richard Antle, was buried. Richard died in 1893 at the age of sixty-three. Courtney, McKinley, Price, and Stevens were also family names.[119] By trade, the Antles were stonemasons and builders.

Figure 91. Gillispie and African American cemetery.

WILLIAM E. AND ANN E. REED BATES HOUSE, FARM, 763 SADIEVILLE-HINTON ROAD. Forest Hill, the farmstead cited on the 1879 Beers & Lanagan map as that of W.E. Bates, continues to be as picture perfect a setting as it must have been in its earliest years when it was owned by Bates and his wife, Diana Reed. Bates, of the Turkeyfoot Bates clan, married Diana Reed in 1860. Diana's father, James Reed, owned an extensive estate said to have extended two miles east from a point one mile east of the Cincinnati road. Her husband was Scott County judge from 1890 to 1898.[120]

---

[117] Deed Book 87-86; other information from Ronald T. Vance.
[118] Deed Books 85-601; 64-191, 140.
[119] Scott County Genealogical Society, *Gone, Forgotten, Now Remembered* (Lexington, 1992), 2, 3. The Antles have an early connection with the Hintons. Deborah Hinton married Peter Antle in Frederick County, Virginia, June 30, 1779, and Solomon Hinton married Nancy Antle in the same county on December 20, 1787. From correspondence, James J. Antle, Naples, Florida, to author March 8, 1982.
[120] Gaines History 1,103.

Ann E. Bates deeded the farm in 1892 to Calvin Gillispie, from whom it passed to Calvin P. Gillispie, a nephew. Gillispie devised all his property to Clyde T. Gillispie and Carrie Bates. In 1960 Gillispie and his wife Virginia deeded the property exclusive of the Gillispie Cemetery and an adjacent African American cemetery to Carrie and Tom Bates. Mr. and Mrs. Bates made their home on the nicely arranged farm, maintaining it impeccably. Mr. Bates and Mrs. Bates died within a month of each other in the fall of 1994. Their son, Dr. Clyde Bates, Georgetown College professor of business, inherited the farm from them. Calvin Thomas and Deborah V. Bates are the present owners.[121]

William E. and Ann E. Bates celebrated their golden wedding anniversary in 1910 at their home on South Hamilton Street in Georgetown. Among their gifts was a gold dollar representing each year of their marriage, a present from the Christian Church. Two hundred guests, including J.F. Gasner, who made their wedding boots, were present. Photo of the Bates house in on page 91.

Figure 92. W.E. Bates barn and dry stone foundation.

Figure 93. James and Diana Reed and J.E. and Martha Vallandingham house.

REED/VALLANDINGHAM HOUSE, 548 ELK LICK CHURCH ROAD. One of the more fascinating houses in the north of Sadieville region is the story and half three bays wide dwelling with gingerbread trimmed porches sheltering the front entrance and the entrance to the ell. An outbuilding with a deep overhanging gable roof built atop a stone cellar is located to the side and rear of the house. An accompanying barn is set on a dry stone foundation and has an artfully designed ventilation system with a raised ridgeline ventilator. The house was originally owned by James and Diana Reed. James Reed bought seventy-six acres in 1839 from John Emison; 128 acres in 1838 from John and Nancy Stewart; 171 acres in 1846 from Ferdinand Flournoy; ninety-two acres in 1845 from Elizabeth Clarke, widow of Cary L. Clarke; 112 acres in 1858 from William Conner; and twenty-six acres and thirteen acres in 1860 and 1865 from John W. Lancaster. In 1875, following Reed's death, commissioners S.T. Connellee, William S. Parker, and R.F. Pack, divided his land, giving Diana the home tract of 128 acres bounded by William Emison and forty acres adjacent to John Lancaster. Other parcels went to children Martha B. Vallandingham, sixty-eight acres; Ann Eliza Bates, sixty-eight acres; Dorcas M. Lancaster, sixty-eight acres; Amanda Steward, thirty-seven acres; and another lot to Margaret J. Connellee.[122]

---

[121] Deed Books 89-110, 155; 45-373; 54-226; 62-378; 329-799; 355-453.
[122] Deed Books P-218, 23; U-248; V-217; 5-56; 7-406; Will Book R-221.

In 1864 Diana Reed deeded seventy-eight acres on Big Eagle to John W. Lancaster, husband of Dorcas Reed. Martha Reed deeded Lancaster her undivided interest in the seventy-eight acres. S.B. Lancaster sold him twenty-three acres; Buford Hall, 109 acres; the Wright heirs, fifty-two acres; James M. Steward, forty-two acres; and W.A. Connellee, fifty-three and ten acres.[123]

John W. Lancaster had previously acquired seventy-two acres from the estate of Lewis Lancaster following litigation of Eliza M. Lancaster versus John W., Mary E., Reuben, Thomas D., James, and S.B. Lancaster. He also purchased thirty-one and seventy-eight acres from Diana and James Reed and others in 1861 and 1864.[124]

Figure 95. Hinton Road School Site. schoolhouse.

From the James Reed heirs the property

Figure 94. Barn on Reed-Vallandingham farm.

passed to J.E. and Martha Vallandingham. The sixty acres that the Vallandinghams deeded to J.B. Robinson in 1912 were returned to Martha B. Vallandingham at the same time, along with ten acres bounded by William E. Bates, Vallandingham, the African American Baptist Church lot, and the old Mulberry Road. Gordon Fightmaster, Opal Skaggs Fightmaster, and Robert K. Fightmaster bought the 134.5-acre tract in 1970 from Valera Marshall, executor of the estate of Edgar B. Marshall, who bought the farm in 1937 from Annie S. Vallandingham, executor of the estate of Voris Vallandingham, who in turn left all his property to his wife, Annie. Vallandingham's title came from his father, J.E. Vallandingham, who in 1925 deeded seven pieces of property to his son. A portion of the farm came through acquisitions by Martha B. Vallandingham.[125]

Figure 96. Reed-Vallandingham smokehouse.

HINTON ROAD SCHOOL SITE. The two-door plan for the one-room schoolhouse built on the Clarence Lancaster farm north of Sadieville recalls the plan of many churches and schools of the nineteenth century. Mrs. Nora Faulconer, teacher in 1926, enjoyed legendary stature at the school, having taught as many as ten other teachers. Later owners of the schoolhouse property included Ethel Lancaster and Clem Fightmaster and their daughter Agnes L. Parrish. The school had the historic name of Locust Grove School.

---

[123] Deed Books 6-95, 7-184, 8-259, 11-320, 13-382, 22-453.
[124] Deed Book 5-304, 76-95, 7-184.
[125] Deed Books 112-65, 62-461, 46-118; 56-119, 42-360 and 366, 15-390, 25-467, 14-275, 25-466, 16-423; Will Book W-253.

Mulberry Properties

Jacob Mulberry House, 1515 Burgess Smith Road.

A two-story house described in PVA files as "unlivable" was not so many years ago a stellar landmark related to the family of the sequence of Jacob Mulberrys. Jacob Mulberry, the progenitor of the Scott County Mulberry clan, was the original owner of the complex that also includes a beautiful variety of dry stone and log structures. Leonard and Estelle Mulberry acquired the interest of other family members in 1917. In 1948 Walter M. Mulberry sold the 297-acre farm to Gilbert and Mary Renaker, who in 1949 deeded 97.58 acres including the house to James Desha and Bonnie Mae Renaker. Mrs. Renaker died in 1972, and in 1989 Mr. Renaker sold 6.56 acres of the total acreage along with the house to James G. and Juanita Dickey and Neal Dickey.[126]

Figure 97. Jacob Mulberry house.

Figure 98. Mulberry-Grigg house.

Mulberry-Grigg House, 930 Luke Pike.

On Joel Mulberry's Luke Pike land are a relatively new house and an ancient ruin of an older house that has intrepidly managed to survive. The picturesque historic home, resting among small saplings and brambles, is three bays wide and has a shed roof sheltered porch spanning the full lower façade. Two large windows are central to the gable ends. The house likely had late nineteenth or early twentieth century origins. The earliest reference in this sequence is special commissioner S.F. Gano's September 1884 deed to Jacob and Hettie N. Mulberry, in which Martha Grigg/Griggs' home at the time of her death (her will was probated June 29, 1935) had been devised to her by her father Joel Mulberry. Grantors for that transaction were J.L. and Elizabeth Antle, Dudley and Kitty Williamson, George T. and Florence Evans, Nannie Evans, Lee Evans, Joseph Grigg, John W. Grigg, and Jophenesse and Ellen Grigg. The property remained with the Mulberry family until the 1973 sale to Carl S. Arthurs, its metes and bounds restated in a 1988 deed by Carolyn Carroway, trustee, to Carl R., William E., and Glenna E. Arthurs for 43.3-acre and 34.9-acre parcels.[127]

The family period of ownership of the farm by Joel Mulberry and his daughter Margaret Griggs continued with purchase of the farm in 1884 by Margaret's brother Jacob Mulberry. Jacob and Elizabeth Mulbery and William V. and Mary F. Mulberry sold fifty-one acres to David Mulberry in 1894 and eighty-five acres in 1912. In 1911 the William V. Mulberrys sold fifty acres to David Mulberry. Mulberry in his will and codicils, dated 1917, 1918, and 1930, stated that his father had requested that his real estate shares be divided among Richie, Miranda Alice, and Nannie May. He willed his home farm of fifty-seven acres to his wife Hettie and at her death to their three children and provided fifty dollars to keep up the family graveyard. In 1933 Richard R. and Esther Mulberry, Nannie Mae and Frank J. Bates, Alice and John M. Campbell, heirs of David Mulberry, deeded to their mother the fifty-one acres minus the 7.5-acre home farm. In 1957 Mrs. Mulberry deeded her interest to the

---

[126] Deed Books 15-390, 25-467, 14-275, 25-466.
[127] Deed Books 16-423; Will Book W-253.

Figure 99. Mulberry-Swinford house.

Bateses. In 1997 Marie Arthurs deeded the same acreage to Glenna E. Arthurs and Floyd A. Crockett. In 1997 Glenna Arthurs sold it to Todd and Glenna Lancaster.[128]

MULBERRY-SWINFORD HOUSE, 1624, 1596, 159 BURGESS SMITH ROAD. A dwelling of American Foursquare design stands close to the Burgess Smith Road near the intersection with the Davis-Turkeyfoot Road. The 80.367 acres on Eagle Creek relate to the farm of eighty-five and 68.5 acres that Richard and Miranda Mulberry acquired from the estate of Jacob Mulberry, whose purchases on Big Eagle also included fifty-nine acres bought from Mary Smith in 1880. The elder Jacob Mulberry willed that the children of Joel and John T. Mulberry receive cash, which if not sufficient, should be made up by the others. This marked the sale of the farm to the Richard Mulberrys, apparent builders of the dwelling. In 1948 Richard Mulberry sold the farm to Raymond Swinford and Edward T. Swinford, who owned it when the writer and Joy Barlow conducted an agricultural building survey in that neighborhood in 1985. In 1989 James Ward and Pamela J. Swinford and other family members sold the farm of 158.9 acres to Edward T. and Etta Ruth Swinford. In 1993 Eastside Truck and Trailer Service purchased the farm and developed a rustic cabin on the back of the farm before selling it to James B. Bevins in 2000. Bevins built a contemporary house on the central part of the farm and sold the farm in 2004 to Donald C. and Felicia A. Silcox of Hollister, California.[129]

Figure 100. Walter V. "Bunk" Mulberry house.

W. V. "BUNK" MULBERRY HOUSE, DAVIS ROAD. In 1894 Jacob Mulberry, Sr., and his wife Elizabeth deeded a forty-eight- acre piece of land to their son William V. Mulberry for $1,536, reserving the graveyard. Other family members transferred title to adjacent land. Mulberry died in 1944, leaving the property to his wife Mollie with remainder to their children, May E. Evans, Sara F. Jones, and William V. Mulberry. Mrs. Mulberry died in 1946, and the next year Mary E. Evans, Sarah and Eric W. Jones, and William D. and Anna Lee sold the 94.7-acre Mulberry spread to Joe and Gladys Lee Eads. The Eads family sold their interest to Noah Eads in 1971 and in 2002 Ann Coleman Eads sold the farm to David A. and Patricia B. Giles and Lloyd D. and Annabel Giles.[130]

The house on the Mulberry-Eads farm is a neat front gable ell dwelling with fish scale trim in the gable; the house rests inside a drylaid stone fence. The foundation is

Figure 101. Walter V. "Bunk" Mulberry cellar/workshop.

---

[128] Deed Books 21-107, 46-537, 42-513, 30-3, 60-99, 122-393, 85-334, 148-700, 206-781, 254-595, 254-595, 227-790; Will Book W-54.
[129] Deed Books 17-255, 21-407, 42-513, 60-103, 73-499, 65-425, 180-103, 180-107, 198-222, 250-800, 286-450, 282-724.
[130] Deed Books 46-541, 42-512, 29-337, 72-412, 116-227, 267-196; W.B. W-378, 1-111. Jacob and Lucinda Mulberry's children included: William V., a farmer who married Mary Frances Burgess; John, a blacksmith, husband of Frankie Neal; Jacob, a farmer, husband of Nannie Northcutt and Lydia Dryden Giles; David, a farmer, husband of Katie Jones, and Hettie Salyers; Leonard, hardware dealer, husband of Essa Keller; and Lucy, wife of Arthur Lancaster, druggist.

laid with coursed squared limestone. Original sash is two-over-two pane. The porch has turned posts and milled cornice detail. In the back yard is a drylaid stone dry cellar on top of which is a workshop clad with vertical batten boards. Also in the yard is a wooden garage with a steeply sloping shed roof. The rock wall lining the lawn and the stone foundation work on the house and outbuilding are outstanding.

LEONARD MULBERRY HOUSE, FARM, 1751 DAVIS ROAD. Also related to the community of Straight Fork/Davis is a one-story house on a stone foundation with a one-story wing, recently acquired along with several neighborhood farms by David and Lloyd Giles. Paul and Betty J. Fuller were recent owners of the Mulberry farm described as including 297 minus 97.58 acres. Owners in more recent times have included J. Stephen and Mary Lee Judy, 1978-1982; Gilbert and Mary Renaker, 1948-1978; and Walter W. Mulberry (parcels acquired between 1912 and 1935 and owned jointly until the 1948 sale to the Renakers). In 1912 Jacob, Sr. and Ann Elizabeth Mulberry deeded the ninety-eight-acre farm, purchased from the William Penn heirs in 1889, to their son Leonard. Subsequent deeds to this and other Mulberry lands were made by the other heirs – W.V. and Mary F. Mulberry, Jacob and Lida Mulberry, Ora Mae and John Rawlston [sic], Grover Mulberry, David and Hattie Mulberry T. Mulberry, Zona B. and George Bassett.[131]

Figure 102. Leonard Mulberry house.

VALLANDINGHAM-NELSON HOUSE, 280 DOUBLE CULVERT ROAD. The carefully constructed log dwelling that was in recent years the home of Mr. and Mrs. R.T. Nelson enjoys a role as one of the centerpieces of the extensive historic Vallandingham farming expanse. The Vallandinghams were instrumental in the early settlement of Scott County, establishing homesteads and farmsteads on both sides of Little Eagle Creek and Cincinnati Road as well as in the region north of Sadieville.

George Vallandingham purchased the farm in tracts of 104.08 and 70.8 acres in 1920 from W.T. Wilhoite. The Double Culvert Road was referred to in the transaction as the Turkeyfoot Road. The dwelling probably relates to the era of John E. Pack or Llewellyn Luke, who are discussed in this volume among the property owners on the Luke Pike, a road extending north from Double Culvert to the Sadieville-Davis road. Luke sold the farm and its previous acreage of 208.16 acres for $5,200 in 1897 to William Holland, who resold it to Luke in 1900 at a reduced cost of $4,950. In 1913 Stephen A. and Lela Gano of New Orleans bought it for an appreciated $11,000, selling it in 1919 to Wilhoite and E.C. McFarland for $20,000. At that point the larger farm was subdivided.[132]

Figure 103. R.T. and Laura Etta V. Nelson log house.

The contemporary Vallandingham vintage of this house, already long established in the Little Eagle Creek region by the settlement period family of George Vallandingham, began in 1920. In 1924 Ettie Vallandingham, widow of George Vallandingham, and Roy Vallandingham and Lucy Mae Vallandingham, transferred 111.84

---

[131] Will Book U-271, 280; Deed Books 61-541, 61-47, 42-514, 54-323, 46-539, 74-7, 138-404, 152-387, 161-757.
[132] Deed Books 31-513; 33-402; 43-228; 49-532; 50-86, 88; 36-321, 322.

acres to J.C. Vallandingham. This land was described as located on Little Eagle and bounded by J.L. Luke and the Turkeyfoot Pike. At the same time J.C. and Fannie Vallandingham and Roy and Lucy Mae Vallandingham transferred title to Ettie Vallandingham on the Cincinnati Pike. Other partitions to the various family members were made at the same time. In the deed relating to the property of Etta Vallandingham was the explanation that J.C. Vallandingham had directed that R.T. Nelson, husband of Laura Etta Vallandingham, his only child and only heir, have a life estate in the property. In 1996 Laura Etta Nelson transferred 174 acres where she and her husband had made their home to Donald R. and Ruby Nelson. The deed described the property as having been willed by Etta Vallandingham to Roy Vallandingham.[133]

Figure 104. McGuirk/Fightmaster house.

McGuirk-Swinford House, 644 Hinton-Sadieville Road. The porch of an older house that is four bays wide and one and one-half stories tall has been enclosed. The house has a tooled central chimney. It relates to the purchase of the farm in 1907 from Margaret McGuirk by J.C.B. Fightmaster, who in 1912 sold seventy-eight acres to George M. and Delilah Swinford for $3,152. The Swinfords sold the portion containing the house in 1913 to George B. Cox. Subsequent owners included Robert L. Fightmaster, Herman D. and Josephine Fields, R.W. Green, C. Reed and Gladys Lancaster, Gerald B. Whalen, Anthony Blackburn, Jack and Iris Blye, and Iris Young, the former Iris Blye.[134]

Figure 105. W.F. Eads house.

W.F. Eads/A.J. and Juanita Lancaster House, 1236 Elk Lick Church Road. One of northern Scott County's finest houses on one of its most outstanding settings is on the farm that was owned by A.J. and Juanita Lancaster from 1957 to 1974, when they sold it to Eura Smith, Jr. and Carla M. Enos.

The spring branch that parallels the lane from Elk Lick Church Road has been landscaped with carefully selected plants and a stone wall. Several outbuildings surround the house, including a dry stone dry cellar with a workshop/storage mounted atop the cellar. Nearby are a raised crib/granary and a large tobacco barn with a continuous raised ridgeline ventilator, along with several modern additions.

---

[133] Deed Books 50-86; 53-320-322; 36-321, 322; 220-524; Will Book W-484; Map of Scott County, 1879.
[134] Deed Books 31-344, 38-174, 43-128, 43-135, 50-216, 72-286, 76-249, 77-278, 204-267, 207-704, 229-40, 207-704, 257-630.

The house is stellar. It is five wide bays wide, two stories tall, and has a one-story ell. The single-story porch shelters the centered entrance with sidelights and the two flanking windows. The foundation is laid of nicely coursed limestone. Two large brick chimneystacks emerge from the gable ends.

The property traces to W.F. Eads, whose approximately 228-acre farm on both sides of the Elk Lick Road was divided among his wife and children in 1912. In 1918 Richard Ignight, who had purchased the interest of several Eads heirs, sold that part of the farm to Alpheus Henry. C.S. and Gertrude Davis in 1919 bought the Henry interest and purchased additional acres from Eads family members. Subsequent owners of this delightful farm included E.C. and Myrtle McFarland (1922-1923), Russell and Maggie Graves (1924-1952), and John M. and Gertrude Bowman (1952-1957).[135]

Figure 106. W.F. Eads landscape features.

Kitchen Properties

John Kitchen House, Davis Road. The lengthy ownership of the 213-acre farm sold in 1988 by Mrs. Carl (Martha Louise) Kitchen to Clabe and Judy A. Mosley began as early as 1869 when John Kitchen bought thirty-six acres of the Elizabeth Peak property on Leeslick and Turkeyfoot roads from James Stucker for $600,

Figure 107. John Kitchen house, smokehouse.

and in 1871 with his purchase of 137 acres at a master commissioner's sale. There was a succession of Kitchens in the line of owners before the close of the century. John and Mary Kitchen sold the home tract of John Kitchen, deceased, to James H. Kitchen; and in 1907 Mary Adams and S.A. Davis sold John W. and Lizzie Kitchen and Peyton and Maggie Kitchen land on the Sadieville-Cynthiana Pike.[136] The land that Mrs. Kitchen sold in 1973 had been owned by the family partnership of Carl, Harold P. and Emery C. Kitchen, children of Roy Kitchen, who died in 1945, and his wife Edna. Carl Kitchen passed away in 1976.[137]

Thomas Kitchen House, 2376 Davis Road. The two-story front gabled house with a wing, remodeled in 1999, was

---

[135] Deed Books 38-580, 47-204, 43-139, 48-205, 48-177, 50-247, 51-579, 53-240, 78-482, 84-567, 126-686; Will Book U-164.
[136] Deed Books 11-122, 10-47, 24-81, 27-476, 101-540, 38-591, 80-165, 511-131.
[137] Deed Books 175-060, 123-204, 51-131, 70-52, 71-218, 58-263.

acres to J.C. Vallandingham. This land was described as located on Little Eagle and bounded by J.L. Luke and the Turkeyfoot Pike. At the same time J.C. and Fannie Vallandingham and Roy and Lucy Mae Vallandingham transferred title to Ettie Vallandingham on the Cincinnati Pike. Other partitions to the various family members were made at the same time. In the deed relating to the property of Etta Vallandingham was the explanation that J.C. Vallandingham had directed that R.T. Nelson, husband of Laura Etta Vallandingham, his only child and only heir, have a life estate in the property. In 1996 Laura Etta Nelson transferred 174 acres where she and her husband had made their home to Donald R. and Ruby Nelson. The deed described the property as having been willed by Etta Vallandingham to Roy Vallandingham.[133]

McGuirk-Swinford House, 644 Hinton-Sadieville Road. The porch of an older house that is four bays wide and one and one-half stories tall has been enclosed. The house has a tooled central chimney. It relates to the purchase of the farm in 1907 from Margaret McGuirk by J.C.B. Fightmaster, who in 1912 sold seventy-eight acres to George M. and Delilah Swinford for $3,152. The Swinfords sold the portion containing the house in 1913 to George B. Cox. Subsequent owners included Robert L. Fightmaster, Herman D. and Josephine Fields, R.W. Green, C. Reed and Gladys Lancaster, Gerald B. Whalen, Anthony Blackburn, Jack and Iris Blye, and Iris Young, the former Iris Blye.[134]

Figure 104. McGuirk/Fightmaster house.

W.F. Eads/A.J. and Juanita Lancaster House, 1236 Elk Lick Church Road. One of northern Scott County's finest houses on one of its most outstanding settings is on the farm that was owned by A.J. and Juanita Lancaster from 1957 to 1974, when they sold it to Eura Smith, Jr. and Carla M. Enos.

The spring branch that parallels the lane from Elk Lick Church Road has been landscaped with carefully selected plants and a stone wall. Several outbuildings surround the house, including a dry stone dry cellar with a workshop/storage mounted atop the cellar. Nearby are a raised crib/granary and a large tobacco barn with a continuous raised ridgeline ventilator, along with several modern additions.

Figure 105. W.F. Eads house.

---

[133] Deed Books 50-86; 53-320-322; 36-321, 322; 220-524; Will Book W-484; Map of Scott County, 1879.
[134] Deed Books 31-344, 38-174, 43-128, 43-135, 50-216, 72-286, 76-249, 77-278, 204-267, 207-704, 229-40, 207-704, 257-630.

The house is stellar. It is five wide bays wide, two stories tall, and has a one-story ell. The single-story porch shelters the centered entrance with sidelights and the two flanking windows. The foundation is laid of nicely coursed limestone. Two large brick chimneystacks emerge from the gable ends.

The property traces to W.F. Eads, whose approximately 228-acre farm on both sides of the Elk Lick Road was divided among his wife and children in 1912. In 1918 Richard Ignight, who had purchased the interest of several Eads heirs, sold that part of the farm to Alpheus Henry. C.S. and Gertrude Davis in 1919 bought the Henry interest and purchased additional acres from Eads family members. Subsequent owners of this delightful farm included E.C. and Myrtle McFarland (1922-1923), Russell and Maggie Graves (1924-1952), and John M. and Gertrude Bowman (1952-1957).[135]

Figure 106. W.F. Eads landscape features.

KITCHEN PROPERTIES

JOHN KITCHEN HOUSE, DAVIS ROAD. The lengthy ownership of the 213-acre farm sold in 1988 by Mrs. Carl (Martha Louise) Kitchen to Clabe and Judy A. Mosley began as early as 1869 when John Kitchen bought thirty-six acres of the Elizabeth Peak property on Leeslick and Turkeyfoot roads from James Stucker for $600,

Figure 107. John Kitchen house, smokehouse.

and in 1871 with his purchase of 137 acres at a master commissioner's sale. There was a succession of Kitchens in the line of owners before the close of the century. John and Mary Kitchen sold the home tract of John Kitchen, deceased, to James H. Kitchen; and in 1907 Mary Adams and S.A. Davis sold John W. and Lizzie Kitchen and Peyton and Maggie Kitchen land on the Sadieville-Cynthiana Pike.[136] The land that Mrs. Kitchen sold in 1973 had been owned by the family partnership of Carl, Harold P. and Emery C. Kitchen, children of Roy Kitchen, who died in 1945, and his wife Edna. Carl Kitchen passed away in 1976.[137]

THOMAS KITCHEN HOUSE, 2376 DAVIS ROAD. The two-story front gabled house with a wing, remodeled in 1999, was

---

[135] Deed Books 38-580, 47-204, 43-139, 48-205, 48-177, 50-247, 51-579, 53-240, 78-482, 84-567, 126-686; Will Book U-164.
[136] Deed Books 11-122, 10-47, 24-81, 27-476, 101-540, 38-591, 80-165, 511-131.
[137] Deed Books 175-060, 123-204, 51-131, 70-52, 71-218, 58-263.

owned during the latter part of the nineteenth century by Thomas Kitchen. Everett McKenney sold it in 1969 to Ezra C. and Naoma R. Bell, giving as sources deeds (1) from George Kitchen on behalf of Martha A. Kitchen, Thomas Kitchen, Mary Alice Kitchen, and others; and (2) Nannie L. Penn, Bessie Penn, and Georgia Lee Sage, all widows. In 1970 the Bells sold the property to Lawrence and Josephine Fister, who in 1996 sold it to Jack and Ruth Bryant.[138]

Figure 108. Thomas Kitchen house.

STONE FAMILY FARM, 555 STONE LANE. State Highway 356 winds its way from Stonewall toward the Hinton-Sadieville and North County Line roads. A bungalow dating back about sixty years and its accompanying barn scan the hillsides of northeast Scott County a short distance past Cincinnati Road and relate to the extensive estate of William Carl (W.C.) Stone of Harrison County, whose 1963 will was probated in late 1964. Stone left all his property to his wife Rachel. After her death, it was to be apportioned to their four children -- Ruth Stone Smith and William Charles Stone (the property in Harrison); and Walter McArthur Stone and James Carlton Stone (the land in Scott).

Figure 109a. The story book-like Mulberry tree in the yard of the Dunaway house may have given historic Mulberry Road its name.

Figure 109. Faulconer-Dunaway Farm.

---

[138] Deed Books 109-216, 29-386, 70-18, 39-264, 111-568, 219-672.

Allotted to sons James and Walter Stone were farms formerly belonging to Wilhoit (101.8 acres); Downing (33.75 acres); the Federal Land Bank (73.24 acres); Parker (55.62 acres); and Hurley (23.75 acres). The north boundary lay along Highway 356, and the southeast, on Elk Lick Pike.[139]

Stone family ownership of the land "goes way back." Deed Book T discusses division of the dower from the J.T. Stone estate, which took place on December 30, 1900. Receiving tracts from their mother's estate were Mary E. Dougherty, twenty-one acres; Lorie Downing, twenty-six acres; Stella B. Merckle, twenty-two acres; John C. Stone, twenty-six acres; Josie Luke, twenty-seven acres; and J.T. Stone, twenty-seven acres. The land was located off the Stonewall county road. J.T. Stone (the second man to bear that name) purchased land from J.C. Stone and J.S. Stone. J.T. Stone in 1920 deeded 260 acres to his son W.C. Stone on terms of love and affection. The elder Stone gave as his sources a thirty-acre spread acquired from J.C. Stone, ninety acres purchased at the courthouse door, fifty-six acres bought from Stella Evans Merckle, and eighty-four acres from the estate of J.S. Stone.[140] James Stone sold the farm in 2015 to North Woods, LLC.[141]

FAULCONER-DUNAWAY HOUSE, 680 STONE LANE. One can't help wondering what the story is behind the storybook-like Mulberry tree that charms the yard of the five-bay house with a central roofline pediment, owned by Hayden and Anna K. Dunaway since 1974. Historically the house, along with a later wing, relates to the extensive family of Richard D. and Eliza Jane Faulconer. Faulconer bought 150 acres in 1877 from J.E. and Sally Adams. He purchased much of the interest of his brothers and sisters and increased that with purchases from his neighbors. In 1941, Mollie Faulconer, along with Odella and John J. Lancaster, Mary Marshall nee Jones and E.B. Marshall, and W.B. Faulconer, sold the property on both sides of the Stonewall and old Mulberry Road to Roy L. and Orva D. Parker. The survey of 297.22 acres referenced land on the Mulberry dirt road, Southern Railroad, an old dirt lane, Scott Downing, McFarland, Stone, and Mrs. Faulconer's dower. Heirs named were Mary E. Jones, 60.33 acres; Orva D. Parker, seventy-two acres; William Boyd Faulconer; Odella Lancaster, 23.88 acres; and the 47.06-acre dower. Faulconer heirs owned the property until the 1974 sale to the Dunaways. Those who held title after Mollie Faulconer included Mary E. and Zemar Jones, Roy L. and Orva Parker, Charles and Christine Jones, and James L. and Charlie Jones.[142]

Figure 110. Mollie and J.E. Faulconer and Lancaster farm.

---

[139] Will Book 1-23.
[140] Will Book T-235; Deed Book 59-408.
[141] Deed Book 371-567.
[142] Deed Books 15-225;66-526; 52-552, 57-498; 75-176; 116-460; 124-324; Will Book U-454-456.

LANCASTER PROPERTIES

LANCASTER HOUSE. A one-story house in an advanced state of decay, with two front doors flanked by deep windows, was owned by Lucy Lancaster. Mrs. Lancaster died in 1942, survived by her husband John Lancaster. Heirs in addition to her husband were her son John, married to Odella; Dorcis L., Lena and Winter Neale; and Laura and Ebon Champion, each inheriting one-fourth interest of the 116.6-acre property. In 1943 Hubert and Stella Morris bought the property; they sold it in 1950 to William and Gwendolyn Lancaster. In 1952 James Webber and Mary Swinford became the owners. The Swinford family owned it until 1978 when they sold it to a partnership of Eugene V. Atkinson, Ronald P. Wells, and Dr. Zahkula Govindarayulu. In 1998 David and Lloyd Giles sold it to John W. and Tonia Sayre.[143]

Figure 111. Richard D. Faulconer house.

LANCASTER HOUSE, 984 STONE LANE. On down Stone Lane/Highway 356 on the same side of the road as the Richard Faulconer house is an extensive L-shaped two-story house with nicely tooled chimneys. It occupies a stone foundation; the siding has been reclad with cream colored vinyl. In 1998 Timothy Franklin sold the house and 21.61 acres to Gregory J. and Debra M. Stearns. Franklin bought the property in 1955 from A.J. and Juanita Lancaster, whose title was derived from Odella and John Lancaster, Orva and Roy Parker, William Boyd Faulconer, and Dorothy, Mary, and E.B. Faulconer, heirs of Mollie and J.E. Faulconer.[144]

JOHN AND PAULINE J. HENRY HOUSE, 120 SOUTH RAYS FORK ROAD. A story and half bungalow, aluminum sided with double windows, its porch once supported by tapered posts typical to the Arts and Crafts period, occupies a setting near the Cincinnati Road and the village of Stonewall. The property has an interesting chain of title, evolving from a gift by Jesse and E.A. Hall of Centreville to John and Pauline J. Henry that included "a tract of land on Rays Fork known as the 'sheep farm' surveyed by Stone at 286 acres." In 1926 T.C. Henry traded the property to J.I. Wilhoite. Containing 401.88 acres, its boundaries included the Stonewall schoolhouse, Edwards, James Smith, a graveyard, and Daugherty. In 1932 C.O. Wilhoite acquired the farm. G.G. and Mabel Lee Willhoite also owned part of the larger farm. In 1945 C.O. and Syble Wilhoite sold 116 acres to J.D. Michael. The seventy-two-acre residue of this farm, including the

Figure 112. John and Pauline Henry bungalow.

---

[143] Deed Books 68-8, 9; 76-134; 77-245; 78-520; 139-115; 234-354; 266-076.
[144] Deed Books 233-433, 215-23, 77-435, 77-385.

Figure 113. Kristine Wilderson and Dorothy Green in the log Stowers house.

house, was sold by the J.D. and Ophelia Michael estate in 1992 to Rhonda Lyons, who sold 116 acres and the house in 2006 to David Inyart.[145]

Stowers and Robinson Farms, 155 and 227 South Rays Fork Road

A pair of similar dogtrot type log houses, standing today rather victoriously on formerly adjacent farms on the north side of South Rays Fork Pike, uniquely underwent similar twentieth century renovations that transformed both with brick faced ranch type exteriors. Both face the eastern reaches of Ray's Fork and the road that parallels the branch for some distance before it strikes north toward the 1870s Cincinnati Southern Railroad and the once densely populated community of Hinton.

Stowers-Wilderson House, 155 South Rays Fork Road. Today's owners of the westernmost residential and agricultural tract on South Ray's Fork Road, earlier known as Hinton Road, are Jeffrey L. and Kristine D. Wilderson, who purchased the farm's 100.5 acres and the house, tobacco barn, and storage building for $225,000 from Dorothy W. Green. Mrs. Green, pictured on this page with Kristine Wilderson, was the popular storekeeper for many years of the grocery at the southeast corner of Frankfort and Payne's Depot roads. She bought the South Rays Fork farm in 1977 from Lewis and Lillis Watson. Prior to the Watsons' ownership, it was owned by W.C. and Lillian Henry (1958-1969) and Lawrence and Edna Scott (1943-1958).[146]

Figure 114. Kristine Wilderson and Dorothy Green and the stone chimney.

When she bought the house, Mrs. Green recalled, "we all knew that there was a log home underneath it. We decided to fix it up and then build on top of the hill." A major exterior clue to the house's antiquity was the stone shouldered chimney on one of its gable ends. Later an old multi-purpose barn, all walnut, collapsed in a storm, leaving the tobacco barn alone to protect the farm machinery and tobacco inventory.

The Greens also built the bridge to spare them from countless creek fordings.[147]

Figure 115. Stowers farmland.

---

[145] Deed Books 20-11, 36-511, 55-356, 55-614, 59-613, 61-404-405, 70-80, 193-517, 298-361.
[146] Deed Books 348-289; 136-153; 85-635; 67-598.
[147] Discussion with Dorothy Wilson Green and Kris Wilderson, September 24, 2013.

Figure 116. Stower-Lowery house.

Figure 117. Photo of Green-Wilderson house.

Previous owner J.R. Stowers bought the farm, on which the westernmost of the pair of houses stood, in three campaigns: eighty-five acres six poles in 1870 from Beverly and Sarah Nelson and George T. Nelson for $2296; seventy-six acres seventeen poles in 1871 from Buford and Nannie Hall; and 127 acres one rod twenty-one poles in 1894 from Buford and Nannie Hall. The dwelling's transformation into a brick faced ranch type house took place circa 1977.[148]

THE ROBINSON-LOWRY FARM, SOUTH RAYS FORK ROAD. Equally and perhaps even more stunning is the Stowers house's neighbor, which dates to acquisition of its 105.09 acre setting and possibly the dogtrot type log house as early as 1850 by Richard A. Robinson and subsequently by his wife Candace Robinson. Robinson purchased 30 ¾ acres in 1850 from William B. Robinson for $307.50. In 1869 Richard Robinson sold seven acres on Rays Fork to Candace Robinson for $120, the property having as a boundary the land of R.A. Robinson. Candace Robinson acquired abutting or nearby parcels from master commissioner Samuel W. Long in 1866 following litigation of N. Warfield vs. R.A. Robinson for $748 (the property had been mortgaged to Warfield); and sixty acres in 1883 from Mariah Jane and Joseph S. Tucker for $1,800. She sold the farm in 1881 to F.W. Davis for $2,712.50. Boundaries were land of Hezekiah Skinner, J.T. Hinton, and Jesse Hall.[149]

Figure 118. Oldest barn on Robinson-Lowery farm.

Figure 118a. Later barns on Robinson-Lowery farm.

---

[148] Deed Books 11-300, 334; 33-6; 348-289; 136-153.
[149] Deed Books 1-428, 15-220, 8-139, 20-207.

Thomas Stowers' title came from Richard Stowers in 1933. In 1900 the heirs of J.R. Stowers divided the seven tracts of their father J.R. Stowers's farm. The several generations of the Stowers family as owners of the farm and possibly the Wildersons' log house as well came to an end in 1943 when Runa, widow of Thomas L. Stowers, who died in 1936, and other family members, sold it to Lawrence Scott.[150]

Carl L. and Doris Lee Fain, who bought the eastern property in 1967 from Audrey J. and Joella Michael, transformed its exterior into that of a brick faced ranch style dwelling. In 1987 they sold a portion of the property to Tim and Kris Lowry, completing the transaction in 1999. The Michaelses bought the property in 1964 from Russell J. and Allie M. Perkins for $23,100. The Perkinses bought it for $17,050 in 1958 from Bessie D. and Morgan Lee. Mrs. Lee inherited it from her mother, who inherited it from her husband F.W. Davis and siblings Lura Lynum and Ernest Davis and their spouses.[151]

Figure 119. Tim and Kris Lowery log house.

The Lowrys meticulously removed the wall coverings with which the two log sections of their home had been covered and preserved the enclosed dogtrot that once provided an open passage between the log sections. Tim used a dental pick to fine tune the cracks in the logs. When they opened the crawl space, Kris maneuvered through it and discovered among the hewn joists a central beam without support on one end, introducing a new mystery to the mix. The Lowrys' three older farm buildings include a large tobacco barn, a smaller general purpose barn, and a third farm building mounted on stacked stone piers which should respond readily to reboxing.

Figure 121. Benjamin and Edna Offutt house.

F.W. AND LUCINDA DAVIS HOUSE, 285 SOUTH RAYS FORK ROAD. A small formerly two door house traces to

Figure 120. Sadieville's Ben Offutt, Spanish American War veteran.

the F.W. Davis family. Windows have six-over-six-pane sash. A stuccoed chimney stack rises from the center of the roof. In 1912 Lucinda Davis sold the house to Lura Lynum, who in 1950 sold it to Lum and George Dixon. Thomas Toohey of Paris is listed as the current owner.[152]

BENJAMIN AND EDNA OFFUTT HOUSE AND FARM, 615 HINTON-SADIEVILLE ROAD. Benjamin and Edna Offutt were the original owners of the Hinton Road bungalow with a wraparound porch supported by classical Arts and Crafts style tapered posts mounted on brick piers with stone caps. Ben Offutt, a stonemason

---

[150] Deed Books 67-598; 65-140; 56-558, 559; 59-420; 35-541; 34-50, 52-58; Will Books T-465, X-389.
[151] Deed Books 105-555, 96-118, 85-613, 19-265, 32-384, 43-483, 44-273, 59-632, 59-482.
[152] Deed Books 43-482, 76-159, 87-565, 263-40.

and an African American, mastered the building trades and brought up his son Harry to also master those trades. The two were responsible for building many of the retaining walls, foundations, and rock walls in and around Sadieville. Both were master carpenters and builders. Offutt, a veteran of the Spanish American War, bought the twenty-three-acre core of the farm in 1915 from Delilah Swinford, wife of George M. Swinford, and according to PVA records, built the house in 1941, although the design and workmanship may suggest an earlier date. Offutt died in 1951, leaving his widow Edna, sons Graham and Harry C., and daughter Mae Etta O. Holmes. Jane L. Tylicki bought the property from Mrs. Offutt in 1988 and sold it in 2004 to David and Nicole Hall.[153]

Figure 122. F.W. and Lucinda Davis house.

Part of Offutt's motivation to purchase the farm accrued from the fact it had been the site of the first Mount Pleasant Baptist Church, a log building. Offutt recalled that the neighborhood's African Americans built a church and had a graveyard there, and that in 1872 they acquired the lot on Sadieville's Pike Street for the relocated church. Nearby they also built a school, and many of Sadieville's African American population established homes nearby.[154]

Harry Offutt, a veteran of World War II, organized an adult farmers group for the veterans' on-farm training program offered via the G.I. Bill, the University of Kentucky College of Agriculture, and high school vocational agriculture teachers. Offutt's group studied with C.F. Esham, teacher at Sadieville and a Veterans Administration supervisor of vocational agriculture. An account in the *Lexington Sunday Herald-Leader* during that period, preserved in the Sadieville archives, points out that Offutt was raising three acres of tobacco and had sizeable herds of cattle, sheep, and hogs. His fifty yearling ewes yielded sixty-five lambs. Jane Tylicki sold this nicely styled and preserved bungalow to David and Nicole Hall in 2004.[155]

BRISE HITEN HOUSE, SADIEVILLE-DAVIS ROAD. A one bay house with a two bay addition traces to the estates of Brise and Letitia Hiten. In her will, written in 1920, Mrs. Hiten left tract number one of thirty-five acres to Lizzie Fields. Other parcels were willed to Carrie Wilson and Orva, Carl, Russell, and Gertrude Dryden. In 1937 Fields and others deeded the property to William T. Smith. Smith died in 1964, his estate transferring title to property on several area roads to his wife Eugenia S. Smith. In 2005 Linda Smith Goepper and others sold the property to David and Patricia Giles and Lloyd and Annabel M. Giles.[156]

HILES, GILES, AND DAVIS HOUSES

HILES-DAVIS HOUSE, SADIEVILLE-DAVIS ROAD. A 250-acre farm with a classic two-door one story house with an end stone chimney, set downhill from the main road and the village known as Straight Fork before its name was changed to Davis, traces to J. Polcer Hiles. Hiles wrote two wills, the second probated August 22, 1877, annulling the first dated January 22, 1874. In the second will, Hiles left to his wife Verinda all his property with instructions to dispose of "the tract on which I reside" to T.B. Hiles.[157]

---

[153] Deed Books 284-840, 177-248, 44-608, 45-117, 62-451, 43-128.
[154] Norman Minch, "Mount Pleasant Keeps the Faith," *Georgetown News & Times*, undated clipping, Collections of Sadieville City Clerk.
[155] Undated clipping (partial), "On Farm Training Program for Vets Improves The Men and Land, Raises Living Standards," *Sunday Herald-Leader,* Archives, Sadieville City Clerk. Deed Book 284-840.
[156] Will Book X-619, Deed Books 51-295-297, 107-355, 102-422, 102-421, 99-103, 297-609.
[157] Will Books R-426 and S-15.

REAL COUNTRY II. NORTHEAST AND EAST CENTRAL SCOTT COUNTY

Figure 123. Polcer Hiles-J.W. Davis house.

In 1892 T.B. Hiles and others sold 156 acres of this property to J.W. Davis for $2,733.28. Davis, a storekeeper and village postmaster, was the man from whom the community got its present name. Excluded from the deed were "new boards on premises and four oak trees suitable for making into boards." Davis also acquired the sixty-two-acre portion of the land left in trust to Thomas B. Hiles for William H. Hiles and his children. Frank Williams purchased the farmland in three tracts from Davis's administrator and other family members, and in 1978 Jane Williams Johnston acquired interest in the property from James G. and Bernice Davis of Dearborn Heights, Michigan.[158] The Davis house has two front doors and a hall-parlor plan.

GILES-REFFETT HOUSE, 2810 DAVIS ROAD. The house and small farm sold by Hez and Emma Giles and Charles Giles in 1959 to Frank and Grace Reffett was earlier part of the Brise and Letitia Hiten property. The house, pictured at right, is a three-bay house with a gabled addition onto the back. The main block has an interesting stone chimney stack at the front roof's ridgeline and is built on a nice stone foundation.[159]

2111 DAVIS ROAD. Signs of antiquity abound for the side-gabled house that is sited downhill, below grade, from the Sadieville-Davis Road. The house has a double hung window lighting the west

Figure 124. Giles-Reffitt house.

side of the upper half story and two large windows lighting the east side. It has a stone foundation, a central door flanked by windows, and slatted shutters. The gabled porch shelter is railed. The house has an ell. It and its twenty-eight-acre setting were sold in 2003 by Michel Kelly to Elizabeth Emery.[160]

KENTUCKY 922/MUDDY FORD ROAD

Though it was known from its earliest days as the Turkeyfoot Road, twenty-first century rural nomenclature indisputably calls the section between the surviving vestiges of the once bustling villages of Muddy Ford and Turkeyfoot the "Muddy Ford Road." The southern segment of this road extends north from the farms on the east side of the road related to historic ownership of the William Nichols and William T. Juett families, discussed in the chapter on Middle Bluegrass Residential and Agricultural Complexes, and further east to the African American community of Boydtown. Entering and leaving the many driveways along Muddy Ford Road's curving hills and hilly

Figure 125. Below-grade house near Sadieville.

curves can be and usually is an extremely nerve-wracking experience. This section of rural road is replete with fascinating history.

Muddy Ford village is discussed in the chapter on Crossroads Villages, Churches, and Country Stores.

---

[158] Deed Book 27-249, 17-183, 39-475, 82-351, 139-440.
[159] Deed Books 42-117, 51-295, 62-408, 49-362, 87-252.
[160] Deed Book 289-636.

REAL COUNTRY II. NORTHEAST AND EAST CENTRAL SCOTT COUNTY

LEE GILKEY FARM, MUDDY FORD ROAD. Lee Gilkey, who made his home on a farm on Anderson Road, acquired 47.54 acres on Muddy Ford Road from B. and Lula Anderson in 1934. On this farm is a compact story and half two door frame dwelling. Anderson purchased a 140.55-acre farm encompassing this acreage in 1914 from Mrs. A.T. Glenn, the acreage a portion of that acquired by Mrs. Glenn from Sarah Risk in 1901.[161]

BARNHILL AND SHARON PROPERTIES

The Barnhill and Sharon families' historic influence for well past two centuries has been and continues to be prominent in the neighborhood north of the Nichols and Cranetown-Boydtown spheres of influence and south of the once bustling village of Muddy Ford. Though he wasn't the first Scott County Barnhill, the name Clinton Barnhill continues to appear and reappear in the annals of Scott County history.

By 1794, Samuel, Robert, and Daniel Barnhill, and by 1797, their sister Jane and her husband, Hugh Sharon, were setting up households and farmsteads along the pattern of southwest forks of Eagle Creek that inspired early surveyors to graphically denominate it "Turkeyfoot." Samuel Barnhill was one of the veterans of the American Revolution memorialized on the 1920 D.A.R.-financed monument above Georgetown's Big Spring and the site of McClelland's Fort. The Scott County Barnhills descended from Robert and Sarah Barnhill, Scots-Irish settlers who moved in a migratory stream to western Pennsylvania and southward into Virginia, North Carolina, Tennessee, and Kentucky. Within this southwesterly flow they contributed in a huge way to the formation of the distinctive Ulster-stamped character of the American midwest.

The Barnhills and Sharons made a special impact in the rural neighborhoods watered by the Sharon, Muddy Ford, Rogers Gap, and West forks of Big Eagle Creek, the latter taking off on its northerly flow just north of the hamlet of Turkeyfoot. Samuel, born in 1761, was the eldest of the Scott County clan; Robert with a birth year of 1769 was next. Daniel came along in 1771, and their little sister Jane was born in 1773. Samuel died in 1844 and is buried in the Vance cemetery near Turkeyfoot on the farm now owned by Ronald T. Vance. Robert's restlessness took him from Scott County to Ohio and then to Indiana, where he died in 1821, having made a significant impact to the development of the Christian Churches along the way. Daniel died around 1820 and was buried in Scott County. Hugh and Jane Sharon left their imprint on the branch of Eagle that bears their name. The Barnhill and Sharon genes mingled with those of their neighbors, leaving generations of successive neighbors with surnames that included Vance, Traylor, Williamson, Antle, Roberts, Muddiman, Wyckoff, Sutton, Pettit, Dozier, Burgess, and McDaniel.[162]

John Barnhill 's heirs received title to seventy-two acres on the west side of the Muddy Ford Road and ninety-two acres on the east side. The dower land of thirty-four acres allotted to his widow Rachel was located near the point that the branch crossed from the east side to the west side of the road. Her one-acre tract of firewood – "there being no firewood on the dower lot" -- was situated on the other side of the road behind John W. Barnhill's seven acres. Others sharing in the division included James Barnhill, Robert Barnhill, Isaiah Barnhill, Clinton Barnhill, Elizabeth Roberts, Sarah McDaniel, Robert and John Barnhill, and John, Clinton, Hugh, Jemima, Thomas, Henry, and Rose Sharon.[163]

---

[161] Deed Books 61-2, 43-622.
[162] The Barnhill story is expertly told by Dwayne Barnhill and Barbara Little in Scott County Genealogical Society, *Families and History: Scott County, Kentucky* (Paducah: Turner Publishing Company, 1996), 147.
[163] Will Books R-54, T-163.

SHEPHERD'S CROSSING/CLINTON BARNHILL HOUSE, 5000 MUDDY FORD ROAD. Unlike its compatriot across the highway, the two-story three bays wide frame house, its lawn at the Muddy Ford Road edge marked by a plank fence, doesn't require a challenging drive for the reaching. Today bearing the pleasant and apt title "Shepherd's Crossing," the house, pictured below, was historically heated with a central chimney. It stands on a

Figure 126. Shepherd's Crossing, Muddy Ford Road: Clinton Barnhill house.

twenty-two and one-half acre division of the lands of the most recent Clinton Barnhill, the same acreage tracing backward to as early as the 1902 subdivision of the lands of the first Clinton Barnhill. This property was sold to Herman Williamson in 1920 by Llewellyn Barnhill, husband of Sarah, who devised it to him after receiving it in the 1902 division of the estate lands of Clinton Barnhill. Others sharing in the earlier Clinton Barnhill's estate on both sides of the Muddy Ford Road included his widow (forty-six acres on the west side of the pike and fifty-four on the east); and, with shares ranging between twenty and twenty-four acres, Sam Barnhill, Sarah Barnhill, J.D. Barnhill, R.S. Barnhill, Laurance and Samuel Harris, Mary McDaniel, J.L. Barnhill, B.T. Barnhill, J.C. Barnhill, and John B. Barnhill. Sarah Barnhill devised her 22 ½ acre tract to her husband Llewellyn Barnhill.

Some eighty-two acres of the first Clinton Barnhill's estate came from Henry and Sarah J.E. Edmundson in 1875, it being "the same tract conveyed to Samuel Salyers" in 1873. In 1877 Barnhill purchased an undivided one-fifth or eighteen acres of the Obediah Pettit farm. In 1891 G.J., Henry, Hugh, James N., N.C., Rosa A., and

Figure 127. Barnhill-Dawson house.

T.J. Sharon deeded to Clinton Barnhill for seventy dollars two parcels – thirty-four acres adjacent to Hugh Sharon, Clinton Barnhill, and Sanford Smith; and one and one-half acres bounded by James H. Williamson, E.T. Burgess, and Dudley Hamon, allotted to Rachel Barnhill in the dower estate of John Barnhill. In 1897 Clinton Barnhill, Sr. purchased at a master commissioner's sale from Martin Nall, Lena Nall, Noble Nall, John Cobb Nall, Nada Nall, and John B. Graves eighty acres conveyed by F.F. Hinton to J.T. Nall, tracts six and seven in the William Hinton division, bounded by Eli Muddiman and known as "the old Cox place." [164]

---

[164] Deed Books 195-295, 238-351, 170-676, 82-75, 50-422, 25-86, 13-338; 16-320, 31-576; Will Books T-276, 285; X-13.

The second Clinton Barnhill wrote his will in 1942; he died in 1948. He left his estate to his wife Lillian "including the buildings and bottom across the road from the house," along with livestock and furnishings. The rest was to be divided among their children: James Barnhill, Willie Lemons, and Mable Lusby. In 1949 Willie B. Lemons and other heirs deeded to Paul and James T. Morris tracts of forty-eight and twenty acres, property that Clinton Barnhill had purchased in 1924 from F.C. Giles.[165]

BARNHILL-DAWSON HOUSE, 5032 MUDDY FORD ROAD. A story and half house with a central chimney and remnants of historic two-over-two-pane-sash is associated in recent history with the family of Ruth Barnhill and William Sanford Dawson, who acquired it 1943 from the family of John E. Barnhill, who died in 1942. In an affidavit dated March 15, 1942, Ward Barnhill enumerated the family of his father, who included Ward's wife Viola Vance, daughter of Joseph Smith Vance; a daughter, Ruth, wife of W.S. Dawson; and the children and heirs of Ethel Barnhill – John E. Barnhill who died in 1924: Lena Mae Dungan, John Thomas Barnhill, Louisa Barnhill, and Tolbert Barnhill. After W.S. Dawson's death, Ruth deeded shares of the property to their children Lillian D. Tucker, William Estill Dawson, and Lorenza Dawson.[166]

BARNHILL-LACY HOUSE, 437 ROGERS GAP ROAD. The stylish one-story L-shaped house became the home of Andrew C. Lacy, William and Edna Lacy, and John A. Lacy. It stands on land derived from the once large settlement period farm of Valentine Rogers. Rogers family members who owned the 184-acre estate from which the Lacy farm was carved were Thomas V. and Annie Rogers; they sold 142 acres in 1909 to W. and Annie L. Southworth. In 1914 the Southworths sold the property to C.D. Winter, who joined by L.E. Winter, sold it to James Barnhill in 1928. Barnhill's widow Grace Barnhill and son George C. Barnhill then inherited it. George and Anita Mae Barnhill sold the farm to A.C. Lacy in 1957. Edna Lacy was director of nurses at John Graves Ford Memorial Hospital during the era of that institution's transition from a private hospital to a publicly owned county institution and finally to a corporately owned medical center. Bill Lacy was a careful and productive farmer. Edna's and Bill's son John was one of Scott County High School's leading vocational agriculture teachers and continues to be a leader in the farm community.

Figure 128. Clinton Barnhill house (see page 108).

---

[165] Will Book X-13, Deed Book 75-22, 53-306.
[166] Deed Books 256-535, 67-495, 35-124, 67-403, 67-495; Will Book 9-474.

BARNHILL-MORRIS HOUSE, 781 GUNNELL PIKE. Old deeds convey a great deal of information about how former country roads with dirt surfaces qualified to become paved roads. Consider Amanda Z. Williams' sale in 1919 of forty-eight acres to John Lemons on "the big road now pike" and twenty acres on the dirt road. Lemons and his wife Alice F. sold the property to John C. Michael. Michael's administrator, N. Giles, sold it to F.C. Giles in 1921, and he in 1924 sold it to Clint Barnhill. Barnhill left it to his heirs: Willie B. Lemons, George C. and Anita Mae Barnhill, Mabel and Joe Lusby, and Lillian and Maude Barnhill. They sold it to Paul and James T. Morris.[167]

Figure 129. Barnhill-Lacy house (see page 109)

On this farm is a compact dwelling three bays wide, the off-center door flanked on one side by a double window and the other by a single window. All windows have six over one pane sash, suggesting an Arts and Crafts period of construction between circa 1910 and 1925. The Morrises sold four acres with the dwelling in 1969 to John D. and Jeannette Hughes, organizers of a neighborhood agricultural subdivision. In 2000 they sold this three-bay house to T.K. Sturgill.[168]

Figure 130. Corda Johnson Reed house.

BURGESS PROPERTIES

MARTHA BURGESS HOUSE, 5219 MUDDY FORD ROAD. Martha J. Burgess, wife of Edward Burgess, acquired the Muddy Ford Road property where a one-story L-shaped house stands in 1872 from B.F. and Eliza Wright. The small farm was allotted to Eliza Wright in the division of the lands of Daniel Lay. In 1894 Martha J. Burgess sold approximately seventeen acres described as on the headwaters of Eagle Creek to Ezra T. Burgess, who in 1894 conveyed a portion of the land to Homer T. Burgess. Homer Burgess died in 1987, and in 1987 Gladys Burgess sold it to Bobby R. Grizzle. At 5219 Muddy Ford Road is a one-story front gabled cottage owned by Bobby Grizzle.[169]

CORDA JOHNSON REED HOUSE, 5343 MUDDY FORD ROAD. In 1934 at a master commissioner's sale, Corda Reed received title to thirty-nine acres that Ida and E.C. Muddiman sold to Daisy and Joseph G. Johnson in 1911. D.R. and Willie A. Reed inherited the property. In 1966 they sold it to John Thomas and Martha Harris. In 1969 David and Linda Lee Harris sold it to E. Leo and Betty Calvert Kettenring, who sold it in 1973 to Morris and Judy Grizzle.[170]

---

[167] Deed Books 25-142, 148; 330-130, 39-535, 48-166, 51-40, 53-306, 90-565.
[168] Deed Books 75-22, 90-565, 109-162, 190-214, 252-745.
[169] Deed Books 12-6, 29-244, 66-561, 224-316; Will Book 5-10.
[170] Deed Books 251-717, 122-449, 109-631, 105-350, 101-106, 60-335, 47-538; Will Book W-66.

Figure 131. Martha J. Burgess house (see page 110)

J.K. "POLK" BURGESS HOUSE, 466 NORTH MOUNT GILEAD CHURCH ROAD. In 1919 the estate of J.K. Burgess was made over to his widow, Susan Ann Burgess, who received a lifetime interest in his estate with remainder to their eight children. Commissioner H.C. Ford deeded tract number one of thirty-two acres and a passway to Ethel Burgess. The children included Flavia Burgess, Scott and Willia Burgess, Frank and Gertrude Burgess, Lula Burgess, and Joe Burgess. In 1960 Ethel Burgess Johnson on behalf of the estate deeded the property to Owen L. Johnson. A later house, owned by Jesse Johnson and Philip and Pam Doan, now occupies the site.[171]

DORCAS AND DARIUS FOXWORTHY AND EDWARD, J.C., SOLOMON BURGESS HOUSE, 513 SOUTH MOUNT GILEAD CHURCH ROAD. A charm of a log house with masterfully crafted stone chimneys and a two-tiered stone retaining wall along the front lawn is recorded as having been built by Darius Foxworthy, an accomplished stonemason. If Foxworthy performed the carpentry of the house that has withstood the ages, he was also a master carpenter. In 1885 the Foxworthys relocated to Coffee County, Kansas, and sold their Scott County farm of 110 acres thirty-nine poles to Edward and Susan Burgess for $2,000. In 1887 the Burgesses sold to J.C. Burgess and Solomon Burgess fifty percent interest in the property.[172]

Figure 132. Darius Foxworthy house.

Burgess family ownership continued until 1950, during which time Martha and J.C.B. Burgess acquired title through a master commissioner's deed. Descendants of J.C.B. and Martha Burgess, who co-signed the 1950 deed to Buford Hall, comprise an interesting list. They include N.M. Burgess, Harold S. and Laura Jane Gano, Frank Gano, Lola G. and Carl Peters, Martha Frances Gano, Lillian Burgess and Walter S. Powell, Burgess and Amelia Gano, Mary Collins, Jimmie Collins, Ray C. Hopper, Paul Collins, Talton K. Stone, Lillian Collins and Eugene Smith, and Laura Gano. Fitzpatrick sold the three-parcel property of 243.85 acres in 1957 to Ora McFarland for $14,400.[173]

During the next nearly half century, owners of the farm and house included Ora and Marietta McFarland, 1957; Forrest and Dona Harmon, 1958 (the three tracts of 243.85 acres); David and Christine Kestel, 1959, three tracts; William E. and Betty O. Faust and Marion and Betty Faust, 1972 (Tract 3); William Marvin, Sr. and Louise J. Lear, 100.11 acres; William Jeffrey and Sandra K. Pribble, 1981, 40.43 acres and 103.31 acres in Harrison and 100.11 acres in Scott, excluding a thirty foot square burial ground. In 1990 the Pribbles sold a part of the farm to Timothy G. Grissom and Bobbi Y. Green, and in 1996, Grissom transferred five acres at 513 Mount

---

[171] Deed Books 52-470, 74-60, 323-749.
[172] Deed Books 22-174, 29-31, 23-272.
[173] Deed Books 23-272, 28-372, 76-206.

Gilead Church Road to Bobbi Grissom. In 1996 the Pribbles sold Mark S. and Bobbie Cain thirty-seven acres, marking the present conformation of the property.[174]

BURGESS/HENDERSON, 5253 MUDDY FORD ROAD. More than half a century ago John and Sally Henderson purchased a twenty-nine-acre farm on the Muddy Ford Road that had been owned by the family of Martha J. Burgess from 1894 to 1953. The Hendersons' 1958 purchase continued the warm feeling that the farm and home communicated to its occupants and they to this nurturing environment. The house is pictured to the right.[175]

Putting together the farm were Martha J. and W.H. Burgess. Martha Burgess purchased tract one for $400 in 1894 from J.N. and Jemima Johnson. Tract 2 was acquired for $202 by William H. Burgess from the estate of A.D. Hamon, who had purchased eight acres for $275 in 1874 from James and Josephine Barnhill. Mrs. Burgess died in 1903. J.R. and George Barnhill witnessed her will. She left her real and personal property to her husband, E.T. Burgess. If he marries, she wrote, the property "shall descend to my two boys immediately as directed below at his death." Son William H. Burgess was to receive "the land on which we reside," defined as nine acres "lying at Muddy Ford" and the twenty acres purchased of J.N. Johnson on the Oxford-Muddy Ford Pike. She willed son Ezra H. Burgess the back portion of the lot (ten acres) purchased of Benjamin F. Wright joining M.L. Hall and the lot purchased of John W. Barnhill adjacent William Gregg (four and one-half acres). She directed that the furniture remain in the house for her husband and son William except one bed, which was to go to grandson George Burgess.[176]

Figure 133. Martha J. Burgess/John, Sally, and Joe Henderson house.

Wary that persons reading her will might interpret her bequests as determining favoritism between her sons, she went on, "I wish to state here that the little differences I have made between my two boys Ezra and William is on account of William remaining with us and spending the best portion of his life working for and waiting on me and not on account of any difference of my affection by any means. I love both of my children alike. They have both been good and dutiful boys to me."[177]

William H. Burgess died in 1934, leaving to his wife Ina their house and land, which at her death was to be divided between their two children John Burgess and Jessie Hehr. In 1950 Jessie and Withers Hehr of Harrison County sold their interest to John and Elizabeth Ann Burgess for $1,065. In 1955 the Burgesses sold the twenty-one and eight-acre parcels to C. Frank and Fenton Allen, who sold it in 1958 to the Hendersons. John and Sally Henderson's son Joseph L., an accomplished vocalist, is trustee of the Henderson Residential Trust.[178]

---

[174] Deed Books 83-448, 85-219, 88-456, 118-162, 138-602, 150-352, 185-642, 216-512, 232-188.
[175] Deed Books 86-139, 82-277, 29-245, 32-493.
[176] Deed Books 29-245, 32-493, 13-80; Will Book T-329.
[177] Will Book T-329.
[178] Will Book W-226; Deed Books 76-221, 82-277, 86-139, 320-296.

6787 MUDDY FORD ROAD. Corda B. Reed in 1934 acquired tracts of thirty-nine and thirty acres that had been deeded to her, her husband John Reed, and Ida and E.C. Muddiman by J.W. Hamilton, master commissioner. The property descended to Willie and Dolphus Reed and Thelma Reed, who sold it in 1962 to Ray and Cephas Tucker.[179] The house on this property, pictured at the right, replaced the original house. It is four bays wide and has an off-center door flanked by one double window on its left and single windows in the end bays, accommodating it to the historic landscape.

MUNSON PROPERTIES

One of the more interesting deeds recorded in the Scott County Clerk's office is a 1785 15,000-acre grant from Patrick Henry, governor of Virginia, to John Young and John Phillips, who sold it then to Samuel Young, a Philadelphia lawyer, for 1,000 pounds. Young sold it to William H. and Agnes Gitt of Dayton, who sold half to Emeline Bundy of Warren County, Ohio, also a Philadelphia lawyer. In 1961 deputy county clerk John A. Cottrell, in the process of devising an indexing system for old deeds, came across the deed to the grant. He described the property located on Eagle Creek near Turkeyfoot in the vicinity of land owned at that time by Buford Munson.[180]

Figure 134. Ray and Cephas Tucker house.

MARGARET MUNSON AND ROLLIE HINTON HOUSE, 1366 ROGERS GAP ROAD. An older two-story house, three bays wide and built on a stone foundation, was the home for many years of Rollie Hinton, son of Richard Hinton, the youngest child of the prolific William and Sarah Hinton. This house originally stood across the road and was moved by Roscoe Vance circa 1950 to its present site. Richard Hinton was born in 1864 and in 1892 married Luizah "Lulu" Vance, their union producing Lottie, Rollie, Roy, Robert, Hallie, Tommie T., Frank, and Ellen. Rollie was born in 1896, grew up on the family farm, and as a young man worked for Southern Railroad. Afterwards, he farmed for the remainder of his life. He and his first wife, Margaret Munson, daughter of Pierce Munson, were parents of Doyle, Nancye and Betsy. After her death he married Wilma Jean Jones, daughter of Charlie and Carrie Havicus Jones; they had one child, Charles.[181]

In 1926 Margaret Hinton became the owner of 55.4 acres of the Munson farm, and in 1963 Rollie and Wilma J. Hinton deeded the historic family property to Betsy and John Reigle, Nancye McNally, and Doyle and Nannie Mae Hinton. In a related transfer, the three children conveyed title to the grantors the seven acres that included this dwelling. Rollie died in 1996 and Wilma, in 2002. Their home and the seven acres passed to Charlie Hinton. In 2003 he and his wife Darcy Head Hinton sold it to Randall and Debra Hammons.[182]

---

[179] Deed Books 92-294, 60-335; Will Book 6-795.
[180] "Deed for 15,000 Acres Found in Scott Records," *The Lexington Leader,* September 22, 1962.
[181] Doris Reed for Rollie Hinton, "Hinton," *Families & History: Scott County, Kentucky* (1996), 193; additional information from Ronald T. Vance.
[182] Deed Books 55-239, 295; 94-323, 326; 203-418, 269-850.

The graceful two-story farmhouse has an upper middle bay without an opening, a central chimney, and a large porch spanning the lower story. Porch posts have been replaced with iron examples. Wide steps provide access from the sidewalk leading from the driveway to the centered front door. The ell is one story high and includes an enclosed back porch.

MUNSON-HINTON-VANCE HOUSE, 1312 ROGERS GAP ROAD. The Munson influence continues to prevail on this section of the Rogers Gap Road in rural Turkeyfoot, evidenced by the landmarks that this historic family left behind. Carl and Thelma Vance in 1968 became owners of ninety-one acres of the former farm of Margaret Munson and her husband Rollie Hinton and the house that completes this very interesting property's landscape.[183]

Figure 135. Margaret Munson and Rollie Hinton house.

Margaret Hinton was a daughter of W.P. and Lena R. Munson and the first wife of Rollie Hinton, son of Richard Hinton, son of Asher Hinton. She became the owner of three parcels of land from the estate of W.P. Munson. In 1926 Lena R. Munson, W.B. Munson, Buford Munson, and Margaret Hinton partitioned their inheritance, the Hintons receiving lot number one of 48.4 acres on Rogers Gap Pike. Also in 1926, W.B. and Ayda (also known as Ada) Munson deeded Margaret seven acres, and in 1950 Ayda Munson, W.B. Munson, Eliene Munson, Kenneth and Geraldine Grant, Betty and James L. Lucas, and Buford and Lottie Munson sold an additional 24.5 acres on the Rogers Gap Pike to the Hintons.[184]

Figure 136. Carl and Thelma Vance house.

---

[183] Deed Book 106-321.
[184] Deed Books 55-239, 295; 76-474; 94-323.

Margaret and Rollie Hinton had three children: Betsy Reigel, Nancye McNally, and Doyle Hinton. After Margaret's death, Rollie Hinton married a second time; they were parents of Charles Hinton. In 1963 the children of Margaret and Rollie's first marriage became owners of tracts one and two, which they sold in 1968 to Carl and Thelma Vance. The property that Charlie inherited after his parents' death is discussed in the previous section.[185]

The three-bay house on this site has a stone foundation and Arts and Crafts style brick piers on which are mounted square posts, replacements for earlier posts that were likely tapered in the spirit of the style. Windows are fitted with six over six-pane sash. The upper level is lighted by windows on the gable ends. A shed roof attachment on the rear facade further expands the dwelling's space.

BRADFORD, PIERCE, AND BUFORD MUNSON HOUSE AND OUTBUILDINGS, 1200 ROGERS GAP ROAD. A major reason that historic Munson presence continues strong in this section of the Rogers Gap Road is the extended life of the log house occupied by Pierce and his heirs continuously from at least the early nineteenth century until the very late years of the century just passed. Here opposite Rogers Gap Branch stands the Pierce/Bradford Munson's log house, approached until recent times by a picturesque walking bridge. The Munson family at this location, as it also did in Little Eagle Creek's Porter neighborhood, made a profound cultural and economic impact on the life of rural Scott County. Other principals among family owners of the spread were successive heads of families Buford Munson and Pierce Munson. This property's Munson era concluded in 1992 with Mark and Karen Vance Wells' acquisition and renovation of the buildings on the historic tract. Their purchase that year included three parcels of the once vast Munson spread, along with the historic Munson home. They proceeded to transform the farm into a creatively organized operation of traditional agriculture

Figure 137. Pierce Munson log house: Shawnee Run Farm.

as well as offering to the buying public from miles around cultivated flowers and garden crops. They christened their estate Shawnee Run Farm, built a new bridge over Rogers Gap Branch, restored the historic log house and its unique root cellar and spring, and therein provided an elegant landmark for an already richly endowed rural neighborhood. Adding additional character to the landscape is the busy Norfolk Southern railroad that cuts across the farm.

---

[185] Deed Books 94-323, 106-321.

The Wellses' three-tract purchase from Buford Munson, the third Scott County sire of the multi-generational family farm, included 131 acres, of which one hundred acres lay across the railroad. W.P. Munson sold Cincinnati Southern Railroad 2.19 acres in the 1870s. Ada (or Ayda) Mae Munson, widow of W.B. Munson, sold Buford Munson 48.5 acres in 1947. In 2001 the Wellses increased their farm with an abutting acquisition from John A. Vance.[186]

Buford Munson acquired his properties in a complex succession of transactions. His lands from W.P. Munson's estate included his own share and those of W.P.'s widow, Lena R. Munson, and his siblings, W. Bradford Munson and Margaret Munson Hinton. Grantors in his 1950 purchase included Ada/Ayda, widow of W.B. Munson; Margaret and Rollie Hinton; and W.S. Munson; Eiliene Munson; Geraldine and Kenneth Grant; and Betty and James L. Lucas, children of Bradford Munson.[187]

Figure 138. Historic photo of Pierce Munson log house.

In 1883 the heirs of Bradford Munson petitioned for a division of their father's 180-acre property. Parties to the action were J. Samuel Munson, Pierce Munson, Evaline Munson, Mary Munson, Lilly Munson, Sarah M. and James Reed, and Emily and Jeptha Bell. In 1884 Pierce Munson purchased 128 acres of Bradford Munson's lands from Emily and Jeptha Bell for $840.[188]

Among Bradford Munson's acquisitions were the 148-acre home place of Robert and Margaret Barnhill on Big Eagle and the old Mulberry Road, its boundaries including lands of Joseph Burgess, Carr, Pitney's old line, and Munson. In 1850 Elizabeth Hall of Fayette County sold him 150 acres for $1,050. In 1860 he purchased for $1,000 the undivided interest of Sandford Munson in his father's estate. Simultaneously he was acquiring land

Figure 140. Bridge over Shawnee Run at historic Munson farm.

Figure 139. Commercial features of Shawnee Run Farm.

---

[186] Deed Books 193-536, 57-266, 55-241, 76-472, 255-80, 254-147, 219-230.
[187] Deed Books 55-241, 76-472, 23-144.
[188] Deed Books 21-189, 23-144.

near Hartwell (present day Porter). Munson's wife Elvissa was a descendant of Sarah and Samuel Penn, significant landowners of that part of Scott County.[189]

A visit to the Munson farm reveals the Vance/Wells family's respect for historic preservation standards. Logs are exposed only on the house's interior, as exterior log walls, once exposed and subsequently weatherboarded, when exposed again will invariably deteriorate and decompose at a rapid rate. Adze and ax hewn beams, mud and lime chinking, and historic upstairs flooring/downstairs ceiling wear the golden tone of aging. The two-story balcony, probably a mid- to late-nineteenth century addition, is beautiful and useable. Visitors cannot help but appreciate the Wellses' sensitivity to the landscape with Shawnee Run's gardens, the branch, the springhouse, and the cellar.

Figure 141. Room of Munson house with logs exposed.

SHELBY MUNSON FARM, 7103 MUDDY FORD ROAD. The lands of nineteenth century farmer Shelby Munson lay near Turkeyfoot on the Rogers Gap-Turkeyfoot Road and the Muddy Ford Road. Part of this real estate is marked today by a large house three bays wide with two two story additions. Though Munson wrote his will in 1884, he continued in his profession as a farmer until 1900. His will was probated on January 21, 1901. He left his wife Rebecca a life estate in family lands after which it was to be apportioned to their children Letha Jane, Mattie, Allie, Inis, and to John Ash Hinton in trust for Josephine and James Barnhill's children – Shelby, Charley, and Stella during the lifetime of their stepfather, Dock Hinton.[190]

The farm hosting the Shelby Munson house has been sold in three tracts since the early twentieth century. In 1902 Inez and W.L. Skinner and others sold ninety acres of the Munson estate to

Figure 142. Shelby Munson house, near Turkeyfoot.

---

[189] Deed Books R-19; V-156, 422, 41; U-416; 1-164, 377; 5-428; 467; 14-293; Will Book S-191.
[190] Will Book T-232, 298.

T.C. and Llewellyn W. White and Daniel B. Dixon for $2,250. White acquired Dixon's title by inheritance and increased it with a 1913 purchase of 39.33 acres and other land bought from G.W. Hinton in 1927. In 1948 White sold 140 acres to J.W. and Stella Roberts, who sold it to Preston Cox in 1958.[191]

PRICE-HILES PROPERTIES, ROGERS GAP/TURKEYFOOT ROAD

PRICE-HILES HOUSE SITE, 1283 ROGERS GAP ROAD.

The confluence of two smaller branches of Rogers Gap Creek provides a perfect setting for the several farms on the westernmost road leading into Turkeyfoot. Here stood a much older house that over the years was taken over by termites. When David and Linda Harris acquired the property, after having searched for some time for a nicely located farm, they elected to rebuild the house, using the same foundation and porch. Their house is the third on the site. The first was the home of William Price, the original settler. Succeeding him as owners/occupants were Thomas Price, William and Ann Price, Martha Price and T.B. Hiles, Lee Hiles, Ed Hiles, Harold Clark, and the Harrises.

Figure 143. House, third on historic Price-Hiles site, was built with sensitivity to history by David and Linda Harris.

The Harrises' resulting house is stunning. Positioned on a rise looking down on the east side of the road and the creek, the Cape Cod style dwelling is a decided enhancement to the rural setting. The vinyl clad house has three dormers and a vinyl wrapped chimney at the front left corner, entirely within the spirit if not the fabric of the earlier era. A one-story porch shelters the main façade's entryway and flanking windows. The house's earlier form and its concrete-plastered foundation and front porch comfortably suggest the antecedent and the reworking of a product of the earlier era. Behind it is a weatherboarded outbuilding on a concrete foundation with likely uses for smokehouse and storage.

Figure 144. Historic smokehouse or storage building on present site of David and Linda Harris house

Ownership of this portion of the rural Rogers Gap neighborhood setting traces to William Price and possibly his settlement period forebears, the family of Thomas and Elizabeth Price. In his will dated August 1873 and probated in September of that year, William Price left his farm in shares to his wife Ann, daughter Martha B. Hiles, and grandchildren Monica and Clay Furnish. Ann Price was to use a portion of the estate funds to buy a

---

[191] Deed Books 35-350, 37-17, 43-300, 56-53, 77-394, 74-193, 86-59.

"nice set of marble to place at my grave." Martha's husband Lee Hiles was to be sole executor. At the sale of Price's personal effects, Erasmus Price purchased farm equipment; J.F. Musselman, four wagons and nineteen mules at eighty-seven dollars each; and Ann Price, a gold watch and chain, saddle, and ten gallons of whiskey.[192]

William Price's land holdings included several tracts purchased during the mid-nineteenth century from other Thomas Price heirs and neighbors. Family members with ownership interest in the farmland were Jacob Price, Dillard Price, George Washington Price, Jackson Price, Rebecca Munson, Ellis Johnson, William Williamson, and Isaac Price. William Price purchased land from the estate of Sanford Munson, Henry Edmondson, John H. and Verinda Barkley, and J.V. Risk.[193]

T.B. and Martha B. Hiles made their home on the stream-enriched property. T.B. Hiles died circa 1900. Succeeding him as owners of the land were T.B. Hiles, Jr. and Lee Hiles. Other Hiles family members inheriting shares in the property included Clay Furnish, A.C. Furnish, Willie Hiles, Cambridge Hiles, and Edward and Pearl C. Hiles. Lee Hiles, who purchased the others' interest, died in 1947, with Pearl C. Hiles succeeding him as owner of the 196.38-acre farm. In 1984 she sold the property to Harold T. and Norma J. Clark, and in 1993, Mrs. Clark sold tracts one, two, and three to the Harrises.[194]

Figure 145. Carl and Thelma Vance's setting of T.C. White historic Turkeyfoot property.

ROBERT A. VANCE HOUSE, 1076 ROGERS GAP ROAD. The two-part house at this address includes a story and half three bay block portion enhanced by a wraparound porch with narrow posts and a stick style balustrade. The two-story section is split-level in concept, with shorter double windows on the lower level and taller also double windows upstairs. Robert A. Vance and his wife Glenda Hammond were the original owners of the house. Birdie White sold the property to the present owners, Carl and Thelma Vance. Earlier owner T.C. White died in 1969, leaving his real property in equal shares to John Sanders and Jimmy Vance and the remainder equally to his sisters Birdie White, Sallie Fields, and Nettie Risk.[195]

RON VANCE HOUSE, 1450 ROGERS GAP ROAD. A modernistic design on an historic ancestral tract is home to Scott County historian Ronald T. Vance and Dick Jackson. Ron sizes up the historic location of his contemporary style home built in 2001: "I live near Turkeyfoot on the property where my third great-grandfather William Vance settled when he came to Kentucky from Berkeley County, Virginia. I was born directly across the road from where I live. William came here in the early 1790s with his father-in-law James Hinton and four other sons-in-law."[196]

Ron's other line of Scott County descent is the Barkley family. His mother was a great-great-granddaughter of Robert Barkley, who lived at Oxford. Robert was born in Kentucky, son of Matthew Barkley, an

---

[192] Will Books Q-375; R-192.
[193] Will Books R-435, 192; S-272, Q-375; Deed Books 11-363; 1-60, 275, 353; 2-250, 300, 425; 3-233; 9-438; 10-242; V-222; 294, 378, 413; 12-418.
[194] Deed Books 36-274; 35-313; 37-501; 34-14, 24, 294; 83-465; 11-157, 160; 156-533; 200-627.
[195] Deed Books 219-230, 254-147, 120-661, 120-663, 120-508; 63-510, 63-234, 8-311; Will Book Z-119.
[196] Ron Vance, email communication, May 10, 2007.

immigrant from Ireland. Ron spent all his first twenty-two years on Eagle Creek, either at Turkeyfoot or Biddle, attending grade school at Oxford and graduating from Scott County High School.

Ron Vance's house is a contemporary dwelling set in one of Scott County's historic communities where his ancestors have farmed and hunted. After farming a couple of years with his father and a couple more years working at Electric Parts Corporation, Ron enlisted in the Air Force and served four years, the first two in training and as a combat crewmember on an Atlas F missile launch crew. He was then transferred to Offutt AFB

Figure 146. Ron Vance, historian, built a contemporary style home on the site of the first Vance house, home of his ancestors, in Turkeyfoot.

as a buyer for two years. While at Offutt, he took several courses on the base through the University of Omaha. After discharge from the Air Force, he completed a degree in political science and history at the University of Kentucky.

For most of his professional life, Ron was involved in administration for Appalachian Regional Healthcare, a not for profit organization formed in the early 1960s to operate ten hospitals built by the United Mine Workers in Eastern Kentucky, Southern West Virginia, and Western Virginia. Ron held several executive positions and retired as senior vice president.

Figure 147. Thomas B. and Nannie Mallory Hiles were individual owners of the Craftsman style house and "wishing well" in the yard.

As a working historian, Ron has been involved in projects in recent years in the reorganization of the Georgetown and Scott County Museum, developing exhibits, and researching the many artifacts that are donated or acquired by the museum. Ron's specialties include the collection and research of historic maps, coin silver, and interpreting and organizing art and photography. His genealogical research has contributed considerably to local families' studies. Ron's home at Turkeyfoot, pictured above, is a contemporary dwelling set in one of Scott County's historic communities where his ancestors have farmed and hunted.

THOMAS B. AND NANNIE MALLORY HILES HOUSE, 1050 ROGERS GAP ROAD. The Princess Anne style frame dwelling dating from the earlier years of the twentieth century relates to the family of Thomas B. and Nannie Mallory Hiles, who married in 1889 after signing a contract that each would own property "in their own right" and that Nannie would "set up no claims to Thomas B. Hiles' property." The Mallory and Hiles families remained close. The Hiles family lived on the 47.5-acre farm throughout their lives and may have been the original owners of the "wishing well" that once adorned the front lawn. Hiles left the property to his infant children with the understanding that it would serve as their home until Jane Hiles should become twenty-one years of age, an event that took place July 15, 1911. In 1908 Joe and Alfretta Mallory sold the farm to Dan Dixon for $1,300 and a $500 mortgage. In 1938 Dixon deeded it to Birdie Dixon, also known as Birdie White, from whom Louella Sanders inherited it.

The picturesque well house was built over the well in the front yard. Historian Ron Vance recalls that the well was drilled and that it had a "pitcher" pump on it. The front room of the house, Vance believes, was originally a toll house and sat next to the road. "After Miss Birdie married Dan Dixon, they moved the building back and added the two back rooms with two rooms over them. In 1986 Mrs. Sanders sold the remaining twenty-six acres described as "near Rogers Gap" to Randy and Debbie Hammons. In 1996 they sold it to Tommy J. and Cheryl F. Hammons, who finished the two upstairs rooms.[197]

Figure 148. Walker and Sally Fields owned the Craftsman era house in Rogers Gap.

WALKER AND SALLY FIELDS HOUSE, 1031 ROGERS GAP ROAD. A transitional bungalow to Cape Cod style house with two large pedimented dormers with double windows, pictured at the left, rises from a stone foundation and was purchased along with its seven-acre lot by Elizabeth Lynn McPherson at a master commissioner's sale in 1997. In 1989 James L. and Anne Laird Horton acquired it from Donald and Sally S. Chowning, who had purchased 27.36 acres from James and Lucy Owen. Dr. Owen bought it in 1982 from Louella and Henry Sanders as part of tracts of seventy-three acres and 49.17 acres. Walter and Sallie White Fields constructed the house in 1938, having purchased 49.17 acres from Lee Hiles' 240-acre farm and seventy-three acres in 1915 from Judith Wilson Duvall, whose title came from her father, Asa G. Wilson, and her uncle, Gilson W. Wilson, both having inherited the farm from their grandmother, Judith Wilson.[198]

BUFORD HALL FAMILY PROPERTIES

BUFORD HALL, II, HOUSE, 383 ROGERS GAP ROAD. A short distance past the intersection of Rogers Gap Road on the Cincinnati Road, the 1879 Beers & Lanagan map designates a dwelling of Buford Hall with the notation "2150 acres." This reference was to Buford Hall, Sr., whose son, after his father's death in 1897, expanded his father's extensive operation, proving to be equally as enterprising and innovative as his father. Buford Hall, Sr. (1827-1896) and Nancy E. "Nannie" Burgess (1844-1914), a daughter of Joseph Burgess, a principal figure in the northern Scott County's Rays Fork, Stonewall, East Fork, and Big Eagle neighborhoods, presided over both sets of parents' inherited lands. The father and son team bred, raised, and marketed sheep, their operation growing to producing

Figure 149. Buford Hall, II, extended and improved his historic family property and built the two story classical revival style house at Rogers Gap.

---

[197] Deed Books 38-614, 61-130, 165-607, 218-594; email communication to author from Ron Vance May 5, 2016.
[198] Deed Books 265-620, 227-266, 178-470, 158-238, 152-487, 45-44, 64-11.

1,000 to 1,200 ewes annually. They expanded their holdings incrementally, usually with very small sections of land. By the early twentieth century the huge Hall farm occupying a generous swath of transitional Inner Bluegrass and Eden Shale lands was not only big, but it was a model operation. For a discussion of its spread of contributing buildings and structures, we refer you to the Chapter 1 with a discussion of the agricultural complexes and buildings."

THE HALL FAMILY. The Hall family that spawned John, William, and Buford Hall and their successive farm families was among Scott County's earliest. Their progenitor was John Hall, who died in 1808. His wife Jane's dower apportionment was one hundred acres on Dry Run, the farm's boundaries being properties of Fielding Bradford, David Kerr, and Ash Emison. John and Jane Hall's sons were John and William Hall. Jane died in 1842, leaving property to daughters Polly, Dorcas, and Jane. To Jane she left the Bradford Smith or Guffey farm of 106 acres near Muddy Ford Road at the headwaters of Eagle, "adjacent Goddard, Roberts, and Barnhill." William Hall's will was probated in June 1859, his wife Malinda receiving their home, or money should she decide to go to Missouri where other family members were planning to move. He asked that his son William be made equal to the others in the will and that his son Buford serve as executor.

The will of John Hall, son of the first John Hall and uncle of Buford Hall, Sr., was, probated in 1874. He called first for carrying out the terms of his sister Dorcas' will that had "failed in law for lack of a witness." Dorcas had directed that $200 be given to Dry Run Baptist Church and seventy-five dollars to John Sherman Offutt, that Buford Hall receive half of joint interest in her estate, and that George Sparrow, an African American, receive thirty acres from the Billy Green land and fifty dollars in cash. Hall's own estate provisions requested burial at Dry Run Baptist Church where his mother and sisters "were deposited" and that he be buried "decently but not extravagantly." Buford Hall, Sr., son of William Hall, was survived by his wife Nancy, their son Buford, and daughters Mrs. Robert Anderson, Mrs. Stucker Offutt, and Miss Mary Hall. The family's home, which burned in 1910, stood on the present Beluga Farm spread near the stone-based water tower. Buford Hall, Jr., bought the Gayle house near Delaplain in 1920.[199]

In 1904 the younger Hall was second among Scott County's largest farmers with 3,700 acres, ranking next to John B. Graves, who had 4,561 acres. T.J. Burgess, Hall's brother in law, owned 3,619 acres. Other large land owners included Warren Graves, brother of John B. Graves, 2,646 acres; Mrs. S.P. Smith (Evaline, sister of Nancy Hall and T.J. Burgess), 1,284 acres; John Osborne, 1,268; and Norman Hambrick, 1,189.[200]

The Hall farm's sheep operation peaked during the Korean War, according to Marion Hall, who succeeded his father as owner and operator. The number of sheep was reduced to about 400 by 1953 and 1954, when increasing numbers of cattle became prevalent on the Hall lands. In its later years Western ewes were crossbred for sale across the Midwest. Suffolk ewes were mated with Hampshire rams as the farm made a transition to an emphasis of mixed wool and mutton.[201]

The impressive classical revival style dwelling and outbuildings on the south side of Rogers Gap Road provided a rural home for the younger Buford Hall. The Halls, in the spirit of many late nineteenth century and early twentieth century farm families, lived in town for most of the year and spent their summers at their country homes. In the case of families with children, the goal was to open the home in the country once school was out for the season. The frame two story five bay dwelling, now vinyl sided, is built on a foundation of molded concrete blocks. The two-story pedimented portico, supported by tall square piers and with a lunette centered in the tympanum, received a balcony during its most recent renovation. The tenant house behind the house has a

---

[199] Will Books A-64, 413, 446, 447; H-72; N-221; O-307, 312; Gaines History 1, 61. In 1874 Buford and Nannie Hall and Will Hall and John Hall of Lafayette County, Missouri, apportioned lands inherited from John Hall; Deed Books 13-314, 318, 320. Reference was made to these lands as late as 1892 in Deed Books 27-232 and 28-38.
[200] Gaines History 1, 41, 61.
[201] Information from Marion Hall.

centered entrance and shuttered windows flanking the central door. Hall's vast agricultural spread lay on the opposite side of the road and extended east toward Turkeyfoot and along the Cincinnati Road to the north.

Buford Hall's lands lay on the both sides of the Rogers Gap and Cincinnati roads, reaching toward Turkeyfoot and Double Culvert roads to the east and north well into the Stonewall and Rays Fork areas. On February 23, 1918, the heirs of Buford Hall, Jr., during a legal action styled Sallie Hall Offutt versus Buford Hall Offutt, sold the 120-acre farm south of Rogers Gap in a master commissioner's sale to Lee Hiles, who, as can be seen in the previous essays, was one of the most prominent landowners in the area. Hiles' bid was $8,287.50; he conveyed the property to C.D. Winter prior to the recording of the master commissioner's deed. Grantors included Sallie Hall, J. Stucker Offutt, Buford Hall, Elinor Hall Offutt, James S. Offutt, E.N. Offutt, and Lee Hiles. Winter and his wife Eva made their home on the estate, and in 1930 Eva Winter conveyed her half interest in the property to Grace Winter Jones, the other half having come via her father's will. In 1937 she and her husband E.E. Jones sold the farm of 97.5 acres and 120 acres to Clark and Mary Guy for $20,000, and in 1940 they sold it to Frank and Viola Martin for $30,000. The Martins kept it for a little more than a year before selling to H.C. and Flo Fain for $30,300. Land values in the transitional soils belt continued to appreciate and the Fains sold the farm in 1943 for $180,700 to Hugh R. Taylor and Ellen Bruner. Taylor and his wife Julia and Ellen and her husband Ernest sold one hundred acres for $220,000 to Homer and Dollie Maybrier. In 1978 I.K. and Jacqueline Nielson purchased the farm for $210,000, making their home there until their sale in 1986 to George and Donna L. Davis for $350,000. In 1996 Robert E. and Treva Y. Alexander purchased all of tract number one of the Davis farm for $162,000 and converted the 50.019 acre spread into a residential farm. Other farm acres are owned by Pat and Monica Juett and Michael Juett as a campground.[202]

HENRY CLAY FIELDS FARM, 123 BARKLEY ROAD. A bungalow with wide steps leading to a deep porch supported by tapered posts set atop brick piers, with joist-end brackets extending across the wide overhang, survives on the historic Henry Clay and Mary Morris Fields farm. Mr. Fields died in 1945, leaving his wife known as "Mommau" in granddaughter Fannee Hilander's book *Hold Back the Spring* (Fields was known to his grandchildren "Poppau") a life estate in the farm that at her death was to be divided among their three children: Nannie Clay Warth, Ann Elizabeth Jarvis, and Woodrow Fields, Fannee's father. Ultimately inheriting the property from Mrs. Warth, wife of Lindsay Warth, was her great nephew Timothy William Fields. Another nephew, William Clay Fields, was executor.[203]

Figure 150. Barkley Road bungalow is historically associated with the Henry Clay and Nannie Morris Fields family.

"They were fine people," recalled their granddaughter. "I always think of Poppau as such a quiet, gentle person. In my memory, he is very dim, fading into the shadows, as indeed he was doing in actuality at the time. He was dying from tuberculosis, and I can remember him in bed as different ones softly looked in on him." Fannee relied on the memories of her aunt, Mrs. Warth, known to her and other family members as Kay, and Mommau. ". . . Kay told me how she was such a tomboy and how she would ride everywhere Dad

---

[202] Deed Books 47-117, 115; 58-497; 63-1; 65-219; 66-243; 68-74; 69-452; 138-72; 164-660; 218-035.
[203] Will Books 4-116, W-529; Deed Books 179-155, 199-42, 201-621; Fannee Hilander, *Hold Back the Spring* (Great Neck, New York: Todd & Honeywell, Inc., 1980), 13.

went, perched behind him on a horse." Her mother recalled for her how "after supper Poppau always liked to sit out on the porch awhile and would ask Mommau to come out too." However, in the spirit of so many housewives, "she always wanted to clean up the kitchen first and by the time she was through and taking off her apron to come out, he was usually ready to go to bed. That always seemed sad to me."[204]

"That porch," recalled Fannee, "in the evening, was truly a pleasant space. Nothing has ever sounded as melancholy and lonesome as those whip-poor-wills calling to one another after dark. Mommau would rock Billy in the swing and wrap her apron around him to ward off the chill that came up from the valley." Mrs. Fields' love affair with her husband didn't end with his death. She would set the table at night for the next morning's breakfast. "She turned the plates upside down over the silverware. I could sense her sadness as I saw her set Poppau's plate every night just as if he had never gone away."[205]

R.H. Williamson Farm, 493 Barkley Road.

Figure 151. Williamson family members owned the sturdily built nineteenth century frame house well into the twentieth century.

A picturesque and comfortable one and one-half story farmhouse, its several features including a one-story porch supported by turned posts and two over two pane sash suggesting possible nineteenth century origins, is set apart from the farm's grassy and tree shaded landscape by a plank fence painted white joining the rock wall in the lower front yard. The porch has turned posts sheltering the three openings. Not far away on sloping ground on a downhill setting is a barn weathered gray from its earlier white coat. The farmstead seems to have had its origin as a ninety-acre operation during the ownership of R.H. Williamson.[206]

In 1911 Dudley Williamson and his siblings deeded their interest in their father's farm to Samuel S. Williamson. At that time, it was bounded on the north by lands of Ira Sutton and Elversa Fields, on the west by Howard Williamson, Jack Parker, and Henry Sharon; and on the south and east by the Muddy Ford and Finnell Road (we call it "Barkley" today). In 1913 Dudley Williamson deeded a ten-acre portion representing one-eighth share of the dower interest "where Nora Williamson and her husband live" to Nora Lee and Howard Williamson and Edgar and Eva May Bailey. In 1919 Howard Williamson and others also transferred their interest in the tract inherited from R.H. Williamson to Nora Williamson. Samuel S. Williamson sold the improved part of the farm to Robert McMillen; his sons, Robert Sharon McMillin, Joe Pat McMillen, and Lyle Bruce McMillen, in turn

---

[204] *Hold Back the Spring*, 13.
[205] Hilander.
[206] Deed Books 79-215, 42-116, 44-386, 49-413.

inherited it. William E. and Karen L. Karrer, who bought it from Joe Patterson and Mary Perkins McMillin, have been the owners since July 2014.[207]

J.T. WILLIAMSON/JAMIE AND JANENE HOFFMAN HOUSE, 1003 BARKLEY ROAD. From the moment that James E. "Jamie" Hoffman purchased a 2.15-acre piece of the historic Williamson properties on Barkley Road, earlier variously known as Giles, Muddy Ford, and Finnell Road, he has had a wonderful time putting together a dream home on the setting. The house ultimately constructed has been the ideal home for Jamie and his wife Janene, who joined her husband in the property's craftsmanship.

Figure 152. Jamie and Janene Hoffman built picturesque house on Barkley Road, using fabric salvaged from demolition of house on Georgetown's North Hamilton and East Washington streets.

Many readers will recall the two-story three bay house on the southeast corner of North Hamilton and East Washington streets in Georgetown, pictured at the left. The house was demolished to make way for another of those ubiquitous urbane urban necessities, parking lots. Observing its demolition, the youngest Hoffman brother seized the moment and secured it – or perhaps we should say its components – and put the pieces together on his picturesque piece of farm country.

The former Georgetown house earlier occupied the site of the eighteenth-century Edward and Lynn West gunsmith shop. George F. Prewitt bought the property in 1878 following litigation styled G.F. Allgaier versus C.H. West. The many creditors who disbursed the sale's returns included Hunnewell [sic], Moore & Hukill; Bayless, McCarty & Company, Greenwood Stove Company, A. Baum & Company, Pomeroy, Peckover & Company; Charles Gooch; Howell Gano & Company, and H.F. West & Brothers.[208]

Figure 153. Historic Lynn West property on North Hamilton and Washington streets survives in the Barkley Road home of Jamie and Janene Hoffman.

The 1879 map shows the building on the lot at that time embracing the sidewalk or street edge and lists its owner as "L.W," easily translated as Lynn West. In 1887, George Prewitt, with a Durango, Colorado address, sold the property to Fannie Barbee, apparently with a new house occupying the gunsmith shop site, for $1,700, stating that before moving, he had rented the property to E.B. Sinclair for a family residence.[209]

The same year Mrs. Barbee sold the house and lot to John Anderson for $1,800. Anderson's death resulted in the sale of the property by his widow, Ann Anderson, on September 1, 1890, to Mrs. Sinclair for $1,800. In 1896, Mrs. Sinclair having died, her husband E.B. Sinclair and

---

[207] Deed Book 79-215, 355-255, 362-723.
[208] Deed Book 17-136.
[209] Deed Book 23-358; Map of Scott County, 1879, Georgetown inset.

Figure 154. View of gable end of Hoffman house looking down Barkley Road to surviving agricultural features from earlier Williamson farm.

parents, John T. and Florrie Johnson of Buckham, Missouri, resold the house and lot to Mrs. Anderson. Mrs. Anderson died in 1898, leaving all her real estate exclusive of the cottage in Georgetown north of her own home on South Broadway to James Anderson of Corryong, Australia, her late husband's brother. She left all her cash to St. John Church.[210]

Now, to return to Jamie and Janene Hoffman's house. Stairs lead from the walkway from the road and the driveway to a wide porch with a centered door flanked by two windows. The first level porch and the balcony above are encircled with square balusters and posts and are elegantly landscaped, as are all the Hoffman lawns. A stone shouldered chimney, laid by the young craftsman, serves the historic mantelpiece inside. Floors are polished poplar from the old house. Star-tipped tie rods are located at various places including the chimneys. Chamfered posts support the shed roof of the house's ell. You quickly recognize the Victorian era style door jambs with their corner blocks as you stroll through the house. Here is an idyllic home, made to the owner's specifications with great skill. It a genuine comfort to know that Hoffman's creativity is still at work in the Eden hills of Scott County.

The property is part of an eighteen-acre parcel that was sold in 1987 by Ricky D. and Bonnie L. Williamson to Susan C. Stephens. Ricky Williamson's title came from J.T. and Gladys Williamson. An earlier J.T. Williamson died in 1932, leaving a large family. Much of this area of Williamson country, connected by several roads that wind around and intersect in this part of Scott County, was or is still owned by Williamson descendants.[211]

Barkley/Grizzle House, 1155 Barkley Road.

In 1936 Lew and Nannie Lee Williamson and other heirs of J.T. Williamson sold for $1,000 to W.M. Barkley a ten-acre tract on the road then designated as Hiles Old Mill Road for $1,000. Williamson in 1868 purchased the farm "where George Tucker now resides and where Harrison Lynn formerly resided" from Harrison and Nancy Lynn for $1,500.

Figure 155. Barkley-Grizzle house, older bungalow with full basement and wraparound balcony.

---

[210] Deed Book 17-136, 23-258, 23-410, 23-410, 26-103, 30-419, 34-172; Will Book T-119.
[211] Deed Books 173-150, 173-278, 16-300.

Figure 156. The part log Dudley Williamson house, thought to date from 1855.

Figure 157. Three friendly dogs greeted passers-by at the Jesse Duncan house, purchased by Stephen E. and Jennifer Gariepy.

Williamson also purchased farmland in the area at a master commissioner's sale and from John Morris. Boundary farms were owned by James Fields, William Williamson, and Harrison Lynn. In 1936 W.M. Barkley bought the small farm from Lew and Nannie Lee Williamson and other heirs, passing title on in 1862 to Richard Allen Barkley. Barbara Barkley and Warren Powers acquired it in 1980 from Allie Clay Vance and other heirs. In 1992 the Powerses sold five acres containing the house to Todd Mitchell Grizzle for $55,400. Other improvements included a shotgun type house now used for storage and a bungalow. Grizzle elaborated the latter dwelling with a wraparound porch and redeveloped and expanded the basement, which is sheltered by an extension of the main level porch. The bungalow has a shed roofed dormer and a large chimney.[212]

WILLIAMSON-DUNCAN HOUSE, 576 HINTON CEMETERY ROAD. The one story five bay house with an impressive stone foundation, an off-center door, and an outstanding stone shouldered gable end chimney, is assigned a 1900 construction date in PVA records. The ascribed date fails to take into consideration the fact that at least part of the front section is log. Pictured on the following page, this interesting house stands on a 145.37-acre farm exclusive of a half-acre graveyard and includes 42.5 acres sold by special commissioner J.C.B. Sebree in 1885 to settle the estate of Joseph W. Peacher.

In 1885 Dudley Williamson bought the acreage then bounded by land of William Hinton and William Price. He later acquired abutting properties in 1913 from J.W. Robertson, in 1915 from J. Price, and in 1918 at a master commissioner's sale. In 1953 Richard Henry Williamson, executor of the Dudley Williamson estate, sold the 80.3-acre farm to Noah Duncan, who sold it in 1983 to Dudley M. and Linda C. Duncan, who sold it in 2016 to David Kelly.[213]

WELLS-DUNCAN HOUSES, 571-577-583 FINNELL ROAD. In 1987 Ellen Gregg Scobey acquired a picturesque piece of folk architecture when she purchased three tracts totaling approximately forty-two acres from Clyde and Dorothy Duncan. The property included, at the 577 Finnell Pike address, a story and half two door house with a stone foundation. Other property transfers in the neighborhood among Duncan family members included: Paul and Corinne R. Duncan to Clyde Duncan, 1958; Paul and Corinne Duncan to Clyde and Dorothy Duncan, 1966; J.D. and Pauline Duncan to Paul Duncan, 1952; and W.B. and Sarah Norton to J.D. and Earl Duncan, 1947. Earlier transactions relate to sale by the J.B. Wells family to John A. and Maggie Pribble, who sold

---

[212] Deed Books 9-203, 13-312, 17-165, 62-5, 93-67, 147-588, 147-694,197-454.
[213] Deed Books 220-119; 47-300, 301, 521; 22-119; 80-134; 264-559; 155-361. Other information from Ronald T. Vance.

the property to Bart S. Padgett. In 1943 Hubert and Betty Hornsby sold it to W.B. and Sarah Norton, who then sold to J.D. and Earl Duncan.

In earlier years, when Bart S. Padgett bought the property from John A. and Maxine Pribble, one of the three comprising tracts, an eight-acre parcel, was described as "the old Sims Place." The Sims Place and fifteen acres were sold to J.A. Garnett in a 1916 court action. J.L. Garnet purchased it from N. Pickett, Ollie O'Neal, Charles O'Neal, Nellie Pickett, Ida Pickett, Albert Pickett, Lewis Pickett, Lucille Pickett, and Mary Pickett. Also involved were thirty-one acres formerly owned by J.B. and Nannie Wells that Lew and Nannie Lee Williamson in 1909 sold to Willie Wells. Pribble bought the property in 1918. The two-bay house is missing from the landscape. Surviving is an older house with battened siding, a picnic shelter labeled "The Home Place Hang Out," and a later house with double windows. Mrs. Scobey passed away in 2017.[214]

JESSE DUNCAN HOUSE, 388 HINTON CEMETERY ROAD. A two door, four bay, one story house on a stone foundation and with two over two pane sash and a central chimney spent many years, possibly all of its existence, in the Duncan family until its sale in 1994 by Paul Duncan to Stephen E. and Jennifer Gariepy. Jesse Duncan purchased it between 1895 and 1903 from James Morris, Alice Robinson, Meredith Price (two tracts), G.W. Hinton, and the Burgess heirs, in small tracts that ultimately comprised the 38.25-acre farm. In 1915 Jesse Sharp sold W.M. Duncan, J.D. Duncan, and Paul Duncan another small parcel. In 1932 the other brothers sold the farm to Paul Duncan who, joined by his wife Corinne R., sold the farm and its nicely preserved house to the Gariepys.[215]

Figure 159. Ellen Gregg Scobey built the family's picnic shelter as a tribute to the Gregg family.

Figure 158. Earlier owned by J.B. Wells, Ellen Gregg Scobey owned the above property at her death in 2017.

---

[214] Deed Books 82-404, 86-5, 101-446, 86-5, 242-363, 169-392; 34-103; 37-487; 40-546, 605; 45-514; 47-108; 48-116, 68-155.
[215] Deed Book 208-527.

Figure 160. Samuel T. Giles house owners include present owners Circuit Judge Paul Isaacs and his wife Anna, also an attorney but at heart a practicing farmer.

SAMUEL T. GILES AND GILES FAMILY PROPERTIES

SAMUEL T. GILES HOUSE II, 1588 BARKLEY ROAD. One of Scott County's premier rural dwellings is the home of Samuel T. Giles, progenitor of the regionally prominent and extensive Giles clan. Many of Giles's descendants established homes on their father's and grandfather's homestead. In 1954 Nancy M. Giles sold the old home place from the F.C. Giles estate to Fred and Beulah Moreland, who sold it to W.E. Hixson in 1956. The deed described the property as located at the intersection of the Giles and Finnell roads.[216]

This house tells the story of Samuel T. Giles and his progeny, all instrumental to life in the surrounding hill country. The stately farmstead presents a pastoral view to persons approaching from several directions. One looks down from the top of the hill formerly known as Giles Hill and envisions youngsters from years gone by sledding or biking down the steep incline. Or as you approach it from the Finnell Pike, you see the Isaacs farmstead cozily nestled in its valley. Around it reside the farm's log crib barn, corn crib, and an older barn.[217]

Samuel T. Giles's accumulated 351.5 acres were parceled out to his heirs on March 21, 1921. Tract one went to Mary A. Milner and S.W. Giles. Tract two was divided among R.P. Giles, D.L. Renaker, and Harvey Giles. Tract three became the property of Frank Giles, Mrs. S.K. Hamon, Nettie Sharp, and Napoleon Giles. At that time the road winding through the farm was called Giles Pike on one end and Harrison County Pike on the other. Roads cutting through east/west were the Sadieville Pike and Finnell Pike.[218]

Several owners of this appealing setting include leading historical figures. Samuel T. Giles, a productive farmer and landowner, carved a niche for himself as one of Scott County's earliest trend setters. Paul Isaacs, present owner with his wife Anna, also an attorney, is a circuit judge for the Scott, Bourbon, and Woodford

---

[216] Deed Books 81-408, 81-409, 83-405.
[217] Deed Books 81-408, 81-409, 83-405.
[218] Will Book U-389.

counties judicial district. Anna conducts much of the farming operation along with her legal practice and sings with a medieval instrumental vocal group.

Andrew N. Lytle, who moved to this farm in 1976 three years after retiring from Sewanee University, was well known as a professor of literature and a novelist, dramatist, and essayist. A graduate of Vanderbilt University, he also studied at Yale University (drama), and taught at The University of the South at Sewanee and the University of Florida. He was a driving force and spokesman for the Southern Agrarians, a movement that included authors Robert Penn Warren and Allen Tate. His first book, *Bedford Forrest and his Critter Company* (1931), a biography, was one of more than a dozen volumes. *The Velvet Horn* (1957) was nominated for the National Book Award. His memoir, the 1973 *A Wake for The Living,* continues to be acclaimed for its "deep religious sensibility" and expansive view of history. After leaving Scott County, he spent his last two decades living in a cabin in Monteagle, Tennessee. He died in 1995 at the age of ninety-two.[219]

Figure 161. Basement entrance to the older log house of the historic Giles family.

The late Woodridge Spears, a friend and literary associate of Lytle, commented:

> Personally, I regard *At the Moon's Inn* as an outstanding Amerian book. I had hoped that he would settle down in Scott and write another book on the Taylor family or the Indians of the Valley. We have talked about this, but – he was having trouble with his eyes. When he was a student at Vanderbilt, he was writing some interesting verse. His "Edward Graves," published in *The Fugitive* by young Andrew Nelson Lytle, is a poem of browning honey-horns and bees, and Pilot Knob, and Edward Graves made old by the flint mill. He went to supper and met a ghost. His wife had run off with the circus freaks. The situation is very like some of the situations in Jesse Stuart's early books. But the tone of the piece is different from Stuart's. The tone is Andrew's own. *W.S.*

Figure 162. The log house occupies a corner of the historic spread.

After owning the property for thirteen years, W.E. Hixson sold the 74.75-acre farm to Charles D. and Jewell Marie Doolin. The Doolins sold it in 1973 to Bronson and Jo Ann Parker, who sold it in 1974 to Richard M. and Susan W. Richards. The Richardses sold it to Dr. Lytle in 1976, and he in 1977 to Judge and Mrs. Isaacs.[220]

SAMUEL T. GILES HOUSE I, 1468 BARKLEY PIKE. This wonderful old house stood on a 47.5-acre tract that the Paul and Anna Isaacs purchased in 1976 from Richard M. and Susan Richards. Like so many of the properties located along what is today identified as Barkley Road, the farm had previously been owned by Samuel T. Giles.[221]

In 1954 Nancy M. Giles, widow of Frank C. Giles, and several nieces and nephews, sold the four parcels that she and her husband had acquired over the years, to Fred and Beulah Moreland. Grantors were J.C. Giles, 49 ½ acres, 1946; thirty-one acres that S.T. Giles purchased in 1922; 15 ¾ acres, number six in the S.T. Giles's

---

[219] "Andrew Nelson Lytle," Wikipedia, the free encyclopedia.
[220] Deed Books 83-405, 109-185, 121-83, 126-232, 133-90, 136-452.
[221] Deed Book 132-594.

division; and 26 ¼ acres bought from G.T. Sharp in 1941. Frank Giles died in 1953. At the time of the acquisitions the road leading from the Turkeyfoot Road along the route was called the Harrison County and Sadieville-Finnell pike.[222]

In 1957 Beulah Moreland Walters and her husband Philip sold the farm to Leon A. and Dorothy E. Fitzpatrick for $8,800. During the next several years purchasers included John and Elizabeth Botkins, 1959; James L. and Sue May Barnett, 1961; Carl Lee and Thelma Bark,1962; Donald L. and Geneva Shepherd, 1968; Richard M. and Susan Richards, 1972; and Anna and Paul Isaacs, 1976.[223]

Figure 163. View of the Samuel T. Giles spread from Giles Hill on Barkley Road.

SAMUEL W. GILES HOUSE, 1495 BARKLEY ROAD. In 1982 Turner and Penny R. Summers purchased a twenty-seven-acre Barkley Road farm from Gilbert and Mary Renaker. Their bungalow dates to 1908-1913. The late Lonnie Williamson discussed working on the house when he was a boy and learning that the plan was a Sears Craftsman plan built with locally acquired materials.

Figure 164. Historic R.P. and Anna Giles house located at the entrance of North Mount Gilead Road.

The farm traces to the larger expanse of Samuel W. Giles, a son of Samuel T. and Eliza A. Giles. Giles's purchase in 1908 of one hundred acres for $2,500 was described as beginning at the crossing of the pike between the Dryden and Pettit lines and bounded by the land of F.C. Giles and the Hiles Mill Pike. In 1913 W.H. and Alleda Lane purchased from Samuel W. Giles the land that he acquired from his parents, which they increased with a 1938 acquisition from J.H. and Mary Rawlins Giles the property that J.H. Giles received in the division of their father S.T. Giles's farm. The Lanes sold their farm in 1943 to Corbin L. and Lucy Wright, who sold the portion of the farm with the dwelling to the Renakers in 1965.[224]

---

[222] Deed Books 71-454; 51-479, 231; 66-92.
[223] Deed Books 81-408, 409; 83-408; 85-338; 90-27; 90-321; 92-122; 106-443; 119-50; 132-594.
[224] Deed Books 153-661; 40-224, 51-235, 43-369, 64-103, 68-137, 98-370, 153-661.

GILES-HUMPHREY HOUSE, 131 NORTH MOUNT GILEAD CHURCH ROAD. It's a wonderful experience when the owners of an historic house and farm receive through the mail a letter introducing them to a former resident, one who grew up on their farm and in their house, and whose son from Minnesota and his family had recently visited the farm, cherishing the opportunity to walk over the yard and the land, reliving memories recalled for them by parents and grandparents. This took place in 1986 when John F. and Anna Humphrey received not only such a memory packed letter from the wife of recently deceased Thomas W. Giles, Sr., but also a poem that her husband had written about the Mount Gilead setting of his youth and the view of that setting from a special hilltop where a young boy could dream away. Mrs. Humphrey treasured the letter – and the poem – as did her sons Gayle and Denver, the latter who passed copies of these treasures on to the author during the winter of 2010-2011, shortly after Mrs. Giles' death.

The picturesque R.P. and Addie Giles's former home faces Barkley Road from a high point at its juncture with the northern branch of Mount Gilead Church Road. The drive leads from Mount Gilead Road with the house on the right and the agricultural complex on the left. The Giles house has two roofline gables on the second level, each with a window with two over two pane sash. On the lower level, sheltered by a long front porch, are the two entries flanked on their outer sides by parlor windows. Supporting the porch are turned posts with upper level trim connecting them to the porch cornice. The side of the house has its own porch, smaller but with similar supports. A smokehouse in the yard has a deep overhang.

In 1958 Thomas W. and Frances W. Giles deeded their interest in the property, described at the time as located on the Turkeyfoot-Boyers Turnpike to John F. and Anna Giles Humphrey. The earlier owners, Richard P. and Addie Giles, had three children: Mary E. Hill, Frank H. Giles, and Thomas W. Giles. The Humphreys' sons inherited the farm. Richard P. Giles acquired the property in three transactions that included a 1904 deed from his parents, Samuel T. and Eliza A. Giles, and 1921 and 1922 deeds from Napoleon and Margaret Giles and others, Ruth and Herman Green, and Bertha T. Renaker.[225]

Mrs. Giles's letter detailed how her husband had written much about the home place and the land he loved. The house, she wrote, "was built by an uncle out of walnut wood cut on the land – the china closet in the dining room was built [from the same] walnut." She continued, "In the corner by the little bridge used to be an old distillery – operated by great grandfather Pemberton –whose daughter married S.T. Giles, my husband's grandfather." She recalled that the present garage was built over an old ice house. Here is the poem that Thomas Giles, Sr., wrote a year before his passing:

Quiet Secure Place
A favorite spot on the old farm place was high on an "Eden Hill"
The place was marked by two walnut trees where I sat and drank my fill –
As I looked all around at familiar things and drank in the artistic scene –
You could never forget the strength you received each visit, either long or lean.
As a boy, then a youth, I would visit this place, the view was old yet new –
I loved the land where my people had worked under skies – oh – ever so blue.
At the foot of the hill just below this spot – was the home of my boyhood friend.
We played together at home and at school, many times after days end.
A look to the north on Dividing Ridge, you could see Coppage school up there –
A place to study and learn and grow with teachers and parents that care.

---
[225] Deed Book 36-97; 51-237, 269; 52-195; 86-24, 68-533, 60-67.

Looking east past two hills was a hallowed place, Mount Gilead Methodist Church –
Where love, devotion, with time and worship, our Creator healed our hurts.
Then looking South was our barn and home – across the creek my grandfather's place –
When I looked at these places I loved so much – it was easy to have a wet face.
Then look to the west on a hill just as high as the one on which I sat
Was the old Burgess graveyard, large cedars on guard, graves covered by a green mat –
To the right of this place you could see at times smoke from a train passing by
Three miles away at our voting place, you could see it when up this high.
A lazy breeze on a summer's day, brought familiar sounds to you here,
The hum of locusts, a killdeer's cry, a thrush's song that seemed very near,
The caw of a crow from the top of a tree, on guard while the young learned to fly,
The baa of the sheep, their lambs at play – a dog barks behind a hill,
A squirrel moves in the walnut tree – while a noisy jaybird grows still.
From our porch comes the sound of a favorite hymn, as my mother prepares our meal,
There was hard work and rest, good food and play, above all there was love that was real.
Sometimes I could hear my father at work as he whistled true and clear,
Strong and upright in all that he did, people loved him from far and near.
As a man, I would pause with my wife and two sons, after mother and father were gone,
Pointing out places and things that were done in the days of muscle and brawn.
So long ago and oh so brief, when measured in God's time –
Even today, when I visit this place --
These memories will always be mine!

T.W. Giles   1/31/86

Figure 165. (a) Willie A. Reed House, a Giles family property owned by Rich A. and Victoria Aurelius. (b) View of the Willie A. Red outbuildings as seen from the house.

WILLIE A. REED HOUSE, 767 MOUNT GILEAD CHURCH ROAD. One of the most positive things that can happen to an historic house would be acquisition by Rich and Victoria Aurelius. Rich is an artist, artisan, restorer, and builder, and Victoria is a teacher. Rich has undertaken renovation of the property and contributed creatively conceived landscape additions. The house looks down on the road from a high point reached by a picturesque winding lane. The house is three bays wide and two stories tall. Its transverse porch is Arts and Crafts style in design, having tapered posts mounted on stone piers. A stone shouldered chimney is on the west end.

Figure 166. Historic photo of Giles-Humphrey Farm, courtesy L. Denver Humphrey, author of contributed poem.

When Samuel T. Giles' estate was formally divided among his heirs in 1921, Mary A. Milner received lot number one of Tract 1's twenty-seven acres and S.W. Giles received lot number two. A sycamore tree, four feet in diameter, standing near the edge of the Harrison County Pike, marked a corner of Mrs. Milner's inheritance. In 1922 the Cynthiana widow sold her acreage to her brother S.W. Giles for $2,500, and in 1923 he sold both tracts to Willie A. Reed for $4,000. About that time Reed built the house where he lived until his death in 1981. At that time John Swinford, his executor, sold it to the Aureliuses.[226]

COPPAGE-GILES HOUSE, 787 HINTON CEMETERY ROAD. A two-story log house on a thirty-acre farm occupied a Hinton Cemetery Road setting purchased in 1879 from Elbert M. and Laura A. Coppage by S.T. Giles. Coppage's title to 172.25 acres came in 1878 from James W. Berry, high bidder at a sheriff's sale involving the estate of S.G. Penn for 39.25 acres "where A. Oder resides."[227]

Giles and his wife Eliza A. Giles sold the farm of 195 acres in 1905 to F.C. Giles. In 1965 F.C. and Nancy Giles sold the then 190-acre farm to John H. Bell, Jr. and Charles M. and Sheila Recones. In 1981 Bell and his wife Betty sold the 196.22-acre farm to Kenneth O. and Shirley T. Houston, who sold thirty acres of the land, including the house, in 1981 to Teresa N. and Robert A. Baggett. The Baggetts sold it to William F. and Gladys J. Lambert, and they sold it in 1994 to Thomas H. and Renee M. Thomas.[228]

SARAH J. SHARP HOUSE, 1889 BARKLEY ROAD. A stepped walkway leading from Barkley Road to an L-shaped house shares a special place in the Mount Gilead neighborhood and as this is written is the home of Buford McDonald. Its lineage traces to the estate of Sarah J. Sharp and the division of her property in 1893 by James B. Finnell, special commissioner, to her heirs James L. Sharp, John M. Sharp, Harriet and Harrison Lynn, Annie and Ely Williamson, Claude Sharp, John Smith, and Martha and John Burgess. Claude M. Sharp acquired the house during the court action.

Figure 167. Sarah J. Sharp house on Barkley Road.

---

[226] Deed Books 51-233, 563; 52-346; 153-893, 894; Will Books U-389, 3-138.
[227] Deed Books 9-268, 16-340, 17-287.
[228] Deed Books 17-287, 37-117, 74-149, 148-831, 149-424, 160-630, 207-786.

In 1943 Fred Williamson purchased the thirty-six-acre farm from Sharp, selling it in 1965 to Lorenza Geary Dawson in 1965. Dawson and his wife Ellen sold it to Martin and Ada Bell Wells in 1967, and they in 1989 to Lloyd Wayne and Linda Martin. In 1991 the Martins sold it to James T. and Jayda Caldwell Lail. Buford McDonald and Shirley Burgess were next to enjoy the property. McDonald told the writer that he very much enjoyed living by the side of the road and sharing the produce of his garden with neighbors.[229]

Figure 168. Coppage-Giles house continues as part of the Giles family landscape.

JOHN REED-HUMPHREY HOUSE, 2024 BARKLEY ROAD. The circuitous Barkley Road reaches its eastern Scott County terminus on the Harrison County line at the "Reed farm," the historic and picturesque property owned by Gayle and Violet Humphrey. Between 1869 and 1978, various members of the Reed family lived here.[230]

Isaac Shuff, who owned a significant amount of property at the convergence of the boundaries of Harrison and Bourbon counties, sold twenty acres in 1869 to John Reed for $400. The Reeds acquired adjacent land from the heirs of William Bennett and Mary E. Bennett. John Reed and his wife Georgia Ann sold this land to John R. Reed on October 14, 1903 for $1,000 and an agreement to provide board for Harrison Reed for one year from the date of the deed. The latter Reed also purchased in 1931 a small tract from the estate of James F. Mockbee, and with his wife Corda bought adjacent tracts from the heirs of Jemima Johnson. In 1913 John and Corda Reed sold a one-acre tract in Scott and Harrison counties to the Harrison County Board of Education for a schoolhouse location. The family's accumulated acreage also included property owned by Mrs. Reed and her family. By his will dated October 25, 1931 and probated April 6, 1932, John Reed left his wife Corda Johnson Reed a life estate. After her death, $1,000 was to go to their son Willie to bring his total allocation from the estate to $3,000. Their son Dolphus was to receive the entire ninety-three-acre farm and two liberty bonds. John Reed requested by

Figure 169. Marie Minus Hamon of the James Amos Hamon family passed the property on to Mattie H. Ewing.

his will that there be no sale of stock or farm implements.[231]

The Humphreys have enlarged the house which contains a two-story gabled section with one story wings. The barn with a shed attachment and a lake are also important features of their farm.

---

[229] Deed Books 28-328, 68-318, 99-431, 104-133, 182-447, 192-46, 238-721; Will Book X-287.
[230] Deed Books 140-556, 36-1.
[231] Deed Books 27-24; 43-437; 60-335; 92-293, 294; 94-147; Will Book X-92.

Finnell Road
Hamon Properties

W.T. and Sue Hamon House, Finnell Road. A two bay two story house occupying a block foundation on an 83.88-acre farm was known from 1939 to 1995 as the home of J.T. Jacobs. It was sold by Jacobs's executor in 1995 to Gaylord B. Hilander. In 1931 W.T. and Sue Hamon of the James Amos Hamon family acquired it, selling it in 1938 to W.K. Sinclair. The Sinclairs sold the farm and house the next year to Mr. Jacobs.

Figure 170. John Reed acquired county line property from Isaac Shuff in 1869. A barn and lake were included in the Shuff to Reed deed.

Mattie H., James K. Ewing House, 850 Finnell Road. A frame house with a front gable and two wings, one side-gabled, was integral to the 178.51-acre farm that became the property of Mattie H. Ewing in the division of the dower lands of Marie Minus Hamon in the James Amos Hamon estate. Mrs. Ewing's title came by way of a 1931 deed from Hamon heirs W.T. Hamon and Delia and H. Frank Milner.[232]

Georgetown National Bank, which acquired the parcel identified as Tract III in Marie Hamon's dower at a master commissioner's sale for $3,748.71, sold it to J. Read and Julia Embry Moore of Wewaha, Oklahoma. In 1939 they sold it to E.W. Walton for $5,560. Walton and his wife Dorothy sold it in 1944 to H.H. and Betty Hornsby for $14,300. The Hornsbys sold it to W.R. and Jessie L. Jennings in 1947. The property value continued to increase and the currency to similarly appreciate when in 1950 the Jenningses sold it to Remus Mason for $23,100. In 1959 Martha P. Mason, executor of the estate of Remus Mason, Sr., sold the farm to Mike and Edith Stephens. Stephens died November 8, 1986, and Mrs. Stephens and James O. Walters sold the subdivided tract with the house and other improvements

Figure 171. William Wells, Sr. and Willie Wells were owners of the Princess Anne style frame house.

---
[232] Deed Books 59-308, 339.

in August 1994 to Philip Hudson. In 2006 Hudson sold the central parcel including the house and 27.54 acres to Dale H. and Minnie S. Wilson.[233]

WILLIAM WELLS, SR., AND WILLIE WELLS HOUSE, 687 FINNELL ROAD. A story and half Princess Anne style house occupies land owned from the 1860s by William Wells, Sr. and his son Willie Wells. The house in more recent times has been owned by Kenneth O. and Margaret Gregory, who bought it in 1975 and sold it and 13.3 acres in 2006 to Heidi and Robert W. Kelm.[234] In 1872 Samuel W. Long, master commissioner, sold William Wells tracts of approximately twenty-seven acres and fifty-nine acres for $1,482.86 at an estate action involving Joseph E. Griggs as administrator for Jane Crawford and Henry Crawford. Other members of the Wells family who owned the property were Willie Wells and Lawrence Wells. In 1955 Lillie Wells, widow of Lawrence Wells, sold the family farm in four tracts to Wesley and Emma Newland Sams; they sold to John W. and Elizabeth McClellan and Owen Clifford and Sandra K. Riggs. The McClellans sold the property to the Gregorys.[235]

Figure 172. O.R. and Gertrude Wells house was left by Nancy Anderson to S.L. Warth in 1901.

WARTH-CONNER HOUSE, 525 FINNELL ROAD. An interesting two-story house, three bays wide with a central gable and an altered end chimney, occupies the farm owned from 1966 by O.R. and Gertrude Wells and deeded by Mrs. Wells in 1976 to her daughter and grandson, reserving a life estate. Mrs. Wells died in 1979, the property passing to Elizabeth Colvin and her son Victor Allen Colvin. In 1994 Elizabeth Colvin Zeigenfuse sold it to James G. and Audrey J. Vickers.[236]

During the farm's earlier history, an interest was sold by J.H. Cannon to S.L. Warth. The 1901 will of Nancy Anderson left all property including eighty acres to her son, S.L. Warth, referring to his obligation to pay her debts and provide board and clothing for her for the remainder of her life, and after her death, to pay one hundred dollars to each of her other children. Other beneficiaries were Sallie Elliott of Lexington, Maggie Paul of Leesburg, and Abe Warth of Finnell. In 1907 Abe and Mollie Warth, David and Sallie Elliott, and John L. and Margaret Paul transferred their title in the Nancy Anderson land to S.L. Warth for $675. In 1909 the Warths sold forty of the eighty acres and five acres adjacent to Collins on the west to Charles C. Conner for $1,000. Purchasers of the land from 1915 to the 1966 Wells acquisition included George W. and Jennie Popham, Lexington, 1915; I.W. Manley, 1916; J.W. and Margaret Pribble, 1919; James W. Bennett, 1918; Nelson and Essie Johnson, 1942; H.H. and Betty Hornsby, 1942; and William E. and Rhoda Hagans, 1943.[237]

Figure 173. W.C. and Noah Hanna, father and son, owned the L-shaped house from 1911 to 1955.

---

[233] Deed Books 88-168, 207-379, 307-089.
[234] Deed Books 7-193, 267, 274,373; 130-86; 299-808.
[235] Deed Books 34-92, 76-168, 38-148, 19-93, 26-457, 51-264, 56-322, 82-322, 99-420, 130-86.
[236] Deed Books 67-602, 102-542, 71-190, 131-634, 206-623; Will Book 2-459, 460.
[237] Will Book T-430; Deed Books 20-176, 38-177, 40-216, 44-422, 45-394, 46-166, 47-109, 65-645, 67-602, 102-542.

Hannah/Hanna

W.C., Noah Hanna House, 423 Finnell Road. Another family integral to the Holdings Mill-Mount Gilead community was the Hanna/Hannah family. W.C. and Noah Hannah, father and son, were owners from 1911 to 1955 of the farm on which a nicely finished one story L-shaped house was erected. The house retains its neatly crafted dry stone foundation, tooled chimney, and turned posts and is today owned by James F. Richardson. W.C. Hanna purchased parts of the small farm on which the house is located from various sources: J.B. Wells, 1911; Willie and Bertha Wells (one acre), 1917; and Lon Hanners, 1913 and 1930. Hanna died in 1954, leaving his property to Noah Hanna and his wife. In 1955 Noah and Hazel Hanna sold the 25.25-acre farm to J.D. and Pauline R. Duncan. Mr. Duncan died in 1994 and in 2001 Pauline R. Duncan sold it to Tim and Shannon N. Frasure, who sold it to James F. Richardson in 2004. [238]

W.C. and Noah Hanna House, 333-339 Finnell Road. On the former W.C. and Noah Hanna farm is a four-bay cottage with a small enclosed pantry on the Finnell Pike. Tony and Betty Medlock purchased the property in 1977 from Ralph and Cleo Bond, who bought it in 1946. Cora Peacher owned it from 1936 to 1940, having bought it from G.F. Hanna. Georgetown National Bank as executor of Lon Hanners sold the property to W.C. and Noah Hanna in 1933. A water gap on the old Hamon dirt road is prominent in deeds of 1931 and 1933.[239]

Shenandoah: Frank and Kay Wiseman Log House and Related Buildings, Finnell Road

Frank Wiseman, longtime chair of the Georgetown College chemistry department and author of the textbook on organic chemistry currently used, and his wife Kay, are eclectic individuals who relish the Wiseman ancestral Shenandoah Valley roots transported to the headwaters of East Eagle on Finnell Road. Travelers are readily drawn to the view of a large log house with full dovetail notching, the banked setting also accommodating a large two car garage. A sign with the farm's name, Shenandoah, and under it "Wiseman" and "Est. 1987" rests on the plank fence.

A woodworking shop adds character to the pastoral setting. The interior offers natural wood walls, reproduction furniture crafted by Dr. Wiseman on this farm, buildings remaining from earlier eras, and a view of the setting. A smokehouse stands adjacent to the driveway on a tall, reworked stone foundation. The battened upper section has a deep overhanging roof supported by large brackets. Walkways and foundations are faced with colorful flagstones.

Figure 174. Sign designating the Wiseman Kentucky spread "Shenandoah" after Wiseman's former home.

Figure 175. Smokehouse/storage with high stone foundation.

---

[238] Deed Books 14-189, 46-593, 58-174, 43-371, 42-214, 59-602, 69-417, 83-37, 258-93, 280-699; Will Book S-243.
[239] Deed Books 135-569, 72-110, 65-124, 62-286, 59-602.

Figure 176. Frank and Kay Wiseman house on Finnell Pike has full dovetail notches, the craftsmanship of Dr. Wiseman.

Figure 177. Shenandoah's rear wing.

A later ranch type house that has been incorporated into the Shenandoah spread is on the north. A portion of the land that the Wisemans purchased in 1987 traces to three tracts including a 155-acre inheritance from John DeGaris to J.T. Boyers and Sarah and Jacob Boyers of Harrison County and three parcels from the Matilda Glenn division.

A portion of the property on Cynthiana Pike southwest of Shenandoah relates to later ownership by the John M. and Randolph R. Rains estate. The transfer from the W.A. DeGaris estate is dated 1901. John M. Glenn's heirs deeded the other tract to Anna E. Glenn, John M. Glenn's widow, in 1895; heirs were Anna C. Glenn, Augusta H. Glenn, James K. and Anna Tee Glenn, Fannie Talbott, Dora E. and Robert S. Gann, and William T. and Anna May Glenn of Livingston County, Missouri. John M. Glenn's source was Matilda Glenn.[240]

Among other earlier purchasers of this Finnell Pike countryside were K.A. Brand, 1905; John Turner, 1911; F.M. McKenney, 1912; Carl and Edith Hamon, 1920; Aura and J.O. Oldham, 1920; Lucy J. and Nora L. King, 1936; and Robert W. and Charlene Tevis.[241]

L.S. MILNER HOUSE, 239 SOUTH MOUNT GILEAD CHURCH ROAD. In 1866 W. Wright and Keziah Allen sold L.S. (Samuel) Milner the farm on the west side and immediately north of Mount Gilead Church. The property included 131 acres two rods twenty perches and excluded the church and two acres, the parsonage lot of one half acre, and the graveyard containing one rod and twenty poles. The deed referenced a lien held by Richard and Fannie Brand and William and Martha Ammerman of Harrison County.

Figure 178. Milner house on adjacent Mount Gilead Road tract.

In 1911 N.C. and Tommie Bailey deeded a nearby tract to Milner. In 1918 Luke S. and Louise Ann Milner sold P.L. Warth a forty-acre parcel excluding a graveyard of .563 acres. In 1919 Milner sold the 117.6 acre land next to the church lot to John Leach for $14,700, boundaries including the Leeslick Turnpike, John Ireland, J.T. McLoney, and George Noel. Leach and his wife Annie B. sold the same acreage the same day to J.E. Luttrell and John

---

[240] Deed Books 171-339, 36-633; 34-286, 29-433, 22-468 19-24.
[241] Deed Books 36-633, 42-127, 42-600, 47-211, 49-608, 61-586, 103-128, 165-80, 219-170, 280-104, 171-335.

A. Roberts. Two years later Luttrell and his wife Iva sold Roberts 55.2 acres from their jointly owned land. The acreage of the remaining parcel remained until 1969 when Robert Hall Smith sold 4.66 acres to John G. and Kathryn Rutledge. In 2000 Jeffrey Stephens sold Jessica Hall and Ruby Lee Hiten Stephens that tract.[242]

Figure 175. Gregory and Elizabeth Trotter House, a present-era Victorian style house with towers and handmade stained-glass windows. Gregory Trotter built the weathervane.

EVA AND HARVE COVINGTON HOUSE, 363 SOUTH MOUNT GILEAD CHURCH ROAD. A one story three bay two pile frame house occupied an eleven-acre one rod fourteen poles tract that was bought in 1945 by Eva and Harve Covington from Etta Hedger Wright for $550. The Covingtons sold it in 1950 to Nannie Wright, and in 1956 Gordon and Nannie Wright sold it to Dorothy E. Wood for $3,000. E.C. and Mary Belle Hixson bought it in 1960, and in 1970, Mrs. Hixson individually and as executor of her late husband's estate sold it to Michael E. and Irene Stephens for $6,200.[243]

GREGORY W. AND ELIZABETH TROTTER HOUSE, 425 SOUTH MOUNT GILEAD ROAD. With enthusiasm engendered from living in an historic Victorian house on Georgetown's Oak Street, Gregory and Elizabeth Trotter decided to build one of their own, central to an idyllic tree studded forestry setting. They found the perfect site on South Mount Gilead Pike and the nearly perfect plan in *Old House Journal*, longtime standard for historic preservation.

Gregory and Liz are mutually committed to historic preservation. Greg is forever taking on new historic detail ventures, such as constructing a stained-glass window in a brick turrett that is one of the crowning achievements of the back yard. The house has three turrets, all with finials. Liz is associated with the American Hemerocallis Association and during the bloom of that American favorite, Rosemont is abloom with prize day lilies. Change of seasons brings wonderful flowers of nature's floral majesty. Greg and Liz acquired the ten-acre site in 1999 from

Figure 176. View of stained glass window crafted by Gregory Trotter.

Greg's parents, James E. and Consatnce Trotter, who live nearby in a contemporary style dwelling. The younger Gregorys began construction of their masterwork circa 2005. It is a combination of a variety of details of Victorian styling. And the work goes on.

---

[242] Deed Books 8-199, 47-198, 42-156, 40-151, 48-186, 48-187, 51-50, 53-531, 59-171, 60-542, 61-74, 62-30, 62-200, 68-70, 74-97, 77-478, 103-227, 109-551, 112-291, 124-322, 139-457, 249-818.
[243] Bevins, *Selected Buildings*, 37; Deed Books 63-629, 69-393, 76-564, 83-587, 85-11, 90-96, 111-520.

This property is a delightful tribute to the creativity of a couple who love the Victorian and are showing their appreciation by recreating it on a perfect setting.

Figure 180. Two views of the Trotter landmark.

HOLLAND-VANCE HOUSE, 715 NORTH MOUNT GILEAD ROAD. A house that appears to have begun its life as an L-shaped one-story dwelling set upon a stone foundation dates from the 1930s and early ownership of Letha J. and John Holland, from whom Stonewall Holland inherited it. Stonewall Holland deeded 34.6 acres and the house in 1938 to Susie and Dewey Lee Vance. In 1939 the Vances sold it to Jesse Lee Johnson, who died in 1941, leaving his wife Ethel, and children J.K. Johnson, Eugenia Johnson Wallace, Owen Lee Johnson, and Martha Johnson Marshall as heirs of the property. Subsequent owners and acquisition dates included Charlie and Carrie Jones, 1959; Harry and Lorraine Jones, 1969; Warren and Anna Barbara Powers, 1987; David and Carla Kelly, 1990; David and Elizabeth Wetzel, 1992; Chad Watts, 1998; and Richard T. and Tina M. Dozer, 2006; and Richard Dozer, 2014.[244]

Figure 177. Letha and John J. Holland's circa 1930 house.

STONEWALL J. HOLLAND HOUSE, 805 NORTH MOUNT GILEAD ROAD. A one and one-half story house retaining two over two pane sash stands on land sold by Ben Pack in 1883 to Stonewall J. Holland. Holland died in 1958 and his wife Ona Duncan Holland, mother of his nine children, died in 1964. In 1964 Bradford and Lucille Holland sold sixty-eight acres and the house to Charlie Jones, who in 1970 transferred title to Charlie and Mary Frances Jones. Jones died in 1995 and Mary Frances in 2000. Raymond L. and Ruth M. Ishmael purchased 52.6907 acres from the Mary F. Jones estate in 2000.[245]

The village of Mount Gilead is discussed in detail in the chapter entitled "Rural Northeast and East Central Crossroads Communities."

BAILEY PROPERTIES

In 1879 the lane that led west from the road that led north from Cynthiana Road, now known as Bailey Road, was densely populated with farms with dwellings. From the intersection of these two rural roads, along the

---

[244] Deed Books 63-387, 455; 64-190; 87-66; 110-632; 170-168; 186-170; 197-744; 210-285; 302-425.
[245] Will Books S-202, 11-151; Deed Books 38-431, 46-130, 44-132, 98-194, 11-194, 253-532, 272-840.

north side of the road were the properties of J. Hamon, the Griggs Estate, a schoolhouse, J. Bailey, J. Wells, and J. Williamson, the latter at the intersection with what we now call Barkley Road. On the south side of that road, proceeding from Finnell Road, were farms labeled W. Smith, J. Hamon, Mrs. Williamson, H. Williamson, W. Williamson, and J.W. Williamson. In a linear north to south pattern south of the Bailey Road are N. Hammond, W. Williamson, T. Johnson, W. Kenny, and W.L. Hammond. A second east-west road cuts across the expanse, merging with what became the Morris Road. Properties along this lane are ascribed to A. Warth, Mrs. P.A. Corbet, W. Tinder, S.W. Regg, and M.T. Gunnell. Midway between the second lane and Cynthiana Road are properties of J. Thompson and A.D. Hammon (note the spelling variations).[246]

GEORGE L. GREGG, AND GEORGE ANN AND JAMES F. BAILEY HOUSE, BAILEY ROAD. Continuing to claim its place on the north side of the Bailey Road is one pen of the two-pen log and timber frame home of George L. Gregg and subsequently of his daughter George Ann and her husband James F. Bailey. George L. Gregg died in 1833 and his wife in 1878. Bailey, born in 1825 a son of John Bailey of the Gunnell Pike, is said to have owned much of the land between Finnell and Muddy Ford roads along the road that bears his name. Bailey and George Ann's children were George William, Mary Adeline, James Paxton, Penelope Ann, Nancy E., Darcus A., Joseph Fisher, Charles Wallace, Hettie E., Noah C., and James S.[247]

Figure 178. Gregg-Bailey house with combined log and timber frame sections.

JOSEPH F. BAILEY HOUSE WEST OF BAILEY ROAD. There's something deep within many of us that loves a ruin. Of course we would prefer a preserved building or structure. Too many times, less ambitious or overly programmed property owners complain that a building or structure is "too far gone" and they almost angrily tell us that there's no point in arguing – it has to go. But there are also those individuals who maintain they can't afford to "fix up" their properties that once attracted admiration. Nevertheless, they refuse to tear them down. As long as it's there, there's an outside chance that it can be restored in kind or similarly. At least it continues to hold on to its ability to recall memories. Such are the remains pictured on this page and the following page of a farm near the west end of the Bailey Road – the decaying collapsing Joseph Fisher Bailey house, the huge propped up smokehouse once joined on the farmscape by an elaborate hog scalding platform, the makeshift current living quarters, and a hospitable owner living with scores of ghosts of the past.[248]

Figure 179. Joseph Bailey log smokehouse propped up for the immediate future.

---

[246] Map of Scott County, 1879.
[247] Information from Doris Bailey Reed.
[248] See Bevins, *Selected Buildings*, 304, 305.

Figure 180. Joseph Bailey house on its "last leg."

The old house, a former five bay dwelling two rooms deep and two stories tall, rests on a dry stone foundation that has held together better than the rest of the house. The house retains its elongated windows, some retaining two over two pane sash, a centered tooled chimney, a portion of hand split lath peeking beneath peeled siding, and an attic opening in and beneath the nearly three bays wide central gable trimmed with diamond shaped shingles. The decorative panels on either side of the front door remain, as does the door with a large screened opening. It is easy to love this house while mourning its coming demise. Sympathetic hands, determined to keep it from falling down, propped up the walls of the log smokehouse joined with V-notches. This is a site where artists could capitalize with a painting with a nostalgic label such as "Old Home Place."

NOAH AND JOSEPH BAILEY HOUSE, 450 MOUNT GILEAD CHURCH ROAD. Set on a high hill on the south side of the road known in earlier times as the Muddy Ford and Finnell Road is a vinyl clad Dutch Colonial Revival house on a stone foundation with a very long extended dormer lighting a high pitch roof. Its earlier twentieth century ownership related to Noah Bailey and Joseph F. Bailey. In 1925 the Noah Bailey heirs, who included J.F. and Talitha Bailey, Noah Bailey's widow Tommie, and Gladys Bailey, Oscar Bailey, Ernest Bailey, Elmo Bailey, and Bertha Bailey, deeded to Anna Kate Faulconer the farm previously owned by Noah Bailey's mother, George Ann Bailey. It had been understood that when George Ann Bailey died, Noah and James F. Bailey would partition her land, Noah taking the portion on the north side of the road and James F. on the south side. Both failed to follow through with deeds or otherwise record the transactions. Noah's portion was bounded on the west by Lou Williamson and others, east by James Amos Hamon and James F. Bailey, and north by Noah Bailey and James Giles.[249]

Figure 181. Joseph and Noah Bailey house on Mount Gilead Road.

Ten years later, in 1936, Mrs. Faulconer sold the farm to James K. Burton, who a few days later sold it to G. Tilford Hambrick and his wife Dorothy and other family members. The family in 1945 sold it for an appreciated sum to Jesse Robert and Dorothy L. Underwood. The next year Underwood sold the 163.08 acres to Howard and Cornelia Stephens, who sold it in 1962 to Robert Hall Smith.[250] This property underwent considerable transfers along with several other parcels by Crest Lawn Memorial

---

[249] Deed Books 54-529, 33-533, 30-184, 38-241, 55-72.
[250] Researching this title is a challenge. Chain of title references prior to sale to Smith's purchase is: Deed Books 55-72, 61-588, 61-598, 19-501, 71-531, 76-247, 92-496.

Gardens in Georgetown, Robert Hall and Clara Jean Smith, Philip Ray Corporation, David and Danny Marcum and Buryl Thompson, USDA, and FHA.

Resolution of ownership of two of the involved tracts, one of 75.69 acres and the other 99.5 acres, came in 1987 with the purchase from David Marcum by Paul F. and Anna H. Isaacs. The house has an extensive screened in front porch sheltering the main façade.[251]

Figure 182. Willis W. Gunnell house was renovated by Ray and Lorrene Alexander.

GUNNELL-ALEXANDER HOUSE, 425 GUNNELL ROAD. Among the earliest settlers in the rural neighborhood north of Oxford were Jesse and Elizabeth Browning, who first settled the farm where today stands a stately dwelling with styling transitional between turn of the century Victorian and early twentieth century Arts and Crafts. Between 1969 and 1990, the house was gracefully renovated and enhanced with a new brick façade by Ray and Lorrene Alexander. When the Alexanders bought the 146.2-acre farm, the road that it faces was referred to as "Gunnell now Sharon Pike." When they sold the house and 21.17 acres to Carl Allen and Glennis Doris Bowers, the road was generally known as Gunnell Road.

One of the earliest dispositions of the farm was the 1851 sale of 104 acres three rods by James Browning and James Hamilton, administrators of Jesse Browning's estate, to James Cummins, reserving one-fourth acre for a graveyard, "a part of which is at present fenced in." In 1860 J.J. and Eliza Browning sold fourteen acres one rod thirty-four poles to William Gunnell for $289, and in 1868 they sold 106 acres to L.D. Mefford for $21.08. There seems to have been a second J.J. Browning whose wife was named Eliza, suggested by legends on the stones of the Jesse and Elizabeth Browning graves: "Elizabeth, Feb 05, 1782-Jun 30, 1835"; "Jesse, Jun 02, 1773-Jun 21, 1818."[252]

Old estate probate documents' capabilities of revealing the culture of their times is carried out in the 1843 will of Jesse Browning. The officials recorded: "There not being a sufficiency of provisions on hand for one year,

---

[251] Deed Books 92-496, 95-553, 108-522, 117-508, 127-460, 156-725, 139-660, 135-269, 165-215, 170-685.
[252] Deed Books 109-106, 189-49, 5-358, 4-495, 6-267; Will Book Q-335; *Gone, Forgotten, Now Remembered* (Georgetown: Scott County Genealogical Society, 1992), 17.

Figure 187. Gunnell-Alexander house Craftsman mantel with over-mirror and historic tile.

Figure 183. Stairwell of Gunnell-Alexander house recalls the Craftsman building era.

we allowed to the widow eight hogs to supply the deficiency." Also set apart for her were a horse, plow, ax, hoe, cow and calves, a coffee pot, and other household and farming items. Among those purchasing items at the sale were William Browning (bureau, bed, lounge, clock, three stone jars, cupboard), F.S. Browning (watch, wagon and harness and, buggy and harness), F.M. Browning (cross cut saw, irons, plows, kettle), James Taylor (two plows), Joel Palmer (sythe and cradle), James Bradley (rifle gun), James Wright (three hoes), and J.W. Fields (double trees and single trees).[253]

Willis W. Gunnell, probably the figure referred to in several deeds as Willie Gunnell, owned the core of the farm from 1880 to 1908, more than likely the era of the house's construction. Gunnell's disposition of the property is, to say the least, quite interesting. On March 2, 1908, Gunnell sold his farm of 288 acres to J.D. Vance, the dwelling's other possible original owner, for $10,150. Gunnell's February 25, 1907 source was W.H. and Lottie A. Franks, the same acreage bringing Franks $7,500. A year earlier, on March 1, 1906, Gunnell traded to Franks other property and therein acquired the 288 acres with a declared value of $10,500. In 1880 Gunnell purchased the farm in four tracts from Jacob and Rebecca Price for $37,036. Price's sources included William H. Salyers, purchaser of 101 acres three rods twenty-seven poles from Joseph Gunnell in 1869. In 1946 Vance's heirs sold the farm to William E. and Lelia Nichols, who twenty years later sold 146 acres and the residential complex to Carl Hurd. In 1966 Hurd sold it to Zenas and Gwendolyn Courtney for $56,340. In 2005 Michael and Hope Goodwin purchased the house and 21.17 acres from Richard Skinner.[254]

---

[253] Will Book Q-335.
[254] Deed Books 39-63, 37-417, 18-96, 10-326, 10-329; 70-127, 101-171, 109-106, 293-063.

RICHARD, WILLIAM GUNNELL HOUSE, 925 GUNNELL ROAD. A log dwelling set well off the road, minus its stone chimney, recalls the settlement period era of circa 1807 when Richard Gunnell was buying land from George Kyger of New Hampshire. In 1808 Gunnell purchased ninety acres from Hurst, who also later acted as Gunnell's executor. Hurst purchased 400 acres of the Josiah Watson 4,000-acre land grant from George Kyger, who acquired 2,000 acres of the grant from Watson's trustee in bankruptcy. In 1833 Gunnell sold land on Eagle Creek and Poplar Fork and bought twenty-three acres from Asa and Polly Williamson. William Gunnell died in 1869, having provided for his wife Maria. A son, Richard, was left five dollars. The remainder of the property was to go to his children, with granddaughters Ann I. Price and Rebecca Shyrock to be considered as one of the children. William W. Gunnell inherited his "wach." S.N. Green was to serve as trustee of Mrs. Gunnell's estate. Children receiving land in the disposition of the estate were Jemima Jane Luke, sixty-five acres; Mary E. Powell, sixty-five acres; Manlius Gunnell, fifty-five acres; Joseph Gunnell, sixty-five acres; Willis Gunnell, forty-six acres; Richard Gunnell, thirty acres; and Ann Price, other property.[255]

Figure 189. Perhaps the original Gunnell log house under camouflaged covering on Gunnell Road.

Jemima Jane Luke's heirs toward the end of the century deeded their portion to A.D. Graves. The heirs were Robert A. and Leah Luke, Victor and Mariah L. Luke, Seth and Hattie Luke, J.W. and Elmer Luke, Vernal

Figure 184. Pastoral view of Gunnell Pike setting of the Gunnell-Alexander farm.

---

[255] Deed Books B-115, 78; C-82, 83; M-19, 15; U-72; 5-358; R-239; V-29; O-139; 3-334; U-72; 9-88; 1-168; Will Books K-215, P-347, Q-50; Bevins, "The Josiah Watson Grant," *Selected Buildings*, 34.

Vance, Mattie Glass, and Dona Luke. In 1901 A.D. and Kitty Graves deeded the farm, still intact, to W.E. Parker. In 1939 Maggie L. Parker sold it to Ollie M. Johnson, who, joined by his wife Anna E., in 1979 sold it to George Steven and Amy Lyon Brannock. In 1985 the Brannocks sold the property to Foster and Connie Covert when the nearby main road was still known as the Sharon Road.

W.T. Juett House, 426 Gunnell Road. L.H. Nichols was the purchaser in 1921 when the widow and children of W.T. Juett disposed of the family property of 101 acres on the west side of Gunnell Road. The farmhouse on the site is a Dutch Colonial Revival style dwelling of early twentieth century vintage with a full extended dormer. With a statement that division deeds were never written, Effie Juett and J.J. Hall, W.E. and Hattie Juett, F.L. and Betsy Juett, Edna J. and L.H. Sherritt, Nellie Juett and Raymond Williamson, and Mabel Juett and Joel Crenshaw sold the farm described as William Nichols' land bought by W.T. Juett. In 1962 W.E. and Lelia T. Nichols of Lexington sold the 202 acres for $38,500 to W.K. Henry, who with his wife Sarah disposed of 82.3334 acres of the total in 2005 for $823,340 to Gunnell Road Development of Loveland, Ohio. A contemporary house occupies the site today.[256]

B.F Sharon House, 866 and 870 Gunnell Road. Hugh Sharon was one of Scott County's earliest settlers, having arrived in Kentucky circa 1797 to claim land and to undertake construction of a two story log house. He developed his farm along a watercourse known as Sharon Branch. The road that was routed across his property was called Sharon Road. Sharon's descendants continued to occupy his land for many years and to develop new homesteads near the once primordial setting. Hugh Sharon died in 1847, leaving four sons and two daughters. His wonderful old log house was on its last leg when volume one of this Scott County architectural history was published in 1981, including a comment from the Reverend Charles T. Egbert, author and Presbyterian minister, regarding its notched and pegged construction system and handmade door latches.[257]

Figure 185. B.F. Sharon house on Gunnell Road.

Benjamin F. "Ben" Sharon became one of the most prominent landowners in the Muddy Ford/Gunnell and Morris Pike neighborhood. In 1870 he purchased the interest of other family members in the lands of James F. Sharon "on Eagle where James F. Sharon died." This included shares owned by William Sharon of Pendleton and John and Maranda Young in land owned by James F. Sharon, Jacob and Rebecca Price, J.M. Sharon, Sam N. Sharon, and W.P. and Almyra Lay in the dower of Nancy Sharon, widow of James M. Sharon.[258]

---

[256] Deed Books 51-406, 70-595, 91-532, 295-029.
[257] Bevins, *Selected Buildings*, 35. This was a landmark visited with Fannee Hilander and Shirley Houston on a field trip following publication of Fannee's *Hold Back the Spring* in 1980.
[258] Deed Books 10-316, 317, 318, 319, 333; 17-387; 20-51; 33-151.

In 1899 for $700 B.F. Sharon purchased fifty acres in three tracts from members of the Luke family, including Robert A. and Leah Luke, Victor and Mariah J. Luke, Seth and Hettie Luke, Andy and Mollie Graves, Al and Catherine Graves, J.W. Luke, Elmer Luke, and G.W. Luke. The primary tract had been owned by James S. Sharon, and tracts two and three were purchased by James S. Sharon from Hugh and John Sharon. Boundaries of the primary tract of eleven acres were farms of G.W. Luke, William Price, and Gunnell.[259]

Figure 186. Dutch Colonial Revival house attributed to W.T. Juett.

The two-story L-shaped house probably dates from the early ownership of the farm by B.F. Sharon, who died in 1916, and his wife Lucy, who passed away in 1932. Their three surviving children, Frank Sharron [c.q.], Allie Barnhill, wife of Joseph D. Barnhill, and Mary E., wife of Carl S. Culbertson of Cincinnati, declared that they agreed to a division of 182 acres that their father had owned "in exclusive and adverse possession at his death." This division alloted fifty acres to Lou Sharron; forty acres to Frank Sharron; 35.08 acres to Mary E. Culbertson; and forty-eight acres to Allie Barnhill. The family graveyard, to which all were to have right of ingress and egress, was included in Allie's part. Culbertson sold the portion containing the two story house in 1943 to Lena Lusby, who joined with her husband Owen in the 1944 sale to J.W. and Lydia Morris. Nelson J. and Lorena Moreland sold the farm to A.E. and Bessie A. Smith, and in 1970 Mrs. Smith's heirs sold it to Thelma J. Elam, the present owner.[260]

Griggs/Gregg Properties

William Griggs/Gregg Farm, 1089 Gunnell Road.

Toward the end of the nineteenth century, William H. Gregg, who also went by the name of Griggs, purchased several parcels of land: from James H. and Emmillee Williamson, 1893; Clinton Barnhill, 1894; N.C. Sharon, 1894; and George H. Williamson, 1901. In 1944 Onie and Annie Bertie Cook sold the property to Halcom and Alice Marshall, who sold tracts of fifty acres, one acre two rods, and a sixteen-foot passway, in 1947, to Ina Smith. Mrs. Smith sold an acre in 1962 to Robert H. and Amileen Piatt. William Mefford and Porter Hoffman purchased and sold the property in 1970 to Herbert Oliver for $4,000. Oliver sold it in 1972 to Lewis E. Simmons. The property in 1894 was described as located on the Muddy Ford-Finnell Road and in 1972 as being on the Gunnell Road. On this farm is a square vinyl clad one story dwelling, three bays wide with a side addition, a block foundation, and a gable roofed porch supported by iron posts.[261]

Figure 187. Square-plan dwelling with hip roof with Griggs-Gregg relationship.

---

[259] Deed Book 33-151 with references to Deed Book 11-182 and 183.
[260] Deed Books 45-356, 59-396, 68-225, 76-263, 76-265, 60-329, 60-330, 86-49, 112-546, 112-547.
[261] Deed Books 29-110, 221; 60-56; 28-105; 68-549; 90-14; 720187; 90-14; 93-198; 111-445; 113-203; 119-33.

GRIGGS HOUSE, ROOT CELLAR, 1153-1155 GUNNELL ROAD. The question of what makes a folksy old turn of the last century house wonderful has been answered by Dorothy Stuard, who, along with her sister and next-door neighbor Carol Wagoner chose to continue living in a house meeting that description. Dorothy, collector of antiques and artifacts from a variety of ancient and not so ancient sources, found living in the three-bay one and one-half story frame house with a brick tooled chimney and milled porch posts – and an impressive stone-faced root cellar in the back yard -- an exciting adventure.[262]

Figure 188. Moody-Morris house has log component.

This delightful house is on a farm bought by William Griggs in 1894 from N.C. Sharon and Clinton Barnhill and in 1893 and 1894 from George H. Williamson and James H. Williamson. In 1894 Sharon sold G. Sharon, Maria Sharon, Maria J. Cox, and George W. Williamson a sixteen-foot passway leading from the Muddy Ford and Finnell Road. Kyle Ramey sold the farm in 1973 to Hubert and Carol Wagoner. He purchased the fifty-one acres along with the passway in 1968 for $14,500.[263]

Figure 189. Dorothy Stuard and the Griggs house and its outbuilding were the perfect match.

MOODY-MORRIS HOUSE, 933 MORRIS ROAD. What more could one wish for rural living than a preserved rambling farmhouse with a log component, beautifully positioned within a pleasant tree shaded lawn on a quiet country road, its antiquity handsomely preserved -- and a host of stories to tell?

Anchoring this pastoral piece of land is a log room served by a large stone chimney that served the ancient fireplace's accommodation for cooking. After its 1875 purchase by John Morris, the log section became an appendage to an impressive two story house that served various members of the Morris family until 1976.

---

[262] Deed Book 122-193.
[263] Deed Books 29-221, 72-187, 93-120, 107-168, 122-193.

William P. Morris, who represented northern Scott County on the fiscal court, and his wife, who explained to this writer years ago the story of gold purportedly hidden in the yard, were the last members of the Morris family to own the property.[264]

The log wing relates to the settlement period family of Thomas and Elizabeth Moody. Thomas Moody died in 1846. As in so many cases in Kentucky's earlier years, before the advent of the 1891 Kentucky Constitution that paved the way for women to have equality as property owners with their husbands, his wife Elizabeth received the typical life estate in the home place and fifty acres. Her husband's will provided that after her death the family's land was to be sold and divided between his two grandchildren, Elizabeth Moody and William Henry Moody, heirs of the late Heroway, also known as Henry, Moody. Other heirs were Thomas, John, Molly Hinton, and William.[265] William Moody continued to live in the home. He was listed in the 1850 census as a farmer, sixty-nine years of age, with $6,675 in real estate – a goodly sum for that time. His household consisted of son Joseph, listed as having no occupation, daughter Martha, and her husband Stanley. Near the time of William's death, in 1859, the census taker cited him as a chair maker.

Joseph was beset by a host of personal problems. In 1843 he married Cynthia Johnson, a neighbor and daughter of William Johnson, and in 1846 they became the parents of James William Moody. Also in 1846, Cynthia filed for divorce, charging cruel, inhuman, life-threatening treatment, and abandonment for one year. Summonses to locate Moody were served in 1846 and 1847. The petition was stricken from the record in November 1849 and no further record of a divorce in Scott County was found. Since Cynthia Moody and her son were not listed in the 1850 census as members of the household of her father-in-law, the estrangement must have continued.[266]

On January 25, 1859, William Moody was murdered. Neighbor J.W. Williamson testified that he came to Moody's house, found the door fastened, called to Joseph Moody, who "came and opened the door." The elder Moody was lying with his feet toward the fire, his feet and clothing badly burned. His son Joseph backed toward "three guns in the corner." Other neighbors arrived, including Joseph Gunnell, who after a scuffle and assisted by another neighbor, Richard Williamson, removed the guns. Williamson, in the ensuing coroner's inquest report, stated that one gun still "had a load in it" and that "one was badly bent." A piece of a gun lying near William Moody's body was covered with blood. Gunnell told how he was forced to knock Joseph Moody to the floor, hitting him with one of the guns. The neighbors tied Moody "as he showed signs of being dangerous." Reuben Morris reported that early in the morning, Williamson had come to his house to tell him that William Moody was murdered. When he went to the house, he reported, Joseph Moody let him in. He said, "Joseph Moody seemed perfectly wild" when knocked down by Gunnell. Dr. Barkley testified that the blow on the head, which fractured the skull about three inches and caused the death, was done with a hard piece of iron. Coroner Granville Clackner noted that loads of the two guns had been fired into different parts of the room, one hitting a desk and the other striking the floor.[267]

The settling of William Moody's estate progressed in the face of attempts to have Joseph Moody declared a lunatic. When the division of his father's lands was made in March 1859, Joseph Moody received "lot number one" containing thirty-three and one-half acres. Others receiving land were Jerry Powers' heirs, 49 and one-half acres; Martha Stanley, thirty-seven acres; Mary and Hugh Bailey, fifty-two acres; William Parker heirs, 40.5

---

[264] Deed Book 132-40, William P. Morris to Marion A. and Judy G. Cox.
[265] Will Book U-300.
[266] Scott County Marriage Register #485; Will Book U-300; Scott County Circuit Court, divorce petition of Cynthia Moody, Circuit Court Order Book 21-67.
[267] "Inquest upon the body of William Moody at 5:00 p.m. 25 Jan. by G.F. Clackner, Coroner of Scott Co." Copy provided by Moody descendants, in files of author.

Figure 191. Mantelpiece in older section of Moody-Morris house.

Figure 190. Decorated stairwell of the Moody-Morris house.

acres; Dorcas Jane and William Johnson; Elizabeth Barnett, ninety-three and one-fourth acres; and Lewis Moody, 82 and one-half acres. In the division of slaves Joseph received Kitty Ann, "valued at "$900."[268]

In the November term of Scott Circuit Court, a jury of twelve declared Joseph Moody a lunatic, explaining "that he had become of unsound mind since his birth by the intemperate use of intoxicating liquors persisting for many years. . . at times he is capable of laboring, at times not." William F. Johnson was appointed trustee and L. Madden as surety. In November William F. Johnson asked to be released as committee and Joseph Gregg was appointed with Henry Edmondson as security. On May 18, 1852 a second jury found that Moody was "incapable of attending to his business." His unhappy life ended in 1875, at which time his son James William Moody became administrator of his father's estate.[269]

It would have been during this period that the legend of the Moody buried gold was given birth. The story persisted that a member of the Moody family, probably Joseph, made his home in a cabin in the yard. One day, Moody emptied a gunnysack containing gold on the floor and announced that he was going to take it to town to put it in a bank. Two hours later – ostensibly not enough time to go to town and back – he reported that he had deposited the gold. Others were certain that he had buried the gold, leading to intermittent attempts among would be gold diggers to pursue that rumor. Years later, when the Morrises were remodeling the porch, they found gold pieces, that discovery resurrecting the gossip.

On March 7, 1875, James W. Moody, then living in Illinois, sold his grandfather's house to John Morris, along with lot number one from the William Moody estate. Morris expanded the size of the farm with eight acres bought in 1865 from Charles Williamson and the Moody tract, thirty acres bought in 1874 from J.N. Johnson, ninety-six acres bought for $1,900 from Thomas H. Morris in 1894, seven and one-half acres from J.M. Fleming in 1895, and nine acres from William Gallahue in 1896.[270]

Morris died in 1902 with an estate that included 213 acres. He left his wife Annie E. a life estate with remainder to his children. In 1924, heirs C.T. and Stella Morris, Preston and Nannie Morris, Emma and H.E. Hurst, and Mary E. and H.C. Fields, sold the property to W.T. Morris, from whom William P. Morris inherited it. In 1970 Morris sold the farm of 155.613 acres (thirty-three acres having been sold to J.W. Robertson) to Marion A. and Judy G. Cox for $90,000.[271]

Bryan T. and Kimberly G. Sageser purchased the house and its 5.68 acre lot in 1995 from Douglas R. and Sandra S. Morrison. During the wedding of Katelyn and Justin Martin, the historic stairway in the house, pictured in this essay, was bedecked with early summer elegance.[272]

---

[268] Will Book N-182-192; Order Book H-226.
[269] Scott County Circuit Court Order Books 25-48, 26-102; Will Book N-182.
[270] Deed Books 7-498; 13-180; 15-246; 13-374, 375; 30-280; Will Book N-182.
[271] Will Books N-182, T-284, Y-322, 2-15; Deed Books 48-115, 53-415, 113-453, 132-40.
[272] Deed Book 212-414.

Hinton Properties, Hinton Cemetery Road

George W. and Dora D. Hinton House, Hinton Cemetery Road. A wonderful setting for a farmhouse and its related agricultural buildings is the crossroads setting for the two-story house accented with a central gable on the main façade's roofline. The dwelling, referenced as "McKinney house," was earlier the home of George W. and Nora D. Hinton, who acquired this piece of farm country from the estate of the family's patriarch and matriarch, William and Sarah Hinton.[273]

Figure 193. Cemetery across road from Fields-Houston house.

Figure 192. Elversia Fields and Fannie Houston house.

Located near Turkeyfoot on the Hinton Cemetery Road at its intersection with the Davis-Turkeyfoot Road are a comfortable rural dwelling on 108.474 acres and a small cemetery measuring seventeen by twenty-five feet. Ricky and Deborah Thompson purchased this property in 1995. Fred E. and Mary E. Sams bought it in 1993 from Chester McKinney, who acquired it in 1961 from Lottie Hinton Munson and other heirs of the George W. Hintons. In 1878 Mandeville Hinton sold George W. Hinton ninety-one and 115 acres. In 1892 the Hinton family estate matter resulted in the allocation to G.W. Hinton of 115 acres or lot number ten of the William and Sarah Hinton lands. The 1892 grantors included James W. Hinton, Nannie and Henry Tucker, John A. Hinton, Aletha and John Holland, Laura and John L. Conner, F.F. Hinton, Martha and John Noel, and Richard Hinton. In 1894 Mandeville and Louisa Hinton sold George W. Hinton seventy-five acres of the dower of Sarah Hinton.[274]

Houston House, 539 Hinton Cemetery Road. The Houston family has long been in command of the pastoral setting of the home across the road from Hinton cemetery on Hinton Cemetery Road. The house was built circa 1910 by Fannie C. and W.L. Houston. Dorothy E. Houston deeded the property that included the three bay two story dwelling with a central gable in 1991 to Kenneth O. and Shirley Houston on terms of love and affection. At the time of the early deeds, boundary

Figure 194. Historic Hinton Cemetery on Hinton Road.

---

[273] Deed Books 212-092, 215-718, 132-627, 200-428.
[274] Deed Books 91-61, 56-382, 27-397, 16-359, 28-437, 49-396, 11-271, 21-97.

properties were owned by Henry Fields, J.T. Williamson, Frank Giles, and the road known as Hinton Turnpike. The cemetery related to this house is located behind the house.[275]

Fannie C. Houston died in 1926, leaving four sons – Paul, thirty; Omera, twenty-six; Harry, twenty-four; and James, seventeen. Between 1899 and 1910 Elversia Fields deeded to Fannie, and in 1910, her husband, W.L. Houston, a fourteen acres two rods property described as located on the Muddy Ford Road. In 1933 Paul Houston transferred title to brothers Omera and Harry L. Houston his one-sixth interest in the fifty-five acres that Mrs. Houston deeded to Kenneth O. and Shirley Houston.[276]

Double Culvert and Luke Roads

Extending northwest from Turkeyfoot to junction with the Cincinnati Road opposite the northern end of Burton-Biddle Road is Double Culvert Road, so named, as related by the Vallandingham family's Betty Carol Kelly, because of the two culverts under the road near its western terminus. The name may have a double meaning if one considers as culverts the two beautifully laid stone-faced tunnels passing under Cincinnati Southern Railway, one on Double Culvert Road and the other nearby on Luke Road. Double Culvert is a short road with an interesting history and interesting landmarks. In its early days it bore the ambiguous name of "Turkeyfoot Road," though it was one of several roads leading into the village and environs that we know as Turkeyfoot. Its present era is dimmed by its role as the route to a landfill that serves a large area.

Figure 195. Older house on Double Culvert Road may relate to William Griffith.

338 Double Culvert Road. An aluminum sided three bay square dwelling with two one story wings and an ell, all on block foundations and shaded by a huge tree, stands near the village of Turkeyfoot. Now occupying 3.43 acres of the host farm, the dwelling was sold to Dennis R. and Carol A. Minter in 1988 by Aetna Casualty Company. This property is located near the designation of "W. Griffeth" on the 1879 map. Thomas E. Cooper and Rebecca S. Walker have owned the property since 1991.[277]

Dr. J.W. and Alice Baird House, 1050 Luke Pike. In 1907 J. Polk and Mary Fields sold Sadieville's Dr. J.W. Baird and his wife Alice 51.75 acres on Big Eagle Creek for $2,000. Boundaries included the lands of R.H. McCabe, Lavina Neale, David Mulberry, and Sallie Paxton. Fields acquired the property as part of tracts of seventy-five and ninety-six acres in 1877 from J.W. Fields, the latter having been part of the dower allotment to Gabriella Fields from the estate of her husband Zephaniah Fields.

Dr. Baird, or his wife Alice, an important property owner in her own right, can be presumed to have been responsible for having the house at this location built, an impressive front gabled dwelling with a lattice trimmed gable. The house is one of northern Scott County's most interesting early twentieth century homes. There are graceful brackets adorning the tapered posts at their connection with the soffit. A shed roof porch shelters the five

---

[275] Deed Book 192-123. The year 1910 is cited in Property Valuation Administrator (PVA) records.
[276] Deed Books 60-129; 37-43; 41-464, 378.
[277] Deed Books 196-286, 190-077, 201-263, 362-256; 385-484; Map of Scott County, 1879.

bays that include a wide central bay and paired end bays. Remaining early fenestration is typical of the Arts and Crafts era of the early twentieth century. The door in the second bay has an historic screen. Railed wooden stairs lead from the lawn to the front porch. A low porch railing extends between the square balusters. This property was sold in 2002 by Josephine Readall to Jeffrey S. and Joyce L. Jackson.

In 1945 Oscar G. Kitchen purchased the 107.5-acre farm for forty-five dollars an acre from the Baird heirs: Elizabeth Griffith and L.C. Baird, James L. Baird, and Griffith and Virginia Baird. Kitchen and his wife Eva shortly afterward sold the farm to H.H. and Nancy Rankin, from whom the Kitchens bought it in 1947. They owned it until 1951 when they sold the 124 acres to June Gayle Simpson, Jr. Clyde and Carol Covington bought it in 1967, selling it in 1982 to Allen and Charlotte Ison, who sold the house and 5.4 acres in 1999 to Sharlene and William J. Cope. Dr. Baird is further discussed

Figure 196. J.L. Luke house ruin provides shelter for modern Charolais herd.

in the chapter about Sadieville. His devotion to Sadieville and the area around it and that of the community to him are legend.[278]

SOWERS-GILES HOUSE, 1075 DOUBLE CULVERT ROAD. A basic two door house with a roof conformation of Cape Cod proportion and the setting relate to early William Hinton family origin. It was part of the William Hinton lands divided in 1892 because of the legal action of L.B. Hinton versus H.M. Hinton and others. In 1945 Kenneth A. and Dorothy K. Hinton sold 106 acres to Fred and Ellen Sowers. In 2001 Bonnie Jean Lugar, Charlene Cheatham, and Carlene and Danny Perkins transferred title to the Ralph C. Giles Trust.[279]

LUKE FAMILY PROPERTIES

J.L. Luke's ownership of the Eagle Creek lands reached by a northerly extension of the Double Culvert Pike became the reason for redesignation of the road toward the end of the nineteenth century when most county roads took the names they presently bear.

Luke, who had a residence in 1879 on this road, as indicated on the Beers & Lanagan map of that date, purchased an accumulated 651 acres in four tracts from Dr. John E. Pack in 1923. Luke paid $23,000 for the acreage. Dr. Pack, who is also shown with a residence on the future Luke Pike in 1879,

Figure 197. Alice Baird and her husband Dr. J.W. Baird were owners of the Luke Pike property.

---

[278] Deed Books 16-41, 86-628, 38-446, 70-158, 70-232, 73-97, 77-585.
[279] Deed Books 27-404, 69-450, 260-652, 282-542.

inherited it from his father, Richard E. Pack. The land that Luke acquired from Pack extended from the Dixie Highway (variously called Cincinnati Road, Dry Ridge Road, and later U.S. 25) and had as listed boundaries the lands of Charlie Thompson, George Vallandingham, Leonard Griffith, Dave Griffith, Southern Railroad, W.T. Hinton, Nannie Tucker, Webb, and L. Price.

In 1926 Luke sold Kendall and Lydia Jones 39.5 acres, "part of the smaller tract." Jones may have been the original owner of the two-story house,. It had several owners prior to its sale by the Henry Evans estate in 1998 to Neal Marshall. Those owners included Jesse B. and Nora Lee Stuard, 1952-1954; Wallace and Betty Courtney, 1952-1956; and Henry C. and Henrietta Evans and their family, 1956 to 1998.

PACK-LUKE HOUSE, 576 LUKE PIKE. The property designated as a residence of Dr. John E. Pack on the 1879 map and part of the parcel deeded to J.L. Luke by Pack in 1923 is a large two story frame house standing near one of the two railroad tunnel underpasses that are the defining landmarks of this area. The house has fireplaces on the interior parlors flanking the walls of the central passage, somewhat typical of the Italianate dwellings of the nineteenth century. Earlier porch supports were turned posts, which have been replaced by the present square posts. The house and its outbuildings and agricultural complex are owned today by Danny R. and Myrl Farmer, whose title relates to a twelve-acre portion of the earlier nearly three hundred acre tract farm that Gilmore N. and Josephine T. Nunn sold to Ralph M. Cooper in 1967. The accumulated acreage of approximately 292 acres lay on both sides of the Luke Pike.[280]

Figure 198. Pack-Luke house on Luke Pike.

Tracts of approximately 109 acres, 115 acres, and sixty-eight acres define the farm as sold in 1967 by the Nunns to Cooper. The 11- acre portion of the original Lewellyn Luke lands was purchased by all-over-Scott County landowner Leander Risk and his wife Kittie in 1896 from J.L. Luke for approximately twelve dollars an acre. The Risks sold this property in 1900 to J.M. Webb, who also purchased sixty-eight acres of the estate in 1919 from S.L. Hutchcraft, who had just acquired it from Willie Hinton, whose title came from the William Hinton 1919 division. Webb paid about forty-two dollars an acre for the land. Finally, in 1925, Elar Webb, Webb's widow sold that portion of the farm to E.S. and Dixie Zeysing. In 1930 the Zeysing heirs, Richard Zeysing, and Lucy and her husband W.A. Thompson, jointly became owners of the other two tracts, which they sold to John and Frances Mefford in 1961 and which the Meffords sold to the Nunns in 1963.[281]

---

[280] Deed Books 135-91, 105-209, 53-275.
[281] Acreage given allows for deductions of the portions of the larger tracts sold to Cincinnati Southern Railroad. Deed Books 53-275, 50-143, 49-33, 40-28, 59-566, 90-344, 93-499, 57-236, 105-209, 135-91; Will Books 2-326, W-385.

Figure 200. Larger house on Luke-Swinford farm.

Figure 199. Older house on Luke-Swinford farm.

LUKE-SWINFORD HISTORIC HOUSE RUIN AND HOUSE, 711 LUKE PIKE. One of two Luke Pike ruins, a relatively large two-story log house occupying a stone foundation on the upper end of the road, stood on the fifty acres sold in 1972 by Roger E. and Opal S. Stephens to Ron W. and Linda Lacy, the present owners. Stephens acquired the farm in 1970 from Edward T. and Etta R. Swinford, whose source was James W. Swinford in 1954. J.L. and Laura Luke sold 14.95 acres in 1924 to Raymond Swinford that was part of Luke's earlier purchase from J.E. Pack. Part of the land also came from W.H. Hall. [282] The second house is three bays wide and two stories tall.

GRIFFITH HOUSE, 213 LUKE PIKE. A nicely detailed three bay one and one-half story house is central to the 24.02-acre farm that George W. and Debra A. Cornett sold in 2007 to James T. Blankenship. The Cornetts purchased it in 1996 from William S. and Betty M. Pribble, owners since 1978. In 1873 Thomas and Nancy L. Griffith deeded one hundred acres on love and affection terms to H. Bascom Griffith. The younger Griffith purchased ten acres three rods in 1890 from J.L. and Laura Luke for $188, seventy-five acres at fifty dollars an acre in 1897 from J.L. Luke, and 102 acres seven poles in 1902 for $3,060 from Henry Bishop. Griffith died in 1914, leaving the property to D.T. Griffith, who deeded it to Addie Penn in 1936. Mrs. Penn died in 1953, her heirs selling the house and one hundred acres to G. Bedford and Helen Brown for $8,800. In 1959 the farm passed from Griffith family connections when the Browns sold it to Belt Brashear for $8,800. Brashear and his wife Louise took a loss in 1959 when they sold the property to Elkhorn Beagle Club for $6,050. The club sold the farm in 1967 to C.L. and Martha Oliver, the name of the road then being Sadieville-Turkeyfoot Road. The Olivers subdivided the property, selling the smaller parcel to the Pribbles. The three bay house has a stone foundation and a half upper story.[283]

Figure 201. House deeded by Thomas and Nancy Griffith to H. Bascom Griffith in 1873.

---

[282] Deed Books 119-240, 112-255, 81-7, 50-82, 49-33, 53-539.
[283] Deed Books 34-443, 20-268, 37-71, 31-568, 35-218, 12-234, 61-68, 80-217, 81-78, 85-134, 88-72, 105-276, 138-591, 218-489; Will Book U-205.

Dividing Ridge Road, North

John Kitchen House, 159 North Dividing Ridge Road.
In 1969 Zoney Soard, a partner in building and restoration with his brother Oney Soard, sold one of Scott County's most picturesque early houses, a four-bay house with a stone shouldered chimney to Chester and Opal Dean Webb, the present owners. Zoney and Mary Soard acquired it in 1968 from Charles and Mary Frances Hutchinson.

John Kitchen purchased 26 ¼ acres in 1869 from James Stucker for $660. The property was described as the Elizabeth Peak tract. In 1871 James E. Cantrill, master commissioner, sold 137 acres one rod thirty poles to Kitchen, with twenty dollars per acre to be paid to the heirs of O.P. Evans, James Stucker, and James L. Adams.[284]

In 1907 Mary Kitchen, widow of John Kitchen and James H. and Nannie Kitchen, deeded the property to Mary Adams and Alice Davis, describing 94 ¾ acres as the home tract, and thirty-two acres one rod three poles as the May tract. The Kitchen family owned it until 1934 when it was bought by J.C. and Harriet Ann Ginn. The road description was the Straight Fork and Twin Creek and Beard's Church Pike and the Cynthiana and Sadieville Pike.[285]

Figure 202. Historic log house owned in earlier years by John Kitchen.

---

[284] Deed Books 24-81, 10-47, 11-222.
[285] Deed Books 38-590, 61-60, 53-122.

Chapter 4
East Central Scott County

Soils in the central belt of Northeast Scott County are very much like those of the southern region, as transition from the Inner Bluegrass Maury McAfee soils underlain with the Middle Ordovician's calcium-magnesium-phosphorous mineral wealth is characteristic. Many of the resources also are of similar strength and character.

Oxford-Muddy Ford Road

The Nichols-Juett Properties. A stretch of farms on the east side of the southern portion of the section on KY 922 vernacularly known as Muddy Ford Road includes farmsteads and farmhouses of members of the family of William T. Juett and his wife Margaret Lou "Maggie" Juett, a daughter of William and Julia A. Nichols. The Nicholses preceded the Juetts as owners of much of this extended sequence of farms. On the west side of the road is Boydtown, earlier known as Boydville, an African American community, that together with the African American Cranetown, provided homes for the post-emancipation community. Boydtown, which falls within the Lowell-Nicholson soils belt, is discussed, along with its Delaplain Road neighbor Cranetown, in the chapter on rural African American communities.

In 1862 William Nichols gave his wife Julia Ann Nichols the eighty-acre home farm with their dwelling, it being "part of the land conveyed to me by William H. Salyers" in 1860. The deed described the property as having as boundaries the Muddy Ford and the Holdens [sic] Church roads as boundaries. Consideration for the transaction was land in Nicholas County conveyed to Mrs. Nichols by Robert E. Miller. Others transferring land to Nichols included Sarah A. and George R. Martin of Carlisle and John A. and Sarah E. Nichols of Bourbon County. In 1884 William Nichols sold W.T. Juett seven acres of the larger Nichols farm. Juett died in 1919, leaving his wife Maggie Lou a life estate in the home place. Son Carl Hendricks Juett was to receive $2,000 toward purchase of a home. After Juett's wife's death, the property was to be divided among the other children – Fred L. Juett, Ward E. Juett, Nellie Juett Williamson, Edna Juett, and Mabel Juett Crenshaw, all for life with remainder to their children.[286]

W.T. Juett and his brother Hugh Frank Juett also owned adjoining lots in Oxford, and in 1880 Hugh Frank and Helen M. Juett sold W.T. Juett for $350 property on the Leesburg Road occupied by John H. Cannon. The deed was described as having been willed by their father Joseph Juett "to our mother Mary A. Cannon, formerly his widow, who married John H. Cannon."[287]

Sherritt House, 4511 Muddy Ford Road. In 1921 Maggie Lou Juett, widow of W.T. Juett, and her other children deeded to their daughter Edna Juett Sherritt the southernmost fifty-five acres of the family spread, designated on the plat of her husband's estate as lot number one. Mrs. Sherritt was to own the property over her lifetime with remainder to her children.

In 1938 Fred G. Sherritt sold the farm to daughter Effie, who married James J. Hall. Effie Hall

Figure 203. Edna Juett Sherritt bungalow on Muddy Ford Road.

---

[286] Deed Books 6-65, 5-242, 38-626, 25-259, 23-97, 24-383; Will Book U-400, 334.
[287] Map of Scott County, 1879; Deed Book 18-12.

died in 1953 and her husband in 1955, leaving five children – Veda Mae Steger of Lexington, James W. Hall of Georgetown, Maggie H. Spradling of Georgetown, Ruth H. Lacefield of Midway, and Mary Elizabeth Patton of Dayton. In 1968 James W. Hall's widow, Betsy Osborne Hall, transferred her title in the farm to James Cary and Janice R. Hall and Margaret Ann and Jack Cook. In 1982 they sold the house and 1.6 acres to Jason J. Gant, and in 1990 Gant and his wife Jo Shirley sold the property to Charles E. and Colette S. Ralph. The dwelling is a bungalow with a block foundation and a central door flanked by double windows. A two light extended dormer with a shed roof is central to the upper level.[288]

EFFIE JUETT HALL HOUSE, 4643 MUDDY FORD ROAD. The fifty-five-acre lot number two of the Nichols-Juett 300 acre spread includes a large pond and an older house that has a stone foundation, two bays on the downstairs level, and a centered bay on the second floor. The house has an end chimney and an ell. It was allotted to Effie Juett Hall by her mother, Maggie Lou Nichols Juett, daughter of William Nichols, and appears to have an edge of antiquity over the other neighborhood dwellings, with the possible exception of the log house on the north end of the family farms owned today by Melissa Johnson. The other Nichols children included Sarah A. Martin, John A. Nichols, Margaret L. "Maggie Lou" Juett, Lewis H. Nichols, and Jane F. Hendricks.[289]

Figure 204. Effie Juett Hall's house is one of the older dwellings of the Juett spread.

In 1880 for $350 Hugh Frank Juett and his wife Helen M. Juett sold to W.T. Juett his interest in a farmland tract on Cynthiana Road occupied by John H. Cannon. The property came to them through the will of their father, Josephus Juett, to their mother, Mary A. Cannon, Josephus Juett's widow and subsequently wife of John H. Cannon.[290]

In 1956 Veda Mae Steger, J.W. and Betsy O. Hall, Ruth H. and Lester Lacefield, and Mary Elizabeth and Henry Patton, for $10,450, deeded the house and the attendant fifty-five acres to Margaret H. and Thomas S. Spradling. The Spradlings left the property to James Cary Hall. A reference to the peach orchard as a boundary is included in the 1956 deed, and a pond is shown on the map. A prominent feature behind the house is a red oak tree (pictured at the right), said to be 200 years old. Claude and Carolyn Lancaster, who acquired the property in 1989, sold the house and 5.024 acres to Debra Faye Woolums. W.R. Bailey and Laura M. Wright, who purchased it in 1998, sold it to Candise A. Henderazaka in 1999.[291]

WILLIAM T. JUETT HOUSE, 4671 AND 4673 MUDDY FORD ROAD. Stellar among the Nichols-Juett dwellings is the log house sold by the Nichols-Juett heirs in 1966 to Elroy S. and Ellen McKinney Mallard. Mallard was president and owner of Georgetown's Mallard Pencil Company,

Figure 205. The red oak tree on the lawn of the Effie Juett Hall house is said to be two centuries old.

---

[288] Deed Books 51-402, 63-301, 83-548, 108-601, 153-170, 184-643; Will Books Y-199, X-195.
[289] Deed Books 83-549, 6-65, 5-242, and 38-626.
[290] Deed Books 18-12.
[291] Deed Books 83-549, 179-180, 200-706, 232-487, and 245-566.

established during World War II and one of the city's earliest contributions to international industry. This dwelling is understood to have been a home of the William T. Juett family. Juett bought it in 1881 from John E. Snell, who acquired it in 1878 from William N. Atkins. Atkins purchased it from Adam J. Miller in 1850. Miller's source was Cary A. Ward, who also owned several pieces of property between Oxford and Muddy Ford.[292]

The nearly overwhelming complexity of William T. Juett's will became apparent during the 1966 sale of his farm to the Mallards. To explain the title exchange, Harriett C. Juett provided the court an affidavit of descent explaining percentages of ownership of the long list of grantors. Juett had devised a life interest in each of six tracts of the farm to six of his children – Fred L. Juett, Ward E. Juett, Effie Juett Hall, Nellie Juett Williamson, Edna Juett Sherritt, and Mabel Juett Crenshaw, and fee interests to their children. In the event that any of the life tenants should die without children, the portion of the estate devised to that child was to be inherited by the various W.T. Juett heirs, that number also including the heirs of his son Carl H. Juett. As part of this inheritance pattern, Nellie Juett Williamson received two parcels, 44.75 acres that were sold and reinvested in 48.692 acres of which she was seven-ninths owner and her husband Raymond Williamson, two-ninths. She died in 1965 with no children. Two other Juett daughters, Edna Juett Sherritt and Mabel Crenshaw, also were childless. Living descendants participating in the sale included granddaughters Veda H. Steger, Ruth Lacefield, Betsy Patton, and Maggie Spradling, all with one-twentieth interest; great grandchildren James Cary Hall, Margaret Hall Cook, Amy Hall, Harriet C. Juett, and Sue Ward Juett, each with one-sixteenth interest; J.C. Juett and Alma Sue Juett with one-thirty-second interest; George W. Cottrell with one-sixteenth interest; Freddie Juett Arnold, one-fourth; Wardna J. Abernathy, Dr. Beverly Juett, and Curtis Juett, with one-sixteenth; and William T. Juett and Marilyn R. Juett, one-forty-eighth interest. Also provided was a list of deceased Juett family descendants.[293]

Figure 206. The stylish W.T. Juett log house became the home of the Elroy Mallard family in 1966.

The log dwelling is four bays wide and has a front roofline gable centered over an upstairs window and the centered front door. An earlier porch, probably added by the Juetts, was stylistically Arts and Crafts supported by tapered posts mounted on square brick piers. In the spirit of older dwellings, the house is served by an ell that contained the kitchen and possibly the dining room. The main block has end chimneys of stone and brick. A contemporary renovation replaced the porch's tapered post configuration with tall narrow examples.

---

[292] Bevins, *Selected Buildings*, 34-35.
[293] Deed Book 101-414.

Figure 207. Ward E. Juett house is a Masonite-sided bungalow on a stone foundation.

JUETT-COTTRELL HOUSE, 4865 MUDDY FORD ROAD. In 1921 Maggie Lou Juett and other family members deeded a life estate to the seventy acre lot number five of the W.T. Juett division to Ward E. Juett with remainder to his children. Juett expanded his holdings with a purchase of forty acres from Josephine Tucker Hall in 1941. In 1951 Ward E. and Sue Ward Juett, and Calvin Gillispie and Zorelda H. Juett deeded the two parcels to Emma Lou J. Cottrell, Harriet C. Juett, and Sue Ward Juett. Ward E. Juett died in 1954. In 1974 Harriet Juett and George W. and Linda N. Cottrell sold the property, minus five acres conveyed to Tammy Gregory, to Lewis L. and Anna S. Oliver. The Olivers sold the farm of 59.67 acres to Jeremy T. and Jacklyne A. Webb in 2003. The dwelling on this subdivision of the W.T. and Maggie Lou Juett spread is a masonite sided bungalow/Cape Cod cottage one and one-half stories tall on a stone foundation. The upper level is lighted by two gabled dormers.[294]

OLD TURKEYFOOT ROAD

INDIAN OIL REFINERY SITE, NORTH HAMILTON STREET/OLD TURKEYFOOT ROAD. The decade between 1905 and 1915 in Georgetown and Scott County was tumultuous, combative, economically hopeful, and distressing as Indiana based Indian Oil Refinery temporarily boomed on a just north of Georgetown site on North Elkhorn Creek. The 1911 *Encyclopedia Britannica* declared, "One of the largest independent oil refineries in the country (that of the Indian Refining Co.) is in Georgetown."[295]

Georgetown's brief role in oil refining was a significant though short lived cog in the wheel of America's response to the need for petroleum products for its rapidly changing industrial and transportation complex. Nestled within a peninsular bend of North Elkhorn Creek, Indian Refining Company was an outgrowth of events originating in the Indiana community of Asphaltum where twenty-three-year-old Richmond M. Levering established Indian Asphalt Company. Levering and his company yielded to pressure of the Georgetown Board of Trade to locate the refinery adjacent to the Cincinnati Southern crossing of North Elkhorn Creek near the site of the historic Prewitt-DeGaris Mill. By 1906 the Georgetown operation, with Levering as president, was refining crude oil and producing byproducts including asphalt, paraffin wax, paint, and axle grease.

---

[294] Deed Books 276-231, 126-483, 78-114, 66-114, 51-403; Will Book U-334.

[295] www.1911encyclopedia.org/Georgetown_Kentucky. The excerpt from *The 1911 Classic Encyclopedia Based on the 11th Edition of the Encyclopedia Britannica*, listed Georgetown's other manufactures as bricks, flour, ice, bagging, and hemp, and discusses "The Remarkable 'Royal Spring,' which rises near the centre of the city, furnishes about 200,000 gallons of water an hour for the city's water supply, and for power for the street railway and for various industries. . . " Successor titles for the firm included Indian Refining Company, Incorporated, Havoline Motor Oil (through 1962), The Texas Company/Texaco Inc. (through 1985); Company History Timeline, Compiled by Jim Hinds, Columbus, Indiana, March 2001, www.oldgas.com/info/texacohist.html

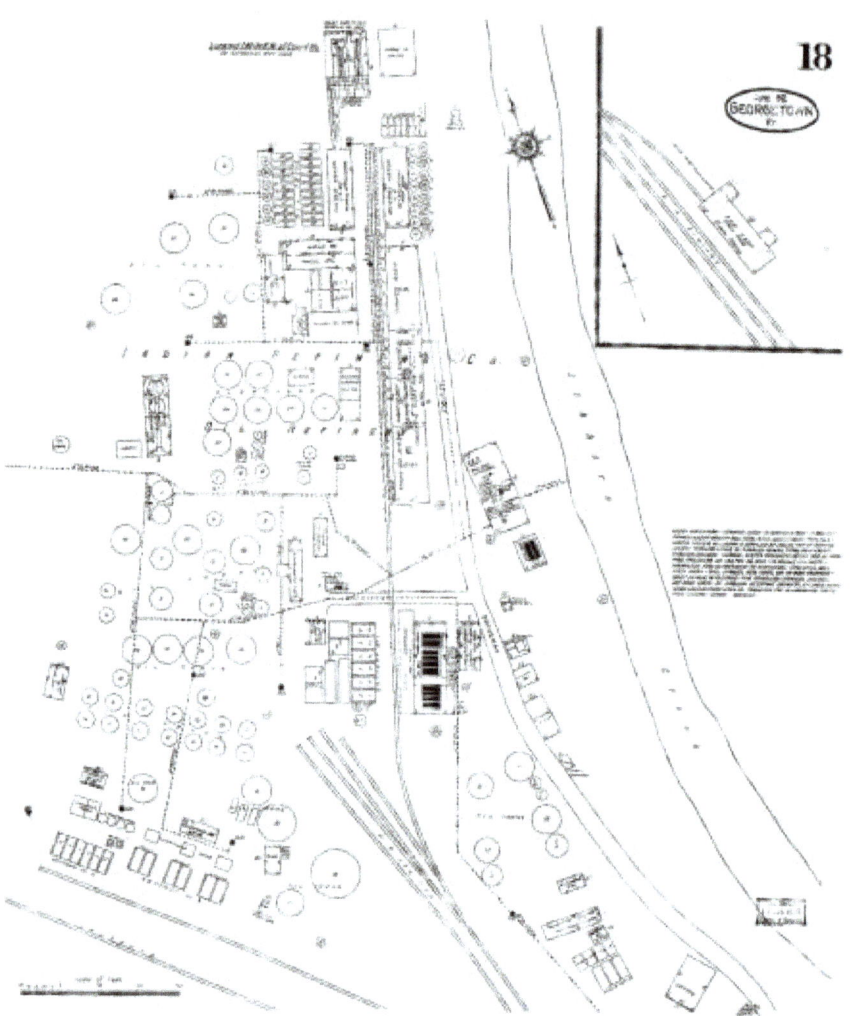

Figure 208. Sanborn map of Indian Oil Refinery recalls one of Georgetown's most exciting eras.

Joining Levering in the operation was his father, J. Mortimer Levering, the company's secretary. In 1907 Indian Refining's Lawrenceville, Illinois refinery became part of the complex.[296]

The Georgetown Board of Trade Commercial Club conducted a major public relations crusade to convince Levering that Georgetown was the right location for Indian Oil's refinery. George Viley Payne, developer of Payne's Addition subdivision immediately north of Georgetown, on March 8, 1905 sold 23.31 acres, excluding the creek, to Indian Asphalt Company. To this parcel, Indian Refining Company, having changed its name, in 1907, added purchases of 14.37 and 38.45 acres from Payne; this land had previously been part of sixty-seven acres acquired by Payne from John A. and Mary C. Gano who had inherited it in 1876 from Stephen F. and Mary Jane Gano. In November 1908, J.H., Mary Belle, and G.A. DeGaris sold Indian Refining 74.77 acres inherited from miller John DeGaris and extending to DeGaris Mill and West Oxford turnpikes, property included in the milling property acquired by the elder DeGaris in 1849 from Henry H. Prewitt. Through the next several years Indian Oil bought and sold various tracts, leaving parcels of 14.37 acres minus .528 acres and 38.45 acres, both conveyed on dissolution of the Georgetown operation to Swift, McNutt and Company, a Boston based demolition firm, in 1915. The Sanborn insurance map of the site as it appeared in 1912 is shown above.[297]

Accompanying Georgetown's euphoria over becoming a leader in the Kentucky and Midwest industrial complex was local drilling of oil wells, which along with spills from the plant frequently coated downstream North Elkhorn Creek with oil, contaminating creek banks, livestock water, and drinking water between Georgetown and Peak's Mill in Franklin County. By the end of 1908, threats of litigation and litigation itself were rampant. Joining industrial accidents punctuating the refinery's success was the competition. John D.

---

[296] Jim Hinds, "Indian Refining Company, Incorporated... Company History Timeline," November 14, 1904 to January 5, 1907, www.oldgas.com/info/texacohist.html
[297] Deed Books 38-415, 19-247, 14-425, Q-234; 39-330, 45-80. See also Deed Books 40-610; 44-57, 196, 199, 200.

Rockefeller's Standard Oil of Indiana ultimately maneuvered a change in railroad rates predicated on a base point system.[298]

Preceding Indian Oil's setting up shop just northeast of Georgetown was a crusade for commitments from property owners in the vicinity to locate and drill oil wells. On September 2, 1901, Scott County Oil & Development Company incorporated with capital stock of $20,000 and a goal "to develop mines for all sorts of minerals and to bore wells for petroleum and other oils and for natural gas, and to store and sell." Incorporators A.C. Cook, J.P. Jackson, J.R. Downing, John S. Montgomery, T.T. Hedger, Thomas Wolfe, and Victor Bradley promptly acquired leases from Joseph S. Rogers (125 acres), C.D. Powell (thirty acres), C. Barnhill (318 acres), R.S. Powell (100 acres), T.T. Hedger (260 acres), Buford Hall (3,200 acres), A.T. Glenn (330 acres), and J.S. Thurman (six and one-half acres). Additional positive response followed the location near Georgetown of Indian Refining.[299]

By the end of August 1906, "Every land owner for several miles have [sic] been approached with a view of securing a lease from them. It is the intention of Indian Refining Company to bore." Interestingly, in August, the company, deciding to drill on its own property ostensibly for water, struck oil. "The first show of oil was found on the land of the Oil Refining Company," reported the *Georgetown Times.* The strike yielded an eight barrel well. L.H. Sublett, a master plumber, put a pump on the well and he and Buford Hall set out to lease additional land in the area. By December, having purchased the Sublett-Hall lease, the company had 7,000 acres under lease for drilling. The *Times* mused in October that while the gasoline pumping apparatus was impressive, "it may prove merely a pocket." In the meantime, Elkhorn Creek was "thickly covered with oil for a considerable distance. It oozes from a fissure in the rocks."[300]

By early 1907 the former farmland sported new buildings, a concrete block plant, a concrete boiler room, foundations for three other buildings, railroad tracks, and a freight switch engine." The 1912 Sanborn Map series depicts a complex with 113 numbered oil tanks, oil pump houses, three battery complexes and condenser, coal bunkers, railroad sidings, a chemical laboratory and dining room with a high roof, an oil pump house, an alkali building, a receiving house, asphalt house, soap kettle house, an agitator building with whistle, an "I.E.P. Engine House," a wax house with two press rooms, a warehouse and press warehouse," a "chill room," a filter house, a barrel house, a car shop, machine shop, store room, great house, cooper

Figure 209. The Indian Oil Refinery office was redone for the home of James R. and Lily May Lewis.

---

[298] *Georgetown Times*, April 20, 1908.
[299] Scott County Articles of Incorporation Book 1, p. 160.
[300] *Georgetown Times*, August 29, September 5, October 17, November 14, 1906.

Figure 210. Rear elevation of Indian Oil Refinery office and an outbuilding.

shop, a system of pipes connecting the various tanks, and other sheds and small buildings.[301]

In 1908, though still operating the Georgetown refinery, Indian Oil moved its offices to Cincinnati and opened a small refinery near East St. Louis, Illinois. In 1909 the firm incorporated under New York laws and purchased the plant producing Havoline Oil, adding Havoline to the Lawrenceville refinery's line of products. In 1910, newly chartered to operate in Louisiana, the corporation opened a refinery in New Orleans. Changes in the chain of command included the death of J. Mortimer Levering in 1909 and the resignation in late 1913 and 1914 of Richmond M. Levering and several other senior officers. Though it closed the Georgetown and East St. Louis refineries in 1915, Indian Oil continued to grow and expand as an independent refinery of petroleum products. By 1931, as the Texaco brand assumed ascendancy in the petroleum industry, the Texas Corporation gained controlling interest in Indian Oil including rights to Havoline.[302]

Industrial accidents plagued Indian Refining's employees and even some visitors. One of the most dramatic incidents occurred when Charlie Mallory, a steam fitter, escaped death as he was fitting a pipe for a whistle in the boiler room. As Mallory got too close to a shaft, a screw caught his overalls and hurled him around at 250 revolutions a minute, shredding his clothing. Mallory threw his arm around an iron brace, which kept him from falling. He suffered serious bruises and a wound to his armpit. On May 13, Leon Anderson and J.J. Mobly received serious injuries from a bursting steam pipe.[303]

Georgetown was the envy of neighboring towns. Population boomed to 10,000 and plant employment grew to 350 persons. All, however, did not bode well. Oil leaks began to show up on Elkhorn, floating west past Georgetown, Great Crossings, Forks of Elkhorn, and Peak's Mill to Main Elkhorn and the Kentucky River. Water supplies and agriculture plainly suffered. In January 1908 the Franklin County grand jury indicted Indian Oil Company after hearing witnesses from Peak's Mill declare that "the surface of the creek is literally coated at times." The Franklin court came up with a fine of $10,000. Frankfort Distilling Company sued in federal court for an injunction and to seek damages. On May 13, 1908, the Scott County grand jury reluctantly issued indictments, declaring, "It is not the purpose of this Grand Jury to oppress this great institution. . . there can be no doubt that the waters of Elkhorn Creek . . . below the plant have been and are polluted by oil from said plant. We know that the company is the greatest source of revenue to the merchants as well as to the working classes; yet the farmers . . . are entitled to the protection guaranteed by law." The jurors, J.G. Shropshire, foreman, J.W. Jameson, J.C.B. Fightmaster, J.K. Foree, Beal Fightmaster, Stephen Gano, F.M. Fitzgerald, George H. Darnaby, W.B. Arnold, E.T. Fleming, G.A. Goddard, and R.L. Wright, gave the company until October "to correct and cure the evil that is being done."[304]

On May 9 Levering told the Board of Trade that nothing but pure water moved from the plant and that the presence of oil was due to accidents. He stressed that on one occasion a pipe broke, causing the loss of 350 barrels

---

[301] *Georgetown Times*, March 6, 1907; Sanborn Map, Georgetown, KY. June 1912.
[302] Jim Hinds, "Indian Refining Company, Incorporated . . . Company History Timeline," 1907 to January 14, 1931.
[303] *Georgetown Times*, April 20, 1908.
[304] *Georgetown Times*, April 20, 1908.

of oil, that the company had invested $240,000 in the plant, and had spent $56,000 in materials, supplies, and wages.[305]

At a mass meeting held at the courthouse, 800 persons signed a petition of support, recalling that Indian Refining had brought to the local railroad station a special train of freight cars daily and that the monthly freight bill was $32,000. Businessmen spoke for the plant, the nation's only independent oil company and one of the Commonwealth's largest employers with a payroll of $9,500. Realtor and developer J.W. Thacker said that property around the plant had advanced twenty-five percent, resulting in the construction of new buildings. "Every man felt the good effects of the payroll... the plant had made Georgetown what it is." J.W. Keller stated that "those injured were few compared to those who benefit." Commercial Club president G.H. Nunnelley queried, "What's the matter with Georgetown?" He commented that the community showed a lack of unity and of life. He explained that the company had bought two million dollars in oil wells in Illinois and that it would cost $1,500,000 to pipe oil here, and the same to relocate. Attorney J.M. Ford appealed to the court "to give the company a chance." J.C. Bradley offered a resolution that "practically everyone signed." Later that month the company hosted an open house, giving guests cakes of wax and small boxes of axle grease as they enjoyed a feast of burgoo, bread, ham, ice cream, and cake. By that time the refinery had an output of 3,000 barrels of oil a day. The work force totaled 350. J.R. Downing, credited for persuading Levering to come to Georgetown, pleaded for public support.[306]

Figure 211. Tower that survived the refinery's demolition.

The company appeared to be gaining control of the pollution and resultant public relations conflict when arch competitor Standard Oil of Indiana won a crucial trade war related to railroad rates. That action caused the local operation to wind down; by 1916 the Elkhorn refinery site was archaeology. Georgetown literally went into depression as hundreds of its citizens found themselves unemployed, new homes not paid for, and a large number of vacant lots, particularly in Payne's Addition.[307]

Closing of the plant brought to Georgetown the Swift-McNutt Building Wrecking demolition complex from Boston. The company was the largest such concern in New England, formed by consolidation of Swift Contracting Co. and Robert R. McNutt, Inc., two powerful demolition companies whose work extended from New England to "large contracts in Kentucky and other states in the Union." The firm employed "skilled foremen" and a "well organized sales department, giving a quick market for material," meeting conditions "no matter how difficult," and completing the work "with little delay and with safety to their employees and the general public." Swift-McNutt assured the owners of the property, the public, and their own employees that the firm had the financial capacity to file a bond of any amount. Completion of their work in Scott County focused on demolishing all but the foundations of the larger buildings, leaving the office and its outbuildings. Their success here added to their reputation of finding "a market for such material which would appear difficult to dispose of..." On June 13, 1916, less than a year after acquiring the plant's complicated acreage, Swift-McNutt sold the main 40.2 acres to J.D. Grover, R.C. Davis, and James Bradley. After selling the City of Georgetown 2.45 acres, the trio sold the remaining 37.75 acres to John and Nellie Bell, who in 1923 sold it to G.A. Hambrick. A master commissioner's sale in 1928 resulted in the purchase of the small farm with its dozens of foundations, earthworks,

---

[305] *Georgetown Times*, May 5, 9, 1908.
[306] *Georgetown Times*, May 5, 29, 1908.
[307] *The Lexington Leader*, April 25, 1915.

and the stylish company office building with a spectacular view of the creek to James R. Lewis and O.H. Prather for $4,530. The historic site then became the farm and home of Lewis and his wife Lily Ice Lewis; there they brought up their daughters and became established as breeders, trainers, and showers of the Tennessee Walking Horse and hunting dogs.[308]

Though James R. Lewis pursued several business ventures, his wife, Lily May Ice Lewis, born in 1907 in Louisville and a resident during early childhood of the Louisville Baptist Children's Home, was the star of the household. She brought new meaning to the Georgetown College student body and to the City of Georgetown beginning in the fall of 1923. She continued to be a brilliant star on the local setting until her passing. Many people recall her in her typical three-inch heels twice daily walking the distance between her home at the end of North Hamilton Street to the Bradley & Bradley law offices where she was legal secretary. She walked home for lunch, back to the office, and not infrequently added to the mix another trek to the public library. Unlike most walkers and runners who tend to be wary of dogs, "she made friends with the dogs," recalled daughter Joy Barlow. As the years passed, Mrs. Lewis spurned a cane but agreed to carry an umbrella, seemingly for shelter from the sun but essentially for support – "only if necessary." She sold the family car after her husband's death in 1976, eliminating that excuse for not walking. She trod the lengthy pathway until the age of ninety-three.

In 1924 Lily May received the college's freshman belle of the blue honors. She had already wowed Louisville by carrying off the lead in her high school senior class play. Dozens of potential beaux pursued her, but Georgetown's James R. Lewis, seven years her senior, was the successful one. At the end of her freshman year Lily May traveled to Akron to spend the summer with a friend. Jimmy got a job there in order that he could continue his pursuit. Ultimately she agreed to marry him only if the orphanage superintendent would grant approval to the marriage. To her surprise he agreed.

"I don't know of anyone who had more fun in life than they did," recalled daughter Joy Barlow "We had the most beautiful mother in the world," she said. Mrs. Lewis is also memorialized as the American Legion Post 24 Drum and Bugle Corps drum majorette in the photograph of the magnificently uniformed Georgetown corps, reproduced on the cover of Arcadia's 1998 Scott County pictorial history, along with the uniformed Corps members. Lewis, then Oldsmobile dealer, raised funds to outfit the corps, and served as drum major. The unit, organized in 1930, won the national Legion competition annually between 1932 and 1937. Mr. Lewis's integral role in the Legion evolved from service with the U.S. Seventh Cavalry in World War I, though he was only sixteen. "He grew up in that war," Joy said. Too old to serve in World War II, he equipped his own plane and patrolled the coast for the Civil Air Patrol.[309]

The Lewises were nationally known for breeding, training, and showing their Tennessee Walking Horses and bird dogs. Lewis was an avid hunter, and Joy recalls her mother declaring, "If you can't beat them, join them," as she became one of the sports' top hunters, equestrians, dog trainers, and shots. At one point the Lewis household had one hundred pups. Their dogs won national competitions year after year. The couple got into breeding, training, and showing horses in the 1940s or 1950s and won four national championships.

When Mrs. Lewis was in her nineties, though "ordered off horses years before," she had a farm employee saddle a horse for her to ride in the Horse Festival parade. Joy recalled looking up from the downtown booth where she was working to see her mother elegantly riding down the street. "She was so proud of herself," Joy said. The writer recalls Mrs. Lewis as one of the most stunning women she has known. Truly elegant, we all held her in great esteem.

---

[308] Deed Books 45-80, 49-482, 53-135, 58-282; Edwin M. Bacon, *The Book of Boston: Fifty Years' Recollections of the New England Metropolis* (Boston, 1916), as quoted on http://brickfrog.wordpress.com/2012/01/01/swift-mcnutt-co-building
[309] Ann Bolton Bevins, Frederick A. Johnston, and Lindsey Apple, *Images of America: Georgetown and Scott County* (Charleston, South Carolina, 1998), front cover, 2; discussion with Joy Barlow.

Joel Penn built the Lewises' barn. Today only vestiges of the buildings, tank supports, and refinery features remain on the site. Concern over ground contamination prevents the peninsular from development. The office building turned residence burned during the years after Mrs. Lewis's death. The farm's acreage has stories to share. Let's hope it can.

PREWITT-DEGARIS MILL, DEGARIS MILL ROAD. One of Scott County's first saw and grist mills was erected on North Elkhorn Creek by Elijah Craig and known as his "upper mill," his "lower mill" having been located near the mouth of Big Spring Branch. A bridge near the dam provided a crossing for the old Turkeyfoot Road. Other settlement period owners associated with the dam and mill site were Craig's son-in-law Josiah Pitts (1799) and entrepreneur Job Stevenson. In 1813 Stevenson sold the mill to Benjamin Stuart Chambers, and in 1813 Chambers sold it to Henry H. Prewitt. With his brother, Levi Prewitt, he expanded the acreage around the mill, and in 1859 sold it to John DeGaris, a carpenter who migrated from the Isle of Guernsey in 1831. In 1912 the DeGaris family permitted Indian Oil Refinery to dismantle the mill and recycle the rock. The dam has been rebuilt several times and provides a back-up water supply for the Georgetown Municipal Water and Sewer Service. The photo was provided by the J.G. Herring Collection, now the property of the Georgetown and Scott County Museum.[310]

Figure 212. Two older postcards' views of DeGaris Mill and the mill dam.

DELAPLAIN ROAD

N.W. HAMBRICK BUNGALOW, 656 DELAPLAIN ROAD. The one and one-half story bungalow of Norman W. Hambrick occupies a stone foundation. The porch is supported by long tapered posts and accompanied on its 10.69 acre setting by a barn and crib at the intersection of Delaplain and Sims roads. It was sold by Mary Lida and Jerry L. Kettelson of Pensacola, Florida, J.T. Conner, and Willard and Edna Conner in 1975 to William F. and Clara Jones for $37,000. The tract was part of the 40.9 acres and 39.8 acres piece of land deeded by Willard and Edna Naomi Conner to J.T. Conner and Willard and Edna Conner in 1952 for $30,800. Willard Conner purchased the same two tracts from Grace L. Risk Carlton in 1950. Mrs. Carlton acquired it for $10,900 from George and Sadie Gray in 1943. The second tract included .2 acres and scales in a scales lot owned in partnership with W.C. Graves. Gray bought the property, part of the land of N.W. Hambrick allotted to Lucy Hambrick, from the Hambrick heirs in 1929, Hambrick's title having come from Cora and Thomas Kelley and Wood Davenport in 1910. Hambrick was most likely the original owner of the bungalow and farm buildings.[311]

Figure 213. Norman Hambrick bungalow.

---

[310] Bevins, *Selected Buildings*, 261; Gaines 1, 17, 109; Perrin, 593.
[311] Deed Books 128-1; 79-546; 76-251; 67-550; 58-124; 41-518; 51-589, 143; 49-628; 28-220, 21-394.

Figure 214. Scott County's last county infirmary has become a comfortable family dwelling.

SCOTT COUNTY INFIRMARY/ "POOR HOUSE," 714 DELAPLAIN ROAD. A product of the late nineteenth to early twentieth century era when citizens and political leaders held to a premise that public buildings should speak to the character of the community that gives them inception and perpetuation, the Scott County Infirmary, vernacularly known as the "poor house" or the "poor farm," has stood since the early years of the twentieth century making such a statement.

"Most of the counties in the State pay little or no attention to provide homes for worthy unfortunate citizens, but such is not the case in Scott County," wrote historian B.O. Gaines in his volume two first published in 1904. He recalled the first poor house, purchased circa 1822, "but we cannot find either records or old citizens

Figure 216. County infirmary's smokehouse was another attractive feature of the operation.

Figure 215. Historic barn associated with county infirmary operation.

stating where it was located." In 1867 the county bought a 213-acre farm near Biddle; in 1903 Thomas Penn, former circuit clerk, bought it for $2,000. The second "poor farm" had several good houses, a recent one having cost the county about $2,500. There were also several other houses. It was well fenced and had an abundance of water. The timber had been cut and the ground "worked so long that it would not have raised black-eyed peas." The county furnished the keeper a house, gave him what he made off the place, and allowed him a ninety-dollar annual allowance fuel, food, and clothes for each of approximately twenty inmates. Among the keepers were Joshua Jones, Asa Southworth, Belfield Glass, W.R. Wright, Jack Adams, and William Adair.[312]

On October 27, 1902, T.T. Hedger sold Scott County Fiscal Court 179.43 acres at the intersection of Oxford and Kincaid Turnpike for $13,457. Boundaries were the land of Graves and James Sharp. Hedger had purchased the land between 1892 and 1894 from Dudley and Eliza Jane Cook (166 acres, $10,794) and J.M. and Annie M. Penn (13 acres, $400). The writer as a student at Georgetown College in the mid-1950s visited the home as part of a Sigma Kappa Sorority gerontology project, taking refreshments and visiting with the residents. The residents dressed in their best clothing for these occasions. The final years of the operation of this institution and others like it were brought about by expansion of the federal welfare system.[313]

The two main buildings on the farm in those days were the relatively posh Arts and Crafts style brick building, the residence for women, and a long wooden building of plain but neat design, for male residents. Residents, referred to as "inmates," were employed in chores such as housekeeping and farming.

The family of Lewis and Lillis Watson is responsible for the renovation of the property which has a resort-like appearance today. The Watsons bought the brick house and 7.84 acres in 1977 from Joe and Lois Ann Brueck, Brueck having purchased the 179.289-acre property from the fiscal court in 1973 for $173,910.33. By that time the deed description referred to the boundary roads as Delaplain and Sims. In 1998 Watson sold the tract to Robert Lewis Watson and George S. and Charmin Watson for $120,000, and in 2003 Robert Lewis and Mary L. Watson transferred their interest on terms of love and affection to George and Charmin Watson. The building consists of a two bay, two and one half story front gabled block, probably the keeper's dwelling, joined to a five bay two story classical revival addition, which served as the dormitory. A brick smokehouse with a pyramidal roof and shed-roofed wing stands in the yard. The barn in the adjacent field is a much added-to structure. The central gabled section is surrounded by a covered walkway. The front part of the barn's one-story section has a gable in the center.[314]

Prompting the 1973 sale was a need for a new location for the county fairgrounds and a park that would also provide a setting for 4-H and FFA and other agricultural events and light recreation. Enhancing the proposal was an offer by owner Mollie Graves, farmer, community leader, and longtime friend of the community, to sell the ninety acre tract lying near the high and junior high schools for $122,000, representing a generous discount for purposes of youth enhancement, a concern that she held. Additional public justification offered by county officials was the possibility of locating on the site a juvenile detention center, county jail, and county garage. The sale of the public property at auction was set for May 19. A neighbor of the proposed project, however, filed a complaint opposing the move, asking for a permanent injunction prohibiting the county from selling the former infirmary farm and investing in the new property. When the injunction was denied, the court rescheduled the sale date for July 21 and Ms. Graves extended the option until August 1. Circuit Judge Robert Hall Smith ruled that "the best interest of the county would be served by selling the said property and reinvesting the proceeds from the sale" and "that other land more suitable for public purposes [than the infirmary property] is available."[315]

---

[312] Gaines History 2, 173.
[313] Deed Books 27-301, 29-39.
[314] Deed Books 122-397, 137-188, 269-100, 277-189.
[315] *Georgetown Graphic,* March 29, June 17, June 24, July 5, 1973.

Meanwhile the fiscal court came up with a proposal to build an 8,000 square foot brick veneer building to be called Brooking Hall in honor of the county judge who was considered father of the plan. Its estimated cost was $160,000, the design to include an auditorium-gymnasium with stage, large kitchen, and restrooms. *Georgetown Graphic* editor Archie Frye joined local opposition to the community center, calling for limiting the park's activities to fair grounds, horse and cattle show facilities, and areas for croquet, tennis, baseball, and other outdoor sports. The proposed measure became a political issue, and in January the new fiscal court eliminated the previous court's public building objectives. Since that time the county garage and the extension office and its large meeting facility have joined the other park and fairgrounds activities.[316]

In time the park expanded to the other side of Long Lick Pike to another portion of the Graves agricultural expanse. In October 2002, the fiscal court acted on a proposal by county agent J.B. Hockensmith to name the park's walking trail in honor of Mollie Graves in recognition of her generous offer of the land for the park and the fact that "the land [was] farmed for many years by Mollie's grandparents, John B. and Mary Jane Graves, her parents Clarence O. and Ann Graves, and by Mollie." Mollie had long been a familiar figure as she worked with the cattle and oversaw the various farming activities.[317]

R. C. MUNTZ RESIDENCE, 892 DELAPLAIN ROAD. R.C. Muntz was one of Scott County's outstanding builders during the Arts and Crafts and Classical Revival building eras. His own home is an outstanding example of the Dutch Colonial Revival style and also of Muntz's ability as a designer and builder. The two story house has a gambrel roof with a full pent roof extending across the main façade, providing shelter for the centered entryway and flanking windows. A shouldered chimney is located on the east end. The wide plank siding has been replaced by green

Figure 217. R.C. Muntz house on Delaplain Road.

vinyl of similar pattern. Metal awnings shelter the various openings. The house is set well back from the road. In 1988 R.C. Muntz, Jr. and Coleen Faye Muntz sold the house and attendant 161.52-acre farm to Thomas G. and Sybil Wood and Kenneth L. and Sarah K. Ramsey. In 1995 Wood sold the Ramseys his interest in the property.[318]

Another well known known Muntz house is the R.W. Thompson house, also Dutch Colonial Revival, located on the Lexington Road, discussed in Volume III of this series.

ROBERT H./CRAWFORD MOORE HOUSE, 1136 DELAPLAIN PIKE. Near the log settlement period house of his father James Moore (1772-1849), Robert H. Moore and

Figure 218. R.H. and Crawford Moore house on Delaplain Road.

---

[316] Georgetown Graphic, Sept. 1, 1973.
[317] Memorandum to Scott County Fiscal Court, Scott County Fiscal Court, Georgetown & Scott County Museum, and Scott County Historical Society, October 2002.
[318] Deed Books 178-92, 209-746.

Figure 219. Annie T. Glenn, C.F. and Martha Glenn, and Remus Mason house.

his wife Nancy Jane, daughter of the Oxford area's James A. Risk, constructed a two story frame house in the Italianate style, the chimneys serving parlors on either side of the central passage. Stylistic features including the entryway with sidelights place it in the late nineteenth century. Robert Moore's brothers, Douglas and Samuel, were also farmers in the Oxford area. The property was inherited by Lavena Johnson, who died in 1948, leaving her husband Frank Johnson a life estate in the property, and after his death, it passed to their children in fee simple.[319]

In 1960 Robert Cannon deeded to Martha Lee Johnson four tracts including the twenty-three acres allotted to R.H. Moore in the division of Crawford Moore on the road then designated as Muddy Ford Road, the eleven acre tract allotted to W.C. Moore in the same division, the seven acre parcel designated for W.O. Moore, and an L-shaped tract on the east side of the Anderson Pike, leaving forty-eight acres of the parent tract. All four tracts were part of the 1935 conveyance from Belle Cannon to R.M. Cannon and part of the 1917 deed from James L. Carrick to Robert M. Cannon. Philip and Santana Perkins acquired the property in 2012.[320]

CARRICK-GLENN-MASON HOUSE, 1290 DELAPLAIN ROAD. A bungalow now occupying a block foundation dates to after 1901 when Sarah Risk partitioned her property to her daughters Annie T. Glenn and Mary Carrick. In 1943 C.F. and Martha Glenn and William and Lois Glenn sold the house and 119 acres to R.W. and Helen Thompson and B.A. Thompson. The property had as boundaries land owned by Murphy, Williams, and Shug Glenn. In 1945 Thompson sold the farm to Remus Mason, Sr., who farmed there until his death. In 1963 his widow, Martha Mason Inguls, his executor, and other heirs – Grace and Frank Black, Jesse and Thomas Ragland, Remus, Jr., and Betty Mason, Joe Mason, and Luther and Ann Nutter Mason, sold the farm in two tracts to William Gilbert and Carrie Hall Green. The Greens then sold their acreage to Luther Mason.[321]

Figure 220. Drawing of Valentine Rogers house on Sims Road by Edith Linn Clifton.

---

[319] "Robert Moore House," Ann Bolton Bevins, *Selected Buildings*, 106, quoting information provided by Mrs. Martha Johnson, late owner of the house. Will Book X-31. Martha L. Johnson, 91, widow of Eldyn Johnson, passed away June 17, 2014. She was born February 19, 1923, a daughter of Emory and June Spradling Moreland. She was active in Muddy Ford's Bethesda Presbyterian Church.
[320] Deed Books 278-361, 89-195, 61-129, 46-523; 343-294; Will Book X-31.
[321] Will Books W-211, X-525; Deed Books 34-341, 68-44, 69-589, 94-215, 94-222, 94-221, 94-219.

REAL COUNTRY II. NORTHEAST AND EAST CENTRAL SCOTT COUNTY

Discussion of Delaplain Road properties continues in the chapter "Rural Crossroads Villages" in the section on Oxford and in the chapter on Dry Ridge Road and Old Turkeyfoot Road.

SIMS ROAD

VALENTINE ROGERS HOUSE, 664 SIMS ROAD. Rogers Gap, Rogers Gap Branch, Rogers Gap Road, and the Valentine Rogers Gap remain to help tell a part of the story of one of Scott County's first families of European derivation. The house is a stately two-story dwelling, five bays wide, and historically heated by stone shoulder chimneys on the gable ends. The doorway with fluted posts provides entry to a central hallway where there is an elegant stairway. Ash floors and pegged windows are part of the defining detail.

Valentine Rogers was a son of William Rogers, who arrived at Bryan Station in the fall of 1783 after the famous battle and aftermath of Blue Licks. He moved to Great Crossings Station in 1785. William Rogers' brother, Joseph Rogers, helped defend Bryan Station and joined the pursuit of attacking British and Indians that ended with disaster as the party attempted crossing the Licking River at Blue Licks. Rogers was an owner of the site of Bryan Station, and he and his wife Annie (Ann Johnson, a sister of Colonel Robert Johnson, founder of Great Crossings) occupied a cabin at the fort and were constituent members of Bryan Station Baptist Church. They began construction of a log house outside the fort in 1796, later adding a two-story brick section. Joseph Rogers died in 1834 at the age of ninety-three. Another brother, Barnett Rogers, a lieutenant, was fatally wounded in the 1782 massacre at Blue Licks.[322]

Several Rogers kinfolk were among the landowners living near Valentine Rogers's house. Joseph Rogers' children included Valentine, John S., Julia (wife of John T. Bates and Snider George), Mildred (wife of Columbus Acuff and later Isaac Coppage), Nancy (wife of Jared Fawkes), Cyrene (wife of Albert Marshall), Elizabeth (wife of William Graves and William Baldridge), William A., Mary (wife of Baruch Hall), Frances (wife of William Rogers), and Joseph. Joseph's home stood somewhat southeast of the later home of Valentine Rogers and is recalled as having been a log building.[323]

Figure 221. R.C. Muntz house on Delaplain Road.

Valentine Rogers's house was later joined in its rural setting by the busy Cincinnati Southern Railway that was completed shortly before his death in 1879. The house stands on the road then known as Rogers Gap Road that led to the roads that we now know as Barkley and Turkeyfoot. The home site is on the headwaters of Dry Run just south of the ridge that separates the waters of Rogers Gap Branch of Eagle Creek from the North Elkhorn Creek watershed. It is part of a parcel patented to Christopher Greenup, Kentucky governor from 1804 to 1808, and sold to George Rogers and Valentine Rogers in 1818 at twelve dollars an acre.

---

[322] Reuben T. Durrett, LL.D., *Bryant's Station and The Memorial Proceedings* (Louisville: Filson Club Publication Number Twelve, 1897), 48, 77, 124, 128, and 229.

[323] Valentine Rogers family Bible courtesy Mabel Brashear; Hattie Scott, *Scott's Papers* (Frankfort: Kentucky Historical Society, 1953), 108-120.

In 1819 the pair divided the tract and sold part of it to Jared Fawkes, husband of Rogers' sister Nancy. Rogers bought other abutting land in the years leading up to his building of his house.[324]

Living nearby were Rogers's brother George, his sister Elizabeth "Betsey" and her husband Jacob Stucker, and his sister Mildred and her husband Isaac Coppage. Jacob and David Stucker and John Rogers died during the battle known as Harmer's Defeat.[325]

Valentine Rogers was a private in Captain Lynn West's Company in the War of 1812, fighting in the Battle of River Raisin and its bloody aftermath at Frenchtown. On February 17, 1825 he married Elizabeth Kelly, daughter of James Yateman and Nancy Noble Kelly. Their seven children were born between 1826 and 1841. Elizabeth died in 1869 and Valentine in 1879. Their homeplace is currently owned by the seventh and eighth generations of Rogers family members, having been first inherited by Joseph Johnson and Cornelia Boulware Rogers, who married in 1853; by their son Theodoric Valentine Rogers, whose son Claude Rogers then passed it on to Milford and Jennings Bryant Brashear; and by them to their daughter Mabel Brashear. The Rogers house is shown on page 174 during its restoration.[326]

ANDERSON ROAD

CRAWFORD MOORE FAMILY PROPERTY, 235 ANDERSON ROAD. An older house that had its origin as an L-shaped dwelling presently enjoys several extensions. Its ownership follows a similar line of title with other properties owned in recent years by Martha L. Johnson and now by her trust of which May Scarborough is trustee. Earlier owners of the land included Crawford Moore, an early settler, and his sons, Samuel Moore and Samuel's wife Annie, R.H. Moore, and W.C. Moore. In 1886 Annie, Samuel's widow, received a small parcel of family property from R.H. and Nancy Risk Moore. R.H. Moore and W.C. Moore each received twenty-three acres of their father's property; and Annie, eleven acres. Adrian Kent Walters became owner in 2006.[327]

Figure 222. Kent Walters house on historic Crawford Moore land.

---

[324] Deed Book I-21, 272, 279.
[325] Draper Manuscript (Shane Papers) 12 CC 197-198; Valentine Rogers Family Bible courtesy Mabel Brashear; Scott, 108-120.
[326] Valentine Rogers Bible; Scott, *Scott's Papers*, 108-120.
[327] Deed Books 23-52, 24-381, 37-57, 33-463, 46-523, 287-188, 277-87, 302-833, 289-043, 207-760; Will Book X-631.

HAMBRICK-GILKEY HOUSE, 315 ANDERSON ROAD. The former Carpenter Gothic style house, its characteristic three front gables with a pitch matching that of the side gable, recently passed through a major façade metamorphosis, a transition from a mid-twentieth century Bedford Stone treatment that in its turn replaced the Carpenter Gothic with gingerbread trim. The spooled porch cornice remained with the twentieth century renovation, a hallmark of the earlier nineteenth century detail, as did the two over two pane sash and the ridgeline's lacelike bargeboards. The contemporary red brick treatment accompanies the façade design change. Ovolo windows pierce the three front gables. An artful one-story appendage on the side adds to the size and spirit of the renovation.

Figure 223. Detail of Valentine Rogers house.

Original owners of the property owned since 1934 by the family of Les and Mabel Gilkey were Margaret "Maggie" and Evermont M. Hambrick. Margaret Hambrick was an heir of the Crawford Moore estate along with R.H. and Nancy Moore, William C. Moore, and Samuel and Anna Moore. In 1877 the Hambricks bought 116 acres at the intersection of the Dry Run Pike and the Muddy Ford dirt roads from the heirs of Wesley Acuff. In 1878 they sold it to Jesse Hambrick. The Gilkeys bought the farm from Bura and Lula Anderson. The line of descent comes from Mrs. A.T. Glenn in 1914 and Sarah Risk in 1901.[328]

Figure 224. Rita Jones house on Anderson Road.

Les Gilkey left his Anderson Road estate to his wife Elzie, and at her death to Lee Gilkey. Mrs. Gilkey died in 1956 and Lee Gilkey in 1992. Lee Gilkey's heirs quitclaimed this portion of the family property to Marcie G. Beatty in 1999. His other heirs were Martha A. and Charles H. Figgs, Emma E. and H.E. Bolton, Darryl K. Gilkey, Marcie G. and Eric Beatty, and Hattie T. Gilkey. Darryl Gilkey inherited the barn on the Anderson Road and the farm on the Muddy Ford Road.[329]

Figure 225. Stairwell of Rita Jones house on Anderson Road.

---

[328] "Moore-Hambrick House" in Bevins, *Selected Buildings* (1981), 215; Deed Books 61-2; 248-561; 43-622; 34-341, 343, 248-361; Will Books X-395, 7-209, 9-746.
[329] Deed Books 61-2, 248-553; Will Books X-395, 7-209 (See figure 226, page 175).

RITA JONES HOUSE, 519 ANDERSON ROAD. One of the stellar surviving features of the home of Rita Jones is the elliptical staircase of 1890 vintage. The main façade of the dwelling has a distinct twenty-first century appearance. However, a closer look reveals a centered entryway with sidelights and transom that are comfortably classical though the portico that shelters it supported by round posts with an extenuated tympanum with a high angled overhang sheltering a large diamond shaped multi-paned window. Large windows flank the doorway; the right-side is angled toward the rear. Also recalling the house's mixed theme of antiquity is a shouldered chimney located toward the back of the right side.[330]

Figure 226. Margaret and Evermont Hambrick, Les and Lee Gilkey, and Marcie Beatty house of several eras.

MUNTZ HOUSE, 328 ANDERSON ROAD. For many years the two story frame house with central gable and Arts and Crafts style porch, owned since 1981 by Belt, Louise, and Jeff Brashear, was associated with Muntz and Giles families. The house has a late nineteenth and early twentieth century floor plan; fireplaces adjacent to the center passage hallway serve the two end parlors. The wooden Arts and Crafts period garage has interlacing doors, each with six windows and two long panels.

The property was sold in two tracts, both relating to Muntz family ownership. In 1933 Russell and Sallie Mae Muntz and Mollie K. Muntz, widow of J.A. Muntz, deeded one tract to Mary Warren Giles, mother of Sallie Mae Muntz, following the 1929 deed of the family property of J.A. Muntz by Mollie K. Muntz, his widow; Russell Muntz; James Harlan and Lena Muntz; Howard and Effie Lee Muntz; and Luther and Loretta Muntz, to Mollie K. Muntz and Russell Muntz. In 1941 Effie D. Rawlins, W.C. and Nellie Mae Rawlins, to settle the estate of Effie D. and H.C. Rawlins, deeded their interest in the property to Mary Rawlins Giles. In 1981 she sold the ninety-acre farm to the Brashears. The present owners are Ann B. Vance and Jeffrey Lynn Brashear.[331]

The property's earlier history found C.T. Hendricks acquiring the 105.18-acre farm at a master commissioner's sale styled Ella Collier Conley versus Vada Collins. Hendricks sold it to R.W. Vance, who sold it to Owen Sams in 1918, Sams to Onie Hardin in 1919, and Hardin in 1921 to J.A. Muntz.[332]

Figure 227. Craftsman period garage of Muntz family on Anderson Road.

---

[330] Deed Book 140-32.
[331] Deed Books 39-114, 42-349, 47-121, 48-240, 51-140, 136-390, 57-380, 60-55, 149-477; Will Book Q-655.
[332] Deed Books 39-114, 42-349, 47-121, 48-240, and 51-140.

CARRICK HOUSE, 590 ANDERSON ROAD. Transitional between Classical Revival and Ranch styles, the frame house with double windows also relates to the Mary R. Carrick and Annie T. Glenn division of the farmland property of their mother, Sarah Risk. In 1901 Mrs. Risk and Mrs. Glenn deeded the portion of the farm on which this house was built to Mary R. Carrick; it included 236.75 acres and 139.91 acres. The road at that time was called the Kinkead and Muddy Ford Dirt Road. James L. and Anne Askew Carrick in 1935 sold 201.97 acres of their inheritance to H.R. and O.O. Taylor, the deed explaining that 236 acres had been inherited from James's parents, Mary R. Carrick and W.O. Carrick. Three acres were purchased from B. Anderson. In 1938 H.R. and Julia Taylor and O.O. and Jennie Taylor deeded the farm to Fred H. Taylor. The Taylor family quite possibly was responsible for construction of this attractive frame house. In 1971 Michael John Taylor and other heirs deeded 331.97 acres to Robert McMillen and Sons and Charles E. and Rebecca Cannon, who subdivided it and sold Tract 5 and the house to Robert L. Cheatham in 1972. Cheatham and his wife Rebecca sold the five acre residential tract to Glynn L. and Lillian D. Tucker in 1994.[333]

Figure 228. Later house on Sarah Risk Farm.

BARKLEY HOUSE, 526 BARKLEY LANE. An interesting house constructed of early twentieth century molded concrete blocks occupies the section of the farm bought by John W. Barkley in 1883 from N.S. and Elvina Anderson. Located on the upper reaches of Lane's Run, in 1895 Barkley added another tract purchased from J.H. and Annie May Giles. This property was inherited by his wife Nannie Barkley and Roy, Guy, and Mattie Clay Barkley. The house dates from that or the next period of ownership. In 1940 Nannie Barkley, Guy and Ethel Barkley, and Mattie Clay and Clyde Hawkins deeded the five-acre farm to Roy Barkley, who devised it to John A. Hawkins, Garth Hawkins, and Guy Allen Barkley. In 1978 those three parties sold the eighty-one-acre farm to Scotty Baesler, who in 1978 sold the portion containing the house to Martin B. Marx. In 2000 Marx deeded it to Martin Boyd Marx, Jr., who in 2003 sold the 6.43-acre tract to Toyota Motor Manufacturing Kentucky.[334]

---

[333] Deed Books 34-623, 34-543, 60-552, 346-23, 34-341, 61-255, 63-626, 114-548, 118-394, 204-669; Will Book W-590.
[334] Deed Books 66-3, 30-171, 22-6, 66-8, 138-98, 139-419, 142-481, 248-211, 270-109.

Chapter 5

Northeast and East Central Scott Crossroads and Railroad Villages

Figure 229. Cincinnati Southern Railroad overpass near Hinton.

Northeast Scott County during the earliest years of non-aboriginal settlement developed much like northwest Scott County, though with a different cast. Establishment of Cincinnati Southern Railroad's north-south trajectory changed much of the earlier pattern as new commerce mandated railroad centers, large and small. We begin our study at the northern Scott County terminus, the village of Hinton.

Hinton

Hinton is one of several communities that emerged as stations and subsequently population centers on Cincinnati Southern Railroad. By the late 1870s Hinton had become a viable small town. It is fascinating to follow the development of these emerging little burgs as their settings began to attract investment prone citizens and a work force. In July 1877 the framework of a hotel under construction for this burgeoning village then known as Butler's Station was the victim of a windstorm. Although the residents preferred the Butler attribution, the railroad ruled the day and named the community Hinton in honor of George W. Hinton, owner of a large farm in the area and a son of Turkeyfoot's Asher Hinton. By 1877 Hinton had several new residences, two stores, and a blacksmith shop. Churches appeared on the landscape as early as 1883. Hinton was incorporated in 1888.[335]

In 1875 G.W. and Millie Hinton were among the Cincinnati Southern Railroad property owners along the railroad who granted rights of way for the new Cincinnati Southern Railroad. The Hintons' sale to the railroad corporation included a wide swath of 3.68 acres through their farm on Mulberry Road. Hinton purchased a small lot on the old Mulberry Road and the Cincinnati Southern Railroad in 1877 from George B. Butler and also bought several small pieces of property in Hinton village, including the acre lot that he sold to School District 17 of Scott and Harrison counties.[336]

Figure 230. McLoney house, no longer standing, near Hinton.

On the east side of the winding road between the road and the railroad tracks, south to north, were homes of B. Sebastian, C. Harp, and M. Flanigan. Slightly to the north stood the blacksmith shop and another building. Mrs. McLoney's property, pictured at the right, stood west of the Hinton Road and southwest of the Rays Fork Road.[337]

B.T. Butler's house stood apart from and north of the other properties east of the railroad. Across the street were two stores, one that included the post office, and the houses of T. Million and Z.T. Sherrin, all south of South Rays Fork Road.

---

[335] *Georgetown Weekly Times*, July 8, August 1, December 26, 1877; Apple, Johnston, and Bevins, *Scott County, A History*, 219, 245, 263; Bevins, *Selected Buildings*, 250.
[336] Deed Books 14-441, 15-415, 30-464.
[337] 1879 Map of Scott County.

Figure 231. Three Hinton houses photographed circa 1980.

Figure 232. Four Hinton Road houses photographed circa 1980.

120 HINTON ROAD, GILLISPIE HOUSE. Houses in the once bustling village of Hinton are "scarce and getting scarcer." Apparently on its last leg when viewed circa 2006 was a three-bay house two rooms deep with early two over two pane sash and a central chimney. It is described as "the M. Gillispie property" on the 1879 map and occupied a .61-acre lot on the Dry Ridge and Friendship turnpike and along the right of way of Southern Railroad. Owners at the time were James E. and Anna L. Smith, who bought it from Chalmer Williams in 2000.[338]

156, 153, 148 CORINTH-HINTON ROAD. The Dixon and Jenkins families owned three houses in Hinton during the early and mid-twentieth century. The house at 156 Hinton Road, located on a relatively steep hill, is L-shaped and has a front gable ell. It is referenced in the 1995 deed from Edward F. Pauley to Harvey and Ruth Hall and stands on the Corinth-Hinton Road and the Friendship-Hinton Pike opposite Granville Scott's property; it is part of 27.26 acres on the Hinton Road leading to U.S. 25. Pauley and his wife, Stella, bought it in 1989 from Ona and Alice Dixon Jenkins. In 1961 Onie and Elbert Jenkins deeded it to Ottis Jenkins, their title having been derived from Lum Dixon. The building at 153 has a low gabled roof porch with turned posts and cornice and was deeded in 1961 by Ottis and Sylvia Jenkins and Elbert Jenkins to Onie Alice Dixon and Elbert Jenkins. At 148 Hinton Road is a three-bay house with an off-center door and a central chimney; it stood on a lot sold by Florence L. Caldwell to George L. Dixon in 1947, who bought it in 1919 from D.K. and Artie Hughes. Title was transferred by Lum and Lula Dixon to Onie Alice Dixon in 1959. Earlier owners of the parent tract included Rufus Lancaster, Hayden Henry, William P. Gardner, and T.H. Daugherty. In 1905 George W. and S.E. Hinton sold Dan Dixon seventeen acres at Hinton Station for $562, Hinton having acquired it from James Morris. (These descriptions followed a 2006 visit to Hinton.)[339]

Figure 233. L-shaped decorated cottage resides on picturesque hilltop.

---

[338] Deed Book 266-154.
[339] Deed Books 37-20. This paragraph relates to research completed in 2006.

Figure 234. Much remodeled Hinton Methodist Church.

LANCASTER-KITCHEN HOUSE, 444 HINTON ROAD. A basic single-story hall parlor plan house with two central doors, a central chimney, and windows in the end bays was part of the 78.96 acre farm bought in 1987 by James N., II, and Laura Beth Stone from Joseph and Elnora Halfhill. The deed description discusses the property's location on the Hinton and Rutland and the Hinton and Stonewall roads with the schoolhouse lot as a boundary. Rufus and Nannie B. Lancaster sold the farm in 1920 to R.S. and Lillie Kitchen. Part of the land came from the 1887 partition of the estate of John Lancaster. Lancaster heirs included Clarence L., Arthur L., and Virgil Lancaster. In 1921 Kitchen sold the farm, then 85.05 acres, to James W. Eads of Hinton. Eads sold it to Richard Faulconer in 1959. The Faulconer family owned it until 1983 when Charles G. Faulconer of Corinth sold it to the Halfhills.[340]

LUTES-WHITSON HOUSE, 561 HINTON ROAD. In the village of Hinton was a story and half vinyl clad house with a central chimney that was acquired by Vooris and Roberta Whitson in 1967 from George Lutes. The one and one-fourth acre lot, once bounded by the schoolhouse lot, was sold in 1896 by G.W. Hinton of Harrison County to W.A. Hinton of Scott County for ninety dollars. In 1899 Hinton and his wife Lillie, for $640, sold a lot and house to Amanda Hinton, who in 1919 sold it to D.K. Hughes. The schoolhouse lot was sold by the Scott County Board of Education in 1926 to Sam Kronenburg. Pestoral Nelson bought it in 1940 at a sheriff's sale and in 1942 she sold it to Vooris Whitson, who deeded it to his wife Roberta.[341]

Figure 235. Hinton house with large windows and picket fence.

RAWLINS-WHITSON HOUSE, 581 HINTON ROAD. Beverly Holland purchased an older house with a central roofline gable in 1998 from James and Vivian Gray. The Grays bought the house and lots in 1993 from Ford and Sandra L. Hounchell, Mrs. Hounchell having inherited it from Amelia Humphrey, widow of Lee Humphrey, who bought the property in 1951 from Pierce and Bertha Fightmaster. Mrs. Humphrey died in 1991. Roberta Whitson bought the house and lot in 1948 and sold it in 1950. The Church of God in Stonewall bought the property in 1923 from the estate of James H. Rawlins. Earlier owners included R.S. Kitchen (1920-1923), R. Lancaster, J.T. and Mary E. Stone, and J.W. and Annie A. Gardner (nee McLoney).[342]

---

[340] Deed Books 24-392, 50-151, 50-190, 87-177, 153-679, and 171-775.
[341] Deed Books 31-314, 33-371, 49-221, 55-86, 104-38.
[342] Deed Books 232-646, 198-697, 88-44, 77-224, 74-214, 73-393, 72-514, 52-465, 50-151, 33-292, 29-240.

Figure 236. Historical photograph of Davis village showing schoolhouse, church, cemetery, and store.

HINTON CHURCH SITES. Gone is the Baptist Church building sold in 1905 by J.T. and Mary E. Stone to trustees Lewis Hurley, Hock Moore, Alex Cavil, and Robert Davis, for one hundred dollars.[343] The Methodist church building at 4646 Hinton Road is among the cultural vestiges of Hinton that have been drastically remodeled with vinyl siding. The country church form remains.

4681 HINTON ROAD. Occupying the crest of a hill and set off from the road by a stone fence with pillars fashioned in the Arts and Crafts style is an attractive cottage with shaped shingles in the gable of the front ell. Since the photograph was taken, the turned posts have been replaced by iron examples. It was recently the property of Kenneth Wilson, who also owned a nearby front gabled building that was once a store.

DAVIS

The village known in earlier years as Straight Fork and in more recent history as Davis, the latter named after a storekeeper/postmaster, is one of those delightful county line communities. Positioned on the Sadieville-Davis and the Dividing Ridge roads, Davis's Scott County waters flow toward Eagle Creek while those on the Harrison County side of the ridge direct themselves to the Licking River watershed. A decided variation in the topography of properties to the east is also discernable. Among Licking River's branches in this vicinity are Pigeon, Twin Creek, and Little Mill Creek. Eagle Creek headwaters include Straight Fork, Hall Branch, Elk Lick Branch, and North and South Rays forks. Among Davis's landmarks on the Scott County side of the Harrison-Scott line are Beard Church and Cemetery, the site of Davis School, two old store buildings, the remnant of grocer Davis's house, and Dr. Sanford's house. The photograph dates from 1985.

DR. M.D. SANFORD HOUSE, 2494 DAVIS ROAD. One of Straight Fork/Davis's more imposing houses is the two-story house with an irregular form that relates to the career of physician M.D. Sanford. The house, which may have originally had detail typical of the Queen Anne style, is finished in the post-Queen Anne style known as Princess Anne. It was built on land that Dr. Sanford bought from Irene Fish in 1895. There is also a possibility that the neighborhood's Dr. Fish and his wife were the house's original owners. In 1896 Dr. Sanford sold fifteen acres of the thirty-eight-acre purchase from Mrs. Fish to C.T. Smith. Dr. Sanford's will, probated in 1950,

---

[343] Deed Book 38-606.

provided that his daughter Eugenia Sanford Smith care for her brother Marvin Sanford. Dr. Sanford left all his property to her "to do with as she may desire." William T. Smith was named executor without bond.[344]

In 1967 Eugenia S. Smith sold Mark Douglas Smith the twenty-three-acre farm and the house; he owned it until 1992 when he and his wife Ruth sold it to Stephen E. and Susan Lawson. In 1992 the Lawsons sold it to Jeffrey L. and Rhonda K. McFarland, who in 2005 sold the house and approximately fifteen acres to Michael and Keni Wendt. In 2013 Sandra Watson sold it to Lonnie R. Watson. The Robert and Sandra Bell Trust are the present owners.[345]

Figure 237. House on Davis property purchased by Dr. M.D. Sanford in 1895.

LAURA CONNER-WILLIAM T. SMITH STORE, 2512 DAVIS ROAD. One of the community stores for the village of Straight Fork-Davis was last operated by Billy Ray Barkley. William A. Hinton, executor of the estate of Laura A. Conner, who died in 1951, sold the property to William T. Smith in 1951. Mrs. Conner bought the site along with the elegantly designed brick community school in 1941 from the Scott County Board of Education. William T. Smith died in 1964. The family sold it to Eugene T. Smith, who with his wife May M. sold it in 1975 to Barkley, who, with his wife Lillian, sold it to Douglas E. Brewer in 2015.[346]

BEARD CHURCH AND CEMETERY

BEARD PRESBYTERIAN CHURCH AND CEMETERY. When Beard Presbyterian Church's richly designed Gothic Revival style meeting house was dedicated on August 30, 1885, it was, chronicled the synod record, "pronounced by all to be the prettiest frame church they had ever seen." During the elegant country church's 175-year existence, others have concurred with the 1885 assessment of the congregation's second building. That year's description of the meeting house also discussed its "fine carpet, elegant walnut pulpit furniture, marble topped communion table, bronzed chandeliers, swinging lamps

Figure 238. Davis Store was purchased by Laura Conner to save the property.

for vestibule and pulpit." Several years ago, participants in a Georgetown and Scott County Museum tour of rural churches agreed, unaware of the 1885 appraisal, that the thirty-four by fifty-two-foot building was the most distinguished frame church seen by the majority of the members of the tour group.[347]

---

[344] Will Book X-104, Deed Book 39-347, 348.
[345] Deed Books 107-36, 192-558, 192-561, 296-255, 323-12, 356-469, 359-1, 361-689.
[346] Deed Books 98-117, 107-355, 129-25.
[347] Charles and Emily Egbert, "History of Beard Presbyterian Church, Scott County, Kentucky," *Kith, Kin, Wee Kirk: History* I (Sadieville, 1995), 2-5; Vivian (Mrs. Paul) Tucker, "Beard's Presbyterian Church," *Scott County Church Histories*, 60-61.

Figure 239. Historic Beard Church at Davis, is said to have been one of the prettiest of such churches.

Beard Church as an institution of worship for northern Scott County since 1828 concluded in September 2004. The congregation of fifteen members, former members, and friends, reduced in size by recent deaths of longtime members, joined by leaders of the Transylvania Presbytery, bade farewell to this jewel of the past. The presbytery gave the building to the Beard Cemetery board. The extensive rural cemetery had grown up since the first church, a little log building, had risen on the hilltop looking down on the cemetery. Nearby Davis School tumbled down several years ago.

Accompanying organization of Beard Church, according to the session record, was "preaching in the forest on the Straight Fork of Eagle Creek during several days by the Reverends John R. Moreland and William H. Forscythe." Hugh Beard hosted the services near his home and afterwards donated ten acres of the elevation looking down on Straight Fork of Eagle Creek. The record continued that "a number of persons made a profession of their faith in Christ" in this forested setting.[348]

The congregation thus formed on September 12, 1828 built a hewn log meeting house measuring thirty-five by forty feet, capable of seating 300 to 400 members. The Reverend Nathan H. Hall preached the dedication sermon in May 1830. For many years, the humble log meeting house remained without weatherboard or plaster. Worshipers sat on "the rudest seats." Forscythe continued as the main supply preacher until his death in 1868. Hugh Beard and Francis Adams, unanimously elected ruling elders, were ordained by the Reverend Moreland. William Emison, son of Ash Emison, was chosen Clerk of the Sessions. The first trustees were Adam Pack, James Cavendar, and William Emison. After Francis Adams's death, William Emison was elected and ordained a ruling

---

[348] Tucker, "Beard's Church," 60; James Wade Emison, Jr., *The Emison Families Revised* (1954), 46.

Figure 240. Exterior detail of Beard Church.

elder, a position he continued to hold for forty-one years until his death in 1875. Other early elders were Joseph Ralston and Luke Adams. William Penn and James Adams also served as trustees during the early years.[349]

Others identifying with the church during its first two years were America Adams, Margaret Adams, Mary Adams, Hugh and Easter Beard, Ann Bailey, George W. Bailey, Elizabeth Chapel, William and Fannie Cogwell, Isaac Evins, Sally Evins, Jane Farior, Gabriella Gallop, Martha Lemon, Cynthia Lindsey, Lucy Mitchell, William May, Polly McCabe, James McCabe, William Ralston, Nancy Reed, and Joseph Watson.

Figure 242. Wooden pews.

Figure 241. Beautiful interior of church.

The Egberts' volume I of *Kith, Kin, Wee Kirk* lists communicants, baptisms, marriages, and deaths, and deacons, elders, and pastors from 1828.[350] It was published before Bob England became Beard's last pastor. Members the church just before it concluded were Joe Cook, Paul Lynn Tucker, Stanley Giles, Mildred Giles, Grace Reffett, Jenny Tucker, Jackson Tucker, Luke Tucker, Ann Tucker, and Jimmie Winkler.[351]

Figure 243. Pulpit area of Beard Church.

Paul Lynn Tucker, who maintained the last session book when it was decided to close the church, said that the presbytery insisted that the book go to the archives at Montreat, a Presbyterian center in North Carolina. Montreat, however, provided Tucker with a photocopy of the book. Tucker descends from church founder and early trustee Francis Adams. Francis and America Adams and other members of their family were admitted to the church on September 14, 1828. Until recent times, Tucker said, "almost everyone who was attending was descended from either Francis Adams or Hugh Beard." His grandson James Tucker represents "the seventh or eighth generation of Adams descendants."[352]

Before the church closed, the congregation had a new roof installed. The cemetery board is considering additional stabilization of the old meeting house.

---

[349] Egbert and Egbert 1: 2, 3; Emison, *Emison Families Revised*, 46.
[350] Egbert and Egbert 1, "Register of Communicants," 6-20.
[351] List provided by Mildred Giles to author.
[352] Discussion of author with Paul Lynn Tucker, 2004.

John Kitchen, speaking for the board, expressed hope for the building's future. Tucker commented that one person has suggested that the building house a museum of country churches.

The board also hopes to erect a historical marker on the site. A sign on the cemetery fence reminds visitors that "the cemetery is maintained by your donations."[353]

DAVIS SCHOOL SITE. Davis School may have been the most attractive survivor of the one and two-room country schools prior to its collapse. It had a projecting entrance pavilion capped with a tower roof of decorative pressed tin. There was a balustraded enclosure for the bell. The roof was typically pyramidal. The raised brick basement with windows providing light for scholars was scored with a band of limestone.[354]

Figure 244. Photograph of Davis School during its last years.

JOSHUA AND JOHN MAY HOUSE, STORE, 2704 DAVIS ROAD. Joseph and Ann E. May sold Thomas Box of Harrison County the twenty-five-acre spread "where Joseph May now resides, better known as the Joshua May place." Box died in December 1889 and in 1907 his many heirs deeded the property to Ella Lucas, wife of Thomas Lucas. In 1919 Samuel D. and Sarah E. Fields sold the property to Clifford and Harriet A. Ginn of Harrison. Mrs. Ginn and her husband J.C. made a deed of part of the property to Tisha Hiten, who had been "in open and notorious possession of said four acres." Tisha died in

Figure 245. Joshua and John May house and store in Davis.

1961. During the intervening years, owners have included Mary C. and Domenico Orsino, Lena Dutton, Jim Wayne Winkler, William R. and Jo Carol Wilson; North Dividing Ridge LLC, and since 2013, Lonnie and Geraldine Smith.[355]

SILAS BOX HOUSE, 2736 DAVIS ROAD. A four bay two door house with a central chimney stood next to the Joseph May place, historically relating to the May and Box families, having been sold in 1907 by Silas and Rebecca Box and other family members to Ella Lucas and others. In 1921 J.C. and Harriet Ginn sold it to Libbie Eads, and her heirs in 1943 sold the half-acre containing the house to Sophia Kitchen. In 1951 the heirs of Sofia Eads Kitchen Courtney including her husband L.B. Courtney sold the property to Garnett and Audrey Florence. Orville Ray Miley bought it in 1957 and sold it in 1971 to Bruce Bryant, seller in 2015 to Lonnie and Geraldine Smith. A new house with Cape Cod features occupies the historic site.[356]

SMITH BUNGALOW, DAVIS ROAD. Across the road from the store and located in the Harrison County portion of Davis village is a distinctive bungalow, now clad in vinyl. Though the house resides in Harrison County, it is a major contributor to the aesthetic view and composition of Davis.

Figure 246. W.T. Smith family house on Davis's Harrison County side.

---

[353] Discussion of author with John Kitchen, 2004.
[354] Bevins, *Selected Buildings*, 179, 180.
[355] Deed Books 25-299, 39-545, 52-119, 52-476, 91-227, 96-486, 294-407, 298-134.
[356] Deed Books 25-299, 39-545, 46-247, 51-433, 53-121, 78-77, 78-351, 85-372, 119-457.

Figure 247. Winding lane leading into village of Alberta on the Scott and Harrison county line.

ALBERTA/BOYERS CHAPEL

Alberta, like Davis, is bisected by the Scott and Harrison county line. The church central to the little community, Boyers Chapel Methodist Church, stands on the Harrison County side of the road. The attractive small county line community has much to share with folk of both counties.

ALBERT AND HARRIET STEVENS HOUSE, 1213 BOYERS CHAPEL ROAD. Facing the Boyers Chapel Road and located across that road from the Methodist Chapel is a two story house with a trio of distinctive front gables in the recessed block, positioned next to a building that may have been the village store for the little crossroads community that came to be called Alberta. The origin of the name is believed to have evolved from landowner Albert M. Stevens, who with his wife Harriet in 1879 deeded thirty-three acres on the headwaters of the North Fork of Eagle Creek to their son Alfred D. Stevens.

Figure 248. Albert and Harriet Stevens's multi-gabled house in Alberta.

Albert M. Stevens died in 1886, arranging for the benefit of his three grandchildren, the children of his deceased daughter Mary Susan F. Hiles, and his three living children, Alfred Dallas Stevens, Sara Ellen Crosthwait, and Harriet Ann Parker. Each was to receive one fourth of the estate. His wife Harriet was to enjoy "the piece of land I got from Isaac Reed of forty-four acres. Crosthwait was to have fifty acres from Billy

Holden's children. The rest of the land was to be rented out for mutual benefit, and at the death of Harriet, to be divided proportionately.[357]

Stevens was a master builder who constructed a home for himself and his family on the Boyers Chapel Pike; the imposing dwelling burned after 1981. The house had an elegant walnut stairway, inlay doors, and hand carved woodwork. Alfred D. Stevens' sale in 1904 to his son in law A.S. Crosthwait brought a price of $54.35. In 1918 A.S. and Lucy A. Crosthwait sold to W.W. Hutchcraft a "lot, shop, and contents in Alberta village on the Sadieville-Boyers Chapel Road and bordered by property of John and George Swinford and A.D. Stevens."[358]

The imposing gabled house is said to have been built after 1904, though its appearance suggests possibly greater antiquity. The section with the two steep front gables has a side porch supported by square posts. The two story front gabled ell section is one bay wide. Most recently the distinctive dwelling has belonged to Michael C. and Joey W. Wiley, who bought it along with the 1.37-acre lot from Clarence and Linda Griffith in 2000, and Bruce Cleary II, purchaser in 2010. In 1947 Oscar and Clarice Jones and Gertrude and Winford Kitchen sold it to Kenneth Hutcherson, along with property located across the road adjacent to the church. They acquired it from Roy and Edna Kitchen and John E. Kitchen. The Kitchens' source was the very interesting Swinford family. In 1926 George M. Swinford, Margaret F. Swinford, and J.E. Swinford "of near Alberta, Scott County. . . brothers and sisters having lived in the same house for many years since the death of our parents and having managed what little property we own in common and for the benefit of all of us, now in order that we may do justice to ourselves and to each other, we hereby covenant to and with each other that in the event of the death of any one of us the other two are to have in fee simple all the property of the one who died, etc." The agreement related to 150 acres in Harrison and two acres across the pike near Alberta.[359]

BATEY-SWINFORD STORE, SHOP, HOUSE, 1227 BOYERS CHAPEL PIKE. At the site next door to the multi-gabled house are the house, lot, and shop in Alberta that S.M. and Iva Jenkins purchased in 1957 from the heirs of Mary B. Crosthwait, who with her sisters Cora A. Whitson and Luna Leach inherited it from Nancy E. and Johnny L. McKenney. Mrs. McKenney's title came from Clarence and Fannie Batey and George Swinford in 1926. Jeffrey F. and Tamela L. Wurtz purchased it in 2006. The shop is pictured at the left.[360]

Figure 249. Alberta's Batey-Swinford Store.

---

[357] Will Book S-228.
[358] Deed Books 40-292, 48-568.
[359] Deed Book 56-173, 249-447, 245-49, 173-28, 172-717, 86-339, 75-57, 70-529, 329-677.
[360] Deed Book 299-727, 98-388, 86-339, 85-208, 55-361.

Real Country II. Northeast and East Central Scott County

BOYERS CHAPEL METHODIST CHURCH. In recent years the historic façade of the Methodist Church that serves the Harrison-Scott County community known as Alberta took on a new appearance, having received a new front porch surmounted with a large gabled roof supported by round posts. A stick balustrade protects the raised porch which has steps and a handicap entry on the right side. The church was built around 1874, replacing an older building destroyed by fire, possibly during the Civil War.[361]

MUDDY FORD

The remnant of the community graphically named Muddy Ford hosted a concrete block grocery store which, not so many years ago, replaced the historic old time wooden store joined on the

Figure 250. Boyers Chapel Methodist Church with later portico.

roadscape by a handful of homes, a school building, and the tiny but powerful Bethesda Presbyterian Church. Muddy Ford lies at a once very busy crossroads near the convergence of the Oxford-Turkeyfoot, Anderson, Gunnell, Hinton Cemetery, and Barkley roads. This trajectory was variously called Hiles Old Mill Road, Muddy Ford-Turkeyfoot Road, and Barkley Road. The 1879 map gives initials of S.B. and J.M. at the location that was or became Muddy Ford. Property owners prominent in this neck of the woods included members of the Muddiman, Barnhill, Burgess, Fields, Morris, Sharon, and Sutton families.

ELIZABETH VANCE-JOE SUTTON PROPERTY, 5411 MUDDY FORD ROAD. Although it probably isn't close to being "one of the oldest properties in the county," the early house on the Muddy Ford Road looks as if it might be a contender for the epithet. Purchased by Todd Grizzle and Holly McKenzie in early 2015, the dwelling house appears to have survived by mere pluck and a lot of patching. Approached by a winding driveway leading into its circa sixteen-acre setting, it stands two stories high, three bays wide, and is approached by five wooden steps. Its porch is railed

Figure 251. Elizabeth Maddox-Joe Sutton house on edge of Muddy Ford.

and shelters the centered doorway and flanking windows. A wooden fence surrounded the house.

As the old house sits awaiting renovation or replacement, it recalls generations of owners including Elizabeth Vance, daughter of Joseph L. Vance and wife of John T. Sutton. After Sutton's death, she married Nelson Hamon. A 1914 deed describes the sale by Frank M. and Evie Sutton, Joseph Sutton, John W. Sutton, and Ira Sutton to Lew Shirley for $300. The small farm's boundaries were the Muddy Ford church on the east, Shirley's land on the north, the schoolhouse lot on the west, and the Muddy Ford and Finnell Pike on the south. In 1924 Addie and Lawrence Adams, Fannie and George Barnhill, and Frank Dixson sold the property estimated at fifteen acres to Joe Sutton. In 1936 four of Sutton's surviving heirs – Cam Sutton; Arthur Sutton; Pearl (wife of

---

[361] "Boyers Chapel Methodist Church," *Scott County Church Histories*, 114.

Roy) Vance; Mary (wife of Howard) Barnhill; and Cindy (wife of George) King -- deeded their interest to Cam Sutton. He willed it to his brother Arthur, who with his wife Christine included their stepson Bennie D. Cox as a joint tenant with them. Arthur died in 1978 and Christine in 2002, leaving real estate to Lula C. Thomas, James Basil Cox, Clara F. Welch, and Ruth O'Leary. Lula Thomas, who received the interest of the other heirs, sold her interest to Grizzle in 2012. Holly McKenzie is joint owner.[362]

Figure 252. Eli Muddiman house in Muddy Ford.

ELI MUDDIMAN HOUSE SITE, MUDDY FORD. An elongated one-story frame house stood near the later popular village store of J.W. Robertson. It dated to the 1888 purchase by Eli Muddiman from J.W. Sutton for $300. The Suttons acquired it from Buford Hall, who bought it in 1884 from Samuel Barnhill. Muddiman's family sold it in 1936. Muddiman, a stone mason, was father of E.C. Muddiman and grandfather of E.E. Muddiman, both masons.[363]

MUDDY FORD/ ROBERTSON STORE SITE, 689 BARKLEY ROAD. In 1893 Lew Shirley announced plans to open a store on a lot bought from E.E. Muddiman. The little community next gained a post office mislabeled Muddy Fork. The surname Muddiman has a sort of phonetic cadence that rings well with the designation of "Muddy." [364]

Figure 253. Muddy Ford Robertson Store as rebuilt following devastating fire.

In 1949 storekeeper J.W. Robertson died, his will stipulating that his property at the death of his wife would go to his six children. Robertson purchased the 129-foot wide lot on which the store and accompanying resources stood in 1928 from W.M. and Lora Z. Shirley for $6,600. Llewellyn and Alice Shirley, who bought one acre in 1893 from Eli and Annie Muddiman for forty dollars, sold it in 1925 to W.M. Shirley for two thousand dollars.[365]

After the Robertsons' deaths, in 1959 John Thomas and Beatrice Robertson and other heirs sold the Muddy Ford store property to Mary Alice Parker; in 1976 she sold it to Timothy W. and Elizabeth L. Sams and Emily Egbert for $20,000. They sold it in 1983 to Carl and Marilyn F. Miller for $35,000, and they, in 1991, to Mark T. and Amy Houston for $53,500. In 1994 Houston sold the accumulated acreage including the 120 by 129 storehouse lot to Stephen W. Wilhoyte for $60,000. The expanded Cape Cod style house on the site has a dormer with a triple window.[366]

Muddy Ford and much of the farm country between Muddy Ford and the historic community surrounding Mount Gilead Methodist Church was immortalized in Fannee Fields Hilander's 1980 *Hold Back the Spring*, an historical/ folk interpretation evolving around the life and times of her mother, born in 1914 as Hazel B "Hash," eighth child of J.W. "Willie" and Fannie Williamson Robertson. Robertson had been well known as a grocer in Lexington, where the family lived at the time of Hash's birth. Over time, Robertson, "Poppa" in his granddaughter's book, and "Momma," operated stores in Lexington on Georgetown Street, Second Street, Upper Street, and South Limestone, in addition to the two at Muddy Ford.[367]

---

[362] Deed Books 43-513, 53-482, 61-520-522, 132-55-57, 304-32, 347-87, 564; 358-309.
[363] Information from Mrs. Lindsay Warth; Bevins, *Selected Buildings*, 104.
[364] Apple, Johnston, and Bevins, *Scott County*, 263; *Georgetown Weekly Times*, December 6, 1993.
[365] Will Book X-61; Deed Books 56-377, 54-194, 28-382.
[366] Deed Books 28-382, 54-194, 56-377, 88-144, 131-299, 151-559, 144-607, 153-539, 191-365, 203-500, 204-613, 359-49.
[367] Fannee Hilander, *Hold Back the Spring* (Great Neck, New York: Todd & Honeywell, Inc., 1980), 8-12.

When Robertson took over the store at Muddy Ford, Hash attended Oxford School where she was graduated in 1934. In 1937, she married high school sweetheart Woodrow Fields, who lived just down the road. They spent the early years of their marriage in Fields's home on the hill with Woodrow's parents, "Mommau and Poppau," Mary Morris and Henry Clay Fields. After Mr. Robertson became ill, the newlyweds returned to the Robertson home. At mealtime and when her father needed to rest, Hash would tend the store. As the young couple's family began to increase, they sought a place of their own, the first being "the Houston Place." There Hash learned to cook. Fannee followed Lowell in the lineup of Fields babies prior to the time that the family moved to Lexington where Woodrow worked for the telephone company. Marking the conclusion of that sojourn was an appeal that he was needed back home, resulting in a return to the hill country and to "the Cox Place" with its "big old front porch – just waiting for us."[368]

Across the road from the Cox place lived Mr. and Mrs. Ira Sutton in the John Bailey log house, who entertained little Fannee with corn bread and jam.[369] After Poppau's death, the Fields family, increased to a count of six, moved in with Mommau at Muddy Ford "so she wouldn't be alone." They moved "to the old familiar white house on the hill; it was the one that felt like home. I'll always love it there. The house with the white rock wall covered with rambling roses, the pear tree, the swing in the back, the chicken house." The family's next move was to Mount Gilead. There they lived in the picturesque log house that survived until recently, owned by the family of Woodrow Fields's sister's husband, Lindsay Warth.[370]

MUDDY FORD STORE FIRE. Fannee's narrative recalled the fire that destroyed her grandfather's store at Muddy Ford. Robertson had long been plagued by destruction by fire of his commercial establishments. "You might say," Fannee wrote, "the last fire destroyed him too." Fannee was spending the night with cousin and best friend Shirley Sharon (later Houston) when "Up in the night we heard Aunt Bea call out, 'Fire, fire.' Shirley and I tumbled out the door into the night before we realized it was not their house that was on fire." As the fire raged, "Poor little Momma came and sat on the front porch; Aunt Bea put a blanket around her while Poppa stood in the yard with a lot of the neighbors, watching, just watching. It was too late to do anything else."[371]

Figure 254. Fannee Fields Hilander posing on the old rock fence by the white house on the hill.

In 1949 most of Scott County was connected to telephone lines, but the only phone in the Muddy Ford neighborhood was in the blazing grocery store. In recent decades the replacement store went the way of the

---

[368] Hilander., 13-16.
[369] See Bevins, *Selected Buildings*, 35.
[370] Hilander., 16, 17, 18. For further discussion of the Mount Gilead properties, refer to the section of this chapter entitled "Mount Gilead."
[371] Hilander, 19.

majority of its sister rural stores due to declining trade occasioned by improved roads leading to a then new and now taken for granted development, the supermarket.

The little store went out of business and gradually disintegrated, its foundations joining the archaeology of the ages. The nearby house with shouldered chimneys of stone with brick stacks, five bays wide, with a wing on the east side and an ell on the back, declined about the same time. The bungalow on the west side of the store continues to serve as a dwelling house. In time the only surviving remnant of historic Muddy Ford was the old church which at this writing is in an abject condition of disrepair.[372]

Figure 255. Muddy Ford School with its large student body.

MUDDY FORD SCHOOL. The photograph of Muddy Ford School earlier reproduced in Charles and Emily Egbert's *Kith, Kin, Wee Kirk: History, Volume 1* reveals a building design used with a variety of modifications by Scott County and other rural public school systems in the early years of the twentieth century. Judging from the ages of students in the photograph, Egbert concluded that the photo would have been taken during the school's infancy in the 1920s.[373]

BETHESDA PRESBYTERIAN CHURCH, MUDDY FORD ROAD. Bethesda Presbyterian Church, located near the crossing of the Oxford-Turkeyfoot and Barkley roads, recalls the mid-nineteenth century period when the Cumberland Presbyterian Church, a product of the Great Revival, and the Methodist Church with congregations in several parts of Kentucky, shared the meeting house. The Great Revival of 1801 had its earliest beginnings in Presbyterian congregations in the Red, Gasper, and Muddy river rural neighborhoods in the summer of 1800 and "caught fire" in 1801 when the enthusiastic meetings, presided over by Presbyterians assisted by Methodist revivalists, occurred in Central Kentucky congregations. The Central Kentucky revivals were coincidental to Barton Stone's ostensibly academic visit to the Red River meetings. Following the revivals, Presbyterians in the Cumberland Valley organized a separate Presbyterian synod. Many of the revivalists in Central Kentucky became part of the united and uniting movement known as the Christian Churches.[374]

The Bethesda congregation originated around 1831, the year that it was listed among the congregations of the West Lexington Presbytery. The church was listed as a contributing congregation to the presbytery also in 1838 and 1839. It ceased to be included in Lexington Presbytery records after 1841, at which time it was aligned with the Methodist-Cumberland Presbyterian brotherhood. The first trustees of record, as reported to Scott County Fiscal Court, were Samuel Sharon, Samuel Barnhill, William Williamson, William Spates, and Samuel Goddard. At that time Hartwell J. Perry was the Methodist minister and Thomas Thomas shepherded the Cumberland Presbyterians. On January 21, 1841, Samuel and Susan Barnhill sold a three-square-rods lot to the congregation for ten dollars. During this period William C. Burgess and Benjamin Neale McDaniel served as lay ministers, performing marriages between 1845 and 1861.[375]

---

[372] Apple, Johnston, Bevins, *Scott County: A History,* 387.

[373] Egbert and Egbert I, 2-53.

[374] D. Newell Williams, *Barton Stone: A Spiritual Biography* (St. Louis: Chalice Press, 2000); Paul K. Conkin, *Cane Ridge, America's Pentecost* (Madison: The University of Wisconsin Press, 1990); Ellen Eslinger, *Citizens of Zion: The Social Origins of Camp Meeting Revivalism* (Knoxville: The University of Tennessee Press, 1999).

[375] Egbert and Egbert, I: 35; Order Book E-89; Deed Book Q-289; O.W. Houston, "Bethesda Presbyterian Church," *Scott County Churches,* 61.

The building used during the period of the joint Presbyterian-Methodist ministry burned in 1872. The schoolhouse on the small lot was used by the church as a meetinghouse until a new church building was constructed circa 1884. The congregation sold the site to the county school board, which sold it in 1938 to storekeeper J.W. Robertson. The schoolhouse pictured in the Egberts' book succeeded a prior school building. In 1884 Samuel Bushrod Barnhill sold John K. Hitner and James W. Williamson, commissioners for the Presbyterian Church in the United States, one half acre for thirty dollars for a house of worship for the Bethesda Presbyterian Church. This location is the site of the present church, constructed for $950 probably shortly after the writing of the deed, by William C. Burgess, Nelson Hamon, Victor Johnson, and George Barnhill. The church basement's construction and installation of a furnace were events of 1958. At the same time the congregation installed hardwood flooring and paneling for the sanctuary and bought pews from Grace Baptist Church in Lexington. The finishing touch was the sign for the front of the church, a project of the congregation's young people. Stephen Wilhoyte of Fordsville purchased the church building and lot in 2012.[376]

During much of the twentieth century, Bethesda Church was yoked with Beard Church at Davis and Providence Church at Oxford, sharing pastors and alternating meeting times. Providence Church closed in 1991 and Beard in 2004. Egbert's account offers an interpretation of why the church, which had once counted upwards of 150 worshipers at its Sunday school and worship services, declined. The reasons parallel those in countless crossroads communities and larger rural trading centers – new job opportunities at large manufacturing centers representing international industry, better roads and easier accessibility to supermarkets and shopping centers, and new residents not interested in the village church. However, a few rural churches such as Bethesda zealously persisted, their congregations reduced in size but not in commitment, until they, too, ceased to exist.

TURKEYFOOT VILLAGE

A shadow of its former self, the village of Turkeyfoot has a powerful heritage of lore and legend. Today the Christian Church meetinghouse alone survives to recall the Turkeyfoot represented on the 1879 map by eight buildings and on the 1965 USGS topographical map by five. The name Turkeyfoot is nearly "as old as the hills" -- or at least as old as our civilization's hills. In 1780 and in 1782, when only the bravest and most foolhardy Kentucky pioneers ventured into what became the future Commonwealth, Robert Patterson, an early settler at McClelland's Fort and a future founder of Lexington, Cincinnati, and Dayton, was thoughtfully involved in a military campaign led by George Rogers Clark. On one of those journeys Patterson noted the merging of several forks – Shawnee, Rogers Gap, West, and Muddy Ford – into a shape

Figure 256. Muddy Ford's Bethesda Presbyterian Church.

resembling a turkey's foot. He and other explorers and surveyors began referring to the stream grouping as "Turkey Foot." During the next few years others corroborated Patterson's observation. Indian scout Jacob Stucker claimed that he first knew the place in 1782 and 1783 and that "Col. Patterson had told him that he had given the place the name of Turkeyfoot." The epithet stuck; the area was to be forever known as Turkeyfoot. Stucker also deposed as to the location of a 2,000 acre survey made in the name of Thomas Bell that "a buffalo

---

[376] Egbert and Egbert I: 35, 36, 52; Deed Book 347-612.

path led from below here to Dry Run" and continued on to the Big Spring in Georgetown and ultimately Bryan Station. Louis Vallandingham testified that he heard the term Turkeyfoot first applied in 1784.[377]

The presence of water at the three-pronged fork on Eagle Creek encouraged the naming of a settlement there as Turkeyfoot," recalls the 1993 *Scott County, Kentucky: A History*. Settlement period neighbors, according to postbellum historian William Henry Perrin, included William Vance, Asher Hinton, Benjamin Carr, Reed, William Price, Abraham Fields, Benjamin Pack, Edward Burgess, Peter Antle, John Gibson, Patrick Watson, John and Polcer Hiles, Cornelius Butler, James Sutton, Joshua Murphy, and Joseph Leach. By the time of the 1879 publication of Perrin's history, Captain Joe Vance was occupying his father's lands, as were Hinton and Carr sons. Ebon Reed located near the Turkeyfoot post office; Thomas Hyles/Hiles settled on the William Price lands; and the enterprising Jacob Price lived nearby. The Hinton family also enjoyed a presence. The Henry Hinton house, pictured here, was a prominent landmark.[378]

Figure 257. Early Turkeyfoot house, possibly the home of Henry Hinton.

An interesting situation reveals itself in a four acre exclusion to a tract of land deeded to Turkeyfoot Christian Church in 1989. Reference was made to property involved in the estate of William Vance. "The decedent [William Vance, father of Buck Vance] had no deed . . . the court adjudges he had possession more than thirty-five years." The property had been assigned to Henry M. Hinton, father of Harrigan Hinton, May 2, 1900, on behalf of the estate of William Vance.[379]

As Turkeyfoot grew, the village accrued a general store, church, tavern, Masonic lodge, and hotel. In 1878 V.F. Bradley, newly elected county school superintendent, reported that Turkeyfoot had no school building though a school was conducted in a rented house with students seated on long benches on either side of a fireplace. However, a school was forthcoming, and in 1911 Turkeyfoot was among several rural communities getting new and stylish brick schoolhouses.[380]

TURKEYFOOT CHRISTIAN CHURCH. In 1842 the Christian Churches, in the first cooperative mission effort jointly sponsored by the Georgetown, Dry Run, and Hebron congregations, dispatched John T. Johnson "to destitute places," a term applied to neighborhoods that lacked churches of the Christian brotherhood. In an 1842 account in Alexander Campbell's *Millennial Harbinger*, the church at Georgetown reported, "We selected brother John T. Johnson for the first mission. He accepted our invitation and repaired to Turkey Foot [in Scott County], where he labored from Lord's Day until Thursday evening following. The meeting was most delightful and triumphant. There was an accession of seventeen members to the good cause. Within a few days, the small congregation at that place was built up and established, and the prospects were good for many more. However, Johnson had a severe attack of sciatica and was compelled to cease his efforts. We hope the example of the brethren in this county will be emulated by the congregations everywhere. . ." John T. Johnson was one of the great early ministers of the Christian Churches.[381]

---

[377] County Lines Book 1; Bevins, *Selected Buildings*, 99-100.
[378] Perrin, *Bourbon, Scott, Harrison, and Nicholas Scott Counties*, 210.
[379] Deed Books 65-327; 91-408, 144-93, 149-068, 181-332; Will Book W-528.
[380] Apple, Johnston, and Bevins, *Scott County: A History*, 249, 263, 317.
[381] John Rogers, *Biography of Elder J.T. Johnson* (Cincinnati: 1861), 183.

Earlier Turkeyfoot village buildings located west/left of the north-facing church, as enumerated by historian Ronald T. Vance were (1) the Mandeville Hinton store; (2) Henry Hinton's house; (3) four acres owned by Fritz Screba (a German), the previous location of White's cemetery, and William Vance's store and bar room where Polk Burgess killed George Bates. The store burned when it was owned by Bill Robertson.[382]

Among Turkeyfoot Christian Church's early members were Pierce Munson, Mandeville Hinton, and Daniel White. Perrin wrote that the first church building was erected in 1854. The first meetinghouse stood just over the hill from the present one. William and Sarah Hinton deeded the site to the church on June 10, 1875; the meetinghouse was constructed in 1880. The present building was dedicated in 1895 with Elder J.T. Sharrard of Paris preaching to a large gathering on the grounds. Early officers of the church included John W. Penn, William H. Hiles, and Tavner Adams.[383]

"Turkeyfoot was what one might call a school for preachers," wrote Suzanne Beckett and Dana Snyder of the Kentucky Young Historians in the 1979 *Scott County Church Histories: A Collection*. "Many ministers have come here for a first class experience of teaching and preaching the ways of God. Once Turkeyfoot Church took in a poor farm boy, Bob Jones, and fed him and sent him to a school for religion. . . Dr. John T. Robinson, minister in 1923, preached for eight or nine years. Under his ministry the church was remodeled in 1924. . . Roy McKinney started as a traveling minister and became full time minister in 1935. . . Bob Jones was minister as a second job when he was going to school." Other young men who served as minister during their student years were Bill Delaney, David Bolton, Dick Ducemberry, and Robert Pelfrey. Earl Simms, professor at the Cincinnati Bible Seminary, preached on occasion at Turkeyfoot. Grayson Ensign, also a professor at Cincinnati Bible Seminary, served the congregation three times – as a student, as a young married man, and after a twenty-year ministry that included three years as a missionary in Jamaica.[384]

Turkeyfoot Christian Church occupies a 5.58-acre lot. The very attractive two door building has a square form with a hip or pyramidal roof. Doors are located in the end bays. The narthex projects from the central block and has a gabled roof with a cornice with returns; it is lighted by two windows. A gable breaks the roofline on the side. The hip roof steeple with arched openings houses the church bell. A contemporary addition provides a fellowship hall and Sunday school rooms, and a sheltered picnic area offers space for warm weather outings. At one time the Masonic Lodge met upstairs in the church building.

Figure 258. Turkeyfoot Christian Church.

---

[382] Information about sequence of buildings from Ron Vance.
[383] Suzanne Beckett and Dana Snyder, "Turkeyfoot Christian Church," *Scott County Church Histories*, 87; Perrin, ed., *Bourbon, Harrison, Scott and Nicholas Counties*, 210; Apple, Johnston, and Bevins, *Scott County: A History*, 263.
[384] Beckett and Snyder, 87.

TURKEYFOOT SCHOOL SITE. "To be restored in 1992" read a note in the Property Valuation Administration office file, referring to Turkeyfoot village's third schoolhouse. The file card indicated that on August 30, 1999, the property was owned by Connie Jackson and Anthony and Darrell Bryant. During the recent past, as this excellent example of a brick early twentieth century schoolhouse was awaiting a hopeful future, it burned, leaving irreparable destruction to the revered site.

Figure 259. Turkeyfoot School was a decorative version of a traditional school design.

Turkeyfoot's first school met in the church. The trustees of School District 20 then built on a one acre lot purchased in 1890 from William and Sallie Hinton. The second building stood on the north side of the stylish brick schoolhouse pictured above. The board of education, having merged several regional schools, sold the building in 1938 for $147.50 to Laura A. Conner, a daughter of the Hintons. In 1947 Mrs. Conner, then a resident of Harrison County, sold the property to Paul and Sally Houston for $1,100. In 1954 the Houstons sold it for $2,200 to Fred Sowers, Rollie Hinton, George Giles, Edward Hiles, Ralph C. Giles, Fred Brewer, and Newland Sowers. The group of former students sold it in 1972 to Lawrence and Louise Bryant for the price that they paid for it seven years earlier. Mr. Bryant died in 1972. In August 1999 Mrs. Bryant deeded it on terms of love and affection to Connie Bryant Jackson, Anthony Bryant, and Darrell Bryant. The title description is the early one. Boundaries include the road from Turkeyfoot to Straight Fork, Louisa Reed, and Conner. Measurements for the one acre lot are 210 by 210 feet.[385]

Figure 260. Iconic photo of Turkeyfoot church.

Figure 261. Photo of second Turkeyfoot school with students grouped in front.

Historian Ron Vance provided identification of some students in the photo at the left. First row: Arthur Bennett, Ed Hiles, Meredith Robertson, Dewey Vance, and Tob Hinton, unknown, Willis Hinton, and Tom Hiles. Second row: Noda Noel, Buford Munson, Raymond Vance, Dick Holland, Cavil Noel, two unknown, Amos Bennett, and the remainder in the second row unknown. Third row, Noah Hinton, Cam Price, Parker Eades, two unknown, Bill Hiles, Chester Robertson, and Mag Munson. Fourth row, Bertha Holland, Lilly Mae Munson, unknown, Sallie Fields, three unknown, and Laura Mae Hinton. Teachers standing in the back are Sarah Creighton and Susie Holland

---

[385] Deed Books 26-51, 63-231, 72-238, 81-533, 91-356, and 244-462. Additional information from Ron Vance.

SHELBY MUNSON HOUSE, TURKEYFOOT ROAD. The Shelby Munson house was on the Turkeyfoot Road on the first farm south of the Fred Skreba lot. According to historian Ronald T. Vance, Skreba, a German, bought his lot from Agatha Parker's heirs. Agatha got it from her father, Thomas Creath White, who apparently got it from William Vance. Shelby's house was directly across the road from Irene Sowers's barn; the Shelby Munson cemetery is on the hill above the barn. Shelby's daughter Almira (Allie) married Ron's great-grandfather Joseph Franklin Barkley, grandson of Robert Barkley of Oxford. Shelby's house burned 1945-1946. His land extended behind his house to the Muddy Ford branch "of the Turkeyfoot" and in front of the house, to Shawnee Run. Muddy Ford Road was the south border. There was another log house on top of the hill on Muddy Ford where Ronnie Courtney now lives; that house was given to Almira. There are no known photos of it. (Photo and information from Ron Vance.)

Figure 262. Historic photo of Shelby Munson house. Third from left is Shelby's daughter Almira (Allie) who married Joseph Franklin Barkley, Ron Vance's great grandfather, grandson of Oxford's Robert Barkley. Shelby's house burned circa 1945-1946.

BARNHILL HOUSE. A house across the road from Turkeyfoot Christian Church was the part of the Shelby Munson estate that became the property of Charles Barnhill, a Munson grandson. In addition to the five daughters of Shelby and Rebecca M. Barnhill mentioned his will were beneficiaries Charles and Shelby Barnhill and Stella Shirley. Munson died in 1900. In 1903 Stella Shirley and her husband Loren Shirley sold a forty-one-acre farm "near Turkeyfoot" to Charles Barnhill for $2,500. In 1975 Anna Mae Means sold the remaining forty acres to Newland and Irene Sowers and Tolbert C. and Sophronia Barnhill, excluding the Shelby Munson family graveyard measuring forty by fifty feet. Munson's house was on a thirty-five-acre tract owned by Billy and Virginia Barnhill.[386]

Figure 263. Rogers Gap village site.

ROGERS GAP

The railroad village of Rogers Gap, one might say, is "all gone but the dust." And we might add, "the dust is pretty much gone, too." The once bustling community with a railroad station was an important rail stop and includes a few remaining examples of railroad personnel housing and a discomforting amount of denuded

---

[386] Deed Books 127-438, 33-438, 35-255, 38-123, 51-267, and 127-439.

landscape. Between 1916 and 1918, E.E. Muddiman, the enterprising builder and storekeeper, who had a stylish brick store a short distance away at the railroad stop at Delaplain, owned a one-fourth acre tract. Through the years, many property owners owned this piece of real estate at the center of the little community. Its resources now include a three-bay dwelling on a block foundation. Historian Ron Vance recorded that there were ten houses in Rogers Gap in 1946, along with two store buildings.

Figure 264. T.R. Clark bungalow at Rogers Gap may date from as late as 1955.

593 ROGERS GAP ROAD. T.R. Clark built the bungalow at this address circa 1955. The seven-acre lot and the house were sold in 1999 by Robert M. and Maria M. Wells to John Michael and Kelly Fay Hogan for $79,500. The Wellses purchased the property in 1988 from Harold T. and Norma J. Clark. The late bungalow has a three-window extended dormer. The lower portion of the house gives the appearance of a full porch having been partially enclosed. A picture window commands the room adjacent to the doorway. The house is pictured at the right.[387]

FIELDS HOUSE, 1031 ROGERS GAP ROAD. Lee Hiles inherited the farm from Martha Bell Hiles that he sold in 1938 to Walter and Sally Fields. The Fieldses chose a design with characteristics of both bungalow and Cape Cod styles for their dwelling. In 1982 Louella and Henry Sanders sold the seventy-three-acre and 49.17-acre tracts to James and Lucy Owen, who in 1984 sold a 27.36-acre parcel to Donald and Susan Chowning, and they, in 1989 to James L. and Anne Laird Horton. Elizabeth McPherson purchased the house and 7.001 acres in 2002.

DRY RUN/DELAPLAIN

Old Turkeyfoot Road, the third major north-south trajectory paralleling the Dry Ridge or Georgetown-Covington Road, was discontinued save for a few sections many years ago. It cut through an area having important natural and built resources, extending north along North Hamilton Street toward DeGaris Mill and on toward the fork in Eagle Creek that inspired explorers to name the setting "turkey foot." The mid and late 1870s Cincinnati Southern Railroad followed the ridge about one-half mile east of the Dry Ridge Road and the same distance west of the Turkeyfoot Road.

Figure 265. Walter and Sallie Fields house at Rogers Gap.

Marking the crossing of the Cincinnati Road and the roads now known as Burton and Delaplain were the 1,000-acre land grants of Ash Emison and James Hogan, the latter purchased early in the settlement period by John and William Bradford. The two grants encroached on each other at a point that included the site of the Dry Run Baptist Church. Waller Rodes and Younger Pitts, trustees in 1800, purchased the one-acre site from Nicholas Long for eight dollars. John G. Bradford also deeded land to the church. The headwaters of Dry Run Creek extended into and

---

[387] Deed Books 22-241, 40-577, 44-207, 48-229, 50-147, and 56-442. Additional information from Ron Vance.

past these grants, the mouth of the creek entering North Elkhorn Creek about a mile upstream from that of Georgetown's Big Spring Branch. This important branch of North Elkhorn defies those who named it "Dry," as it retains its flow during dry seasons well after the companion streams, excluding Big Spring Branch but including Lane's, Cherry, and Boyd's runs, have tended to "run dry."[388]

Figure 266. Third building of Dry Run Baptist Church was built in 1958.

DRY RUN BAPTIST CHURCH, 2109 CINCINNATI ROAD. Dry Run Baptist Church (pictured above), chartered in 1801 by the Great Crossings Baptist Church, mother church of the area, and the Dry Run cemetery, provided an early social nucleus for the early Dry Run neighborhood. Constituent members included the Reverend Joshua Leatherer, J. Withers, Waller Rodes, Jacob Neal, Younger Pitts, Sr., William Jones, and Louden Snell. After about fifty-six years, the log building was replaced by a frame meetinghouse that burned. Its successor burned circa 1903. The present building dates from 1958. Families prominent in the congregation have included Hambrick, Glass, Thomasson, Neal, Nutter, Pitts, Smith, Brown, and Triplett.

---

[388] James Wade Emison, Jr., and W.T. Smith, map, 1942, "Original Land Patents (1774-1816) in Georgetown Area, Scott County, Kentucky," in Emison, *Emison Families, Revised,* 33-36; Deed Book 34-89.

GREEN ACRES GASOLINE STATION, CINCINNATI PIKE. A gasoline station built by Joe Harp in the Craftsman style on a poured concrete foundation in the 1930s recalled increasing numbers of vehicles traveling the Dixie Highway. The building had an overhanging porch with a hip-on-gable roof to shelter vehicles seeking services provided by the station. The station's banked basement related to the slope of land to the east and Dry Run. A guest cottage stood nearby, its ruins visible until the 1980s. The main block of the station had a centered entry with windows on either side. A three bay gabled addition on the south was somewhat balanced by the frame addition on the north and had an entry near the north end and a double window on the opposite end.

Figure 267. Dry Run School on Cincinnati Road.

DRY RUN SCHOOL, CINCINNATI ROAD. Master Mason Kelly Linn is credited with construction of the brick school building at Delaplain on Cincinnati Road. It is five bays wide with a wide classical entry with multi-paned transom and sidelights. Sheltering the door is an open pediment supported by Tuscan style columns. Three steps lead to the small portico. Windows are double hung. The building earlier had end chimneys. It is similar in plan to the former school building by the lakeside at White Sulphur on Frankfort Road. For many years after it served as a school, it was the home of William Edgar Sharpe, a former student.[389]

Ruth West, later head art consultant in program development for the Kentucky Department of Education, taught for three years at the Dry Run School after getting her start as a teacher at Risk School near Josephine. Afterwards she taught at Newtown, Stonewall, and "all over the place until 1955."

E.E. MUDDIMAN STORE SITE, DELAPLAIN, NEAR FORMER CINCINNATI RAIL DEPOT. Missing from the railroad and crossroads Delaplain setting is a formerly notable store building built by E.E. Muddiman, brick and stone mason and a literal "chip off the block" of his father, E.C. Muddiman. The Delaplain store was trimmed with decorative iron and had a stepped parapet across the front. The entryway leading from the porch was set in the cut-off corner. At the time that it was visited by this writer, during the 1970s, two bays of the main façade had been boarded over. It is easy to imagine the earlier plate glass windows. The building was constructed around 1913, according to Muddiman's daughter, the late Mrs. J.R. Wyatt.[390]

Figure 268. E.E. Muddiman store at Delaplain had a distinguishing design.

---

[389] Bevins, *Selected Buildings*, 282.
[390] Bevins., 302.

HIRAM WOOD HOUSE SITE, DELAPLAIN ROAD. A two story five bay brick house with exterior end chimneys and elaborate interior woodwork was the home of Hiram Wood, Kentucky legislator from 1855. Wood probably built the house shortly after his 1837 purchase from Levi Smith and Benjamin Emison in 1832. At the time of his death, in 1865, Wood owned almost four hundred acres in the neighborhood. The Delaplain station was first called "Kinkead" in recognition of the property's ownership by Louisa Kinkead at the time of construction of Cincinnati Southern Railroad. At her death it was divided among heirs Cora Kelly, James Y. Kelly, Cora Fleming, and Sally Davenport. In 1886 Cora Wood and C.J. Fleming sold 13.8 acres at Kinkead to Neal Delaplain, after which Kincaid Station took on the name Delaplain.[391]

Figure 269. Hiram Wood house at Delaplain.

The house, already in disrepair, was further damaged by the 1974 tornadoes that ransacked much of the area, and by an earthquake. The house's fluted woodwork was outstanding. The house measured forty-six by twenty-two feet and had an ell twenty-two by eighteen feet and a porch nine feet deep.[392]

The log crib central to the barn on the site had earlier been a dwelling. It was moved to the village of Oxford by carpenter Martin Congleton as the site was cleared for construction of the Toyota plant. Congleton also saved the pegs joining the heavy timbers and the braces. On the other side of the interstate was a 1930 nine bent tobacco barn built by Charles Perkins, a leading area builder.

HOLDINGS MILL/MOUNT GILEAD INNER COMMUNITY

Scott County's eastern edge with its several significant farmsteads or parts of farmsteads and a picturesque rural cemetery skirts along the northeast Scott/Harrison county line. The various properties share social demographics of the faded heritage of Holdings Mill, later known as Finnell and Star and today as Mount Gilead. Centerpieces of the rural community are Mount Gilead Methodist Church and the community cemetery, separated by the Finnell Road that bends to the east leading into Harrison County. Wrapping around the extensive tract on the Harrison County side of the line at Mount Gilead is a large section of land understood to have been a land grant historically and presently owned by members of the McLoney family, located within a quasi-circular sequence of roads that include Finnell, KY 3044, Coppage, and Mount Gilead Church roads. The community of Finnell most likely was named after Benjamin W. Finnell, a son-in-law of early major landowner Lon Sutphin and his wife Sally. Sutphin specified in his will the Finnell share in the estate be given to his children Sally Ann and James William.[393]

---

[391] Bevins and Powell, "Hiram Wood House," Individual Inventory Form SC64, December 16, 1987.
[392] *Selected Buildings*, 302.
[393] Will Books I-13, L-81, M-709, September 24, 1825, probated in February 1845.

MOUNT GILEAD METHODIST CHURCH. Properties in the immediate vicinity of Mount Gilead Church and cemetery collectively tell the story of a community where residents maintain close ties to each other and the church. The church was established, according to tradition, in 1834 on land donated by Lindsay Holding, a member of the family that established the community first called Holding's Mill. In 1887, the congregation's first building, a brick meetinghouse, was torn down due to weakened walls and was replaced by the present church building, a stylish frame meetinghouse. Set on rising ground with a stone retaining wall on the edge of the front lawn, the meetinghouse has a rough faced cut stone foundation. Paired brackets are lined up under the front eaves and single ones are grouped along the sides. Three pointed arched windows light the long sides of the building. The basement with Sunday school rooms, dug in the fall of 1949, was dedicated in 1950. The façade design is front gabled, three bays wide, and has a double centered entrance with pointed arched tracery in the large transom. In more recent times the congregation added a small concrete portico with steps leading from both sides. On the east side of the building is a recently constructed one story wing, four bays wide and three bays deep. The cross atop the spire bears a symbol used by Methodism to recall the tongues of fire that descended on persons gathered in Jerusalem at the first Pentecost.[394]

Figure 270. Mount Gilead Methodist Church served the community known sequentially as Holdings Mill, Finnell, Star, and Mount Gilead.

MOUNT GILEAD CEMETERY. Titles to land on the east side of Finnell Road, along with the original church building, are helpful to understanding the history of Holdings Mill. The oldest grave in the beautiful pastoral cemetery is that of Nancy Holding, wife of Thomas (1789 to 1826). Buried next to her is James D. Holding, whose date of birth is given as June 30, 1844. A note in the Scott County Genealogical Society cemetery study states that his stone was broken and that he was a "son of J.E. and E." The stone of Lutitia H. Hamon (1821-1891) states that she was the wife of Nelson Hamon and that the "H" stands for Holding.[395]

---

[394] Lisa Stephens, "Mount Gilead Methodist Church," *Scott County Church Histories A Collection* (Georgetown: Scott County Bicentennial Committee), 108.
[395] *Gone, Forgotten, Now Remembered: Scott County, Kentucky Cemeteries* (Georgetown: Scott County Genealogical Society, 1982), 112.

Among the other nineteenth century burials at Gilead Cemetery were those of Elizabeth Penn (1818-1857) and John Penn (1814-1859); John H. Stout (1798-1859); Ane-Bth [sic] Stanla (1856-1876); Mary Ann Hamon, wife of W.E. Hamon (1857-1879); James Fields (died in 1881 at the age of sixty-two); Henry Warth (died in 1883 at the approximate age of sixty-five); Eliud Hamon (1806-1894); John F. Giles, Jr. (1862-1894); Samuel W. Pavy (1834-1897); Martha J. Tinder nee Hamon (1876-1882), Mamah D. Tinder (1876-1897); and George Ann Bailey, wife of James F. (1833-1898). Several members of the Anderson family who died in the late nineteenth century – James W. (1824-1886); French B. (1856-1889); Margaret Ann, wife of James W. (1829-1890); and Dona D. 1867-1894) are also buried at Mount Gilead Cemetery. Numerous early twentieth century burials took place here during the era when rural family life enjoyed a numeric peak.[396]

Figure 271. Rhoda Gregg Roehrig, since deceased, and Judy McLoney McDowell check out the tombstone of their ancestor Lutitia Holding Hamon in the Mount Gilead cemetery.

THE HOLDINGS. This premier family involved in the industrial and cultural life of the early Finnell Pike neighborhood has nearly been lost in time. Holding, the name of the family that provided the land for the Mount Gilead Church and cemetery, was also spelled "Holdin" and "Holden," sometimes in the same record.

Division of the lands of William Holding was made by the county court on November 18, 1846, following directions given in his will. Forty-eight acres comprised the widow's dower. It was bounded by the land of Benjamin Holding and William Lilly. Small tracts were laid off for (1) Mary Simpson (four acres two rods) bounded by Benjamin Holden; (2) James Holden (four acres two rods); (3) Margaret Greenwell (four acres two rods); (4) Amanda Holden (one acre); (5) Joel S. Holding, four acres two rods; (6) John W. Holden, four acres two rods; (7) William M. Holden, three acres two rods; (8) Harriet McMillen (three acres two rods); (9) Ruth McMillen (three acres two rods); (10) Theophilus Holden (three acres two rods); (11) Valentine Holden (three acres two rods); (12) Ann Eliza Holden (three acres two rods); and (13) Elizabeth Holden (three acres two rods). Making the apportionment were Isaac Shuff, James Griffith, and John Curry. J.M. Ewing was surveyor.[397]

William M. Holding was principal descendant who worked out the division of his father's lands in the mid-1850s. In 1854 he deeded to Mary E. Holding, A.Y. Holding, William P. Holding, Lorenzo D.W. Holding, Stephen Holding, Joseph L. Holden Frances A. Holding, and Sarah A.A. Holding land located between Witherspoon's link with Nutter and William Holding. On October 20, 1854 he sold to Lewis B. Offutt parcels 1, 2, 3, and 4 at thirty dollars per acre of the dower land of Robert Brock. The same day he and Sarah Holding sold

---

[396] *Gone, Forgotten*, 111-113.
[397] Will Book K-8.

William H. Salyers an undivided interest in the allotment of Eliza Holding in her father's land. On October 7, 1856 William and Irene E. Wood, William and Sarah M. Holding, and James H. and Mary E. Stewart sold to James Warf (as spelled in the deed) 22 ½ acres on Holding Mill Road bounded by Widow Lemons, Herbert Burke's lot, and the dower. On January 16, 1855, Joseph Peacher, S.F. Peacher, and T.T. Peacher sold to William H. Holding for fifty dollars five to six acres from the Robert Brock lands.[398]

By his will dated July 14, 1875 and probated June 27, 1877, Joseph D. Holden left his estate except for one hundred acres sold to John Conner to his niece Mary E. Holden, "now living with me." John W. Penn was executor; and witnesses were Penn, John Kitchen, and William Penn.[399]

GRANGERS HALL SITE. At the time that Beers & Lanagan of Philadelphia published its 1879 Map of Scott County, a Grangers' Hall stood on the east side of the church.

WARTH HOUSE, 1351-1395 FINNELL ROAD. An impressive two-story house on a stone foundation, with two front doors and two Venetian style dormers along the front roofline, and a barn on the east side, greets the traveler heading east on leaving the cemetery. PVA files state that the house dates from 1860. For many years and perhaps for its entire existence, if built by Amanda M. Penn Warth or her husband Henry Warth, it has since been owned by members of the Penn and Warth family and their descendants. It is likely that the ancient log house that stood behind the Warth house was the home of John and Elizabeth Penn, whose graves are the oldest in the Mount Gilead cemetery. The property during the more recent late twentieth century was the home of Nannie Clay Fields Warth ("Kay" in Fannee Hilander's *Hold Back the Spring*), and her husband, Lindsay. Mr. Warth, who died in 1977, left his property to his wife; Mrs. Warth died in 1985. She left the farm to her brother Woodrow Fields' son William Clay Fields. In 1993, Fields'

Figure 272. Two-story house of Amanda M. Penn or her husband has been owned by the family since construction.

administrator Cheryl Fields Hammons and Aileen Fields, guardian of Dylan Jude Fields and Bronston Cable Fields, sold it to their aunt, Fannee Fields, and her husband, Gaylord Hilander.[400]

---

[398] Deed Books 2-141, 437, 494-496; 4-187; 1-290.
[399] Will Book S-1.
[400] Deed Books 7-36, 8-176, 203-414, and *Gone, Forgotten*, 113, 114. According to Mount Gilead Cemetery records, Amanda, wife of Henry Warth, was born in 1837 and died in 1906. Henry Warth died in 1883.

The house has an impressive early history. In 1863, George E. Prewitt, master commissioner, acting on behalf of the heirs of John Penn, deeded the property to Amanda M. Warth late Penn; the deed described the

Figure 273. Fannee Fields Hilander and Shirley Houston check out a log house that they visited frequently in childhood.

sixty-one acre and an adjacent twenty-one-acre parcel as near the Mount Gilead Meeting House adjacent James Holding, Richard Bond, and J. Corban. In 1866, B.N. and Sarah S. McDaniel sold a twenty-six-acre tract adjacent to that of John Penn and Berry for $1,200.47. Members of the Warth family continued to buy adjacent tracts. In 1903 John H. and Lee Warth and James W. and Georgie Warth deeded land bounded by Mrs. Smith and William Berry to Daisie and J. Smith, the deed stating that all the parties were heirs of Henry Smith. In 1916 Daisie and J.W. Smith of Harrison County sold to Pleasant L. Warth the same sixty-one acres five poles mentioned in the 1866 deed from Penn to P.L. Warth. Other parties' interest in Amanda Warth's dower was acquired from Mary E. and James A. Hampton.[401]

WARTH FARM LOG HOUSE SITE. The compact log house that until very recent times occupied the high point behind the Warth house may have been an early home of a member of the Holding family or of the Penns. Here the brood of Woodrow and "Hash" Fields spent an appreciable share of their youth as described in Fannee's folk history *Hold Back the Spring*. Mrs. Warth was a popular and well known teacher and along with her husband Lindsay considered the Fields children and grandchildren their own. "I guess I'd have to say that the happiest I, or we, ever were, was when we made our next move to the little house 'up the hollor' behind Kay and Lindsay's house. To me and to my simple child's mind at the time, life was perfect. I loved it there," wrote Fannee.[402]

Figure 274. Early house in Holdings Mill community possibly originally owned by Penn or Holding family and discussed in Fannee Hilander's *Hold Back the Spring*.

The house, she wrote, "eluded a certain ageless dignity that accompanies the tired grace of an old log cabin. Old it was; tired it was. Boards had given up, like old bones, creaking with age until they finally collapsed and fell, unnoticed. . . The massive chimney on the side, surely once a monument to the house, had succumbed to the elements of the years, crumbling slowly. However, a transformation took place once the rooms were filled with 'a real live family.' The old house came alive; it seemed to smile."[403]

By day, "as we romped and squealed, its walls seemed to expand to accommodate five rowdy kids; at night, when all was quiet and the coal-oil lamps were lit (the electricity was not hooked up until a few weeks

---

[401] Deed Books 37-56, 64; 38-463; 42-280; 45-304; 50-315.
[402] Hilander, 18.
[403] Hillander, 18.

later), its windows shone with a golden glow. . . Outside, close to the back porch door, the peach tree hung heavy with fruit, the apple trees were on a little knoll, ready for the picking. Lilacs and honeysuckle bloomed, as if for the first time; tricycles and stick horses appeared out of nowhere. The old house was now a home."[404]

Fannee would have done well as an architectural historian. Her and Gaylord's son Tracy is impressive in his professional quality avocational restoration work with his and his family's collection of historical properties. She continued, "Remember the steep little stairway that led to our playroom upstairs? Daddy used to point out to people that the door had wooden pegs (or hinges) – a real testament to its antiquity. . . There was the first room you entered with its door leading into the tiny little room beside the chimney – then there was the middle room with the huge rock chimney which covered the whole wall. At least it was that way in my mind . . . But this spring when we all took a trek up there to relive old memories, after a picnic at Kay's, to my dismay I found that the huge fireplace had, shall we say, shrunk? It was considerably smaller than what I remembered it to be. But I too am a different size than what I was then; perhaps that is the answer. . . Then the next room was the kitchen. There used to be a little bird that came to the window all the time – we'd put crumbs out for it."[405]

When Alice Dean, the fifth Fields child, was born on July 13, 1949, Poppa (Mr. Robertson) decided to have a celebration and "with Momma walked from the 'Cummins Place' to our house [see Cummins house discussion below]. He carried a large watermelon all the way. And Poppa was 76 years old." Sometime during the next week, in the middle of the night, Poppa passed away. "All her married life Momma had been well taken care of by Poppa. He protected her from life, amused her with his rambunctious ways and together they had enjoyed the love and respect heaped upon them by their offspring. Poppa's death was a profound moment for the family and the many farm folk who had identified with his store at Muddy Ford." Fannee wrote that his funeral was the largest held at Johnson Funeral Home at that time."[406]

Fannee's *Hold Back the Spring* captures that age and its moments in a spellbinding way. Her tribute to Mrs. Warth is touching: "Kay was always good to us; we could depend on her for anything. She was 'there' and we knew it. It meant a lot."[407]

Growing up in the unspoiled countryside in those days involved immersion in seasonal pursuits and activities. "Then came the fall and we were all through the thickets and bushes in pursuit of walnuts, persimmons, and pawpaws. How strange that our kids today hardly know what we are talking about when we mention pawpaws. Not that they were much to miss. . . Then came the winter and the little potbellied stove seemed to be ready to burst with its efforts, rising splendidly to the occasion of warming us and keeping the ever present pot of beans or vegetables to simmering. . . We would fight with snowballs and ride dishpans down the hillsides and skate precariously on the thin iced ponds. . . We used to run across the top rails of the barn and even play tag up in there. What in the world would we do if we saw our kids doing that? I would immediately chalk it up as either a serious lack of intelligence or a self-destructive attitude, yet we had neither of those motives or excuses; we were simply running wild and having fun doing it. . ."[408]

Soon the family left the idyllic setting above Mount Gilead Church to move back to the home place on the hill – "not a 'mansion on the hill' but considerably better than where we were. The move was made because Mommau (Mrs. Fields) could no longer live there alone." Though Fannee missed the old log house, "We were happy and carefree at Mommau's, too. I remember how we played. My, how we played. There was no TV – no phone and we didn't go many places – so we played together. . .

---

[404] Hilander, 18.
[405] Hilander, 19.
[406] Hilander, 21, 22.
[407] Hilander, 22.
[408] Hilander, 23.

"In the spring, roses bloomed in profusion on the rock wall out front, plums hung from the tree by the kitchen window and the old neglected orchard strained to make a showing."[409]

One wonders if such carefree pursuits might have gone by the wayside as we take for granted our super-organized existences that mandate driving into to town to shop, to participate in organized recreation and other disciplines, and to hurriedly grab supper at a fast food establishment.

JOHN F. GILES FARM/ CUMMINS/ROEHRIG HOUSE, 1353 FINNELL ROAD. The home of Joseph V. and Rhoda Gregg Roehrig from 1991 to 2015, the year of Joseph Roehrig's death, marked the couple's retirement and their decision to accomplish Mrs. Roehrig's dream of "going back home." The setting is idyllic. Rhoda grew up on a farm south of her and Joe's Mount Gilead home. To get to their home from Finnell Road, one crosses a small branch via a bridge leading from the road that in turn leads from Mount Gilead Cemetery, which the Roehrigs also cared for. The lane leads either to their garage, the Cape Cod style house, the nearby "den," or the four-bent barn painted white.

Several years ago, Rhoda Roehrig guided me and her cousin Judy McDowell on the circular route surrounding the historic McLoney farm of their shared ancestry, returning by way of the church to the cemetery, where Rhoda's parents, Claudie Gregg (1886-1944) and Pelagia E. Gregg (1893-1941) lay buried in a lot next to W.H. McLoney (dates not legible) and Nannie, daughter of W.H. and S. McLoney. Rhoda and Judy were descended from John T. McLoney and his wife Carrie. John T. owned and operated the large family farm north of the line of Mount Gilead properties, mostly in Harrison County, before moving to Georgetown where among other projects he and his wife Carrie owned and operated the KOA Camp Grounds on the Cynthiana Road. Later they moved into Georgetown and a large frame house on Gano Avenue where Carrie's bountiful meals accrued a mouth watering reputation.

In more recent years Rhoda and close neighborhood friend Mildred Gregory (see 1284 Finnell Road) traveled to Georgetown to oversee the clothing room of Scott County's interdenominational AMEN House. Joe Roehrig took great pleasure in farming the county line land and herding cattle from one county into the other, all in view of his home. He and Rhoda purchased the Scott County portion of the McLoney land when they were living on their home farm bought in 1991 from Spring Valley, Inc., which in turn purchased it from Burgess and Monnie Rea Drake in 1972. The Drakes acquired the farm in 1968 from C.B. and Ona May Cummins, and they in 1934 in a

Figure 275. The John F. Giles complex later owned by the Cummins and Roehrig families.

---

[409] Hilander, 23-25.

Figure 276. Gothic Revival house in Finnell relates to businessman/farmer James Amos Hamon.

Figure 277. James Amos Hamon barn in Finnell/Star had showy horizontal siding.

Figure 279. Robert and Mildred Gregory's front-gabled house. The Gregorys were farmers and leaders in the Mount Gilead and Scott County community.

Figure 279. James Amos Hamon's "Cheap Store" was preserved overtime by Robert Gregory.

court action related to the estate of Leander Giles. The Cumminses were likely builders of the house and related buildings.[410]

The land traces to John F. and Elizabeth J. Giles estate. On March 18, 1907, heirs Llewellyn Giles, Hiram Giles, Frank Giles, Susan Giles, Stella Maddox, B.C. McDaniel, Noble McDaniel, Lizzie Daugherty, Joseph Giles, and J.T. Giles, deeded seventeen acres and a twelve-foot passway to Leander Giles, who purchased adjacent acreage from Charles and Maude McMillan.[411]

ROBERT AND MILDRED GREGORY FARM, JAMES AMOS HAMON STORE, AND RELATED PROPERTIES, FINNELL PIKE. Finnell Store or the Amos Hamon Store shows the scars of time as it rests on Scott County's northern reaches of Finnell Road, continuing in its place due to the honor accorded it by owner Robert M. Gregory. Gregory underscores its architectural and historic significance, resulting in his refusal to remove it from the landscape.

Hamon secured post office privileges for the community first called Finnell in 1886 in honor of Judge James B. Finnell, subsequently Prohibition candidate for President of the United States. One of those properties that Property Valuation Administrator Timothy Jenkins' field team marks "unlivable" in their card files, Hamon named his store "St. John's Cheap Store." Hamon and his sister, who married John T. McLoney, were children of Nelson Hamon and his first wife, Letitia Holding. In travels searching for historic landmarks over the past half century, the writer has sadly observed many older Scott County properties disappearing from the landscape. One such lost landmark was the early twentieth century gasoline station that reminded us to turn north from Cynthiana Road toward Finnell. Such ruins mark the way of many memories. Much thanks is due Robert and Mildred Gregory for allowing Amos Hamon's store to remain so long for the rest of the world to enjoy.[412]

James Amos Hamon was a late nineteenth and early twentieth citizen who helped define the county. He was a farmer and stock breeder and trader all his life and owned a saddle stallion bred and trained by Richard Pack. His farm, much now owned by Robert and Mildred Gregory, was known as East Eagle Stock Farm. As magistrate from the Turkeyfoot district, Hamon served on the building committee that let the contract for the 1890 jail. He represented Scott County in the Kentucky House of Representatives from 1893 to 1898. His first wife died in 1905.

After her death Hamon married Marie Minus. He died in 1930. By his will, dated 1924, he made bequests of $300 to his tenant Claude Wells and $400 to family servant Gertrude Morris. He left

---

[410] Deed Books 192-126, 117-58, 107-153, 67-334, 61-569,
[411] Deed Books 38-326, 352, 581; 55-410.
[412] *Georgetown Weekly Times*, September 30, 1885, August 11, 1886; Gaines History 1: 175.

one-fifth shares in the balance of his estate to his wife Marie and children W.T. Hamon, a Cynthiana merchant; Delia Milner; Edith Stewart; and Mattie Ewing. According to his biographical sketch in *B.O. Gaines History of Scott County*, he also had a grandson, James K. Ewing. Mrs. Hamon on November 11, 1931, acceding to her option under Kentucky law, renounced her husband's will, declaring her intention to take the statutory amount allowed by law. Hamon's Gothic Revival dwelling, which burned a couple of decades ago, is pictured at the top of the previous page, along with a showpiece barn with horizontal siding that continues to command the landscape.[413]

Figure 280. Hilltop barn of James Amos Hamon in Mount Gilead community.

The estate division mandated by the statutory division of Amos Hamon's property was resolved in 1931 when Marie Hamon deeded to W.T. Hamon, Mattie H. Ewing and Delia Hamon Milner her dower in three tracts: (1) 146.96 acres on Finnell Road, boundaries including Cummins, Faulconer, and Mrs. T. Bailey; 275.90 acres on Finnell Road bounded by Mrs. N. Bailey, Warth, Paul, Skinner, and Gallihue; and (3) 178.5 acres on Finnell Road, the land of Neddie Sharp and Faulconer being adjacent. Also included were a house in Georgetown on North Hamilton and Jefferson streets and "any stores and properties at the intersection of the Finnell and Sadieville Pike." In conjunction with the settlement, W.T. Hamon, Delia and Frank Milner, and Mattie Ewing divided Hamon's property. Mattie H. Ewing came into possession of the 178.51- acre tract in 1934.[414]

Hamon began acquiring property in the area as early as 1870 when he bought forty-five acres from John F. Giles, Sr., for $22.50 an acre. In 1872 he bought a small parcel from B.N. McDaniel. The Gregory land on the west side of Finnell Road retains an ancient barn with part of its clapboard siding. The barn and an Italianate style house that burned several years ago were associated with Hamon's saddlebred operation. Gregory and his wife Mildred have been a part of the Finnell neighborhood since 1949 when they purchased 150 acres from Arnold and Lillie Watson previously owned by Hamon and subsequently by his widow Marie M. Hamon, later the wife of S.C. Doggin. In 1944 Mrs. Hamon sold the 150.02- acre farm to E.R. and Emma Wilmoth, who in 1946 sold it to Roland and Okla Motley.[415]

Bertha Bailey in 1933 quitclaimed to Elizabeth Bessinger her interest in forty-five acres exclusive of a fifty-by-seventy-foot graveyard earlier deeded to N.C. and Bertha Bailey by William T. Hamon, son of Amos and Marie Hamon. Elizabeth Bessinger willed her interest to her husband, William, who willed it to Carey and Harvey Bessinger. They in turn, with Carey and Ada Bessinger, deeded the property in 1958 to the Gregorys. The Gregorys also acquired a parcel of land in 1966 from Royce W. and Lona H. Ladd on Mount Gilead Road, earlier part of the Matthew and Minnie Lee Middleton estate.[416]

---

[413] Gaines History 1, 6; Will Book W-51 and W-62.
[414] Deed Books 59-339; 60-, 551; 65-67; 68-462; 72-234; 77-39; 88-168; Will Books X-525, 4-368.
[415] Deed Books 59-310, 75-188, 75-103, 68-498.
[416] Deed Books 86-197, 89-532, 59-264; Will Books W-265, X-393.

Chapter 6
Oxford Village

Oxford's years as an incorporated city may have been short lived, but the little burg of several eras was indeed at one time a corporate entity.

Located at the crossing of the Lexington/Newtown/Muddy Ford/Turkeyfoot road with the road from Georgetown to Cynthiana, Oxford retains impressive integrity-loaded components of the early crossroads village. In fact, all but four of the existing buildings – the two one story Greek Revival period brick residences on Oxford Village Lane, the Masonic Lodge building, also on the lane, and the Ward-Hendricks house on Muddy Ford Road -- are late nineteenth and early twentieth century in origin. Three brick church buildings survive. Oxford Christian Church, home to an active Disciples of Christ congregation, is filled weekly and oftentimes several times a week. The former Presbyterian church building serves as an antique shop, and the Methodist church building is a private home.

Figure 281. Oxford sidewalks are believed to have been the work of E.C. and E.E. Muddiman.

Other vestiges of the past include the Greek Revival period tavern/Masonic Lodge, three former stores, two Greek Revival period dwellings, several Victorian period homes, a brick one room early turn of the nineteenth into the twentieth century schoolhouse, and a larger Arts and Crafts era six grades to high school building that is now home to a lumber yard. A relocated log house now occupies the site of a former five bay brick house, the owner's family having lived in the north four bays. A tavern was located in the south gable end.

Oxford's earliest designation was Patterson's Crossroads, possibly an allusion to Colonel Robert Patterson's earlier affirmation of the turkey foot contours of Eagle Creek's branches to the north. Then it became Hamilton's Crossroads, in recognition of Charles Hamilton's early mill about a quarter mile north of present Oxford and Hamilton's dwelling in the village. Robert Barkley is said to have accorded Oxford the designation of Barkley's Crossroads. It was next incorporated as Marion, for whom we know not, or at least are not certain, and finally, as Oxford.[417] Lewis Collins' 1847 *Historical Sketches of Kentucky* listed Scott County with five towns: Georgetown, Great Crossings, Marion, Newtown, and Stamping Ground. Marion, Collins wrote, "is a small village, having a population of about fifty souls – with one Methodist and one Christian church, one school, one physician, and five mechanical trades." An interesting photograph published in the Scott County Genealogical Society's *Families & History* features a gathering of Oxford's leading citizens posed in front of the home of Dr. Francis Marion Cannon, along with a suggestion that the village name may relate to the doctor's story.[418]

---

[417] Perrin (ed.), *Bourbon, Harrison, Scott, and Nicholas Counties,* 211, 212; Gaines History 2:175. Deed Book M-442: On March 16, 1825 and March 28, 1833, the heirs of William Warren sold 200 acres on Lane's Run at Hamilton's Crossroads to Job Stevenson. Deed Book 7-356, March 12, 1865, Joseph and M.E. Barkley sold to James Risk, Sr. for $7,029, eighty-two acres on Lane's Run, Georgetown Road corner to R. Barkley, Muddy Ford Road, Atkins, and J. Risk. Deed Book 9-365: On September 16, 1868, George M. Tilford, commissioner in the case of Robert Barkley versus John T. Anderson, sold to James Risk for $568 a house and lot bounded on the south by the Leesburg Road, east by the Turkeyfoot Road, and north and west by James Risk, "occupied by J.F. Anderson, sold by him by title bond by Robert Barkley."

[418] Lewis Collins, *Historical Sketches of Kentucky* (Cincinnati and Maysville, 1847), reprinted in 1968 as *History of Kentucky by Lewis Collins* (Lexington: Henry Clay Press, 1968), 594; *Families & History,* 15.

Oxford was a popular location for representatives of the medical profession. Dr. Joseph Barkley was a grandson of Matthew Barkley and a son of Robert and Mary Cooper Barkley. Matthew Barkley with his family had been denied refuge from a downpour of rain in an already too crowded fort at Lexington. Matthew Barkley, Jr., married Margaret, daughter of Hugh and Mary Baird Emison. Mary inherited family land near Oxford and the mill property north of Sadieville. Dr. Joseph Barkley was born in 1820; he married Mary E. Kimbrough and practiced in Oxford and Leesburg. Dr. John Barkley in 1888 bought and lived in the Ward-Hendricks house.[419] Dr. William H. Paxton bought the William Gray house in 1850 from Dr. B.F. Elliott, who had acquired it in 1850. Dr. C.T. Hendricks first lived in the Gothic Revival Ward-Hendricks house across the road from the James Risk family, whose daughter he married. In 1887 Jane and C.T. Hendricks built their expansive Italianate style house on Oxford's southwest corner.[420] Dr. James T. Johnson and his wife Nannie M. bought the Helen F. Juett house in 1885 and sold it in 1887 to Sep M. Anderson. Dr. Frank Collins, born in Kenton County and graduated from Centre, Ohio, Medical School, began practicing in Scott County in 1897 as a partner with Oxford's Dr. Hendricks.[421] Dr. R.A. Moore was born in Scott County to James and Sallie Allen Moore, his grandfather James having been one of Scott's earliest settlers. Dr. W.G. Moore lived in the brick house east of the Presbyterian Church prior to selling it in 1894 to the Presbyterians. He worked with Dr. Francis M. Cannon on various cases.[422]

Dr. F.M. Cannon was born in 1832 to hatter and farmer J.J. Cannon and Martha Hester Ford. Cannon was one of fourteen children. Educated at Stamping Ground Academy, he taught four years prior to studying medicine with Oxford's Dr. W.B. Paxton before entering the Kentucky School of Medicine in Louisville. In 1868 he married Mary A. Sidener of Lexington; their children were Alonzo and Mary Frances. The doctor was described as having been six feet six inches tall. The journal that he kept between 1893 and 1907 provides an interesting study of the turn of century era and particularly of his medical practice, the village of Oxford, the breeding and buying of trotting horses, the Christian Church, and the Masonic Lodge.[423] Dr. Boyers, in 1893, newly graduated by the Kentucky School of Medicine, located his office in the corner storeroom of Jacob Price's building.[424]

Oxford also had a generous share of attorneys. J.Q. Ward of Cynthiana was born in 1838 to Cary A. Ward. A printer by trade, Ward, an 1858 graduate of Georgetown College, had been editor of a newspaper in Oxford, Ohio, and subsequently became a farmer and merchant. He studied law under Georgetown's celebrated Marcellus Polk.[425]

As this is written, there is great concern about the traffic that takes advantage of Oxford's location. Just east of Oxford is the still growing thousands of employees Toyota manufacturing establishment. Next door to it is the City of Georgetown's industrial park conceived to provide opportunities for companies that might help Georgetown and Scott County rely less on the automotive industry. Seated well within the boundaries of the industrial park is an old "Penn plan" two story three room log house with added kitchen wing, built by surveyor Joseph Ewing in the 1790s. It is protected by a sheathing of corrugated steel as it awaits a better day when it can be properly restored. The redevelopment of U.S. 62 between Georgetown and Cynthiana bypassed and in some ways protected historic Oxford but also influenced some stagnation.

One of the four roads leading into Oxford is now known as Oxford Village Lane. Leading from the new Cynthiana Road, it deadends after you pass the historic buildings lining it. Another entrance is provided by KY 922, the old Lexington-Newtown-Muddy Ford Road. Its traffic generally moves more rapidly than it should

---

[419] Perrin (ed.), 720; James Wade Emison, Jr., *Supplement to The Emison Families, Revised (1954)* (Vincennes, 1962), 111.
[420] Gaines History 2:175.
[421] Gaines History 2:175.
[422] Perrin (ed.), 572.
[423] Dr. F.M. Cannon, Journal Notes, January 1, 1893 to July 9, 1907, Scott County Public Library; Perrin (ed.), 639.
[424] Dr. Francis M. Cannon Journal, July 3, 1893.
[425] Perrin (ed.), 687.

toward the four-way stop signs at the old Oxford crossroads. Drivers sometimes zoom through the intersection before they realize that they have violated a traffic sign. Another entryway is the old Delaplain Pike that leads into the village after it passes the former grade and high school, the former custodian's residence, and the brick Future Farmers of America building. The best way to study Oxford is to examine its buildings. We begin at the east terminus of Oxford Village Lane.

OXFORD VILLAGE LANE, NORTH SIDE

OWENS-FLEMING-RAINS HOUSE SITE, 2780 OXFORD VILLAGE LANE. W.C. Owens represented the Central Kentucky district in the United States Congress. His candidacy was supported by village physician Dr. F.M. Cannon, who commented on Oxford native son's victory over incumbent W.C.P. Breckinridge in the 1894 election. Owens' victory by 730 votes was declared on September 15. Dr. Cannon wrote, "My large farm bell and that of James W. Renaker and Will Carrick's simultaneously sent forth the joyous news of the great Owens victory." Earlier that year, Owens had held a campaign rally at the Oxford schoolhouse, several other speakers having journeyed to Oxford to campaign for him.

The two-story L-shaped house occupies the land that Jacob and Rebecca Price sold to John W. Fleming in 1884 after buying it from W.C. Owens in 1881. Randolph Rains inherited the Oxford property from his mother and willed it to Garnett Wayne Rains.[426]

The house during its very early years had multi-paned sash and changed it during the Victorian era to two-over-two pane double hung sash before passing into oblivion. During its later years, vinyl frames replaced the earlier mitre-joined wooden frames.

Figure 282. Rains home in Oxford was a former home of W.C. Owens, winner of the 1894 Congressional election.

OLD OXFORD SCHOOL, 2782 OXFORD VILLAGE LANE. Few Scott County country school districts were able to pay the high cost of having their one room schoolhouses constructed of brick. The Oxford example with an elegantly corbelled gable and a porch supported by turned posts is unexcelled among early Scott County schools. Master brick and stone mason E.C. Muddiman, responsible for building the three community churches, several houses, and the stone village sidewalks, built the schoolhouse from bricks left over from construction of the Christian Church across the street.

The former schoolhouse adapted well to its second life as a dwelling. Randolph R. Rains bought the property in 1968 from Jessie May Combs and in 1998 gifted it to his son and daughter-in-law

Figure 283. Former Oxford School.

---

[426] Deed Books 21-400, 18-332.

Garnett Wayne and Hazel Darlene Rains. The schoolhouse converted into a dwelling recently enjoyed an attractive renovation and addition.[427]

BAILEY-PRICE HOUSE, PRESBYTERIAN MANSE, 2758 OXFORD VILLAGE LANE. Charles Hamilton was an original owner of a central lot in the village once known as Hamilton's Crossroads. Hamilton's farmland came from the 4,000 acre Josiah Watson land grant. Village shoemaker Isaiah Bailey purchased the land from Hamilton's heirs in 1851 for ninety dollars and sold the house and lot in 1869 to Jacob Price, a community leader, for $500.50. A favorite piece of Oxford lore is the story of Price's daughter Helen climbing out of the rear east window to elope with Hugh Frank Juett. In 1884, Helen Juett's daughter, Rebecca, and her husband Jacob Price sold the property to S.M. and Betty Anderson. Sallie E. Moore bought it in 1894. Sallie and her husband, W.G. Moore, sold it to Dr. J.A. Coyle in 1894 for $859.[428]

Figure 284. Shoemaker Isaiah Bailey's house was bought by Jacob Price and later was Presbyterian manse.

Coyle's sale of the house and its one-acre lot for $825 to the West Lexington Presbytery trustees took place in 1895. In 1927 the presbytery deeded the property to the church trustees – Belle Cannon, W.C. Murphy, and Robert Cannon. Not quite one hundred years later, the trustees of the Transylvania Presbytery, successor to the West Lexington Presbytery, sold the manse for $30,000 to Joe W. Jarvis, III.[429]

Figure 285. Cast iron steps of Presbyterian Church were inherited from Cynthiana Christian Church.

---

[427] Deed Books 239-245, 107-156, 67-462, 49-263, 48-236, 40-32.
[428] Egbert and Egbert, I,62; Deed Books 21-413, 24-64, 29-77, 29-370, 56-227, 196-325. Charles Hamilton was probably the individual for whom the crossroads was named. See also Bevins, *Selected Buildings*, 171.
[429] Deed Books 26-370, 56-227, 196-325.

Figure 286. Oxford Presbyterian Church was an outstanding design of E.C. Muddiman.

Former Providence Presbyterian Church/Jarvis Antiques, Oxford Village Lane

Architecture of Oxford's former Presbyterian Church places it among the best Victorian era brick churches. Large rough faced stones are laid with rounded mortar joints to face the foundation. Brick sidewalks remain beneath the grassy area in front of the church. The two-door Tudor arched entryway is set within a tall corbelled Tudor arch flanked on both sides by round headed arches. Stained glass fills the six Tudor arched windows. A large stained-glass window lights the pulpit area. The genius behind the beautiful design and brickwork of Providence Church, which after 1991 became the home of Jarvis Antiques, was master mason Eli C. Muddiman. The heavy cast iron steps were retrieved from the demolition of the second building of Cynthiana Christian Church following its final service there in 1899.[430]

Oxford's settlement period antecedents reflected the Presbyterian faith of many families who settled nearby. To the south on Miller's Run, according to the early county order book, were "little tents," small wooden structures from which qualified communicants at the early Presbyterian preaching and communion events received tokens to present prior to receiving the bread and wine. The church constructed on or near the Miller's Run site a meetinghouse known as Beatty Church, an antecedent of Barkley Church, which in 1830 at its new location in Oxford was renamed Providence Presbyterian Church.[431]

---

[430] Egbert and Egbert 1, 61.
[431] Egbert and Egbert, 56-63.

In 1831, according to research of the Reverend Charles Egbert, Matthew and Margaret Barkley sold one acre of land for twenty dollars to trustees Jacob Miller, W.W. Allen, and A.D. Offutt for a school house and a meeting house popularly known as the Sugar Ridge Meeting House. The Presbyterian congregation used the meetinghouse until its successor was erected about one-half mile to the east in Oxford village. In March 1835 the trustees of Oxford White School District #15, C.J. Ward, Joel Ammerman, and H.S. Anderson, sold the one acre Sugar Ridge School House property to Jones Risk. Among the groups who had earlier used the meetinghouse was the Christian Church. Evangelist John T. Johnson, according to his biography, preached at Sugar Ridge as early as 1832. John Rogers and "Raccoon" John Smith visited Sugar Ridge in March 1834 to formally announce the union of the Christian Churches led by Barton Stone with the Disciples of Christ led by Alexander Campbell.[432]

The Presbyterian Church's 1836 rebuilding followed donation to trustees Jehoshaphat Polk and Scott C. Moore by Samuel and Mary Moore of the two acre site where the congregation was already meeting. The meetinghouse was constructed with bricks made from clay dug behind the church and kilned on church property. Building committee members were Columbus Ward, Robert Moore, William Finley, Belle Cannon, Sally Carrick, and Bettie Moore.[433]

The two-door church had a U-shaped balcony. The building was used until its floor caved in from termite damage. E.C. Muddiman, mason and carpenter, constructed the 1893 building. Dr. H.C. Hendricks, Oxford physician, spearheaded the movement for the building of the Victorian masterpiece. Bricks from the old building and additional bricks kilned near the back of the building were used to craft the walls. A large stained glass window was positioned on the rear wall and three windows pierced each of the sides. The pump organ and communion table chairs were saved from the first building; the organ was replaced when musician Mabel Fleming found it too difficult to pump, at which time Minnie Cannon bought a piano used until replacement by an electric organ purchased in 1961 in memory of Robert Cannon. Dr. Hendricks covered the cost of church pews, the communion table, three large pulpit chairs, and a large pulpit made to order in Cincinnati. Gano May is said to have delivered the furnishings from the Delaplain station in his "jolt wagon." Dr. Edward O. Guerrant preached the dedication sermon on October 19, 1893 to an estimated 1,000 persons; the celebration continued with morning and evening services through Tuesday. The church's first set of wooden steps with wooden hand rails on each side, painted gray, was replaced by iron steps with handrails from the Cynthiana Christian Church when the latter church was discontinued in 1899. E.C. Muddiman installed the steps.[434]

On March 1, 1895, the West Lexington Presbytery purchased the former home of Dr. J.A. Coyle on the east side of the church for a rectory for $825. The Cherry Spring Church at Newtown contributed $165 toward the project with the understanding that the Providence pastor would provide services for the Newtown congregation. The Presbytery contributed $640 from the sale of the manse at Leesburg and on September 29, 1927 for one dollar deeded the Oxford manse to the Oxford church. By this date the Cherry Spring Church had disbanded. The first resident pastor, the Reverend J.W. Tyler, was granted permission to raise a garden and pasture his horse on the lot. The design of the house is impressive. The entryway has a transom. Cupboards closed with Greek Revival style long panels occupy both sides of the gable end fireplaces. Original doors, including those in the hall, have Greek Revival twin panels.[435]

---

[432] Egbert and Egbert, I, 59-60; John Rogers, *The Biography of Elder J.T. Johnson*, second edition (Cincinnati: published for the author, 1861), 80; Barton W. Stone and J.T. Johnson (eds.), *The Christian Messenger* VIII, No. 1, 49.
[433] Egbert and Egbert, 60, 61.
[434] Egbert and Egbert, 62.
[435] Egbert and Egbert, 62, 63.

Sunday school classes met in the manse prior to the January 1971 donation by George May of the Masonic Lodge building on the church's west side. In December 1971 Mr. May also donated to Providence Church the old Methodist Church building that he had converted into a duplex. His purpose in making the gift was for the church to have financial means to underwrite the minister's salary with rental income.[436]

Figure 287. Oxford's Masonic Lodge was the work of Hartwell E. Boswell.

The congregation, reduced to three communicants, voted on April 14, 1991, to petition the Transylvania Presbytery to dissolve Providence Church, allowing members to transfer to other congregations. Eldyn Johnson, clerk of the session, signed the petition. The presbytery dissolved the church on September 19, 1991. The pulpit furniture, communion table and two chairs, and the pedestal stand were given to Bethesda Church at Muddy Ford. Joe and Sue Jarvis and Joe W. Jarvis, III, purchased the church building for conversion into an antique shop, and the manse, which became the home of Joe Jarvis, III.[437]

MASONIC LODGE, TAVERN, STORE, POST OFFICE, CHURCH EDUCATION BUILDING, OXFORD VILLAGE LANE. The stylish Greek Revival period commercial building, three bays wide on the lower story and two on the second, is an upscale example of a tavern and village store building. Its original owner was Hartwell E. Boswell, who later built the historic Ashland House in Lexington and the Elliston at Covington. Boswell, who married Rebecca, daughter of John B. and Catherine Emison Sutphin in 1840, also operated a tavern at Leesburg from 1852 to 1857. In 1832 Matthew Barkley sold the property to James W. Smoot and Ruben (Reuben) Anderson. Several property owners owned the stylish rural village property before the Free and Accepted Masons, Oxford Lodge 176, bought it in 1852. Lodge trustees were James H. Jewett, John Shelley, Moses Risk, William Gano, and William Penn. The lodge used the second floor of the building while the lower story was a store and post office.[438]

Oxford's post office was established as Marion in 1836; its name was changed to Oxford in 1846. The post office, discontinued on November 16, 1877 and reestablished on December 12 the same year, was permanently discontinued March 31, 1902. Cary A. Ward was the first postmaster, serving from 1836 to 1843. An interesting development was installation of a burglar alarm in the lodge building in 1927 or 1928 by Jack Rains. It was connected to the bedroom of storekeeper Hugh Frank Juett's house. Rains used all local parts except the wire. George May purchased the building in 1941, renting the ground floor as a store and the second as a dwelling. He then gave the building to the church for its education annex. The property reverted to the May heirs after the church ceased to exist.[439]

---

[436] Deed Books 66-391, 116-539; Egbert and Emily Egbert 1, 64.
[437] Egbert and Egbert, 65.
[438] Perrin (ed.), 559; James Wade Emison, *Supplement*, 58.
[439] Egbert and Egbert 1, 63,64.

Figure 288. Reuben Anderson house and tavern with entrances from Muddy Ford Road (house) and Cynthiana Road (tavern).

REUBEN ANDERSON HOUSE/TAVERN SITE, 2740 OXFORD VILLAGE LANE. A relocated historic log house that had faced the long abandoned Old Turkeyfoot Road several miles to the west now occupies a corner of the large lot where Reuben Anderson's brick dwelling/tavern formerly stood. Before its relocation to Oxford village by Martin and Eileen Congleton, the log dwelling was central to a log crib barn on the former farm of Hiram Wood. As the site was being cleared for construction of the Toyota plant, Congleton numbered and removed the logs. Schermbeck of Redondo Beach, California purchased the relocated log house in 1996. Bruce and Cary Williams bought it along with the former lodge building in 2011 and have since made additions.[440]

Reuben Anderson was the original owner of the five-bay house that hugged the sidewalk beside the Oxford-Leesburg Road from the time of its construction circa 1835 to 1840 to its demolition in the 1980s. Anderson operated a tavern in the house's two end bays, entered by the gable end entrance. Anderson descendant Ruby Crenshaw recalled family tradition that Anderson built the house and tavern and a storehouse on the eastern part of his lot before going broke.

Civil War tales abound regarding the old house, including the story of the Anderson children hiding under their mother's skirt to avoid being seen by soldiers passing through. After the Anderson era, Jacob Price and his daughter Helen Juett had a

Figure 289. Removal of the Anderson building provided a lot for the relocation of a log house from the barn of Hiram Wood.

---

[440] Bevins and Powell, Survey Form SC64, Hiram Wood House, December 16, 1987; Deed Book 341-001.

vineyard and winery on the site. The Juett family's ownership concluded in 1969.[441]

JAMES RISK HOUSE, 2720 OXFORD VILLAGE LANE. James Risk is shown on the 1879 Beers & Lanagan map as the owner of two of the corner houses in the village of Oxford, one of which is pictured at the left. This two-story house on the northeast corner of the crossroads faces the road we now call Oxford Village Lane.

The Risk house has a central gable over the central bay, the remains of an early porch, multiple paired brackets in the eaves, and tooled chimneys flanking the centered passage. The *Georgetown Weekly Times* remarked in December 1873 that "James Risk is completing a fine building in the northwest corner" of the town.

The house was left to Jane F. Hendricks by her father, and in 1902 was sold by Mrs. Hendricks and her husband, Dr. C.T. Hendricks, to Annie T. Glenn. Sarah Risk, widow of James Risk, and Mary Risk and her husband, W.O. Carrick, in 1901 deeded another Risk property on the Muddy Ford Road to Mrs. Glenn. In 1945, Mrs. Glenn's heirs sold their 230.25-acre farm on the Muddy Ford and Cynthiana roads to George T. Beckett, Jr. The Becketts left four children, William G. Beckett, Martha Beckett Graves, Betsy Beckett Mahoney, and George T. Beckett, III, who in 2002 sold the five-acre tract and the house to Lorette Raymon.[442] The large smokehouse with wide horizontal siding is pictured at left.

Figure 290. James and Sarah Risk's Italianate style house and interior chimneys and brackets in the soffit.

OXFORD VILLAGE LANE, SOUTH SIDE

WILLIAM GRAY HOUSE, 2769 OXFORD VILLAGE LANE. The five-bay single story brick house with an attractive brick ell was an 1840 accomplishment of grocer William Gray, who maintained a ledger with the building's construction details. Briefly, the bill for materials came to $649.65 ¼. Henry McDonough received $200 for labor, and in 1841, twenty-five dollars for building the porch. Gray bought the 140-acre farm in 1838 from Cary Ward, sold it in 1850 to Dr. B.F. Elliott, and almost in the same instant, he sold it to Dr. William H. Paxton.

Ward family members are among later owners via inheritance from Meredith Anderson. Anderson purchased it in three parcels: 101 acres in 1857 from W.B. and E.F. Paxton; one acre and thirty-six poles in 1860 from W.B. and H.E. Payne; and in 1861, seventy-eight acres from John Shelley in partnership with C.J.

Figure 291. Greek Revival period house of William Gray dates from 1840.

---

[441] Bevins, *Selected Buildings*, 176, 177.
[442] Map of Scott County, 1879; Deed Books 64-571, 34-576, 34-343, 70-55, 263-124, 267-764; *Georgetown Weekly Times*, December 17, 1873.

Ward. Anderson died in 1888, leaving his former home to his grandchildren, Sally Jane Carrick, Robert Q. Ward, Joseph B. Ward, and Mary E. Ward Allen. The Wards deeded their interest to W.T. and Sally Jane Carrick and their three children, Jim Bob Carrick, J. Ward Carrick; and Mollie C. Herndon. In 1968 Jim Bob Carrick sold the family farm to Charles E. and Rebecca Lear Cannon, who two years later sold it to Marion A. and Judy G. Cox. Judy Cox currently owns this stellar village dwelling.[443]

OXFORD CHRISTIAN CHURCH, OXFORD VILLAGE LANE. The second of Oxford village's three brick late Victorian meeting houses was built in 1900 and 1901 on the site of the village's second historic church, the Christian Church. The picturesque building, pictured on this page, has pilasters separating the three-pointed arched windows on each side, and three corbelled blind Tudor arches in the front gable. The entryway's pointed arched opening has double doors surrounded by corbelled patterning.

Figure 292. Oxford Christian Church is another masterpiece of E.C. Muddiman.

Oxford Christian Church was established in 1831 at the old Sugar Ridge Meetinghouse, the former Presbyterian church and schoolhouse. In 1847, four years before buying the site from Cary Ward, the congregation built a meetinghouse on the site where the successor building was to rise in 1900 and 1901. More than likely the first meetinghouse was a two-door church, a customary evangelical style that traditionally called for pews facing the entrance with the pulpit located between the doors. The one-acre lot cost one hundred dollars. Trustees were James Moore, William McMillin, Charles Herndon, and Remus Payne. In 1895, four years before beginning its third building, the congregation arranged to relocate the pulpit to the south end of the church and wainscoted the walls to sill level. Dr. Francis M. Cannon, physician and church member, in his 1893-1907 journal, graphically detailed the church's construction.[444]

Funding for building the church was accomplished by July 1899. On June 8, 1900, a team of brick makers, African American, from Georgetown, removed the sod from the church yard to have a place to dry the brick before burning. J.P. Jarvis furnished the wood and Dr. Cannon's team hauled the fifty cords to the site. Master mason E.C. Muddiman began constructing the walls on December 6 and in March undertook to "run up" the gable end in the rear. On June 22 Dr. Cannon wrote, "I walked around the new Christian Church where they are putting the windows in, which are beautiful, costing $225 with wire screens." On June 30 Dr. Cannon recorded his thoughts of the dedication, the crowd numbering 2,000, "the largest ever in Oxford." The offering of $580 was short of the $1,762.20 building debt. On October 11, 1901, "the ladies moved the church stoves in."[445]

---

[443] Will Book S-28, Deed Books 3-372, 5-521, and 5-396.
[444] Deed Book V-562; Dr. Cannon's journal; John G. Trefzger, "A History of the Oxford Christian Church, Oxford, Kentucky," MSS, June 9, 1950; John Parker Jarvis, "History of Oxford Christian Church," *The Georgetown News*, August 26, 1977.
[445] Dr. Cannon's journal; John G. Trefzger, 1950.

THOMAS C. PEACHER HOUSE, 2733 OXFORD VILLAGE LANE. Two houses that appear to have been interposed parenthetically into Oxford's south line of buildings include a Cape Cod style house with hip roofed gables lighting the loft, and an L-shaped house on the west. In an 1895 litigation of R.J. Hamon versus Jasper Hamon, the lot containing the brick house and adjacent commercial building was partitioned into two parcels, Henry Hamon receiving the lot just east of the brick community store. Hamon sold it the same year to Thomas C. Peacher, who at his death in 1904 passed it on to his daughter Lottie Barkley. In 1906 she and her husband A.J. deeded the property to her sister Fannie Cannon. In 1961 Ida May Flinn and others deeded it to Amos Fightmaster, whose estate sold it to Franklin D. and Delores Smith in 1995.[446]

Figure 293. Thomas C. Peacher passed on his home to daughter Lottie Barkley. The Barkleys deeded it to her sister Fannie Cannon.

LOTTIE BARKLEY HOUSE, 2731 OXFORD VILLAGE LANE. The older of the two buildings interjected into the brick streetscape is the L-shaped dwelling on the lot that Fannie Cannon sold to Lottie M. Barkley in 1906, describing it as "one half the lot willed by Thomas C. Peacher." Mrs. Cannon's lot lay on the east. On the west was the property sold by L.H. Nichols to the Misses Hamon. That year following Barkley family litigation, J.B. Wells bought the property. By 1908 J.W. Hiten owned the house and lot, his family holding title until 1922 when Mary C. Hiten and others sold it to Georgia Sharp.

Figure 294. By 1908 J.W. Hiten owned the L-shaped frame house and lot in central Oxford

Other owners have included S.B. and Annie E. White, 1924 to 1930; A.H. and Annie Hambrick, 1930-1935; C.S. and Coraline Muir, 1935-1945; Willis Combs, 1945-1954; John E. and Elizabeth A. Burgess, 1955-1973; and Charles K. and Florence Carpenter, 1978-1985 and 1988 to 1996. Dean and Donna Bedient purchased in 1996, and Dean Bedient, Jr. sold it to Randolph T. and Christine A. Harrison in 2010.[447]

---

[446] Deed Books 29-411, 78-489, 29-465, 37-335, 90-553, 213-144; Will Book T-345.
[447] Will Book T-345; Deed Books 37-336, 38-6, 38-585, 38-635, 39-400, 52-36, 53-194, 58-218, 69-66, 61-219, 70-325, 80-584, 82-280, 120-696, 128-629, 132-128, 139-413, 161-317, 177-140, 218-309, 334-506.

MUDDIMAN/HAMON/EWBANK HOUSE, 2727 OXFORD VILLAGE LANE. The picturesque brick house on Oxford's southeast corner is doubly significant – for its stylistic attributes, and its yard as the location of the town's village well. Early deeds to the lot and the adjacent lot fronting on the Newtown Pike exclude the village well from the title with these words: "but in this conveyance the well lot upon the said premises is not conveyed... being a well belonging to the people generally." [448]

Figure 295. Jim and Wilma Ewbank owned the brick Italianate style house possibly built by E.C. Muddiman.

This charm of an early Victorian dwelling was the work of master mason Eli Muddiman and rented by him to Washington Allen on November 3, 1894. The central bay of the two-story brick house extends forward and contains the centered entry. Flanking the three bays of the façade is a stylish porch with a forward extension serving the entrance pavilion. Square posts rise from square bases to milled crowns connecting them to the porch's concave soffits. Elegant milled brackets are positioned under the soffits. The flare provided by the brackets joins the gingerbread cornice that has cut-out trim with a toothed border. Double hung windows with single pane sash have segmental arched lintels and stone sills. Muddiman shows up twice in the lot's lineage, first as purchaser at a master commissioner's sale involving the daughters of A. Dudley Hamon: Mary, Frances, and Lida Bell. Lida Bell married a Tinder. Muddiman again bought the property in 1894 from Nelson Hamon for $952.70.

Figure 296. E.C. Muddiman probably built the stylish country store that Wilma and Jim Ewbank christened "The Wee Shop of Oxford."

Muddiman and his wife then owned it for four years before selling it to L.H. and Nettie Nichols in 1898. Muddiman may have been the builder and original owner of the equally captivating brick storehouse on the east side of the house. The three-bay store has a double entry flanked by large store front windows with four large single pane sash components. Brackets join the porch roof to the narrow, chamfered columns mounted on small square bases. The picket fence surrounding the yard has arrow tipped points. It is positioned next to the stone curbed sidewalk apparently built by Muddiman connecting the village's three Muddiman-built churches.[449]

The title for the lot traces to William and Matilda Spates' 1859 deed to Jacob Price, who also deeded the house and lot "formerly occupied by Isaiah Bailey as a shoe shop," purchased at a master commissioner's sale in

---

[448] Deed Books 4-532, 5-66.
[449] Deed Books 29-181, 29-182, 32-295; Dr. Francis M. Cannon, Journal, November 3, 1894..

the case of James E. Cannon and others versus Walter C. Glinn. In 1868 Price sold the two houses and lots to William C., Samuel, and Douglas P. Moore. In 1871 Moore and his wife Nancy F. sold the properties to A. Dudley and Eliza Hamon for $525. Members of the Hamon family were prominent among the property's owners for all but a few years prior to 1920.[450]

Ambrose Dudley Hamon farmed in the Oxford area. He was born in Woodford County in 1818, son of a stonemason. He married Eliza Jane Hardesty in 1848; their children were Hannah Lucy, Sally Henry, Fanny Lee, Mary, and Ducker. For twenty years Hamon, frequently signed as "A. Hamon," worked as a wagon maker and blacksmith. Perrin's history recalled, "Although advanced in years, Mr. Hamon is one of the most energetic of men and he has by industry and economy reared a family of highly cultivated children." Family members were recalled as "Baptists and Democrats."[451]

Of Nelson Hamon, Gaines wrote that he was ninety-two years of age in 1906 and was as active as most men in their sixties. "Mr. Hamon a few years ago was quite wealthy," Gaines wrote, "but in recent years he has given considerable property to churches and institutions under a contract that he is to receive 10 percent annually of its value during his life."[452]

During ownership of James L. and Wilma E. Ewbank, the house that they painstakingly renovated became an important cultural and social center and was made available for several historic house tours and other special events. Leslie Ann Perkins is the present owner.

Figure 297. In the 1980s and 1990s Oxford hosted annual festivals in the fall. (The building at left was a Jacob Price outbuilding.)

---

[450] The circuit court case of Mary Hamon and others versus Lida Bell Tinder resulted in the 1892 sale for $810 to Muddiman, who for $952.70 transferred his bid to Nelson Hamon. Hamon resold it in 1894 to Muddiman. In 1898 Muddiman sold it to L.H. and Nettie Nichols, who sold it in 1919 to W.T. and Florida Nelson and Thomas Nelson for $6,000. Subsequent purchasers included Lizzie and W.B. Anderson, 1920; F.O. and Mary Bell Redford, 1933; Charles Cannon and Robert McMillin, 1970; James L. and Wilma E. Ewbank, 1970; and Leslie Perkins, the recent owner (2009). Deed Books 12-207, 29-181, 46-162, 29-182, 32-395, 48-534, 50-599, 59-588, 112-279, 197-37, 257-597.
[451] Perrin (ed.), 639.
[452] Gaines History 2: 175.

Figure 298. Jane Frankie Risk and her husband Dr. W.T. Hendricks had the Victorian Italianate building as their home. Outbuildings at the right relate to the farm and Dr. Hendricks's medical practice.

JANE FRANKIE RISK AND DR. W.T. HENDRICKS HOUSE, 2721 OXFORD VILLAGE LANE. James Risk purchased from Mary A. Ford in 1879 the corner lot where his daughter, Jane Frankie, and her husband, Dr. W.T. Hendricks, built their imposing Italianate style dwelling. Mrs. Ford, whose husband was Jesse Ford, bought thirty-eight acres in 1865 from Joseph and Mary Elizabeth Barkley at the Oxford crossroads to which the Barkleys had given the name of Barkley's Crossroads. Mrs. Ford disposed of several parcels of this and other farmland lying along the Oxford-Newtown and Oxford-Georgetown pikes. Others to whom she sold small tracts at that time were F.M. Cannon, John R. Ewing, W.G. Moore, Helen M. Juett, Aaron Gaylor, Charles Ford, and John Lucas. Mrs. Ford was also on the buying end of other transactions, acquiring parcels from Edwin Ward (sixty-five acres in 1878) and W.G. and Sallie Moore (16 ½ acres in 1890).[453]

At this location Dr. Hendricks had a doctor's office along with several outbuildings. The richly embellished main house is L-shaped and mounted on a foundation of rough faced stone laid with rounded mortar joints. Its front gable ell has double windows with a sunburst between them. The gable contains fish-scale shingles and is sheltered by an elaborate milled skirt. All the main openings have gabled hoodmolds. The front porch supports are tooled posts with flared capitals beneath a tooled cornice with quatrefoils and triangular toothing. Paired brackets are positioned along the cornice. Chimneys are neatly tooled. Surviving outbuildings include a garage and storage buildings.

In 1919 Dr. and Mrs. Hendricks sold the property to Theodore Marshall, apparently a speculator, who sold it the same month to G.B. and Belle Cannon, for whom the seven-acre tract became a longtime family property. C. Frank and Fenton Allen bought it in 1951. Mr. Allen sold it in 1996

Figure 299. Aaron Gaylor owned the house at the left and the store later owned by W.E. Davis.

---

[453] Deed Books 12-394, 237, 455, 239, 455; 16-340, 26-225, 21-204, 19-202, 17-53, 14-188, 6-473, 28-473.

to the present owners, Donald W. and Sandra Allen.[454]

BLACKSMITH SHOP/GROCERY, HOUSE SITE, 2693 OXFORD VILLAGE LANE. Davis Grocery and its adjacent repair shop was a favorite Oxford landmark in recent years. The 1879 Beers & Lanagan map shows a blacksmith shop on the site. The old storehouse had a long history of serving the people of Oxford and the traveling public. W.E. Bush in 1908 purchased at a master commissioner's sale the property that had been owned by Aaron Gaylor, an early Oxford settler. In 1913 Emery Bush also bought a small tract near Oxford.[455]

The late Nancy Belle Bush recalled a blacksmith named Hervey Jones as having had his shop on the site.

Figure 300. The partial house was known as the Bradford Holland garage.

In 1977 William J. Davis, who with his wife Tempie purchased the property in 1950 from Noah and Hazel Hanna, gifted it to their daughter Elizabeth Jane Davis. Tempie Davis died in 1975, and William J. Davis in 1989. In 2004 Elizabeth Davis Doolin sold the property to Dwight Wayne Gillispie, Sr. A two-story frame house is also associated with this site.[456]

BRADFORD HOLLAND GARAGE, 2616 OXFORD VILLAGE LANE. The old saying of architects and designers, "Form follows function" might be reversed when trying to describe the house turned garage that continues to mystify travelers along the road leading into Oxford. The building is minus its original gabled roof and upstairs balcony. Two wide drive-in doors flank the almost centered single-entry door and the window with six-over-six-pane sash to its side. On Charles Egbert's map of Oxford, this property is referred to as "Bradford Holland's garage." Its title history goes like this. In 1928 Howard and Effie Lee Muntz sold the lot measuring 110 by 140 feet to Joe T. and Lelia Mae Owens, who twenty years later sold it to Lelia Mae Owens. The price was represented by fifty dollars in deed stamps. In 1966 Louise Davis, widow of James G. "Bud" Davis and her children sold the .264-acre tract to William J. and Tempie L. Davis for $5,000. Various members of the Davis family continued to own the

Figure 301. W.S. Dickerson constructed the Cape Cod style house on 195 acres that he purchased in 1944. Billy and Carrie Hall Green were recent owners.

---

[454] Deed Books 48-441, 442; 77-431, 449; 218-692; Will Books W-576, 8-742.
[455] Deed Books 39-192, 43-274.
[456] Deed Books 70-358, 136-588, 76-97, 283-436; Will Books 1-407 and 5-609.

property and in 1989 Elizabeth Davis Doolin and other family members sold it for $20,000 to Dale and Betty J. Gifford. In 1992 David G. Monhollin bought it from Dale Gifford.[457]

DICKERSON-GREEN HOUSE, 2609 OXFORD VILLAGE LANE. In 1944 Harry G. and Virginia Dickerson sold their Cape Cod style house with several outbuildings to William Gilbert "Billy" and Carrie Hall Green. The house and lot and two and one-half acres on the east side of the highway were part of the nineteen acres that B.R. and Aura Oldham sold to Lottie Barkley in 1915. In 1928 W.S. Dickerson bought the 19.5-acre tract at a master commissioner's sale following litigation of Charles W. Barkley versus Annie Lee Crenshaw and others. The neatly defined dwelling has an interior chimney with tooled stack and on the east side a bay window. The barn used for many years by the Greens has on its long side facing the road a quilt square designed and painted by the Stamping Ground Buffalo Gals Extension Homemakers. Mrs. Green passed away in 2013, leaving the farm to her children.[458]

Figure 302. James G. Davis owned the house of John and Lena True for three decades.

JOHN W. AND LENA TRUE HOUSE, 2507 OXFORD VILLAGE LANE. A recent remodeling removed the central chimney stack from the older one-story house standing east of the Juett-Cannon farm. The farmland traces to an early subdivision of a farm owned by Mary A. Ford. In 1902 W.H. and Lottie A. Franks sold five acres to Dr. C.T. and J.F. Hendricks. The Hendrickses sold it to John W. and Lena True, who in 1918 sold it to J.W. and Luna Kimbrough. Mrs. Kimbrough sold the property in 1913 to B.R. and Aura Oldham, who the same year sold it to Lottie Barkley. After her marriage to J.M. Chinn, the former Lottie Barkley sold two and one-half acres including the house to J.T. Barkley. In 1951 with the sale by G.N. and Anna Mae Smith to James G. Davis, the property entered a period of almost three decades owned by the Davis family. In 1995 Floyd R. and Denita Isaacs owned it from 1995 to 2007, when they sold it to W.J. and Amy Diane Bailey.[459]

Figure 303. Lula Ethel Juett and her son Hugh Frank Juett willed their home to farm manager James W. Cannon.

JUETT-CANNON HOUSE, 2489 OXFORD VILLAGE LANE. Lula Ethel Juett and her son Hugh Frank Juett willed their interest in their home farm to each other and to James W. "Jimmie" Cannon, who managed the property for them. The house on the property is a two-story dwelling on a stone foundation and having a stone shouldered chimney. Mrs. Juett died in 1965, and her son, in 1969. In 1973 Cannon and his wife Geraldine sold seven of the thirty-five acres to Russell and Jewell M. Moody. In 1999 the Moodys sold a lifetime interest to Charles E. Moody.[460]

---

[457] Charles and Emily Egbert, *Kith, Kin, Wee Kirk* 1: 83, 84; Scott County Deed Books 54-326, 63-551, 72-177, 103-143, 182-431, 230-596, 197-320.
[458] Scott County Deed Books 57-39, 102-101, 68-469; Will Book 20-584.
[459] Scott County Deed Books 24-35, 38-122, 39-542, 40-589, 43-152, 44-2, 44-421, 55-316, 79-507, 133-35, 150,864, 150-867, 187-469, 212-321.
[460] Scott County Will Books Y-245, Z-174; Deed Books 122-151, 239-268, 243-458.

Figure 304. The two houses on Newtown Road were sold by A. Dudley Hamon to Douglas P. and Mary F. Moore.

Oxford-Newtown Road

G.B. AND BELLE CANNON HOUSE, 4313 NEWTOWN ROAD. Another brick house with a tradition of having been built by Eli C. Muddiman, the master mason responsible for building much of Victorian Oxford, is the two-story dwelling just north of the former Methodist Church. On January 1, 1894, C.W. and Mattie L. Allen sold it to G.B. and Belle Cannon for $1,900. In 1919 the Cannons sold the house to Fred and Kate Peters for $3,600.[461]

In modern parlance, the dwelling is referred to as "the brick Cannon house." Members of the Cannon family appear frequently in its history, the most recent having been the line of family members that began with the purchase in 1944 by Frances C. Gaines from J.E. and Laura B. Ferrell. Mrs. Gaines was the daughter of Dr. Francis M. Cannon; in his journal he referred to her as "my beloved Fannie." Mrs. Gaines and her husband John W. Gaines, both of Lawrenceburg, sold the house to John Francis Cannon in 1945. Cannon and his wife Mildred sold it to Thomas and Patricia Lutz in 1970, and they to John Francis Cannon, Jr. and Diane L. Cannon in 1974. They owned it until 1981 when it was sold it to James C. and Marilyn Phipps.[462]

This was the home of Doctors James R. and Audrey Rooney between 1984 and 1995. Dr. James Rooney was director of the University of Kentucky's Gluck Equine Research Center. Audrey completed her Ph.D. work in history with the University of Kentucky and her dissertation about Germany's Magdeburg Cathedral. Their contributions, personally and financially, to their home village of Oxford, to Georgetown, Scott County, and particularly to the Georgetown and Scott County Museum and the Scott County Arts Consortium, merit remembrance forever. David and Jamie Keesling purchased the property in 1995.

Figure 305. E.C. Muddiman may have built the brick house owned in recent years by Doctors James R. and Audrey Rooney.

MOORE-HAMON HOUSES, 4347 NEWTOWN ROAD. In 1871 Douglas P. and Nancy F. Moore sold to A. Dudley Hamon for $1,575 "for the exclusive use and benefit of Eliza J. Hamon as an estate separate from that of her husband," two houses and lots that had been conveyed to Douglas P., William C., and Samuel Moore. Excepted from the deed was the "well situated on the property which is a public

---

[461] Deed Books 28-416, 48-515.
[462] Deed Books 69-158, 80-301, 112-368, 125-73, 150-397, 157-218.

well for the use of the people generally with the privilege of going to and from said well."[463]

One Moore-Hamon house is a charming one and one-half stories – with a tall upper half story -- three bay village dwelling with a gable with an attractive lunette window centered over the front door. A one-story porch shelters the three downstairs bays. The roof slopes in saltbox fashion to enclose a kitchen and pantry.

The three Hamon daughters – Mary and Frances Hamon and Lida Bell Tinder – joined in litigation regarding the two-acre tract, resulting in its sale to Nelson Hamon. Hamon also purchased from J.F. and Michie Parker the interest of four of the five Aaron Gaylor heirs and promised to set aside one fifth of the purchase price should a fifth son be discovered. Gaylor's ownership came from his purchase of the land in 1875 from Mary A. Ford. In 1894 Nelson Hamon deeded the property to Mary and Frances Hamon, and in 1917 Frances Hamon sold it to W.H. Garnett. In 1975 Charles Allen and Edna Garnett sold the property to Shirley B. McQueen. Sheila and John R. Murphy acquired it in 1998.[464]

An interesting chain of property transactions played themselves out during the early years of the houses, the older of which which appears to have been built for G.B. and Belle Cannon before 1901. That year the Cannons sold a house and lot and shop on the property to Kate M. Furnish, wife of H.C. Furnish. The Cannons bought the larger lot from Cris W. Allen. Mrs. Furnish willed the property to Ina M. Johnson, wife of W.L. Johnson, who sold it in 1905 to the Cannons, declaring that the first party was compelled to sell the lot to discharge a mortgage and Furnish's funeral expenses. In 1907 the Cannons sold the house and lot to J.H. Giles for $650.[465]

4031 NEWTOWN PIKE. Annite T. Moore purchased the property in 1915. In 1923 she wrote her will, leaving G.B. and Belle Cannon's son Robert "the picture of my deceased husband Samuel Moore, also my KuKu clock." Other property owned at the time of her death was to be divided among the children of her brother John Thurman and the children of her deceased husband's brothers, Robert and Douglas Moore. The fifteen heirs deeded the house and lot and barn to Cecil E. Parker, whose family owned it until its sale in 1967 to George May. In 1970 Russell and Jewell Moody bought it, selling it in 1986 to William T. and Willette Bryant.[466]

Figure 306. Dr. F.M. Cannon house has Carpenter Gothic styling and a later addition.

F.M. CANNON HOUSE, 4330 NEWTOWN ROAD. Long associated with the family of Dr. F.M. Cannon (1832-1908), the two-story frame house facing the Oxford-Newtown Road from the west seems to represent at least two building campaigns, the first having produced a pointed style Carpenter Gothic house. The second added a front gable ell joined to the Gothic style house by an older porch that recalls stylistically the porch on the Hamon/Ewbank brick house built by Eli C. Muddiman. The square posts supporting the porch have a square base, paneling on the lower level, and cut-out brackets tying the posts to the cornice. The

---

[463] Deed Book 12-207.
[464] Deed Book 29-181, 34-464, 35-188, 46-162, 46-164, 47-260, 50-181, 130-483, 140-213, 149-122, 167-537, 234-555.
[465] Deed Books 34-467, 37-223; Will Book T-407.
[466] Deed Books 38-602, 41-583, 58-459, 58-521, 60-446, 65-50, 103-501, 107-233, 111-526, 126-80, 131-207, 167-753.

cornice has toothed edging and diamond detail. Nicely tooled brick chimney stacks rise from the two sections of the house.

Dr. Cannon willed his property to his daughter Mary Frances Gaines with remainder to his son Lonnie. In 1968 Mary Cannon McDowell willed her interest in the house to John Francis Cannon, Sr. In 1993 Cannon's wife Mildred deeded the property on love and affection terms to John Francis Cannon, Jr.[467]

Dr. Cannon's title to this property came from Mary Ann Ford, wife of Jesse Ford, who in 1865 purchased thirty-eight acres at the Oxford crossroads from Joseph and Mary Elizabeth Barkley. Her sales to Dr. Cannon included ten acres in 1873 bounded by Alisse Jarvis and Ford; fourteen acres by Cannon, Edwin Ward, Aaron Gaylor, and J.R. Ewing; three acres in 1879 by Cannon and Ford; and sixteen and one-half acres in 1894 by Gaylor, S.M. Anderson, J.H. Barkley, and W.W. Allen.[468]

During his lifetime Dr. Cannon became a legend to the people of Oxford and Scott County. His journal survives to give a moving picture of his life as physician, saddle horse breeder, farmer, Presbyterian, and Mason.

Dr. Cannon's grandson, John Francis Cannon, had an illustrious career as pitcher and outfielder with the Cincinnati Reds from 1936 to 1940. He was born in 1915, a son of Lonnie and Mary Andrew Lockridge Cannon. He was graduated from Oxford High School and attended Georgetown College where he was a member of Pi Kappa Alpha fraternity. He was also a member of the Lawrenceburg Christian Church. Paul Derringer, a Reds' scout, recognized Cannon's baseball ability when the young man from Oxford was pitching for the Georgetown Athletics semi-pro team.[469]

Figure 307. Dr. C.T. Hendricks may have been the original owner of the Carpenter Gothic style house facing Muddy Ford Road.

While with the Reds, Cannon roomed with the popular pitcher John Vandermeer. During the 1940 spring training schedule, Cannon pitched against the Boston Red Sox's Ted Williams. Cannon was with the Reds two weeks prior to being traded to the Yankees. He pitched for the Binghamton farm team of the Yankees and in one game struck out fifteen or sixteen batters. An injury to his left elbow resulted in his retirement to his farm in Oxford. However, in 1943 Cannon pitched for the Man-o-War Colts team in Lexington, as Georgetown did not have a team during World War II. Cannon also brought in Vandermeer to pitch a game for the Colts. He coached Little League baseball for many years and was an avid hunter and fisherman.[470]

Cannon married Mildred Richardson; they were parents of John F. "Johnny" Cannon, recent owner of the family home with his wife Jennie Pat; Betty Lou Cannon Tutt, and Ann Cannon Williamson. He was a member of the Oxford Christian Church. John Francis "Johnny" Cannon was a leading farmer.

---

[467] Deed Books 108-221, 126-97, 173-328, 108-221, 236-368, 291-820, and 236-368.
[468] Deed Books 12-237, 239, 394; 28-473.
[469] Information about John Francis Cannon's baseball career from news story, "John Francis Cannon dies," *Georgetown News-Graphic*, January 4, 1989.
[470] "Farmer J.F. Cannon Sr., ex-minor leaguer, dies," *Lexington Herald Leader*, December 31, 1988; *Georgetown News*, January 4, 1989.

FORMER OXFORD METHODIST CHURCH SOUTH, 4303 NEWTOWN PIKE. Oxford village's third church, the 1905 Southern Methodist Church, bears the hallmarks of the handwork of mason Eli C. Muddiman. The pattern of flagstone sidewalks leading from church to church recalls the turn of century years when village residents visited each other's church and Sunday school services. The former Methodist Church occupies the site of an older building.[471]

In 1955 the trustees of the Kentucky Annual Conference of the Methodist Church – C.D. Harsh, W.P. Fryman, and S.W. Funk -- sold the church property to George May for $2,200. May converted it into two apartments to be leased by Providence Presbyterian Church with rental income to contribute to the pastor's salary. In 1971 May conveyed the property to the Presbyterian trustees, stipulating that it be designated to Bellewood Presbyterian Home for Children in Anchorage, Kentucky, in the event of the church's demise or disuse. In 1992 the Presbytery deeded the sixty-eight by 150 foot lot to The Bellwood Home, which sold it four months later for $30,000 to Michael and Tina Schnurr. Tina Schnurr as Tina Wirtz became sole owner in 2002.[472]

Figure 308. Oxford Methodist Church was a 1905 masterwork of E.C. Muddiman.

MUDDY FORD ROAD

HENDRICKS-BARKLEY-HOLLAND HOUSE, 4381 MUDDY FORD ROAD. Either Cary Ward or Dr. C.T. Hendricks was the original owner of the frame or Carpenter Gothic house that for so many years was one of the oldest and best high styled houses in the historic Oxford. Although Hendricks acquired the two-acre lot for $300 in 1888 from members of the Ward family: C.J., J.Q. and Mary E. Ward, Edwin and Lizzie Ward, Reuben Thompson, Asa Allen, Cary Allen, and Georgia Allen, he was shown as householder on the site on the 1879 map. In 1890 the doctor and his wife, J. Frankie, sold the lot, complete with improvements, for $2,200 to John H. Barkley. Members of the Barkley family called the attractive pointed styled dwelling home until 1911 when A.J. Barkley, W.O. and Fay Barkley, M.L. and Herbert Zeysing, and W.D. and Ida Barkley sold it to Betty and Cora Peacher for $4,400. In 1952 Charles W. and Alice Barkley sold the two-acre tract to Lucille M. Holland. The house became intimately identified with Mrs. Holland and her husband Bradford for more than a half century until their deaths in 2008 and 2009.[473]

Among the most notable features of the house were the pointed arches sheltering the upper story windows, the bargeboard trim of milled curved detail and point-centered down arrows, and the porch with trefoil

---

[471] Apple, Johnston, Bevins, eds., *Scott County, Kentucky: A History*, 105; Bevins, *Selected Buildings*, 270.
[472] Deed Books 88-480, 116-539, 193-792, 195-338, and 262-846.
[473] 1879 Map of Scott County; Deed Books 24-340, 24-182, 42-486, 78-569; Will Book X-131.

spandrels sheltering the single front door. Round posts mounted on square brick piers rose to pointed arched spandrels. Milled brackets were positioned at the corners.

Delaplain Road

Mattie A. and Charlie Smith House, 1463 Delaplain Road.

A many times remodeled older house with two front gables, the peaks of which are accented with milled trim, stands near the intersection of Oxford Village Lane and Delaplain Road. The land traces to an 1878 deed by the heirs of James Risk (James R. Risk, William Risk, Rebecca J. Barkley, Nancy J. and Robert H. Moore, and Martha A. Risk) of forty acres to Mattie A. and Charlie Smith, who in 1911 sold a one acre lot on the corner of the Oxford-Kincaid Road and the Oxford-Georgetown Road to Booth and Laura Anderson for $250. The lot with the house increased in value by the time of its 1919 sale by W.B. and Lizzie Anderson to M.L. and Claudie Hughes. Charlie Smith again came into ownership of the property in 1922. Between 1925 and 1955, J.A. and Howard Muntz owned it. Dorsie and Lula Bell Sargent and their family owned it from 1944 to 1983, when they sold it to Donald W. and Betty F. Green, who owned it until 1995. Wallace R. and Melissa Parrish are the present owners.[474]

Figure 309. Mattie A. and Charlie Smith house has two front gables with soffit trim at the gables' apex.

Vocational Agriculture/FFA Building, 1442 Delaplain Road.

During the early years of the University of Kentucky's College of Agriculture Extension Service Smith-Hughes program of agricultural education and the associated Future Farmers of America program, the corps of vocational agriculture teachers and their students gained practical experience by designing, financing, building, and finishing their own shops, classrooms, and meeting places. Under the leadership of E.W. Walton, the Oxford students dismantled the former brick school building at Great Crossings and hauled the materials to the northwest side of Oxford school for their projected FFA building. The students designed the building in the prevailing classical revival style. Walton's successor teacher was Conrad Haynes. The Oxford FFA students won state honors in 1949 for the best overall farm shop exhibit.[475]

Figure 310. Oxford's vocational agriculture chapter house was built by students of E.W. Walton using bricks from former Great Crossings schoolhouse.

---

[474] Deed Books 16-391, 42-136, 44-426, 49-522, 50-166, 51-523, 53-202, 54-46, 54-326, 68-453, 153-285, 214-675, 256-542; Will Book U-209.

[475] Ann Bevins, "Oxford Community grows as school opens its doors," *Georgetown Graphic*, October 22, 1967.

Figure 311. Oxford's Craftsman Style school building began with four rooms constructed in 1928.

OXFORD HIGH SCHOOL, GRAVES LUMBER YARD, 1446 DELAPLAIN ROAD. The long two story plus basement public school plan was popular for an extended era. The traditional "Collegiate Gothic" style morphed into "collegiate classical" or "collegiate arts and crafts" or "collegiate art deco" or simply "collegiate Italianate" or "collegiate plain." Those of us who attended school in these spacious buildings will remember the large stairways at the ends of the halls; the cafeterias and gymnasiums and restrooms in the basements; the lower grades classrooms on the main story and the upper grades with principals' offices and teachers' lounges upstairs. Air conditioning came along as populations became less tough or more affluent. The buildings had capacity to grow and to be redecorated to accommodate changing tastes and pupils' and teachers' tendencies to be spoiled.

Such was the building at Oxford. Early in the twentieth century, Oxford and the school district became aware that the small brick building across the road from the Christian Church built with bricks left over from construction of the Christian Church was ready to be replaced by a much larger facility.

Few nineteenth century buildings were equal to twentieth century educational demands. However, school boards across the state were "hard strapped" by bonded indebtedness limits imposed by the 1893 Kentucky Constitution for building adequate school buildings. Not until Georgetown city superintendent J. Wilbur Lancaster and attorneys V.A. and Craig Bradley combined Lancaster's idea of a bonded holding company with their legal expertise did Kentucky schools have a device for circumventing the state constitution's economic straitjacket. Their concept of a process to organize civic bonded holding companies to sell bonds for school construction, build the schools, and apply taxes annually to debt retirement breezed through the court systems. Georgetown's Garth School and the means to make it happen became the prototype for schools across the Commonwealth. V.A. Bradley, Sr. explained in a 1963 series of interviews that the Bradleys' Georgetown offices were kept busy supplying local districts with the legal information necessary to solve their financing needs. Ultimately, in exasperation, the state board of education relented and set up a public legal process to accomplish the same task.[476]

In 1914, much of eastern Scott County seemed unalterably opposed to consolidation of their schools. Oxford was included in subdistrict number one that incorporated schools at Oxford, Newtown, Pleasant Point, Oakland, Muddy Ford, and Finnell (also known as "Star"). Public pressure forced candidates for county superintendent to deny that they saw a future for consolidation. Meanwhile, tiny schools continued to be built and

---

[476] Interview, 1963, with V.A. Bradley, Georgetown, Kentucky, notes in author's vertical files; see Survey form and National Register form for Garth School.

maintained. Perennial conflicts with the department of health and the Civic League/Woman's Club continued to grow, as did Oxford's enrollment, which climbed to 192 in 1923.[477]

Finally, however, in 1928, the new Oxford School's first four rooms were ready for students about the same time that the Harrison County school system withdrew support from the previously jointly supported county-line Coppage School. This left several Scott County students without a school. J.K. Feeback, a parent, offered to provide a pickup truck and outfit it with seats and a tarpaulin to haul the children to Oxford, if the school would accept them, which it did. In 1932 two more rooms were added above the gymnasium to accommodate expanding enrollment. Shortly afterwards children and parents of the Muddy Ford neighborhoods, through which the student-hauling conveyances passed, agreed that they, too, would like to be part of the larger school at Oxford. Therein began not only consolidation but a scheme for pupil transportation, which county educators theretofore had avoided.[478]

By 1938, when Oxford School had one teacher for each grade, Louise Adams declared that she "had all she could take in the first grade." At that time a wing was added to the north end of the building. In 1939 the school added a model vocational agriculture program led by E.W. Walton and subsequently Conrad Haynes. In short order, additional students came from Dry Run and Oakland. Newtown's two-year high school was closed with its students matriculating to Oxford. In 1951 Superintendent Hood conceded for a mixed seventh and eighth grade class to be established for the overflow enrollment. About that time, the twelve-grade school building was condemned. The new superintendent, M.L. Archer, and the state superintendent decided that repairs would come at too high a cost and that it was time to consolidate all four county high schools. The new Scott County High School opened in 1955. At that time the Oxford and Newtown lower grades also consolidated. The four one room and one two room schools for African American students closed in 1957 as other schools absorbed their enrolments. Thus the 1928 Oxford school became a relic of the past and was purchased by the Charles "Pete" Graves family for a lumber company.[479]

"Pete" Graves, founder of Graves Lumber Company housed at the former Oxford School, is a jovial businessman who "used to play ball on the floors." He has supplied Scott County builders, particularly those doing finishing work, with choice wood for their projects, adding to the "historic dust" that complements the décor. Graves Lumber Company is a family business that seems to be well on its way to perpetuating itself.[480]

The old school building retains its earlier form and detail. It combines Art Deco and Arts and Crafts detail in the organization and trim of its various wired brick facades. We should be thankful that demolition was not the solution when Oxford School's school days ended. Hopefully, in the future, a new use can be found that will encourage a tasteful and useful renovation. The many memories evoked by old school buildings and their solid construction demand their preservation.

---

[477] Record of Scott County Board of Education, 1914 through 1923, records stored at county school bus garage in 1991.
[478] Ann Bevins, "G.W. Cassity remembers origins of school system" for "Making the Grade Series," *Georgetown Graphic*, October 15, 1987; M.L. Archer, former superintendent, column for "Two Hundred Years of Education" series, *Georgetown News & Times*, October 13, 1987, 11; Ann Bevins, "Oxford community grows as school opens its doors" for "Making the Grade" series, *Georgetown Graphic*, October 23, 1987.
[479] Archer, October 13, 1987, 11; Bevins, *Georgetown Graphic*, October 23, 1987.
[480] Vicky Broadus, "Outside the Cube: Old School Lumber Company: Pete Graves' Family Business Adapts Without Disturbing the Dust," *Lexington Herald-Leader*, May 28, 2012.

HELEN F. JUETT HOUSE, DELAPLAIN ROAD. Perhaps the most elegantly detailed house in Oxford is the one-story dwelling on the Delaplain Road that shows off with aplomb the artistry of its designer and builder, hampered somewhat by modern embellishments that include a picture window. The L-shaped home of Helen F. Juett, one of the village's most interesting and productive characters, has two tall brick chimneys and a modern era color scheme of blue and white. The gable of the front gable ell has a pattern of shaped shingles and a cornice with returns. Large brackets or consoles join to enclose the top of the shingle filled angled cutaway that leads inward to the porch. The porch shelters the entryway and the window to its left. The turned posts are beautifully scored and rise to support a toothed cornice decorated with a snowflake design. Above them are the finishing contributors to the house's

Figure 312. Helen F. Juett's house is richly embellished with Victorian trim. The picture window is an addition.

rising symphony – chic spools connecting with the soffit. Mary B. Ford was an early owner of the land where the house resides. Mrs. Juett sold it in 1885 to Dr. James T. Johnson and his wife Nannie M., who sold it in 1887 to Sep M. Anderson.

OXFORD HISTORIC DISTRICT. Oxford Historic District's thirty-six buildings and structures, of which thirty-one were considered contributors, were listed in the National Register of Historic Places in 1979. Since that time the Reuben Anderson house, the John Fleming house, and the Hendricks/Barkley house have been demolished.

Chapter 7
Sadieville

Figure 314. Early Sadieville buildings lining Pike Street are across the road from the modern city park.

Figure 313. Light recreation can be enjoyed at Warring Pavilion

The future site of Sadieville was not northern Scott County's most logistically ideal location for a railroad center for the Cincinnati Southern Railroad as the line's construction progressed in the 1870s. However, this improbable setting near the railroad's junction with the Connersville Road and Eagle Creek without a doubt had the most influential, determined, and enterprising team of property owners contending for the depot site.

Initiating the emerging postbellum Big Eagle commercial community were T.J. Burgess of the Joseph Burgess clan and the area's major landowner; Richard F. Pack, owner of a vast amount of acreage in the vicinity; and S.T. Connellee, from whom Burgess and Pack purchased about twenty-five acres with the intention of having the rail station established there. Silas Jones' and Polk Fields' properties abutted the land of the other three, giving them significance as well among the developers of commercial and residential tracts.[481]

Incorporators of Sadieville, which was formally organized in 1881, were T.J. Burgess, Douglass Stewart, T.T. Hedger, and John Kaley (also spelled Caley). J.W. Truitt became the first police judge and L. Penn the first marshal. Organized shortly after the community began developing was the fire department, of which E.B. Braun was chief. Within a few years an enthusiastic talented citizenry had organized a brass band equipped with nickel and silver plated instruments ordered at a cost of $250. Edward Baldwin was director; musicians were Joe L. Mulberry, A.L. McCabe, C.S. Davis, E.P. McKenney, T.F. Sherritt, C.W. Rose, W.W. Mansfield, Levi Craig, A. Lemons, W.A. Maines, and Grover Maines. The city erected a bandstand in the park on the corner of Pike and Main.[482] The year 1886, a decade after completion of the laying of the track, found the city installing

Figure 315. Sadieville's relocated depot is now City Hall.

---
[481] Apple, Johnston, and Bevins, *Scott County, Kentucky: A History*, 36.
[482] Gaines History 2, 167, 168.

streetlamps, brick pavements, and stone street crossings.

Sadieville's undertaker and furniture store operator J.K. Northcutt purchased a hearse in 1889, and John A. McCabe's lumber yard and hardware store was doing a booming business. Baptists' competition for numbers of members came from the Methodists in 1887 and the Christians in 1893. The city's Deposit Bank opened its doors in 1893 and the next year the new mill made its first flour.[483]

During construction of the Cincinnati Southern rail line through this part of Scott County, railroad engineers and executives made frequent stops at the Pack home, providing Pack and Burgess with connections that would aid them as proponents for the strategically important rail stop. They were determined to name the town that would blossom around the station "Sadieville" in honor of Mrs. Pack. Rail officials agreed to the location of the station on grounds that if Pack "wanted a depot, he must build it, and then it was to be under the control of the railroad company."[484] Mrs. Pack, for whom the depot setting and the consequent town were named, was highly revered throughout her life. When she died in 1895, Sadieville's principal business houses closed their doors out of respect for her. Historian B.O. Gaines wrote that she was "one of the most beloved and highly honored citizens of Scott County. She was, without a doubt, among the best women God ever made. She was the mother of Dr. John E. Pack, of Georgetown, and Mrs. Luke H. Paxton, of Sadieville."[485]

The succession of T.J. Burgesses, all instrumental in Sadieville's development, began with the 1849 birth of T.J. Burgess, I, who died in 1923. He married Josephine "Josie" C. Pack, daughter of Richard F. and Sarah Martha "Sadie" Emison Pack. The couple lived on the Pack estate farm, "Charity Hill," located east of Sadieville. Their daughter Laura Stevenson (1882-1936) married her first cousin once removed Noble Moses "Mose" Burgess (1880-1953). Mose Burgess was a farm manager, businessman, promoter, and store and warehouse owner in Sadieville. Mose and Laura were parents of T.J. "Jed" Burgess, II (1936-1972), who like his predecessors bearing his name was among Scott County's chief landowners. He married first Pauline Giles (1904-1939). After her death he married Louise Mulberry Osborne. T.J., III "Tommy," born in 1942, managed the family's

Figure 316. Sadieville's leading resource may be the railroad underpass with a view of the mill. Photo by Sandra Whelan, former city clerk.

---

[483] "The Sadieville Sunshine: Special Edition for 'Sadieville in September,'" September 10, 1988, 2.
[484] Apple, Johnston, and Bevins, 217, quoting the *Georgetown Weekly Times*, January 24, February 14, May 25, 1877.
[485] Gaines History 2, 166.

land of approximately 3,000 acres.[486]

Perhaps the overpass on which trains of Southern Railroad roar into Sadieville is the kingpin of the city's landmarks. The historic mill that grew up with Sadieville likewise shares priority in Sadieville's story. The depot, though not in its original location, is exceedingly significant, both for its historic association and for its present use as City Hall.

Close behind in priority of time is the row of businesses that grew up along Pike Street. Coeval with the Pike commercial neighborhood were some of the Main Street commercial and institutional buildings and on up the street, some of the city's classiest dwellings. One might designate it "Big Bug Hill" in the spirit of a similar neighborhood in Red Lodge, Montana.

The Beers & Lanagan census map of 1879 shows a row of properties extending from west to east along the south side of Pike Street, beginning with the underpass, as having included: White and Blacksmith Shop; W.W. Jones; J.W. Jones; Store and P.O.; Hotel; J. Kaley; J. Cottenham; S.T. Connellee; and F.M. Price. Behind those buildings, essentially commercial, was a building owned by F. McGinn. The map also cited in this space near the tracks on one or both sides J.P. Fields's 155 acres and T.B., probably Thomas J. Burgess. Extending along a dirt road – now Main Street -- leading from Pike to Eagle Creek and the 150-acre farm of S.T. Connellee were business properties of "Mrs. Kaley, Kaley, T. J. Burgess Store, and Penn." Nearby and north of the Elk Lick Church road was the Emison Estate and Mill, that road wrapping around the bend in Eagle Creek and connecting with the mill road as it joined the present Hinton Road. Silas B. Jones was also active in the early development of Sadieville. Jones owned the farm located within the large horseshoe bend of Eagle Creek just west of Sadieville. An L-shaped dwelling in the center of the southern part of the tract was cited as Jones's. The property had earlier belonged to James Hammond.[487]

In 1904, when historian Gaines published his two-volume history of Scott County, 216 cars of stock, logs, and tobacco left the Sadieville shipping yard. The region's hunters and trappers profited that year in the sum of $13,000 for hides and other products.[488]

A small building with the form of a typical one room schoolhouse of the nineteenth century survived until the early 1980s Urban Renewal program found it dispensable. The building may have housed John McCabe's 1878 subscription school and later served as the community "telephone house." A photograph included in the 1983 survey form prepared by Proctor-Davis-Ray Engineers showed it to have had a centered chimney and a porch with turned posts and milled trim.[489]

SADIEVILLE RAILROAD UNDERPASS. Drivers are justifiably cautious as they launch passage from either side through the railroad underpass, parts of which relate to the earliest period of construction. Cincinnati Southern

Figure 317. Cincinnati Southern Railroad became Cincinnati New Orleans and Texas Pacific and is now known as Norfolk Southern. It is a very busy railroad.

---

[486] Burgess, *House of the Burgesses*, 54-59. Mrs. Burgess (Louise) continued until recently to live on the family farm in the attractive high style bungalow with a splendid view of surrounding farmland and the road leading into Sadieville.
[487] Incorporation Articles of Sadieville," August 9, 1881, Scott County Will Book S-123.
[488] Gaines History 2, 167.
[489] McCabe School/Telephone House Building, Kentucky Survey Form SC22.

secured a charter from the Kentucky legislature to run the line from Covington south through the state. Scott County was the first county to acquire rights of way as the county provided subscriptions for land not donated. Workers dwelling in makeshift communities along the route created their own brand of excitement. The roadbed from Lexington to Cincinnati was completed in 1876 and iron was laid in 1877. This west gateway into Sadieville was constructed of huge blocks of rusticated limestone. Sections of drylaid limestone can be observed at the sides of the bridge along the track. With this new engineering and architectural feature as a sort of crown, by 1879 Sadieville could be said to have been booming. The railroad has been integral in ways both positive and negative to Sadieville since the beginning. The city entered a continuing decline as the railroad abandoned its station in 1937.[490]

SADIEVILLE MILLING COMPANY/NEW ERA MILLING COMPANY, 350 PIKE STREET. One of the keys to industrial and commercial success was the mill that Daniel Gano established on an Eagle Creek tract adjacent to the railroad crossing of the Connersville Turnpike. Gano, son of Captain Daniel Gano of Revolutionary War renown, and his wife Phebe, sold to the Sadieville Milling Company a house and lot and stable at this setting in 1874 for $690. A new mill on the site began grinding grain into flour in July 1894, soon developing a possibly apocryphal reputation of producing more flour and meal than any other mill in Scott County. In 1902 Gano sold the same firm two and three-quarters acres for $750. Nine years later the company, its directors including S.P. Smith (father of Burgess Smith), president; Burgess Smith; Jacob Mulberry; and C.T. Covington, sold the three-acre tract to Burgess Smith. Smith was one of the region's more progressive farmers (refer to his Burgess Smith Pike farming operation discussed elsewhere in this volume). Through a series of transactions J.W. Collins, F.C. Collins, N.M. Burgess, and C.S. Davis became owners of the mill. At the time of the fire in January 1919, J.W. and F.C. Collins were owners.[491]

Figure 318. The current Sadieville Milling Company succeeded the original mill on nearby Eagle Creek.

We can conjecture, based on descriptions of other mills, how the first mill would have appeared. Basically, there would have been a large dam to impound the waters of Eagle Creek and a drylaid stone foundation and possibly a stone first level, above which would have been one or two wooden stories and an attic with a high pitch roof. There would have been a millpond enclosed by drylaid stone walls.

On March 14, 1919, following the fire, the partners sold the mill site to W.W. McCabe, who with his wife Nannie J. sold it the next year to the Sadieville Milling Company. The new corporation's partners were W.W. McCabe, A.L. McCabe, and P.L. Congleton. They rebuilt the mill, which was to be operated by an alternative to water power, adjacent to the road and next to the railroad crossing, certainly an advantageous situation. They

---

[490] Ann Bevins, *One Hundred Years at First and Four Component Banks* (Georgetown: First National Bank, 1983), 9, 10, 24-29.
[491] Deed Books 32-66, 36-435, 37-483, 42-99, 42-100, 44-585, 50-336; "The Sadieville Sunshine, Special Edition, 1988."

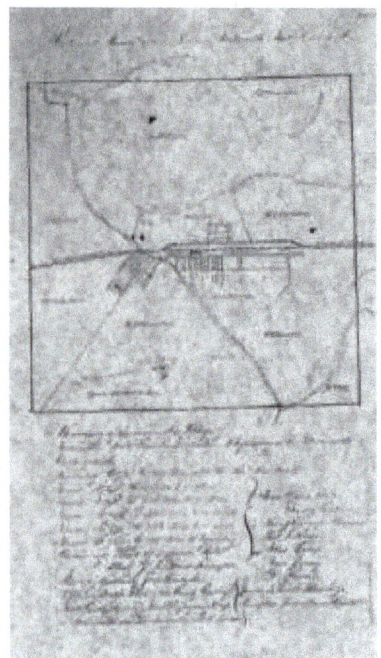

Figure 319. Plat of Sadieville as filed in Scott County Will Book S.

chose the prevailing Arts and Crafts style for the mill's exterior. Occupying a full basement and two and one-half brick stories high, it had a sheltered scales area at the entrance. Two years later the title to "the mill, machinery, accounts, and indebtedness" was transferred to the New Era Milling Company which, after two years assigned the property to W.A. Hinton, president of the local bank, who held an auction in 1925 and sold the mill, its brands and equipment to Laura Conner for $7,505. Mrs. Conner, an astute businesswoman, owned the mill until 1945.[492]

Pat May Mudd, who grew up in Sadieville, recalls the Coca Cola sign on the gable end of the mill, pictured on the previous page, when the paint was bright and fresh. In 1945 Laura Conner sold the mill to J.S. Burgess and R.L. Burgess. In 1961 Joe S. and Nell M. Burgess, along with Helena Burgess, Jessie Burgess Shirley, and Mary Alma and G.H. Thomas sold the mill and all the machinery in the mill buildings on the three-acre tract to Vivian Burgess, from whom title passed to Josie Chowning, who sold it to Herman and Josephine Fields in 1965. Donald and Geneva Shepherd were the next to buy the mill, its "machinery and inventory and all goodwill of the business," which they sold in 1982 to Barbara and Logan Sagester. At that time the mill carried out custom grinding and mixing and sold farm and home supplies.[493]

MAIN STREET – "DOWNTOWN"

Main and Pike streets together comprised Sadieville's downtown. Pike had the edge in priority of time, as it was and is the highway along which the pieces of real estate that became Sadieville stand. Main Street began its existence as a muddy lane paralleling the new railroad track, but shortly after the "depot decision," it became the setting for several impressive business houses, residences, and churches.

SITE, FORMER "CORNER HOUSE" – MARSHALL-MCCABE FURNITURE STORE.

The house that cornered on Main and Pike Streets, pictured in an earlier section of this chapter, was at one time an important hallmark of Sadieville commerce. During its early existence, it served as a furniture store and was owned by G.B. Johnson. In 1895 Johnson traded it to Cyrene Marshall for

Figure 320. The former Pike Street building known as the "Corner House" no longer stands.

thirty-two acres. Its nearest neighbors included the store that had belonged consecutively to A. Lancaster and L. Mulberry. When Mrs. Marshall sold it to Nannie J. McCabe in 1917, she reserved a portion occupied as a barber shop. In 1921 Mrs. McCabe sold the property to W.S. Parker for $1,000. Parker sold it in 1930 to Nannie J.

---

[492] Deed Books 50-485, 52-51, 52-520, 54-219, 74-543.
[493] Deed Books 74-543, 91-212, 100-205, 151-778, 151-781; Gaines History 2: 168; Kentucky Survey Form SC522, Sadieville Milling Company, 1988; see also flyer for Shepherd's Farm Store & Feed Mill, Absolute Auction, author's collection.

Figure 321. Warring Picnic Pavilion is a gathering place for Sadieville events.

McCabe, and W.W. McCabe sold it in 1945 to Russell L. Fightmaster. Emma K. Fightmaster sold it in 1973 to Annie F. and M. Frances King. The building has been demolished for some time.[494]

WARRING PAVILION, CITY PARK, BANDSTAND SITE, FIREHOUSE SITE. Graciously welcoming visitors and townsfolk alike is the city park that occupies the site of much of Sadieville's earlier hoopla, including the firehouse that was owned by the railroad well into recent times. Remaining is the historic gong mounted on the front of the gable of the picnic pavilion. A red caboose is also positioned in the park. Historian B.O. Gaines at the turn of the twentieth century wrote of the city's famed volunteer fire department:

Figure 322. Arthur Lancaster's drug store during earlier years had a railed balcony.

Figure 323. Leonard Mulberry owned the large store that became Sadieville Baptist Church.

"When the large gong, recently purchased at cost of $50, sounds the alarm of fire, the chief, followed by all of the male citizens of the town, is soon on the spot and with hooks, ladders and buckets . . . and extinguishers, owned by the citizens of the town, the fiery fiend is soon at the mercy of the daring and determined individual who is as determined to save his neighbor's property as he would be to save his own. In one or two instances the boys have proven themselves heroes, saving valuable property which any sane person would have considered an impossibility."[495]

---

[494] Deed Books 29-463, 51-258, 51-623, 63-29, 70-194, 123-87.
[495] Gaines History 2, 168.

123 MAIN STREET – LEONARD MULBERRY STORE/SADIEVILLE BAPTIST CHURCH. Several Sadieville businesses occupied the choice Main Street commercial lots across Main from the Cincinnati Southern depot that the church trustees deeded to the Elkhorn Baptist Association in 1987. As a business property, it was identified with Leonard Mulberry and other members of his family from 1910 to 1946, when heirs Walter W. and Matsy Mulberry sold it to Calvin W. Gillispie, who in turn sold it to A.L. McCabe and Walter W. McCabe. In 1892 William H. McCabe, J.W. McCabe, and R.N. McCabe bought the lot between Lancaster's Drug Store and Northcutt's Furniture Store for $250. Two years later William H. and Lavina McCabe sold the property to Arthur Lancaster for $700, Lancaster selling it in 1910 to S.S. and S.B. Jones. The Joneses appear to have enlarged or replaced the building before selling to Mulberry in 1910 for $1,200. In 1952 A.L. McCabe transferred ownership to C.P. Gillispie, who at his death willed it to Clyde T. Gillispie and Carrie Bates. After purchase by the church, the congregation revised the building by extending the first story to the edge of the sidewalk and capping it with a shed roof and cladding it with Bedford stone. The building retains its segmental arched windows on the second level. In 1979 under the pastorate of the Reverend Bradford Landry, the congregation had 152 members.[496]

Leonard Mulberry, wrote Professor Joe L. Mulberry in the account published by B.O. Gaines, "is enjoying a large trade and is at home in his new and spacious brick building and keeps a full line of hardware and lumber, also saddles, harness, etc. 'Rusty' is a careful buyer, quick sales and small profits being his motto."[497] This property is today owned by Eagle Creek Baptist Church.[498]

125 MAIN STREET – ARTHUR LANCASTER DRUG STORE. Professor J.L. Mulberry in early twentieth century historian B.O. Gaines' history described Arthur Lancaster as "our popular druggist . . . a young man of fine business qualities. He handles a stock of goods which covers every conceivable article found in a first-class drug store." Lancaster's store was one of Sadieville's first stores. The frame building like its neighbor to the northwest was a uniquely picturesque component of the Main Street streetscape prior to the enclosure of its porch and balcony. Both levels were designed with porches supported by turned posts connected by railings with balusters. Under the bracket supported cornice, which extended from the front of the sloping roof, was a row of louvered attic vents.

Lancaster bought the lot and a building in 1892 from T.J. and Josie Burgess and an extension of the lot in 1894 from W.H. and Lavina McCabe. In 1910 Lancaster sold the property to S.B. Jones, who as a resident of Orlando, Florida, in 1913 sold it to Dr. J.M. Henry, who left it to Robert M. Gillispie, owner until 1985. Dr. Henry was one of the city's three early twentieth century

Figure 324. Harriet Kaley Hotel in earlier years attracted railroad travelers.

---

[496] J.K. Northcutt operated a furniture store and funeral business in the early twentieth century, selling it to W.A. Hinton. Gaines History 2: 170; Deed Books 27-197, 31-354, 41-288, 42-515, 71-195, 71-317, 79-403, 90-491, 171-239; Edna Evans, "Sadieville Baptist Church," *Scott County Church Histories*, 41.
[497] Gaines History 2, 170.
[498] PVA files.

physicians. Bobby Tucker has owned the historic store since 2013.[499]

127 MAIN STREET – HARRIET KALEY HOTEL. The diminutive house on a neat dry stone foundation intervenes in the Sadieville streetscape as a large scale doll house. It dates from Sadieville's beginnings when Harriett Kaley operated it as a boarding house or as a hotel in line with the more inclusive application of the word "hotel" in those days. Mrs. Kaley's building was shown on both the 1879 Beers & Lanagan map and on the plat of the City of Sadieville filed with the county clerk. In 1885 Lucinda, wife of John Kaley, became the owner. The house was superbly designed, having a recessed entryway set within an alcove and sharing its main façade space with two windows sheltered by hoodmolds, and a centered gable with a louvered octagonal vent. The chimney heating the front block is nicely tooled. A porch that sheltered the ell has been partially enclosed. The Kaleys, who were well known in the hostelry trade, sold the property to Millard T. Griffith and T.J. Luke. William Mulberry owned it from 1893 to 1903 when he sold it to S.B. Jones. R.E. Lee, who operated a general store, was the owner from 1905 to 1946. The property must have been a welcome and romantic scene for weary travelers embarking from the Cincinnati Southern trains. Jamie and Jillian B. Donovan purchased this charming property in 2005.[500]

Figure 325. Sadieville Deposit Bank was designed and built by African American builder James Bailey.

133 MAIN STREET – DEPOSIT BANK. The noted African American designer/builder James Bailey, described as an architect in a Cincinnati builders' guide, is identified as the designer and builder of Sadieville's bank building. Bailey rode the train daily in 1890 from Georgetown to supervise the building's construction. Unfortunately, that contract was to represent Bailey's last active role in the execution of his very fine designs. On mounting the train to ride home to Georgetown, the craftsman was thrown from the train's entry platform as it lurched forward, throwing Bailey into the ditch. For a time it was feared that he would not recover from his injuries, though he continued to work in a supervisory position for several years.

Incorporators of Deposit Bank of Sadieville, originally capitalized at $50,000, included Richard F. Pack, president, Thomas J. Burgess, Millard F. Griffith, Dr. Thomas H.

---

[499] Bevins, Survey Form SC231, July 29, 1988; Gaines History 2, 170, 160.
[500] Bevins, Survey Form SC232, July 29, 1988; Scott County Will Book S-123, August 9, 1881, Sadieville incorporation; PVA files.

Daugherty, F.T. Mansfield, W.T. Mefford, and Daniel Gano. When the bank opened for business, Pack, Mefford, Burgess, and Daugherty, joined by J.J. Rogers, J.L. Luke, and Stephen Gano comprised the first board of trustees. On May 21, 1890, the trustees purchased from Millard F. and Sallie Griffith a thirty by one hundred-foot lot on Main and contracted with Bailey to design and build the bank. A distinguished building it was, entered by a double door with a deep transom and lighted by two four-pane windows on either side with kickplates beneath. A street level door to the upper story was positioned to the right of the banking façade. The main façade of the upper level was lighted by four shuttered windows with two over two pane sash. There were round attic vents above. Beneath the cornice were paired brackets. The bank's early presidents included Pack, S.P. Smith, Dr. Daugherty, R.H. McCabe, and William A. Hinton.[501]

Sadieville's second bank, Farmers Bank of Sadieville, opened on October 20, 1899 and was capitalized at $15,000. Organizers included S.B. Jones, G.B. Johnson, R.E. Lee, W.W. McCabe, E.S. Zeysing, Jacob Mulberry, Jr., and John A. Gano. Lee, whose business career included operation of a general store, was its first and only president. The two banks merged in 1918. Capital assets of both banks came to more than $600,000, and deposits amounted to more than $500,000. New stock certificates worth $40,000 were issued, making the two banks equal in their new association. W.A. Hinton assumed the role of cashier. Charlie Fields returned from his role with Farmers Bank in Georgetown to serve as assistant cashier. R.H. McCabe was president and G.B. Johnson, vice president.[502]

In 1929, W.T. Warring, who was teaching school in the Porter community, began working as a clerk in Farmers-Deposit Bank at sixty dollars a month. While R.H. McCabe was still president, Hinton as executive vice president and chief executive officer, was in charge. The bank's assets totaled a half-million dollars. Though the agricultural and commercial communities of the region suffered economically as the Great Depression wore on, the bank remained so sound that it did not need to apply for remedies from Reconstruction Finance Corporation. During the "bank holiday" declared by United States President Franklin D. Roosevelt, bank officials were at the bank daily. Though the bank was closed, they were committed to being on hand to answer customers' questions and to reassure them of its financial stability.[503]

Sadieville's only bank robbery took place in 1933 as Warring arrived for work. The robber had been holding a pistol in the face of cashier Charles Fields. Warring set out in pursuit of the robber and was soon joined by Fields carrying an old pistol until he remembered that he had left the bank unattended and the safe open. He handed the pistol to Warring. Meanwhile, other Sadieville residents joined in pursuit and cornered the bandit in an empty building. Theodore Adams grabbed a sixteen-gauge shotgun in Mulberry's hardware store and tried to cram twelve-gauge shells into it. Another person carried out two pistols, one of which worked. When the bank's pistol was tested, every chamber misfired.[504]

W.A. Hinton's leadership continued to be important as Sadieville and the surrounding farm country weathered the Depression. By 1949 the bank was lending $25,000 each month. On November 22 of that year, Hinton wrote of the importance of helping all farmers who need money for improvements "over a period of months so that they will not impoverish their working capital. . . The public should know our willingness to more effective cooperation." Sadieville's bank was also a leader in designating female employees for executive positions: Vera Hinton Van Cleve became an assistant cashier in 1940, along with Warring. In the 1950s Edna Evans was elected assistant cashier. The little bank continued to keep its region at heart so that when Garvice Kincaid was building his banking empire, he looked to the Sadieville bank and its president William T. Warring for leadership in the Scott County phase of his effort. Warring became president of Georgetown's First National

---

[501] Bevins, *One Hundred Years*, 26-28.
[502] Bevins, *One Hundred Years*.
[503] Bevins, *One Hundred Years*, 27-28.
[504] As told by Warring, reported in Bevins, *One Hundred Years*, 28.

Figure 326. Leander Risk's popular hotel dated from 1885. The photo depicts a 1970s festival.

Bank. Elmo Cushman was designated assistant cashier as Farmers-Deposit Bank merged with the new Georgetown First organization.[505]

In 2016, the City of Sadieville, which received the bank as a gift from Whitaker Banks, auctioned the property. It was bought by Randy and Carolyn Wilson, whose proposal for the property is to develop it as a full line decorative accessory and home décor store. "Our vision is to create a wonderful country shop where people can come in and find country décor, small furnishings, and unique items handcrafted by local vendors. We want to bring a Gatlinburg type décor shop here in Sadieville. We are excited to fill both the lower and upper level with unique and beautiful items. As a lifelong resident of Sadieville, our family is excited to bring new life to Main Street."[506]

137 MAIN STREET – LEANDER RISK HOTEL. Sadieville's several restaurants, hotels, and boarding houses benefitted in lucrative ways from their location near a major depot and regional commercial center, but perhaps none of them did as well as the brick hotel constructed and operated by Leander Risk. Risk's high style operation was known far and wide for its dining and lodging opportunities. As travelers and salespersons embarked from the Cincinnati Southern Pullman cars, one of their first views was Risk's hotel. Once registered, many clients would rent horses and buggies to visit the crossroads commercial centers and stores to peddle their wares.

In 1885 Risk bought a fifty by 150-foot lot "known as the Zeysing property" from T.J. and Josie Burgess. The incorporation plat of Sadieville corroborates this property as the one where Risk erected the hotel building with two store fronts on its lower level. Brick was laid with contrasting mortar very neatly in a running bond pattern. The five-bay second story featured a center balcony entrance flanked by two tall windows having matching stone lintels and sills. In recent years the windows have been retrofitted with smaller windows and the voids above and beneath them filled with plywood. The attic is lighted by five small circular windows with headers patterning circles around them. The left store front survives relatively intact. It is entered by a double door

---

[505] Bevins., 28-29.
[506] Deed Books 378-282, 349-109.

flanked by two large windows, each having four lights. The transoms of the various openings are filled in. The storefront on the other side of the door leading to the stairway has been altered with a picture window and an entryway flanked by two tapered posts.[507]

Risk and his wife Mary K. sold the hotel in 1919 to E.J. and Maggie Jones, who five years later sold it to Farmers Union Supply Company for $750. In

Figure 327. George B. Johnson house was built following an historic Sunday morning fire.

1930 the farm store and its president, Finley Gano, sold it to N. M. "Mose" Burgess. Heralding the 1977 auction of the property by Burgess' heirs was a *Lexington Herald* story recalling the history of the building following the closing of the depot by the railroad – "the financial bottom fell from under the Risks as well as Sadieville . . . one of the state's largest rail road shipping yards . . . a large relay station for Southern Rail Road. . . a major livestock selling location."

Banker William T. Warring was quoted as recalling how in the 1920s "the dining room and saloon were packed every night." With the change in commercial activity, the owner replaced the two once popular hotel and dining features with racks for clothing and hardware items." Orville Burgess inherited the property from Mose Burgess, one of the city's major promoters. Faced with a large inheritance tax, he

Figure 328. John M. Theobald house dates from 1888.

"closed up shop, vowing never to reopen it." Orville Burgess died in 1974 and heirs Louise Burgess, T.J. Burgess, and Jane Leslie Burgess sold it at auction to Kenneth and Detta Wilson.[508]

Main Street Residential Block

207 Main Street – George B. Johnson House.
Known locally in the recent past as the Wilson Hotel is a house on a lot bought in 1892 by G.B. Johnson from T.J. Burgess. At the time Johnson also bought two nearby

---

[507] Deed Book 26-164.
[508] Deed Books 49-259, 53-585, 61-600, 126-697; Malcolm L. Stallons, "Sadieville's Once Fancy Risk Hotel Goes on Auction Block," *The Lexington Herald*," May 14, 1977.

lots, relating to a pattern of householders to have back lots for gardens, stables, and other secondary purposes. The house is said to have been rebuilt following a fire.[509]

Perhaps the fire reported in W.A. Marshall's historical account relates to this property. Sadieville had a volunteer fire department that received alerts regarding fires by the striking of the large gong that cost the city fifty dollars, and which is today a fixture in the Warring Pavilion. At such times male citizens gathered with hooks, ladders, and buckets. The department had an array of round bottom buckets that couldn't be set down, typical of early American firefighting equipment. On a winter Sunday morning as Sadieville residents were leaving for church, the house, which was used as a boarding house or hotel known as the Neale Boarding House, burst into flames.

Firefighters lined up between the railroad water column and the house, passing filled buckets from man to man to the fire, and then handing them to women and children who took them to the starting point. This process continued for two and one-half hours, damaging the Sunday best clothes of the firefighters. At one point, the owner of the building was observed standing nearby in overcoat and fur hat "enjoying the scene." Someone called, "G.B., why don't you give us a lift and help us carry water – we are all worn out." G.B. is said to have replied, "I can't help you; my health is worth more than all my property and money. It would make me sick to do what you fool people are doing." Wrote Marshall, "the men immediately gathered up their buckets and let the building burn to the ground." However, in defense of Johnson, it must be said that Professor J. L. Mulberry opened his historical account published in B.O. Gaines' 1904 history by declaring, "One of the most energetic and successful businessmen of Sadieville is Mr. G.B. Johnson. Mr. Johnson runs a general merchandise store and is one of the strongest candidates for the patronage of the public that can be found in the town."[510]

Johnson and his wife Maude sold the rebuilt house in 1937 to John H. and Opal Shirley, who owned it until 1947 when they sold it to R.H. Rogers. Rogers converted it into a funeral home. In 1990 Matthew Vance sold it to Brian and Miriam I. Reese. The house which occupies a beautifully laid cut stone foundation has a stately two-story form with a two story bay window on the south end. The front gable ell is crowned with a lattice like bargeboard. Brick chimneystacks are nicely tooled. Late twentieth century fabric covers the original wood siding and standing seam metal roof.[511]

211 MAIN STREET – JOHN M. THEOBALD HOUSE. Application of late twentieth century materials and removal of late nineteenth century fabric and trim have somewhat altered the appearance of the house of John M. Theobald. Theobald bought the improved lot in 1888 from T.J. and Josie Burgess. In 1910 Thomas D. and Sallie D. Theobald sold their family home for $1,520 to N.J. McCabe, the deed relating that the property had been occupied by John M. Theobald and then by his widow until her death prior to inheritance by their son. Mrs. McCabe and her husband, W.W. McCabe, sold it to Ford and Katherine Whitson in 1939 for $2,600. In 1992 Ronnie Cannon sold it to David and Fairlena J. Woolums. The house rests on a nicely laid stone foundation.[512]

---

[509] Deed Book 28-56; other information from W.T. and Frances Warring, 1988.
[510] W.A. Marshall, "The Classic City of Sadieville," undated typescript; Professor J.L. Mulberry, "The Business People," Gaines History 2,170.
[511] Deed Books 62-541, 72-423, 107-275, 184-011; Bevins, Kentucky Survey Form SC234, July 29, 1988; other information from Frances and W.T. Warring, 1988.
[512] Deed Books 18-255, 41-208, 63-26, 64-340, 197-620.

215 Main Street – F.T. Mansfield/W.T. and Frances P. Warring House. F.T. Mansfield, according to W.A. Marshall's account, operated Sadieville's first business house in a building constructed by J.W. Jones. J.L. Mulberry's account comments on Mansfield's general merchandise store: "Mr. Mansfield is a close student in all matters pertaining to his business, understanding it in every detail, and by close attention to business affairs receives his share of trade." Mansfield's store must have stood on Pike Street in the building that he sold to William H. McCabe in 1898. The property was adjacent to that of S.T. Connellee, the latter reserving the storehouse and five feet in the rear and half the space between the store and the dwelling house.[513]

Figure 329. F.T. Mansfield, business leader, lived here until 1937. W.T. and Frances Warring became owners in 1956.

In 1889 Mansfield bought the improved lot at this site for $2,000 from T.J. Burgess. He built a three bay two story house in the spirit of the traditional "I-house," (a house form popular in states with names beginning with "I"). In 1891 Fannie Taylor, W.W. Mansfield, and Laura and J.L. Luke sold the property to James W. Neale, whose executor, John Scarborough, deeded it to Lucy Neale for $1,525, Neale selling it shortly afterwards to Charles P. and Morah Fields and the Fieldses to J.O. Rose, a merchant and entrepreneur whose saloon on Pike Street was popular in its time. In 1922 Rose and his wife Laura sold it to the Sadieville Christian Church whose trustees, A.D. Stevens, William A. Hinton, and E.S. Zeysing, in 1932 sold it to Annie T. Lancaster. Lancaster sold the property in 1938 to Roy L. Parker, who with his wife Orva D. sold it to William Thomas Warring in 1956. Don Piggins of Paris has been owner since 2007.[514]

Figure 330. R.E. Lee bought the lot for this house in 1898. Joseph and Nell Burgess bought it in 1936.

219 Main Street – R.E. Lee/J.S. and Nell Burgess House. Fellow storekeepers Robert E. Lee and F.T. Mansfield were best friends and neighbors, as were the two recent owners of their nineteenth century homes at 219 and 215 Main Street, Nell Burgess and Frances

---
[513] W.A. Marshall, "Sadieville"; J.L. Mulberry, "The Business People," Gaines History 2, 170; Deed Book 28-187.
[514] Deed Books 25-357, 36-627, 46-557, 47-4, 52-19, 59-456, 59-460, 63-418, 86-379; PVA files.

Warring. Mrs. Burgess and Mrs Warring as students rode the train into Georgetown in the wee hours of the morning to complete high school and returned the same way to Sadieville in the evening. They later taught together. Mansfield, who was an original or early owner of the former Warring home, sold the lot next door to R.E. Lee in 1898 for $360. In 1925 Lee and his wife Mary G. Lee sold the house to C.T. Smith for $4,250. In 1936 Orpha Smith and other heirs of C.T. Smith sold the property to Joseph C. Burgess and in 1961 Vivian Burgess and others deeded it to Joe S. Burgess. Joe Burgess' wife Nell left it to Julianna Lafleche, the present owner.[515]

Figure 331. Rodham and Fannie Fields were the original owners of the house at 223 Main Street.

Of R.E. Lee, Professor J.L. Mulberry wrote in his account of Sadieville's business people, "Another man in the whirl and confusion of mercantile life is Mr. R.E. Lee. Mr. Lee keeps a general store. Possessing the energy and pluck that all business men must have, Polly commands his share of the public patronage." Lee was founding president of Farmers Bank of Sadieville and served as such until the bank merged with Deposit Bank in 1918. Lee's house has a front gable ell with shaped shingles in the attic pediment, the lower portion of a former tower, and a complex of interesting rear façade additions. There is a stylish smokehouse in the back yard. In recent years the front porch was enclosed to accommodate a sunroom.[516]

223 MAIN STREET/RODHAM AND FANNIE FIELDS HOUSE. Citing themselves as "R. and Fannie Fields," the original owners of the circa 1888 house bought the lot for $200 from T.J. and Josie Burgess and sold it in 1890 to George T. Nelson for $1,500. Fields operated a store on Pike Street. In 1917 Nelson sold the two story three bay house with central roof pediment to Dr. John M. Henry, who several months later sold it to David Mulberry. In 1931 Hattie Mulberry and other heirs sold it to J. Finley Gano, who sold it in 1966 to Finley Gano. Edmond C. Aldridge bought the property in 2001. Marvin D. Woolums and Fairlena J. Woolums are the current owners.[517]

The stately two-story house has undergone several changes of exterior fabric in recent years. Its earlier porch supported by turned posts with a milled cornice beneath its flat roof now is carried by tall square posts and has a plain soffit. The windows have nine over nine pane sash. Chimneys positioned on the inside wall of the two parlors on either side of the center passage retain their decorative tooling, and the central pediment breaking the roofline at mid-point retains its original shaped shingles. A stable stood on the lot behind the house.

---

[515] Deed Books 31-628, 55-566, 61-423, 102-405, Will Books 7-61, 10-686; other information from Frances Warring.
[516] J.L. Mulberry, Gaines History 2, 170; Bevins, *One Hundred Years*, 26, 27.
[517] Deed Books 25-195, 34-133, 46-616, 47-263, 63-250, 101-209, 259-477; PVA files.

231 Main Street – Mefford/Daugherty/Hinton House. Some of Sadieville's most influential, versatile, and interesting property owners lived in the two-story dwelling with a central roof pediment and an Arts and Crafts era porch. The porch may have been a later addition. Approached by eight concrete steps positioned between stepped brick antepodia with stone slabs on top, its tapered posts are mounted on brick piers with stone slabs. Stone ledges connect the piers on either side of the entry steps, providing additional space for seating in addition to the porch swing. The porch has a flat roof with a central pediment. The dwelling retains its two over two pane sash.

Figure 332. Vera Hinton later Van Cleve stands in foreground of the earlier W.A. Hinton home.

Apparently built for W.T. Mefford, who bought the lot in 1886 from T.J. and Josie Burgess, the house was first sold to Dr. Thomas H. Daugherty, a physician who made it his home until 1906 when he moved to Georgetown and constructed a brick Princess Anne style dwelling on South Broadway. Dr. Daugherty had earlier practiced at Stonewall. He sold the house and lot to Sadieville entrepreneur and banker William A. Hinton, whose story is told above in the history of the Sadieville bank, and Hinton's wife Lillie. In 1959 Mrs. Hinton sold the family home to the couple's daughter, Vera Hinton (Mrs. Jack) Van Cleve, who had made an important contribution to banking history by becoming one of the first female bank executives in this part of the state in 1940. In 2000 Margie Veatch sold the property to Matthew Vance.[518]

Sadieville Christian Church – 241 Main Street, and Christian Church Parsonage, 245 Main Street. Sadieville Christian Church is the sole survivor of the group of churches that once enhanced Sadieville's north end and which gave the present Gano Street its earlier name of Church Street. The Methodist church and the former Baptist church have long been gone from their moorings, the former having closed, and the latter having moved to the south end of Main Street in a former commercial building. The Christian Church, however, occupies the same lot that it did at the time of its founding and construction in 1893.

Figure 333. W.T. Mefford built the two-story house in 1886.

Moses E. Lard, one of the most illustrious preachers of the early American indigenous movement known as the Christian Churches, was the founding minister of the Sadieville congregation. A Lincolnian sort of man in appearance and at least in part in philosophy, Lard left Missouri under pressure during the Civil War because of his refusal to take a pro-Southern oath of allegiance. It was not long after his arrival in Georgetown that the pacifist Lard was not allowed to continue to preach. For part of the war he found life more

---

[518] Deed Books 26-178, 37-617, 64-77, 95-173, 247-587; Bevins, *One Hundred Years*, 24-29, 18-19.

comfortable when he lived in Canada. After the war Lard returned to Central Kentucky where he was associated with congregations in Scott County, including Georgetown and Sadieville.[519]

In 1893 Lard, along with Mr. and Mrs. E.S. Zeysing, Mr. and Mrs. W.W. McCabe, and John A. McCabe, organized the Sadieville Christian Church. The first trustees, G.B. Johnson, A.D. Stevens, and E.L. Zeysing, bought the building lot that year from John T. Mulberry and A.F. Mulberry for $250. The

Figure 334. Founded and constructed in 1893, Sadieville Christian Church has long been served by outstanding ministers.

congregation began construction of stylish meetinghouse that year, modeling it after the Mount Olivet Church on the Cincinnati Pike, a progenitor.

The church has a cross gable roof pattern. A bell tower once occupied the northwest corner. The 2,000-pound bell is now mounted on a stand in front of the church after having hung in the top of the tower just under the steeple. Former minister Frank Veatch related that the huge size of the bell contributed to its having cracked the plaster when the large gong struck the metal. Eventually the tower was removed and the bell was mounted in its place of honor in front of the church. You can still ring the bell, but it is advised that you use ear plugs before striking it. Veatch recalled that the congregation hired a wrecker to move the bell to the church's front yard. "When he hooked it up, the front wheels came off the ground," he mused.[520]

Another leading architectural feature of the church is the large pointed arched window on the south main façade of the building. It has

Figure 335. Judith A. Stone's one-story house dates from 1897.

---

[519] Ann Bolton Bevins, *The First Disciples/Christian Church* (Georgetown, 1981), 42; Gaines History 2: 168; Jennifer Justice and Teresa Bannister, "Sadieville Christian Church," *Scott County Church Histories*, 98-99.
[520] Norman Minch, "Sadieville Church hopes to gain from Toyota growth," *Georgetown News & Times*, March 11, 1986.

decorative mullions separating its twelve variously shaped panes. The large window is flanked by a pair of smaller double hung pointed arched windows.

Figure 337. Historic photo of Main Street and Sadieville's early commercial life.

311 MAIN STREET—JUDITH A. STONE HOUSE. In 1897 Millard F. and A.B. Griffith sold Judith Stone a house and one-half acre lot for $600. The one-story house has a hall-parlor plan and chimneys with brick stacks set inside the end walls. The former lattice porch has been changed to a porch with plain posts. Stone died in 1900, leaving the property to her two grandchildren, Lutie Paxton Downing and Nannie Downing, daughters of her daughter Lora. Owners following sale of the house in 1911 by Lutie D. Whitson and other heirs were J.W. Baird, 1933; Lillie McMillen, 1944; Bruce McKenney, 1974; Clarice Cheek; and Randall and Carolyn Wilson, 2003. Kay and Michael Bechel are the current owners.[521]

PIKE STREET - SOUTH SIDE

CORNISH HALL, 205 PIKE STREET. Sadieville businessman Charles W. Cornish provided funds in his will to enable the city's two lodges "to build in Sadieville a suitable hall that shall be jointly owned." His son-in-law Leander Risk served as his executor. On January 27, 1905, Leander and Mary K. Risk made a joint deed to the I.T. Martin Lodge Number 459 Free & Accepted Masons, and the Big Eagle Lodge Number 120 Knights of Pythias, for $500, the lot with a building. Its boundaries included the south side of Pike Street, property owned by J.D. Mulberry's shop, and Vine Street.[522]

Figure 336. Earlier view of Sadieville City Hall and Cornish Hall next door.

The lodges forthwith began construction of Cornish Hall. Of Italianate persuasion, the street front level provided store space for the lodges to produce income to maintain the building, their organizations, and to carry out charitable work. The street front retains its early twentieth century design with plate glass windows, glazed transoms, molded frames, and show windows. The double entryway has a doorway transom. Above the three bays are large transoms. The upper level has four bays. A wooden canopy shelters the sidewalk in front of the lower story. The building has a basement.

Figure 338. Charles W. Cornish provided funds in his will for a joint hall for Sadieville's two lodges. The building dates from 1895.

Midway between the lintels and the elaborate metal cornice is a horizontal band. Emblazoned on the cornice is the lettering, "F&AM/K of P/Hall/1905." The interior retains its wooden floor. For sixty-eight years the lodges controlled the property.

---

[521] Will Book T-206; Deed Books 34-72, 45-632, 60-315, 52-562, 69-298, 126-579, 159-189, 272-629; PVA files.
[522] Deed Book 36-567.

Shop keepers included Herman Fields and Elmo Cushman. The Warring-Parker Insurance Agency was also located here. In 1973 the Grand Lodge of Kentucky, Knights of Pythias, and Mount Vernon No. 14 Masonic Lodge, F&AM, sold the impressive two-story brick building to Albert and Mary Lee Goepper for $5,000. The Goeppers operated an antique store in the building. In 2005 Todd Goepper sold the building to Kenneth A. Wilson.[523] On Vine Street west of the lodge stood Leander Risk's livery stable that operated in association with his brick hotel on Main Street, providing horses and buggies to take guests into the countryside. After school bus transportation became general around 1920, buses were stored here.[524]

Figure 339. Jimmie Jones's house was perhaps Sadieville's first store.

Queen City Railroad Depot/Sadieville City Hall.

Sadieville's large shipping yard and depot were located between the tracks and the burgeoning Main Street line of businesses and dwelling houses of some of the city's most enterprising citizens. Until use of automobiles became standard and until state and federal highway systems rendered rail shipping and travel comparatively less popular, Sadieville thrived as a shipping and travel center. Its taverns and other entertainment halls along with smaller boarding houses and livery stables took care of travelers, traveling salespersons, and the local population.

After the depot closed in 1937, T.J. Burgess, grandson of the T.J. Burgess who founded Sadieville, moved it to another location and ultimately to its present site on the east side of Cornish Hall. A movement to salvage the depot and to use it for expanding city government offices (though the old city hall/jail building still held a place of historic honor) was successful into the late 1980s and early 1990s. In July 1989 Nell (Mrs. Joseph S.) Burgess sold the City of Sadieville the .2732-acre lot and the former depot. Its renovation as Sadieville's city hall got underway in 1996 when Carl Jones was mayor. The project began under the previous mayor Diana Vest.[525]

Figure 340. Older view of Jimmie Jones's house.

Concurrently a bright red caboose was restored as an addition to the city park. It stands at the edge of Pike and Main streets. The city commission accepted a bid in May 1996 for $91,200 from Georgetown Sheet Metal for renovation of the old depot. Larry Jones, well known metal worker and carpenter, was in charge.[526]

---

[523] Kentucky Survey Form SC229, Cornish Hall; Deed Books 36-567, 293-489.
[524] Kentucky Survey Form SC520, 1988; other information from Frances Warring, 1988.
[525] Kentucky Survey Form SC45, Queen City Railroad Depot, 1988; information from W.T. and Frances Warring, 1988.
[526] Derek Armstrong, "Renovation under way on old Sadieville depot," *Georgetown News-Graphic*, June 6, 1996.

Figure 341. The former depot was relocated by Joseph Burgess and turned into City Hall.

JIMMIE JONES DWELLING AND STOREHOUSE, 615 PIKE STREET. Reputedly the first business house in Sadieville, the three-bay frame side gabled building next door to city hall served as a general store during the city's early years. This and the house just to the east were sold jointly by Elbridge Price in 1890 to F.T. Mansfield for $350, the deed referring to the property as "Jimmie Jones dwelling and storehouse." Like other buildings of its era, the building has a dry stone foundation, the rear portion necessarily tall due to the steep slope. Part of the north abutment of the town's footbridge to Vine Street is on the east side of the lot. In 1905 Mansfield's heirs sold the store to L. Price, and in 1909 he and his wife Nannie sold it to L.V. Jenkins. Jenkins sold it in 1914 to A.L. McCabe, who sold in 1930 to John W. Adams. In 1938 Lucy Ellen Adams sold it to Sallie Wright. Charles K. and Gwendolyn Eberhart, who bought the property in 2006, are the present owners.[527]

PIKE STREET 1901 FOOTBRIDGE ABUTMENT SITE. In 1901 the citizens of Sadieville raised $200 to provide access to "downtown" from the residences along Vine Street. The footbridge was five feet wide, 300 feet long, and fifty feet high, and had a high railing on both sides. The stone abutments were capped with concrete. The Vine Street house west of the bridge had its own small footbridge that connected with the municipal one. Polk Fields' deed to W.W. and Nannie McCabe for a Vine Street house and lot referred to the twelve foot reserve for "Poke's Alley" or bridgeway with reversion to the former property owner whenever "it ceases to be used as a bridge way, street, or alley . . ." The upper portion of the bridge site is shown at the right.[528]

Figure 342. Site of the 1901 foot bridge.

Figure 343. The well organized Kaley Hotel advertised on the 1879 Beers & Lanagan map.

JONES DWELLING HOUSE, 621 PIKE STREET. A picturesque three bay cottage with a relatively high-pitched roof, a stone foundation, a classical entryway and interior chimney on the main block's east end, and a one bay wing on the east side had its beginnings as Jimmie Jones's dwelling house. S.B. Jones sold it in 1898 to W.H. Truitt for $575. In 1915 Truitt and his wife Sadie sold the property to John A. McCabe for $600, and in 1828 McCabe and his wife Frances sold it to J.W. Baird, suggesting the building's possible use as a

Figure 344. Jimmie Jones's dwelling house on Pike Street.

---

[527] Kentucky Survey Forms SC67, SC241, 1988: Jimmie Jones Dwelling and Storehouse; 1881 plat; 1879 Map of Scott County; Deed Books 25-356; 38-365; 44-296, 557; 56-177; 58-555; 63-223; Gaines History 2: 167.
[528] Deed Book 38-254; Gaines History 2, 167.

doctor's office. Dr. Baird sold the building in 1833 to Russell Fightmaster, who with his wife Emma K. sold it to Sallie Wright in 1954. Mrs. R.M. Carlisle purchased it in 1972 from J.W. Wright. Annie F. King and Frances McDuffy acquired the building in 1983. Charles and Gwendolyn Eberhart bought it in 2006.[529]

JOHN KALEY HOTEL, 625 PIKE STREET. John Kaley, a Sadieville incorporator whose name was sometimes spelled Caley, bought his fifty foot one-sixth acre hotel site from S.T. Connellee for fifty dollars in 1877. The deed from Connellee refers to a boundary as having been "Fields old line near Polk Fields store house occupied by John Kaley." The building is well designed, having a street level entrance from the sidewalk as well as wooden steps leading to a porch sheltering the centered entrance on the long side. Another set of stairs leads from the sidewalk to the lower level.[530]

Figure 345. Jasper Rose bought the former brick hotel at auction in 1906. It was one of the city's most popular destinations.

Kaley's notice on the 1879 Beers & Lanagan map read, "Accommodations First Class. Livery Stable attached. Fine Wines, Liquors and Cigars always on hand." C.W. Cornish later bought the hotel and attached barber shop and willed it to his daughter Mary K. Risk and her husband Leander Risk. Later owners included Nannie J. and W.W. McCabe, Hedgie and David Covington, Russell Fightmaster, and Sallie and John W. Wright.[531] Virginia Dickey of Corinth has been listed as owner since 1991.[532]

JOHN COTTINGHAM BUILDING, 631 PIKE STREET. John Cottingham paid fifty dollars for the fifty-foot lot that he bought from S.T. and Lucy A. Connellee in 1877.[533] The frame house has a raised section of sidewalk that suggests a former porch. The central entrance retains its transom. Some windows, including the second story window centered under the roofline gable, retain original two over two pane sash. The roof cladding is standing seam metal, and the somewhat small brick chimney stack is neatly tooled.

Thomas C. Moore of Georgetown, Cottingham's devisee, sold the property in 1880 to Catharine Vance Kenney. She sold it in 1891 to Ellen Reddick, and in 1892 William Reddick sold it to Catherine Connellee. Later buyers included J.V. and Mary Ellen Mulberry, 1892, 1904; W.C. Faulconer, 1919; Farmers Deposit Bank, 1936; Theodore Adams, 1936; Opal and Welcome Wilson, 1938; Russell Fightmaster, 1956; Barbara F. Bourgeois; Emma K. Fightmaster; 1973; Cammy Middleton, 2012; Richard D. and Angela D Bryant, 2012.[534]

---

[529] Deed Book 33-385, 44-456, 58-5, 108-212, 119-173, 153-715, 299-367; Will Book 3-164.
[530] Deed Book 15-432.
[531] 1879 Map of Scott County; Kentucky Survey Form SC519, 1988; Will Book T-310; Deed Books 15-432, 24-37, 63-28, 70-196, 81-543, 84-354, 122-642.
[532] Deed Books 189-665.
[533] Deed Book 15-432.
[534] Deed Books 18-20, 20-90, 26-542, 28-4, 30-268, 51-279, 61-627, 61-628, 113-510, 122-617, 342-166, 349-715..

BARNES-ROSE HOTEL (AND SALOON), 639 PIKE STREET. Bought by Jasper O. Rose in 1903 from S.W. Collins and other assignees of Mary E. Barnes, the Rose Hotel and Saloon became one of Sadieville's most popular destinations. John and Mary E. Barnes were early owners, John Barnes having bought the lot in 1900 from S.T. and Lucy A. Connellee for $180. In 1906 Mary E. Barnes acquired the property, which she sold to Rose at auction for $1,212. Rose was owner when the men and boys of Sadieville posed in front of the building with Edward Burgess. Rose sold the property in 1918 to W.C. Faulconer for $1,108. In 1923 Edgar B. and Mary Marshall acquired it, which they sold to John O. and Ora Downing in 1946. Lucille Henry sold it in 1996 to Kathryn Anne Olson. Ronald A. Wilson is the present owner.[535]

Figure 346. John Cottingam's house before recent renovation.

643 PIKE STREET – CONNELLEE-CROSTHWAIT DWELLING AND STORE. It's tempting to consider the former nearly picture perfect connected dwelling house and store building as having been owned and operated by Sadieville founders S.T. and Lucy A. Connellee. In 1904 Mrs. Connellee sold the property on Pike described as a house and lot to John P. Crosthwait for $350. Crosthwait was referred to by Professor Joe L. Mulberry as "Sadieville's clever jeweler," who is "active and energetic and a close student in all matters pertaining to his business, having learned it in the hard, stern school of practical experience." Connellee's estate was divided in 1905 among his wife, daughters Mary Ellen Boon and Dixie Zeysing, and grandchildren Richard and Lucy Zeysing. Also apportioned was a large red stained box made by Connellee's grandfather, Thomas Wood.[536]

Figure 347. Former S.T. and Lucy Connellee dwelling and store house.

Crosthwait sold the property to the Deposit Bank of Sadieville in 1912 for $1,020. The bank sold it to L.V. and Minnie Jenkins, who the next year sold it to M.B. and B.J. Neale. J.T. Cunningham bought it in 1916 and owned it until 1921 when he sold it to Lee R. Huffman. The value of the property increased to $4,000 in 1947 when Lee R. Huffman sold it to J.T. Hamilton, Elizabeth Hamilton, and D.L. Sheehan. Later purchasers have included Hannah S. and Holly W. Johnson (1950), Chester B. Vance (1971), Lucille I. Henry (1971), and

---

[535] Bevins, Johnston, Apple, editors, *Images of America: Georgetown and Scott County* (Charleston, S.C.: Arcadia Publishing Company, 1998), 46; Deed Books 34-134; 38-40, 41; 36-56; 39-77; 37-280; 55-366, 71-392, 221-281.
[536] Deed Book 41-491; Will Book T-366, 402; Gaines History 2, 170.

Kathryn Olson (2003). Ronald A. Wilson acquired it in 2010.[537]

667 Pike Street – Mabel Gann House Site. Mabel Gann is a current era folk figure whose indomitable spirit inspired the rest of us to speak up for what we believe. In 1931 Granville Kelly purchased the lot at auction that had been earlier owned by J.O. Rose, hotel and tavern owner. In 1958 Mable Gann, Granville and Fannie T. Kelly, and other heirs sold the house and lot on the site to Mrs. Gann for $5,000. Bordering the property were lots owned by W.M. Brashears, S.B. Jones, and L. Craig. When Urban Renewal marked Mrs. Gann's house for demolition, she resisted, complained to the authorities, and tried her utmost to save her house. Nevertheless, the agency built a new house for Mrs. Gann. Those of us who would have liked to help her could only offer admiration, as the urban renewal agency was determined to condemn all properties that sat below grade, as hers did. The replacement house on the site is three bays wide and has an unfinished concrete block basement. Mrs. Gann now lives in Lexington.[538]

Figure 348. House sold in 1910 by Lucille and B.B. Barnett to Emma Nelson.

683 Pike Street – Nathaniel McLoney House. A three-bay house with a shed roofed porch supported by square posts connected with a railing close to the sidewalk recalls two early deeds, including one relating to a house and lot sold in 1921 by Nathaniel T. McLoney of Harrison County to W.W. and Susan Hutchcraft for $300. McLoney bought the property from R. and Fannie Fields in 1896. Several of the parcels contributing to the boundaries refer to Fields Branch. Other owners associated with the property include J.O. and Laura Rose, Albert and Veria McCoy, J.W. and Alice Baird, B.J. Edwards, Ida Kelly Edwards Whitton, Walter R. and Juanita Edwards, James and Ivy Clark, and Paula and Curtis Works. Eric and Kristina Johnson have owned the property since 2006.[539]

Figure 349. The Nathaniel McLoney-W.W. Hutchcraft house.

Figure 350. John Crosthwait bought this house in 1900.

685 Pike Street – Barnett-Nelson House. A basic one story three bay two door house that Walter W. McCabe, Sr. sold to Cecil and Ora Doan in 1952 has antecedents that trace to a house and lot sold in 1910 by Lucille and B.B. Barnett to Emma Nelson. The house, pictured at the upper right, has two centered doors flanked by deeply set windows, and a central chimney. There is also an entrance on the east end. Other owners through the years included Mary Etta Covington, Bessie Perkins Covington, Thomas and Marcella Reeves, W.H. Morgan, Cecil B. and Myrtle B. Crosthwaite, Ronnie M. and Thelma Bates, Lonnie and Ben Romans, Aaron Middleton, and Christopher and Amber Owsley.[540]

---

[537] Deed Books 41-492, 44-514, 44-538, 45-406, 51-286, 74-59, 77-285, 114-128, 116-516, 270-263.
[538] Deed Books 86-639, 60-561,562; PVA files.
[539] Deed Books 31-152, 39-163, 52-104, 52-103, 42-382, 55-362, 70-570, 146-590, 178-457, 178-457, 220-037.
[540] Deed Books 43-607, 60-227, 71-248, 74-367, 73-526, 75-589, 76-42, 78-470, 79-16, 329-285, 336-275.

Figure 351. Building with shop relates to 1915 sale by R.H. McCabe to E.S. Baldwin.

695 PIKE STREET – COMMERCIAL BUILDING. A three-bay front-gabled building with an attached shop was sold by James L. Jones to Kenneth and Detta Wilson in 2001. The property was sold in 1915 by R.H. McCabe to E.S. Baldwin.

697 PIKE STREET – COMMERCIAL BUILDING. East of the shop is another tall frame vinyl sided commercial building.[541]

723 PIKE STREET – BAILEY-ROBERTSON HOUSE. An L-shaped house on a rebuilt block foundation with a steep slope was sold in 1996 by Stella Jones to Ronald G. and Audrey L. Jones. Its history dates to 1931 when G.C. and Selah Bailey sold the lot to G.M. Robertson. In 1938 Robertson sold it to Theo and Lloyd Adams. In 1940 Adams sold the property to J.S. and R.L. Burgess. Joe and Nell Burgess and others sold it to Vivian Burgess in 1961. Josie Chowning sold it to Herman and Josephine Fields in 1965, with Robert McKenney buying it in 1965. Michael A. and Regina K. Mizell bought it in 2012.[542]

Figure 352. Front-gabled ell style house was sold in 1931 by G.N. Robertson.

PIKE STREET - NORTH SIDE

662 PIKE STREET – CROSTHWAIT-RISK HOUSE. The lots on the north side of Pike Street called on builders to adjust their designs for an upward incline on the backs of their lots. The easternmost of two larger houses that date to Sadieville's early eras is a one and one-half story house, three bays wide, occupying a rebuilt block foundation. An attractive asset is a steep central roofline gable positioned over the centered front door. A deck has replaced the original front porch. The house has an enclosed back wing. At the turn of the nineteenth century into the twentieth, George B. Johnson sold the lot to John Crosthwait. Three years later J.P. and Monie Crosthwait sold the house and lot on the site to Lee and Mary K. Risk. The Risks sold the improved property in 1928 to Russell Fightmaster, who with his wife Emma in 1969 sold it to Lillie Mae Downing, a widow, who died in 1991. Orva Hiten then sold it to Roy Cannon in 1991, and in 1991 Cannon sold it Green A. Hillard, guardian for William J. Hillard. Wendt Properties became the owner in 2002.[543]

Figure 353. Manlius Price bought the small outlying farm from R. and Fannie Fields.

668 PIKE STREET – PRICE-PARKER HOUSE. Next door to 662 Pike is a two-story house that has experienced considerable expansion and alterations as times have moved on. Its setting is reached by an extensive array of concrete steps. The house has a centered tooled chimney and a central roofline gable lighted by a small six-light double hung window. Manlius Price appears to have been the original or an early owner. Price sold the small agricultural lot deeded to him by R. and Fannie Fields in 1900 to W.S. and Addie Parker. The Parker-Davis family sold it in 1959 to Albert Goldey. Later purchasers include

---

[541] Deed Books 62-568, 82-455, 257-031.
[542] Deed Books 59-328, 64-609, 59-328, 52-520, 65-581, 91-212, 200-205, 100-205, 100-530, 217-748, 346-845.
[543] Deed Books 33-631, 45-484, 59-521, 110-473, 190-270, 201-12, 266-103.

Charles Hager, 1964; Glenda Sue Kidwell, 1966; Martha Tom Perkins, 1971; and Ronnie A. and Genevieve Cannon, Sr., 1972.[544]

730 PIKE STREET – FAULCONER-ROBERTS HOUSE. A tall two-story house three bays wide with a steep lot sloping downward to a stone fence along the Connersville Road, occupies a lot sold in 1906 to Mount Faulconer by T.J. Burgess. Faulconer and his wife Lottie sold it to Frank and Vena Johnson in 1906 and they to Cinda and Richard Roberts in 1909. The Robertses owned the property until 1936 when they sold it to Mary K. Gillispie, who owned it until 1968. More recent owners were Martha T. Jones, Stella E. and Ray Jones, Sadieville Urban Renewal, David and Deborah Short, and Woody and Josephine White, the latter who bought it in 1986.[545]

Figure 354. The tall unembellished house occupies a lot owned by Mary K. Gillispie in 1936.

VINE STREET – SOUTH SIDE

117 VINE STREET -- NEALE-WILLHOITE HOUSE. One of Sadieville's most distinguished houses, a three bay two story dwelling with a flair of antiquity, occupies a seventy-two-acre portion of the original farm of Zephaniah Fields. Location of the home of Thelma J. Willhoite from 1965 to 1999, it is owned today by her son and daughter-in-law, William Lane and Barbara Jean Willhoite. The house and farm are located on the southwest side of the city and date to the purchase of four parcels of farmland by C. Lawrence Neale beginning in mid-1888.

Figure 355. The Neale house is near the site of the Zephaniah and Gabriella Fields log house.

The Neale acquisitions included (1) two parcels containing six acres purchased for $360 in 1888 by Lawrence and Joel M. Neale from John W. McCabe, representing tracts one and two of the division of the land of Lemon Mulberry; three acres bought in 1889 from C.H. Neale for seventy dollars; and twenty acres purchased in 1893 for $1,410 from J.P. and Mary J. Fields. The property included a half-acre burying ground and one and one-half acres of the dower of Gabriella Fields. C.L. Neale owned the property at the time of his death, at which time it was inherited by his daughter, Lucy Mae Vallandingham, wife of Roy Vallandingham.[546]

STABLE/GARAGE SITE ON VINE. Between 1946 and 2001, members of the Burgess family owned the building that was used over its lifetime as a stable and school bus garage. It and its predecessors enjoyed several other commercial purposes during the city's earlier years when the owners were S.B. Jones, A.D. Graves, George S. and A.F. Goodnight, John A. McCabe, A.L. and Mary Covington McCabe, J.T. and Frankie Mulberry, C.W. Cornish, L. and Mary K. Risk,

Figure 356. C. L. Neale house.

---

[544] Deed Books 33-500, 62-542, 33-500, 96-17, 88-181, 96-19, 101-496, 116-409, 118-647.
[545] Deed Books 166-477, 206; 158-604; 110-310; 108-74; 105-3; 82-520, 326; 41-479; 40-314; 37-571.
[546] Deed Books 33-200, 25-226, 33-606, 48-583; 98-495, 99-367.

John and Lucy Adams, O.D. and Bertha Hamilton, Calbert Anderson, B.B. and Jeanette S. Welch, J.W. Jewett, and Kepple Roland. Joseph S. and Richard L. Burgess bought part of the lot for $550 in 1946 from Calbert Anderson, and in 1953, for $1,200, from J.W. and Lula Juett and others. Joe Burgess gained clear title in 1961 and owned it until his death in 1984, when he devised it to his wife Nell M. Burgess and their daughter, Julia Ann LaFleche. Ronnie and Genevieve Cannon bought the property in 2001.[547]

J. Polk Fields House, 151 Vine Street. Long recognized as Sadieville's oldest house is the enlarged home of James Polk Fields, who acquired the lot from J.W. Fields, who inherited it from the estate of Zephaniah and Gabriella Fields. The property included the lands allotted to Gabriella Fields as dower. The historic log house of the Fieldses collapsed in recent years, according to historian Ron Vance. Mary Jane Fields, widow of J.P. Fields, sold the house and acreage to Walter W. and Matsy Mulbry [c.q.] in 1923, who sold it in 1947 to John C. and Blanch Fields. Subsequently it was home to Elmo B. and Alma L. Cushman and remained in the Fields-Cushman family until 2002, when Mrs. Cushman sold the house and twenty acres to Nancy Stone Farley.[548]

Figure 358. The Marshall family house's early deeds called for "room to turn a team."

Fields-Marshall House, 137 Vine Street. Recalling a day gone by are references in several early Sadieville deeds of "room to turn a team" within the conveyed property. One such lot, associated with the Marshall family from the 1920s through 1973, contains an attractive L-shaped house with a later picture window and replacement iron posts on the porch of the main façade. The dwelling was originally owned by J. Polk and Mary J. Fields and sold in 1907 to Richard Ignight for $450 and a house and lot on the pike. The room to turn a team persisted as part of the title through the 1973 sale of the property by George E. and Letha Marshall to Bessie and Wilma J. Pivonka, the current owners. An alley on the south side of the lot was also included within the boundary. The house occupies a steep hillside that requires a tall banked foundation.[549]

Owners prior to the various members of the Marshall family were J.C. Green, Ray Franklin Green, and Jennie E. and Charles Cunningham. In 1924 H.S. Marshall sold the property to James H. Covington, who in 1929 sold it to E.C. Marshall of Grant County. J.K. Marshall acquired it from them in 1932. It was deeded in 1963 subject Marshall's life estate; he passed away in 1972.[550]

Figure 359. Polk Fields house was long considered Sadieville's first house.

C.S. Davis House, 141 Vine Street. A three bay L-shaped house clad in blue vinyl occupies a dry stone foundation on the crest of a low hill extending south from Vine Street. It has a replacement porch of stained wood. The house retains the original transom over the front door and the stained-glass transom over the parlor window. J. Polk and Mary J. Fields sold the lot in 1905 to C.S. Davis for $175. Davis and his wife Gertrude sold the house and lot to Sadieville Baptist Church. The property then sold to Gertrude Davis, who in 1971 sold it Alex

---

[547] Deed Books 33-34, 38-140, 58-290, 72-16, 33-264, 58-249, 66-12, 74-453, 73-596, 80-215, 102-405, 266-162; Will Books X-531, 3-722.
[548] Deed Books 16-41, 15-341, 56-148, 73-629, 75-112, 16-41, 62-511, 268-664; Will Books U-314, Z-656.
[549] Deed Books 39-395, 48-607, 120-299.
[550] Deed Books 49-357, 50-454, 53-138, 53-337, 58-55, 86-592, 103-182, 120-299.

and Paul Jones. Subsequent purchasers were William Lane Wilhoite, 1972; Michael W. and Jennie West, 1979; Norman L. and Yvette Wilson in 1981; and Paul K. and Edith D. Pelley, 1985. Jankie Jackson bought it in 2008 and sold it in 2017 to Greta S. Peak and Brenda J. McMillen. [551]

EDGAR B. MARSHALL HOUSE, 145 VINE STREET. A nicely preserved house with a double window in the front gable ell and an Arts and Crafts style porch with tapered posts mounted on brick piers occupies a lot sold for $150 by J. Polk and Mary J. Fields in 1898 to Leonard Mulberry. The house is popularly identified with Edgar B. Marshall, who purchased it in 1933 and whose estate sold it in 1970 to Vernon and Phyllis Welch Morris. During its earlier years, Leonard Mulberry and his wife Stella sold the house in 1905 to S.S. Jones for $1,000. Jones sold it in 1910 to Arthur and Lucy Lancaster in 1910. Later purchasers included Charles P. and Morah W. Fields, 1912; J.R. and Ollie Swinford, 1928; and Beckham and Pearl Hughes, 1933. Morris Vernon is the current owner.[552]

Figure 360. The former home of Scott County Sheriff R.H. McCabe is one of Sadieville's best designs.

J.W. HAMILTON HOUSE, 211 VINE STREET. Retaining one of Sadieville's earliest porches is an L-shaped house which, with vinyl recladding, bears likeness to the house described as "the beautiful cottage of J.W. Hamilton on Vine" in historian B.O. Gaines's 1904 account of Sadieville. Gaines considered the homes of J. Polk Fields and Hamilton as exemplary along with those of "R.E. Lee, L. Risk, G.T. Nelson, G.B. Johnson, R.H. McCabe, T.H. Daugherty, and W.H. McCabe." The two bays of its recessed block are sheltered by a porch with turned posts and a spooled cornice with a border of tiny triangular dentils. The front lawn is separated from the streetside sidewalk by a drylaid stone fence and concrete steps that lead to the sidewalk.[553]

Figure 361. J.W. Hamilton house is pictured in B.O. Gaines's History of Scott County.

James W. and Nancy S. Brooks sold this house in 1995 to Bonnie Rowland. The Brooks ownership evolved from the estate of Linda H. Brooks, who acquired interest in the larger rural tract of O.H. and Linnie Brooks, which they purchased from W.C. and Rachel Stone, who in turn bought 132.6 acres from William A. and Lillie Hinton. The Hintons sold additional land to the City of Sadieville adjacent to the Knights of Pythias Cemetery. C.S. and Gertrude Davis sold 18.065 acres to William A. Hinton in 1918, "embracing all the land [fourteen acres] on the east side of the Pythias Pike [the cemetery road]." Bonny and Steve C. Parrish have owned the house since 2008.[554] Nancy Brooks was a

Figure 362. House on lot sold by Polk Fields to C.S. Davis in 1905.

---

[551] Deed Books 37-367, 70-2, 81-171, 114-39, 119-711, 144-204, 149-99, 161-489, 319-398, 384-398.
[552] Deed Books 33-141, 37-229, 60-72, 112-141, 41-216, 42-387, 56-341.
[553] Gaines History 2: 169.
[554] Deed Books 211-325, 119-650, 74-58, 73-417, 63-459, 49-175, 44-438, 18-98, 17-364, 318-735.

columnist for the *Georgetown News & Times*, delving into and sharing the background of the fascinating community of Sadieville.

GRANVILLE AND FANNIE KELLY HOUSE, 215 VINE STREET. The heirs of Granville Kelly, who died in 1948, and Fanny T. Kelly, who died in 1954, deeded the small L-shaped house on a slight rise south of the Vine Street sidewalk in 1958 to William H. Morgan. In 1963 Morgan conveyed his interest to Esther Jane Morgan, who directed her interest to John H. Mulberry, who was married to Juanita Florence. In 1964 the Mulberrys transferred the title to Roy B. and Pearl Vance. In 1976 they sold it to Harry C. Offutt, who the same year sold it to Thomas and Virginia M. Gentry. Cammy W. Middleton and Agnes Middleton, his mother, bought it in 1979. Linda C. Humphrey is the present owner. The lot extends from Vine and Bridge streets.

Figure 363. Polk Fields sold the lot for 145 Vine Street to Leonard Mulberry.

R.H. MCCABE/BOB DAVIS HOUSE, 219 VINE STREET. One of Sadieville's best designed and most historic residences occupies a large lot set above a stone terrace on Vine Street. It is one of two early Sadieville dwellings featured in the account of Sadieville in the second volume of *B.O. Gaines History of Scott County*.

Gaines's 1904 photograph pictures the house with a simpler porch than the present one. Both the historic porch pictured here and the present porch retain large Arts and Crafts style tapered posts mounted on tall stone piers. The one-story dwelling has a centered room-size semi-octagonal bay window flanked by wings on either side. An enclosed gable rests at the center of the roof above the bay window. The porch, revised in recent years, now has a high balustrade that continues along the sides of the eight steps leading from the sidewalk and lawn. A pattern of trellises that shelters the area beneath the porch is retained; The house has replacement windows.

Figure 364. Early house of Granville Kelly.

Gaines referred to the house as the dwelling of Ex-Sheriff R.H. McCabe. McCabe made several turn of century purchases on this section of Vine: a lot fifty by 150 feet bought in 1898 from Henry Craig for $200; a lot bought in 1900 from S.B. Jones, measuring fifty by 150 feet; and a house and a one hundred by 150 foot lot purchased for $500 from J.W. Hamilton in 1901. The purchases gave McCabe 200 feet frontage on Vine for his own home and for other residential lots. Hamilton's title came from Cora L. Hamilton. McCabe's heirs included Mary E. McCabe, Edith McCabe Davis, and Ernest Davis, Edith's husband. In 1916 John A. and Frances McCabe sold their interest in the family property to R.H. McCabe and Ernest Davis, retaining the rights to the cistern for their residence. In more recent times Ernest's son, Bob Davis, a popular farmer and northern Scott County landowner, lived in the house and farmed the adjacent land. In 2001 Brenda and Ronnie R. Cannon sold the house and its .3

Figure 365. Early McCabe house became the home of Elizabeth Craig.

acre lot to Ronnie Cannon, Sr. and Genevieve Cannon. Matthew D. and Lacrecia McKenney purchased it in 2015 from Donald Bruce Ledman, II, and Tanisha Cherie Ledman.[555]

Figure 366. The Marshall family were longtime owners of the L-shaped house on Vine Street.

At the time that R.H. McCabe was building houses and developing his farmstead on the south side of Vine Street, he and his brothers, W.H. McCabe and J.W. McCabe, were also partnering in the development of business lots on Main Street and Eagle Creek's milling potential.[556]

Behind the house is the McCabe-Davis farmstead site carved from the Polk Fields farm. Among the outbuildings included in the urban/rural setting was a dry cellar built into the hill and surmounted with a boxed structure with metal roofing, a garage, an outhouse, and a woodshed mounted on wooden posts, retaining boxing with early up and down saw marks. On top of the ridge was a barn described by Bob Davis in 1987 as having been rebuilt in the 1920s or 1930s "by Bill Spears and Robinson or Holcraft" following a fire. The five-bent barn had one ventilator door per bent and large round metal ventilators. The stripping room, built a year after the barn, had a dry stone foundation. The complex included a stock barn "for teams and milking cows" with four tall stalls on each side of the narrow central drive, a buggy section, and a high loft. A hen house stood to the side of the barn. Two of the agricultural buildings are pictured on the following page.[557]

McCabe-Marshall House, 223 Vine Street. The Marshall family has had a lengthy association with the L-shaped house poised on its lawn above an interesting concrete block retaining wall with a rounded upper edge. The wall is broken by seven steps with curved concrete edging. In 1963 J.K. Marshall deeded the property to George E. Marshall, and in 1982 Marshall transferred a lifetime interest in the property to May Daisy Truitt with remainder to George E. and Letha L. Marshall. The Marshalls sold the property in 1983 to Clarence W. and Jackie Ann Pickett, who sold it in 1986 to William R. and Ann Wilson for $27,000. Ronnie and Brenda Cannon bought it in 2004 for $40,000. Carl McIntyre purchased the property in 2005.[558]

Figure 367. John A. and Frances McCabe bought the lot for this house in 1898.

---

[555] Deed Books 33-243, 92-87, 64-199, 46-3, 259-059, 296-322, 336-177, 339-63, 345-435, 366-691, 382-411; Gaines History 2: 169.
[556] Deed Books 27-197, 36-566.
[557] Joy Barlow, notes made during agricultural building survey, June 5, 1985.
[558] Deed Books 151-011, 103-18, 155-812, 165-707, 174-617, 194-350, 199-506, 240-658, 225-288, 289-747.

Figure 368. The McCabes' cellar with a storage building above occupied the back of their Vine Street lot.

JOHN A. AND FRANCES MCCABE HOUSE, 225 VINE STREET. Continuing to convey design and construction fitting the description of "pretty as a picture" is a square three bay house mounted on a nicely dressed dry stone foundation. The porch is supported by turned posts carrying a cornice with pointed dentils. The porch also retains an early railing of wooden square wooden balusters. A wide roofline gable with shaped shingles adds additional interest to the hipped roof. The house occupies one of three Vine Street lots sold in 1898 by S.B. Jones to John A. and Frances McCabe for $400.[559]

Frances McCabe was next to own the property. From her it passed to Mary E. McCabe, Penelope Gano, and John H. Penn. In 1941 Richard S. Hayden sold it to Finley Gano, husband of Penelope Gano, with whom he sold it in 1942 to Mollie Faulconer. Over the next four decades, owners included Odella Lancaster, Leroy and Wanda Faulconer, Roy and Lucy Vallandingham, J.W. Rodgers, Bertha Dunn, and James Paul and Ivy Clark. Albert Plucknet and Sowkam Leong purchased the property in 2015.[560]

Figure 369. The McCabes' barn served farmland adjacent to their Sadieville lot.

MCCABE-GLASS HOUSE, 229 VINE STREET. Carved from the three lots that S.B. Jones sold John A. and Frances McCabe in 1898 was the setting for the frame L-shaped house and its fine stone foundation. In 1930 J.W. Hamilton, commissioner for a family action styled W.W. McCabe versus Frances McCabe, sold the property to Gordon and Annie E. Glass, who then sold it to Elizabeth Craig. Other parties who owned the property included J.C. and Leona Craig, Thelma Craig Bates, Roscoe M. Bates, Pleasant McKenney, Agnes McKenney, R.B. and Hazel Rose, Roger L. and Beverly Sue Stevens, Norman and Yvette Wilson, and Michael and Linda Jones. The Joneses have owned it since 1983.[561]

Figure 370. Lavina McCabe was the original owner of the house at 229 Vine.

LAVINA MCCABE HOUSE, 239 VINE STREET. In 1900 another McCabe joined the host of family members who owned, developed, and lived in Vine Street properties, when fellow developer S.B. Jones sold to Lavina McCabe, wife of W.H. McCabe, the lot where she had built for herself an L-shaped house that was later enlarged. The old and later sections of the house are distinguished by their foundation materials, the older section having a finely crafted stone foundation.

---

[559] Deed Book 32-367.
[560] Deed Books 32-367, 65-184, 65-180, 67-283, 70-155, 78-54, 97-110, 102-3-269, 102-273, 132-462, 155-299, 172-349.
[561] Deed Books 32-367, 58-291, 58-368, 70-204, 90-571, 113-216, 111-257, 124-513, 135-69, 155-36.

Mrs. McCabe willed the property to Robert H. McCabe, who died in 1939, survived by his widow, Mary E. McCabe, and daughter, Edith McCabe Davis. In 1976 Bob Davis, acting in behalf of his mother, sold the house and its .2690-acre lot to Gary H. and Judy W. Fuller for $6,000. The house has an interesting brick shouldered chimney on the west end and an interior chimney with a tooled brick chimneystack between the rooms of the front gable ell. The recessed portion of the older section has a bay window and a tapered post joining post supports of the flat roofed porch. A balustrade encloses portions of the porch and leads to the sidewalk. The section of the house appended on the east end has a concrete block foundation. Windows of both blocks of the house have two over two pane sash. Not conveyed with the deed was the McCabe-Davis family's "right of maintaining and keeping in operation the water pike leading from the cistern situated on these premises to their residence." The deed continued the second party's privilege of "running a water pike from the cistern through the first party's property, to be sunk underground six inches if required."[562]

Figure 371. Hotel owner J.O. Rose and his family owned the property from 1925 to 1935.

JACOB MULBERRY HOUSE, 247 VINE STREET. A tract purchased in 1918 by Jacob Mulberry from S.F. Dutton of Hamilton, Ohio, and willed by him to Ira Otis Mulberry, yielded four lots on Vine Street where there was ultimately built a front gabled house on a stone foundation accommodating the steep slope of the setting. Steps lead to the full front porch which is supported by four tapered posts. The driveway from Vine Street leads to the garage. Mulberry sold the lots to L.T. Dryden and Shelby Dutton for $932, who in 1925 sold to J.O. Rose, Sadieville tavern keeper, the various surveyed properties. The Roses retained the property until 1935, when Laura Rose and other heirs sold the tracts to N.M. Burgess and Ed Evans. In 1975 Louise and T.J. Burgess and Bill and Jane Burgess deeded the property to Matthew Vance and Corinne Duncan. In 1985 Matthew and Trina Vance sold the property to Nancy L. Waldman for $26,000, and in 2015 she sold it to Albert Plucknett and Sowkam Leong.[563]

Figure 372. The Robert Carlisle family owned the property on the north side of Vine.

VINE STREET – NORTH SIDE

ROBERT M. AND ELLA NORA CARLISLE HOUSE, 152 VINE STREET. Two abutting lots and a strip of land relating to Sadieville's once famous subscription-built foot bridge, described in one of the deeds as having "ceased to be used for such purposes in 1955," were included in the property owned in recent years by Ella Nora and Robert M. Carlisle, Sr. Hugging the street on its north side is an L-shaped house that retains several early features including a large parlor window with transom in the front gable ell to which has been appended a second entrance bay to the house. The earlier recessed porch is now supported by iron posts painted burgundy to match the vinyl shutters of the revised vinyl clad façade. The original shouldered chimney also recalls the construction era. A second house similarly situated with a steep banked rear foundation was previously owned by C.S. Davis. It, too, has vinyl cladding.[564]

---

[562] Deed Books 78-373, 34-147, 131-637, 46-3.
[563] Deed Books 47-264; 51-289; 60-42; 61-534; 127-610; 149-387, 389; 161-692.
[564] Deed Books 221-344.

Ella Nora and Robert M. Carlisle and their son Robert M. Carlisle, Jr., have been identified with this house and the adjacent property for much of the just passed half century. Robert M. and Betty Carlisle, who lived in Maysville, sold the combined tracts in 1996 to Verna L. and Phyllis Morris.[565]

Sallie Wright and other family members sold the first described house in 1947 to the elder Carlisles for $4,400. C.D. Winter purchased a house and lot on this site for $500 in 1913 from J.M. and Nartie Henry and a lot from J.O. and Laura Rose. Eva Winter sold the abutting tract in 1946 to Eugene Marshall. In 1920 J.O. and Laura Rose sold a parcel of land included in the larger Carlisle tract to C.S. Davis, who also in 1920 bought a house and lot from Mrs. N.S. Hamon. Mrs. Hamon purchased the latter property in 1913 from James E. Polk and Mary J. Fields, whose title came from a 1910 purchase from J.C. and Lettie Swinford. Reuben and Vivian Davis and Gertrude Davis sold their interest in other property including the old Kaley Hotel to the Carlisles in 1953 and 1955.[566]

Figure 373. C.W. Cornish bought the lot for this house in 1899 from S.B. Jones.

C.W. CORNISH HOUSE, 210 VINE STREET. Three families have enjoyed extended ownership of the L-shaped house with a later picture window in the recessed block. Naomi Rachel and Jan Southworth are the present owners. In 1975 William R. and Luetishie Wilson sold Sam O. and Nellie Vance Wood the house and lot and adjacent Vine Street lot to their daughter Rachel and her husband Jan Southworth. The Wilson family ownership began in 1960 when Cordie Lee Jones and other family members deeded the house and lot to Lula K. Wilson. The property's early history involved S.B. Jones in 1899 selling the lot for ninety-five dollars to C.W. Cornish, who left his property to Leander and Mary K. Risk. They sold it 1919 to S.E. Marshall. In 1923

Figure 374. Hamilton and Sheehan sold this house in 1924 to J.T. Cunningham.

Marshall and his wife Ethel sold the house and lot for $1,650. In 1945 Mrs. Davis sold it to W.H. and Juanita Morgan, who sold it in 1947 to Frank and Lavina McCoy. The McCoy heirs sold it in 1954 to Sally Houston, who sold it in 1957 to Kendall and Cordie Lee Jones.[567]

---

[565] Deed Books.
[566] Deed Books 73-284, 43-266 and 267, tracts 1 and 2; 39-509, 50-588, 51-509, 42-328, 41-386, 39-124 (tracts 3 and 4); 84-354, 73-283 and 286, tracts 5 and 6.
[567] Deed Books 215-781, 156-396, 135-429, 130-208, 95-142, 88-365, 85-100, 81-532, 73-406, 69-544, 53-72, 50-418, 34-136; Will Book X-61.

HAMILTON AND SHEEHAN HOUSE, 214 VINE STREET. During the early years of the twentieth century, the steep lot on the north side of Vine Street was the setting for a stable that was sold in 1902 by John and Mary E. Barnes to Abraham and Margaret J. Steward. In 1903 Nannie J. McCabe bought the stable for $1,400 and an adjacent lot from Bernard and Virgie Hinton for one dollar and other considerations. In 1911 Nannie J. and W.W. McCabe sold the lot to Hamilton and Sheehan, who in 1924 sold a house and lot on the site to J.T. Cunningham. Other purchasers have included: J.D. and Hattie Nunnelley, 1930; Roy and Lucy Vallandingham, 1940; Lula K. and Raymond Wilson, 1951; Jimalee Reed, 1995; and Jimalee R. and Matthew Fitzpatrick, since 2001. The house is a three-bay story and half house built on a hall-parlor plan atop a banked basement foundation. A picture window has replaced the original single hung window on the west side of the front door. A porch shelters the three bays of the lower story and a central tooled chimney pierces the center of the roofline.[568]

Figure 375. This was the home of historian and mail carrier W.A. "Bill" Mashall.

W.A. "BILL" MARSHALL HOUSE, 220 VINE STREET. Sadieville and northern Scott County enjoy considerable historic information due to the work of W.A. "Bill" Marshall, regional historian and also well known rural mail carrier. Whenever we needed an answer to a question about northern Scott County, it was Bill Marshall to whom we turned. His

Figure 376. Silas B. Jones sold this house to blacksmith and handyman W.A. Maines and William McCoy.

contributions to the 1979 book *Scott County Church Histories: A Collection* were rich with lore and history. Remnants of his many stories survive in Sadieville's recorded history. His work merits collection and publication as fragments of it resurface.

In 1957 Marshall purchased the house at 220 Vine Street from F.C. and Leona Anderson. There he did much of his writing on an old model typewriter of the sort that was both blessing and bane to many of us who did a great deal of our productive work during those pre-computer years. In 1987 his wife Mary Betty Marshall sold the house and lot to Stacy Norris for $14,600. Earlier owners of Marshall's three bay house mounted on a banked basement and having a central tooled chimney and shed roof porch included Herman and Josephine Fields and Viona and Theodore Adams.[569]

---

[568] Deed Books 37-397, 35-341, 38-630, 38-74, 42-193, 51-287, 58-460, 62-56, 65-456, 77-533, 211-138, 262-267.
[569] Deed Books 84-498, 172-622, 68-219, 67-298.

J.O. AND LAURA ROSE HOUSE, 222 VINE STREET. The story of Hubert and Stella Morris's marriage and their taking into their family young Wilson Faulkner, an orphan, is told in the couple's deeds relating to the attractive L-shaped house on Vine Street. The house rose around 1900 on a lot deeded that year by Silas B. Jones to W.A. Maines, who did general repairs and was also a blacksmith, and William McCoy. The dwelling retains two over two pane sash and a brick chimneystack. In 1900 Maines and his wife Belle deeded to William and Stella McCoy "the remainder of the lot" sold to them by Jones. The McCoys sold the house and lot for $500 to J.O. and Laura Rose, which they sold in 1920 to Elizabeth F. Craig, Mrs. Rose's mother. Eleven years later the Craig heirs sold the property to Kate and Russell Beard. Beard, who was active in the hardware business, sold the Vine Street house in 1945 to C.P. Gillispie, who a year later sold it to Herman and Josephine Fields. In 1946 Mrs. Fields deeded it to Duard E. and Naomi P.

Figure 377. J.C. and Lottie Swinford sold this house in 1930 to Roy Fightmaster.

Bayless and in 1950 the Hubert Morrises bought it. Mrs. Morris in her will designated that "as Wilson Faulkner is an orphan, that is why I feel he is due to have whatever is left after funeral expenses." She explained that she and her husband had reared Faulkner. She left Lucille Jacoby her marble top table and family Bible.[570]

McCABE-SWINFORD HOUSE, 228 VINE STREET. The prominent Sadieville and northern Scott County family names of McCabe, Swinford, and Fightmaster have been associated with the four bay one story house on Vine with a full porch supported by turned posts. In 1930 J.C. and Lettie Swinford sold the house and lot to Roy Fightmaster, also requesting John A. McCabe "to open the pipeline from the kitchen sink, this residence having been made by him when he sold the property." McCabe and his wife Frances sold the property to the Swinfords in 1921. In 1974 Roy and Edith Fightmaster deeded the property to Wallace Baird and James Warren Fightmaster, who later deeded it back to their mother, Edith Fightmaster, on terms of love and affection. In 2005 Mrs. Fightmaster deeded it to Warren Fightmaster.[571]

Figure 378. Granville and Fannie Kelly were longtime owners of the house at Vine and Bridge.

GRANVILLE AND FANNIE KELLY HOUSE, 403 VINE STREET. An older hall-parlor plan house, four bays wide with two centered front doors, occupies a banked setting at the convergence of Bridge and Vine streets. The lot was sold in the action of Ernest Davis and others versus Mary Michael for a high bid of $213.06 to Granville Kelly. The Granville and Fannie T. Kelly heirs sold it at an estate auction for $1,650 in 1958 to William H. Morgan. In 1963 Morgan sold it to Esther Jane Morgan, who sold it to John H. Mulberry. In 1964 Mulberry sold it to Pearl H. Vance, who sold it to

---

[570] Will Book 1-533, Deed Books 82-182, 76-212, 71-594, 71-291, 69-566, 59-299, 50-297, 47-496, 34-606; Gaines History 2: 170.
[571] Deed Books 51-508, 52-396, 125-554, 125-556, 275-691, 159-521, 301-268.

Figure 379. J.M. Henry sold the T-shaped house to Dixie Zeysing, mother of Richard W. Zeysing.

Harry C. Offutt in 1976. Offutt sold it to Thomas and Virginia Gentry for $3,400, and they in 1979 to C.W. and Agnes D. Middleton for $5,500. The Middletons sold it in 1993 to Cecil C. and Oma F. Doan and Evelyn Johnson, third party. The present owners, Diane and Danny Strong, acquired it in 2011.[572]

CHURCH STREET/GANO AVENUE

Present Gano Avenue was earlier known as Church Street due to the location there of the several Sadieville churches. This early section of town might have been considered a cultural hub of the city due to its location just north of the Methodist Church, northwest of the Baptist Church, northeast of the Christian Church, and briefly north of the earlier city school. Surviving is a neighborhood of several early one-story houses which with selected renovation could present an elegant housing rhythm.[573]

Figure 380. The Methodist Episcopal Church was Sadieville's first church.

SADIEVILLE METHODIST CHURCH SITE. Trustees Thomas J. Burgess and his wife Josie, B.G. Kissman, Richard D. Faulconer, and Joseph May in 1886 deeded Sadieville's new Methodist Church building to the Methodist Episcopal Church South. The church, constituted in 1876, is believed to have been the first church established in Sadieville. The congregation disbanded in 1978, and in early 1979 the old meeting house was dismantled. The building with round arched openings provided classical presentation.[574]

Figure 381. Lucy Thompson's house has a high dry stone foundation.

FIRST SADIEVILLE BAPTIST CHURCH SITE. Organized, interestingly, in 1899 in the Sadieville Methodist Church, the city's Baptist Church was received into the Elkhorn Association the same year. The congregation constructed a large frame building with a steeple that in 1902 included a bell tower. In 1960 under the leadership of Dr. David P. Haney, the congregation voted to move from the Church Street location to the former hardware store originally owned by Leonard Mulberry on Main Street. They bought and remodeled the building at a cost of $30,000 and dedicated it in 1963.[575]

FORMER METHODIST CHURCH PARSONAGE, 109 GANO AVENUE. Just north of the corner lot that once housed the Sadieville Methodist Church is a three-bay house with end chimneys and a stone foundation. This house occupies a lot sold by Leander and Mary Risk in 1913 to J.F. and P. Gano. The Gano family owned the lot until 1941, when the heirs sold it to Jesse B. Stuard. Sam and Odella Perkins and other family members sold it to the trustees of the Salem, Sadieville, and Hinton Methodist Churches for $2,750 in 1948. They

Figure 382. Sadieville Baptist Church was a large building with a balcony and a large bell tower.

---

[572] Deed Books 62-584; 86-631, 634; 93-441, 442; 95-293, 295, 534; 132-604, 661; 144-718; 202-433; 338-449.
[573] The source relating to the following four buildings is entitled the Kentucky Historic Resources Neighborhood Inventory Form SSC4, incorporating properties numbered SC526 through SC529 on Gano Avenue in Sadieville.
[574] "Sadieville Methodist Church," *Scott County Church Histories: A Collection*, 113-114.
[575] Edna Evans, "Sadieville Baptist Church," 41.

jointly owned it until 1951. In 1995 Edward and Catherine Tyree sold it to Carl E. and Bonnie D. Jones.[576]

Figure 384. The Church Street house during its later years.

Figure 383. The west wing of the house at 216 Church Street briefly served as a schoolhouse.

PAMELIA PARKER HOUSE, 113 GANO AVENUE. The three-bay dwelling with a stone foundation has a centered entrance and off-center chimney. It earlier had two over two pane sash, as did its neighbor at 109; the present fenestration includes a picture window. Known during its earliest years as the Pamelia Parker house, it was sold by her heirs to R.W. Chowning in 1906. Dr. C.M. Stokeley owned the house and lot prior to sale by his heirs to R.E. Zeysing, Jr. In 1995 Billy Ray Barkley sold it to David R. Norton.[577]

Figure 386. The Methodist Church parsonage was jointly owned by the trustees of the Salem, Sadieville, and Hinton congregations.

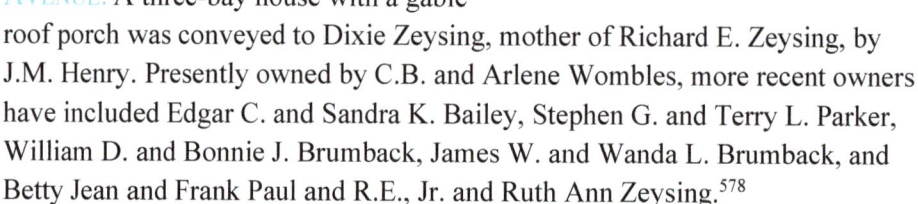

Figure 385. R.W. Chowning bought the Pamelia Parker house in 1906 from her heirs.

HENRY-ZEYSING HOUSE, 122 GANO AVENUE. A three-bay house with a gable roof porch was conveyed to Dixie Zeysing, mother of Richard E. Zeysing, by J.M. Henry. Presently owned by C.B. and Arlene Wombles, more recent owners have included Edgar C. and Sandra K. Bailey, Stephen G. and Terry L. Parker, William D. and Bonnie J. Brumback, James W. and Wanda L. Brumback, and Betty Jean and Frank Paul and R.E., Jr. and Ruth Ann Zeysing.[578]

LUCY THOMPSON HOUSE, 123 GANO AVENUE. The dwelling known for many years as the Lucy Thompson house occupies a tall dry stone foundation. The earlier cornice had returns and the earlier porch posts were turned. Replacement windows have taken the place of the earlier two over two pane sash. In 1998 Edgar Bailey sold the house and lot to Thomas D. Hargis.[579]

117 GANO AVENUE – DR. BAIRD HOUSE. Dr. J.W. Baird, a popular northern Scott County physician for some sixty-four years, occupied the Arts and Crafts style house, its earlier stylish refinements having been obscured by recladding with vinyl siding. These included pointed door and window openings. The house had two

---

[576] Deed Books 33-183, 44-107, 45-204, 66-247, 66-283, 70-506, 75-452, 78-241, 78-377, 86-184, 160-470, 211-107.
[577] Deed Books 37-328, 81-153, 103-73, 154-903, 210-156.
[578] Deed Books 71-312, 314; 144-98; 149-415; 159-517; 211-151; 327-342; 227-338, 342.
[579] Deed Book 218-224.

over two pane sash. It retains its Princess Anne hipped roof section and Arts and Crafts style porch with tapered posts mounted on brick piers. The porch is approached by wooden steps.

In 1951 the Sadieville Lions Club paid tribute to Dr. Baird, then eighty-five years of age, at a dinner at Hayden's Restaurant at Stonewall. The doctor was honored with recognition of having at that time practiced medicine for fifty-nine years and "still serves the Sadieville community." Dr. Baird "often made long weary miles by horseback, in the dead of night, in the winter's snow and blizzards, to attend those who he knew, when he left his fireside, could not pay for his services. Yet he answered those calls until age and rheumatism stiffened his joints and made long trips and night calls impossible." Dr. Baird told the gathering that "he wished a young doctor would come to this community and take up his practice so that he could retire and still feel that the people he has known and loved for so many years would not be left unattended." The faithful physician, it was said, had delivered 2,000 babies, "unassisted by nurses or modern facilities."[580]

Figure 387. Dr. J.W. Baird's house shares features of the Craftsman and Princess Anne styles.

In 2004 the partnership of E. Sisco and K. Hathaway sold the house and lot to Cyril I. Kendrick. In 2013 Gary Afterkirk sold it to Brian A. Tyler.[581]

SADIEVILLE DISTRICT 13 SCHOOL, 216 CHURCH STREET. The west wing of the Victorian house with a distinguishing sunburst in the pediment over the bay window of the main façade served Sadieville's School District 13 as a public school. In 1892 T.J. and Josie Burgess sold the school board the lot for fifty-six dollars. The trustees in 1899 – Dr. J.W. Baird, chair, C.E. Mallory and W.V. Mulberry -- sold the improved property to Leander Risk for $300. In 1913 Risk sold the property along with a house on lot on Gano Avenue to J.F. and P. Gano. In addition to its dramatic extended bay window on the main façade, the house retains several pieces of porch detail including its turned posts, milled post capitals, and balustrade.[582]

MOSE BURGESS BARN. A large barn on the north side of Sadieville housed various items brought into the city to await shipping on the Southern Railroad once shared the streetscape of north Sadieville. It was an important landmark, its vertical boards battened and retaining some of its former red paint. N.M. Burgess purchased the "lot [65-by-160 foot] with a barn thereon" in 1920 from John A. and Sarah H. Gano, the latter having acquired it from J. Finley Gano, and he in turn in 1908 from S.B. Jones. Jones purchased the property in 1906 from J.D. Fields. The large barn recalled an important era in the life of Sadieville, as had the nearby school and churches that also ceased to survive.[583]

Figure 388. Mose Burgess's large barn served as warehouse for items to be shipped on the railroad.

---

[580] Deed Book 210-156; "Sadieville Lions honor Dr. J.W. Baird, 1951," from collected articles related to Sadieville circulated under the title "The Sadieville Sunshine" during the 1988 Sadieville festival.
[581] Deed Books 284-217, 320-138, 354-752.
[582] Kentucky Survey Form SC530, July 29, 1988.
[583] Deed Books 50-408, 46-239, 42-410, 38-75.

JAIL -- "TEMPLE OF JUSTICE," CORNER OF CHURCH (MULBERRY) AND JOHNSON ALLEY. Strategically located at the corner of the former Church Street and an alley connecting Church/Gano to Pike Street is the well built, compact structure designed at the opening of the twentieth century to accommodate the needs and duties of city government. The city bought the small lot for seventy-five dollars in 1901 from J.P. and Mona Crosthwait and constructed the building for $2,000. Government offices occupied the upper level, using the entrance from Church/Gano. The jail with an entrance on the south side occupied the banked basement level. As early as 1987, brick on three sides was damaged by water entering through the cornice. More recently protruding late model concrete blocks were applied over the former foundation of rough faced stone laid with a fine mortar joint. Upper level windows originally had two over two pane sash; those on the lower level have bars. The windows are capped with stone lintels. A 1980s wooden deck has an entrance to the upper level and wraps the side of the building, providing steps that lead to the jail entrance.[584]

Figure 389. In Sadievlle's early years, this building housed city hall upstairs and the jail downstairs.

COLLEGE STREET

It was not uncommon during the late nineteenth and early twentieth century for towns and cities to designate the hilltops and streets on which they built their schools as "College Hill" and "College Street." The large square schoolhouse that stood at the top of College Street hill, and its brick successor that grew over several campaigns that began in 1924, were the pride of the city.

SADIEVILLE SCHOOLS. We must remind today's young people that prior to circa 1954, in most Kentucky communities, African American and non-African American young people attended separate schools. Sadieville's first school for non-African American students is said to have been a "subscription school," meaning that parents provided tuition and other costs for a period of three to six months. Sadieville's first subscription school is believed to have opened in 1878 in a building on Pike Street that later became the telephone building. John McCabe was the teacher. A successor subscription school was located on Church Street and was taught by E.S. Baldwin. A Mr. Rollins is recorded as teacher of a Sadieville school in 1882. Joel L. Mulberry, later

---

[584] Crosthwait bought the lot from G.B. Johnson. Deed Book 34-494; Kentucky Survey Form SC533; Gaines History 2: 168.

superintendent of Sadieville schools, taught a subscription school, also on Pike Street, in 1884-1885. Others listed as subscription teachers were Mollie Lemons, 1886; Mattie O'Hara, 1887; a Mr. Spencer, 1889; Mrs. Essex, 1889; and W.A. Gano, 1893. Meanwhile, the people of the growing city clamored for a public school. School commissioner L.H. Paxton called for schools not only in Sadieville but in various parts of northern Scott County.[585]

In 1887 Polk Fields, recently elected school trustee for Sadieville, along with H.C. Penn and Rodham Fields, were appointed a committee to select a lot and secure bids for a new Sadieville school. This may have been the "old school" that the trustees of "White District # 13" sold in 1899 to Leander Risk for $300. Its property description places it on Mulberry Street adjacent to the Methodist church and Baird's Alley. Risk bought an adjacent lot at the same time from G.B. Johnson. At that time the school trustees were Dr. J.W. Baird, chairman; and C.E. Mallory and W.V. Mulberry, trustees. Trustees elected in 1906 were W.A. Maines, J.O. Rose, and T.J. Burgess.[586]

A major change for public education in Sadieville followed the donation by T.J. Burgess in 1898 of a school site on the top of College Street in his newly developing Burgess Heights subdivision. The two story building, pictured below on this page, cost an initial $2,500. It had two rooms on the first floor and a large open room on

Figure 390. George and Letha Marshall were among the Sadieville young people who became lifelong sweethearts after high school.

the second. The second floor was later partitioned to include two rooms and a hall. Here Professor Joe L. Mulberry taught an eight-month school and a nine month school for advanced students, with Ed Baldwin teaching the lower grades. Other teachers were Louis Baird, Clarence Davis, Bessie Fields, and Eva McKinivan. Some eighty students attended the lower grades on the first floor and thirty-six were enrolled in the two-year high school, which opened in 1911 with Miss Jennie Quinn as teacher. The first graduates of the two-year high school were

Figure 391. This historic photo of College Street shows Sadieville School at the apex and to the east the J.W. Burgess barn that was a landmark in deeds to neighborhood properties.

Sammie T. Bowman, Maygene Covington, Vera Hinton, Anna Neale, George Parker, and Ruth Price. Succeeding

---

[585] Geneva Southworth and Nell Burgess, "History of the Sadieville School," MS, 1987, 2.
[586] Deed Book 33-181, 183.

Miss Quinn as principal after her resignation in 1917 were Walter Jackson, W.O. Lewis, and Paul Arnold. In 1922 the high school added a new teacher and junior and senior classes.[587]

SADIEVILLE CITY SCHOOL. By 1924 the Sadieville population was calling for a bigger school that would provide larger classrooms and space for courses that would prepare students for college or post high school success. Even the students were crusading for an educational structure with space for amenities such as

> a lab to assist in instruction of Physics, Chemistry, Botany, General Science and Biology, as well as Agriculture. We had excellent equipment but because we had no place to keep them they have been stolen or ruined. Cooking utensils have vanished and the stove has decayed. The whole building is in sad need of repair. It would cost a lot of money to make it inhabitable next year, so why not save and put it on a new building since this one might blow down any night, or even during the day when the children are there. More people need to realize the need of training the body as well as the mind."[588]

Figure 392. Sadieville's 1904 school building during its later years.

Succeeding the $2,500 two story square building with hipped roof and projecting entrance and bell tower was the partially surviving and seriously neglected nine bay two story functionally designed east facing building with minimal trim. Inspiring the new building were two events – the increase of student enrollment to 250, and passage by the Kentucky legislature of the 1908 Sullivan School Act that established county boards of education as the administrative unit and required one or more high schools with free tuition in each county.

Professor Joe L. Mulberry was the force behind the early development and refinement of Sadieville's educational structure for white students. Historian B.O. Gaines wrote of Mulberry: "It is due to him more than to anyone else that the town erected and maintains such an educational institution as this."

In 1924, with Ebon Champion as principal, the county authorized the razing of the old schoolhouse and construction of the brick replacement, providing space for the enlarged school as well as a four year high school that graduated its first class that year. Frank Hood, who became principal in 1926, was elevated to the position of county superintendent in 1932, at which time Lawrence Welch became principal. Under Welch's leadership, several additions were made to the school and partitions were added to provide for a library and restrooms. The vaulted roofed gymnasium rose in 1937; a subsequent addition accommodated a lunchroom. In 1941 Charles

---

[587] Cheryl Jones, "School days at Sadieville Elementary," *Georgetown News-Times*, March 3, 1985, and Geneva Southworth and Nell Burgess, "History," 1987, 1.
[588] "New School Building, 1922," from *The Green and White*, Sadieville School newspaper, Paul Mansfield, editor in chief; Lucille Fightmaster, news editor; Angus Parker, sports editor; and J.T. McCabe, distribution manager. Subscription was fifty cents a year. Reprinted in "The Sadieville Sunshine, Special Edition for September 10, 1988," 3.

Barrett led the development of a vocational agricultural program, with Hazel Martin taking on the organization of the home economics program in 1946. Lester Cooper succeeded Welch as principal in 1949 and he in turn was succeeded by William Stevens, "the last of the [Sadieville] high school principals."[589]

Scott County merged its four high schools in 1955 at the new Scott County High School in the building later taken over by Scott County Middle School. Students from Oxford, Great Crossings, and Stamping Ground joined Sadieville students in the new school. Seventh and eighth graders transferred to Scott County Junior High School in 1965 in the building that later became the Scott County Alternative School. In 1980, the sixth grade moved to the new middle school as the middle school system was adopted by Scott County schools.

Figure 393. Sadieville School's vaulted-roofed gymnasium was built in 1957.

In 1987 the county board of education decided to provide a new elementary school for northern Scott County. In spite of organized and spirited concern expressed by Sadieville residents and others, and in spite of the generous offer by Mrs. T.J. Burgess and her son Tom Burgess for a new gift of land, the board accepted the proposal of the Mallard Point planned unit development for the school site.[590]

James Allen Justice spoke for many Sadieville residents when he wrote for the August 21, 1989 *Georgetown News & Times*:

> An era is passing in Sadieville. The Sadieville Elementary School is closing its door midway through the school year and fading into the past. . . This August 24th my son Jake will become the 4th generation to begin his education at this school. . . I have since returned to Sadieville so that my children can have what I had: the security, safety, and warm feelings of a small community along with a solid education." Justice went on to question "why this move was considered beneficial by the Scott County School Board. After all, Garth Elementary has been renovated in the past and is currently being upgraded again." He pointed to the board's decision to build a community school "miles from Sadieville.[591]

---

[589] Southworth and Burgess; Gaines History 2: 169; Kentucky Survey Forms SC536 and SC530.
[590] Kentucky Survey Form SC536.
[591] *Georgetown News & Times*, August 30, 1989.

On December 11, 1991, the Scott County Board of Education, having declared the Sadieville school surplus property, sold the 2.863-acre site to John B. and Mary C. Jeter for $48,300. Over the next several years as the property went into serious decline, Sadieville residents tried in vain to work with the owners to make the property once again useful and valuable to the community. In the meantime, Jeter passed away. City clerk Cindy Foster and Jeter's son Mark worked for a time on a solution, though Mark's younger brother declined to join the effort in view of the city's earlier attempts at condemnation and demolition. Although the city qualified for grant money to have the property assessed, the Jeter family decided to sell it with an approximate starting price of $200,000. A walk-through with the Brownfield and EPA personnel revealed the building to be structurally sound. Jeter continues to own the property.[592]

Figure 394. A.H. Creighton house on College Street has a Craftsman style porch.

A.H. CREIGHTON HOUSE, 224 COLLEGE STREET.

Living in the neighborhood of a city school has always been a plus for families with children. When T.J. and Josie Burgess decided to subdivide their property west of the railroad, south of the turnpike and north of the newly developing school, they found a ready group of buyers. Among these was A.H. Creighton, who paid one hundred dollars in 1902 for one of the Burgesses's newly available lots. Creighton was responsible for constructing the L-shaped dwelling on a dry stone foundation, banked to accommodate the grade, and finished with an Arts and Crafts style porch with tapered posts resting on stone capped brick piers. Creighton and his wife Bertha sold the lot and the house they built upon it to Tom Mulberry for $425. In 1984 Geneva and Grant E. Southworth purchased the property. In 1998 Southworth sold it to Brian and Anna Mae Ishmael. Jo Carol and William R. Wilson bought the house in 2014 and in 2015 sold it to Gina M. Jennings.[593]

Figure 395. Stafford and Nancy Hughes's house on College Street.

STAFFORD AND NANCY HUGHES HOUSE, 228 COLLEGE STREET.

Thomas Mulberry paid $135 for a ninety-five by 150 foot lot that he later divided. The portion of the lot on which a three-bays wide one story house arose was sold by Ruth A. Middleton in 1999 to Roy D. Cannon; she and her late husband Robert had bought it in 1969 from Stanley and Pauline Underwood, whose family had owned it since 1957. Earlier owners included Robert B. and Bertha Elmo Gillispie, 1951-1957; Zelma Fields Riddle, 1947-1951; Charles P. and Morah W. Fields, 1924-1947; and Stafford and Nancy J. Hughes.[594]

Figure 396. J.H. Truitt house on College Street.

---

[592] Deed Books 192-603, 186-733; email correspondence with Cindy Foster, Sadieville city clerk/treasurer, May 11, 2009.
[593] Deed Books 366-608, 361-736, 231-187, 214-361, 159-404, 36-205, 353-1.
[594] Deed Books 241-266, 111-32, 85-82, 78-462, 77-581, 72-533, 53-169, 52-269, 38-501.

J.W. TRUITT HOUSE, 236 COLLEGE STREET. T.J. and Josie Burgess sold the lot on the corner of College and Cunningham to J.B. Robinson, who in 1899 sold the fifty by 150-foot tract to J.W. Truitt for ninety-five dollars. Truitt, apparent builder of the charming one and one-half story house with a steep central gable, sold it in 1913 to Kendall Jones. In 1919 Jones sold the property to Charles P. Fields, who in 1932 sold it to Ida N. Mulberry, wife of Joe L. Mulberry, to whom she devised it. Mulberry in turn left it to Frances Burgess White who died in 1959. Her heirs sold it to Norman Vance, whose only daughter, Nellie V. Wood, inherited it. In 1986 her husband, Sam O. Wood, sold it to Robert and Donna Florence. Florence sold it to Casey and Krystal McIntyre in 2007.[595]

T.F. SHERRITT - BROOKER HOUSE, 302 COLLEGE STREET. One of Sadieville's most notable dwellings was constructed by and for T.F. Sherritt and his wife Carrie. Sherritt is variously known as a farmer, builder, general store owner and operator, and developer. He was a son of Thomas Frank and Sallie Nutter Sherritt. His father, known as Frank, was farm manager of Blue Grass Park, the internationally renowned horse breeding establishment of Alexander Keene Richards on Georgetown's West Main and South Broadway. Sallie Sherritt continued to live in Sadieville after her husband's death and owned property near that of her son and his wife.

Gracefully representing the Craftsman style, the Sherritt house is three wide bays wide and two stories high. An attractive roof gable shelters a triple window with a stone lintel and stone sill. The centered roof gable is patterned like that of the porch roof; both are accented by rectangular brackets. On the main façade's lower level, a pair of double hung windows with tracery in the upper sash are positioned on either side of the centered entrance. The house's roof and that of the porch have deep overhangs. Tapered posts mounted on stone-capped brick piers meet stone ledges. Three windows and triangular attic vents, all with stone lintels and sills, pierce each of the gable ends. Mortar contrasts with the brick and matches the sills and lintels.

Figure 397. One of Sadieville's stellar dwellings is the Craftsman style brick house of T.F. and Carrie Sherritt on College Street.

---

[595] Deed Books 310-421; 167-316; 88-484; 91-64; 66-195; 48-39, 40; 43-463, 523; 33-383; 34-266.

In 1899 T.F. Sherritt purchased from L. and Nannie Price a lot on the street that led to the tobacco barn of T.J. Burgess, a prominent landmark in west Sadieville. In 1903 Sallie Sherritt, wife of the first T. Frank Sherritt, bought a lot on College Street measuring fifty by 150 feet from T.J. and Josie Burgess. In 1905 T.F. Sherritt purchased a house and lot from Burgess Smith. The lot was bordered by the turnpike and the property of Adeline Moritz. Sherritt, who wrote his will in 1932 and died in 1942, left most of his property to his daughter Hazel L. Brooker and the residue to his wife Carrie Sherritt, who was to serve as executrix without bond. Carrie Sherritt's will was probated in 1956; she left $1,000 to her sister Gertrude Davis, $500 to the Sadieville Christian Church, fifty dollars to Grayson School, fifty dollars to Sadieville Christian Missionary Society, and the residue to her daughter, Hazel Sherritt Brooker.[596] In 1972 the Sherritts' daughter Hazel L. Brooker sold the Craftsman style Sherritt/Brooker house to Albert and Mary Lee Goepper. Mrs. Goepper was a daughter of Sadieville's first citizen, J. Polk Fields. The Goeppers made this grand house their home, and in 2006 John Goepper sold it to Kenneth A. Wilson.[597]

Of Sherritt, Professor Mulberry in his account published in *B.O. Gaines History of Scott County* wrote, "Tom keeps a full line of dry goods, groceries and notions, and although young in the business he has, by energy and pluck, proven that he is well fitted for the business and commands a large trade."[598]

Figure 398. Stylish A.L. McCabe house was the family's home from 1905 to 1962.

A.L. MCCABE HOUSE, 306 COLLEGE STREET. The three-bay story and half house with a single window with two over two pane sash in the centered gable above the front door was long known as the home of the family of A.L. McCabe. The slightly sloping porch roof is now carried by decorative iron posts. Silas B. Jones, who sold the McCabe family the lot, was an active investor and dealer in land in south and west Sadieville. His purchases included lots bought in 1880 and 1883 from T.J. and Josie Burgess. In 1900 he sold R.H. McCabe a lot that may have included the house that McCabe sold in 1905 to A.L. McCabe for $425. Here the latter McCabe made his home; he died in 1952 and his wife Mary in 1961. In 1962 the McCabe heirs, Valeria and Douglas McCabe, Hubert and Mary McCabe, John and Eleanor McCabe,

Figure 399. Lucy Lancaster family home from 1899 to 1984.

---

[596] Will Books W-440, Z-417.
[597] Deed Books 45-209, 45-210, 27-227, 34-266, 33-594, 38-366, 304-226.
[598] Gaines History 2:170.

Walter and Urso McCabe, sold the property to Buford Perkins. After Perkins' death in 1968, his heirs sold it to Flo Hughes. Her heirs sold it in 1980 to Marge and Herman Crisp. The Crisps sold it in 1998 to James S. and Bertha Roberts. Daniel W. and Jennifer R. Maudlin bought it in 2007.[599]

LUCY LANCASTER HOUSE, 308 COLLEGE STREET. Lucy E. Lancaster and her descendants long enjoyed calling the tall two-story vinyl clad L-shaped house home. Among the dwelling's surviving refinements is a diamond shaped stained glass window on the second level and turned posts supporting the porch. Mrs. Lancaster bought the house and lot in 1899 from Darius and Lida Jones for $900. It is interesting to compare the prices attached to houses in Sadieville to those in other communities. It was a much better bargain to live in Sadieville.[600]

Figure 400. Sallie Sherritt's American Foursquare style house.

The house was probably built by Leander and Kitty Risk, who acquired the lot in 1895 from the Joneses and sold it later that year for $700. Four years later, the lengthy ownership by Mrs. Lancaster and her descendants took root. In 1952 Lucy Lancaster and Winter Neale, Laura Lancaster and Ebon Champion, and Dorcas Lancaster deeded the house and lot to John Lancaster, who in 1984 in company with his wife Odella deeded it to Juanita Lancaster. In 1995 Juanita and A.J. Lancaster sold the property to Juanita Murphy, and in 2014 she deeded it to Michael Murphy.[601]

SALLIE SHERRITT HOUSE, 312 COLLEGE STREET. Sallie Sherritt, wife of the first T. Frank Sherritt and mother of Sadieville entrepreneur T.F. Sherritt, was the original owner of the lot where either she or her children erected a frame house in the American Foursquare style. Her children who sold the house and lot for $400 to J.W. Collins in 1916 included T.F. and Carrie Sherritt, Nannie and L. Price, Josie and R.E. Chowning, and Carrie and Joe C. White. Three years later Collins sold it to Dave T. Griffith, who in 1934 sold it for $800 to Edna Craycraft and W.D. Price. The house's value rose to $37,000 in 1943 when the Prices sold it to Edgar Evans, who devised it to his wife Edna Margaret. She lived here until 1991 when she sold it to Jimmie and Lee Ann Mullikin. Michael Mizell purchased it in 2015.[602]

Figure 401. W.H. and Sadie Truitt house, circa 1894.

316 COLLEGE STREET. William H. and Sadie Truitt bought three lots between 1894 and 1896 from T.J. and Josie Burgess.

Figure 402. Pike Street commercial building of W.H. and Sadie Truitt.

---

[599] Deed Books 20-442, 20-439, 18-5, 18-7, 35-566, 41-158, 93-342, 110-529, 148-111, 230-523, 309-605.
[600] Deed Book 33-352.
[601] Deed Books 33-352, 30-44, 87-449, 156-587, 213-432, 365-211.
[602] Deed Books 45-209, 45-295, 48-596, 60-423, 68-169, 191-554, 308-680, 363-88, 368-392; Will Book X-161.

They sold the adjacent fifty by 150-foot lot and the house in 1915 to John A. and Frankie McCabe for $600.[603]

318 COLLEGE STREET. In 1896 Leonard Mulberry paid $500 for a house and lot that two years later was to become the home of Adelia H. Mortz of Corinth, who paid $625 for it. The house is a three bay dwelling banked in the rear. It was heated by a chimney on the east end. Two over two pane sash and a small porch supported by round posts complete the exterior picture. Mrs. Mortz lived there until 1920 when she gave the property to William Nelson of Lexington for taking care of her during her life and for arranging for her burial. In 1975 Eugenia Sanford Smith, committee for Marvin Earl Sanford, deeded the property to Doris Johnson, who sold it in 1987 to Herman W. and Marge Irene Crisp. Chris and Amanda Neaves bought it in 2001 and sold it to C.B. Wombles.[604]

WILLIAM H. AND SADIE TRUITT COMMERCIAL BUILDING, 326 COLLEGE STREET. The business building on the corner of Pike and College is two stories tall with frontage on the pike. A small block building stands next to the larger frame building. William H. and Sadie Truitt appear to have been the original owners. In 1988 Dorothy Faulconer sold it to Carol Faulconer Walters.[605]

CUNNINGHAM AVENUE

In 1880, on the heels of Sadieville's incorporation as a city, Silas B. Jones sold T.J. Burgess the forty-three-acre farm that he had purchased from Joel M. Neale. Neale's title accrued from a commissioner's sale of land owned by Charles E. Neale in 1878. Burgess subdivided the farm and named the addition Burgess Heights. Sadieville School, aptly situated at the top of College Street Hill, was an attraction for homes for teachers, administrators, and families with children. Most of the dwellings erected in the neighborhood date from the early years of the twentieth century.[606]

Figure 403. Sadieville's unique lodge building and movie theater.

LODGE BUILDING, THEATER, 213 CUNNINGHAM AVENUE. One of the most significant features of early Cunningham Avenue is a fascinating one-story dwelling with a hip roof and small double hung windows on one end and a bay window on the other. The building enjoys the tradition of having housed Sadieville's movie theater. During the early twentieth century, movies were on the minds of many Americans as the nation's fledgling silent movie industry morphed into movies accompanied by sound. The world's first commercial motion picture exhibition took place in 1894 in New York City. The first movies, unaccompanied by sound, were phased out in the 1920s by the new rage of "talkies."

---

[603] Deed Book 44-456.
[604] Deed Books 44-456, 31-622, 33-138, 30-386, 33-142, 33-143, 49-523, 128-110, 169-692, 210-705, 210-708, 225-280, 225-283, 227-338, 257-314.
[605] Deed Book 44-456, 177-395.
[606] Deed Book 17-464.

In December 1913 the lodges of Winalansit Tribe # 125 IORM and IOOF#234, both of Sadieville, purchased from T.J. and Josephine D. Burgess a lot in Burgess Heights for seventy-five dollars. Trustees were John Marshall, E.B. Braun, Ben Covington, J.H. Hatton, and Beal Fightmaster. During its early years the property is said to have been used as a movie theater. The lodge sold the building in June 1919 to Lillie H. and William A. Hinton for $840. Ben Covington purchased an adjacent lot in 1919 which he then sold to the Hintons. The next year the Hintons sold the property described as a house and lot to Ruth L. Congleton for $1100, which Mrs. Congleton and her husband Porter sold in June 1925 to N.J. McCabe. McCabe along with W.W. McCabe in 1942 sold the property to George Evans. George and Laura M. Evans were parents of Juanita Zumwalt, Geneva Driskell, and Julia Rowland. Juanita Zumwalt traded the property for a rural lot. Brian Eads, who acquired the property in 2007, sold it to Pamela J. Price in 2016.[607]

Figure 404. J.C. and Lettie Swinford's Dutch Colonial Revival style house, circa 1914.

Figure 405. Llewellyn Price house dates from early twentieth century.

TRUITT-WARRING HOUSE, 203 CUNNINGHAM AVENUE. The Classical Revival style house that occupies the lot that Theresa Marshall deeded to Vance P. Marshall in 1947 and that Addie Penn and subsequently her heirs acquired from Marshall has been attractively remodeled. In 1953 Addie Penn's heirs – Annie Cox; Oscar Sharon; Eunice, Helen, and Charles Fain; and H.T. Sharon sold the property to Clem and Ethel Fightmaster, from whom it was inherited by Agnes L. and Andrew M. Parrish. Betty Lou Romans purchased it in 1999, and Randall and Carolyn Wilson acquired it in 2008.[608] The house's earlier history found W.H. and Sadie Truitt selling the property to W.C. Warring for $600. Warring and his wife Lena R. sold it in 1907 to Llewellyn Price for the same price.[609]

J.C. AND LETTIE A. SWINFORD HOUSE, 219 CUNNINGHAM AVENUE. J.C. and Lettie A. Swinford purchased a banked lot for their Dutch Colonial Revival home in 1914 from J.P. and Mary J. Fields for fifty-five dollars. In 1920, L.B. and Frankie Craig bought the property improved with the house for $1,000. Subsequent purchasers included:

Figure 406. R.E. Chowning house, circa 1919.

---

[607] Deed Books 17-464; 43-525, 539; 49-171, 173; 50-12; 63-30; 67-343; 81-551, 552; 308-225; Will Book U-189.
[608] Deed Books 73-258, 80-217, 56; 80-217, 89-94, 80-218, 148-880, 245-642, 246-296; 320-578, 379-870; Will Book 1-299.
[609] Deed Books 38-105, 366; 73-258; 356.

L. and Nannie L. Price, 1923; Roy and Ruth Mallory, 1930; Farmers Deposit Bank, 1939; Charles and Mary Catherine May, 1938; Ayda Smith, 1962; Donald R. and Beverly J. Cooper, 1995. Charles and Mary Catherine May owned it for twenty-three years, from 1938 to 1961. The neatly designed house has a high stone basement that is artfully built, particularly on the chimney side. A stone dividing wall marks the side of the lot. Owners Miranda K. and Jon M. Lamont acquired it in 2006.[610]

Figure 407. W.C. and Nettie Faulconer house on Cunningham Avenue.

R.E. CHOWNING HOUSE, 239 CUNNINGHAM AVENUE. The historic house at 239 Cunningham has a special charm that speaks through its early stone foundation and two-story bay window. Its site is advantageous to showing off the house's two facades. This dwelling occupies a lot that was sold in 1919 by T.J. and Josie Burgess to R.E. Chowning for one hundred dollars. At the time of the sale, the neighborhood was known as Burgess Heights with Cunningham Avenue having the name of Burgess Avenue. The Chowning deed encompassed lots numbered twenty-one and twenty-two as well as lot number nineteen to the north. The land had been part of a larger sale from Silas Jones to Burgess. The property remained in the Chowning family until 1968 when W.T. Warring, executor of the estate of Josephine Chowning, sold it to Clem Fightmaster. Fightmaster died in 1975, leaving it to his daughter Agnes, wife of Andrew Parrish, who left it to her daughter Dianna F. Vest. In 1997 Diane Vest individually and as executor, and Philip W. Vest, sold the property to S.B. Sherman. Richard Stephen Seals was a recent owner. Christopher S. and Amanda L. Neaves are the present owners.[611]

FAULCONER HOUSE, 204 CUNNINGHAM AVENUE. The many years that the ruggedly endowed L-shaped one-story house had pursued when viewed in 2007, representing the time spanned since its original or at least early ownership by W.C. and Nettie Faulconer, tell the house's story. Changes have included the partially enclosed porch, the shaped shingles cladding the front gable ell, the shingled lower level, and the vertical boards enclosing part of the porch. The house has a nice brick sidewalk.

Richard and Sallie Ignight purchased the lot in 1914 from Lucinda Robinson and sold it in 1916 to W.C. Faulconer, who in 1920 with his wife Nettie sold it to Maggie Kitchen for $1,600. Ms. Kitchen owned the property for nine years and sold it in 1929 to Mary A. Michael, whose executor in 1939 sold it to Emory S. Davis. Mr. Davis died in 1953, leaving his wife Minnie who subsequently married a Woodrum, and sons Emory and Robert L. Davis. In 1977 Mrs. Davis and a host of descendants – Robert Lewis and Linda Davis, John Warring and Shirley Davis, William Emory and Rochelle Davis, Clay Parker and Patricia Davis, Harold Reed Davis, Brenda Gail Davis and Raymond Gerald Burns, Randy Edward and Connie Colleen Davis, and Roger Lee Davis – sold it to Martha Tom Perkins. She sold it ten years later to Sharon Dailey Sharp. Successive purchasers have included Bobby G. and Teresa L. Ison, 1987; Mark and Judy Farrow, 1988; William D. and Simiko Y. Coleman, 1988; and Charlene English, 1994.[612]

---

[610] Will Book U-189, 314; Deed Books 43-526, 328; 44-56,57; 50-519; 520-519; 53-33; 58-227; 63-624, 625; 151-259; 155-260; 91-182; 211-103, 3-5-068.
[611] Deed Books 50-276, 277; 132-505, 226-262, 228-691, 294-277, 239-116.
[612] Deed Books 45-369, 49-155, 50-224, 58-107, 64-579, 135-706, 172-257; 273-666; 174- 669; 219-484.

Figure 408. Lorena Hamilton house, circa 1914, is one of Sadieville's most attractive dwellings.

MARY E. MULBERRY HOUSE, 208 CUNNINGHAM AVENUE. The three-bay two story house occupying Burgess Heights lot number twenty-eight has a distinctive rural flair. T.J. and Josie Burgess sold the lot in 1913 to J.L. Neale. In 1925 Lorena Hamilton sold it to Mary E. Mulberry, mother of Carrie Sherritt and Gertrude Davis, who in 1951 sold it to Andrew M. and Agnes Lee Parrish. Andrew Parrish died in 1983, leaving his interest to his wife and daughter Diana F. Vest. In 1997 Diana Vest as executor sold the property to Kenneth W. Elswick and Stephen Brentley Schureman for $35,000. Succeeding owners have included Rodney A. and Peggy A. Petty, 1999; Associates Home Equity; Harold G. and Blanche Moran, 2000; Kami Kattelus, 2012; Kenneth Isaacs Interior Inc., 2013; and Geri L. and Nicholas D. and Geri L. Price, 2014.[613] Renovation, some apparently necessitated, included addition of vinyl siding and vinyl windows and replacing the early stone foundation. The square tapered posts supporting the porch recall the Arts and Crafts era.

LORENA HAMILTON HOUSE, 214 CUNNINGHAM AVENUE. Lorena Hamilton was the original owner of the distinguished two-story house with a central roofline gable lighted by two double hung windows. The roof has a deep overhang with large stick style brackets; its pitch is matched by that of the porch, which is supported by turned posts. The main level has a double window flanking the entryway.

Mrs. Hamilton purchased the lot in 1914 from J.L. and Mary E. Neale for one hundred dollars, sold it to Neale in 1922 for $3,700, and reacquired it along with abutting acreage in 1924

Figure 409. Lorena Hamilton sold this house to Mary E. Mulberry, mother of Carrie Sherritt and Gertrude Davis.

for $3,200, giving her possession of Burgess Heights lots thirty-three, thirty-four, and thirty-five and two other parcels adjacent to the city school property.[614]

It is interesting to observe how inflation and renovation assisted this property's acceleration in value. In 1967 Elizabeth and D.L. Sheehan sold it to John C. and Blanche Fields, Mrs. Fields selling in 1977 to Mark R. and Donna M. Goss.

Figure 410. Charles and Mamie May's house has a unique high roof.

---

[613] Deed Books 17-464, 43-578, 54-589, 78-037, 226-259, 226-259, 240-87, 249-429, 253-779, 328-848, 342-260, 357-455, 362-129.
[614] Deed Books 43-578, 44-286, 52-17, 53-357,

The Gosses lived there until Goss' transfer by Merrill Lynch in 1981. By that time the house was worth $38,550. The next year Judy F. Cox purchased the property. Judy and Norman Sinkhorn renovated the house and in 1991 sold it to Roy and Jennifer Rutledge for $52,000, who sold it in 1994 for $53,000 to Allen K. and Angela Smith. The Smiths sold it in 2003 to Ira H. and Sandra Combs for $80,000.[615]

Figure 411. Masons and builders Herbert and George Antle, Charley May, and John Neal are shown building the foundation of a house for Tom Hamilton's mother, Lorena Hamilton. Photo courtesy Ron Vance.

220 Cunningham Avenue. In 1914 Lorena Hamilton sold Burgess Heights lots number thirty-three and thirty-four to Charles and Mamie May, Mrs. Hamilton having purchased the lots in 1913 from T.J. Burgess for eighty-five dollars. In 1957 Harold and Helen S. May and family members Edna Withrow, Patricia May and W.C. Mudd, and Alton May, by W.T. Warring, sold Burgess Heights lots thirty-three and thirty-four to Clem and Ethel Fightmaster. The May family owned the property from 1917 to 1957. The Fightmasters were parents of Agnes Parrish and Ed R. Fightmaster, the latter inheriting this house. In 1980 William and Diana Fightmaster and other heirs deeded the property to John L. and Elizabeth S. Botkins. Later purchasers included Beulah Sinclair, 1981; Nannie Vance, 1983; Ken and Judy Elswick, 1998; Richard S. and Paula Seals and Ken Isaacs Interiors, 2004. William R. and Jo Carol Wilson acquired this very interesting house in 2015 and sold it in 2016 to Amanda Ciejko.[616]

Railroad Lane

C.T. Covington House, Railroad Lane. In the late 1980s Frances Parker (Mrs. W.T.) Warring recalled how the C. Thompson Covingtons had expanded their new home after their honeymoon. Covington purchased his five-acre lot in 1884 from T.J. and Josie Burgess. Around 1900 the Covingtons added the upper story to the house, distinguishing it with a pair of roofline gables.

Figure 412. C.T. Covington house on Railroad Lane.

The Covingtons had a romantic view from the west of the railroad, giving them a more protected opportunity from the prevailing winds to watch trains and activity in town than did those who lived in Sadieville and were faced with constant smoke from trains and dust from the stockyard. Covington owned a hardware store. In 1974 Karl M. and Bertha Baker purchased a 2.6 acre piece of land and the considerably remodeled two story house. In 1941 the Covington heirs sold the family home to Mary McCabe, who left it to her daughter Valerie Guy and sons Hubert, John, and Walter McCabe. Mrs. Guy sold it in 1970 to C.C. Cook. In 2006 Karl Baker, Sr., sold the property to Jankie Jackson, who in 2015 sold it to McDeevits Fresh Goods LLC. Cynthia Holbrook became owner in 2016.[617]

---

[615] Deed Book 103-429, 153-223, 166-51, 188-323, 208-573, 273-060.
[616] Deed Books 45-77, 43-524, 51-457, 85-15, 128-171, 146-460, 149-848, 154-154, 252-573, 233-106, 285-359; 372-726.
[617] Deed Books 22-25, 93-338, 66-284, 113-382, 119-95, 254-174, 126-682, 305-813, 370-686, 381-586; Kentucky Survey Form SC534; other information from Frances Warring, 1987.

FORMER SECTION HOUSE. Cincinnati Southern Railroad built the Section House as the dwelling for the railroad section foreman who took care of the track. According to the late William A. Marshall, Sadieville historian, two of the earlier occupants were named Corrigan and Crawley. The two story house and its outhouse had tongue and groove siding much like that applied to older railroad depots. Marshall said that prior to and during railroad construction, the residence of S.T. Connellee stood near the site of the Section House.[618]

About 500 feet north of the Section House was a small gable roofed building used for storing service wagons for the railroad and control equipment. The building was faced with siding like that of the Section House.[619]

EAGLE BEND ROAD – THE SADIE BURGESS WHITNEY ESTATE

CLARENCE S. AND GERTRUDE DAVIS HOUSE, 105 EAGLE BEND DRIVE. Exquisitely patterned Arts and Crafts style blocks of white Kentucky marble form the exterior facades of the Dutch Colonial Revival dwelling originally owned by Clarence S. and Gertrude Davis. The Davises in 1925 and 1927 bought 216.649 acres of the estate of Sadie Burgess Whitney, whose address was at that time Buffalo, New York. The acreage was richly surrounded by picturesque bends of Eagle Creek a short distance from the Cincinnati Southern overpass that leads into Sadieville.[620]

Figure 413. Clarence and Gertrude Davis house was constructed of Tyrone limestone in a Dutch Colonial Revival style.

After Davis's death, in 1954 Gertrude Davis sold the family home to Lawrence Rogers. In 1963 Rogers and his wife Lucille sold the property to John N. and Glenda L. Ross and Vera K. Ross. The next year they sold it, with six exceptions, to Jessie T. and Mary M. Allison. Harry and Lorraine Jones's 1994 sale to Doug and Doris Smith embraced tract number one extending from the Sadieville Turnpike, the water gap on the west side of Eagle Creek, and with the creek bordered with land formerly owned by Charlie Fields and Gordon Fightmaster.

The City of Sadieville water plant was one of the exceptions. The Smiths sold the house and lot in 1997 to Gerald D. and Debra L. Meltons.[621]

An earlier dwelling on the bend of Eagle Creek is shown on the 1879 Beers & Lanagan map as having been the home and farm of "J. Hammond."[622]

---

[618] Kentucky Survey Form SC21.
[619] Kentucky Survey Form SC535.
[620] Deed Books 53-638, 55-83, 65-84, 82-17, 93-349, 96-176, 205-213, 224-672; Will Book X-80.
[621] Deed Books 82-17, 93-349, 96-176, 205-213, 224-672.
[622] 1879 Map of Scott County.

Figure 415. Gauging station on Eagle Creek related to Sadieville's earlier water works.

Figure 414. Sadieville water tower, dismantled in 2016.

SADIEVILLE WATER WORKS. Sadieville was in line with other municipalities when the little city of the sixth class established its municipal water works in 1938. The City received a direct grant of $14,000 from the federal government and issued $23,000 in revenue bonds. In August 1961 Sadieville voted 200 to three to sell its 150-customer water plant to the rural Scott County Water District. At that time a dam was built across Eagle Creek to supply water for much of that part of rural Scott County. Recalling that era, the dam and the gauging station (pictured above) stand beside Eagle Bend Road in the subdivision that grew up around the Clarence Fields house.[623] The large water tank that occupied a high point, looking down on Sadieville, the railroad, and Knights of Pythias Cemetery, "past its time," was torn down during the summer of 2016.

KNIGHTS OF PYTHIAS/ SADIEVILLE CEMETERY. Another cardinal feature of this neighborhood is the Knights of Pythias/Sadieville Cemetery, which the lodge deeded to the Sadieville Cemetery Company, Inc. on June 7, 1960. K of P's Big Eagle Lodge 120 trustees A.L. McCabe, T.F. Sherritt, and E.P. McKenney purchased for the cemetery for $637 a four and one-half acre tract beginning at the ridge corner in the west edge of the street extending to the CNO&TP Railroad on December 12, 1913. Land which became the cemetery had been part of the parcel purchased by the Burgesses in 1880 from Silas B. Jones. The cemetery has decorative gateposts and a lane leading through and around the graves.[624]

Figure 416. Entrance to Sadieville Knights of Pythias Cemetery.

---

[623] Interview with William T. Warring, 1961, notes in author's vertical files.
[624] Deed Books 89-11, 4-469.17-464; *Gone, Forgotten, Now Remembered*, 139-147.

Conclusion

During many of the years discussed in detail in this chapter, Sadieville, which originally encompassed one square mile, was governed by a city council, W.T. Warring reported during to an interview with this writer in 1963. The council consisted of the mayor, Bob Davis, and four councilmen, Elmo Cushman, John Lancaster, E.B. Vance, and W.T. Warring. All were appointed by the governor on recommendation of the county judge. "People were satisfied," Mr. Warring said, "and never called for an election."[625]

The reader is asked to understand that as this work was completed, discussed properties continued to be sold and bought.

Figure 417. Early view of Cincinnati Southern railroad station and Main Street.

---

[625] *Gone, Forgotten.*

GLOSSARY

abacus – the square at the top of a Doric column

acanthus – Corinthian column capital detail inspired by leaf of Greek plant native to the Mediterranean region

acroteria – summit or extremity ornaments on a pediment, as on the top of a Grecian or Roman temple

antebellum – the period of American history after the Settlement Period and before the Civil War, circa 1825 to 1861

antepodium, antepodia – extended projections from a platform, porch, or basement

anthemion – the Greek honeysuckle motif

arch – a structural device, especially of masonry, forming the curved, pointed, or flat upper edge of an opening; also a support as in a bridge or doorway

arch types --
    -jack arch or splayed flat brick arch – a flat opening support composed of voussoirs the sides of which radiate from a common center
    -round headed arch – a 180 degree arch over a window
    -segmental or segmented arch – a curved support of less than half a circle, or ellipse
    -Tudor arch – a pointed arch

architectural style -- a definite type of architecture, distinguished by special characteristics of structure, ornament, and time period. Architectural styles include:

-Adamesque – neoclassic style of furniture and architecture originated by Robert and James Adams. A feature of finely detailed Early Kentucky homes.

-Art Deco, the first American style to break with revivalist tradition; used low relief geoemetric designs such as zigzags, chevrons, stylized floral motifs. Examples include movie theaters, and the telephone company building on Georgetown's East Main Street.

-Art Nouveau –architectural style dating from circa 1885-1890 among European architects to establish a new style in opposition to the prevailing eclectic, emphasizing the "willowy curve," based on nature, flowers imitated in wrought iron, colored glass, stucco, plaster paint, and enamel

- Arts and Crafts – also called Craftsman, a style popular during the early twentieth century distinguished by right angles, natural woods, "close to ground" forms. The bungalow and American Foursquare plans evolved during this period and are often grouped under the general heading.

-ashlar – hewn or squared stone

- baroque – a flamboyant style of art or architecture dating from 1550 to 1700 with elaborate and ornate scrolls, curves, and other overstated and ostentatious decoration

- beaux-arts – the fine arts, a school of architecture influenced by the European Ecole des Beaux Arts, classically inspired and long lasting

- bungalow – an architectural style with Asian origin usually featuring a balanced one story façade with a side gabled roof and having an extended dormer at mid-roof, wide porches. The best bungalows have fine craftsmanship, materials left as much as possible in their natural state

- Carpenter Gothic – Gothic Revival Style carried out in wood

-Classical Revival – academic revival of the classical, evolving from Beaux Arts interpretation of classicism

- Colonial – an American architectural style prevalent in the American colonies before and during the American Revolution

- Dutch Colonial Revival – style usually associated with gambrel (two pitch) roof, balanced symmetry

- Federal – an American style "for the common man as well as the privileged…Americans had different materials to work, less use for decoration, and a need to economize on labor and materials." Carole Rifkind, *A Field Guide to American Architecture*

-Georgian – characterized by rigid symmetry, axial entrances, geometrical proportions, hipped roofs, and sash windows

- Georgian Colonial – style evolving from Georgian England with high style classicism, balanced façade, lintels, use of many paneled surfaces

- Early Kentucky – a building style popular during the Settlement periods in Kentucky, tenoned joints, stressing interior and exterior balance, use of chairrail, understated woodwork style

- Egyptian Revival – use of Egyptian detail in columns, friezes

- Federal – the Scots Adamesque style recalling Renaissance and Palladian forms, the French rococo, and classical architecture of Greece and Rome, characteristic of the Early American period featuring balance, use of elliptical and round arches, carved mantels with panels, sunbursts, applied columns

- Greek Revival – style inspired by architecture of ancient Greece with characteristics of balance, use of pediments, twin panel doors, flat arches. Also hallmarks of the style are columns and pilasters, bold simple moldings, pedimented gables, heavy cornices with unadorned friezes, horizontal transoms (not arches) above entrances

- Gothic Revival – European romantic movement-influenced style using asymmetry, pointed arches, crenellation, steep gables and roofs, lacy bargeboards, bay and oriel windows, tracery leaded stained glass

-High Victorian Gothic (or Ruskinian after John Ruskin), use of brick and stone, used in public buildings, schools, libraries, and churches. Georgetown Baptist Church is an example.

- Italianate – derived from the rural Italian, with broad roofs, ample verandas, round and segmental arches, hoodmolds, decorative cast iron features, decorative brackets, wide eaves, entrance towers, pressed metal in commercial buildings

-Period Houses – revivals of farm or rural buildings including English cottages, English Gothic, popular for residential architecture and estate houses during first third of twentieth century

- Richardsonian Romanesque – an American style drawn from Henry Hobson Richardson's (1838-1886) fascination with utilitarian use of Romanesque arches surrounded by rock faced stonework

-Prairie Style – essentially horizontal with broad hipped or gabled roof and wide overhanging eaves, popular before 1920, curveless, large plain exterior chimneys, use of multiple built-ins

- Romanesque Revival – late nineteenth century style derived from Richardsonian Romanesque using round arches and mixed materials

- Second Empire – a late nineteenth century style with Italianate influence and a mansard roof; vernacularly called the General Grant style

- Shingle Style – emphasis on the surface, the shingle covering uniting all parts of the building. The interior plan was Queen Anne defined by openness and informality

-Stick Style, wooden construction with intersecting boards applied over weatherboarding to "express the inner structure of the house through exterior ornament."

- Victorian Italianate – a mid to late nineteenth century style especially popular in city streetscapes and commercial neighborhoods reflecting use of balance, hoodmolds of various shapes, segmental and round headed arches, elaborate trim

- Victorian – ". . . America's most versatile and creative period, exuberant and uninhibited in its expression and the originator of ideas . . ." Mary Mix Foley, *The American House*

- Queen Anne – a late nineteenth century Victorian style having multiple forms evolving from a generally central hip roof, front gable ells, and voluptuously trimmed towers, turrets, windows, lots of stained glass, and picturesque chimney organization

- English Cottage – a style that developed in the same neighborhoods as Arts and Craft buildings

- architrave – the bottom member of an entablature; also the molding around a door or window balloon frame

bead – a half or three-quarters round molding; a line along the edge of a molding

baluster – a vertical often vase-shaped or rhythmically curved member of a balustrade

balustrade – a series of upright members framing a stairway or porch

banister – the handrail or balustrade of a staircase

bargeboard – a decorated member, pendant to an overhanging gable

baroque – the flamboyant style of seventeenth century European architecture

batten – an upright component of an architectural structure such as a door or wall covering. A battened barn is clad with vertical boards with narrow strips enclosing the spaces between the boards.

batter – receding upward slope of wall

battlement – a toothed roofline structure, right angled, with high and low points reflecting military protection

bay – one unit of a building width

bead and reel – a pattern of Greek trim composed of a round bead joined to a vertical oval form or reel

belt course – a band of masonry or wood (in the case of a frame building) delineating a level of a building

bent – a vertical and horizontal division of a barn

blind arch – an arch without a window or door set against or indented within wall

bracket – a vertical member providing support to a horizontal member

capital – the elaborated head of a column

center passage – a central hallway with rooms spaced on both sides

chamfer – a surface formed by cutting away the edge of two perpendicular panes

chinking – the filling of mud, rocks, and other materials between logs in a log wall

clapboard – sawn horizontal timbering joined to cover the sides of a building, also known as weatherboarding

classical – pertaining to architecture of Greece or Rome

clerestory – the upper part of the nave, transcepts and choir of a church containing wndows or other opening

colonnade – an arrangement of columns

colonnette – a small slender column

composite capital – capital composed of acanthus and Ionic scrolls

console – a large bracket usually scrolled at either end

corbel – bracket or block projecting from face of wall generally supporting a cornice, beam, or arch

Corinthian – the classical order distinguished by elaborate acanthus ornaments on capitals of columns

cornice – the projecting topmost member of an entablature

coursed masonry – wall with continuous horizontal layers of stone or brick

crenellation – a battlement

crown molding – a projecting molding at the top of a cornice

cupola – a superstructure on a roof, usually with windows for admitting light

dentil – one of a series of small blocks in an entablatlure, resembling teeth in an entablature

denticulated/dentilled – an entablature or band of detail with dentils

dependency – a building subordinate to the main building

distyle – having two columns

dogtrot – a breezeway or open space between pens of a log house

Doric – the Greek order characterized by heavy channeled shafts and plain capitals

dormer – a vertically set window on a sloping roof; extended dormer – a wide dormer, usually characteristic of the roof of a bungalow

double-hung window – a window with two sash, one above the other, arranged to slide vertically past each other

double portico – a two story porch with columns and possibly a pediment egg and dart -- a band of detail of Grecian art often included in a frieze

engaged pier – a classic support usually with the design of the columns, placed flush with a wall

entablature – the full crowning of a colonnade or wall, consisting of an architrave, frieze, and cornice

entasis -- the swelling of a classic column of the Doric order about a third of a way up the shaft

eyebrow dormer -- a low dormer in which the arched roofline forms a reverse curve at each end

fabric – the physical material of a building, structure, or city, connoting an interweaving of component parts

façade – a wall of a building; the front of a building is the main façade

fanlight – a lunette, half round, or half elliptical opening filled with glass, usually leaded, to admit light, often on top of a doorway or complex window

fee or fee simple—full ownership conveyed

fenestration – plan of window or door openings

finial – ornament at the top of a spire, gable, or pinnacle

fluted – concave curves giving a decorative surface to a column or framing

foliated – decorated with leaf ornamentation or design of arcs or lobes

footing – the side and end supports for a building connecting the building to the ground, vernacularly referred to as "footer"

fret – an ornamental network of slender bars with a right angle patterning, popular in Greek trim; also known as Greek key

gable – the triangular space at the end of a pitched roof

gambrel – a roof of two slopes, the lower being more steeply pitched

garret – attic

girt – the horizontal member in the outer frame of a building that supports the ends of the upper floor or ceiling joists

glazed-- filled with glass

Greek ear – a projection on the sides near the upper corners of doors, windows, or fireplace casings, typical to the Greek Revival period of architecture

Greek key – fretwork, featuring slender bars at right angles

Half-timbering – wall constructon in which the spaces between spaces of timber frame are filled with brick, stone, mud, or other material

hall/parlor – a floor plan featuring two main rooms, sometimes each with its own exterior entrance, or one with an exterior entrance and the other with an interior entrance

hewn and pegged – a frame construction system in which beams are hewn with an adze and joined by large wooden pegs

hexastyle – having six columns

hipped roof – a roof with four uniformly pitched sides

hoodmold – an ornamental or structural member over a door or window

in antis – a doorway set behind the flanking columns

Ionic – the classical order characterized by volute capitals

joist – a horizontal floor or ceiling support

lamb's-tongue – a reverse-curve transition between the square and octagonal sections of a chamfered post

land measurements
    acre- a land area equaling 160 square rods, 4,840 square yards, or 43,560 square feet
    pole – a rod: 30 ¼ square yards; an area equal to a square rood
    rod – a linear measure equal to 5.5 yards, 16.5 feet, or 5.3 meters

lancet – a narrow pointed arch

lantern – a structure on top of a roof with open or windowed walls

log crib barn – a barn built around or including one or more log structures or pens

lozenge – a diamond shaped decorative motif

mansard roof – roof with two slopes on all four sides

masonry bondings --
    -Flemish bond – the pattern of bricks or stone with ends and long sides laid alternately
    - American bond – several rows of stretchers patterned with a single row of headers
    - common bond – a pattern of brick with several rows of stretchers laid alternately with one row of headers
    - English garden bond – a pattern of brick with bricks placed artistically horizontally and vertically in an elaboration of Flemish bond
    - running bond – a pattern of bricks with all bricks facing horizontally

massing – organization of the shape of a building

measured drawing – an exact scale drawing based on measurements of a building

medallion – a ceiling centerpiece; an object resembling a large medal or coin

metope – the space between triglyphs in a frieze, usually in the Doric order, sometimes filled with relief carvings as in the Parthenon

modillion – a trim supporting a cornice that is more elaborate than a dentil and less elaborate and smaller than a bracket or console

molded concrete blocks – early concrete blocks crafted in special molds, often with decorative profiles

mortise and tenon – a system of wood joinery with a projecting member inserted into a receiving member, often secured with a peg

mullion – a vertical strip dividing the panes of a window, door, or panel

muntin – slender window bar supporting panes of glass

nave – the long narrow main part of a church

nogging – brick or mud used to fill the space in a timber house frame

obelisk – a tall four-sided shaft that is tapered and crowned with a pyramidal point

order – a combination of a column and entablature of a given style, e.g., Doric, Ionic, Corinthian, Composite, Tuscan

Palladian design – giant pilasters at corners, two-story portico, central pavilion with pediment and plasters, five-part composition (central block with connected wings), belt course

Palladian window – arched central window flanked by narrower rectangular windows

parapet – a low solid wall or railing along the edge of a roof or balcony

patera – a circular ornament recalling a Greek wine cup

pavilion – part of a building projecting from the rest; an ornamental structure in a garden

pediment – the triangular form of a classical gable

pedimented – having a pediment

pen – a division of a log structure

pier – a square or multi-sided upright support larger than a post

pilaster – an upright form projecting from a wall resembling a flattened column

plinth – the base of a pedestal, column, or statue

podium – a low platform on a base

polychromy – the use of many colors

porch – an area, sometimes enclosed, providing a receiving area for an entryway

portal – the main entrance of a structure

porte cochere – a large covered entrance porch through which vehicles can drive portico – a formal porch with roof supported by classical columns

postbellum – the period of American history following the Civil War

press – a recessed opening with shelves, often located in the interior space provided by a mantel serving an enclosed chimney

pressed metal – sheets of metal molded into decorative designs used to cover interior walls and ceilings

proportion – the relation of one dimension to another, such as width to height, front area to side depth

prostyle – having a portico spanning the front of a building

quatrefoil – a symbol with four leaves resembling a four-leaf clover

quatrastyle – having four columns

quoin – units of stone or brick accenting the corners of a building

rack barn -- a tobacco barn with timbering for hanging tobacco extending across the driveway

reeding – decoration of parallel convex moldings

remainder – specification that conveyed property is entailed to another party

reredos – an ornamental screen behind an altar

reveal – the vertical side of a door or window opening between the frame and wall surface

rhythm – regular recurrence of elements

rinceau – a continuous scrolled relief of intertwined stems and leaves

rococo – the decorative style developed from the baroque, characterized by delicacy, light colors, and a general reduction in building scale

rosette – stylized floral decoration

rustication – masonry cut in large blocks separated from each other by deep joints

saltbox – a gable-roofed house with the rear slope much longer than the front

sash – moveable portions of double hung windows

scale – the relative size of a building or other element in relation to other elements, structures, or open spaces

shotgun – a house style with a narrow front bay and rooms extended laterally, thought by some sources having been brought to Louisiana by free Haitian blacks in the early nineteenth century

sidelights – detail on the sides of entryways with windows

soffit – the underside of an overhanging cornice, door, window, or staircase

spandrel – the space between adjacent arches and the horizontal molding above them

spindle – a turned wooden element often used in screens, stair railings, and porch trim

station – a fortified house or houses, usually of the early settlement period

streetscape – the distinguishing and pictorial character of a particular street as created by width, degree of curvature and paving materials, design of street furniture, and forms of surrounding buildings

stringcourse – a narrow continuous ornamental band on the face on a building

style – an art form that reflects the philosophy, intellectual currents, hopes, and aspirations of its time (Poppeliers, Chambers, and Schwartz, *What Style Is It* (NTHP, 1983).

sunburst -- artistic detail elaborating the design of the sun with rays

swag – a festoon in which the object suspended resembles a piece of draped cloth

terra cotta – a fine grained brown-red fired clay used for roof tiles and decoration

tie rod -- a metal rod designed to provide support to a wall, usually with exposed ends having decorative detail such as stars

timber frame -- a type of construction consisting of usually heavy timbers with mortised and tenoned joints

trabeated – post and beam construction

tracery – the curved mullions of a stone-framed window; ornamental work in or on a screen or window glass

transom -- the upper portion of an entryway that opens and closes and allows for ventilation

trefoil – a design of three lobes similar to a cloverlear

trigliph – an ornament in a frieze with three channels (as in a Doric entablature)

truss –a framework of wooden beams or metal bars often arranged in triangles to support a roof, bridge, or similar structure

turret – a small slender tower usually at the corner of a building often containing a circular stair

tympanum – an enclosed triangular structure

vault – an arched ceiling of masonry

vernacular architecture – "those indigenous, more humble buildings everywhere . . . intimately related to environment and to the heart life of the people." Frank Lloyd Wright, "The Sovereignty of the Individual" (1951).

volute – having a spiral shape, as in an Ionic capital, or the end of a stair rail

voussoir – a wedge shaped member of a masonry arch

water table – a molded setback in an outside wall usually at the first floor level

wattle and daub – mud mixed with straw held together by inserted sticks in a house frame

winder – a wedge shaped step in a corner of a winding staircase

window arrangements
    -double window – two windows joined at the center
    -lunette – a half moon shaped window
    -oculus – a round window or opening at the apex of a dome
    -Palladian window – a three part window, the central portion arched
    -triple window – a three part window, the central portion being wider than the two flankers

vault – a ceiling arched in various ways

BIBLIOGRAPHY

Adams, Alicestyne. *Rosenwald Schools in Kentucky.* Georgetown: African American Forum, Inc., Georgetown College, and Underground Railroad Research Institute, 2007.

Antle, James J., Naples, Florida. Correspondence to author, March 8, 1982.

Apple, Lindsey; Frederick A. Johnston; Ann Bolton Bevins, eds. *Scott County, Kentucky: A History.* Georgetown: Scott County Historical Society, 1993.

Archer, M.L. Column for "Two Hundred Years of Education" Series. *Georgetown News & Times*, October 13, 1987.

Armstrong, Derek. "Renovation under way on old Sadieville depot." *Georgetown News-Graphic,* June 6, 1996.

Axton, W.F. *Tobacco and Kentucky.* Lexington: University Press of Kentucky, 1975.

Bacon, Edwin M. Bacon. *The Book of Boston: Fifty Years' Recollections of the New England Metropolis.* Boston, 1916. Quoted http://brickfrog.wordpress.com/2012/01/01/swift-mcnutt-co-building.

Barlow, Joy. Field Notes, Agricultural Buildings Study, 1985.

Barnhill, Dwayne and Barbara Little. "Barnhill." In Scott County Genealogical Society, *Families and History: Scott County, Kentucky.* Paducah: Turner Publishing Company, 1996.

Beckett, Suzanne and Dana Snyder, "Turkeyfoot Christian Church." In Bevins and Snyder, *Scott County Church Histories.* Georgetown: Scott County Bicentennial Committee, 1979.

Beers, D.G. and J. Lanagan. Map of Scott County. Philadelphia, 1879.

Bevins, Ann. "G.W. Cassity remembers origins of school system." In "Making the Grade Series." *Georgetown Graphic*, October 15, 1987.

Bevins, Ann Bolton. "Historical Development of Agricultural Buildings With Specific Focus on Agricultural Resources of Scott County, Kentucky." Report prepared for Kentucky Heritage Council, 1985.

Bevins, Ann Bolton. *History of Scott County As Told By Selected Buildings.* Georgetown: Kreative Grafiks, Ink., 1981.

Bevins, Ann Bolton; Frederick A. Johnston, Lindsey Apple. *Images of America: Georgetown and Scott County.* Charleston, S.C.: Arcadia Publishing Company, 1998.

Bevins, Ann Bolton. Notes from minutes of Scott County Board of Education, Office of the Superintendent, Scott County Schools, various years.

Bevins, Ann. *One Hundred Years at First and Four Component Banks.* Georgetown: First National Bank, 1983.

Bevins, Ann. "Oxford community grows as school opens its doors." "Making the Grade" series. *Georgetown Graphic*, October 23, 1987.

Bevins, Ann Bolton. "Robert Moore House." In *A History of Scott County As Told By Selected Buildings*, 106, quoting Mrs. Martha Johnson, late owner of the house.

Bevins, Ann Bolton. *The First Disciples/Christian Church*. Georgetown: First Christian Church, 1981.

Bevins, Ann Bolton and J.B. Hockensmith. Memorandum to Scott County Fiscal Court, Georgetown & Scott County Museum, and Scott County Historical Society. October 2002.

Bevins, Ann Bolton, and J. Robert Snyder (eds.). *Scott County Church Histories: A Collection*. Georgetown: Scott County Bicentennial Committee, 1979.

Birdwhistell, Ira. *The Baptists of the Bluegrass: A History of Elkhorn Baptist Association, 1785-1985*. Berea: Berea College Press, 1985.

"Boyers Chapel Methodist Church." In *Scott County Church Histories*, 1979.

Bradley, V.A. Interview, 1963, by author. Notes in author's vertical files.

Brashear, Jeff. Tour of Buford Hall farm for Helen Powell and Ann Bevins. October 1988.

Brooks, Nancy. Welcome to Sadieville Column. *Georgetown News & Times*, September 28, 1988.

Burgess, M.R. *The House of the Burgesses*. San Bernardino, California: Borgo Press, 1983.

Cannon, Dr. F.M. Journal. January 1, 1893 to July 9, 1907, Scott County Public Library.

Carter, Deane G. *Farm Buildings*. Fourth Edition, Rewritten. New York: John Wiley & Sons, 1954.

Cheves, John. "Land sale sweet for political donor." *Lexington Herald Leader*, December 19, 2011.

Clackner, G.F., Coroner of Scott Co. "Inquest upon the body of William Moody at 5:00 p.m. 25 Jan." Copy provided by Moody descendants. Author's vertical files.

Collins, Lewis. *Historical Sketches of Kentucky*. Cincinnati and Maysville, 1847, reprinted as *History of Kentucky by Lewis Collins*. Lexington: Henry Clay Press, 1968.

Conkin, Paul K. *Cane Ridge, America's Pentecost*. Madison: The University of Wisconsin Press, 1990.

Davidson, J. Brownlee, A.E. *Agricultural Machinery*. New York: John Wiley & Sons, Inc., 1931.

Davis, Darrell Haug. *Geography of the Blue Grass Region of Kentucky*. Frankfort: Kentucky Geological Survey, 1927.

"Diamond Dave." Email message entitled "Asher Hinton" to Jim Bevins, August 31, 2009.

Deaton, Gayle. "Sadieville buys historic church." *Georgetown News-Graphic*, August 11, 2008.

"Deed for 15,000 Acres Found in Scott Records." *The Lexington Leader,* September 22, 1962.

Draper Manuscript (Shane Papers) 12 CC 197-198

Durrett, Reuben T., LL.D. *Bryant's Station and The Memorial Proceedings.* Louisville: Filson Club Publication Number Twelve, 1897.

Egbert, Charles and Emily Egbert. "History of Beard Presbyterian Church, Scott County, Kentucky." In *Kith, Kin, Wee Kirk: History* I. Sadieville, 1995.

Eslinger, Ellen. *Citizens of Zion: The Social Origins of Camp Meeting Revivalism.* Knoxville: The University of Tennessee Press, 1999.

Emison, James Wade, Jr. *Emison Families Revised.* Vincennes, Indiana, 1954.

Emison, James Wade, Jr. *Supplement to The Emison Families Revised (1954).* Vincennes, Indiana, 1962.

Emison, James Wade, Jr., and W.T. Smith. Map, 1942: "Original Land Patents (1774-1816) in Georgetown Area, Scott County, Kentucky," in Emison, *Emison Families, Revised,* 33-36.

Evans, Edna . "Sadieville Baptist Church." In *Scott County Church Histories.* Georgetown: Scott County Bicentennial Committee, 1979.

"Farmer J.F. Cannon Sr., ex-minor leaguer, dies." *Lexington Herald Leader, December 31, 1988* and *Georgetown News,* January 4, 1989.

Foster, Cindy, Sadieville City Clerk/Treasurer. Correspondence with author. May 11, 2009.

Gaines, B.O. *B.O. Gaines History of Scott County* 1 and 2. Georgetown: B.O. Gaines Printery, 1904, reprinted in new format by Frye Printing Company, 1981.

Georgetown Graphic. March 29, June 17, June 24, July 5, 1973.

Georgetown News & Times. August 30, 1989.

Georgetown Times. December 6, 1993; August 29, September 5, October 17, November 14, 1906; March 6, 1907; April 20, May 5, 9, 13, 19, 25, 1908.

Georgetown Weekly Times. September 10, October 22, 1873; January 24, February 14, May 25, July 8, August 1, December 26, 1877; September 30, 1885; August 11, 1886.

Gone, Forgotten, Now Remembered: Scott County, Kentucky Cemeteries. Georgetown: Scott County Genealogical Society. 1982.

Gossey, Ethel M. "Mount Olive Baptist Church, Dry Run." In Bevins and Snyder (eds.), *Scott County Church Histories.* Georgetown: Scott County Bicentennial Committee, 1979.

Green, Dorothy Wilson Green and Kris Wilderson. September 24, 2013, at Wilderson home, South Rays Fork Road, Sadieville, Kentucky.

Herring, Mary Barkley. Letter, copy presented to Sisters of the Visitation at Cardome by Evelyn Herring Harman of the Cardome Academy Class of 1942 and provided to the writer by Mother Jane Frances Blakely of the Visitation.

Herring, J.R. Collection, Georgetown and Scott County Museum, made available to author by historian Ron Vance.

Hilander, Fannee. *Hold Back the Spring.* Great Neck, New York: Todd & Honeywell, Inc., 1980.

Hinds, Jim. "Indian Refining Company, Incorporated. . . Company History Timeline," November 14, 1904 to January 5, 1907, www.oldgas.com/info/texacohist.html

Houston, O.W. "Bethesda Presbyterian Church." In *Scott County Church Histories*. Georgetown: Scott County Bicentennial Committee, 1979.

Information from:
    Jeffrey Gillispie, grandson of Frank Gillispie.
    Marion Hall.
    Burgess (Mrs. Felix) Swope.
    Ronald T. Vance.
    Frances (Mrs. W.T.) Warring.
    Mrs. Lindsay Warth

Jarvis, John Parker, "History of Oxford Christian Church." *The Georgetown News*, August 26, 1977.

"John Francis Cannon dies." *Georgetown News-Graphic*, January 4, 1989.

Jones, Cheryl. "School Days at Sadieville Elementary." *Georgetown News-Times*, March 3, 1988.

Justice, Jennifer and Teresa Bannister. "Sadieville Christian Church." *Scott County Church Histories.* Georgetown: Scott County Bicentennial Committee, 1979.

Minch, Norman. "Sadieville Church hopes to gain from Toyota growth." *Georgetown News & Times*, March 11, 1986.

Kentucky Historic Building Inventory Forms:
    Bevins and Powell, SC45, Queen City Railroad Depot, 1988.
    Bevins and Powell, SC232, July 29, 1988.
    Bevins and Powell, SC234, July 29, 1988.
    Bevins and Powell, SC472 and SC472A-M "Buford Hall Farm,", November 20 - December 4, 1987.
    Bevins and Powell, SC474 "Mount Olive/Dry Run Missionary Baptist Church,", December 4, 1987.
    Bevins and Powell. SC64 "Hiram Wood House,", December 16, 1987.
    Bevins and Powell, SC67, SC241 Jimmie Jones Dwelling and Storehouse, 1988.
    Bevins and Powell, SC522, Sadieville Milling Company, 1988.
    Bevins and Powell, SC530, July 29, 1988.
    Bevins and Powell, SC533.
    Bevins and Powell, SC534; other information from Frances Warring, 1987.
    Bevins and Powell, SC535.
    Bevins and Powell, SC536 and SC530.

Kentucky Historic Building Survey (early forms):
    Kentucky Survey Form SC21.
    Kentucky Survey Form SC22, McCabe School/Telephone House Building.

Kentucky Historic Neighborhood Inventory Form SSC4, incorporating properties numbered SC526 through SC529 on Gano Avenue in Sadieville.

Lancaster, Clay. *Antebellum Architecture of Kentucky.* Lexington: University Press of Kentucky, 1991.

Lee, Rebecca Smith. *Mary Austin Holley, a Biography*. Austin: University of Texas Press, 1962.

Lexington Leader, April 25, 1915.

"Lytle, Andrew Nelson." Wikipedia, the free encyclopedia.

Marshall, William A. "Elk Lick Particular Baptist Church." *Scott County Church Histories: A Collection.* Georgetown: Scott County Bicentennial Commission, 1979.

Marshall, W.A.. "The Classic City of Sadieville." undated typescript.

Minch, Norman. "Mount Pleasant Keeps the Faith." *Georgetown News & Times*, undated clipping. Collection of Sadieville City Clerk.

Moody, Cynthia. Divorce Petition. Scott County Circuit Court. Circuit Court Order Book 21, 67.

Mulberry, Professor J.L. "The Business People." Gaines History 2, 170.

"New School Building, 1922." *The Green and White* : Sadieville School newspaper. Reprinted in "The Sadieville Sunshine, Special Edition for September 10, 1988."

"On Farm Training Program for Vets Improves the Men and Land, Raises Living Standards," *Sunday Herald-Leader.* Archives, City Clerk, Sadieville, Kentucky.

Perrin, William Henry, ed. *History of Bourbon, Scott, Harrison, and Nicholas Counties.* Chicago: O.L. Baskin, 1882.

Raitz, Karl B. and Peter C. Smith. "Negro Hamlets and Agricultural Estates in Kentucky's Inner Bluegrass." In *Geographical Review 64.* Lexington: University of Kentucky.

Reed, Doris for Rollie Hinton. *Families & History : Scott County, Kentucky.* Paducah: Turner Publishing Company for Scott County Genealogical Society, 1996.

Reed, Kathy. "Reed/Bailey" and "Reed/Lusby." *Families & History: Scott County, Kentucky.* Paducah: Turner Publishing Company for Scott County Genealogical Society, 1996.

Rogers, John. *The Biography of Elder J.T. Johnson*, second edition. Cincinnati: published for the author, 1861.

Rogers, Valentine. Family Bible courtesy Mabel Brashear.

Royden, Nancy. *Georgetown News-Graphic*, July 17, 2012.

Sadieville, Kentucky. Incorporation Articles," August 9, 1881.

"Sadieville Methodist Church." *Scott County Church Histories: A Collection.* Georgetown: Scott County Bicentennial Committee, 1979.

"Sadieville Sunshine: Special Edition for 'Sadieville in September.'" September 10, 1988.

"Sadieville Lions honor Dr. J.W. Baird, 1951." "Sadieville Sunshine." September 10, 1988.

Sanborn Map, Georgetown, Kentucky. Sanborn Map Company, June 1912.

Scott County Genealogical Society. *Gone, Forgotten, Now Remembered.* Lexington, Kentucky. 1992.

Scott County, Kentucky. Articles of Incorporation Book 1.

Scott County, Kentucky. Deed, Will, Order Books, Office of the Scott County Clerk, Georgetown, Kentucky.

Scott County, Kentucky. Lines Book 1.

Scott County, Kentucky. Property Valuation Administrator (PVA) records.

Scott, Hattie Scott. *Scott's Papers.* Frankfort: Kentucky Historical Society, 1953.

"Shepherd's Farm Store & Feed Mill." Absolute Auction flyer. Author's collection.

Southworth, Geneva and Nell Burgess. "History of the Sadieville School." Typescript, 1987.

Stallons, Malcolm L. "Sadieville's Once Fancy Risk Hotel Goes on Auction Block." *The Lexington Herald*," May 14, 1977.

Stone, Barton W. and J.T. Johnson (eds.). *The Christian Messenger* VIII, No. 1, 49. Published in Georgetown, Kentucky.

Trefzger, John G.. "A History of the Oxford Christian Church, Oxford, Kentucky." Typescript, June 9, 1950.

Tucker, Vivian (Mrs. Paul). "Beard's Presbyterian Church." *Scott County Church Histories.* Georgetown: Scott County Bicentennial Committee.

Williams, D. Newell. *Barton Stone: A Spiritual Biography.* St. Louis: Chalice Press, 2000.

www.1911encyclopedia.org/Georgetown_Kentucky

www.oldgas.com/info/texacohist.html

Index

A

Abrams, David, 63
Acuff, Columbus, 172
Acuff, Wesley, 174
Adair, William, 169
Adams, 60–61, 254, 291
   Francis, 182–83
   Jack, 169
   James, 183, 284
   James L., 157
   John W., 250
   Lawrence, 187
   Lloyd, 254
   Louise, 230
   Lucy, 255
   Luke, 183
   Margaret, 183
   Mary, 98, 157, 183
   Sally, 100
   Theodore, 240, 251, 264
Addie Penn House, 76
African American, 50, 52–53, 55, 57–58, 61–62, 92, 104, 106, 122, 158, 217, 239
   Community's, 64
   First, 59
   Neighborhood's, 105
Afterkirk, Gary, 267
Aldridge, Edmond C., 245
Alexander Campbell's Millennial Harbinger, 192
Alice Baird House, 153
Allen
   Asa, 227
   Carl, 144
   Cary, 227
   Charles, 225
   Curtis, 54
   Mattie L., 224
   Phyllis, 57
   Sandra, 222
   Virgie, 53–54
   Willie D., 56
Alley, Johnson, 268
Allgaier, 125
Allie, 117, 195
Allie Clay Vance, 127
Allison, Mary M., 281
Alma, Mary, 236
Amileen Piatt, 148
Ammerman, Joel, 213
Ammerman, Martha, 139
Amos, 207
Amos Hamon Store, 206
Anchorage, 227
Anderson, 107, 126, 176, 187, 208, 213–17, 220, 226
   Ann, 125
   Betty, 211
   James, 126
   John, 125
   John T., 208
   Laura, 228
   Leon, 164
   Leona, 263
   Lizzie, 228
   Lula, 106, 174
   Meredith, 216
   Nancy, 137
   Reuben, 215, 231
   Robert, 122
   Sep M., 209, 231
Anderson Building, 215
Antle Cemetery, 91
Antle-Driskell House, 91
Appalachian Regional Healthcare, 120
Arcadia Publishing Company, 252, 291
Armstrong, 291
   Derek, 249
Arnold, 164, 207
   Paul, 270
Arthur Lancaster Drug Store, 238
Arthurs
   Carl S., 94
   Glenna, 95
   Glenna E., 94
   Marie, 95
Arvin, Anne M., 79
Associates Home Equity, 279
Atkins, 54–55, 160, 208
   William N., 52
   Fannie, 55
   William N., 160
Aurelius, Victoria, 133
Aureliuses, 134
Austin, 75, 294
Austin Harp Masonry, 75

B

Bach, Fred, 79
Bacon, Edwin M., 166, 291
Baesler, Scotty, 176
Baggetts, 134
Bailey, 68, 142–43, 159, 183, 207, 239–40
   Ann, 183
   Bertha, 143, 207
   Elmo, 143
   Ernest, 143
   Gladys, 143
   Hugh, 151
   James F., 142
   Isaiah, 219
   James, 239
   James F., 143
   John, 142, 189
   Joseph, 142–43
   Joseph F., 143
   Noah, 143
   Oscar, 143

Sandra K., 266
Talitha, 143
Throwing, 239
Tommie, 139
Bailey House, 142
Bailey-Price House, 211
Bailey Properties, 141
Bailey Road, 141–42
Bailey-Robertson House, 254
Baird, 153–54, 248, 250–51, 267, 269, 295
   Alice, 154, 253
   James L., 154
   Louis, 269
   Wallace, 264
Baird Heirs, 154
Baird House, 267
Baird's Alley, 269
Baker, Bertha, 280
Baker, Karl, 280
Baldridge, William, 172
Baldwin, 254, 268
   Edward, 232
Banks, Jessie, 64
Bannister, Teresa, 247, 294
Baptist Church, 57–58, 80, 197, 265
Barbee, 125
   Fannie, 125
Bark, Thelma, 131
Barkley, 68, 85, 124, 126–27, 134, 150, 172, 176, 181,
   188, 208, 218, 221, 223, 226–28
   Alice, 227
   Barbara, 127
   Charles W., 223
   Ethel, 176
   Fay, 227
   Ida, 227
   John, 209
   John H., 52, 227
   John W., 176
   Joseph, 209
   Lottie, 223
   Lottie M., 218
   Margaret, 213
   Mary, 293
   Matthew, 119, 209, 214
   Nannie, 176
   Robert, 119, 195, 208
   Roy, 176
Barkley Children, 85–86
Barkley Church, 213
Barkley-Grizzle House, 126
Barkley House, 176
Barkley Lane, 176
Barkley Mill Operation, 85
Barkley Pike, 130
Barlow, 291
   Joy, 73, 78, 95, 166, 259
Barnes, 252
   John, 252

John L., 55
Mary E., 252, 263
Barnett, 253
   Elizabeth, 151
Barnett-Nelson House, 253
Barnhill, 86, 89, 107–8, 110, 122, 148, 163, 187–88, 291
   Allie, 148
   Carrie H., 88
   Charles, 195
   Clint, 110
   Clinton, 108–9, 148–49
   Daniel, 107
   Dwayne, 107
   Ethel, 109
   George, 112, 187, 191
   James, 109, 117
   John, 107–8
   John B., 108
   John E., 109
   John W., 112
   Josephine, 112
   Leonard, 88
   Louisa, 109
   Margaret, 116
   Maude, 110
   Rachel, 108
   Rebecca M., 195
   Robert, 107
   Ruth, 109
   Sam, 108
   Samuel, 107, 188, 190
   Sarah, 107–8
   Shelby, 195
   Son George C., 109
   Susan, 190
   Ward, 109
Barnhill-Dawson House, 108–9
Barnhill House, 195
Barnhill-Lacy House, 109–10
Bassett, George, 96
Bates, 92–93
   Angela, 58–59, 63
   Ann E., 92
   Carrie, 92, 238
   Clyde, 92
   Deborah V., 92
   Frank J., 94
   John T., 172
   Roscoe M., 261
   Thelma, 253
   Tom, 92
Bates Barn, 92
Bates House, 91
Batey, Fannie, 186
Beard, 183, 191, 264
   Hugh, 182–83
   Russell, 264
Beard Cemetery, 182
Beard Church, 181–83, 191

Beard Church and Cemetery, 180
Beard Presbyterian Church, 181, 292
Beard's Church, 182
Beard's Church Pike, 157
Beatty, Eric, 174
Beatty, Marcie G., 174
Beatty, Margie, 174
Beatty Church, 213
Bechel, Michael, 248
Beckett, George T., 216
Beckett, Suzanne, 193
Beckett, William G., 216
Becketts, 193, 216, 291
Beckham, 257
Bedford, 156
Bedford Forrest, 130
Bedford Stone, 80, 238
Bedient, Dean, 218
Bedient, Donna, 218
Beers, 291
Beers & Lanagan, 69, 78, 92, 154, 202, 216, 222, 234, 239, 250–51, 281
Belfield Glass, 169
Bell, John H., 134
Bell, Morris, 59
Bell, Nellie, 165
Bell, Thomas, 191
Bell Cannon, 211
Belle, Mary, 162
Belle Cannon House, 224
Bellewood Presbyterian Home For Children In Anchorage, 227
Bellwood Home, 227
Bennett, Amos, 194
Bennett, Arthur, 194
Bennett, James W., 137
Bennett, Mary E., 135
Bennett, William, 135
Berkeley County, 119
Bernard, 263
Bernardino, San, 68, 78, 292
Berry, 203
　James W., 134
　William, 203
Bess Dallas, 60, 63
　Childhood Home Of, 62
　Home Of, 62
Bessinger, Ada, 207
Bessinger, Elizabeth, 207
Bessinger, Harvey, 207
Bess's Sister Cora Frye, 60
Bethesda, 191
Bethesda Church, 191, 214
Bethesda Congregation, 190
Bethesda Presbyterian Church, 187, 190–91, 293
Bevins, 55, 57, 94–95, 140, 142, 146–47, 177, 188–90, 192–93, 227, 230, 232–33, 239–40, 245–46, 291
　Ann, 228, 230, 235, 292
　Jim, 87, 292

　Robert, 84
Bevins And Powell, 58, 199, 215, 294
Big Bug Hill, 234
Big Eagle, 58, 75, 93, 95, 116, 121
Big Eagle-Connersville Pike, 73
Big Eagle Creek, 72, 81, 83–84, 107, 153
Big Eagle Lodge, 282
Big Spring Branch, 167, 197
Big Spring In Georgetown, 192
Bill's Son John, 109
Bishop, 85
　Henry, 156
　Zelma, 53
Black, Frank, 171
Black, Jacob, 51
Black, Mary, 50–51, 53
Black, Thomas, 50
Black, William, 51–52
Blackburn, Anthony, 97
Black/Happy House, Wide, 52
Black Neighborhood, 51
Black's Ability, 51
Black's Lane, 51
Blacksmith Shop/Grocery, 222
Blankenship, James T., 156
Blue Licks, 172
Blye, Iris, 97
Bolton, 174
　Ann, 291–92
　David, 193
Bond, Cleo, 138
Bond, Richard, 203
Bonnie, 88
Bonnie Jane Lugar, 88
Bonnie Jean King, 63
Bonnie Mae Renaker, 94
Borgo Press, 68, 78, 292
Boston, 165–66, 291
Botkins, Elizabeth, 131
Botkins, Elizabeth S., 280
Bourbon, 68, 70, 129, 192–93, 208, 295
Bourbon County, 78, 158
Bourbon County Line, 67
Bourgeois, Barbara F., 251
Bowman, Gertrude, 98
Bowman, Richard, 64
Bowman, Sammie T., 269
Boyd, 52, 197
　Wesley, 52–55
Boydsville, 52–53
Boydtown, 50, 52–55, 106, 158
Boydtown Church, 56
Boydtown Community, 52–53, 106
Boydtown Districts, 55
Boydtown Methodist Chapel, 52
Boydtown Methodist Church, 54
Boydtown Ongregation, 54
Boydtown Properties, 53
Boydtown School, 55–56

Boydtown Schoolhouse, 54
Boydtown's Church, 52
Boydtown Site, 55
Boydtown's Rosenwald School, 54
Boydtown United Methodist Church, 53
Boydville, 158
Boyers, 68, 139, 209
  Jacob, 139
Boyers Chapel Methodist Church, 185, 187, 292
Boyers Chapel Pike, 186
Boyers Chapel Road, 69–70, 185
Boyers Chapel Road Properties, 70
Boyers Methodist, 69
Bradford, 115, 141
  John G., 196
  William, 196
Bradford Holland Garage, 222
Bradford Munson's Lands, 116
Bradley, 165, 192, 229, 292
  Craig, 229
  James, 145, 165
  Victor, 163
Branch, Sharon, 147
Brand, Fannie, 139
Brashear, Jeff, 175
Brashear, Mabel, 172–73, 295
Brashears, 156, 175, 253, 292
  Alma, 64
Braun, 232, 277
Brenda, 259
Brenda Gail Davis, 278
Brewer, Douglas E., 181
Brewer, Fred, 194
Brian, 243, 272
Brise, 105–6
Broadus, Vicky, 230
Brock, Robert, 201
Bronston, Anna B., 77
Brooker House, 273
Brooks, 63–64, 292
  Adeline, 63–64
  Linda H., 258
  Nancy, 60, 258
  Nancy S., 258
  Robert, 64
  Roy, 64
Brooks Farm Buildings, 64
Brown, Helen, 156
Brownfield, 272
Browning, 144–45
  Eliza, 144
  Elizabeth, 144
  James, 144
  Jesse, 144
  William, 145
Brumback, Bonnie J., 266
Brumback, Wanda L., 266
Brumley, Bill, 81
Bruner, Ellen, 123

Bryan Station, 172, 192
Bryan Station Baptist Church, 172
Bryant, 80, 194
  Anthony, 194
  Bruce, 184
  Darrell, 194
  Louise, 194
  Ruth, 81, 99
Bryant's Station, 172, 292
Buford, 57, 77, 82, 103, 114, 122, 135
Buford Hall Family Properties, 121
Buford Hall Farm, 294
Buford Hall Offutt, 123
Buford Hall Set, 163
Buford Hall's Lands, 123
Buford Munson House, 115
Bugle Corps, 166
Bundy, Emeline, 113
Burgess, 64–65, 68–69, 73–74, 77–78, 80–83, 111–12,
    121–22, 232–36, 242, 244–45, 249, 254–56, 268–
    72, 276, 292–93
  Edward, 68, 77–81, 110, 192, 252
  Elizabeth A., 218
  Ella, 81
  Ethel, 111
  Ezra T., 110
  George, 112
  Gertrude, 111
  Gladys, 110
  Helena, 81, 236
  Homer, 110
  Homer T., 110
  James G., 79
  Jane, 261
  Joe, 81, 111, 256
  Joe S., 245
  John, 134
  John C., 79
  Joseph, 69, 71, 78–79, 82, 116, 121, 232, 250
  Joseph C., 245
  Josephine D., 277
  Josie, 61, 64, 73, 238, 241, 243, 245–46, 267, 272–75,
    278–80
  Lillian, 111
  Louise, 82
  Lula, 111
  Martha, 111–12
  Martha J., 110–12
  Mose, 63, 82, 233, 242, 268
  Orville, 242
  Richard L., 256
  Sallie, 73
  Scott, 75, 89
  Shirley, 135
  Solomon, 111
  Son William H., 112
  Susan, 111
  Thomas J., 234, 239
  Vivian, 81, 236, 245, 254

Wife Sarah E., 79
Willed Son Ezra H., 112
William C., 191
William H., 112
Burgess Avenue, 278
Burgess Barn, 269
Burgess Bungalow, 82
Burgess Family, 255
Burgess Family Ownership, 111
Burgess Farms, 61
Burgess Heights, 277–78
Burgess Heights Lots, 279
Burgess Heirs, 128
Burgess/Henderson, 112
Burgess Homestead Site, 77
Burgess House, 81, 111, 244
Burgess House, Small, 78
Burgess/John, Martha J., 112
Burgess Properties, 77, 110
Burgess Property, 74
Burgess Schoolhouse, 77
Burgess Smith, 69, 78–79, 94, 235, 274
Burgess Smith Home Site, 79
Burgess Smith Road, 69, 79, 86, 89, 91, 95
Burgess Stone Walls, 73
Burke, Herbert, 202
Burton, 196
  James K., 143
Burton-Biddle Road, 153
Bush, 222
  Emery, 222
Butler, 177
  Cornelius, 70, 192
  George B., 177
  John K., 69
Butler's Station, 177

C

Caesar, Edward, 78
Cain, Bobbie, 112
Calbert Anderson, 255–56
Caldwell, Florence L., 178
Calvin, William, 78
Campbell, Alexander, 213
Campbell, John M., 94
Cane Ridge, 190
Cannon, 137, 171, 209–10, 217–18, 221, 223–26, 254, 292
  Belle, 171, 213, 221, 224–25
  Brenda, 260
  Charles, 220
  Diane L., 224
  Fannie, 218
  James W., 223
  Francis M., 209, 217, 219, 224
  Genevieve, 255–56, 259
  James E., 220
  Jimmie, 223
  John H., 158–59
  Johnny, 226
  Mary A., 159
  Mother Mary A., 158
  Rebecca, 176
  Robert, 171, 211, 213
  Robert M., 171
  Ronnie, 243, 259
  Ronnie R., 259
  Roy, 254
  Roy D., 272
Cannon Family, 224
Cannon House, 225
Cantrill, 85
  James E., 157
Cardome Academy Class, 85, 293
Carlisle
  Betty, 262
  Robert M., 262
Carlisles, 158, 251, 262
Carpenter, Charles, 63
Carpenter, Florence, 218
Carr, 116
  Benjamin, 192
  Joe B., 63
Carrick, 176, 210, 216
  James L., 171
  Mary, 171
  Mary R., 176
  Sally, 213
  Ward, 217
Carrick-Glenn-Mason House, 171
Carrie, 88, 92, 205, 275
Carroway, Carolyn, 94
Cary, James, 159
Cason Neighborhood, 69
Cavendar, James, 182
Cavil, Alex, 180
Centreville, 101
Chapel, Elizabeth, 183
Charlie Smith House, 228
Cheatham, 176
  Charlene, 88, 154
  Robert L., 176
Cheek, Clarice, 248
Cherry Spring Church, 213
  Ike, 54
  Isaac, 54
  Mary, 54
Chowning, 266, 275, 278
  Sally S., 121
Chowning Family, 278
Chowning House, 277–78
Christian Brotherhood, 192
Christian Church, 208
Christian Churches, 92, 107, 190–92, 209–10, 213, 217, 229, 246, 265
Christian Church Parsonage, 246
Church Of God In Stonewall, 179
Church Street/Gano, 265

Ciejko, Amanda, 280
Cincinnati Bible Seminary, 193
Cincinnati Road, 56–57, 69, 71, 82, 90, 92, 96, 99, 101, 121, 123, 153, 155, 196–98
Cincinnati Southern, 161, 233, 235, 238–39, 281, 283
Cincinnati Southern Tunnels, 67
City Of Georgetown, 165–66
City Of Sadieville Water Plant, 281
Civic League/Woman's Club, 230
Civil Air Patrol, 166
Civil War, 50, 58, 71, 85, 187, 215, 246, 284, 289
Clarke, Cary L., 92
Clarke, Elizabeth, 92
Clay, Henry, 123
Clay, Mattie, 176
Coffee County, 111
Cole, Preston, 56
Collins, 137, 208, 235, 252, 275, 292
  Frank, 209
  Jimmie, 111
  Lewis, 208, 292
  Lillian, 111
  Mary, 111
  Paul, 111
Colvin, Elizabeth, 137
Combs, Sandra, 280
Combs, Willis, 218
Congleton, 199, 215, 235, 277
  Eileen, 215
  Ruth L., 277
Conkin, 292
  Paul K., 190
Connellee, 63–64, 73, 93, 232, 234, 244, 251–52, 281
  Catherine, 251
  Lucy, 252
  Lucy A., 63, 251–52
  Margaret J., 93
Conner, 76, 86, 90, 167, 181, 194, 236
  Charles C., 137
  Edna, 167
  John, 68, 202
  John H., 68
  John L., 89, 152
  Laura, 77, 86, 88–89, 91, 181, 236
  Laura A., 76, 181, 194
  Lewis, 68
  Willard, 167
Connersville Road, 232, 255
Connersville Turnpike, 235
Conrad, Benjamin, 68
Conrad, William, 68
Cook, Jack, 159
Cook, Joe, 183
Cooper, Beverly J., 278
Cooper, Lester, 271
Cooper, Ralph M., 155
Cooper, Thomas E., 153
Cope, William J., 154
Coppage, 199
  Isaac, 172
  Laura A., 134
Coppage-Giles House, 134–35
Coppage School, 132
Coppage's Title, 134
Cora Frye House, 62
Corda Johnson Reed House, 110
Corinth-Hinton Road, 178
Cornett, Debra A., 156
Cornish Hall, 248–49
Cornish House, 262
Corrigan, 281
  Pat, 63
  Susie, 63
Cottingam, John, 252
Cottingham, John, 251
  Emma Lou J., 161
  George W., 160
  Linda N., 161
Courtney, 79, 91, 184
  Betty, 155
  Charles, 68
  Gwendolyn, 145
  Rodney, 79
  Ronnie, 195
Covert, Connie, 147
Covington, Carol, 154
Covington, David, 251
Covington, James H., 65, 256
Covington Heirs, 280
Covington House, 280
Covingtons, 65, 140, 214, 235, 277, 280
Cox, 189
  Annie, 277
  Basil, 188
  Edna, 77
  George B., 97
  Judy, 217
  Judy F., 280
  Judy G., 150–51, 217
  Maria J., 149
  Preston, 118
  Stepson Bennie D., 188
Coyle, 211, 213
  Craig, 58, 63, 253
  Elijah, 167
  Elizabeth, 259, 261
  Elizabeth F., 62, 264
  Frankie, 277
  Henry, 259
  Leona, 261
  Levi, 61, 63, 232
Crane, 55–56
  Albert, 56–57
Cranetown-Boydtown Spheres, 107
Cranetown Lane, 56
Crawford, Henry, 137
Crawford, Jane, 137
Crawford Moore, 170–71, 174

Crawford Moore Family Property, 173
Crawford Moore House On Delaplain Road, 170
Craycraft, Edna, 275
Creighton, 272
  Sarah, 194
Creighton House, 272
Creighton House On College Street, 272
Crenshaw, Joel, 147
Crenshaw, Mabel, 160
Crenshaw, Ruby, 83
Crenshaws, 83
Crest Lawn Memorial Gardens In Georgetown, 144
Cris, 225
Crisp, Herman, 275
Critter Company, 130
Crockett, Floyd A., 95
Cross, Rhonda, 88
Crosthwait, 185–86, 252, 268
  Ellen, 185
  John, 253–54
  John P., 252
  Lucy A., 186
  Mary B., 186
  Mona, 268
Crosthwait, Myrtle B., 253
Crosthwaite-Risk House, 254
Cube, 230
Culbertson, 148
  Carl S., 148
  Mary E., 148
Cumberland Presbyterian Church, 190
Cumberland Presbyterians, 190
Cumberland Valley, 190
Cummins, 205–7
  James, 144
Cummins House, 204
Cummins Place, 204
Cummins/Roehrig House, 205
Cunningham, 252, 263, 273, 278
  Charles, 256
Cunningham Avenue, 276–80
Curry, John, 201
Curtis Works, 253
Cushman, 241, 256
  Alma L., 256
  Elmo, 249, 283
Cynthia, 150, 294
Cynthiana, 68, 157, 208–9
Cynthiana Christian Church, 211–13
Cynthiana Democrat, 70
Cynthiana Merchant, 207
Cynthiana Pike, 139
Cynthiana Road, 50–53, 55, 141–42, 159, 205–6, 215–16
  New, 209
Cynthiana Widow, 134
Cyrene, 172
Cyrene Marshall, 236

D

Dallas's House, 63
Darnaby, George H., 164
Daugherty, 101, 178, 240, 246, 258
  Lizzie, 206
Davenport, Sally, 199
Davis, 69, 71, 76, 83, 91, 103–6, 180, 182, 184–85, 221–22, 232, 235, 257–58, 262, 278
  Alice, 157
  Bernice, 106
  Bob, 259, 261, 283
  Clarence, 269
  Clarence S., 83
  Donna L., 123
  Edith, 64
  Emory S., 278
  Ernest, 104, 259, 264
  Gertrude, 98, 257–58, 262, 279, 281
  James G., 223
  Jeffrey, 79
  Linda, 278
  Louise, 222
  Lucinda, 104–5
  Patricia, 278
  Robert, 180
  Robert L., 278
  Rochelle, 278
  Shirley, 278
  Stella H., 65
  Vivian, 262
  William J., 222
Davis/Crenshaw House, 83
Davis-Crenshaw/Mrs, 83
Davises, 83, 281
Davis Family, 104, 222–23
Davis Farm, 123
Davis House, 105–6, 257
Davis Property, 181
Davis's Administrator, 106
Davis School Site, 184
Davis's Landmarks, 180
Davis's Scott County, 180
Davis-Turkeyfoot Road, 69, 77, 80–81, 90–91, 95, 152
Davis Village, 180, 184
Dawson, 109, 135
Dawson's Death, 109
Dayton, 113, 159, 191
Dean, 56, 218
  Alice, 204
Dearborn Heights, 106
Deaton, 292
  Gayle, 62, 68
Degaris, 162
  John, 139, 167
Degaris Estate, 139
Degaris Family, 167
Degaris Mill, 167, 196
Degaris Mill And West Oxford, 162
Delaney, Bill, 193
Delaplain, 67, 122, 167, 169–70, 196, 198–99

Neal, 199
Delaplain Road, 50, 158, 167–68, 170–72, 199, 228–29, 231
Desha, James, 94
Deshay, 56
  George, 54
Dianna, Sarah, 71
Dickerson-Green House, 223
Dickey, Juanita, 94
Dickey, Neal, 94
Dividing Ridge, 71, 132, 180
Dividing Ridge Road, 67, 73
Dixon, 121, 178–79
  Daniel B., 118
  George, 104
  George L., 178
  Lula, 178
Dixson, Frank, 187
Doan, 253, 265
  Pam, 111
Dougherty, Mary E., 100
Douglas, 151, 171, 224
Dozer, Richard, 141
Dozer, Tina M., 141
Dryden, 131, 261
  Gertrude, 105
Dry Ridge Road, 155, 172, 196
Dry Run, 55, 57–58, 84, 122, 172, 192, 197–98, 230, 293
  Lower, 84
Dry Run Baptist Church, 122, 196–97
Dry Run Creek, 196
Dry Run/Delaplain, 196
Dry Run Pike, 174
Dry Run School, 198
Ducemberry, Dick, 193
  Anna K., 100
Duncan, 128, 138
  Clyde, 127
  Corinne, 127, 261
  Corinne R., 127
  Dorothy, 127
  Earl, 127–28
  Jesse, 127–28
  Linda C., 127
  Mary E., 79
  Noah, 127
  Paul, 127–28
  Pauline, 127
  Pauline R., 138
  Sheri, 91
Dungan, 69
  James, 69
Dunn, Bertha, 260
Durango, 125
Durrett, 292
  Reuben T., 172
Dutton, 261
  Lena, 184
  Shelby, 261

Duvall, Wilson, 121

E

Eades, Parker, 194
Eads, 98, 179
  Brian, 277
  James W., 179
  Noah, 95
Eads/A, 97
Eagle Bend Road, 282
Eagle Creek, 68–69, 72, 76–77, 80, 84, 86–87, 89, 107, 110, 113, 180, 182, 232, 234–35, 281–82
Eagle Creek Baptist Church, 238
Eagle Creek Lands, 154
Eagle Hills, 68
Eberhart, Gwendolyn, 250–51
Eden Shale Lands, 122
Edgar, 79, 124, 252, 257
  Duke Penn, 79
Edgar's Wife, 79
Edger Bailey, 267
Edmondson, Henry, 119, 151
Edmundson, 108
  Henry, 50
Edward, 77–78, 95, 101, 111, 119, 156, 253, 266
  Randy, 278
Edwards, Juanita, 253
Edwards, Katie S., 56
Effie Juett Hall House, 159
Egbert, 183, 190–91, 211–12, 214, 292
  Charles, 222
  Emily, 181, 188, 214, 223, 292
  Norma, 55
  Reverend Charles T., 147
Elam, Thelma J., 148
Elizabeth, 144, 172–73, 279
  Emma, 53
  Mary, 159
Elkhorn Baptist Association, 238
Elk Lick Particular Baptist Church, 80, 294
Elk Lick Pike, 100
Elk Lick Primitive Baptist Church, 69, 78
Elko-Bell Lane, 67
Ella Nora Carlisle House, 262
Ellen, 90, 113, 123, 292
  Helena, 81
Elliott, 70–71, 209, 216
  Sallie, 137
Ellison, Raymond, 53
Elswick, Judy, 280
Elswick, Kenneth W., 279
Emery, Elizabeth, 106
Emison, 84–85, 183, 197, 292
  Benjamin, 199
  James E., 83–85
  John, 92
  Nancy, 80
  Sadie, 72, 85
  Thomas, 84

William, 83–85, 93, 182
Emison-Barkley House, 84
Emison-Barkley Mill, 85
Emison Dwelling, 84
Emison Estate And Mill, 234
Emison Families, 197, 209, 292
Emison Families Revised, 84–85, 182–83, 292
Emison Mill, 86
Emison Miller's House, 84
Emison Mill Site, 84
Emison Mills Properties, 83
Emison's Mill, 69, 83
Emison's Mill Road, 84
Emma, 54, 151, 174, 237
Emma Jean Adams, 81
Emma Newland Sams, 137
Emma Nichols Wilson, 53
Emmillee Williamson, 148
Emory, 171
   William, 278
Engine House, 163
English, Charlene, 278
English Cottages, 285
Enos, Carla M., 97
Eric, 253
Ernest, 64
Esham, 105
Eslinger, 292
   Ellen, 190
Essa Keller, 95
Essex, 269
Etta, Mae, 61, 65
Eubank, Wilma, 219
Eugene, 101
Evans, 95, 157, 261, 292
   Edgar, 275
   Edna, 238, 240, 265
   Florence, 94
   George, 277
   Henrietta, 155
   Henry, 155
   Laura M., 277
   Lee, 94
   Mary E., 95
   Nannie, 94
Evins, Isaac, 183
Evins, Sally, 183
Ewbank, Jim, 219
Ewbank, Wilma, 56
Ewbank, Wilma E., 220
Ewing, 201, 226
   James K., 207
   John R., 86, 221
   Mattie, 207
   Mattie H., 135–36, 207
Ewing House, 136

F
Fain, Charles, 277
Fain, Flo, 123
Fancy Risk Hotel, 242, 295
Fannie Kelly House, 258, 264
Farior, Jane, 183
Farmers Bank In Georgetown, 240
Farmers Bank Of Sadieville, 240, 245
Farmers Deposit Bank, 251, 278
Farmers-Deposit Bank, 240–41
Farmers Of America Building, 210
Farmers Of America Program, 228
Farmers Union Supply, 242
Farrar, Chasity, 71
Farrow, Judy, 278
Faulconer, 100–101, 143, 207, 251–52, 255, 278
   Charles G., 179
   Dorothy, 276
   Mollie, 100, 260
   Nettie, 278
   Richard, 101, 179
   Richard D., 101, 265
   Wanda, 260
Faulconer And Lancaster Farm, 100
Faulconer/Dunaway Farm, 99
Faulconer-Dunaway House, 100
Faulconer Family, 179
Faulconer Heirs, 100
Faulconer House, 278
Faulconer House On Cunningham Avenue, 278
Faulconer Of Corinth, 179
Faulconer-Roberts House, 255
Faulconer's Dower, 100
Faulkner, Wilson, 264
Faust, Betty, 111
Faust, Betty O., 111
Fawkes, Jared, 172–73
Fayette, 67
Fayette County, 116
Federal Land Bank, 100
Feed Mill, 236, 295
Fender, Henrietta E., 53
Fenton, 112, 221
Ferrell, Laura B., 224
FFA, 169
FHA, 144
Fielding Bradford, 122
Fields, 73, 77–78, 83, 123, 145, 151, 153, 202–4, 240, 244–45, 251, 256–57, 264, 268, 272
   Charles P., 83, 273
   Mary J., 255–57, 262, 277
   Nancy E., 90
   Sarah E., 184
Fields Branch, 253
Fields-Cushman Family, 256
Fields Family, 189
Fields House, 78, 83, 196
Fields-Houston House, 152
Fields-Marshall House, 256
Fields Road, 67–69
Fields's Home, 189

Figgs, Charles H., 174
Fightmaster, 62–63, 83, 93, 97, 164, 237, 264, 277–78, 280
  Alonzo, 69
  Amos, 218
  Bertha, 179
  Diana, 280
  Edith, 264
  Emma K., 251
  Ethel, 280
  Gordon, 83, 93, 281
  Robert L., 97
  Lucille, 270
  Richard, 90
  Roy, 264
  Russell, 251, 254
  Russell L., 237
  Warren, 264
  Zelma, 88
Finley, William, 213
Finnell, 137, 199–200, 206, 229
  Benjamin W., 199
  James B., 134
  Judge James B., 206
Finnell And Muddy Ford, 142
Finnell And Sadieville Pike, 207
Finnell Neighborhood, 207
Finnell Pike, 127, 129, 138–39, 187, 206
Finnell Road, 124–25, 127, 129, 136–38, 142–43, 149, 199–200, 202, 205–7
  Present, 51
Finnell/Star, 206
First Christian Church, 291
First Disciples/Christian Church, 247, 291
First Elk Lick Particular Baptist Church, 80
First Methodist Church Of Boydtown, 53
First National Bank, 235, 291
First Sadieville Baptist Church Site, 265
Fish, 180
  Irene, 180
Fisher
  Corinne, 53
  Hallie, 69
  James, 53–54
  James K., 53
  Jimmy, 56
  John C., 57
  Joseph, 142
  Sally, 70
  Stella, 54
Fisher's Camp, 69
Fister, Josephine, 99
Fitzgerald, 164
Fitzpatrick, 111
  Dorothy E., 131
  Matthew, 263
Flanigan, 177
Flanking, 219
Flavia Burgess, Included, 111
Fleming, 151, 164, 199
  John W., 210
Florence, 273
  Audrey, 184
  Donna, 273
  Juanita, 258
Flournoy, 51
  Ferdinand, 92
Floyd, 65, 223
Footbridge Abutment Site, 250
Ford, 111, 165, 179, 221, 223, 226, 243
  Charles, 221
  Jesse, 221, 226
  Mary A., 221, 225
  Mary B., 231
Ford Road, 106, 187
Fordsville, 191
Foree, 164
Fork/Davis, 96
Forrest, 77, 111
Forrest Baker, Bertha L., 65
Forscythe, 182
Forsythe, 85
Foster, Cindy, 63, 272
Fox, Cynthia, 57
Fox, Dave, 54
Foxworthy, Darius, 111
Foxworthys, 111
Frances, 62, 68, 172, 219, 243–44, 293
  Emma, 61
  Mary, 141, 209
Frances Burgess White, 273
Frances Mccabe House, 260
Frank, 79, 90, 106, 111–13, 123, 138, 141, 145, 187, 221, 255, 263, 273
  Hugh, 158
  Thomas, 273
  William, 65
Frankfort, 102, 172, 295
Frankfort Distilling Company, 164
Frankfort Road, 198
Frankie, 227
  Jane, 221
Franklin, 67, 101, 218
  Timothy, 101
Franklin County, 162, 164
Franklin Court, 164
Frank Lloyd Wright, 290
Franks, Lottie A., 145, 223
Frasure, Shannon N., 138
Fred, 87–88, 129–30, 152, 154, 176, 224
Frederick County, 91
Free & Accepted Masons, 248
French Rococo, 285
Frenchtown, 173
Friendship-Hinton Pike, 178
Friendship Turnpike, 178
Frye, 60
  Archie, 170

Cora, 62–63
Frye Printing Company, 293
Fryman, 85, 227
Fuller, Betty J., 96
Fuller, Judy W., 261
Funk, 227
Furnish, 119, 225
  Clay, 118
  Kate M., 225

G

Gabriella Fields, 153, 255–56
Gaines, 167–68, 220, 224, 233, 237–38, 243, 258–59, 270, 293
  Frances C., 224
Gaines History, 55, 62, 122, 206–9, 232–34, 236–39, 243–45, 247, 250, 252, 258–59, 268, 271, 274, 293–94
Gaines Printery, 293
Gaines's History, 238, 257
Gallahue, William, 151
Gallop, Gabriella, 183
Gann, 253
  Mabel, 253
  Mable, 253
  Robert S., 139
  Samuel, 64
Gano, 94, 235, 266–67, 269
  Amelia, 111
  Daniel, 86, 235, 240
  Finley, 242, 245, 260, 268
  Frank, 111
  John A., 240
  Laura, 111
  Lela, 96
  Mary C., 162
  Penelope, 260
  Sarah H., 268
  Stephen, 164, 240
  William, 214
Gano Avenue, 205, 265–67, 294
Gano Family, 266
Gano Street, Present, 246
Gant, 159
  Jason J., 159
Gap Road, 114, 119, 121
Gardner, Annie A., 179
Gardner, William P., 178
Gariepy, Jennifer, 127–28
Gariepys, 128
Garnet, 128
Garnett, 128, 184, 225
  Edna, 225
Garton, Hiram, 70
Gary, 89, 261
Gaskins, 62
Gasner, 92
Gasper, 190
Gayle, 135, 292

Gayle House, 122
Gaylor, 226
  Aaron, 221–22, 226
Georgetown, 55–56, 58, 84–86, 125–26, 159, 161–67, 192, 200, 205, 207–9, 224, 239–40, 245–47, 251–52, 291–95
  Downtown, 67
  Listed, 161
Georgetown & Scott County Museum, 170, 181, 292
Georgetown And Peak's Mill, 162
Georgetown Area, 197, 292
Georgetown Athletics, 226
Georgetown Baptist Church, 285
Georgetown Board, 161–62
Georgetown City Superintendent, 229
Georgetown College, 55, 92, 138, 169, 209, 226, 291
Georgetown College's Alicestyne Adams, 55
Georgetown College Student Body, 166
Georgetown College's Underground Railroad Research Institute, 60
Georgetown-Covington Road, 196
Georgetown-Cynthiana Road, 67
Georgetown-Frankfort Road, 67
Georgetown Graphic, 169–70, 228, 230, 291, 293
Georgetown Municipal Water, 167
Georgetown National Bank, 136, 138
Georgetown News, 217, 226, 293
Georgetown News & Times, 60, 105, 230, 247, 258, 271, 291–94
Georgetown News-Graphic, 62, 68, 226, 249, 291–93, 295
Georgetown News-Times, 60, 270, 294
Georgetown Indian Refining, 163
Georgetown Road, 208
Georgetown's Big Spring, 107
Georgetown's Big Spring Branch, 197
Georgetown's Boston, 51
Georgetown's East Main Street, 284
Georgetown's First National, 240
Georgetown's Garth School, 229
Georgetown Sheet Metal For Renovation, 249
Georgetown Site On North Elkhorn Creek, 161
Georgetown's Mallard Pencil Company, 159
Georgetown's North Hamilton, 125
Georgetown's Oak Street, 140
Georgetown Street, 188
Georgetown's West Main And South Broadway, 273
Georgetown Times, 163–65, 293
Georgetown-Turkeyfoot Road, 68
Georgetown Weekly Times, 71–72, 177, 188, 206, 216, 233, 293
Georgian Colonial, 285
Georgian England, 285
Geraldine, 116
Germany's Magdeburg Cathedral, 224
Gertrude Davis House, 281
Gibson, John, 74, 192
Gifford, Betty J., 223
Gifford, Dale, 223

Gilbert, 63, 68, 94, 96, 131
　William, 171, 223
Gilead Cemetery, 201
Gilead Church Road, 111
Gilead Methodist Episcopal Church, 87
Giles, 76, 79, 95, 105, 109–10, 125, 129–34, 143, 206–7, 225
　Addie, 132
　Anna, 131
　Annabel, 75, 95
　Annabel M., 105
　Charles, 106
　Deceased Thomas W., 132
　Eliza A., 132
　Elizabeth J., 206
　Emma, 106
　Frances W., 132
　Frank, 129–30, 153, 206
　Frank C., 130
　Frank H., 132
　George, 89, 194
　Harvey, 129
　Heirs Llewellyn, 206
　Hiram, 206
　John F., 201, 205
　Joseph, 206
　Leander, 206
　Lillian, 76
　Lloyd, 96, 101
　Lloyd D., 76
　Margaret, 132
　Mildred, 76, 183
　Nancy, 134
　Nancy M., 129–30
　Napoleon, 129
　Patricia, 75–76, 105
　Ralph C., 87–88, 194
　Richard P., 132
　Samuel T., 129–31, 134
　Samuel W., 131
　Stanley, 183
　Susan, 206
　Thomas, 132
　Thomas W., 132
　Wife Eliza A., 134
Giles And Finnell Roads, 129
Giles Family Properties, 129
Giles Farm, 87, 205
Giles Hill, 129
Giles Hill On Barkley Road, 131
Giles House, 87, 130–32
Giles House Ii, 129
Giles-Humphrey Farm, 133–34
Giles Pike, 129
Giles-Reffett House, 106
Giles-Reffitt House, 106
Giles's Descendants, 129
Giles Trust, 154
　Ralph C., 87–88

Gilkey, Darryl, 174
Gilkey, Darryl K., 174
Gilkey, Hattie T., 174
Gilkey, John, 55
Gilkey, Lee, 106, 174
Gilkey, Mabel, 174
Gilkey, Martha, 54
Gilkey, William, 55
Gilkeys, 57, 174
Gillispie, 74, 80, 92, 238, 264
　Calvin, 92, 161
　Calvin P., 92
　Calvin W., 238
　Christina, 80
　Christine, 80
　Clyde T., 92, 238
　Frank, 73–74, 293
　Jeffrey, 74, 293
　Mary K., 255
　Robert M., 238
Gillispie Cemetery, 92
Gillispie House, 80, 178
Gillispie Property, 178
Gillispie's Family, 74
Ginn, 184
　Harriet, 184
Gitt, Agnes, 113
Glass, Annie E., 261
Glass, Mattie, 147
Glenn, 107, 163, 174, 176, 216
　Anna C., 139
　Anna E., 139
　Annie T., 171, 216
　Augusta H., 139
　Daughters Annie T., 171
　John M., 139
　Lois, 171
　Martha, 171
　Matilda, 139
Glenna, 95
Glinn, Walter C., 220
Goddard, 164
　Samuel, 190
Goepper, John, 274
Goepper, Todd, 75, 249
Goeppers, 249, 274
Goldey, Albert, 254
Gooch, Charles, 125
Goodnight, 255
Gordon, 140, 261
Goss, Donna M., 279
Gosses, 280
Gossey, 57–58, 293
　Ethel M., 57
　Willie, 58
Gothic Revival, 76, 206, 285
Grace Baptist Church, 191
Graham County, 60
Grangers' Hall, 202

Grant, Geraldine, 114
Grant, Kenneth, 116
Grant County, 67, 256
Granville, 253, 258, 264
Graves
  Ann, 170
  Catherine, 148
  Cora, 52
  Edward, 130
  Howard, 54
  Howard M., 53
  John B., 108, 122
  Kitty, 147
  Maggie, 98
  Martin, 52–53
  Mollie, 148, 170
  William, 172
Graves Lumber, 229
Graves Lumber Company, 230
Gray, Sadie, 167
Gray, Vivian, 179
Gray Dates, 216
Grayland Farm/K, 81
Grayland House, 81
Grays, 167, 179, 216
Grayson Ensign, 193
Grayson School, 274
Greatbatch, John L., 63
Great Crossings, 55, 164, 172, 208, 228, 271
Great Crossings Baptist Church, 197
Great Crossings Station, 172
Great Neck, 123, 188, 293
Griffin, Wyatt, 57
Griffith, 154, 156, 239, 248
  Dave, 155
  Dave T., 275
  Elizabeth, 154
  James, 201
  Leonard, 155
  Linda, 186
  Millard F., 239
  Nancy, 156
  Nancy L., 156
  Sallie, 240
  William, 153
  Younger, 156
GRIFFITH HOUSE, 156
Grigg, Ellen, 94
Grigg, John W., 94
Grigg, Joseph, 94
Griggs, Martha, 94
Griggs, 148
  Joseph E., 137
  William, 149
Griggs Estate, 142
Griggs/Gregg Properties, 148
Griggs House, 149
Grissom, 111
  Bobbi, 112

Great Nephew Timothy William Fields, 123
Great Revival, 190
Grecian, 284
Grecian Art, 287
Greece, 285–86
  Ancient, 285
Greek Revival, 74, 213, 285
Green
  Betty F., 228
  Bobbi Y., 111
  Dorothy, 102
  Dorothy W., 102
  Henry, 86
  Herman, 132
Green Bay Packer, 59
Greenberry Fields, 78
Greenup, Christopher, 172
Greenwell, Margaret, 201
Green-Wilderson House, 103
Greenwood Stove Company, 125
Gregg, 142, 205
  George L., 142
  Joseph, 151
  William H., 148
Gregg-Bailey House, 142
Gregg Family, 128
Gregory, 101, 137, 140, 206–7
  Margaret, 137
  Mildred, 206
  Robert, 206
  Tammy, 161

  Timothy G., 111
Grizzle, 127, 188
  Bobby, 110
  Bobby R., 110
  Judy, 110
  Todd, 187
Grocery, Davis, 222
Grover, 165
Guernsey, 167
Guerrant, Edward O., 213
Guffey Farm, 122
Gunnell, 142, 145–46, 148, 150, 187
  Joseph, 145, 150
  Martha A., 55
  Richard, 146
  William, 144, 146
  William W., 146
  Willie, 145
  Willis W., 144–45
Gunnell-Alexander Farm, 146
Gunnell-Alexander House, 144–45
Gunnell Family, 56
Gunnell Now Sharon Pike, 144
Gunnell Pike, 110, 142
Gunnell Pike Setting, 146
Gunnell Road, 144, 146–49
Gunnell Road Development Of Loveland, 147

Gunnell's Estate, 146
Guy, Mary, 123

H

Hagans, Rhoda, 137
Haggin, Linda H., 53
Halcom, 148
Halfhill, Elnora, 179
Hall, 51, 57, 82, 101, 112, 122–23, 147, 156, 213, 229, 248, 269
  Amy, 160
  Betsy O., 159
  Buford, 73, 93, 121–23, 163, 188, 292
  Effie, 158
  Elizabeth, 116
  Entertainment, 249
  Fellowship, 60, 193
  James W., 159
  Jane, 122
  Janice R., 159
  Jesse, 51, 103
  John, 51, 89, 122
  Joint, 248
  Marion, 122, 293
  Married James J., 158
  Nancy, 122
  Nannie, 103, 122
  Nicole, 105
  Reverend Nathan H., 182
  Robert, 144
  Ruth, 178
  William, 122
Hall Branch, 180
Hambrick, 85, 165, 167, 174
  Annie, 218
  Included, 197
  Jesse, 174
  Lucy, 167
  Margaret, 174
  Norman, 122, 167
  Norman W., 167
Hambrick Bungalow, 167
Hamilton, 113, 211, 252, 258–59, 261, 263, 279–80
  Bertha, 255
  Charles, 208, 211
  Cora L., 259
  Elizabeth, 252
  James, 144
  Lorena, 279–80
  Tom, 280
Hamilton House, 257–58
Hamilton's Crossroads, 208, 211
Hammond, 51, 142, 281
  James, 234
Hammons, Cheryl F., 121
Hammons, Debbie, 121
Hammons, Debra, 113

Hamon, 112, 129, 136, 142, 200–201, 206–7, 218, 220, 225, 262
  Amos, 206–7
  Dudley, 108, 219, 224
  Edith, 139
  Eliza, 220
  Eliza J., 224
  Frances, 225
  Henry, 218
  Jasper, 218
  Marie, 136, 207
  Mary, 220
  Nelson, 191, 200, 206, 219–20, 225
  William T., 207
Hamon Family, 220
Hamon Heirs, 136
Hamon Properties, 136
Hampshire Rams, 122
Hampton, James A., 203
Haney, David P., 265
Hanna, 138
  Hazel, 138, 222
  Noah, 138
Hannah, Noah, 137–38
Hanna/Hannah Family, 138
Hanners, Lon, 138
Happy, James, 54
Happy, William, 52–54
Happy Lane, 51
Hardin, 175
Hargis, Thomas D., 267
Harlan, James, 175
Harmer's Defeat, 173
Harmon, Dona, 111
Harold, 63, 65, 98, 111, 119, 196, 279–80
Harold Reed Davis, 278
Harp, 177
  Joe, 198
Harriet, 71, 134, 184, 186
Harriet Kaley Hotel, 238–39
Harriet Stevens House, 185
Harrigan Hinton, 192
Harris, Linda, 118
Harris, Martha, 110
Harris, Samuel, 108
Harrises, 118–19
Harrison, 64, 67–68, 70, 73, 99, 111, 126, 135, 184, 186, 192–93, 208, 295
  Christine A., 218
  Henry, 62
  John, 62
Harrison County, 68–69, 81, 90, 99, 112, 131, 139, 179, 184, 194, 199, 203, 205, 230, 253
Harrison County Board, 135
Harrison County Lands, 68
Harrison County Line, 67, 69, 135, 185
Harrison County Line Communities, 71
Harrison County Pike, 129, 134
Harrison County Portion, 184

Harrison County's Connersville, 68
Harrison County Side, 180, 185, 199
Harrison County's Unity Precinct, 68
Harrison County Turnpike, 75
Harrison-Scott County, 187
Harrison-Scott Line, 180
Harry, 61, 63, 105, 141, 153, 223, 265, 281
Hartwell, 117, 214
Harve Covington House, 140
Harwood, Margaret, 84–85
Hash, 188–89, 203
Havoline Motor Oil, 161
Havoline Oil, Producing, 164
Hawkins, Clyde, 176
Hawkins, David, 86
Hawkins, Garth, 176
Hawkins, John A., 176
Hawkins, Karen D., 89
Hayden, 100
  Richard S., 260
Hayden's Restaurant, 267
Haynes, Conrad, 228, 230
Hazel Darlene Rains, 211
Hazel Sherritt Brooker, 274
Hedger, 163, 169, 232
  Mary, 70
Hehr, Jessie, 112
Henderson
  Barney, 54
  Charity, 63
  Edmund, 55
  Joe, 112
  John, 55–56
  Sally, 112
Henderson Residential Trust, 112
Hendersons, 56, 112
Hendricks, 175, 209, 213, 216, 221, 223, 226–27
  Jane F., 159, 216
Hendricks-Barkley-Holland House, 227
Hendricks/Barkley House, 231
Hendricks House, 221
Henry, 63–64, 101, 108, 147, 150, 155, 238, 265–66
  Hayden, 178
  James, 78
  John M., 245
  Lillian, 102
  Lucille, 252
  Lucille I., 252
  Nannie J., 64
  Patrick, 113
  Pauline, 101
  Pauline J., 101
  Sally, 220
  William, 295
Henry Bruce Drake, 78
Henry Clay Fields, 189
Henry Clay Fields Farm, 123
Henry Clay Press, 208, 292
Henry Families, 65

Henry Fields, 153
Henry Hobson Richardson, 285
Henry House, 101
Henry Mitchell Hinton, 86, 89
Henry Sherman Sowers, 88
Henry-Zeysing House, 266
Herman, 97, 236, 254, 264, 276
Hernandez, Gilbert, 63
Hernandez, Kathy, 63
Herndon, Charles, 217
Herndon, Mollie C., 217
Heroway, Late, 150
Herring, 293
Herring Collection, 84–86, 167
Hickman, 58–60
  Daniel, 58–59
  Left, 59
Higgins, Diane, 55
Higgins Family, 55
Hilander, 189, 203, 293
  Gaylord B., 136
Hiles, 86, 105–6, 118–20, 193–94
  Bill, 194
  Edward, 194
  Jane, 120
  Lee, 118–19, 121, 123, 196
  Martha B., 119
  Pearl C., 119
  Thomas B., 106, 120
  Tom, 194
  William H., 106
  Willie, 119
Hiles-Davis House, 105
Hiles Families, 120
Hiles, 119
Hiles Mill Pike, 131
Hiles Old Mill Road, 126, 187
Hill, Charity, 71, 82, 85, 233
Hill, Forest, 92
Hill, Mary E., 132
Hill, Zion, 55
Hillard, 254
  William J., 254
Hinds, 293
  Jim, 161–62, 164
Hinton, 69, 86–87, 89–91, 102–3, 113–14, 118, 152, 154–55, 177–80, 236, 238, 240, 244, 246, 277
  Amanda, 179
  Benjamin F., 86
  Bernard, 87–88
  Billy, 87
  Charles, 115
  Charlie, 113
  Deborah, 91
  Dick, 90
  Dorothy K., 88, 154
  Doyle, 115
  Ferdinand, 86, 89–90
  Ferdinand F., 86

George, 86
George W., 86–87, 89–90, 152, 177
Henry, 192–93
Henry M., 86, 192
James, 90–91
James W., 86, 89
Jean, 90
John A., 87, 89, 152
Kenneth, 87
Laura, 86
Lillie, 258
Louisa, 152
Lula, 87
Margaret, 113–14
Marian, 90
Millie, 177
Molly, 150
Noah, 194
Nora D., 152
Richard, 89, 113–14, 152
Richard M., 86
Sallie, 194
Sarah, 113, 152, 193
Sold George W., 152
Solomon, 91
Thomas, 86
Vera, 246, 269
Village Of, 67, 69, 177–79
Virgie, 263
William, 80, 86–89, 91, 127, 155
William A., 76, 181, 240, 258, 277
Willie, 155
Willis, 194
Wilma J., 113
Hinton And Carr Sons, 192
Hinton And Stonewall Roads, 179
Hinton/Cam Skinner, 90
Hinton Cemetery, 187
Hinton Cemetery On Hinton Cemetery Road, 153
Hinton Cemetery Road, 127–28, 152–53
Hinton Cemetery Road Setting, 134
Hinton Communities, 69
Hinton Congregations, 266
Hinton Descendant Doris Reed, 91
Hinton-Doris Reed, 90
Hinton Family, 87–88, 192
Hinton Family Estate Matter, 152
Hinton Family Influence, 86
Hinton Family Lands And Heritage, 87
Hinton Family Properties, 86
Hinton Heirs, 88–89
Hinton Home, 246
Hinton House, 152, 179
Hinton Methodist Churches, 266
Hinton Property Owners, 177
HINTON-REED HOUSE, 90
Hinton Road, 61, 69, 93, 102, 104, 152, 178–80
  Present, 234
Hinton Road And Southwest, 178

Hinton Road School Site, 93
Hinton Road South, 67
Hinton-Sadieville And North County Line, 99
Hinton-Sadieville Road, 61, 97, 104
Hinton Station, 179
Hinton-Stonewall, 69
Hinton's Wife Lillie, 246
Hinton-Tucker House, 89
Hinton Turnpike, 153
Hiram Wood House, 199, 215, 294
Hiten, 105, 218
  Letitia, 105–6
  Mary C., 218
  Tisha, 184
Hitner, Sold John K., 191
Hix, Merit, 57
Hixson, 129–30, 140
Hobbits, 59
Hockensmith, 170, 292
Hock Moore, 180
Hoffman, Jamie, 125
Hoffman, Porter, 148
Hoffman Brother, 125
Hoffman House, 126
Hoffman Lawns, 126
Hoffman's Creativity, 126
Hogan, James, 196
Holbrook, Cynthia, 280
Holcraft, 259
Holden
  Amanda, 201
  Benjamin, 201
  Elizabeth, 201
  James, 201
  John W., 201
  Joseph D., 202
  Niece Mary E., 202
  Valentine, 201
  William M., 201
Holdens, 158, 201
Holding
  Benjamin, 201
  Eliza, 202
  James D., 200
  Joel S., 201
  joseph L. Holden Frances A., 201
  Letltla, 206
  Lindsay, 200
  Mary E., 201
  Nancy, 200
  Sarah, 201
  Sarah M., 202
  Stephen, 201
  William, 201
  William M., 201
  William P., 201
Holding Land, 201
Holding Mill Road, 202
  Holding's Mill, 200

Holdings Mill, 199–200, 203
Holdings Mill-Mount Gilead, 138
Holdings Mill/Mount Gilead Inner Community, 199
Holland, 79, 141, 227
  Bertha, 194
  Beverly, 179
  Dick, 194
  Jane, 86
  John, 141, 152
  John J., 141
  Lucille, 141
  Lucille M., 227
  Susie, 194
  William, 96
Holland House, 141
Holland-Vance House, 141
Hollister, 95
Holmes, 61, 65
  Mae Etta O., 105
Hood, Frank, 270
Hopper, Ray C., 111
Hornsby, Betty, 128, 136
Hoskins, George, 77, 79
Hoskins, William, 77
Hounchell, 179
  Sandra L., 179
Houston, 153, 188–90, 194, 293
  Amy, 188
  Dorothy E., 153
  Fannie, 152
  Fannie C., 153
  Harry L., 153
  Paul, 153
  Sally, 194, 263
  Shirley, 147, 153, 203
  Shirley T., 134
Houston Family, 153
Howard, 143, 175, 188, 222
Howell Gano & Company, 125
Hubert, 101, 128, 149, 264, 274
Hudson, 137
  Philip, 137
Huffman, Lee R., 252
Hugh, 107–8, 148, 183, 209
Hughes, 179
  Flo, 275
  Jeannette, 110
  Nancy, 272
  Nancy J., 272
  Pearl, 257
  Ralph, 78
Hugh Frank Juett, 159, 211
Humphrey
  Amelia, 179
  Anna, 132
  Denver, 133–34
  Lee, 179
  Linda C., 258
  Violet, 135

Humphreys, 132, 135, 179
Humphreys' Sons, 132
Hurd, 145
  Carl, 145
Hurley, 53, 65, 100
  Alex, 54
  Alexander, 53
  Ann, 64
  Charles, 54
  Elizabeth, 63
  Julia, 53
  Louisa, 54
  Reuben, 53
  William, 61
Hurley House, 53, 64
Hurst, 146, 151
Hutchcraft, 155, 186
  Susan, 253
Hutchcraft House, 253
Hutcherson, Kenneth, 186
Hyles/Hiles, Thomas, 192

I

Ignight, Richard, 98, 256
Ignight, Sallie, 278
Ignight, Sally, 63
Ignites, 63
Incorporation Articles Of Sadieville, 234
Incorporators Of Deposit Bank Of Sadieville, 239
Incorporators Of Sadieville, 232
Indian Oil, 162, 164
Indian Oil Refinery, 162–64
Inner Bluegrass, Transitional, 122
Inner Bluegrass Maury Mcafee, 158
Innis, 50
  Dick, 50
  Richard, 50–51
  William, 50–51
Innis In Rush County, 50
Inyart, David, 102
Ireland, 51, 120
  John, 50, 139
Isaacs, 71, 130
  Anna, 130
  Anna H., 144
  Kenneth, 279
  Paul, 129, 131
Ishmael, Ruth M., 141
Ison, Charlotte, 154
Ison, Teresa L., 278
Italianate, 74, 285
  Collegiate, 229
Italianate Brackets, 80
Italianate Dwellings, 155
Italianate Influence, 285
Italianate Persuasion, 248
Italianate Style, 171
Italianate Style Dwelling, 72, 221

Italianate Style House And Interior Chimneys And Brackets, 216

J

Jackson, 51, 163
  Connie, 194
  Dick, 119
  Joyce L., 154
  Walter, 270
Jacob, 73, 94–96, 136, 145, 147, 173, 210
Jacob Mulberry County Road, 73
Jacob Mulberry House, 94, 261
Jacob Price's Building, 209
James, 53, 71, 90, 92–95, 121, 135–37, 139–40, 142–43, 148–49, 178–79, 196, 201–3, 216–17, 220, 222–24
James Allen Justice, 271
James Amos, 206
Jameson, 164
James Polk Fields, 256
James Risk Family, 209
James Risk House, 216
James Wade Emison, 84, 182, 197, 209, 214
Janene Hoffman House, 125
Jane Williams Johnston, 106
Jankie Jackson, 257, 280
Jarvis, 217, 293
  Joe, 214
  Joe W., 211, 214
Jean, Betty, 266
Jeffrey, 102, 154, 181, 186
  William, 111
Jeffrey Lynn Brashear, 175
Jemima, 108
Jemima Jane Luke, 146
Jenkins, 186, 250
  Elbert, 178
  Minnie, 252
  Sylvia, 178
Jennings, Gina M., 272
Jennings, Jessie L., 136
  Jeptha Bell, 116
  Jeremiah, 90
  Jeremy, 161
  Jeret Smith, 57
  Jerusalem, 200
  Jesse, 101, 144, 171
Jesse Duncan House, 128
Jeter, 272
  Mary C., 272
Jeter Family, 272
Jeter's Son Mark, 272
Jewell Marie Doolin, 130
Jewett, 256
  James H., 214
Jimmie Jones Dwelling, 250, 294
John Cottingham Building, 251
John Graves Ford Memorial Hospital, 109
John Kaley Hotel, 251
John Kitchen House, 98, 157

John Nichols House, 53
John Reed-Humphrey House, 135
Johnson, 112, 141–42, 151, 173, 192, 213, 225, 236, 240, 242–43, 247, 258, 268–69, 295
  Ann, 172
  Doris, 276
  Ellis, 119
  Essie, 137
  Evangelist John T., 213
  Evelyn, 265
  George B., 242, 254
  Hannah, 62
  Holly W., 252
  Ina M., 225
  James T., 209, 231
  Jemima, 112, 135
  Jesse, 111
  John T., 192
  Joseph, 173
  Joseph G., 110
  Kristina, 253
  Linda, 71
  Martha, 171, 291
  Martha L., 171
  Melissa, 159
  Ollie M., 147
  Owen L., 111
  Richard M., 59
  Victor, 191
  William, 150–51
  William F., 151
Johnson Funeral Home, 204
Johnson House, 242
Johnston, 52, 68, 177, 188, 190, 192–93, 227, 232–33, 252
  Frederick A., 166, 291
Jones, 63, 73, 95, 100, 234, 238–40, 244, 250, 253, 255, 257, 259–62, 264, 268, 273
  Audrey L., 254
  Bob, 193
  Bonnie D., 266
  Carl, 249
  Carrie, 141
  Charlie, 100, 141
  Cheryl, 270
  Christine, 100
  Clara, 167
  Clarice, 186
  Edith C., 64
  Eric W., 95
  Frankie, 52
  James L., 254
  Jimmie, 249–50
  Joshua, 169
  Katie, 95
  Kendall, 273
  Larry, 249
  Linda, 261
  Lorraine, 141, 281

Lydia, 155
Maggie, 242
Martha T., 255
Mary, 63
Mary E., 100
Mary F., 141
Paul, 257
Ray, 255
Rita, 174–75
Silas, 232, 278
Silas B., 234, 263–64, 274, 276, 282
Stella, 254
Stephen, 52, 54
Steve, 54
William, 197
Jones Dwelling House, 250
Joneses, 238, 261, 275
Joseph, 112, 142–43, 146, 148, 150–51, 172, 179, 184, 205, 208, 221, 226, 244, 249, 256
Joseph Bailey House, 143
Joy, 166, 291
Juett, 147–48, 158–61, 223, 231
   Betsy, 147
   Beverly, 160
   Curtis, 160
   Edna, 158
   Effie, 147
   Fred L., 158, 160
   Harriet, 161
   Harriet C., 160–61
   Harriett C., 160
   Hattie, 147
   Helen, 211
   Helen F., 209, 231
   Helen M., 158, 221
   Lula, 256
   Mabel, 147
   Maggie, 158
   Michael, 123
   Monica, 123
   Nellie, 147
   Ward E., 158, 160–61
   William T., 158, 160
Juett-Cannon Farm, 223
Juett-Cannon House, 223
Juett House, 147, 159, 231
Juett Log House, 160
Junction City, 60
Justice, Jennifer, 247

K
Kaley, 234, 239, 251
   Harriett, 239
   John, 232, 239, 251
Kaley's Building, 239
Kansas, 57–59, 63, 111
Kansas National Park Site, 60
Kansas Suburb, 57
Kay Wiseman Log House, 138

Keene, Mollie, 64
Kelley, Thomas, 167
Kelly, 77, 199
   Carla, 141
   David, 127
   Fannie, 264
   Fannie T., 253
   Fanny T., 258
   Granville, 253, 258–59, 264
   Michel, 106
   Samuel, 64
Kelm, Robert W., 137
Kendrick, Cyril I., 267
Kerr, David, 122
Kestel, Christine, 111
Kettelson, Jerry L., 167
Kimbrough, 223
   Luna, 223
   Married Mary E., 209
Kincaid Station, 199
Kincaid Turnpike, 169
King, 63, 188
   Annie F., 251
   Frances, 237
   Nora L., 139
   William, 57
Kinkead, 199
   Louisa, 199
Kinkead And Muddy Ford Dirt Road, 176
Kissman, 265
Kitchen,
   Carl, 98
   Edna, 186
   Emery C., 98
   George, 99
   James H., 98
   John, 98, 157, 184, 202
   John E., 186
   Lizzie, 98
   Maggie, 278
   Martha A., 99
   Mary, 98, 157
   Nannie, 157
   Oscar G., 154
   Roy, 98
   Sophia, 184
   Thomas, 99
   Winford, 186
Kitchen Properties, 98
Kitchens' Source, 186
Kith, 181, 183, 223, 292
Knights, 282
Knights Of Pythias, 248–49
Knights Of Pythias Cemetery, 258, 282
Knights Of Pythias/Sadieville Cemetery, 282
Kronenburg, Sam, 179
Kroness, Lucille, 83
Kyger, George, 146

L

Lacefield, Lester, 159
Lacefield, Ruth H., 159
Lacy, 109
  Andrew C., 109
  Bill, 109
  Edna, 109
  John A., 109
  Linda, 156
Ladd, Lona H., 207
Lamont, Jon M., 278
Lancaster, 68, 73, 80–81, 86, 93, 101, 179, 236, 238, 244, 275
  Annie T., 244
  Arthur, 95, 237–38
  Carolyn, 159
  Clarence, 93
  Deeded, 93
  Eliza M., 93
  Gladys, 97
  Glenna, 95
  Gwendolyn, 101
  John, 93, 101, 179, 275, 283
  John J., 100
  John W., 93
  Juanita, 97, 101, 275
  Laura, 275
  Lewis, 93
  Lottie, 264
  Lucy, 101, 257, 275
  Lucy E., 275
  Nannie B., 179
  Virgil, 179
  Wilbur, 229
Lancaster Farm, 100
Lancaster Heirs, 179
Lancaster House, 97, 101
Lancaster-Kitchen House, 179
Lancaster's Drug, 238
Lane, William, 255
Langley Derossitt, 91
Lard, 246–47
  Moses E., 246
Lavina McCabe House, 261
Lawrenceburg Christian Church, 226
Lawrenceville Refinery's Line, 164
Lawson, Susan, 181
Lay, Daniel, 110
Leach, 140
  John, 139
  Joseph, 192
  Luna, 186
Leander, 248, 262, 266, 275
Leander Risk Hotel, 241
Lear, Louise J., 111
Lee, 104, 174, 239–40, 244–45, 254, 258, 294
  Anna, 95
  Carl, 131
  Fanny, 220
  Fellow Storekeepers Robert E., 244
  Mary G., 74
  Morgan, 104
  Nora, 124
  Owen S., 74
  Robert E., 74
  Wife Mary G., 245
Lee Gilkey Farm, 106
Leesburg Road, 158, 208
Lee's House, 245
Leeslick And Turkeyfoot Roads, 98
Leeslick Turnpike, 139
Lemon, George, 68
Lemon, Martha, 183
Lemon Mulberry, 255
Lemons, 85, 110, 232
  John, 110
  Mollie, 269
  Willie, 109
  Willie B., 109–10
Lena, 101, 114, 223
Leonard Mulberry House, 96
Levi Craig House, 63
Lew, 126–28
Lewis, 57, 64, 102, 161, 166, 169, 270, 292
  Georgetown's James R., 166
  James R., 166
  Joseph, 57
  Robert, 169, 278
Lexington, 68, 72, 91, 137, 147, 159, 188–89, 191, 208–9, 214, 226, 235, 253, 292, 295
Lexington And Rogers Gap, 68
Lexington Herald, 242, 295
Lexington Herald Leader, 226, 292–93, 113, 165, 292, 294
Lexington/Newtown/Muddy Ford/Turkeyfoot, 208
Lexington Presbytery, 190
Lexington Road, 170
Licking River, 172, 180
Lida, Mary, 167
Lida Bell, 219
Lilly, William, 201
Lilly Mae Munson, 194
Lindsay's House, 203
Lindsey, 291
  Cynthia, 183
Linnie Brooks, 258
Little, Barbara, 107, 291
Little Eagle, 97
Little Eagle Creek, 96
Livery Stable, 249, 251
Lizziebeth Fight/Fightmaster, 91
Lizzie Fields, 105
Locust Grove School, 93
Log House
Long
  Nicholas, 196
  Samuel W., 137
Long Lick Pike, 170

Lonnie, 184, 226, 253
Louisville Baptist Children's Home, 166
Lucas, Ella, 184
Lucas, James L., 114, 116
Lucas, John, 221
Lucas, Thomas, 184
Lucinda Davis House, 104
Lucy, 95, 139, 155, 267
    Hannah, 220
Lucy Lancaster House, 275
Lucy Mae Vallandingham, 96–97, 255
Lucy Zeysing, 252
Luke, 73, 86, 96–97, 139, 146, 148, 154–56, 239–40, 244
    Dona, 147
    Elmer, 146, 148
    Hattie, 146
    Josie, 100
    Laura, 156
    Leah, 146, 148
Luke Family, 148
Luke Family Properties, 154
Luke-Swinford Farm, 156
Lusby, Joe, 110
Lusby, Lena, 148
Lusby, Mable, 109
Lutes, George, 179
Lutes-Whitson House, 179
Lutz, Patricia, 224
Lynch, Merrill, 280
Lynn, Harrison, 126–27, 134
Lynn, Nancy, 126
Lyons, Rhonda, 102
Lytle, 130, 294
    Andrew N., 130

M

Mabel Gann House Site, 253
Maddox, Stella, 206
Mae, 96
    Nannie, 94
Maggie Kitchen Land, 98
Mahan Farm, 78
Main And Pike Streets, 236
Main Elkhorn, 164
Maines, 232, 263–64, 269
    Grover, 232
Main Street Line Of Businesses And Dwelling Houses, 249
Main Street Residential Block, 242
Main Street/Rodham, 245
Mallory, 84–85, 120, 164, 267, 269
    Charlie, 164
    Mary, 84–85
    Ruth, 278
Mamah, 201
Man-O-War Colts, 226
Mansfield, 232, 240, 244–45, 250
    Paul, 270
Mansfield's Heirs, 250

Marcum, Danny, 144
Marcum, David, 144
Marshall, 80, 86, 100, 236, 243–44, 252, 256–57, 260, 262–64, 277, 281, 294
    Albert, 172
    Alice, 148
    Bill, 263
    Edgar B., 93
    Eugene, 262
    George E., 260
    Historian William A., 80
    John, 277
    Late William A., 281
    Letha, 256, 269
    Mary, 100, 252
    Neal, 155
    Theodore, 221
    Theresa, 277
    Vance P., 277
    William F., 79–80
Marshall Family, 256, 260
Marshall Family House, 256
Marshall-Mccabe Furniture, 236
Martha Burgess House, 110
Martin
    David, 87–88
    George R., 158
    Hazel, 271
    Included Sarah A., 159
    Justin, 151
    Linda, 135
    Viola, 123
, 123, 135, 215
Marvin, William, 111
Marx, 176
    Martin B., 176
Mason, Betty, 171
Mason, Jesse, 58
Mason, Joe, 55, 171
Mason, Joseph, 57
Mason, Luther, 171
Mason, Martha P., 136
Mason, Sallie, 55–57
Masonic Lodge, 192–93, 209, 214, 249
Masonic Lodge Building, 208, 214
Matilda Glenn Division, 139
Maudlin, Jennifer R., 275
May, Ann E., 184
May, Helen S., 280
Maybrier, Dollie, 123
Mccabe, 88, 232, 235–38, 240, 243–44, 247, 250–51, 254, 257–59, 261, 263–64, 270, 274, 277, 282
    Douglas, 274
    Eleanor, 274
    Frances, 259–61
    Frankie, 276
    Included Mary E., 259
    James, 183
    John, 268

John A., 250, 255, 264
John W., 255
Lavinia, 261
Mary, 65, 274, 280
Mary E., 64, 260
Nannie, 250
Nannie J., 236, 263
Polly, 183
Robert H., 261
Valerie, 65
Walter, 280
Walter W., 238, 253
William H., 238
Mccabe/Bob Davis House, 258
Mccabe-Davis Family, 261
Mccabe-Davis Farmstead Site, 259
Mccabe Family, 274
Mccabe Heirs, 274
Mccabe House, 274
Mccabe-Marshall House, 260
Mccabes' Barn, 260
Mccabes' Cellar, 260
Mccabe School/Telephone, 234
Mccabe School/Telephone House Building, 234, 294
Mccabe's Heirs, 259
Mccabe's Lumber, 233
Mccabe-Swinford House, 264
Mccarty & Company, 125
Mcclellan, Elizabeth, 137
Mcclelland's Fort, 107, 191
Mcclellans, 137
Mcconnell, Lawrence, 64
Mccoy, Stella, 264
Mccoy, William, 263–64
Mccoy Heirs, 263
Mccoys, 264
Mcdaniel, 107, 206–7
  Mary, 108
  Noble, 206
  Sarah, 108
  Sarah S., 203
Mcdeevits Fresh Goods Llc, 280
Mcdonald, 135
  Buford, 134
Mcdonough, Henry, 216
Mcduffy, Frances, 251
Mcfarland, 96, 100, 111
  Marietta, 111
  Myrtle, 98
  Rhonda K., 181
Mcginn, 234
Mcguirk, Margaret, 97
Mcguirk/Fightmaster House, 97
Mcguirk-Swinford House, 97
Mchatton, Elizabeth, 50
Mcintyre, Carl, 260
Mcintyre, Krystal, 273
Mcintyre, William, 51
Mckenney, 73, 139, 232, 282
  Agnes, 261
  Bruce, 248
  Everett, 99
  Johnny L., 186
  Robert, 254
Mckenney's Title, 186
Mckenzie, Holly, 187–88
Mckinivan, Eva, 269
Mckinley, 91
Mckinney, Chester, 152
Mckinney, Roy, 193
Mckinney, Tommie, 90
Mckinney House, 152
Mcloney, 205, 253
  John T., 205
  Married John T., 206
  Nathaniel T., 253
  Nee, 179
Mcloney Family, 199
Mcloney House, 177
Mcloney Land, 205
Mcloney's Property, 178
Mcmillan, Maude, 206
Mcmillen, 248
  Brenda J., 257
  Harriet, 201
  Robert, 124, 176
  Ruth, 201
Mcmillin, Robert, 220
Mcmillin, William, 217
Mcnutt, 162
  Robert R., 165
Mcpherson, Elizabeth, 196
Mcqueen, Shirley B., 65, 225
Medlock, Betty, 138
Mefford, 144, 155, 240, 246
  Frances, 155
  William, 148
Mefford/Daugherty/Hinton House, 246
Meltons, Debra L., 281
Merckle, Stella B., 100
Methodist Church, 52, 54, 187, 190, 208, 227, 246, 265–66, 269
Methodist Church Building, 180
Methodist-Cumberland Presbyterian, 190
Methodist Episcopal Church, 265
Methodist Episcopal Church South, 265
Methodist Minister, 190
Methodist Revivalists, 190
Methodists, 208, 233
Michael, 101, 140, 145, 181, 186, 227, 254, 257, 261
  John, 196
  John C., 110
  Mary, 264
  Mary A., 278
  Ophelia, 102
Michael John Taylor, 176
Middleton, Aaron, 253
Middleton, Agnes, 258

Middleton, Agnes D., 265
Middleton, Ruth A., 272
Middletons, 258, 265
Mildred Gregory Farm, 206
Miley, Lula, 75
Milford, 173
Millard, 239–40, 248
Miller, 212
   Adam J., 160
   Marilyn F., 188
   Robert E., 158
   Valeria, 65
Milner, 139
   Delia, 207
   Frank, 136, 207
   Mary A., 129, 134
Milner House, 139
Minch, 294
   Norman, 105, 247
Minter, Carol A., 153
Missionary Baptist Church, 57
Mitchell, 51
   Lucy, 183
   Nancy, 89
Mizell, Michael, 275
Mizell, Regina K., 254
Mockbee, James F., 135
Monhollin, David G., 223
Montgomery, John S., 163
Moody, 150–51, 223, 294
   Charles E., 223
   Cynthia, 150
   Elder, 150
   Elizabeth, 150
   James W., 151
   Jewell, 225
   Jewell M., 223
   Joseph, 150–51
   Lewis, 151
   Thomas, 150
   William, 150–51, 292
Moody - Morris House, 149, 151
Moody's House, 150
Moody Tract, 151
Moon's Inn, 130
Moore, 63, 171, 173, 209, 211, 217, 220–21, 225
   Anna, 174
   Bettie, 213
   Douglas, 225
   Douglas P., 220
   Emily, 57
   Marvin, 63
   Mary, 213
   Mary F., 224
   Nancy, 174
   Nancy F., 224
   Robert, 213
   Robert H., 170, 228
   Sallie, 221
   Sallie E., 211
   Samuel, 173, 224
   Scott C., 213
   Thomas C., 251
   William C., 174
Moore & Hukill, 125
Moore-Hambrick House, 174
Moore-Hamon Houses, 224–25
Morah Fields, 244
Moran, Blanche, 279
Moreland, Beulah, 129–30
Moreland, James, 90
Moreland, Lorena, 148
Moreland, Reverends John R., 182
Morgan, 253, 258, 265
   Juanita, 263
   William H., 258, 265
Moritz, Adeline, 274
Morris, 110, 151, 187, 264
   James, 128, 179
   James T., 109–10
   John, 127, 150–51
   Lydia, 148
   Mary, 189
   Nannie, 151
   Phyllis, 262
   Reuben, 150
   Stella, 101, 151, 264
   Thomas H., 151
   William P., 150–51
Morrises, 110, 151
   Hubert, 264
Morris Family, 150
Morrison, Sandra S., 151
Moses, Noble, 82
Mosley, 77
   Judy A., 98
Mount Faulconer, 255
Mount Gilead, 134, 141, 189, 199–202, 205–7
Mount Gilead Cemetery, 200–202, 205
Mount Gilead Church, 139, 199, 204
Mount Gilead Church And Cemetery, 200–201
Mount Gilead Church Road, 111, 132–33, 143
Mount Gilead Meeting House, 203
Mount Gilead Methodist Church, 132, 199–200
Mount Gilead Road, 132, 140–41, 143, 207
Mount Gilead Setting, 132
Mount Olive, 56, 58
Mount Olive Baptist, 57
Mount Olive Baptist Church, 57, 59, 293
Mount Olive Church, 57–58
Mount Olive Congregation, 58
Mount Olive/Dry Run Missionary Baptist Church, 58, 294
Mount Olivet, 60
Mount Olivet Church, 59, 247
Mount Pleasant Baptist Church, 60–61
Mount Vernon No, 249
Mount Zion Chapel Methodist, 68

Mount Zion Church, 68
Muddiman, 67–68, 107, 110, 113, 187–88, 196, 198, 208, 210, 212–13, 217, 219–20, 224, 227
  Annie, 188
  Eli, 109, 188
  Eli C., 224–25
Muddy Ford, 106–7, 125, 142, 158–60, 174, 187–91, 195, 204, 214, 229–30
Muddy Ford and Cynthiana Roads, 216
Muddy Ford and Finnell Pike, 187
Muddy Ford and Finnell Road, 124, 143, 149
Muddy Ford Church, 187
Muddy Ford Dirt Road, 176
Muddy Ford-Finnell Road, 148
Muddy Ford/Gunnell, 147
Muddy Ford Road, 52–54, 106–10, 112–13, 117, 122, 153, 158–59, 161, 171, 174, 187, 195, 208, 215–16, 226–27
Muddy Ford Robertson, 188
Muddy Ford's Bethesda Presbyterian Church, 171, 191
Muddy Ford School, 190
Muddy Ford Section Of Turkeyfoot Road, 50
Muddy Ford-Turkeyfoot Road, 187
Muddy River, 190
Mulberry, 64, 73, 79–80, 94–96, 236, 238, 243–45, 247, 258, 261, 265, 267–70, 273–74, 294
  Billy, 80
  David, 94, 153, 245
  Estella, 64
  Estelle, 94
  Esther, 94
  Frankie, 255
  Grover, 96
  Hattie, 245
  Ida N., 273
  Jacob, 80, 94–95, 235, 240, 261
  Joel, 94
  Joe L., 232, 238, 252, 269–70, 273
  Joel L., 268
  John H., 258
  John T., 95
  Leonard, 96, 237–38, 257–58, 265, 276
  Lucinda, 95
  Mary E., 279
  Mary F., 94, 96
  Miranda, 95
  Son William V., 95
  Thomas, 272
  Tom, 272
  William, 80, 239
Mulberry Cellar/Workshop, 95
Mulberry Dirt Road, 100
Mulberry-Eads Farm, 95
Mulberry Family, 94
Mulberry Farm, 96
Mulberry-Grigg House, 94
Mulberry House, 95, 279
Mulberry Lands, 96
Mulberry Road, 93, 177
Mulberrys, Richard, 95
Mulberrys, William V., 94–95
Mulberry's Account, 244
Mulberry's Hardware, 240
Mulberry's Luke Pike Land, 94
Mulberry's Shop, 248
Mulberry Street, 269
Mulberry-Swinford House, 95
Mulberry Tree, 99–100
Mulbery, Elizabeth, 94
Munson, 70–71, 114–17, 194–95
  Bradford, 116
  Buford, 90, 113–14, 116, 194
  Historic, 115
  Lena R., 114, 116
  Lilly, 116
  Lottie, 114
  Mae, 116
  Margaret, 113–14
  Mary, 116
  Rebecca, 119
  Samuel, 116
  Sanford, 70, 119
  Shelby, 117, 195
Munson Estate, 117
Munson Family, 115
Munson Farm, 113, 117
  Historic, 116
Munson Grandson, 195
Munson-Hinton-Vance House, 114
Munson House, 117
Munson Properties, 113
Munson's Estate, 116
Munson's House, 195
Muntz, 170, 175
  Howard, 228
  Lena, 175
  Loretta, 175
  Mollie K., 175
  Russell, 175
Muntz And Giles Families, 175
Muntz Family, 175
Muntz Family Ownership, 175
Muntz House, 175
Muntz House On Delaplain Road, 170
Muntz Residence, 170
Muntz's Ability, 170
Murphy, 171, 211
  John R., 225
  Joshua, 192
  Juanita, 275
  Michael, 275
Murray, Margaret, 54
Musselman, 82, 119

N
Nall, 108
  Lena, 108
  Martin, 108

Nada, 108
Noble, 108
Nancy Hughes House, 272
Nannie Mallory Hiles House, 120
Nannie Roberts House, 65
Neal, 197
   Frankie, 95
   Jacob, 197
   John, 280
Neale, 244, 252, 255, 276, 279
   Anna, 269
   Charles E., 276
   Jacob B., 80
   James W., 244
   Joel M., 255
   Lawrence, 255
   Lucy, 244
   Mary E., 279
   Winter, 101, 275
Neale Boarding House, 243
NEALE-WILLHOITE HOUSE, 255
Neaves, Amanda L., 278
Nelson, 83, 96–97, 137, 148, 245, 258
   Andrew, 294
   Emma, 253
   George T., 103, 245
   Laura Etta V., 96
   Ruby, 97
   Sarah, 103
   Thomas, 220
   William, 73, 276
New Era Milling Company, 236
Newtown, 198, 208, 213, 229–30
Newtown Congregation, 213
Newtown Pike, 219, 225, 227
Newtown Road, 224–25
New Zion, 55–56
Nicholas, 279
Nicholas County, 158
Nichols, 53, 107, 147, 158, 218
   Cora, 53–54
   Emma, 53
   John, 53
   John A., 159
   John K., 54
   Julia A., 158
   Lelia, 145
   Lelia T., 147
   Lewis H., 159
   Nettie, 219–20
   Norma, 53
   Russell, 53
   Sarah E., 158
   William, 106, 158–59
Nichols Children, 159
Nichols Farm, 158
Nichols-Juett, 159
Nichols-Juett Dwellings, 159
Nichols-Juett Heirs, 159
Nichols-Juett Properties, 158
Nichols Property, Sold, 53
Nicodemus, 57–60, 63
   That Is, 59
Nicodemus African Methodist Episcopal Church, 58
Nicodemus National Park Service Visitor Center, 59
Nielson, Jacqueline, 123
Noah Hanna House, 138
Noel, 89
   George, 140
   John, 152
   John C., 89–90
   Laura F., 89
   Lela, 90
   Martha, 86
Noel Family, 88
Noland, Nancy, 78
Nora, Ella, 262
Norfolk Southern, 115, 234
Norris, Stacy, 263
North, George, 79
Northcutt, 233, 238
   Nannie, 95
Northcutt's Furniture, 238
North Elkhorn, 197
North Elkhorn Creek, 67, 84, 161, 167, 172, 197
North Fork Of Eagle Creek, 185
North Fork Pike, 73
North Hamilton, 125, 207
North Hamilton And East Washington Streets In Georgetown, 125
North Hamilton Street, 166, 196
North Hamilton Street/Old Turkeyfoot Road, 161
North Mount, 111, 141
North Mount Gilead Church Road, 132
North Mount Gilead Road, 131, 141
North Rays Fork Road, 69
North Scott's Lone, 71
North Woods, 100
Norton, David R., 266
Norton, Sarah, 127–28
Nunn, Josephine T., 155
Nunnelley, 165
   Hattie, 263
Nunnelley-Berman Heirs, 83
Nutter, 197, 201
   Elizabeth, 61
   Jane, 54

O

Oaks, Dawn, 89
Obediah Pettit, 108
Odella, 100–101
Odella Lancaster, 100
Offutt, 61, 63–65, 104–5, 120, 123, 213, 265
   Chris, 61
   Edna, 61, 65, 104
   Harry, 61, 65, 105
   Harry C., 258

James S., 123
Lewis B., 201
Offutt AFB, 120
Offutt Heirs, 73
Offutt House, 65
Offutt's Group, 105
Offutt's Motivation, 105
O'Hara, Mattie, 269
Oil Refining Company, 163
Oldham, 139, 223
Old Turkeyfoot Road, 161, 167, 172, 196
O'Leary, Ruth, 188
Oliver, Anna S., 161
Oliver, Herbert, 148
Oliver, Martha, 156
Olivers, 148, 156, 161
O'Neal, Charles, 128
O'Neal, Ollie, 128
Onorato, Emily, 76
Orva Hiten, 254
Osborne, 85
  John, 122
Owen, Lucy, 121, 196
Owens, 67, 71, 121, 210
Owens Baptist Church, 58
Owens-Fleming-Rains House Site, 210
Owsley, Amber, 253
Oxford, 50, 52, 55, 119–20, 169, 172, 191, 195, 208–10, 212–14, 216–20, 222, 224, 226, 228–31

Oxford And Muddy Ford, 160
Oxford Area, 171, 220
Oxford Area African American Communities, 50
Oxford Christian Church, 208, 217, 226, 293, 295
Oxford Church, 213
Oxford Community, 228, 230, 291
Oxford Crossroads, 221, 226
Oxford Example, 210
Oxford FFA Students, 228
Oxford-Georgetown Pikes, 221
Oxford-Georgetown Road, 228
Oxford High School, 226
Oxford Historic District, 231
Oxford-Kincaid Road, 228
Oxford-Leesburg Road, 215
Oxford Lodge, 214
Oxford Manse, 213
Oxford Methodist Church, 227
Oxford-Muddy Ford Pike, 112
Oxford-Muddy Ford Road, 52, 158
Oxford-Newtown And Oxford-Georgetown Pikes, 221
Oxford-Newtown Road, 225
Oxford Presbyterian Church, 212
Oxford School, 228, 230
  Attended, 189
  Former, 230
  New, 230
Oxford Schoolhouse, 210
Oxford's Craftsman Style, 229

Oxford's Enrollment, 230
Oxford Settler, Early, 222
Oxford Sidewalks, 208
Oxford's Location, 209
Oxford's Masonic Lodge, 214
Oxford's Post Office, 214
Oxford's Southeast Corner, 219
Oxford's Southwest Corner, 209
Oxford Stone Sidewalks, 67
Oxford Students, 228
Oxford-Turkeyfoot, 187, 190
Oxford Village, 199, 208–9, 213–17, 227
Oxford Village Lane, 208–12, 215–19, 221–23, 228
Oxford White School District, 213

P
Pacific Theater, 64
Pack, 71–72, 93, 141, 154–56, 232–33, 240
  Adam, 182
  Benjamin, 192
  Included, 240
  Included Richard F., 239
  John, 71, 74, 80
  John E., 73, 96, 154–55, 233
  Josie C., 82, 233
  Married Richard F., 85
  Polly, 69
  Richard, 86, 206
  Richard E., 155
  Richard F., 71–73, 83, 232
  Sadie, 72
  Sallie, 84
  Sarah, 84–85
  Sarah M., 73
Pack Estate Farm, 233
Pack Farm, 73
Pack Home, 85, 233
Pack-Luke House, 155
Pack Property, 72
Pack's Estate, Divided, 72
Pack Smokehouse, 72
Padgett, Bart S., 128
Paducah, 71, 107, 291, 295
Paired Brackets, 70, 72, 200, 221, 240
  Multiple, 216
Palladian Design, 288
Palladian Forms, 285
Palladian Window, 288, 290
Palmer, 54
  Joel, 145
Pamelia Parker House, 266
Pam Faye Courtney, 79
Paris, 78, 104, 244
Parker, 100, 147, 236
  Addie, 254
  Cecil E., 225
  Clay, 278
  Frances, 280
  George, 269

George E., 62
Jack, 124
John, 293
Josie, 77
Maggie L., 147
Roy, 101
Roy L., 244
Tammy, 53
Terry L., 266
William, 73, 151
William S., 93
Parker-Davis Family, 254
Parrish, Agnes L., 63, 93
Parrish, Andrew M., 277
Parrish, Melissa, 228
Parrish, Steve C., 258
Patterson, 191
   Joe, 125
   Journeys, 191
   Robert, 191
Patterson's Crossroads, 208
Patton, Betsy, 160
Patton, Henry, 159
Paul, 53, 96, 109–10, 127, 130, 144, 153, 181, 194, 207, 257, 295
   Frank, 266
   James, 260
   Maggie, 137
   Margaret, 137
   Edward F., 178
Pavy, Samuel W., 201
Paxton, 209, 216, 269
   James, 142
   Luke H., 233
   Sallie, 153
   William H., 209, 216
Payne, 162, 216
Payne's Addition, 162, 165
Payne's Depot, 102
Peabody College, 54
Peacher, 202
   Cora, 138, 227
   Joseph, 202
   Joseph W., 127
   Thomas C., 218
Peacher House, 218
Peak, Greta S., 257
Peak's Mill, 162, 164
Peckover & Company, 125
Pelagia, 205
Pelfrey, Robert, 193
Pelley, Edith D., 257
Pemberton, 68
Pendleton, 147
Penelope, 79, 82
Penn, 72, 74–77, 79, 134, 156, 202–3, 232, 234
   Addie, 76–77, 156, 277
   Amanda M., 202
   Annie M., 169
   Belle, 76
   Bennie, 77
   Bessie, 99
   Elizabeth, 201–2
   George M., 76
   Henry C., 74
   Included John W., 193
   Joel M., 74
   John, 201, 203
   John B., 80
   John H., 260
   John W., 75, 202
   Katie, 79
   Late, 203
   Mary E., 74
   Millard F., 74
   Miranda, 78
   Nannie, 77
   Nannie L., 76, 99
   Richard F., 74
   Samuel, 74, 117
   Thomas, 169
   William, 74–75, 96, 183, 202, 214
Penn And Rodham Fields, 269
Penn And Warth Family, 202
Penn-Courtney Tract, 79
Penn Family Houses, 75
Penn Family Properties, 71
Penn Farm, 79
Penn Farms' Burgess Smith, 79
Penn Heirs, 77
Penn Plan, 209
Penn Side, 76
Penn Warth, Amanda M., 202
Perkins, Allie M., 104
Perkins, Buford, 275
Perkins, Charles, 199
Perkins, Danny, 88, 154
Perkins, Elizabeth, 73
Perkins, Leslie, 220
Perrin, 68, 167, 192–93, 208–9, 214, 220, 295
Perry, 55, 190
Peters, Kate, 224
Pettit, 107, 131
Petty, Peggy A., 279
Peyton, 98
Philadelphia, 59, 202, 291
Philip Ray Corporation, 144
Phillips, John, 113
Phipps, Marilyn, 224
Phyllis Welch Morris, 257
Pickett, 128
   Albert, 128
   Ida, 128
   Lewis, 128
   Lucille, 128
   Mary, 128
   Nellie, 128
Pierce/Bradford Munson, 115

Piggins, Don, 244
Pi Kappa Alpha, 226
Pike, Anderson, 171
Pike, Luke, 94, 96, 153–56
Pike, Morris, 147
Pike Street, 61–64, 234–36, 244–45, 248, 250–55, 268–69, 275
  North Side Of, 64, 254
  South Side Of, 234, 248
Pike Street Building, Former, 236
Pilot Knob, 130
Pivonka, Wilma J., 256
Pleasant Mckenney, 261
Pleasant Point, 229
Pleas Smith, 54
Plucknet, Albert, 260
Plucknett, Albert, 262
Poke's Alley, 250
Polk, 111, 153, 256–57
  James E., 262
Polk Fields, 232, 250–51, 256, 258–59, 269, 274
Polk Fields And Hamilton, 258
Polk Fields House, 256
Polly, 90
Popham, Jennie, 137
Poplar Fork, 84, 146
Poppeliers, 289
Porter Community, 240
Powell, 58, 163, 199, 215, 294
  Helen, 292
  Mary E., 146
  Ruben, 85
  Walter S., 111
Powers, Jerry, 151
Powers, Sallie, 79
Powers, Warren, 127
Powerses, 127
Preaching, Early Presbyterian, 212
Presbyterian Center, 183
Presbyterian Church, 191, 209, 211, 213, 227
  Renamed Providence, 213
Presbyterian Church Places, Former, 212
Presbyterian Congregations, 190, 213
Presbyterian Faith, 212
Presbyterian Manse, 211
Presbyterian Minister, 147
Presbyterians, 190, 209, 226
Presbyterian Synod, 190
Presbyterian Trustees, 227
Present Gano Avenue, 265
Prewitt, George, 125
Prewitt, George E., 203
Prewitt, George F., 125
Prewitt, Henry H., 162, 167
Prewitt, Levi, 167
Prewitt-Degaris Mill, 167
  Historic, 161
Pribble, Betty M., 156
Pribble, Maggie, 127

Pribble, Margaret, 137
Pribble, Maxine, 128
Pribble, Sandra K., 111
Pribbles, 111–12, 128, 156
Price
  Ann, 118–19
  Elizabeth, 118
  Granddaughters Ann I., 146
  Isaac, 119
  Jackson, 119
  Jacob, 119, 192, 211, 215, 219–20
  Martha, 118
  Meredith, 128
  Nannie, 274
  Nannie L., 278
  Pamela J., 277
  Rebecca, 145, 147, 210
  Ruth, 269
  Thomas, 118–19
  William, 118–19, 127, 148, 192
PRICE-HILES HOUSE SITE, 118
Price-Hiles Properties, 118
Price-Parker House, 254
Price's Daughter Helen, 211
Princess Anne, 75–76, 120, 180, 267
Priscilla Griffith Sinclair, 87
Proctor-Davis-Ray Engineers, 234
Prohibition Candidate For President, 206
Providence, 227
Providence Church, 191, 212, 214
Providence Pastor, 213
Pugh, Amos, 56
Pythias, 248–49, 282
Pythias Cemetery, 258, 282
Pythias Pike, 258
Pythias/Sadieville Cemetery, 282

Q

Queen City Railroad Depot, 249, 294
Queen City Railroad Depot/Sadieville City Hall, 249
Quiet Secure Place, 132

R

Rachel, Naomi, 262
Ragland, Douglas L., 81
Ragland, Thomas, 171
Railroad Lane, 280
Railroad Villages, 177, 195
Rains, Jack, 214
Rains, Randolph, 210
Rains, Randolph R., 139, 210
Ralph, 87, 138, 154
  Colette S., 159
Ralston, 183
  Joseph, 183
Ramey, Kyle, 149
Ramsey, Sarah K., 170
Ramseys, 170
Randall, 113, 248, 277

Rankin, Nancy, 154
Rawlins, 175
   Effie D., 175
   James H., 179
Rawlins-Whitson House, 179
Rawlston, John, 96
Ray, 113, 144, 289
Ray's Fork, 67, 102
Rays Fork, 69, 101, 103
Rays Fork Areas, 123
Rays Fork Road, 178
Readall, Josephine, 154
Recones, Sheila, 134
Reddick, Ellen, 251
Reddick, William, 251
Red Lodge, 234
Redondo Beach, 215
Red River Meetings, 190
Reds, 226
Reed, 70–71, 86, 97, 113, 135, 192, 295
   Ann E., 70
   Diana, 91–93
   Doris, 89, 113
   Elder, 70
   Harrison, 135
   Isaac, 185
   James, 86, 92–93, 116
   John, 135–36
   John R., 135
   Kathy, 71
   Louisa, 194
   Martha, 93
   Nancy, 183
   Samuel, 71
   Sold James N., 70
   Thelma, 113
   Thomas, 70
   Willie A., 110, 133–34
Reed/Bailey, 71, 295
REED BATES HOUSE, 92
Reed/Bates Properties, 91
Reeder, Charles J., 53
Reeder, Wendy, 53
Reed Family, 135
Reed Farm, 135
Reed-Garton Homesite, 70
Reed Hill In Turkeyfoot, 71
Reed House, 133
Reed House, Former Willie A., 133
Reed/Lusby, 71, 295
Reed-Munson Graveyard, 70
Reed's Death, 70, 93
Reed's Father, 70
Reed Tract, 136
Reed-Vallandingham Farm, 93
Reed/Vallandingham House, 92
Reed-Vallandingham Smokehouse, 93
Reese, Miriam I., 243
Reeves, Marcella, 253

Reffett, Grace, 106, 183
Reigel, Betsy, 115
Reigle, John, 113
Remus, 171
Remus Mason, 136, 171
Remus Payne, 217
Renaissance, 285
Renaker, Adam, 68
Renaker, Bertha T., 132
Renaker, James W., 210
Renaker, Mary, 94, 96, 131
Renakers, 94, 96, 129, 131
Reuben, 93, 214, 262, 292
Reuben Anderson House/Tavern Site, 215
Reverend Anthony Roberts, 62
Reverend Bradford Landry, 238
Reverend Charles, 57
Reverend Charles Egbert, 213
Reverend Don Hickman, 57
Reverend Joshua Leatherer, 197
Reverend Josiah Whittaker, 68
Reverend Moreland, 182
Reverend Morris Bell, 57
Reverends Felix Ross, 54
Reverends Jessie Scott, 54
Reverend William Nutter, 54
Revolutionary War, 78, 235
Richard Allen Barkley, 127
Richards, Susan, 130–31
Richards, Susan W., 130
Richard-Sadie Pack, 72
Richardson, 85
   James F., 138
Riddle, Larry, 88
Ridge Road, 67, 157
Rifkind, Carole, 284
Riggs, Sandra K., 137
Riley, Jack, 57
Risk, 55, 86, 119, 155, 176, 208, 241–42, 254, 258, 267, 269
   James, 208, 216, 221, 228
   James R., 228
   Kitty, 275
   Leander, 241, 249, 267, 269
   Martha A., 228
   Mary, 216, 266
   Mary K., 248, 254–55, 262
   Moses, 214
   Nettie, 119
   Sarah, 107, 171, 174, 176, 216
   William, 228
Risk House, 216
Risk Property, 216
Risk School, 198
Risk's Hotel, 241
River Raisin, 173
Road, Anderson, 68, 106, 173–76
Road, Davis, 63, 71, 74, 76, 95–96, 98, 106, 180–81, 184
Road, Morris, 142, 149

Road, Sharon, 147
Roads, Luke, 67–68, 153
Robert, 62–64, 76, 80, 107–8, 113, 116, 119, 122–23, 134, 146, 148, 206, 209, 225, 262
  Jesse, 143
  Sold, 140
Robert Brock Lands, 202
Roberts
  Alice, 64
  Annie, 64
  Bertha, 275
  Elizabeth, 108
  James, 64
  John A., 140
  Laura L., 83
  Nannie, 65
  Nannie C., 63
  Richard, 255
  Stella, 118
Roberts Family, 64
Roberts Lane, 60, 64–65
Robertson, 127, 151, 188–89, 191, 204, 254
  Beatrice, 188
  Bill, 193
  Chester, 194
  Meredith, 194
Robertson Home, 189
Robertsons' Deaths, 188
Roberts-Williams House, 64
Robinson, 93, 103, 259, 273
  Alice, 128
  Candace, 103
  James F., 85
  John, 57
  John T., 193
  Kentucky Governor James F., 85
  Lucinda, 278
  Richard, 103
  Richard A., 103
  William B., 103
Robinson Farms, 102
Robinson-Lowry Farm, 103
Roehrig, Joe, 205
Roehrig, Joseph, 205
Roehrig, Rhoda, 205
Roehrig Families, 205
Roehrigs, 205
Roehrig's Dream, 205
Roger Lee Davis, 278
Rogers, 114, 119, 121, 156, 172–73, 196, 240, 243, 261, 281, 295
  Annie, 109
  George, 172
  John, 173, 192, 213
  Joseph, 172
  Joseph S., 163
  Lawrence, 281
  Valentine, 109, 171–73
  William, 172

Rogers Family Members, 109, 173
Rogers Gap, 68, 107, 121, 123, 172, 191, 195–96
  Near, 121
Rogers Gap And Cincinnati Roads, 123
Rogers Gap Branch, 115, 172
Rogers Gap Creek, 118
Rogers Gap Pike, 114
Rogers Gap Road, 109, 113–15, 118–22, 172, 196
Rogers Gap-Turkeyfoot And Cincinnati Roads, 57
Rogers Gap/Turkeyfoot Road, 118
Rogers Gap-Turkeyfoot Road, 117
Rogers House, 173
Rogers Kinfolk, 172
Rogers's Brother George, 173
Ronvance, 196
Ron Vance House, 119
Rooney, Audrey, 224
Rooney, James, 224
Roosevelt, United States President Franklin D., 240
Root Cellar, 149
Rose, Hazel, 261
Rose, Jasper, 251
Rose, Jasper O., 252
Rose, Laura, 64, 253, 261–62, 264
Rosenwald, 54–55
  Julius, 54
Rosenwald Fund, 52, 55
Rosenwald Fund For Colored Schools, 55
Rosenwald Funding, 61
Rosenwald Fund Requirements, 55
Rosenwald School, 52
Rosenwald Schoolhouse, 59
Rosenwald Schools, Preserving, 62
Rosenwald Schools In Kentucky, 55, 60, 291
Ross, Glenda L., 281
Ross, Vera K., 281
Rowe, Galen R., 65
Rowland, Bonnie, 258
Rowland, Julia, 277
Royal Spring, 161
Roy Brooks House, 63
Royce, 207
Royden, 295
Ruben, 214
Run, Cherry, 51
Rush County, 50
Ruskin, John, 285
Ruskinian, 285
Russell, 53, 98, 104–5, 175, 223, 225
Russell Clay Givens, 53
Rutledge, Jennifer, 280
Rutledge, Kathryn, 140
Rutledge, Taylor, 89

S

Sadie Emison Pack, 82, 233
Sadie Truitt Commercial Building, 276

Sadieville, 60–63, 69, 71, 80–85, 91, 93, 104–5, 154, 232–50, 252, 254–58, 262–71, 273–77, 279–83, 292–95
  Account Of, 258
  City Of, 62, 83, 85, 239, 241, 249, 258
Sadieville African American Neighborhoods, 59
Sadieville African Americans' Role In Settling And Developing Nicodemus, 60
Sadieville And Secondary Station, 69
Sadieville Archives, 105
Sadieville Area, 61
Sadieville Bank, 240, 246
Sadieville Banker, 83
Sadieville Baptist Church, 237–38, 257, 265, 292
Sadieville-Boyers Chapel Road, 186
Sadieville Buys Historic Church, 62, 68, 292
Sadieville Cemetery Company, 282
Sadieville Christian, 247
Sadieville Christian Church, 244, 246–47, 274, 294
Sadieville Christian Missionary Society, 274
Sadieville Church, 247, 294
Sadieville Churches, 265
Sadieville City Clerk, 105, 294
Sadieville City Clerk Cindy Foster, 63
Sadieville City Clerk/Treasurer, 272, 293
Sadieville City Hall, 83, 248
Sadieville City School, 270
Sadieville Column, 292
Sadieville Columnist, 60
Sadieville Commerce, 236
Sadieville Community, 258, 267
Sadieville Congregation, 246
Sadieville-Connersville Road, 69, 80
Sadieville-Connersville Turnpike, 69
Sadieville-Cynthiana Pike, 98
Sadieville-Davis, 75, 180
Sadieville-Davis Road, 69–71, 73–76, 96, 105–6
Sadieville-Davis Turnpike, 73
Sadieville Deposit Bank, 239, 252
Sadieville District, 267
Sadieville Elementary, 270, 294
Sadieville Elementary School, 271
Sadieville-Finnell Pike, 131
Sadieville-Hinton Pike, 89
Sadieville-Hinton Road, 92
Sadieville Knights, 282
Sadieville Lions, 267, 295
Sadieville Methodist Church, 265–66, 295
Sadieville Milling Company, 235–36, 294
Sadieville Mount Pleasant Baptist Church, 59
Sadieville Pike, 129, 157, 207
Sadieville Railroad Underpass, 234
Sadieville Region, 92
Sadieville Rosenwald School, 60
Sadieville's African American Community, 60
Sadieville's African American Population, 105
Sadieville's Bank, 240
Sadieville's Bank Building, 239
Sadieville School, 61, 74, 268–71, 276, 294–95
  New, 269
Sadieville's City Hall, 249
Sadieville's Downtown, 236
Sadieville's Mount Pleasant Baptist Church, 60
Sadieville's Pike Street, 61, 105
Sadieville's Rosenwald School, 61, 63
Sadieville's Undertaker And Furniture, 233
Sadieville Sunshine, 63, 233, 235, 270, 294–95
Sadieville-Turkeyfoot Road, 156
Sadieville Turnpike, 281
Sadieville Urban Renewal, 63, 255
Sadieville Water Plant, 281
Sadieville Water Tower, 282
Sadieville Water Works, 282
Salem Chapel Methodist Church, 68
Salem Church, 68
Sallie Sherritt House, 275
Sallie Sherritt's American Foursquare, 275
Sams, 175, 266
  Elizabeth L., 188
  Mary E., 152
  Owen, 175
Sanborn Map, 163–64, 295
Sanborn Map Company, 295
Sanborn Map Of Indian Oil Refinery, 162
Sanchez, Leonardo, 63
Sanders, 121
  Henry, 121, 196
  John, 119
  Louella, 121
Scarborough, John, 244
Schelldonald T, Lois J., 71
Schnurr, Tina, 227
School, Davis, 180, 184
School, Garth, 229
School, Perry, 55
Scots-Irish Settlers, 107
Scott, 67–68, 70–71, 99, 111, 129–30, 135, 173, 177, 185, 192–93, 208–9, 257, 295
  Edna, 102
  Elizabeth, 52
  Hattie, 172, 295
  Lawrence, 104
  William, 63
Scott Circuit Court, 87, 151
Scott County, 58–59, 67–69, 107, 119–20, 125–26, 164–68, 177–79, 188–90, 192–93, 205–7, 209, 226–27, 232–35, 291–93, 295
Scott County Alternative School, 271
Scott County Articles, 163
Scott County Arts Consortium, 224
Scott County as Told By Selected Buildings, 291
Scott County Barnhills, 107
Scott County Bicentennial Commission, 294
Scott County Bicentennial Committee, 200, 291–95
Scott County Board, 55, 61, 80, 179, 181, 230, 272, 291
Scott County Burgess Families, 77
Scott County Churches, 190

Scott County Church Histories, 53–54, 57, 61, 80, 181, 187, 193, 238, 247, 265, 291–95
Scott County Church Histories A Collection, 200
Scott County Circuit Court, 150, 294
Scott County Circuit Court Order Books, 151
Scott County Clerk, 113, 295
Scott County Country School Districts, 210
Scott County Deed Books, 223
Scott County Fiscal Court, 170, 190, 292
Scott County Genealogical Society, 71, 91, 107, 144, 200, 291, 293, 295
Scott County Genealogical Society's Families, 208
Scott County High School, 109, 120
Scott County Historical Society, 170, 291–92
Scott County Infirmary, 168
Scott County Junior High School, 271
Scott County List, 55
Scott County Marriage Register, 150
Scott County Middle School, 271
Scott County Mount Olive, 58
Scott County Mulberry, 94
Scott County Museum, 84–86, 120, 167, 224, 293
Scott County Oil, 163
Scott County Portion, 205
Scott County Public Library, 209, 292
Scott County's Chief Landowners, 233
Scott County School Board, 271
Scott County Schools, 55, 291
Scott County Sheriff R, 257
Scott County Side, 180
Scott County's Mount Olive Church, 58
Scott County Students, 230
Scott County Will Book, 236
Scott County Will Book S-123, 234, 239
Scott County Will Books Y-245, 223
Scott Downing, 100
Scott-Harrison County Line, 50, 52
Scott Records, 113, 292
Scott's Papers, 172–73, 295
Screba, Fritz, 193
Scruggs, Jerry, 57
Seals, Paula, 280
Seals, Taylor, 54
Sears, 54
Sears Craftsman Plan, 131
Seventh Day Adventist Church, 80
Shane Papers, 173, 292
Sharon, 107–8, 147–49, 187, 277
  Henry, 124
  Hugh, 108, 147
  James F., 147
  James M., 147
  James S., 148
  Jane, 107
  John, 148
  Maria, 149
  Nancy, 147
  Oscar, 277
  Sam N., 147
  Samuel, 190
  William, 147
Sharp, Claude, 134
Sharp, Claude M., 134
Sharp, James, 169
Sharp, James L., 134
Sharp, Jesse, 128
Sharp, John M., 134
Sharp, Nettie, 129
Sharp, Sarah J., 134
Sharron, Frank, 148
Sharron, Lou, 148
Shaw, Mattie, 56
Shawnee Run, 67–68, 116–17, 195
Shawnee Run Farm, 115–16
Sheehan House, 263
Shelby Munson Family Graveyard, 195
Shelby Munson Farm, 117
Shelby's House, 195
Sheley, John, 214
Shelley, John, 216
Shepherd's Crossing, 108
Shepherd's Crossing/Clinton Barnhill House, 108
Shepherd's Farm, 236, 295
Sherritt, 86, 147, 158, 232, 273–75, 282
  Carrie, 273–75, 279
  Frank, 274–75
  Fred G., 158
  John E., 85
  Sallie, 273–74
Sherritt House, 158, 273
Shirey, Lisa W., 79
Shirley, 188–89
  Alice, 188
  Jessie, 81
  Lora Z., 188
  Opal, 243
  Stella, 195
Shirley's Land, 187
Short, Deborah, 255
Shropshire, 51, 53, 164
  James, 56
Shuff, Isaac, 135–36, 201
Shyrock, Rebecca, 146
Siegel, Julie, 76
Silcox, Felicia A., 95
Simmons, Lewis E., 148
Simms, Earl, 193
Simpson, Mary, 201
Sims, 169
  Mary, 57
Sims Place, 128
  The Old, 128
Sims Road, 167, 171–72
Sinkhorn, Norman, 280
Skinner, 117, 207
  John R., 90
  Richard, 145
Skreba, 195

Fred, 195
Smith, 57, 63–64, 73, 79, 82, 105, 142, 148, 180–81, 197, 203, 235, 240, 245, 280–81
- Angela, 280
- Anna L., 178
- Bessie A., 148
- Bradford, 122
- Charlie, 228
- Clayton, 91
- Daughter Mariah, 50
- Delores, 218
- Doris, 281
- Eugene, 111
- Eugene T., 181
- Eugenia S., 75, 181
- Geraldine, 184
- Hazel C., 65
- Henry, 203
- Ina, 148
- James, 86, 101
- John, 134
- Levi, 199
- Lewis, 57
- Linda, 75
- Mary, 95
- Mother Eva B., 79
- Naomi, 52, 54
- Rebecca, 294
- Ruth, 65
- Sanford, 108
- Wife Eugenia S., 105
- William T., 105, 181

Smith Bungalow, 184
Smith Family House, 184
Smith Family Landmarks, 69
Smith Road, 91, 95
Smith's Heirs, 148
Smith's Home, 79
Smith's Purchase, 143
Smoot, James W., 214
Snell, John E., 160
Snyder, 57, 193, 291, 293
- Dana, 193, 291

Soard, Mary, 157
Solomon Burgess House, 111
Southern Methodist Church, 227
Southern Railroad, 88, 100, 113, 155, 178, 234, 268
Southern Rail Road, 242
Southern Railroad
- Building Cincinnati, 68
- New Cincinnati, 85, 177
- Sold Cincinnati, 116

South Hamilton Street In Georgetown, 92
South Limestone, 188
South Mount Gilead Church Road, 139–40
South Mount Gilead Pike, 140
South Ray's Fork, 69
South Rays Fork, 102–4, 180
South Rays Fork Pike, 102

South Ray's Fork Road, 69, 102
South Rays Fork Road, 101–2, 178, 293
Southworth, 109, 271–72, 295
- Annie L., 109
- Asa, 169
- Jan, 262

Sovereignty, 290
Sowers, Constance, 88
Sowers, Ellen, 154
Sowers, Fred, 194
Sowers, Irene, 195
Sowerses, 88
Sowers-Giles Farm, 88
Sowers-Giles House, 154
Sowers Heirs, 88
Sowkam Leong, 260, 262
Spanish American War, 51, 104–5
Sparrow, George, 122
Spates, Matilda, 219
Spates, William, 190
Spears, 61
- Bill, 259
- Late Woodridge, 130

Special Edition, 233, 235, 270, 294–95
Spencer, 269
- Marie, 57

Spradling, Maggie H., 159
Spradling, Thomas S., 159
Spradlings, 159
Springfield, 54
Spring Valley, 205
Stafford County, 78
Stafford Howard, 62
Stallons, 295
- Malcolm L., 242

Stamping Ground, 55, 208, 271
Stamping Ground Academy, 209
Stamping Ground Buffalo Gals Extension Homemakers, 223
Stanley, 76, 272
- Martha, 151

Stearns, Debra M., 101
Stephens, Cornelia, 143
Stephens, Edith, 136
Stephens, Irene, 140
Stephens, Jeffrey, 140
Stephens, Lisa, 200
Stephens, Opal S., 156
Stephens, Susan C., 126
Sterling Paul, 82
Sterling Price Smith, 69
Steven, George, 147
Stevens, 91, 186, 244, 247
- Albert, 70
- Albert M., 185
- Alfred D., 186
- Harriet, 185
- Landowner Albert M., 185
- Son Alfred D., 185

329

William, 271
Steward, Amanda, 93
Steward, James M., 93
Steward, Margaret J., 263
Stewart, Douglass, 232
Stewart, Edith, 207
Stewart, Mary E., 202
Stewart, Nancy, 92
St. John Church, 126
St. John's Cheap, 206
St. Louis, 190, 296
  East, 164
Stone
  Barton, 190, 213, 296
  John C., 100
  Judith A., 247
  Mary E., 179–80
  Rachel, 258
  Walter, 100
Stone Family Farm, 99
Stone House, 248
Stone Lane, 69, 99–101
Stone Lane/Highway, 101
Stonemason Bill Spears, 62
Stonewall, 69, 71, 99, 101, 121, 141, 179, 198, 246, 267
Stonewall and Hinton Communities, 69
Stonewall and Old Mulberry Road, 100
Stonewall and Rays Fork Areas, 123
Stonewall County Road, 100
Stonewall Holland, 141
Stonewall Jackson Holland, 141
Stonewall Roads, 179
Stonewall Schoolhouse, 101
Store, Davis, 181
Stout, John H., 201
Stowers, 102–4
  Richard, 104
  Thomas L., 104
Stowers Barns, 103
Stowers Family, 104
Stowers Farmland, 102
Stowers House's Neighbor, 103
Stowers Log House, 102
Stowers's Farm, 104
Stowers-Wilderson House, 102
Straight Fork, 72, 74–75, 105, 180, 194
Straight Fork And Twin Creek And Beard's Church Pike, 157
Straight Fork Branch, 76
  Small, 76
Straight Fork/Davis, 71, 180
Straight Fork-Davis, 181
Straight Fork In Honor, 69
Straight Fork Of Eagle Creek, 72, 182
Strong, Danny, 265
Stuard, Dorothy, 149
Stuard, Jesse B., 266
Stuart, 130
  Jesse, 130

Stucker, 191
  David, 173
  James, 98, 157
Stucker Offutt, 122–23
Students, Non-African American, 268
Sturgill, 110
Sublett-Hall, 163
Sue Hamon House, 136
Sugar Ridge, 213
Sugar Ridge Meeting House, 213
Sugar Ridge Meetinghouse, Old, 217
Sullivan School Act, 270
Summers, Penny R., 131
Sunday Herald-Leader, 105, 295
Sutton
  Arthur, 187
  Evie, 187
  Ira, 124, 187, 189
  James, 192
  Joe, 187
  John T., 187
  John W., 187
  Joseph, 187
Sutton Families, 187
Sutton Property, 187
Sutton's Surviving Heirs, 187
Swift Contracting Co, 165
Swift-Mcnutt Building Wrecking Demolition, 165
Swinford, 95, 97, 105, 186, 264, 277
  Edward T., 95
  Etta R., 156
  George, 186
  George M., 186
  James W., 156
  Margaret F., 186
  Mary, 101
  Ollie, 257
  Raymond, 95, 156
Swinford Family, 101, 186
Swope, 78, 293
  Burgess, 77
Syble Wilhoite, 101

T
Talbott, Fannie, 139
Taylor, 79, 123, 176
  Fannie, 244
  Hugh R., 79–80, 123
  James, 145
  Jennie, 176
  Julia, 176
Taylor Family, 130, 176
Temple Of Justice, 268
Tennessee Press, 190, 292
Tennessee Walking Horses, 166
Tevis, Charlene, 139
Texaco Inc, 161
Texas Pacific, 234
Texas Press, 75, 294

Theobald, 243
　John M., 242–43
　Sallie D., 243
Theobald House, 243
Thomas, 71, 108–9, 118, 120, 132, 134, 150, 156, 236, 239, 243, 246, 253, 258, 265
　Amanda, 53
　Calvin, 92
　John, 110, 188
　Lula, 188
　Lula C., 188
　Renee M., 134
　Thomas, 190
Thomas Black Settlement, 50
Thomas Creath White, 195
Thomas Jefferson Burgess I, 82
Thomas Kitchen House, 98
Thompson, 51, 142, 155, 171
　Charlie, 155
　Deborah, 152
　Edna M., 57
　Helen, 171
　Louis, 57
　Lucy, 266
　Reuben, 227
　William A., 51
Thomson, 81–82
　Zachariah, 85
Thornton Williams, 57
Tilford, George M., 208
Timberlake, Abe, 57
Timberlake, Harriet, 57
Timothy, 188
Tinder, 142, 201, 219
　Martha J., 201
Todd, 95
　Robert, 69
Todd & Honeywell, 123, 188, 293
Tomlinson, Herbert, 77
Toohey, Thomas, 104
Topeka, 60
Toyota Motor Manufacturing Kentucky, 176
Toyota Plant, 199, 215
Transylvania Presbytery, 182, 211, 214
Trefzger, 295
　John G., 217
Trotter, Elizabeth, 140
Trotter, Gregory, 141
True, Lena, 223
Truitt, 232, 250, 273
　Sadie, 275–77
Truitt House, 273
Truitt-Warring House, 277
Tucker, 75, 89, 181–84, 295
　Ann, 183
　Bobby, 239
　Children Lillian D., 109
　George, 126
　Henry, 152
　Jackson, 183
　Jenny, 183
　Joseph S., 103
　Lillian D., 176
　Luke, 183
　Nannie, 86, 89–90, 155
　Sallie B., 89
　Willie, 89
Tucker's Heirs, 89
Tucker's Lands, Nannie E., 89
Turkeyfoot, 68, 70–71, 77–78, 86–87, 106–7, 113, 117–20, 123, 152–53, 172, 191–94
Turkey Foot, 70, 191–92, 196
Turkeyfoot And Double Culvert, 123
Turkeyfoot Area, 71
Turkeyfoot Bates, 92
Turkeyfoot-Boyers Turnpike, 132
Turkeyfoot Christian Church, 192–93, 195, 291
Turkeyfoot Church, 193–94
Turkeyfoot District, 206
Turkeyfoot Neighborhood Circa, 90
Turkeyfoot Pike, 88, 97
Turkeyfoot Post Office, 192
Turkey Foot Precinct, 70
Turkeyfoot Road, 50, 96, 98, 106, 131, 153, 195–96, 208
　Long Abandoned Old, 215
Turkeyfoot's Asher Hinton, 177
Turkeyfoot School, 194
Turkeyfoot School, Second, 194
Turner Publishing Company, 71, 107, 291, 295
Tyler, 213
　Brian A., 267
Tylicki, Jane L., 105
Tyree, Catherine, 266

U
Underground Railroad Research Institute, 55, 291
Underwood, 143
　Dorothy L., 143
　Pauline, 272
Utica, 74

V
Valentine Rogers Family Bible, 172–73
Valentine Rogers Gap, 172
Valentine Rogers House On Sims Road, 171
Vallandingham
　Annie S., 93
　Etta, 97
　Fannie, 97
　George, 96, 155
　Louis, 192
　Lucy, 260, 263
　Martha, 92–93
　Martha B., 93
　Roy, 96–97, 255
Vallandingham-Nelson House, 96
Vallandingham's Title, 93
Vance, 90, 113, 121, 141, 145, 175, 188, 283

Buck, 192
Chester B., 252
Dewey, 194
Elizabeth, 187
Historian Ronald T., 193, 195
Jimmy, 119
John A., 116
Joseph L., 187
Lee L., 64
Matthew, 243, 246, 261
Nannie, 280
Norman, 273
Pearl, 258
Pearl H., 265
Raymond, 194
Robert A., 119
Ron, 67, 91, 119–21, 193–95
Ronald T., 68, 80, 86, 91, 107, 113, 119, 127, 293
Roscoe, 113
Roy, 62
Thelma, 114–15, 119
Trina, 261
William, 192–93, 195
Vance Cemetery, 107
Vance House, 119
Vance's Heirs, 145
Vance/Wells Family, 117
Van Cleve, 246
Vandermeer, 226
Veatch, 247
  Margie, 246
Veda Mae Steger, 159
Vest
  Diana, 279
  Diane, 278
  Philip W., 278
Vickers, Audrey J., 137
Victor, 146, 148
Village Lane, 218
Vocational Agriculture/FFA Building, 228

W
Wade, 65
  James, 292
Wagoner, Carol, 149
Waldman, Nancy L., 262
Walker, Rebecca S., 153
Wallace, 155, 228
  Charles, 142
  Paul, 63
Walter Mcarthur Stone, 99
Walters, James O., 136
Walters, Kent, 173
Walton, 136, 228, 230
Ward
  Cary, 216–17, 227
  Cary A., 160, 209, 214
  Columbus, 213
  Edwin, 221, 226
  James, 95
  Joseph B., 217
  Lizzie, 227
  Mary E., 227
  Robert Q., 217
  Allen, Mary E., 217
Ward-Hendricks House, 209
Warf, James, 202
Warren, 141
  William, 208
Warren County, 113
Warring, 62, 68, 240, 243, 245, 277–78, 280, 283, 293
  William T., 282
Warring Home, Former, 245
Warring House, 244
Warring-Parker Insurance Agency, 249
Warring Pavilion, 232, 237, 243
Warring Picnic Pavilion, 237
Warring Set, 240
Warth, 123, 137, 139, 142, 202–4, 207
  Abe, 137
  Amanda, 203
  Amanda M., 203
  Henry, 201–2
  Lee, 203
  Lindsay, 123, 188–89, 293
  Mollie, 137
Warth-Conner House, 137
Warth Family, 202–3
Warth Farm Log House Site, 203
Warth House, 202–3
Washington, 54, 219
  Booker T., 54
  George, 61
Watkinsville, 55
Watson, Joseph, 183
Watson, Lillie, 207
Watson, Lonnie R., 181
Watson, Patrick, 192
Watson, Sandra, 181
Watsons, 169
Watsons' Ownership, 102
Watson's Trustee, 146
Watts, Chad, 141
Wayne, Lloyd, 135
Weakley, Harriet, 70
Weakley, Jeremiah, 70
Webber, James, 101
Wee Kirk, 181, 183, 190, 223, 292
Welch, Clara F., 188
Wells
  Bertha, 138
  Claude, 206
  Gertrude, 137
  Laura H., 91
  Lawrence, 137
  Lillie, 137
  Maria M., 196
  Nannie, 128

Ronald P., 101
William, 137
Willie, 128, 137
Wells-Duncan Houses, 127
Wesley, 137
Thomas, 50
West, Jennie, 257
West, Lynn, 125
West, Ruth, 198
West & Brothers, 125
Western Virginia, 120
West Forks, 107
West Lexington Presbytery, 190, 211, 213
West Oxford, 162
Wetzel, Elizabeth, 141
Wewaha, 136
Whalen, Gerald B., 97
Whelan, Sandra, 233
White
Annie E., 218
Daniel, 193
Joe C., 275
John, 56
Josephine, 255
Sally, 56
White's Cemetery, 193
White Sulphur On Frankfort Road, 198
Whitney, 83
Whitson, 248
Katherine, 243
Roberta, 179
Sisters Cora A., 186
Wilder, Henry, 80
Wilderson, Christine, 102
Wilderson, Kris, 102, 293
Wilderson, Kristine, 102
Wilderson, Kristine D., 102
Wilderson Home, 293
Wildersons' Log House, 104
Wiley, Joey W., 186
Wilhoyte, Stephen, 191
Wilhoyte, Stephen W., 188
Willard, 167
Willhoite, Thelma J., 255
William, 79–80, 92–95, 111–13, 118–19, 139, 152, 158–59, 171–72, 182–84, 193–94, 202, 219–20, 224–25, 275–76, 280
George, 142
James, 199
William Gray House, 209, 216
William Griggs/Gregg Farm, 148
William Gunnell House, 146
William Hinton Division, 109
William Hinton Family, 80
William Hinton Lands, 154
William Hinton's Lands, 86
William Innis Farm, 50
William Nichols' Land, 147
William Penn House Site, 74

William Price Lands, 192
William Price's Land Holdings, 119
Williams, Amanda Z., 110
Williams, Cary, 215
Williams, Frank, 106
Williams, Susie, 62–64
William Sanford Dawson, 109
Williamson, 86, 107, 124, 126–27, 142, 149–50, 153
Bonnie L., 126
Charles, 151
Dudley, 124, 127
Fred, 135
George H., 148–49
George W., 149
Gladys, 126
Herman, 108
Howard, 124
James H., 108
James W., 191
Kitty, 94
Lou, 143
Nora, 124
Polly, 146
Raymond, 147
Richard, 150
Ricky, 126
Samuel S., 124
William, 119, 190
Williamson Descendants, 126
Williamson-Duncan House, 127
Williamson Family Members, 124
Williamson Farm, 124
William Thomson House, 81
Wilmoth, Emma, 207
Wilson, 54, 57, 121, 249
Aaron, 57
Ann, 260
Asa G., 121
Carolyn, 241, 248, 277
Carrie, 105
Emma, 56
Jeremiah, 54
Judith, 121
Kenneth, 180
Kenneth A., 274
Lula K., 262
Minnie S., 137
Raymond, 263
Ronald A., 252–53
Vivian, 53–54
William R., 272
Yvette, 257, 261
Winalansit Tribe, 277
Winburn, Stuart, 76
Winkler, Jimmie, 183
Winter, Eva, 123, 262
Wirtz, Tina, 227
Wiseman, 138–39
Frank, 138

Kay, 138, 141
Wolfe, Thomas, 163
Wombles, 276
  Arlene, 266
Wood
  Cora, 199
  Dorothy E., 140
  Hiram, 199, 215
  Irene E., 202
  Nellie V., 273
  Sam O., 273
  Sybil, 170
  Thomas, 252
Woolums, 243, 245
  Marvin D., 245
Wright, 80, 139, 164, 169, 251
  Benjamin F., 112
  Christine, 62
  Earl, 80
  Eliza, 110
  James, 145
  John W., 251
  Laura M., 159
  Lucy, 131
  Nannie, 140
  Sallie, 250–51, 262
Wright Heirs, 93
Wurtz, 186
Wyatt, 198
Wyckoff, 107

Y

Yateman, James, 173
York Smith House, 63
Young, Iris, 97
Young, John, 113
Young, Samuel, 113

Z

Zephaniah, 255–56
Zephaniah Fields, 255
Zeysing, 240, 244, 247, 266
  Richard E., 266
  Richard W., 265
Zeysing Heirs, 155
Zumwalt, Juanita, 277

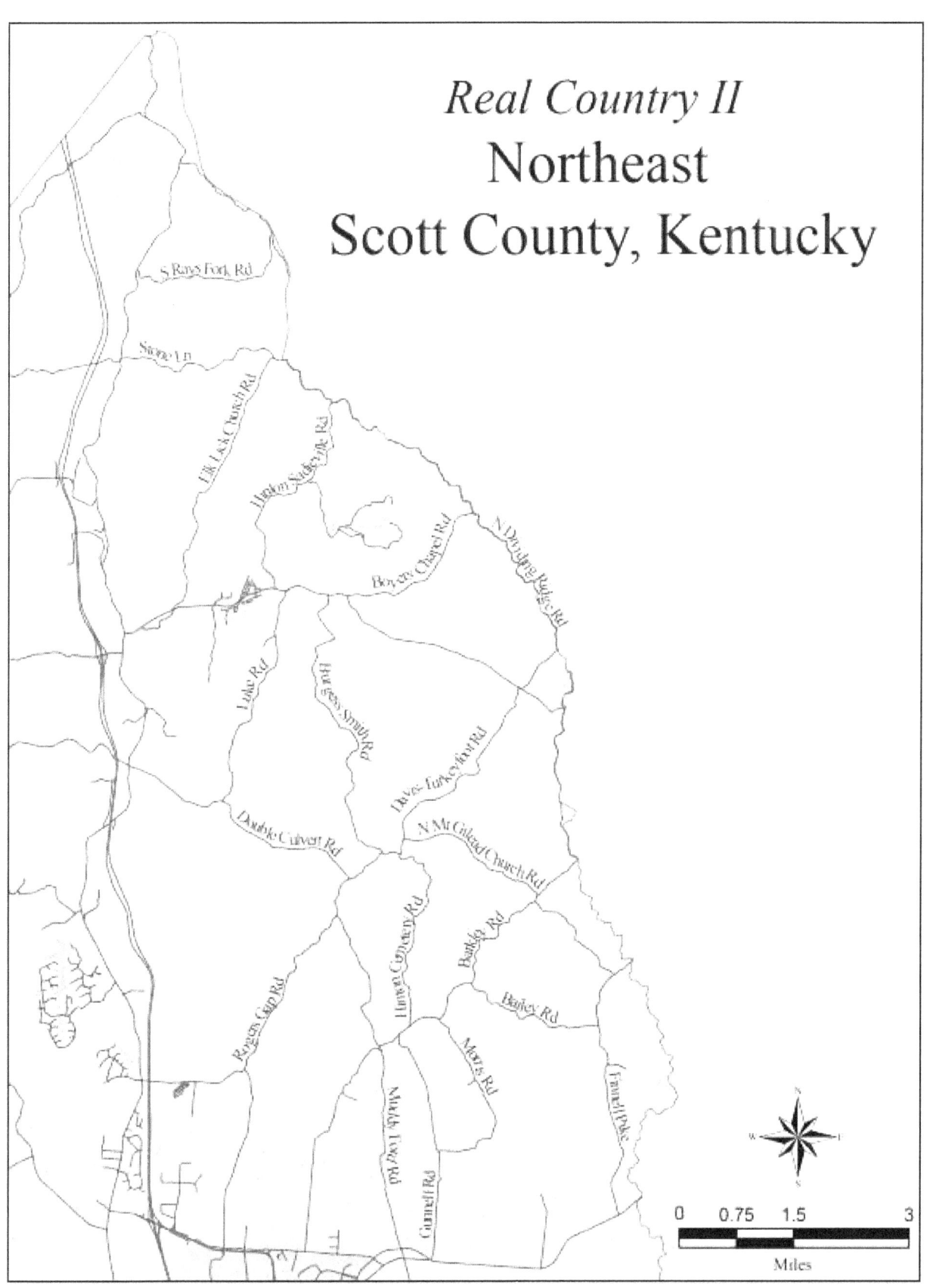

Real Country II
Northeast Scott County, Kentucky

www.ingramcontent.com/pod-product-compliance
Lightning Source LLC
Chambersburg PA
CBHW060502240426
43661CB00006B/889